Journalism Matters

◆ **JAMES SCHAFFER**
Nebraska Wesleyan University

◆ **RANDALL MCCUTCHEON**
Albuquerque Academy

◆ **KATHRYN T. STOFER**
Hastings College

National Textbook Company
a division of NTC/CONTEMPORARY PUBLISHING GROUP
Lincolnwood, Illinois USA

Acknowledgements begin following the index, which is to be considered an extension of this copyright page.

Student Edition ISBN: 0-538-43111-3
Teacher's Annotated Edition ISBN: 0-538-43112-1

Published by National Textbook Company,
a division of NTC/Contemporary Publishing Group, Inc.,
4255 West Touhy Avenue, Lincolnwood, Illinois 60712-1975 U.S.A.

01 02 03 04 05 06 07 08 09 QB 0 9 8 7 6 5 4 3

CONTENTS

SECTION 3
WRITING THE NEWS   111

BYLINE:
Mario Garcia, Newspaper Design Consultant 331

THIS JUST IN: PORTRAIT OF A YOUNG JOURNALIST
Craig Pursley, Assistant Art Director, *Orange County Register* 335

THIS JUST IN: PORTRAIT OF A YOUNG JOURNALIST
Dennis Ortiz-Lopez, Type Designer 360

BYLINE:
George Rorick, Director of Graphics for Knight-Ridder 368

PREFACE

*J*ournalism," wrote Matthew Arnold, "is literature in a hurry." And "hurry" may be what's on the minds of most teachers as they approach a journalism course. No matter how important the big picture—the use or misuse of information, for example—these teachers are eager to quickly train students to take on the responsibilities of school newspapers, magazines, yearbooks, even television and radio programs.

Nearly all the chapters in this book are designed as resources to do just that, to bring students up to speed as working journalists. These chapters train students to write well—to summarize information, describe observations and accurately record the views and comments of others. They also cover interviewing, sports writing, feature writing, and the special demands of column and review writing. Still other chapters cover the knowledge and skills required to bring a product to the public's attention.

While only a few of our students will actually find careers in the news media someday, all of them will become lifelong news-consumers. *Journalism Matters* provides chapters that touch on those concerns, too, by analyzing how students can make good, informed decisions about their concerns and causes, their interests and passions. Indeed, the future of our democratic society depends upon the ability of a new generation of citizens to participate fully and effectively in the exchange of information.

The theme of *Journalism Matters* is simply that journalism plays a vital role in the creation, development and continuing good health of democratic communities. Within that overarching theme are three separate but intertwined threads. The first emphasizes journalism's role as a marketplace of ideas. The print and broadcast media provide a crucial "party-line" for both large and small communities. At their best the news media enable a community to hold conversations with itself.

This thread highlights the intensely communal nature of journalism. "All stories are local stories," the saying goes. Journalists must always keep the interests of their immediate audience in mind. They must strive to satisfy their readers' and listeners' needs for timely, accurate and relevant information. Throughout the text, students will encounter frequent examples of journalists engaged in community-building activities.

A second thematic thread is the multi-cultural nature of journalism. Journalists have no greater responsibility than to seek out their community's many diverse voices. You won't, however, find a "multi-cultural" chapter. One isolated chapter could never do justice to this critical aspect of journalism. Instead, students will find multi-cultural concerns raised throughout the book. Special

> " Journalism is literature in a hurry."
> — Matthew Arnold

> " A newspaper that does not look like a cross-section of the community it serves will not—and cannot— serve the community as it wants to be served."
>
> — Newspaper Editor

attention is paid to how the press itself, both professional and scholastic, is becoming increasingly diverse. As one editor puts it, "A newspaper that does not look like a cross-section of the community it serves will not—and cannot—serve the community as it wants to be served."

The third thread in the book's theme is a concern for ethics. Journalism, as many of its practitioners are fond of saying, is a craft, not a profession. But it is a craft with a strict code of ethics. Students need to learn about that code from the very beginning because virtually every activity—from a short phone call to check facts to a lengthy off-the-record interview—raises questions of trust and confidentiality. You'll find the importance of journalistic ethics reflected in the positioning of an entire chapter devoted to the subject early in the book. That thread continues in the form of learning activities, discussion questions and open forum "scenarios" where we challenge students to solve ethical dilemmas through role-playing situations.

A brief word about methodology. Traditional texts generally devote a chapter to the history of journalism. Because history should be smoothly integrated throughout the text rather than studied for its own sake, this book takes a much different approach. The major milestones in the history of journalism are featured throughout the textbook as "Datelines." Because they relate to the content of each chapter, they do not appear in chronological order. The highlights of each milestone appear in chronological order as a separate timeline preceding Section 1 of the text. The chapter in which the complete Dateline appears, or to which the timeline entry applies, is in parentheses following the summary.

Journalism teachers are sometimes in a quandary as to whether to draw examples from the professional media or the scholastic press. Both are important. The examples and anecdotes in each chapter are chosen equally from professional and student media. The professional examples offer glimpses of excellence—the standard to strive for, in other words—while student examples give students insights into applying what they have learned to topics that interest teenagers.

Journalism Matters offers students a lively, engaging text, one filled with rewarding activities and compelling examples. The text can work well for the teacher who seeks to provide a broad overview of the news media and for the teacher who wants a practical hands-on guide for producing student media. Toward this end, we have provided a Stylebook and Editor's Handbook following the last chapter. *The Stylebook* combines the best of the AP rules and scholastic style sheets from across the country. *The Editor's Handbook* provides numerous practical tips for organizing and managing a student staff. Also included is a complete *Glossary* with alphabetized definitions for all the marginal terms in the book.

Journalism Matters will provide significant help and sound ideas for both new and veteran teachers. As we move into the 21st century, journalism and the role it provides in communities—both local and global—will become increasingly significant. Journalism Matters gives today's students the skills and factual background they need to become active participants in their communities today and throughout their lives.

◆ **James Schaffer**
◆ **Randall McCutcheon**
◆ **Kathryn T. Stofer**

◆ ACKNOWLEDGEMENTS ◆

James Schaffer would like to thank Julie Hoyt for her insights, research and marvelous curiosity into First Amendment issues; Merry Hayes for her good humor, brilliant prose and inspiring example; wonderful colleagues at Lincoln East High School and Nebraska Wesleyan University; Peggy Ruprecht and many, many students whose devoted effort has made being a publication adviser so worthwhile. He would also like to thank Mary Lynn Schaffer for her unwavering support; and Suzanne, Sarah and Stephen for their patience when their father was too busy to hear a piano program or play catch.

Randall McCutcheon would like to thank the following individuals for their assistance: Jane Durso for her immeasurable contributions; Todd Cooper, Jenn Crouse, Jane Holt—for their invaluable input on chapter rough drafts; Molly Dunn, Julie Gasseling, Andrea Goldberg, Laura Hochla, Dr. Michael McElroy, Emily Voth—for their assistance and generosity.

Kathryn T. Stofer gratefully acknowledges the generous contributions of John W. Wood, whose computer expertise and moral support made this project possible; Steven R. Lincoln and Brian A. Rosenthal, for their professional expertise on chapters 5 and 7; Sharon Behl Brooks for research and editing assistance; Lottie Fryer, Matt Helm, Emily P. Wagner, Lisa Maupin, Jarolyn Forney, Chris Jacquin and Melissa James for creative assistance; Hastings College students and the Hastings College *Collegian* for examples; Steven R. Lincoln, Michael Hancock and Chris Schukei for *This Just In* interviews.

◆ DEDICATIONS ◆

To Dolores, for her faith; to Debra, for her friendship; and to Tom, for his love of language
◆ *James Schaffer*

To my grandmother
◆ *Randall McCutcheon*

To Woody, Mimi, Tammie and Jeanne for their encouragement and their patience.
◆ *Kathryn T. Stofer*

REVIEWERS

The authors greatly appreciate the efforts of these reviewers:

Judy Babb
  Highland Park High School
  Dallas, Texas

Laurie Bielong
  Belleville West High School
  Belleville, Illinois

Mark Billingsley
  Travis High School
  Austin, Texas

Lynn Boshart
  Garden Grove High School
  Garden Grove, California

John Bowen
  Lakewood High School
  Lakewood, Ohio

Barclay Burrow
  Victoria High School
  Victoria, Texas

Danise Chandler
  George Washington High School
  San Francisco, California

Sister Mary Anne Coughlin
  Nazareth Academy
  Rochester, New York

Mary Ann Downs
  Bardstown High School
  Bardstown, Kentucky

Melanie Durfee
  Brighton High School
  Salt Lake City, Utah

Sue F. Farlow
  Asheboro High School
  Asheboro, North Carolina

Pat Graff
  La Cueva High School
  Albuquerque, New Mexico

Margaret Gregory
  Greenway High School
  Phoenix, Arizona

James D. Hand
  Harrison High School
  West Lafayette, Indiana

Stacey Hipps
  Hopewell High School
  Hopewell, Virginia

David Humpal
  Calallen High School
  Corpus Christi, Texas

Jim Jordan
  Del Campo High School
  Fair Oaks, California

Barbara Juliano
  Waldwick High School
  Waldwick, New Jersey

Jack Kennedy
  City High School
  Iowa City, Iowa

Deanne Kunz
  Westlake High School
  Austin, Texas

Andrea S. Martine
  Taylor Allderice High School
  Pittsburgh, Pennsylvania

Margaret Naples
  Holland Central High School
  Holland City, New York

Katherine Pekel
  Cambridge High School
  Cambridge, Minnesota

Geri Siener
  Taft High School
  Woodland Hills, California

Tony Sipp
  Cherry Hill High School East
  Cherry Hill, New Jersey

Diane Stanley
  Agoura High School
  Agoura Hills, California

Kathy Stockham
  Valley High School
  Valley, Nebraska

Shelley Straits
  Buckeye Valley High School
  Columbus, Ohio

Kathleen Swift
  Newton High School
  Sandy Nook, Connecticut

Carolyn Tillema
  Southeast High School
  Greensboro, North Carolina

E. Graham Ward
  Brooks School
  N. Andover, Massachusetts

John R. Williamson
  Johnson Central High School
  Paintsville, Kentucky

TIMELINE REMINDER

For a concise overview of significant milestones in the history
of journalism refer to the timeline on the following six pages.

3000 B. C. — BABYLONIA (now in Iraq), 3000 B.C.—Clay, stone and wooden tablets are used by the residents of Babylonia to advertise their businesses. (17)

THEBES, Egypt, 500 B.C.—Egyptians make papyrus, a form of paper, from the stems of the papyrus plant. (8)

Pre- A.D. — POMPEII, pre-A.D. 79—Merchants use stone or clay sings to advertise what they are selling. (14)

100 A.D. — CHINA, 100 A.D.—Paper and ink were developed by the Chinese more than 1000 years before Europeans began using them. (15)

1400 — STRASBOURG, Germany 1438—Johann Gutenberg begins working on a method of printing using moveable type. (15)

LONDON, 1480—William Caxton publishes the first advertisements in English. (17)

1600 — LONDON, 1614—Signs attached to buildings or swinging over doorways identify local inns and taverns. These signs are the forerunners of modern billboards. (17)

CAMBRIDGE, Mass., 1638—The first printing press is brought to America to print religious texts, such as the *Bay Psalm Book of 1640*, for students at Harvard College. (1)

BOSTON, Mass., September 25, 1690—Benjamin Harris publishes *Publick Occurences: Both Forreign and Domestick*, a four-page newspaper. (2)

1700 — BOSTON, Mass., August 7, 1721—James Franklin establishes *The New England Courant*. (2)

PHILADELPHIA, Pa., 1732—The first foreign language newspaper in the United States, the Philadelphia *Zeitung*, is printed by Benjamin Franklin. (1)

NEW YORK, N. Y., August 4, 1735—John Peter Zenger, editor of *The New York Weekly Journal*, is found not guilty of "raising sedition" against the government through columns printed in his newspaper. (2)

CHARLESTON, S.C., January 4, 1737—Elizabeth Timothy becomes the first woman publisher in the colonies when her husband Louis Timothy, an apprentice for the weekly *Charleston South Carolina Gazette*, is accidentally killed. (6)

PHILADELPHIA, January 1741—Printers Benjamin Franklin and Andrew Bradford race to put the first American magazine into print. (18)

PHILADELPHIA, Pa., May 9 , 1754—The first cartoon appears in the *Pennsylvania Gazette*. (11)

PHILADELPHIA, Pa., July 6, 1776—The *Pennsylvania Evening Post* is the first newspaper to print the Declaration of Independence. (2)

PHILADELPHIA, May 30, 1783—On this day, the Pennsylvania Evening Post became the first daily paper in America. (2)

— 1800

1807—President Thomas Jefferson is the first person who officially uses the term "public relations" in his *Writings*. (20)

NEW ORLEANS, 1808—The first Spanish-language newspaper in the United States, *El Misisipi*, is published. (1)

— 1810

LONDON, 1814—For the first time, the London Times used a steam-driven press. The press could print up to 1,100 sheets an hour. (15)

NEW ECHOTA, GEORGIA, 1818—The Cherokee Phoenix, printed partly in an 86-character Cherokee alphabet, became the first Native American newspaper. (1)

— 1820

NEW YORK, N.Y., March 16, 1827—The first black newspaper, *Freedom's Journal*, is published. Founded by John B. Russwurm and the Rev. Samuel E. Cornish, *Freedom's Journal* is a response to racist attacks by other newspapers. (4)

— 1830

NEW YORK, N.Y., September 3, 1833—The *New York Sun* is the first penny paper. A paper for common working folk, it carries mostly sensationalized human interest news with a touch of humor. (9)

NEW YORK, N.Y., 1835—Regular Pony Express service is established between New York and Philadelphia by the postmaster. (4)

— 1840

BALTIMORE, Md., May 24, 1844—"What hath God wrought?" The first electromagnetic telegraph message is transmitted over a telegraph line from Baltimore to inventor Samuel F. B. Morse who receives it in the U. S. Supreme Court chamber. (4)

NEW YORK, N.Y., January 11, 1849—The first cooperative news gathering service, Harbor News Association, is formally organized by six New York daily newspapers. (4)

— 1850

LONDON, August 16, 1858—"Glory to God in the highest, on earth peace, good will toward men," is the first message sent over the Atlantic Cable connecting London and the United States. (7)

— 1860

USA, 1866—The completion of the Atlantic Cable enabled an American wire service, the New York Associated Press, to exchange news with a British wire service, Reuters. (4)

— 1870

PHILADELPHIA, 1874—One of the most famous American editorial cartoonists, Thomas Nast, introduced the elephant as the symbol of the Republican Party in a cartoon in Harper's Weekly. He also made the donkey popular as a symbol of the Democratic Party. (11)

BOSTON, Mass., March 10, 1876—Alexander Graham Bell successfully demonstrates his system for transmitting voices over wire by sending for his assistant, Thomas A. Watson, in their Boston laboratory. (5)

MENLO PARK, N.J., 1877—"Mary had a little lamb . . " Thomas Alva Edison shouts the nursery rhyme against the recording diaphragm of a model phonograph his assistant constructed from Edison's sketch. (7)

1880 —

GERMANY, 1887—In laboratory experiments with what would become known as "Hertzian waves," physicist Heinrich Hertz proves the existence of radio energy and measures the length of a radio wave. (13)

NEW YORK, N.Y., 1889—Started by Charles H. Dow and Edward D. Jones as a financial news service for Dow Jones and Company, the *Wall Street Journal* has the largest circulation of any traditional newspaper in the United States. (11)

NEW YORK, 1889—Richard Outcault's cartoon character, the "Yellow Kid," gives a journalistic style practiced in the last decades of the 1800s its name: *yellow journalism*. (6)

1890 —

NEW YORK, 1895—William Randolph Hearst, heir to a wealthy California family, bought the *New York Journal* and brought his own version of "Gee-whiz" journalism to the East Coast. (8)

LONDON, 1896—Italian inventor Guglielmo Marconi, registers a patent in London for instruments to send and receive communications by wireless telegraphy. (5)

NEW YORK, N.Y., August 18, 1896—"All the News That's Fit to Print" becomes the motto of *The New York Times* when Adolph S. Ochs is editor. (3)

1900 —

NEW YORK, N.Y., 1904—Former *New York Times* and *New York Journal* reporter Ivy Ledbetter Lee opens a publicity firm dedicated to honest and truthful promotion of clients in New York. (20)

1904—Magazines become instigators for social reform in the early twentieth century, and their style of investigative reporting is labeled "muckraking" by President Teddy Roosevelt. McClure's Magazine becomes the leader in the muckraking efforts with the publication of exposes on the Standard Oil Company by Ida M. Tarbell. (9)

BRANT ROCK, Mass., December 24, 1906—Using the same waves Marconi used, Canadian Reginald A. Fessenden broadcasts music and Christmas messages. (8)

NEW YORK, N.Y., December 1906—The father of modern radio, Lee de Forest, patents the key element of radio, the Audio tube, but it takes another decade to perfect the circuitry to make it work. (19)

USA, 1907—The word "television" is first used in an article in *Scientific American* magazine. (6)

SAN JOSE, Calif., 1909—The first radio station to have a regular schedule of programs is experimental station FN owned by Charles D. "Doc" Herrold. (19)

— 1910

NEW JERSEY, 1911—French film maker Charles Pathe introduces the silent newsreel to American theatres. (4)

NEWFOUNDLAND BANKS, April 14-15, 1912—The Wireless Ship Act, the first U. S. Radio law, passed in 1910 required a radio and operator on all ocean-going passenger vessels; unfortunately it could not save the Titanic when it struck an iceberg on its maiden voyage. (10)

NEW YORK, November 7, 1916—Despite the fact that he got the result wrong, Lee de Forest broadcast the first presidential election results. DeForest estimated that Charles E. Hughes had defeated Woodrow Wilson. (19)

USA, 1919—Coast-to-coast telephone service became possible, less than 50 years after the invention of the telephone. (5)

— 1920

USA, 1920-1950—Known as the Golden Age of Broadcasting, these decades bring news and entertainment into American homes via sound. (1)

PITTSBURGH, Pa., November 2, 1920—KDKA, the first fully licensed commercial station for standard broadcasting, goes on the air from a studio in East Pittsburgh with a broadcast of returns from the Harding-Cox presidential election interspersed with live banjo and phonograph music. (11)

NEW YORK, N.Y., August 16, 1922—Station WEAF goes on the air on August 16 as the first commercial radio station. (17)

WASHINGTON, D.C., 1923—President Warren G. Harding's face is immortalized through wireless transmissions when Charles Francis Jenkins sends likeness of Harding to Washington from Philadelphia by wireless transmission. (14)

1923—Vladimir K. Zworykin, known as the "Father of Television," immigrates from Russia to the United States. Four years later, working as an engineer for Westinghouse, Zworykin patents the first electronic camera pickup tube. (9)

LONDON, January 26, 1923—The first instantaneous moving pictures transmitted and demonstrated by Scotsman, John Logie Baird. (5)

NEW YORK, N.Y., November 15, 1926—The National Broadcast Company goes on the air with a four and one-half hour broadcast of music and comedy. (10)

SAN FRANCISCO, Calif., 1927—The first electronic television pictures are transmitted by a self-taught 21-year-old American inventor, Philo T. Farnsworth; he calls his new scanning and synchronizing system "image dissection." (11)

USA, 1927—Philco makes the first automobile radio. (1)

WASHINGTON, D.C., 1927—Herbert E. Ives, working in the Bell Telephone Laboratories, sends a picture with synchronized sound of then Secretary of Commerce Herbert Hoover's voice from Washington to New York. (14)

USA, September 18, 1927—The Columbia Broadcasting Company, later known as CBS, began broadcasting with a music variety show. (10)

NEW YORK, N.Y., 1928—A new show, called *Newscasting*, is introduced by radio station WOR. (6)

1930 —

LONDON, November 2, 1936—The British Broadcasting Company goes on the air with the world's first open-circuit TV broadcasts. The BBC is the first television station in the world to offer regular programming. (13)

GROVER'S MILL, N.J., October 30, 1938—H. G. Wells' novel, "The War of the Worlds," is adapted as a radio drama by Mercury Theater of the Air. The drama includes simulated news bulletins announcing that aliens are invading the countryside. (10)

NEW YORK, N.Y., April 30, 1939—David Sarnoff chooses the World's Fair to launch regular television broadcasting by the National Broadcasting Company. The first telecast from the fair featured President Franklin D. Roosevelt, the first president to appear on television. (20)

NEW YORK, May 17, 1939—The first televised sports event, a baseball game between Princeton and Columbia universities, was carried on NBC. (6)

1940 —

NEW YORK, N.Y., July 1, 1941—Commercial television is born when both NBC and CBS were granted licenses on the same day for their New York stations. That same year CBS began televising sporadic news reports shortly after the U.S. entered World War II. The first regularly scheduled network news was broadcast on NBC in 1945. (10)

MAY, 1946—A government freeze on the construction of new stations and a halt in the production of television sets during World War II slows the momentum of the developing television industry. (19)

JUNE, 1948—Three Bell Laboratory engineers, John Bardeen, Walter Brattain, and William Schockley, demonstrate the transistor, a tiny, solid, crystal block which would replace the fragile, bulky tube construction in radios and televisions. (9)

MAHONEY, Pa., 1948—The first cable antenna television (CATV) system starts when local appliance dealer, John Walson, erects a television antenna atop a mountain and, for a hook-up fee and monthly payment, grants user rights to his neighbors. (13)

1950 —

USA, 1954—Small, easily portable transistor radios went on the market. (9)

1959—Two engineers working separately, Jack Kilby and Robert Noyce, invent the integrated circuit, or computer "chip." Each man's invention has advantages the other lacked, but Kilby eventually won the patent rights to the invention. (16)

MOSCOW, April 12, 1961—Soviet space officials held the first radio talks with a human in space when cosmonaut Yuri Gagarin circled the earth for one hour and 48 minutes. (7)

July 10, 1962—Telestar I, an experimental communications satellite, is launched by the U.S. National Aeronautics and Space Administration. Telestar I relays telephone calls and sends the first trans-Atlantic broadcast making live telecasts between Europe and the United States possible.

MOON, July 20, 1969—"That's one small step for man, one giant leap for mankind," Astronaut Neil A. Armstrong announces as he steps from the Eagle onto the surface of the moon. (7)

1970—The television industry downsizes equipment until reporters can cover on-the-spot news with portable cameras and send pictures back to the station via microwave or satellite relay. (3)

USA, 1970—Computers began replacing typewriters in newsrooms in the 1970s, touching off a revolution in journalistic technology. (16)

1972—Sony introduces the video cassette recorder (VCR) for educational and business uses.

COLUMBUS, OH., 1977—Residents are introduced to QUBE, an interactive cable television system which allows viewers the ability to talk to cable operators who forward information to the source of the programming. (1)

USA, 1982—The FCC agreed upon rules for using direct broadcast satellites, and rooftop dishes on homes became a reality. (1)

WASHINGTON, D.C., September 15, 1982—*USA Today* becomes recognized as the first successful national general interest newspaper. (3)

LONDON and PHILADELPHIA, July 13, 1985—An estimated world-wide audience of 1.5 billion tune in to the 16-hour Live Aid concert broadcast simultaneously from London and Philadelphia. The Live Aid campaign raises pledges of over $70 million for African famine relief. (18)

USA, 1988—For the first time, more than half of all U.S. homes had VCRs. (18)

SWITZERLAND, 1990—The World Wide Web is developed, enabling anyone with a computer to establish a home page on the Internet. (1)

USA, 1995—The sale of home computers exceeded the sale of television sets in the United States for the first time, less than 50 years after the first computer component was invented. (16)

SAN FRANCISCO, August 7, 1996—Over 6 million Internet customers were left stranded when America Online computer system crashed. Service finally resumed about 19 hours later. (1)

— 1960

— 1970

— 1980

— 1990

SECTION 1

Thinking Like a Journalist

Chapter 1
Community Voices

"At our best, we try to bear witness to the truth . . . give voice to the voiceless . . . present heroes, fools and villains and all the surprises that entails."

—Shelby Coffey, newspaper editor

KEY TERMS

In this chapter, you will learn the meaning of these terms:

weekly newspaper
daily newspaper
journalism
journalist
credibility
verify
objectivity
First Amendment
commentary
public journalism

LEARNING OBJECTIVES

After completing this chapter, you will be able to:

◆ discuss how journalism can contribute to a sense of community,

◆ identify the roles and responsibilities of journalists,

◆ discuss why valuing diversity makes journalistic efforts stronger.

◆

J ournalism, the effort to gather and report news, is a vital force in your life and in the life of your community. The news media (newspapers, magazines, television, radio and computer networks) help people communicate with one another. They give voice to community members who applaud and complain, compliment and criticize, suggest and apologize.

Journalism enables people to maintain an ongoing conversation about who they are and what they want their communities to be. Most high schools give voice to their communities through newspapers, electronic broadcasts or both. Howard K. Smith, a former commentator for ABC News, estimated that at least four-fifths of what the average citizen learns about the world "comes filtered through observations of the journalist." If what Smith said is true, then journalists help shape our perception of reality. They have an enormous responsibility to be truthful, fair and ethical. They also must compete with a great number of distractions.

In this chapter, you will learn how journalists help people determine the important issues and concerns in their communities. You will learn about the different roles and responsibilities journalists exercise and gain insight into how journalists provide a way for all people to be heard and understood.

▲THE VALUE OF VOICES

Have you ever found yourself surrounded by so much noise that you could hardly think? *Weather 100 times a day . . . SportsCenter . . . CNN . . . People . . . "You give us 22 minutes, we'll give you the world" . . . MTV . . . the Comedy Channel . . . Sharper Image catalog . . . the computer bulletin board . . . the phone in the car, plane and toilet . . . the fax paper unrolling . . . the pager chirping . . .* At times this babble can be deafening. We sometimes feel as if we are drowning in a sea of messages. "Ours is the age of distraction," notes writer Bill McKibben.

One consequence of all this noise is that we often don't hear what is actually important. When so much is being said, we find it difficult to sort out what is genuinely meaningful from what is merely superficial. Furthermore, some voices are lost in the scramble for airtime, and some voices are never even heard.

Regardless of how "electronic" we have become, consumers still want to read. This college student pauses to buy the local paper even though he can access news on the Internet in his dorm.

Much of this dismaying distraction comes from the media—the roar of cable television, talk radio, worldwide computer networks and tabloid newspapers. Yet the journalistic portion of all this noise—the news media—offers our best hope for finding meaning amid all the din. That's why responsible journalism is crucial to the success of our democracy. By enabling citizens to exchange both news and views, journalists provide a means for communities to achieve an understanding of competing points of view, and perhaps to reach consensus on the critical issues of the day.

Weekly Newspapers Serve Communities

Small-town **weekly newspapers** play an important role in helping us cope with today's world. They are published once a week and can generally be found in towns with populations of 5,000 or fewer. "CNN is not going to come in here and cover the local spelling bee," says Terry Sholin, editor of the *Hobbs Flare* in rural New Mexico. "But we're going to be there, and we're going to take a picture of the winning kid, and we're going to publish it." The object of weekly papers, Sholin explains, is to provide a showcase for life's small victories. "There's a sense of intimacy between the community and a weekly paper," he says.

At a time when many **daily newspapers** (papers published every day, with the exception in some cases of weekends) are struggling to keep subscribers and advertisers, weekly newspapers are thriving. According to the National Newspaper Association, more people (about 66 million) read weekly papers than dailies, and usually at a cheaper price—the average cost of these papers is less than fifty cents a week.

weekly newspaper

a paper published once a week, usually in a small town

daily newspaper

a paper published once a day (except in some cases on weekends), usually in a large town or city

Weekly newspapers typically cover the day-to-day activities of their readers—often in intimate detail. A dog with its head stuck in a drainpipe merits a story and a follow-up, but the only way the president could get an obituary would be to die right in town. "You can find out who found a snake in their garden, who died and the time of their death in relation to when their spouse died," explained Howard Smith, a devoted reader of the *Guntersville (Ala.) Advertiser-Gleam.* "It's what's what" (*American Journalism Review*).

Here, for example, are some items from one week's edition of the *Gleam:*

- A man who tried to pry his change from a Pepsi machine spent hours with his arm trapped inside.
- The keys to the city were stolen.
- The vandal who had been striking the fire chief's office turned out to be a squirrel.

Elsewhere in the paper you might find photos of the ostrich races at the county fair, a report on water levels in local lakes and highlights of the Pee Wee baseball league games. If you read a weekly paper, you know what all your neighbors are doing.

In many ways, weekly papers resemble high school newspapers. Both provide information about things that are going to happen or have happened—public auctions and bake sales, city council and student council meetings, grocery specials and who made homecoming court.

THIS JUST IN: *Portrait of a Young Journalist*
Julienne Gasseling, editor, Minden (Neb.) Courier

One month after she took over as editor of the *Minden (Neb.) Courier,* Julienne Gasseling, 25, was embroiled in controversy. The school board was being sued over possible violations of open meeting laws as well as its bid-letting procedures. The *Courier* needed to report the stories accurately and at the same time provide the voice of reason through its editorials.

As the new editor of a small-town newspaper, Gasseling covers everything from ribbon cuttings to retirements. The *Courier* even features a "resident of the month" at retirement homes. Gasseling has already given the paper a facelift. She changed the masthead and layout style to make the *Courier* more "engaging and enjoyable to its readers."

Gasseling's career in journalism began with a three-week internship at the *Alliance Times Herald,* a small daily in western Nebraska. She knew that working at a small newspaper would allow her the opportunity to better learn the business. "You've got to love what you're doing," Gasseling says, "or you're never going to make it."

What lies ahead for Gasseling and the *Courier?* She plans to add county court news. The newspaper hasn't carried court news for years, and county officials are reluctant to make the information available. Gasseling points out, however, that "the first thing people want to know is who's in trouble."

Making Connections

Most high schools resemble communities—communities with many roles and niches. The principal acts a bit like the town mayor, the student council resembles a group of community leaders, and everyone else is busy pursuing a wide array of interests. In a high school, a good newspaper, radio program or television broadcast reports on all those activities, keeping the members of the community in touch with one another.

The transmission of this feeling of being connected to one's neighbors is ultimately what makes journalism important. No other endeavor can do as much to help people talk about the political, social, environmental and personal choices they face in an increasingly impersonal world. Small weekly papers connect local communities, whereas large daily papers connect metropolitan areas and statewide communities.

National papers, such as the *Wall Street Journal* and *USA Today,* provide a sense of connection for a national community. Connectedness on a global scale is rapidly becoming a reality. Cable News Network (CNN) is a television network that provides 24-hour news coverage and is reportedly a favorite of political leaders worldwide. The Internet functions as an information superhighway that can link a computer in Delaware with another in New Delhi.

A high school student delivers the results of the student council election during a student-produced radio program.

1. Discuss with classmates your sources for news. Where do you learn new information about school events and activities, about fads and fashions, about your friends and acquaintances? Are you a news source yourself? How often? For what kind of information?

2. Keep a media diary for a week in which you record every time you use any news medium—including newspapers, magazines, radio and television, friends, teachers and acquaintances. At the end of the week, compare your diary with those of other students. Can you determine whether some kinds of information are more reliable than others?

THE ROLES AND RESPONSIBILITIES OF JOURNALISM

journalism
> the gathering and reporting of the news

Journalism is traditionally defined as the gathering and reporting of the news. In other words, journalism represents a search for truth.

journalist

> a person who gathers and reports the news (for example, reporters, TV anchors and radio correspondents) or who provides the financial, managerial and technical support that is necessary to transmit the news (for example, publishers, station owners, directors and camera operators)

credibility

> the belief that what someone says is true

verify

> to check for accuracy

Journalists include both those who gather and report news (reporters, TV anchors and radio correspondents) and those who provide the financial, managerial and technical support that is necessary to bring the news to the rest of us (publishers, station owners, directors, camera operators and so on).

The Responsibilities of Journalists

Whether we believe what we hear through the news media or not depends on the **credibility** of the source. Credibility refers to the degree to which the public believes what it reads and hears. That is why absolute accuracy is the most important responsibility journalists bear. No excuse can be accepted for sloppy or inaccurate reporting because journalists pay a huge price for being wrong: people no longer listen to them.

People decide how credible a source is in many ways, but a source's attention to detail is certainly high on the list of factors people consider. A good journalist always double-checks names for correct spellings and numbers for the correct decimal points. Reporters **verify** a fact (check it for accuracy) by finding two or more people who can confirm it. For example, although one witness to an explosion might say that it happened at 10 p.m., a good reporter would not be satisfied until he or she had sought out at least one more witness—perhaps a police or fire department official—to confirm the time.

The news media's credibility is at stake now more than ever. A study by the Center for the People and the Press reveals that the public often looks on the press with the same disdain and cynicism it usually reserves for politicians. Seven out of 10 Americans, according to the study, think the press "gets in the way of society solving its problems."

Print and broadcast journalists often compete with one another to get a fast-breaking news story.

Accurate reporting, however, is not enough. Journalists must also strive to be fair, balanced and objective. To be fair to all sides in a controversy, for example, the media must give each side its chance to be heard. Balance requires that the reporter always consider what the minority view might be (for instance, a reporter might seek a comment from someone on the losing side in a community vote to build a new school). **Objectivity,** perhaps the most difficult quality to achieve in covering the news, means that the reporter keeps all personal feelings and bias out of the report. To the greatest extent possible, reporters work to present the facts in a straightforward and neutral manner. Interpretations, views and opinions are reserved for the editorial page.

objectivity
> a lack of personal feelings or bias

The Roles of Journalists

The news media are frequently accused of representing a particular political point of view, but the truth is that most journalists strive for a high standard of objectivity. They conduct their work in a professional and ethical manner—gathering and then spreading information with accuracy, objectivity, fairness and balance. Journalists provide society with a spotlight. They use their privileged status and access, guaranteed by the **First Amendment,** to shine the light of scrutiny on various areas of public activity. The First Amendment is the first of ten amendments to the Constitution included in the Bill of Rights. It guarantees, among other things, freedom of speech and freedom of the press.

Journalists also provide a database for their communities. A typical newspaper, for example, provides an enormous amount of information that can be sampled by easy browsing. In addition to major local, state, national and international developments, papers often provide "briefs"—short tidbits of news to help the average reader. These items can include school lunch menus, street closings, winning lottery numbers, obituaries, TV and movie listings, and the weather, including pollen counts and "sneeze" indexes.

The third part of what journalists do is provide an open forum through which members of a community can discuss what they find important, significant or simply fun. Like the forum in ancient Rome, journalism today provides a place for people in communities, large and small, to converse with one another as they share news, tips, ideas and personal stories. In other words, journalists keep democracy in motion. As members of a community, when we write letters to the editor, call in to talk radio, tune in to a local cable television program, or log on to an online chat group, we are participating in journalism.

First Amendment
> amendment to the U.S. Constitution that provides a right to free speech and a free press

Journalism as a Spotlight.   For better or worse, journalism provides a spotlight to examine people and events. Journalists set an agenda for public issues by the choices they make regarding what stories to cover and what stories to ignore. They also give greater priority or prominence to some stories (by placing them on the front page or at the beginning of a broadcast) than to others. These decisions are largely

Hope Journalism

Burned out on crime and fed up with the antics of celebrities? Relief may be at a newsstand near you. A new magazine and wire service have started offering hope journalism—news about real people who make a difference.

"There are a quarter of a billion people in this country. If you read the paper, you get the feeling that most of them are involved in drugs and mayhem, crime and disaster," said Paul Martin Du Bois, who founded the American News Service. "A significant proportion of this quarter-billion population are also involved very constructively in addressing the issues of education, housing, the environment, integration, inadequate human services and poverty."

So with unsung heroes in mind, the American News Service and *Hope* magazine are delivering a different kind of news. "I think that we both want to call attention to the extraordinary acts and efforts of ordinary individuals," said Jon Wilson, editor and publisher of *Hope*. His magazine looks chiefly at the accomplishments of individuals. One issue, for example, featured articles about a cellist who played in the streets of Sarajevo during a bombing, a former drug addict who now runs an outreach program for gang members in Boston, and a carpenter who built his new wife a house as he was dying of cancer.

related to the journalist's efforts to be the citizen's advocate in examining the activities of public officials and organizations.

Providing Information.   The news media seek to provide accurate, up-to-date information on events that affect the lives of their audience, whether those events happen nearby or around the world. Newspapers keep their readers current on daily and weekly events, whereas television and radio bring those events to life through sights and sounds.

For example, when several teens who were avid users of computer bulletin boards disappeared, the media turned its spotlight on a significant threat: "A 13-year-old Kentucky girl, apparently lured away from home by an electronic computer message nearly two weeks ago, was taken into protective custody in Los Angeles after she contacted authorities" *(Los Angeles Times)*. Meanwhile, in the high school press, reporters seek out stories that help students with their problems. For example, "Twenty percent of all high school students fall asleep during school, according to the National Parent Information Network" (*West Wind,* Bellevue, Nebr.).

Acting As A Lookout.   Journalism also acts as a spotlight to protect the rights of citizens. Journalists routinely report on the activities of business, government and other areas of society that might have an impact on our lives. They investigate and expose wrongdoing when they believe the government may not be acting in the best interests of the people.

What started as a class project for some Northwestern University journalism students resulted in the release of three prison inmates wrongfully charged with a brutal rape and murder. This remarkable accomplishment began when Professor David Protess described a few controversial legal decisions in his investigative reporting class. One court case in particular intrigued three seniors in the class. It involved a man who had recently been executed. Hours before his death, the man had made Protess promise to do his best to save the life of a fellow death row inmate he believed was innocent. That man's case was the one that seniors Stacey Delo, Laura Sullivan and Stephanie Goldstein chose to investigate for their class project.

Legwork and determination led the students across Chicago to Ford Heights, the area where the three inmates had lived. Sometimes with their professor, sometimes on their own, the women asked questions of those who knew the men or knew someone who knew them. The students talked to crack dealers, ex-convicts and ordinary people. "It's kind of a weird version of the college road trip," Goldstein said.

Eventually, the students found a man who said he knew the real killers. The students' discoveries persuaded prosecutors to agree to conduct deoxyribonucleic acid (DNA) tests on the men who were serving time for the crime. The results showed that none of them had committed the rape. "That three people are walking out of a prison where they've been sitting for 18 years, and to know you had some direct impact on that is a good feeling," Delo said.

Journalists also act as sentries. They stand on the watchtowers of society, looking for future trends. They alert us to exciting and sometimes dangerous possibilities. For example, student journalists in Chicago reported the following: "In Chicago, a rash of shootings in and around high schools has prompted Mayor Richard Daley to offer metal detectors free to city schools. As violence in schools becomes more frequent around the country, administrators have been tightening security—locking doors, hiring guards and installing metal detectors" (*U-High Midway,* University High School, Chicago).

Journalism as a Database.

A second role journalism fills is to provide communities with a database. A database typically contains a large amount of information that can be accessed in a variety of ways. You might think of a library as a database, for example, or perhaps a CD-ROM version of the encyclopedia. A typical daily newspaper contains a wide variety of informative items beyond the regular news stories. These items can include the following:

- Box scores and standings to help sports fans find out how their favorite teams and players are doing.
- Weather forecasts to help travelers learn what they can expect at their destinations.
- A new partner for the lonely or lovelorn in the Personals section.
- Current mortgage interest rates for home buyers.
- Details of governmental budgets for concerned taxpayers.
- Maps to help readers understand where events are taking place.
- Charts and graphs to help turn numbers into meaningful ideas.

Learning how to use these data effectively is part of becoming an efficient, media-savvy consumer. Many newspapers now offer online services to help readers. The *Washington Post,* for example, routinely refers readers to its site on the World Wide Web. When the *Post* ran a story on the "compliment man," an unemployed cook who had spent the last five years offering rapid-fire flattery to the milling crowds outside some of Washington's busiest restaurants and hotels, it offered readers this note at the conclusion of the story:

> FOR MORE INFORMATION
> Have you heard from the Compliment Man? Post your story on the *Post's* site on the World Wide Web at http://www.washingtonpost.com (*Washington Post*)

Other stories in the *Post* refer readers to the Web site for background information on international stories, for maps or charts, or for access to other information in the *Post's* extensive database.

A similar but more traditional way to think of this journalistic role is to consider the news media as a marketplace of ideas. In this market, the goods are usually ideas—bits of information, news and opinions. In some shops reporters tell the news; in others, editorialists interpret

---

DATELINE

BOSTON, Sept. 25, 1690—The first newspaper in the American colonies appeared on the streets of Boston. The paper, called *Publick Occurrences Both Forreign and Domestick,* was scheduled to appear "once a month (or if any Glut of Occurrences happen, oftener)." The paper measured just 6 inches by 10¼ inches and was printed on three pages. The fourth page was left blank for readers to add their own items before passing the paper along to other readers.

The newspaper's publisher, Benjamin Harris, was an English printer whose London newspaper had been shut down years before by government authorities. He was eventually exiled to the colonies, where he opened a coffeehouse and bookshop in Boston.

Publick Occurrences included both local and foreign news. Articles reported that "Christianized Indians" had declared a day of thanks for the harvest, and some Mohawk Indians were treating French prisoners too harshly. The paper also reported that an epidemic of "Fevers and Agues" had left many people too sick to work.

As interesting as all this sounds, however, the first issue was the last. The royal governor ordered the paper permanently closed. Massachusetts Bay officials found the paper "in bad taste," and Harris had failed to get the required printing license.

events and tell us what they think the events will mean. All of us, in one way or another, are shopping for news and information.

As you turn the pages of a newspaper or switch channels on your radio or TV set, imagine you are moving from shop to shop. Some of the merchants shout at you in loud voices, whereas others wait quietly for you to come to them. At some shops you buy things. At others you just browse and move on. You pass by some shops without a second glance.

Everyone has a voice in this marketplace, and the marketplace is open to all who want to walk through. This role of journalism includes several important responsibilities: to interpret and explain, to entertain and amuse, and to keep a permanent record of the community's activities.

Interpreting and Explaining.   Journalists help their readers and listeners to understand and interpret the stories of the day. The following story, for example, helps readers understand the implications of a new scientific study:

> For centuries expectant mothers have been seeking simple ways to predict the sex of their babies. Researchers have found a clue: Women who suffer severe morning sickness early in pregnancy are more likely to have a girl.
>
> The finding by epidemiologists at Stockholm's Karolinska Institute may give credence to an observation once made by Hippocrates, physician to the ancient Greeks and the father of Western medicine.
>
> He said that a woman carrying a female baby has a pale face, whereas if she is carrying a male baby, she has a healthy tone to her skin. (*Associated Press*)

commentary

a personal view offered in a radio or TV program

Those in charge of newspapers and broadcast stations have opinions just as everyone else does. Radio and television programs often offer personal views, usually called **commentaries,** to help shape public opinion. Newspaper editors share their opinions on the editorial page. For example, here is the beginning of an editorial on a problem nearly every teenager can recognize:

> Every teen has faced at least one encounter with age discrimination. There are the sales people who happen to follow young people around, as if they are just waiting for them to steal something. There are also job applications. They are often filled with great references and honest answers; yet, that empty employment past always manages to turn the manager's expression into a scowl.
>
> Is this ageism? No, not exactly. Ageism, according to *USA Today*, is the prejudice against older people. Yet, shouldn't this definition also include the younger people so often ignored and avoided? (*Saguaro Sabercat,* Saguaro High School, Scottsdale, Ariz.)

Newspapers also invite interested readers to respond to editorials or to express their opinions in the form of letters or guest columns.

Entertaining and Amusing.   Surveys show that readers look to the news media for entertainment as well as information. We all like to be diverted occasionally from the serious issues of the day. Comics, cross-

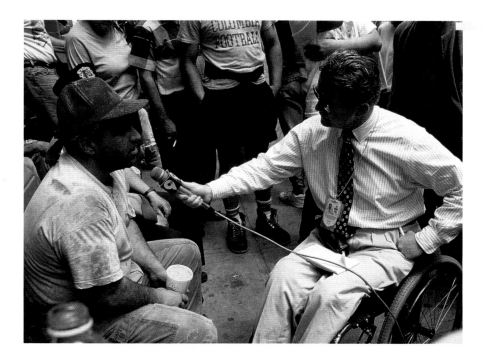

Shop with This Speciality Newspaper

"Be on the lookout and keep your camera ready—celebrity sightings run rampant at Mall of America." At least that's what it says in *Best of the Mall*, a unique newspaper printed weekly by the Mall of America in Bloomington, Minnesota. Not many malls are large enough to have their own newspaper, but this mall could hold seven Yankee Stadiums. By another measure, it's five times larger than Red Square in Moscow.

The *Best of the Mall* is an eight-page, full-size color paper with features on upcoming events, celebrity visits, tips for covering the mall's 4.2 million square feet, and articles on fashion trends. You can also find a directory for the mall's 14 movie screens and a map of Camp Snoopy, the mall's amusement park. Now if you're too tired to shop any more, you can read about it.

word puzzles and even advice columns provide entertainment and give a lighter side to the news. For example, one reporter decided to investigate the funny, odd or just bizarre messages people leave on their answering machines:

> The answering machine is 25 years old—more than enough time for owners to come up with the most annoying, buoying or cloying messages to amuse or offend callers' ears.
>
> Half of all households now sport answering machines. Sales of the devices rang up $1.1 billion in 1995 alone, according to the makers of Casio PhoneMate.
>
> One local resident uses this mystifying message: "Hi! You have reached the number you dialed. If this is a wrong number, please hang up and consult your directory. If this is the number you intended to reach, please call back when I'm here and we'll have a lovely chat! 'Til then, so long!" (*Lincoln Journal-Star*)

Journalists also provide reviews of various kinds of entertainment including movies, CDs, concerts, and even haunted houses:

> Halloween's right around the corner, and you and your friends are trying to decide which haunted house to go to first. Survey says: The Fright Zone, located on 17th and California streets.
>
> Talk about scary. A word to the wise: If you have to use the restroom before going, please do. That's how scary it was. (*Central High School Register*, Omaha, Nebr.)

Television and radio news programs are often as entertaining as they are informative. The CBS News program *60 Minutes,* consistently one of the most watched shows on television, proves that well-told news stories can be fascinating. National Public Radio frequently brings listeners many delightfully interesting and informative programs; one of them is *Car Talk,* a show devoted to car repair.

Keeping A Record. Journalists engaged in creating a community database have one other important, but unglamorous, role: to keep track of everything. Newspapers serve future historians by keeping accurate records. All the details of public life—elections, births, deaths, weddings, anniversaries, crimes and court records—are duly recorded and thus preserved for our children and grandchildren. Sometimes those records require some explanation: "Don Furcillo, 86, who claims to be actor Jack Nicholson's dad and is dying in a Florida hospital, wants to see the movie star before he departs, but Nicholson isn't having it. The actor, born to an unwed mother, was raised by his grandmother. Furcillo said Nicholson once acknowledged the paternal connection in a phone call years ago but told him not to write any more letters and go away" (*Miami Herald*).

The New York Times prides itself on being the paper of record in the United States. The *Times* is careful to print the complete text of important speeches.

Journalism as an Open Forum.

A third role journalism plays is to act as an open forum. At a time when so much divides us, what draws people together? How do we create a sense of belonging, a sense of being part of a community? One basic way is to share our hopes and dreams. This is where the role of journalism as a forum becomes significant.

Communities are those places where we live, work and play. A family is one kind of community. A neighborhood is another. You might think of communities as a series of larger and larger concentric circles, each with you as the midpoint. Thus, you belong to your home, your neighborhood, your town, your county, your state, your region, your country, your hemisphere and so on.

A character in Thornton Wilder's famous play *Our Town* ponders her sense of community as she studies the return address on a letter. The address first lists the character's name (Jane Crofut), then her home (Crofut farm), her town (Grover's Corners), her state (New Hampshire), her country, her planet, her solar system and finally "the mind of God." In this dramatic sense, our community is our return address, the place where we tell others that we can be reached.

But living in a community is not the same as belonging to one, and that's where journalism fits in. A new style of journalism, called **public journalism,** seeks to revitalize public life, to promote a sense among ordinary folks that their institutions belong to them. The idea of this style of journalism is to help turn inhabitants into citizens.

In the past, "old-style" journalism tended to focus on political horse races (who's ahead, who's gaining and who's losing). It covered battles

public journalism

a style of journalism that seeks to revitalize public life and to promote a sense among members of the public that their institutions actually belong to them

among political leaders and self-styled experts, all in the name of the public interest. But this kind of journalism often left out a vast number of ordinary people, who began to feel a sense of isolation from the public life of their communities. Public journalism goes beyond politicians, experts and special interest groups to find out what ordinary people think about the issues discussed in the media and what they think are the real issues. Public journalists look for a complexity of opinion, not just for a pair of adversaries.

A superb example of public journalism ran on the front page of the *Miami Herald* a few months after a ValuJet airplane crashed in the Florida Everglades. The story profiled Mitch Bridges, a guide and airboat operator who assisted law enforcement officials in locating the remains of the plane and its passengers in the swamps of southern Florida. Bridges not only helped search parties steer clear of alligators and water moccasins, but also showed an uncanny ability to distinguish one patch of the Everglades from another. "I could take them back to the same blade of grass where we stopped the day before," he said. "They couldn't understand how I did that." Local officials did appreciate his efforts, however. The Metro-Dade Police Department awarded Bridges and his son the Silver Medal of Valor, its highest civilian award.

Keeping Democracy in Motion. During the past few years a number of newspapers across the country have launched public service projects that go beyond reporting and editorializing to provide hands-on community leadership. The *Battle Creek (Mich.) Enquirer,* for example, organized a town meeting on the problem of teens and drinking. Relying on an advisory group of high school students and parents for help, the paper developed stories outlining the problems. The town meeting lead to community education and intervention programs.

Two of the most popular items in the *Bloomington (Ind.) Herald-Times* invite the active involvement of readers. One is a reader-response column called Hotline. Readers call or write in with questions about credit cards, health, sexual harassment, local building projects and much more. Answers are published five days a week at the back of Section A. Another popular feature with readers is the Neighbors section, published twice a week. Readers submit news items and photos on school events and other happenings in the community that would otherwise not get covered.

We can get a good sense of how journalism can serve a community by taking a close look at what a yearbook staff in a small town did for a class project. Forty journalism students in Nebraska's Elkhorn High School, together with their adviser and 15 local residents, decided to do something special to commemorate the 50th anniversary of their school. They decided to record virtually everything that happened in the life of their community on just one day. The result was a display of 220 photographs and 40 essays that detail the life and character of their hometown.

"I got the idea from the book *A Day in the Life of America,*" explained the students' adviser, Penny Sander. "It was a collection of photographs

Building a Better Newspaper

Throughout history, leading thinkers have offered proposals to change newspapers to better meet the needs of their communities:

◆ Thomas Jefferson suggested that editors divide their newspapers into four sections: Truths, Probabilities, Possibilities, and Lies.

◆ The poet Johann Wolfgang von Goethe thought that in order to avoid trivial affairs, one should let newspapers age for a month before reading them.

◆ The novelist Albert Camus suggested creating a "control newspaper," which would publish reviews of articles from other newspapers, and estimate their accuracy and bias. "But," Camus wondered, "do people really want to know how much truth there is in what they read? Would they buy the control paper? That's the most difficult problem."

Source: Adapted from Stephen Bates' *If No News, Send Rumors,* Holt.

taken on one day by hundreds of photographers highlighting people and places across America. The students spent two months on the project. They first wrote letters telling of the project and asking participation by faculty members and residents," Sander said. "They collected the essays and scheduled photo assignments so there would be no duplications. They coordinated everything on computers."

The display, entitled "A Day In the Life of Elkhorn," was first shown at Elkhorn Manor, a senior center, and was then moved to several local meeting places. Many residents who saw the display said it captured the warmth and spirit of Elkhorn, and some are working to turn the project into a book.

These high school students approached their town as if it were a group of families, and that is often the way public journalism works. The fact is, even the largest paper is still about community. The stories and articles tell readers who's doing what and when and how and why. They provide just the kind of information that keeps a family, and in the case of a large paper, a community together.

1. Find newspaper articles that you think represent each of the following major roles of the press: to inform, to act as a lookout, to interpret, to explain, to entertain, to amuse and to keep a record. Clip and label each article. Share your articles with the class. Can some articles overlap two or more roles?

2. Conduct your own public journalism experiment. Ask five nonstudents how they think your school affects the quality of life in the community. Discuss what you discover with classmates.

3. Contact the local media outlets—newspapers, radio stations and television stations, for example—and ask what community projects they have undertaken in the last year. Discuss with your classmates how effective these projects were.

▲MANY CULTURES, MANY VOICES

Journalists involved in public journalism need to report, write and edit news for the entire community. Their news stories need to represent the various segments of their communities. But how well do the people reporting these stories reflect the ethnic and racial make-up of their communities? According to the American Society of Newspaper Editors, in 1999, people of color represented about 11.5 percent of the journalists employed by daily newspapers. That means that of roughly 55,000 professional journalists, just over 6,300, were members of cultural or racial minorities.

Reporters and editors have been concerned about diversity in the newsroom for a long time, but improvements have been slow in coming. In 1968, following a series of riots in major cities throughout the United States, a national advisory board known as the Kerner

BYLINE

CHUCK STONE
ON AFRICAN-AMERICAN NEWSPAPERS

"When I was growing up, during World War Two," explains Chuck Stone, former editor-in-chief of three African-American newspapers and now a professor of journalism, "my mother took the *Pittsburgh Courier* even though we lived in Hartford, Connecticut. That was really the only way to find out what the black troops were doing."

In those days, the African-American press provided African-American readers with virtually their only source of news about themselves. It also gave African-American journalists virtually their only source of employment. In the 1940s, the *Pittsburgh Courier's* circulation soared to a nationwide readership of 400,000. The *Courier's* circulation stands now at about 35,000. The postwar years have been hard on African-American papers, Stone said: ". . . They've become partly victims of their own success. . . . African Americans have been hired in substantial numbers by other newspapers. . . . There are black columnists everywhere now. It's like the Negro Leagues in baseball, or why the top black students now go to Harvard, Yale, and Princeton. The price of integration is the failure of black institutions."

Yet, a number of African-American newspapers still survive—such as New York City's *Amsterdam News*, the *Baltimore Afro-American*, and the *Los Angeles Sentinel*—providing a voice for many who might otherwise be silent.

Commission criticized the American news media for "basking in a white world, looking out of it, if at all, with a white man's eyes and a white perspective." The press, the commission insisted, "must make a reality of integration—in both their product and their personnel."

Steady but Slow Progress

Some progress toward true racial integration in the field of journalism has been made over the years, but not nearly enough. "Newspapers can't do business as usual any more if they hope to present an accurate report of the increasingly diverse communities they serve," commented Edward Seaton, president of ASNE. His organization reported that in 1999, 5.4 percent of journalists were African American, 3.5 percent Hispanic, 2.3 percent Asian American, and .4 percent Native American. The same study showed that women make up 37 percent of the newsroom staff of daily papers.

The basic stumbling block in more fully integrating the members of the press has been a lack of minority applicants. As one editor put it, you can't hire minority graduates if they aren't there. The Kerner Commission stated the challenge this way: "It must become a commitment to seek out young [minority] men and women and inspire them to become journalists. Training programs should be started at high schools." Thus, high school journalism programs can become the launchpads for sending a new generation of journalists of all races and backgrounds into professional journalism.

The fact that few minority students are on their school media staffs has meant an absence of their views and voices. To be inclusive, newsrooms—and journalism classrooms—must develop a welcoming environment. Educators and student editors can demonstrate their interest in making school media more diverse by learning about minority history, literature and other experiences.

Journalists are also becoming more concerned about gender equality. Although women have taken significant strides into public life, the national forums of public debate—opinion pages, political magazines, public affairs talk shows and newspaper columns—remain largely male dominated. As recently as 1992, just 13 percent of the opinion or editorial pieces published in the *Washington Post* were written by women. With the emergence of talk radio in the mid-1990s, a new opportunity beckoned. But of the National Radio Association's roster of 900 talk show hosts, only 50 are female. "Think of women as a suburb you don't cover very well," said Nancy Woodhull, a trustee of the Freedom Forum, as she addressed a group of editors.

The challenge for the journalism industry goes beyond the hiring of women and people of color. The communications media are striving to create a feeling of ownership in everyone, both in and out of the newsroom. All people need to feel that the newspapers and broadcast stations in their community "belong" to them.

Sam Fulwood, an award-winning national correspondent for the *Los Angeles Times,* says that despite the fact that overt racial barriers have fallen, the color line is still very much a fact of life. Fulwood recalls a white *Washington Post* editor who asked him in an interview, "Are you black first or a reporter first?" Fulwood said the assumption was apparently that he could not be both.

Suggestions for
Making Publications More Diverse

One of your challenges as a high school journalist is to make each group and individual genuinely feel a part of the school. You can begin by recognizing the diversity of voices in your community. Marcia Kovas, a journalism teacher and adviser at James Whitcomb Riley High School in South Bend, Indiana, has given a great deal of thought to this subject. She offers the following suggestions to students working on school papers or broadcasts to help their efforts to build community:

+ First, encourage a "diversity is special" mentality. All staff members should be sensitive to cultural differences in their reporting. Student reporters could examine, for example, the fairness of minority scholarships or the importance of including African American history in the curriculum.
+ Second, banish all cliques and become comrades-in-arms. When the overriding goal of the entire staff is a great product, differences tend to fall aside.
+ Third, use diverse talent in creative ways. "Several years ago a talented editor joined the staff," Kovas explained.

"He enjoyed creative writing, and rather than pressure him to change his style, I encouraged him to create a column which would critique a black fashion fad or trend in each issue. Our readers loved the column, and best yet, we didn't discourage or alienate a talented writer who had much to offer."

✦ Finally, turn anger into ideas. Help those students who feel alienated to find a forum for their opinions. Kovas relates the following example:

Several years ago, two female staffers who enjoyed dressing in the punk style came to class irate. They were convinced that the security guards had accosted them because their hair was spiked and their jackets were leather.

I suggested that rather than arguing, they objectively examine the guards' treatment of students in an article for the paper. The staffers set up five scenarios in which a student might encounter an authority figure: walking in the halls without a pass, sitting on the lawn during school hours, talking loudly in a library, playing with squirt guns in the mall, and carrying a soft drink into a clothing store.

On the first week of the investigation, the girls dressed in preppy attire: they wore their hair in ponytails, donned penny loafers, wore clean jeans and crew neck sweaters. They found that their behavior went largely unnoticed by those in authority. Not so the next week. Dressed 'all out' as punkers, the reporters were verbally chastised each time.

Their article went on to win a Gold Key Award from Quill and Scroll. They were thrilled with the reader response and the knowledge that they could make a difference (*Death By Cheeseburger,* p. 41).

Cultural barriers can be broken down, but students first need to feel a sense of community, a sense that what they think matters, a sense that they will be listened to and that their voices will be heard. Journalism is one important way that a school can give everyone that sense.

1. The term *politically correct* (PC) usually refers to a word choice that avoids offending a particular group of people. The *Los Angeles Times* banned the words *deaf, handicapped* and *alien* from its stories. Instead of *deaf,* for example, reporters refer to *an individual who cannot hear.* Although being culturally sensitive is common courtesy, some writers feel the PC movement goes too far. Author Chris Cerf says that someday looters may be called *nontraditional shoppers.*

Compile a list of 10 terms that you feel have been made politically correct. For example, instead of saying *drug addict,* we might say *substance abuser.* The list might also include terms you think might be replaced in the future. To what degree should the news media be politically correct?

2. Does your community have newspapers or radio or television programs produced in a language other than English? If so, what does this suggest about the different kinds of communities in our states and regions? What purpose do newspapers and programs in other languages serve?

CHAPTER REVIEW

KEY TERMS

Show that you know the meanings of the following key terms by correctly using them in complete sentences. Write your answers on a separate sheet of paper.

weekly newspaper
daily newspaper
journalism
journalist
credibility

verify
objectivity
First Amendment
commentary
public journalism

OPEN FORUM

Discuss the following situations in small groups. Try to reach a consensus about what you think should be done.

1. You are the advertising manager of the school paper. A group called Friends and Parents of Gays and Lesbians has called you and asked to place an ad in the school paper. The ad shows an open door and is promoting a meeting on a local college campus in a few weeks. The purpose of the meeting is to help high school students find support for unpopular or unusual lifestyles. The principal thinks the ad is outrageous and insists that it be refused. What should you and the newspaper staff do?

2. The mother of one of your friends is upset about a book her daughter brought home from school. The book is about a teenager who becomes an unwed mother and a substance abuser. The mother thinks that the book should be removed from the school's library and plans to bring the matter to the school board. You have read the book and think that it has a valuable message. What role could the school media play in discussing this issue?

3. You are all members of the student council. One day some students approach you with a request. They have noticed that a cafeteria dishwasher has tattoos that feature the Nazi swastika and the letters KKK. The tattoos can be seen easily because the worker always wears short-sleeved shirts. The students want the council to ask the principal to have the dishwasher fired. What action, if any, should you take?

FINDING THE FLAW

Much has changed in the past hundred years. The following stories appeared in newspapers in 1885. How would the same news be covered today? What would be different about how the stories were written?

Cleveland in the Mountains

President Cleveland is now camping out at Willis Pond, one of the most inaccessible spots in the Adirondack mountains. The president was ill for the first few days in camp, but has now fully recovered. He generally fishes during the day and in the evening enjoys a social game of euchre. Orders were given to the proprietors of the Prospect house at Saranac Lake that no newspaper man should be allowed to engage rooms there. The president has not yet decided when he will return to Washington.

The Police Raid a Lair That Has Hitherto Been Undisturbed

Sam Buswitz's gambling rooms in Barker's block, under the Y.M.C.A. rooms on 15th street between Farnam and Harney, were raided last night between 9 and 10 o'clock and the proprietor and seven young men were arrested. The chips, cards, and other paraphernalia were captured and taken to the police headquarters. Officer Matza upon opening the door was recognized as a policeman and the door was slammed violently, his hand being caught between the door and casing and quite badly injured. Several other policemen guarded the exits. The house has been running for some time, but so quietly that it had not been placed on the police list for fines. The sportive ones who frequented it might have passed for good young men going to the Y.M.C.A. reading rooms. All of the visitors were taken, however, and tried this morning.

 MEDIA WATCH

1. Compare how newspapers and television news shows cover the same story. What differences do you find? Notice, especially, the degree of prominence given each story and the length of time (or amount of space) devoted to each. What conclusions can you draw about these differences?
2. Monitor your local media for a week, tracking stories about minority groups. To what degree are these groups covered? Does the coverage seem fair?

◆ **MEDIA WATCH,** CONTINUED

3. Evaluate a recent issue of your local newspaper from a geographic perspective, as follows. Divide your community into neighborhoods (or several small towns, as the case may be), and count the number of articles that concern each neighborhood. Are some areas of town better covered than others? Why might that be? You might also want to try this with the school newspaper to see which groups or activities are being covered and which ones are not.

String Book

1. In *Alice's Adventures in Wonderland,* before tumbling down the rabbit hole, Alice asks, "What is the use of a book without pictures or conversations?" Was Alice, in a sense, predicting the difficulties facing newspapers of the future? Write a short editorial (an article based on fact but carrying the writer's opinion) discussing how newspapers can compete with television's reporting of news stories.

2. Thomas Jefferson had this to say about newspapers before he became president: "Were it left to me to decide whether we should have a government without newspapers, or newspapers without government, I should not hesitate for a moment to prefer the latter." After he became president, he said this: "Even the least informed of the people have learnt that nothing in a newspaper is to be believed." Write an essay in which you explain which of those two views you share, and why.

Chapter 2
Making Ethical Choices

"Right is right, even if everyone is against it and wrong is wrong, even if everyone is for it."

—William Penn

In this chapter, you will learn the meaning of these terms:

ethics
confidentiality
censorship
obscenity
copyright
libel
slander
prior review
off-the-record
retraction
student expression policy
publication board

LEARNING OBJECTIVES

After completing this chapter, you will be able to:

◆ discuss the three major Supreme Court cases affecting free speech in school,

◆ explain the important points contained in a professional code of ethics for journalists,

◆ list some of the policies and procedures students can use within their schools to help protect their right to a free press.

◆

ournalism, as many of its practitioners like to say, is a craft, not a profession. But it is a craft with a strict code of ethics. A large part of learning to be a journalist is learning to make ethical decisions because virtually every activity—from making a short phone call to checking the facts in a long off-the-record interview—raises questions of trust and confidentiality.

In this chapter, you will learn how making ethical choices can benefit you as a student journalist. You will examine the basic legal concepts of journalism and read about three Supreme Court cases that have had an impact on the rights of high school students. In addition, you will study a professional code of ethics and apply what you learn to situations other students have faced. Finally, you will consider some practical advice about what you can do when faced with tough ethical choices.

◢LEGAL AND ETHICAL BOUNDARIES OF STUDENT JOURNALISM

If someone were to ask you to describe yourself, how would you answer? Would you say you were athletic, intelligent, always nice, fairly funny and, of course, the most considerate person around? What if that same person asked, "Well, those are all fine qualities, but would I be able to say that you are ethical?" How would you respond?

Without even realizing it, the issue of ethics has been staring you in the face since the day you were born. Don't you remember all those moral dilemmas in your life? Should you sneak a cookie from the cookie jar before dinner even though you were told not to spoil your appetite? Should you lie at the movie theater about your age? Should you pretend to be sick and stay home from school on the day of a big test and go to the mall instead? What about covering up a crime you saw a friend commit?

Briefly stated, **ethics** can be defined as the branch of philosophy that deals with right and wrong. In other words, it is ethics that helps you decide whether to return a wallet you found or resist the temptation to plagiarize an English paper.

ethics

the branch of philosophy that deals with right and wrong

Just like everybody else, journalists are faced with ethical questions every day. Should a reporter promise a source **confidentiality** (a promise of secrecy for restricted information)? If a reporter knows the police are searching for the very same robber who is telling her how burglars case a house before breaking into it, can she go back on a promise of secrecy? Should she have made the promise in the first place? Should a photographer stage a picture? After all, having a person fake some tears might be an easy way to capture that award-winning shot on film.

You might not want to admit it, but you too are faced with ethical questions every time you put pen to paper. Yet often without realizing it, you already have the basics of ethics figured out; you just might have to search a little for the reasons for your decisions.

confidentiality
the assurance of secrecy for restricted information

Avoiding Censorship

Unlike other aspects of journalism and reporting, ethics is not something that comes with a list of how-to's. Your parents, teachers or even the authors of this textbook can advise you on how to respond in certain situations, but that is as far as they can go. Then it is up to you to decide for yourself how to act. You have to evaluate each situation, search your conscience and decide how you will act. No one else can do this for you.

Ethical conduct is your best defense against the most persistent enemy of high school journalism—**censorship.** Censorship occurs when officials prevent the printing or broadcasting of material that they consider objectionable. You are far less likely to have something censored if you follow your own sense of fair play and a set of ethical guidelines shaped by legal decisions, professional codes and practices established by other student journalists.

censorship
removal or prohibition of material by an authority, usually governmental

In *Freedom to Publish,* David Kennedy, the president of the American Society of Journalists and Authors, makes the following comment about censorship: "A country that tolerates censorship of the press cannot be truly free. Only when citizens can exercise their thoughts in an unfettered manner can they claim to be truly free." Fortunately, we live in a country that does not tolerate censorship of the press. Our country's stance on this issue was made evident when the First Amendment was ratified on Dec. 15, 1791. Article I of the Constitution states: "Congress shall make no law respecting an establishment of religion, or prohibiting the free exercise thereof; or abridging the freedom of speech, or of the press; or of the right of the people peaceably to assemble, and to petition the government for a redress of grievances."

Because of this constitutional provision, Americans are guaranteed freedom of the press, which includes everything from newspapers, magazines, periodicals and pamphlets to radio, television and motion pictures. But as we will soon see, although the First Amendment gives you a great opportunity to speak and write, it does not protect everything. Some kinds of material, such as obscenity, are still off-limits. The Supreme Court also has determined that schools have special powers in some cases to restrict what students can say or write.

Freedom of speech is a right protected in most democratic societies; this student prepares to give a speech to his classmates.

obscenity

> material that offends local community standards and lacks serious artistic purpose

copyright

> the exclusive rights to something a person has written or otherwise created

libel

> the printing or broadcasting of false information that damages someone's reputation

slander

> a spoken falsehood

A Lesson on Libel

Despite the "guaranteed freedoms" of the First Amendment, the Supreme Court still recognizes a few categories of speech that are not protected—expressions that can be lawfully prohibited and regulated by the government. The following are some of those categories:

- *Obscenity.* **Obscenity** means more than just impolite words. It refers to material that offends local community standards and lacks any serious artistic purpose. In some communities, movies, books, posters and even songs have been judged to be obscene.
- *Fighting words.* So-called fighting words are usually racial, ethnic, gender or religious insults. Because such words can cause fights, school officials are permitted to ban them from campuses. By the same reasoning, some schools outlaw certain kinds of clothing that might be gang related.
- *Invasion of privacy.* The Supreme Court has consistently supported certain protections for private information. In school, for example, this means that a student's medical and academic records are kept confidential.
- *Copyright violations.* A **copyright** gives a person exclusive rights to something he or she has written or otherwise created. Any kind of plagiarism, such as a reporter's copying a paragraph from *Time* without citing a source, is a violation of copyright law.
- *Libel.* **Libel** occurs when false information that damages someone's reputation is printed or broadcast. Libel is considered much more serious than **slander** (a spoken falsehood), because it is more permanent and thus can have long-lasting effects.

Although it is important for students to avoid all forms of unprotected speech, they would be especially wise to steer clear of anything that could be considered libelous. According to the Student Press Law Center, libel is "any printed communication—words or pictures—which tends to expose one to public hatred, shame, contempt or disgrace or damage one's reputation in the community or injure the person." Because libel can cause permanent harm, juries have awarded huge settlements—in the millions of dollars—to libel victims. Libel is so potentially dangerous that students should make a special effort to understand how it can find its way into their journalistic products.

To better understand the concept of libel, consider the following scenario: While working in your school's journalism lab after class, you overhear two teachers discussing an upcoming basketball tournament. You recognize the voice of one of the teachers, who is asking the other if she would like to "put money in the pot." The second teacher declines, but this does not discourage the first teacher from pushing the issue. "It's only $50," he says. "Winner take all. Five thousand tax-free dollars. It could be yours if you play and win. Think about it." "I don't know," she says. "The city has been cracking down on gambling lately and how can I tell my students that gambling is wrong and then turn around and do it myself?" They continue to talk until she relents. She asks if she can write a check for $25 and pay him the balance tomorrow. He agrees, and the two then leave the lab.

You suddenly realize you have been handed the lead story for Friday's paper. Gambling has been a big problem among students at your school, but teachers? What a twist. The only problem is how you can write the article and identify the teacher without being charged with libel.

If there is a way to verify (prove) that the teachers in your school do have a pool going for the upcoming tournament, then your statement that "Mr. Jack Doe is using his math ability to do more than teach geometry" would be true. If a statement is true, it is not libelous even though it might be damaging.

However, if you can't verify what you have just heard, you will certainly want to reconsider your "proof" before you go to print. Although legal interns at the Student Press Law Center say that the chances of your being sued for libel are small, they recommend that students be careful when taking on sensitive material and abide by the following suggestions:

+ Check and recheck all facts. Always try to find more than one source before publishing material that could be viewed as damaging. Responsible journalists seek two or more sources that are independent of one another, credible and in a position to know and tell the truth.
+ Remember that fairness dictates that reporters contact the individual about whom they are writing. By contacting the subject of the story, reporters obtain both sides of a controversial issue and often avoid printing incomplete or incorrect information.
+ Exercise good judgment. Would printing a story about the teachers' basketball pool be in the school's best interest? Generally, editors rather than reporters worry about these kinds of questions, but an ethical reporter should consider the possible implications of printing or televising a particular story.

It might take longer to follow these rules, but the guidelines help you report in the most ethical way—a goal that all journalists should share.

How would you write a story about this Lacrosse game if you thought that the rumors of a "fixed" game were true?

Court Decisions and the Rights of High School Journalists

Learning how to avoid a libel suit and knowing how to exercise good news judgment will put you on the high road to principled journalism, but those abilities by themselves won't give you a full understanding of the boundaries of responsible journalism. You need to turn to three United States Supreme Court decisions that have examined students' rights. These decisions have redefined what free speech means in school.

Tinker v. Des Moines.   Prior to the 1960s, the Supreme Court had said very little about students' free speech rights. But that situation changed dramatically as a result of protests over the Vietnam War.

In the winter of 1965, a group of students in Des Moines, Iowa, decided that they would wear black armbands during the Christmas season to protest the war. Meanwhile, in an effort to prevent disruptions in school, the Des Moines principals adopted a policy that prohibited students from wearing armbands. Despite the policy, three students—13-year-old Mary Beth Tinker, 15-year-old John Tinker, and 16-year-old Christopher Eckhardt—wore armbands to school and were suspended. They did not return to school until their planned period for wearing the armbands had expired in January. Eckhardt explained:

> "I wore the black armband over a camel-colored jacket," recalled Eckhardt. "The captain of the football team attempted to rip it off. I turned myself in to the principal's office where the vice principal asked if 'I wanted a busted nose.' Then he called my counselor in. She asked if I wanted to go to college, and said that colleges didn't accept protesters. She said I would probably need to look for a new high school if I didn't take the armband off."

To dramatize the unfairness of their suspensions, the three students sued the school district, stating that their First Amendment rights had been violated. Although school officials maintained that the armbands were "substantially disruptive" to other students' studies, the Supreme Court eventually ruled 7-2 in the students' favor. In the majority opinion, Justice Abe Fortas wrote, "It can hardly be argued that either students or teachers shed their constitutional rights to freedom of speech or expression at the schoolhouse gate."

A quarter-century later, Mary Beth Tinker, now a nurse in St. Louis, says she doesn't remember much about the case but is committed to "do whatever I can to give kids a voice. It's interesting that school newspapers are being used a lot now to let kids talk about AIDS, sex education, pregnancy prevention—important topics like that."

With the decision in *Tinker v. Des Moines,* students became confident that their rights, just as those of other Americans, would be protected both on and off school grounds. More important to student journalists, the ruling established students' constitutional rights to voice their ideas and opinions, even those that might be viewed as unpopular or controversial.

THIS JUST IN: *Portrait of a Young Journalist*
Mark Goodman, Executive Director of the Student Press Law Center

One of the most important places students can find help when they face dilemmas involving freedom of speech is the Student Press Law Center (SPLC), an independent, nonprofit corporation located in Washington, D.C. The center provides free legal advice and information to students and advisers.

Mark Goodman, the center's first and only executive director, says his organization receives about 2,000 calls each year, often from upset students. "In many cases," Goodman says, "they'll call us in extreme frustration, often in times of anger and fear. They are trying to do their jobs as journalists and are facing roadblocks."

Nearly half of the calls the SPLC receives from public high schools are about censorship. Staff members at the center—usually law and journalism interns from different colleges—take the calls and provide on-the-spot legal advice. These interns also undertake research to provide more thorough and comprehensive answers when needed. The center operates a formal Attorney Referral Network of approximately 150 lawyers across the country who are available to provide free legal representation to local students when necessary.

Goodman attended high school in Versailles, Missouri, and then earned a journalism degree at the University of Missouri and a law degree at Duke University. He said that his journalism major was an excellent preparation for law school. "To a certain extent, I think I was better off than a lot of my law school classmates because I was used to writing under strict deadline pressure. I was used to constant writing every day and every week. Also, writing journalistically teaches one certain logical thought processes—that's valuable in law school and in being a lawyer."

Goodman served an internship at SPLC between his second and third years in law school. During his senior year, Goodman was asked to apply for the executive director's position, and he was later hired. "I knew I would have the chance to make a difference to a certain extent. I realized there weren't many positions in which I could do something I like as much as I could do here."

When asked about today's student journalists, Goodman said,

"I find most of the high school editors are not necessarily the ones who are intending to make journalism their careers, but are those who are most involved in their school activities.

"Generally, they're interested in doing a good job in turning out a professional product and in having a newspaper they can be proud of. They want something that's not only going to be timely and read by the students, but also the kind of thing they believe to be worthwhile by contributing to it.

"Though they don't necessarily see journalism as a career, they see the important function of what they are doing and are serious about being involved in that function." (*Quill & Scroll*)

For the next 17 years, students and advisers believed that because of the ruling, only articles that were libelous, obscene or disruptive to the operation of the school could be censored. The *Tinker* decision became, as columnist Nat Hentoff called it, "the Magna Carta of scholastic journalism." Thanks to *Tinker,* high school journalists enjoyed a great deal of freedom. But in 1986 a more conservative Supreme Court made another ruling that limited the free expression rights of students.

Bethel School District v. Fraser.   Approximately 600 fellow students were on hand that day in April 1983 when 17-year-old Matthew Fraser delivered a speech nominating another student for president of the student body of his high school near Tacoma, Washington. Although the speech was given at an assembly to which attendance was voluntary, Fraser had been advised by teachers not to deliver it because of its lewd content. Throughout his speech, Fraser referred to the candidate in an elaborate sexual metaphor that included such phrases as "I know a man who is firm—he's firm in his shirt, his character is firm" and "Jeff is a man who will go to the very end—even the climax—for each and every one of you."

It was not surprising that school administrators looked unfavorably on Fraser's speech. The following day, Fraser was notified by the principal that he had been suspended from school for two days for violating the school's "disruptive conduct rule." In addition, his name was removed from a list of candidates for graduation speaker.

Feeling that his rights had been violated, Fraser decided to take his case to court. When a lower court ruled in Fraser's favor, school officials appealed to the United States Supreme Court. Eventually, the Supreme Court ruled in favor of the school. The Court's decision stated that "schools, as instruments of the state, may determine that the essential lessons of civil, mature conduct cannot be conveyed in a school that tolerates lewd, indecent, or offensive speech."

Unlike the *Tinker* decision, which focused on the importance of enforcing the rights of students, this decision put some control back into the hands of school officials. The ruling indicated that the constitutional rights of students are not the same as those of adults. It also indicated that the school board had the authority to decide what was offensive speech. Student reporters and their advisers viewed this ruling as a hint that the climate had changed, a view that would soon prove correct when the Court made a more sweeping decision.

Hazelwood School District v. Kuhlmeier.   In May 1983, students in the Journalism II class at Hazelwood East High School in suburban St. Louis were shocked when their school paper, *The Spectrum,* came back from the printer with the middle two pages missing. The students learned that a substitute teacher had shown page proofs of the paper to principal Robert Reynolds for approval. Reynolds's approval was necessary because Hazelwood East had a **prior review** policy. Prior review occurs when a principal or other official reviews a proof of the paper before it goes to press.

After reviewing the paper, Reynolds told the substitute that he objected to two articles. One of the articles dealt with the impact that

prior review
the review of a proof of a newspaper by an official before it goes to press

Due to recent Supreme Court rulings, students do not have the same constitutional rights as adults. In most schools, there is generally a prior review policy by either the principal or a designated school official before going to press.

divorce has on students. The other discussed three students' experiences with pregnancy. The latter story began this way:

> Sixteen-year-old Sue had it all—good looks, good grades, a loving family and a cute boyfriend. She also had a seven pound baby boy. Each year, according to Claire Berman *(Readers Digest),* close to 1.1 million teenagers—more than one out of every 10 teenage girls—become pregnant. *(The Spectrum,* Hazelwood East High School, Hazelwood, Mo.)

The article continued with personal accounts of three pregnant Hazelwood students, who were given fictitious names:

> **Terri:** I am five months pregnant and very excited about having my baby. My husband is excited too. We both can't wait until it's born. . . .
>
> **Patti:** I didn't think it could happen to me, but I knew I had to start making plans for me and my little one. . . .
>
> **Julie:** At first I was shocked. You always think "It won't happen to me." I was also scared because I did not know how everyone was going to handle it. *(The Spectrum,* Hazelwood East High School, Hazelwood, Mo.)

When asked about his objections, Reynolds said he believed that pregnancy was not an appropriate topic for a high school newspaper, and that the three girls in the article would have been recognized by fellow students. Reynolds further stated that the article that dealt with divorce (in which a student criticized her father for not spending more time with his family) violated journalistic fairness because the father was not given an opportunity to defend himself.

As a result of Reynolds's decision, student editor Cathy Kuhlmeier and members of the newspaper staff concluded that their First Amendment rights had been violated, and they sued the administration. Five years later the Supreme Court ruled against the students, defending the principal's right to censor articles. By a 5-3 majority vote, the Court decided that because the student newspaper at Hazelwood East High School was not a "forum for public expression," it could be censored. The newspaper was not considered a forum because it was produced as part of the school's curriculum. In their ruling, members of the Court agreed that high school administrators have a right to censor student publications if they can "present a reasonable educational justification" for the censorship. In the future, the Court added, administrators would have the right to censor stories that were "ungrammatical, poorly written, inadequately researched, biased or prejudiced, vulgar or profane, or unsuitable for immature audiences."

With this ruling, it became apparent that school administrators could tighten the control they have over what students can and cannot publish. Mark Goodman, an attorney who directs the Student Press Law Center, says that the *Hazelwood* decision has had a chilling effect on the willingness of student journalists to write about serious issues and the problems that teenagers face today. However, some schools have actually been allowed to start school papers because principals and school boards now feel they can have at least some say in the articles the papers contain.

1. Invite the principal to your class for a discussion of students' free speech rights. What are the principal's policies, for example, toward student dress codes, theatrical productions and newspaper articles?

2. Legislative bodies in a number of states, including California, Colorado, Massachusetts, Iowa and Kansas, have passed laws guaranteeing student journalists the right to determine the content of school publications. Other states are considering such laws. Does your state have any laws affecting free speech for students? (*Hint:* Consult your school district's attorney.)

3. Has censorship ever been an issue at your school (consider library books, drama productions and literary magazines, as well as school newspapers, yearbooks and broadcast programs)? How were those issues resolved? Did any policies change as a result?

▲PROFESSIONAL GUIDELINES AND CODES OF ETHICS

Pretend for a minute that this is a perfect world. You can sneak a cookie before dinner without spoiling your appetite, movie tickets can be purchased at half price, and you can go to the mall instead of school any day. Now imagine that your school administrators and the court system decide to let you print whatever you want. How would you react? Would your own code of ethics change?

Odds are that even though you might want to take advantage of your new-found journalistic freedom, you would not. Most likely, being who you are, you would still want to practice ethical reporting. You would probably choose to follow a few simple guidelines that were established as part of a code of ethics for professional journalists.

Code of Ethics

One of the most widely used and respected sets of guidelines for professional journalists is the Code of Ethics developed by the Society of Professional Journalists (also called Sigma Delta Chi). The code was first adopted in 1926 and then completely revised in 1996. It covers four key principles that seek to explain "why we do what we do and what we believe in," according to ethics chair Jay Black of the University of South Florida. Those principles are: Seek truth and report it; Minimize harm; Act independently; and Be accountable. The society hoped the code will educate and inspire journalists so that they can avoid ethical lapses. (See Figure 1.1 for the complete code.)

Responsibility.   According to the code, the duty of journalists is to serve the truth. Journalists do so by satisfying the public's right to know regarding events of public importance. Journalists who use their professional status as representatives of the public for selfish or other unworthy motives violate a high trust.

One of the most impressive examples of a student journalist's taking this responsibility seriously involved Jeff Lovell, a student reporter at Northrop High School in Fort Wayne, Indiana. Lovell stirred up controversy when he uncovered suspicious behavior on the part of the tennis coach. While checking into the school's spring sports programs, Lovell discovered that the girls' tennis team was practicing on some indoor courts at the coach's apartment complex. That was not unusual—it was too cold to practice outdoors in February. When Jeff learned that each girl on the team was paying $65 to rent the space, however, an alarm went off in his head. "Doing a quick estimate—there were 22 girls on the tennis team—it sounded like an inordinate amount of money to be paying at an apartment complex where the coach lived," Jeff said.

He did a little more checking and discovered that, in fact, it wasn't costing the tennis team anything to practice there. "If you play with a

NEW YORK CITY, Aug. 4, 1735—John Peter Zenger, editor of the *New-York Weekly Journal,* was found not guilty of "raising sedition" against the government through columns printed in his newspaper. Zenger had been asked by a group of businessmen to represent their interests against those of Gov. William Cosby of New York. He responded by publishing a series of articles attacking Cosby and the government's policies.

Zenger was arrested on Nov. 17, 1734, and charged with "Scandalous, Virulent and Seditious Reflections upon the Government." In court, Zenger's lawyer did not deny that Zenger had printed the articles. He argued, however, that "the words themselves must be libelous—that is, False, Malicious, and Seditious—or else we are not guilty." Although Zenger's facts made the government look bad, they were correct. He had written the truth.

For nine months while her husband awaited trial, Anna Zenger published the paper.

A jury of his peers found Zenger not guilty because what he had printed was true, and they would not condemn a person for telling the truth. The verdict did not change libel law for half a century, but it was the first case to establish truth as a defense. No colonial printers were charged with libel after 1735.

FIGURE 1.1
CODE OF ETHICS—SOCIETY OF PROFESSIONAL JOURNALISTS

PREAMBLE

Members of the Society of Professional Journalists believe that public enlightenment is the forerunner of justice and the foundation of democracy. The duty of the journalist is to further those ends by seeking truth and providing a fair and comprehensive account of events and issues. Conscientious journalists from all media and specialties strive to serve the public with thoroughness and honesty. Professional integrity is the cornerstone of a journalist's credibility.

Members of the Society share a dedication to ethical behavior and adopt this code to declare the Society's principles and standards of practice.

Seek Truth and Report It

Journalists should be honest, fair and courageous in gathering, reporting and interpreting information.

Journalists should:

- Test the accuracy of information from all sources and exercise care to avoid inadvertent error. Deliberate distortion is never permissible.
- Diligently seek out subjects of news stories to give them the opportunity to respond to allegations of wrong doing.
- Identify sources whenever feasible. The public is entitled to as much information as possible on sources' reliability.
- Always question sources' motives before promising anonymity. Clarify conditions attached to any promise made in exchange for information. Keep promises.
- Make certain that headlines, news teasers and promotional material, photos, video, audio, graphics, sound bites and quotations do not misrepresent. They should not oversimplify or highlight incidents out of context.
- Never distort the content of news photos or video. Image enhancement for technical clarity is always permissible. Label montages and photo illustrations.
- Avoid misleading re-enactments or staged news events. If re-enactment is necessary to tell a story, label it.

- Avoid undercover or other surreptitious methods of gathering information except when traditional open methods will not yield information vital to the public. Use of such methods should be explained as part of the story.
- Never plagiarize.
- Tell the story of the diversity and magnitude of the human experience boldly, even when it is unpopular to do so.
- Examine their own cultural values and avoid imposing those values on others.
- Avoid stereotyping by race, gender, age, religion, ethnicity, geography, sexual orientation, disability, physical appearance or social status.
- Support the open exchange of views, even views they find repugnant.
- Give voice to the voiceless; official and unofficial sources of information can be equally valid.
- Distinguish between advocacy and news reporting. Analysis and commentary should be labeled and not misrepresent fact or context.
- Distinguish news from advertising and shun hybrids that blur the lines between the two.
- Recognize a special obligation to ensure that the public's business is conducted in the open and that government records are open to inspection.

Minimize Harm

Ethical journalists treat sources, subjects and colleagues as human beings deserving of respect.

◆ FIGURE 1.1, **continued**

Journalists should:

Show compassion for those who may be affected adversely by news coverage. Use special sensitivity when dealing with children and inexperienced sources or subjects.

- Be sensitive when seeking or using interviews or photographs of those affected by tragedy or grief.
- Recognize that gathering and reporting information may cause harm or discomfort. Pursuit of the news is not a license for arrogance.
- Recognize that private people have a greater right to control information about themselves than do public officials and others who seek power, influence or attention. Only an overriding public need can justify intrusion into anyone's privacy.
- Show good taste. Avoid pandering to lurid curiosity.
- Be cautious about identifying juvenile suspects or victims of sex crimes.
- Be judicious about naming criminal suspects before the formal filing of charges.
- Balance a criminal suspect's fair trial rights with the public's right to be informed.

Act Independently

Journalists should be free of obligation to any interest other than the public's right to know.

Journalists should:

- Avoid conflicts of interest, real or perceived.
- Remain free of associations and activities that may compromise integrity or damage credibility.
- Refuse gifts, favors, fees, free travel and special treatment, and shun secondary employment, political involvement, public office and service in community organizations if they compromise journalistic integrity.
- Disclose unavoidable conflicts.
- Be vigilant and courageous about holding those with power accountable.
- Deny favored treatment to advertisers and special interests and resist their pressure to influence news coverage.
- Be wary of sources offering information for favors or money; avoid bidding for news.

Be Accountable

Journalists are accountable to the readers, listeners, viewers and each other.

Journalists should:

- Clarify and explain news coverage and invite dialogue with the public over journalistic conduct.
- Encourage the public to voice grievances against the news media.
- Admit mistakes and correct them promptly.
- Expose unethical practices of journalists and the news media.
- Abide by the same high standards to which they hold others.

(SOURCE: *Editor & Publisher*, 1996)

DATELINE
DATELINE
DATELINE

BOSTON, Aug. 7, 1721—James Franklin established the *New England Courant*. His brother Benjamin, apprenticed as a printer's assistant, was Franklin's helper and a contributing writer.

Most newspapers of the time prominently displayed the term "by Authority" to indicate that the editor had been given permission by the British government to print the paper. The *Courant* was the first newspaper continuously printed in America without the explicit permission or editorial approval of any government officials. Thus, James Franklin was the first to exercise the privilege of editorial independence. His actions set the tone for a free press in America.

James Franklin's courage and independence, however, caused him to be jailed in 1722 for criticism of the government and religious authorities. During that time, he continued to publish his paper by naming his 14-year-old brother Benjamin editor. "During my brother's confinement," Ben would later write, "I had the management of the paper. I made bold to give our rulers some rubs in it, which my brother took very kindly, while others began to consider me in an unfavorable light, as a young genius that had a turn for libeling and satire." Eventually James was forbidden by the General Court to print the *Courant* or any similar publication.

member," explained the apartment manager, "it's free." Jeff then talked to each member of the team to confirm the amount he thought they were paying. He also found that the coach had told the players that "he was not making any money on this."

Word gradually leaked out that Jeff was doing an article on the team. At one point the coach called Jeff out of class and asked what he was doing. "I don't have a problem with you," Jeff replied. "I'm doing an investigative story and would like to talk to you." The coach, however, never agreed to an interview.

Jeff was careful to discuss his progress with both newspaper adviser Wendy Kruger and school principal H. Douglas Williams. And Jeff thought he had their approval, that is, until the final moment. "I took it [the completed story] to the principal at which time he said that 'This is well written, it is factual, it is not libelous. Yet this article will never be printed.'" Williams said he had decided to pull the article because it was "an attack on an individual and would have damaged student-teacher relationships."

Both Jeff and his adviser were shocked. They learned later that the article had been used as a bargaining chip—the coach agreed to resign in part because the principal promised to kill the article.

Where was justice for Lovell? By covering the incident to the best of his ability, he had the satisfaction of knowing that he had handled the situation in a professional manner. Although his article was not printed, Lovell had practiced ethical journalism and, in the process, saved his fellow students a considerable amount of money. The power of the freedom of the press had worked after all, but in a strange way.

Freedom of the Press.   Journalists guard their right to speak unpopular opinions and the privilege to disagree with the majority. They fight so-called gag rules that restrict what the public can know about sensitive legal cases. They also maintain the right to criticize those in power. Opinion columns and political cartoons frequently call attention to our leaders' shortcomings, an exercise in democracy that is not always honored elsewhere in the world.

Some community newspapers have supported a free student press by offering to print items censored by the school. A photo of a student smoking off campus was scheduled to run with a front-page story about school smoking regulations in the *Bagpipe* at Highland Park High School in Dallas. Even though the student had chosen to be in the photo, his parents threatened to sue if the photo was printed. The school superintendent told the newspaper staff to remove the photo from the paper. He changed his mind, however, when the *Dallas Morning News* said it would run the photo and the censorship story. The photo ran as planned in the *Bagpipe*.

Ethics.   The code calls attention to the fact that journalists must never accept gifts, favors, free travel or special treatment. You might think student journalists never face such temptations, but they do. For example, would you accept free movie tickets if you planned to review a film? Would you accept a free meal at a restaurant you intended to

BYLINE

ALAN OTA
WASHINGTON CORRESPONDENT FOR THE (PORTLAND) OREGONIAN

I was always a shy person in school. In my high school journalism class I discovered that by assuming the role of a journalist it was much easier to talk with people about their lives and experiences. Not all the experiences were good ones. I can still remember a vice principal who used derogatory racial references to Japanese while recounting his experiences in World War II in one of my journalism classes. As a Japanese American, I took his comments personally. I wrote a story and quoted his comments. It was much later in college and while working as a young journalist that I learned to separate my feelings from my professional goal of being objective. I discovered that stories could be a way to counteract discrimination by educating people. (*Death by Cheeseburger*, Freedom Forum)

critique? Suppose you were a sports writer who needed to miss class occasionally to attend games. What would you do if the assistant principal told you he would be glad to excuse you, and by the way, be sure to write a positive story? Would you report on a student's cheating or plagiarism, people drinking at the prom or friends using steroids? Journalists must be free of any obligation to anyone with an interest in the stories they cover, or their credibility is jeopardized.

The code also cautions against conflicts of interest. Journalists should be wary of information from "private sources." Someone who refuses to be quoted and instead asks to go **off-the-record** may have an ax to grind. Off-the-record comments are usually intended to give the reporter some background information or help the reporter find the right angle for a story. But the source may have selfish reasons for wishing to keep his or her identity secret. A reporter who agrees to keep comments off-the-record is promising not to use the comments or reveal who said them.

On the other hand, journalists sometimes should protect the identity of their sources. For example, employees sometimes fear for their jobs and refuse to discuss safety hazards or misuse of public money without a guarantee of anonymity. In school, however, you should promise to keep a source secret only in very rare cases. No doubt, some students will fear bad grades, poor recommendations or public embarrassment if they tell you something, but most of the time you are safer with sources you can reveal to your audience.

off-the-record
comments made to a reporter as background information and not for publication

Accuracy and Objectivity.
Ethical reporters should always strive for accuracy when covering events. Reporters have no excuse for inaccuracies or a lack of thoroughness. For example, if you cover a school board meeting and are not sure how to spell the superintendent's name, you should check it in your school's directory. If you need to

retraction

a correction in a subsequent issue of a publication

double check who won first place in the student art show, call the chair of the art department.

Remember that it's easier to take an extra minute to get the facts right before your article is printed than it is to run a **retraction,** a correction in a subsequent issue. Retractions are necessary but occasionally embarrassing for the newspaper staff.

The code also encourages reporters to be objective. In other words, unless you are writing an editorial (or certain kinds of feature stories), keep your opinions to yourself. Although you might think the jazz band performed better than the pep band at the All-City Music Contest, don't say so in a news story. The judges' marks will indicate this. Wouldn't you be better off not commenting on the football team's weight problem? Let the coach's comment that the team would be more agile if some of the linemen dropped a few pounds speak for itself.

Fair Play. Finally, the Code of Ethics emphasizes that journalists should always show respect for the dignity, privacy, rights and well-being of the people they encounter while gathering and covering news. If you plan to report that your school's janitorial staff has not been doing a good a job of cleaning, be sure to present all sides. Take the time to interview the supervisor. You might learn that he or she has fewer staff members this year because of budget cuts. By giving the supervisor a chance to respond to your initial charges, you are getting the true story and not hurting someone's professional reputation.

Now that you understand the basics of the Code of Ethics of the Society of Professional Journalists, it should be easier to know what to do in sticky situations. Consider the following situations high school students have encountered, and decide what you would do if faced with the same problems.

Working with a tape recorder insures accurate reporting when you conduct an interview.

Maintaining High Standards

Two students attending Moses Lake High School in Washington accused their principal of violating their First Amendment rights after he confiscated the results of a survey they had conducted. The students, Lisa Segura and Stacey Dennis, became upset after their school principal, Larry Smith, demanded that they give him the results of a survey regarding the sexual experiences of their classmates. The two had planned to use the survey as a sidebar to a story on teenage pregnancy for the *Chief Events,* the student newspaper.

The problem for Segura and Dennis began after they wrote the survey and distributed it to a senior history class. After they collected the completed surveys, the history teacher started to worry about whether the students had the authority to conduct a survey and then contacted the principal. Smith questioned and scolded the two students before calling the newspaper's adviser, Lynda Maraby, into his office. Maraby said she wished she had seen the survey before it was distributed. She backed the students, however, saying the survey results would be a good addition to the article. Despite Maraby's show of support, Smith refused to let the survey run in the paper.

Why did Smith confiscate the survey's results? Did he think the survey was in poor taste, or did he object for some other reason? If Smith did not like the subject matter, why would he let the article on pregnancy run? If the students had shared the survey with their adviser in the first place, could some of their difficulties with the principal have been avoided?

Matters of Taste

How many times have you read a newspaper or magazine article that caused you to do a doubletake or wrinkle your nose in disgust? As much as reporters want to use gritty realism to capture their readers' attention, they have to remember to be tasteful, too. The problem with taste is that something that might be acceptable to one person could be highly offensive to another. Learning to use good judgment in such matters is not an exact science. It takes experience and maturity.

Consider this case: When an unusual visitor invited himself to lunch at St. Albans School in northwestern Washington, headmaster Mark Mullin and newspaper adviser Wallace Ragan did not want to hear any more about him, let alone read about him in the school paper. The visitor was a cockroach who had shown up in a plate of chicken nuggets during lunch in the school cafeteria. Staff members of the *St. Albans News* heard about the incident and decided to investigate it for the next issue.

After reviewing the proposed article, Mullin told Ragan that the article was not "fit to print" at the prestigious private school and advised him to pull it before the paper ran. Instead of calling his decision censorship, however, the adviser defended the principal's actions as a "question of good taste and sensitivity." Mullin further stated that he wanted to have the article pulled in an attempt to set higher standards

A Yearbook of Turmoil

Life in many small towns revolves around the local schools. So when people in Auburn, Neb., saw the 1995-96 high school yearbook, the one with a National Enquirer-style theme, controversy was sure to follow.

What no one expected was that the controversial yearbook would eventually cause the principal and the yearbook adviser to both resign. Craig Fredin, the yearbook adviser and a guidance counselor, said the yearbook staff members meant no harm. "We used satire," Fredin said. "Some people in the community misinterpreted what was put in the book. It's a small town. That kind of thing causes an uproar."

One student, Kara Vaughn, asked for a refund. On the "Psychic Predictions Page," hers said she would be "speaking to students about teen-age abstinence." Ms. Vaughn, then Kara Bowman, graduated at midterm, pregnant, and married to classmate Andrew Vaughn. "It's totally disgusting that the teacher let it slide by," she said. "A high school yearbook is supposed to be about good things."

Principal Jerry Beach said he resigned because ultimately he was responsible for whatever happened in his building. "The annual published this year was something that some people considered as being hurtful. When you accept a position like this, things that come out of my building are mine. It's part of the job."

(*Omaha World-Herald*, Dec. 10, 1996)

for the newspaper. He was not putting a stop to aggressive reporting but rather giving students a chance to report "within the standards of decency," he said.

Could the students have covered this incident in an ethical manner and avoided the issue of poor taste? Perhaps they could have written an article on food preparation and health standards. Rather than dwelling on one sensational happening, they might have used that event to lead to a more serious issue. In addition to focusing on their own cafeteria, for example, they could have checked the health standards of local fast-food restaurants. By doing so, they would have used the cockroach incident to develop a newsworthy issue—something with which few administrators could find fault.

1. Do other professions have codes of ethics? Ask your teacher what code of ethics educators use. Check with your parents and relatives to see if they know about professional standards of behavior for different career fields. Your guidance counselors may be able to help, too.

2. One of the most important areas of journalistic ethics involves an accused person's right to a fair trial. What steps can a judge take to safeguard the presumption of innocence? How do the media cover routine court cases? How do they cover sensational cases? What ethical considerations should a journalist covering a court case keep in mind?

◢ PRACTICAL POLICIES AND PROCEDURES

No more pretending. As much as we would like to believe the world is a perfect place, we can't. Sometimes crumbs are all we find in the cookie jar, the person selling movie tickets knows how old you really are, and your mother always calls from work to see how you are feeling if you stay home. Furthermore, school administrators and the court system certainly will not allow you to print whatever you want to about anything.

Don't panic. By recalling what you have learned about ethics, you can still write hard-hitting articles for your high school newspaper or broadcast programs. Tough, uncompromising, fair-minded journalism is still an option, and you are not expected to tackle tough issues alone. Your adviser, principal and fellow staff members are there to help.

Journalism Advisers

Just as you go to your math teacher with a tough algebra problem, you should seek out your journalism adviser for help with ethical questions. Many advisers have extensive journalistic experience and want to share their expertise with you. But remember, your adviser can't help you if you don't share the problem. Remember, too, that your adviser will be the one most likely to back you up when you encounter censorship issues. The following example illustrates a case in which students could count on their adviser for support.

Members of the Upper Arlington High School newspaper staff in Arlington, Virginia, ran into a question of ethics and censorship when they decided to gather information on local police tactics by staging a party. The idea for a story called "Police versus Parties" began when members of the local police force refused to comment to student reporters on allegations that the police had entered high school parties without probable cause. Probable cause in this case meant the police had reason to believe the students were engaging in unlawful behavior.

According to reporter Chad Kister, the staff "wanted to give the police the benefit of the doubt," so they decided to hold a nonalcoholic party to see what the police would do. They held the party at the home of the paper's photographer and called in a complaint that a party at that address was too loud. Responding to the complaint, the police officers approached the house, and without knocking or obtaining permission to enter, they went inside.

The reporters who were staging the party immediately identified themselves to the police officers. The reporters said that because the officers had entered the house without permission, they were violating the students' protection against unreasonable search and seizure guaranteed to them by the Fourth Amendment. The city attorney, who later investigated the incident, said the officers followed "proper procedure, consistent with the law," but Kister said he and other reporters still wanted to let people know what the police were doing.

The students' journalism adviser, Sarah Ortman, could have chosen to censor the article because the information was gathered in a questionable fashion. She decided not to, however, and the article was published.

What do you think? Would things have been different if the students had discussed their plans with their adviser before staging the party?

High School Principals

A journalism adviser is not the only person students can turn to for help with tough journalism issues. Many high school principals are willing to assist student reporters and do as much as they can to help members of the newspaper staff practice ethical journalism and avoid censorship.

At Central High School in Tennessee, student reporters have developed a professional working relationship with their principal that has benefited the entire school. Principal Thomas Harrison has told the students that they can cover whatever they choose as long as they don't write anything irresponsible. By all accounts, the students appreciate their journalistic freedom and abide by Harrison's request.

"I don't think that [censorship]'s wise," Harrison said. "I think the students take the paper more seriously if they don't view it as some mouthpiece or some public relations effort of the administration. Even students know when they are being manipulated."

In choosing to take a hands off approach to their students' newspapers, as Harrison did, high school principals know that they may face controversy. Administrators, members of the teaching staff and people in the community are not always going to agree with what students are covering, and they will go to the principal with their complaints. This was the case in Missouri at Kirkwood High School when principal Frankie McCallie backed her students' rights to cover controversial issues.

McCallie felt pressure to censor the student newspaper when staff members decided to run a Planned Parenthood advertisement. The ad, which listed a telephone number for counseling and referral, said, in part, "It's not enough to 'just say no.' Say KNOW." Birthright, an anti-abortion organization, asked to run its own ad. That ad said, in part, "Make no mistake about it. The abortionist doesn't perform choice. He kills a baby." The students ran that ad too.

As expected, McCallie received many requests from parents and other members of the community for both ads to be pulled. In fact, Kirkwood High eventually received 300 phone calls and 121 letters. There were also pickets at meetings of the school board. But because the school's policy stated that the students control their newspaper's content, McCallie decided the students should choose whether or not to continue to run the ads. "If there's going to be a free press, it's up to the students to decide how to handle difficult situations," McCallie said. "I would have supported whatever decision the staff made. . . . It's the right way to educate."

How would your principal react to these situations? Would he or she back the decisions made by student staff members? What can student journalists do to improve or develop a working relationship with their schools' administrators?

student expression policy
a written directive approved by the school board or established by a school publication board to protect the rights of student expression and to establish limits on expression where needed

publication board
a committee set up to help guide and advise student publications

Publication Boards

One other step that students can take to avoid censorship is to make sure that their high school has a policy stating the rights of student reporters. If your school does not have a policy concerning student publications, urge your adviser to help you work toward getting one established. Your adviser could play an important role in encouraging your principal, superintendent or school board to create a policy protecting the right of student reporters to make their own content decisions. **Student expression policies** can take the form of written directives approved by the school board or be established by individual school publication boards.

A **publication board** is basically a committee set up to help guide and advise student publications. In some cases, the publication board plays a role in selecting staff members, selecting the kind of computer equipment the publication will buy, providing a forum for those with complaints against a publication, revising publication policies and in handling disputes between staff members and the school administrators. Publication boards often include the publication advisor, student editor, representatives of student government, other interested students, a parent and an assistant principal. In many cases students make up the majority of the board's members.

At Bigfork High School in Montana, the *Norse Code* had been in the habit of stirring up controversy. In the past, complaints concerning some of the editorial cartoons and what community members viewed as racist comments in the student newspaper had caused Principal Vernon Pond to put his foot down. The "last straw," Pond said, occurred when one student wrote a story entitled "How to Kill a Cat" and another student came up with a story on self-mutilation. Although the articles were intended to be satiric, Pond said they were "admittedly in poor taste."

Pond's solution was to create a publications board. The purpose of the board (which would consist of Pond, two teachers, two community members and three students) was to make sure that articles in the paper were not obscene or libelous. A publications board, however, can also be a positive force by helping recruit and select staff members, screening complaints and settling disputes between student editors and the adviser.

Student expression policies or publication boards offer several protections. In particular, they allow a school district to commit itself to supporting free expression. Publication boards won't work for every school, but one might be an asset at your school.

....

1. Find out if your school has a publications board. How are disputes about censorship handled within the school? Are there avenues for students to appeal an adviser's decision? The principal's decision?

2. Suppose your yearbook staff decides to accept senior pictures by student choice rather than those chosen by a designated professional photographer. What guidelines should the yearbook staff establish besides specifying size and other technical matters? For example, would student-drawn self-portraits be accepted? What about pictures that include hats, pets or unusual poses? What kinds of problems does freedom of choice create for the staff in this case?

CHAPTER REVIEW

KEY TERMS

Show that you know the meanings of the following key terms by correctly using them in complete sentences. Write your answers on a separate sheet of paper.

ethics	libel	student expression
confidentiality	slander	policy
censorship	prior review	publication board
obscenity	off-the-record	
copyright	retraction	

OPEN FORUM

1. Imagine that you and your classmates have inherited an island where you will establish the rules, rights and freedoms that will prevail. One of the first decisions you island citizens will make is whether or not to allow a free press. What are the pros and cons of each position? Which position does your class prefer?
2. A common conflict in student journalism occurs when a reporter has too little time before a deadline to double check the facts in a story. Are there times when meeting a deadline is more important than making an ethical decision?
3. Professional journalists sometimes see themselves as "adversaries" of governmental officials. Is such an attitude appropriate or wise for professional journalists? For student journalists? Why or why not?
4. Suppose you're a reporter covering a major criminal case. You visit the prosecutor in his office and ask a few questions. The prosecutor answers "no comment" to all your questions. Then the prosecutor is called out of his office. You realize that a file you're interested in is lying on his desk. What do you do?

FINDING THE FLAW

1. Find an example of political doublespeak in the news media. Politicians use doublespeak when they say one thing but mean another. Doublespeak comes in handy especially when presenting bad news to the public. (Election campaigns are especially good times to look.) Can you find a flaw in facts, logic or reasoning?
2. Read the following story, and decide whether it is ready for print. Does it contain the writer's opinions? Is any of it libelous?

◆ FINDING THE FLAW, continued

Calculus Teacher Gives Students the Shaft

Juniors and seniors who have taken Honors Advanced Algebra and are thinking of taking calculus should think again.

Not all the students who are presently enrolled in the course are doing well or happy with what they are learning. Six of the 13 students taking the course said it's okay; three said they don't like it but are determined to see things through because the course will look good on their transcripts; and the other four said they are not getting what they expected.

Their frustration could be summed up by the comments of Mary Sanchez, senior. She said that the teacher, Mr. Harry Howard, "is incapable of explaining calculus to students who are not familiar with the subject." She said she is often lost in the lectures and that she does not get enough help from Howard.

When Howard was asked about the dissatisfaction of some of his students, he said, "Students of limited ability, like Mary, have difficulty grasping subjects as difficult as calculus and probably cannot earn above a 'C' in my course."

Howard has been teaching here at Slippery Falls for five years. He is a graduate of Sand Dunes State in California, where he earned a 2.5 GPA. His college grade in calculus was a D+.

At Slippery Falls he tried to start a calculus club, but no one joined. Students say he will help them if they go to him, but he seems reluctant to offer assistance and almost never encourages them to stop by his classroom for help.

Students who expect to enroll in calculus should discuss their plans with other teachers in the math department. We need a new calculus teacher!

 MEDIA WATCH

1. Watch an investigative news program such as *60 Minutes, 48 Hours, 20/20* or *Hard Copy*. Discuss with your classmates how ethical you consider the investigation to have been.
2. Buy a few copies of the supermarket tabloids. Analyze whether the stories are libelous or unethical.
3. Angry journalists shredded the reputation of Joe Klein, a political columnist for *Newsweek* and a commentator for CBS, when he admitted he was the anonymous author of *Primary Colors,* a political novel. The novel dramatizes the exploits of a charming, womanizing southern governor and presidential candidate named Jack Stanton, who bears an uncanny resemblance to Bill Clinton. Journalists didn't mind Klein's decision to disguise his authorship, but they did object to his repeated denials to the media. "For God's sake," Klein had told the *New York Times*, "definitely I didn't write

◆ MEDIA WATCH, CONTINUED

it." But Klein did write it, as a handwriting analysis of the manuscript proved. He then paid a price. CBS accepted his resignation, and *Newsweek* suspended his column. What do you think? Is it ethical for journalists to use "Anonymous" as a byline?

String Book

1. Examine the daily paper or a daily news broadcast to find a possible ethical dilemma. Write a short essay detailing the dilemma, and explain how you would handle it.
2. Draft your own personal code of ethics for journalism. Refer to it from time to time to check whether you have been consistent in following your principles.

Chapter 3
What Is News?

"The primary office of a newspaper is gathering of news . . . comment is free, but facts are sacred."

—Charles Prestwich Scott

KEY TERMS

In this chapter, you will learn the meaning of these terms:

news
gatekeeper
timeliness
run
prominence
proximity
conflict
impact
human interest
wire service
tip
budget
top story
news hole
news flow
cut
deadline
column inch
news judgment
beat
local angle
localize
futures file

LEARNING OBJECTIVES

After completing this chapter, you will be able to:

◆ define news, and explain its characteristics,
◆ identify characteristics that make a story newsworthy,
◆ recognize other factors that influence news,
◆ find story ideas.

◆

"All the good stories, I call 'em *'Did 'ja stories,'* because people say *'Did 'ja hear* about this?' or *'Did 'ja hear* about that?'" says *New York Daily News* reporter Michael Daly.

How many times have you heard someone begin a conversation with "Did 'ja hear about"? Maybe you've even done it yourself. When friends want to communicate information, they often begin that way. When television newscasters or newspaper reporters want to communicate information, they don't begin with "Did 'ja hear," but they do convey information to an audience. When someone wins the lottery, an earthquake damages California freeways, a movie star gets married or multitudes of people die from hunger in Africa, journalists tell people about it, and people talk to one another about it. They call it news.

In this chapter we will look at different ways news has been defined, at the characteristics that make stories news, and at the other things that influence what is news on any given day. We will also give you some tips that will help you start finding news for your newspaper or newscast.

◆ DEFINING NEWS

News is all of the following:

  ◆ information, especially information you haven't heard before,
  ◆ something interesting or important to you,
  ◆ something that has or will have an impact on you and others,
  ◆ what the media report.

Putting it all together, we say **news** is information we haven't heard before that is delivered through a mass medium and has some impact on our lives.

Every day hundreds, perhaps thousands, of pieces of information could be news. From all that information, certain individuals select the few pieces that will be called news for their communities. Directors and producers select the stories and plan the news shows for radio and television. Editors select and prioritize the items for each page of the newspaper. The individuals who determine what stories will be news for their communities have been called **gatekeepers** because of their role

news

information not previously known that is delivered through the mass media and has some impact on the audience

gatekeeper

a label put on those individuals, such as newspaper editors and broadcast news directors, who determine what stories will be news for their communities in selecting what they believe to be the important stories and rejecting what they believe to be the less significant stories.

As they look over all the possibilities, the producers and editors must feel like we all do when we stand in front of a candy store window and look at all the possible goodies we could have. But imagine that today you have been designated to buy one kind of candy to treat all your classmates. You are in charge of deciding what the most people will like.

As you watch, you notice that some people go past the candy display without buying anything. You observe that of those who buy, most select the chocolate fudge. You also notice that a few choose the peanut butter fudge or the chocolate-covered cherries. The really adventurous buy the macadamia nut mix. Some buy a little of each. You prefer the chocolate mints, but you compromise with the one the most people are buying, the chocolate fudge.

The front page of a newspaper is like a candy store window. People look in quickly. If there's nothing there that tempts them in the first 15 seconds, they go on by. They may stop only long enough to read the tastiest news, or they may stop to sample several stories.

The stories that the gatekeepers choose to put on the front page or at the beginning of the newscast are chosen because they are like the fudge in the candy store: they come closest to being of interest to the most people. The editors and producers, like the candy makers, have identified them as being the ones that will attract the largest number of people, and they have put them in the 'window.'

Professional Journalists Define News

Longtime NBC news anchor David Brinkley said news is "what I say it is. It's something worth knowing by my standards." A professional journalist who has spent his career defining news, Brinkley speaks as one of the key people who make the judgments about what will be news each day.

A more colorful definition of news was offered by Stanley Walker, editor of the *New York Herald Tribune,* in the 1930s. He said news revolved around the three W's—"women, wampum, and wrongdoing." Although today we might consider Walker's remark politically incorrect, we can understand that he meant people are interested in stories about sex, money and crime. He believed that those were the topics people secretly desired to read about.

Walker was using metaphors to define news, but the categories he identified still dominate the news in today's media. As we move into the 21st century, sex stories deal with more than celebrity romances. They focus on pay equity, sexual harassment, women's rights, divorce, abortion, AIDS and babies born addicted to crack cocaine. Money stories deal with the economy, unemployment, taxes, bond issues, and the Dow Jones and NASDAQ averages. Crime stories deal with child and spouse abuse, gangs, bombings, shooting sprees and computer hackers. Some stories, like natural disasters and the weather, are harder to fit into Walker's categories.

News is . . .

◆ "Anything that will make people talk."—Charles A. Dana, editor, *New York Sun*

◆ "The glue that binds free societies together."—Allen H. Neuharth, founder, *USA Today*

◆ "Anything that makes the reader say, 'Gee Whiz!' "—Arthur McEwen, editorial writer, *San Francisco Examiner*

◆ "A business, but it is also a public trust."—Dan Rather, CBS News

◆ "What a chap who doesn't care much about anything wants to read."—Corker, a character in *Scoop*, a novel by Evelyn Waugh

◆ "What is news? It is *information* only."—Walter Cronkite, news anchor, CBS News

◆ "What makes it a cover story? It sells papers."—Erin Moriarty, reporter, CBS News

DATELINE DATELINE DATELINE

NEW YORK, Aug. 19, 1896—
"All the News That's Fit to Print"
has been the motto of the *New
York Times* since shortly after
Adolph S. Ochs became editor
in August 1896. In his first editorial, Ochs wrote:

"It will be my earnest aim
that the *New York Times* give the
news, all the news, in concise
and attractive form, in language
that is parliamentary in good
society, and give it as early, if
not earlier, than it can be
learned through any other reliable medium . . . to make of the
New York Times a forum for the
consideration of all questions of
public importance."

Asked what news was unfit to
print, Ochs replied, "What's
untrue."

Today the *New York Times* is
considered the newspaper of
record, the source for complete,
fair and accurate news of the
day, for the United States. It
earned the title because of its
tradition of thorough coverage
of the news events that make
history: national politics; the
administration; Congress; government agencies; foreign policies; news from abroad of significant governmental change;
wars; and certain general topics
in the news such as finance, science and the press.

Its reputation for accuracy,
completeness and honesty, as
well as its policy of carrying the
complete texts of important
speeches, reports, documents
and presidential news conferences, has made it a reference
source for historians and
researchers.

Over a century ago, John B. Bogart, an editor at the *New York Sun,*
said, "When a dog bites a man, that is not news, because it happens so
often, but if a man bites a dog, it's news." Bogart was implying that in
order for an event to be news, it had to be slightly out of the ordinary.
Bogart's definition is still being tested, if some recent headlines are any
indication:

"Man charged after biting dog"
"Police dog bites handler's wife"
"Burglar bites off part of man's ear"

An executive producer of ABC's *Evening News* recently said that people are interested in stories that tell them how safe the world is, how
safe their families are and how safe their money is. This definition
implies that people are concerned about more than just what they
secretly desire to read. They're concerned about the impact of what's
happening in the world. People want to know how the news will affect
their own security and that of their families.

When the gatekeepers at the television networks plan the content of
their newscasts, they make selections that fit their definition of news.
Thus, stories that will be news on the newscasts today are determined
by a few key people, but these people determine what becomes the
news for everyone.

Consumers Define News

As a consumer of news, you are your own gatekeeper. You have a limited amount of time to spend reading or watching news. Your interests
and preferences guide you to set your own agenda. From what the
media gatekeepers choose to offer, you narrow what you will call news
to the stories or sections of the paper or newscast that you'll spend time
investigating.

Each individual has a reading strategy. Maybe you read the sports
first and never look at the editorial page, or you check out the front
page and the comics but don't look at the sports
or weather reports. Your grandparents may
watch the weather report and ignore the sports.
They might read the obituaries and the editorial
page. Your little brother looks at only the
comics. He watches his favorite
weekly show and ignores the news
altogether. He doesn't even know
what an editorial is.

Your parents, friends and
neighbors all want to read or listen
to some parts of the news more than
others, but not necessarily the same
parts. Because the media report on
an event, doesn't make it news to
everyone.

CHARACTERISTICS OF NEWS

People, events and information that are newsworthy share common, identifiable characteristics. Not all characteristics are present in every news story, but every item that is newsworthy will have one or more of these characteristics: timeliness, prominence, proximity, conflict, impact and human interest. The importance of each characteristic differs from story to story. Most stories have elements of more than one characteristic.

Timeliness

News is timely the day it happens. In other words, **timeliness** is a characteristic of a news story about an event that is reported as soon as it happens. An accident, a fire, the signing of a peace treaty or the result of an election is news when it happens. It appears on that day's front page or newscast. Many stories only **run,** or appear in the media, one day—the day they happen. Others continue to be timely news as long as there is new information to add and the audience is interested in knowing more about the topic.

School newspapers usually do not come out frequently enough to carry truly timely news. The time and cost involved in producing and printing the school paper means that several days or weeks may elapse between the time the reporter writes the story and the reader reads it—long enough for much of the news to lose its timeliness. Most stories in school newspapers, therefore, are written as preview stories, timeless features or consequence stories (stories that are news now as the result of earlier events). Sports coverage is particularly challenging for school

timeliness

> a characteristic of a news story about an event that is reported as soon as it happens

run

> to appear in the media. A story is said to run the day it appears in the media: "The story will run in the Sunday edition."

newspapers when several games are played between issues (see Chapters 10 and 13).

Prominence

prominence

a characteristic of a news story about someone whose name or job (such as the president of the United States) is well known and easily recognized by the public

Prominent persons are those whose names you recognize. The president of the United States, rock stars, actors, actresses and Mickey Mouse all have **prominence.** Prominent persons do not have to be international celebrities. Every community has prominent persons. The mayor, the police chief, local radio or television personalities, and business leaders are generally recognized throughout the community. They are the people whose names, pictures and voices appear before the public on a regular basis and who have the power to influence public opinion by their actions or attitudes.

Prominent persons exist in your school community, too. Members of the board of education, administrators, faculty, the quarterback of the school football team and the president of the student council are some of the prominent persons your readers and listeners will recognize. These people are in positions to make decisions or express opinions that affect everyone in your audience. People expect to see the names of these leaders in headlines and to hear their voices in newscasts.

Proximity

proximity

a characteristic of a news story that happens close to home

The word **proximity** refers to being close by. If a hurricane destroys a small town in Florida, everyone in the United States is interested, because their fellow citizens are involved. But people in Florida are more interested than those in Oklahoma, because it happened in their state. If a tornado blows away a small town in Oklahoma, however, people in Oklahoma are more interested than those in Florida.

If a team in your school conference or district violates the rules and must forfeit the games they played the first half of the season, the story of the penalty is more newsworthy in your paper than in a school paper outside your conference or district. If one of the forfeited games was against your school, the proximity factor is even greater for you.

Emotional proximity may also make a story news to you. You listen for details when you hear a story about Fargo, North Dakota, if you have relatives there. You look closely at pictures of Yellowstone National Park in the Sunday entertainment section because you've vacationed there. You are attracted to a story about a child with leukemia because a classmate has a terminal illness.

conflict

a characteristic of a news story that involves two sides engaged in a 'battle' from which one will emerge the winner, such as a story about war, an athletic competition or an election

Conflict

Conflict involves opposing forces and the tension and suspense that is created when two sides meet. These forces may be physical, emotional or philosophical. The extreme and classic example of conflict is war. When opposing forces meet in battle, there is physical conflict, and one side usually emerges victorious. The conflict, however, may have begun as a philosophical disagreement between two governments long before their forces met.

A common example of conflict is an athletic competition. Two teams or several individuals meet to compete. One side or one person wins. Another common example is an election. Elections are conflicts in that two or more persons with different philosophies about how a job should be done compete for votes, and the one with whom the most people agree gets elected. Stories about contests, debates, peace negotiations between nations, contract negotiations between teachers and boards of education, and fights in the school parking lot are all based on conflict.

Impact

The effect or consequence a story has on the audience is its **impact.** Readers' interests are directly related to the degree of impact the subject of the story will have on their lives. Stories about the environment, for example, have an impact on everyone. A story about a nuclear waste dump's being built in your county has more immediate impact on you than one about the deforestation of the jungles in Brazil, yet both have consequences that will eventually affect you.

News of a tax increase has an impact on all who will pay the tax and all who will benefit from the money collected. You may not feel that an increase in the property tax has consequences for you, because you do not own any property and will not have to pay the extra tax. However, if the money is going to go to build a new school, it may affect your younger brother or sister.

Imagine that your state legislature passes a bill limiting students' freedom of expression. Your community paper gives it a couple of paragraphs on page 15 of the first section. However, your school newspaper prints a front-page story on what the bill will mean to your readers and to your newspaper. The story has quotes from your state senator, your newspaper adviser and the principal. The editorial cartoon is about the bill, and an editorial explains the impact of the bill on your readers. The difference in the amount of coverage given to the story in each publication is a reflection of the consequence, or impact, the story has on the readers of that publication. Few general readers will feel the impact of such a bill, but all students will feel it.

impact
a characteristic of a news story based on the effect or consequence the story will have on the audience

Competition equals impact and interest, especially with sporting events.

BYLINE

DAN RATHER
CBS NEWS

I was in the CBS studios in New York on April 4, 1968, the night the bulletin from Memphis hit the wire that Martin Luther King had been shot. I had long since left the civil rights beat, had served a turn at the White House, gone overseas, and covered the war in Vietnam.

But I remembered Memphis.

The instant someone tore the copy off the wire and read the paragraph out loud, I picked up the phone and dialed from memory the police station in Memphis. There wasn't time to look up the number or go through an operator. The switchboard would be jammed almost immediately. I had to get and keep an open line, if I could.

A reporter half ran through the newsroom asking if anyone had any sources. I shouted back, "I'm on the line to the Memphis police now." The cop on the switchboard knew nothing. When I said, "This is Dan Rather, with CBS News, in New York," he almost hung up on me. He didn't want to be involved. New York. CBS. Red flags everywhere.

Finally he said, "I can't keep this line open. If you want to talk to someone, tell me now."

I said, "Give me the police chief."

"He's not here."

"Then give me homicide."

What went through my mind was this: If I could talk to someone who knew what had happened, I thought I could judge whether he was telling me the truth and how serious the situation was. The questions were like a stepladder. Was Dr. King seriously wounded? If so, was he critical? If critical, was he now dead? You ran it up just that way. The police-beat experience came into play automatically, like a computer tape activating.

I was switched to homicide. I identified myself. The cop at the other end said, "There is not a thing I can tell you."

I said, "I know that. But I only want to know one thing. Is he dead?"

He repeated, "There's not a thing I can tell you."

The second time he said that, I knew King was dead. I asked him to transfer me to the chief's office. A spokesman assigned to handle calls from the press got on the line. I told him, "I know Martin Luther King is dead and I simply need to verify that fact."

He said, "I'm not the one to verify it."

I said, "In that case I must ask you to deny it."

He said, very quickly, "I'm not denying it."

"Then it is true, I take it."

"You take it any way you want."

In the meantime I had obtained the name of the hospital from the officer in homicide, and I had another reporter contact the doctors. We soon verified that King was dead.

I walked over to Casey Davidson, who was helping supervise the newsroom. I said, "Casey, here's the situation: King is dead, but I don't think we ought to go with that as step one. You better prepare a bulletin though, because I'm telling you he's dead."

He asked me how I knew. I told him I had talked with two people at the police station, no denials. Another reporter had received the same response from the hospital. Casey started to turn to someone to ask them to prepare a standby bulletin—we had writers on duty for that sort of thing—but I said, "No, I'll write one." And I did, very straight:

> Dr. Martin Luther King, Jr., is dead.
> Dr. King was shot by an assailant, or assailants, at approximately 7:15 p.m. Eastern time tonight at a motel in Memphis.

We were the first to confirm on the air the death of the man who had led the battle to win the rights promised his people one hundred years before. He had died as many, including Dr. King, expected he would.

Rather, Dan with Mickey Herskowitz, The Camera Never Blinks: Adventures of a TV Journalist, *Morrow & Co.: New York. 1977. pp. 104–105.*

Human Interest

A story that tugs at your heartstrings or satisfies your curiosity about other people and what happens to them has the news characteristic of **human interest.** Ever since cave dwellers began gathering around fires to talk about who killed the largest mastodon, or who had been killed by one, people have wanted to know about other people. Whether a message about the life of another human being comes in a letter, by phone or through your computer's electronic mail system, everyone is interested. The common interest in what happens to others is what makes us seek out friends for conversation during a refreshment break or buy *People* to read in our spare moments.

When a little girl got caught in a well in Texas, millions of people watched to see if she would be rescued. When the *Challenger* space shuttle exploded, people everywhere grieved with the families of the astronauts and the civilians who died. When a young family with a baby was stranded in the mountains in a snowstorm and the father walked for two days to get help, people followed the story and rejoiced when the family was found alive. When a flood in Mississippi or a hurricane in South Carolina destroys homes and injures or kills people, other people rush to help or send food and clothing because they care that human beings are suffering.

Children and adults doing normal activities in some slightly unusual way are topics for human interest stories. A high school student who does taxidermy as a hobby, a teacher in Missouri who spends summers in Alaska running a salmon-fishing business, a graduate of your school who celebrates a 100th birthday, and a young person who overcomes an injury or handicap are all subjects for human interest stories for your newspaper.

Some stories are news because they are about unusual things that happen to people. Consider a story that happened in Munich, Germany, and appeared in American newspapers:

> A Munich robber used instant-setting glue and an electric cable Friday to render his victim helpless after following the man home from a bank.
>
> According to police in this Bavarian city, the unidentified robber pulled a pistol on the 25-year-old house painter just outside the painter's apartment door and demanded $2,700.
>
> When the painter, who had just made a withdrawal from a bank, resisted, the robber forced him into the apartment. He then glued him to the toilet seat and shocked the painter until he fainted.
>
> By the time the painter recovered, the robber had fled with the cash. *(AP, Omaha World Herald.)*

People are held up at gunpoint everywhere, so conflict alone does not make this story newsworthy. Only the unusual twist of the robber's gluing his victim to the toilet seat makes it news as far away as the United States.

Like the story of the German painter, many stories have more than one characteristic of news. Proximity, for instance, varies in importance depending upon the location in which the story occurs. When the

human interest
a characteristic of a news story about people, usually those involved in some emotional struggle

president makes a speech to Congress, it is news to everyone in the United States, because he is the president. If he makes a speech in your state, it is more newsworthy to the people in your state, because someone with prominence is also in close proximity to you. If the president comes to your city or town, proximity is an even more important characteristic of news for the story, because your readers or viewers have a very high degree of interest in the event. The day the speech is delivered, the story will be timely news in many distant locations where proximity is not a factor but where the president has prominence.

YOUR BEAT

1. List the characteristics that make each story on the front page of yesterday's newspaper or on last night's half-hour newscast newsworthy. Indicate the characteristic you feel is the most significant for each story. Explain your choice.
2. Find stories that you think do not fit any of the characteristics of news listed in the chapter. Add characteristics to the list to fit the stories you found (for example, *consequence* or *bizarre*). Define your characteristic or characteristics, and give examples. If you were writing the list of characteristics, which characteristic or characteristics would you omit?

Explain your rationale for each omission. Are there characteristics on the list that might be combined? Which ones would you combine? Give examples for each combination you create.

3. Make a list of the prominent people in your school and their credentials or areas of interest. Compare your list to those of others in the class. As a group, make a master list of the prominent people who might be contacts for stories. Include their telephone numbers, office or room numbers, and homeroom teacher or counselor (if applicable) for ease in contacting them. Post your master list where everyone can use it, or keep a copy handy in your notebook for future reference.

CNN editors are surrounded by information sources in their workplace. Video feeds and time zone clocks keep them aware of up-to-the minute developments for their stories.

◢DETERMINING NEWS

From events happening locally, from the **wire services** (membership organizations that gather news from around the world and distribute it to local members) and from their reporters' ideas, or **tips,** editors and producers set a **budget.** A budget is a list of stories that will be news in their papers or on their newscasts for the day.

Journalists draw on their knowledge of their community and its values and interests when selecting the stories they believe will interest and affect people. They understand that some stories are of more interest to their readers and viewers, and that some have greater impact on the community's economic or political future. Each staff selects the stories it feels will be most important to its audience.

Fact, Interest and Audience

One way producers and editors decide which stories are news today is by considering fact, interest and audience. The *facts* are the material for the story itself: the words, numbers and pictures that make up the story. The facts must be adequate, accurate and timely. *Interest* indicates how much meaning the story has to the readers or viewers. What will it mean to their lives, their pocketbooks and their safety? The *audience* is the people who will be watching or reading the story and their values and interests. Within the audience are minority groups or subgroups whose interests need to be considered in today's multicultural society. Fact, interest and audience are not always of equal importance, but each should be considered for every story.

Every day's front page carries the stories the editors deem most important to the largest number of their readers. Let's analyze a front page using the fact, interest and audience formula.

Stories available today include the president's trip to Naples, Italy, to attend an economic conference with heads of state from 20 countries, a vote that will double the rates at the local landfill, the announcement of the state's decision on school funds allocations for the coming year, confirmation hearings for a Supreme Court nominee, and the story of a cat that escaped from its pet carrier on a flight from New York to Los Angeles.

Looking over the shoulders of the editors in Anytown, USA, as they consider each story in terms of fact, audience and interest, we can see how the newspaper editors might weigh each story and each factor. The president's trip to Europe is timely. The results of the conference with other heads of state will affect international relations and trade between the United States and 20 other countries for decades to come. The facts of the story are accurate, and the impact of the trip, both on current international relations and on the long-term economy of many governments, is momentous. No question, the editors think, of the importance of this story. Everyone should care about an event with such long-term international implications. Besides, the wire service has provided pictures of the president and his wife greeting foreign dignitaries in front of historic sites that readers will recognize.

wire service

a membership organization that gathers news from around the world and distributes it to local members; the way most local media outlets receive national and international news

tip

an idea for a story. A tip may come from a reporter, from the public or from a beat source

budget

a list of the stories for the next newspaper or news broadcast. Budgets are determined by editors or producers

Even though the president's trip is an important event, the gatekeepers know that not everyone will be interested in reading this story. Most readers will glance at the picture and maybe read the headline, but many will skip to another story. They will not care enough to read the details and weigh all that it may mean to them in the distant future. A few readers—those whose jobs are dependent upon international trade, or those who have been in Naples at some time, or those whose professions depend upon their knowledge of economic issues, for example—will care enough to read the whole story.

The second story on page one, about a raise in rates at the local landfill, has already brought an outcry from the public. People have been talking about the issue, and now city council members have voted to double the present rate. This story is timely and has immediate impact on residents. Because the money will come directly out of the pockets of homeowners and business owners, nearly everyone in the community will care. The editors are certain their readers will want to know about this immediately. However, fewer than half the subscribers live in the city. The others live in surrounding communities, where rates are not affected, so they likely will not care much about the story. The half of the audience who will pay the increase has a very high interest level; the other half has very little interest.

The third story involves something that occurs every year: the state allocates school funds. Because children and tax dollars are involved, the story is news every year, but the editors must ask whether there is anything that makes the story different this year. They discover that a new formula is being used to calculate the amount given to each school. Some schools will get more than they did last year; some will get significantly less. The local school is among those to receive less, but several schools in the area will receive more. The editors reason that everyone who pays taxes has a stake in this story, because it is his or her tax dollars being doled out by the state legislature. Some parents will be disappointed to see that the state is giving less support to the school their children attend. Others will be happy that their schools will get more. Teachers will fear that their salaries are in danger of being cut. Nearly everyone cares about this story.

The fourth story is about the confirmation hearings of a Supreme Court justice. Here the editors shake their heads, remembering that the last confirmation hearings took several months. The nominee must be approved by the Senate Judiciary Committee after a public hearing. The committee is very thorough in its investigation, because those appointed to the Court serve for life, and their decisions may influence national policy for many years.

Previous committee hearings have been televised, sometimes for days at a time. This nominee, a chief judge of the First Circuit Court of Appeals, has sailed quietly and almost unchallenged through four days of committee hearings. The public is hardly aware anyone has been nominated, let alone is about to be approved. The editors believe their readers need to know that this important vote is about to take place even though few seem to care. They decide to run the story on the front page with a photo of the nominee testifying at the hearing.

Finally, there is the story about the cat. A 3-year-old striped calico named Tabitha, missing for almost two weeks since she escaped from her pet carrier in the cargo hold of a Boeing 747, has been found frightened but alive in the false ceiling of the luggage compartment. During the 12 days Tabitha was missing, the plane had flown more than 32,000 miles and had been searched several times.

New York papers have been carrying the story for a week with daily "Pet Watch" updates, and several animal protection organizations have been pressuring the airline to find the cat. The story drew the attention of the national media when Tabitha was rescued, and the wire service sent a story and several photos to newspapers around the country.

The editors nod, knowing that there is little information of any value in the story but that everyone who picks up the paper will look at this story, because everyone seems to care about people and animals rescued from danger. A color picture of Tabitha and her happy owner will draw readers to the front page.

Now let's analyze a local television news lineup for the same day. The producers would probably use the same stories. The state school funds allocation story might come first, because it will have the most immediate effect on the largest number of local viewers. The TV reporters can tell the story with pictures of local schools and students whom viewers will recognize. Graphics can be added to show how the local allocations compare with others in the area. However, if it is a school break and there are no students in the halls, or if the graphics are just dull pie charts, the editors may move the story out of the lead position because it lacks visual impact.

Because of its immediate impact on local viewers, the landfill story will be a close competitor for **top story,** the most important story on the newscast or the front page. It can be shown through pictures of trucks collecting residents' garbage and dumping it at the landfill. News of the president's trip and the Supreme court nominee's hearing would lead the national news segment. The story of Tabitha's rescue would probably be the last story of the evening in order to leave listeners with a good feeling about the news.

top story

the most important story of the day, usually placed at the top of the front page or at the beginning of the newscast

Fact, Interest and Audience for School Media

School news staffs go through the same decision-making process in selecting the stories they will cover. They choose the stories they print or broadcast based on how much interest readers will have in the story and how much impact the news will have on them.

The fact, interest and audience formula works for school news, too. A story like the one above about state school funds allocations probably would not be covered in the school newspaper when it happened. Even though it was timely, the main reading audience, students, would not be interested in reading it. It would seem to them like a lot of big, meaningless numbers.

Two months later, however, when the school board announces a plan to remodel the gym and the fine arts wing with the money your school has received from the allocations, the story has much more proximity and impact for your readers. Students are interested, and editors choose to cover the story. By the time the page is designed, the architect's drawing is available to use as a graphic, and the reporter has quotations from school district officials. The story becomes the top story and the topic of the student opinion page.

Take the top story in the Jan. 14, 1994, issue of the student newspaper at Homestead High School in Cupertino, California (Exhibit 3.1). This story in the *Epitaph,* about a change in school starting time, was a good editorial choice. The story had timeliness, proximity and impact for the readers at Homestead High. The headline, "Students to Start School Late Mondays," should have gotten the attention of every student reader. The story was timely, too, because it appeared just before the beginning of the spring semester, when the late start time would go into effect. The student comments in the story and in an accompanying student opinion feature revealed the human interest side of the story.

Another story on the same front page was based on an interview with the district superintendent, who had been on the job only three weeks. Readers were curious to learn about her as a prominent person in their school community. They also wanted to know how the decisions she would be making would affect them. The feature and the question-and-answer format of the story kept the three-week-old news timely.

The third story on the page, "District adopts state's new transfer policy," was also chosen for the impact it would have on students in the future. The story localized a state legislative action allowing students to transfer among schools in the district. The quotes in the story from parents and school administrators showed that there had been favorable reaction to the new policy.

1. Look at the stories on the front page of a recent edition of your local newspaper. Using the fact, interest and audience formula, analyze each story. Why do you think the editor chose to put these stories on the front page? Who is the audience for each story? How much interest do people have in each story? Look through the rest of the paper. Are there other stories you would have chosen for the front page if you were the editor? Why?

2. Using the fact, interest and audience formula, analyze the stories in the last issue of your school newspaper. Who is the audience for each story? Is it everyone in the school or only a portion of the students? Are there stories that represent the interests of smaller groups within the audience? Look at the other news stories in the issue that might have been on the front page. Which one would you have chosen for the front page? Why?

3. Try substituting the word *impact* for the word *interest* in the *fact, interest* and *audience formula.* Instead of looking at how much interest readers have in a story, look at the impact or consequences the story will have on the readers. Analyze who the readers are and how much impact the story will have on them. Does this formula work as well? Would it change how the editors evaluate stories for the local paper? For the school paper? Choose either *interest* or *impact,* and write a persuasive paragraph convincing readers why it is the better choice.

FIGURE 3.1
CHOOSING APPROPRIATE FRONT PAGE STORIES

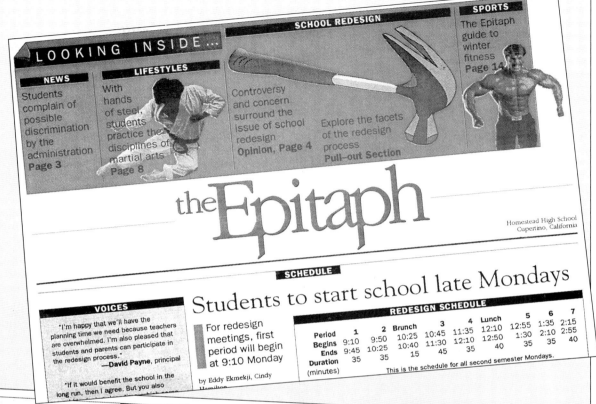

LOOKING INSIDE...

NEWS
Students complain of possible discrimination by the administration Page 3

LIFESTYLES
With hands of steel, students practice the disciplines of martial arts Page 8

SCHOOL REDESIGN
Controversy and concern surround the issue of school redesign Opinion, Page 4

Explore the facets of the redesign process Pull-out Section

SPORTS
The Epitaph guide to winter fitness Page 14

the Epitaph

Homestead High School
Cupertino, California

SCHEDULE

Students to start school late Mondays

VOICES

"I'm happy that we'll have the planning time we need because teachers are overwhelmed. I'm also pleased that students and parents can participate in the redesign process."
—**David Payne**, principal

"If it would benefit the school in the long run, then I agree. But you also...

For redesign meetings, first period will begin at 9:10 Monday

by Eddy Ekmekji, Cindy Hamilton

REDESIGN SCHEDULE

Period	1	2	Brunch	3	4	Lunch	5	6	7
Begins	9:10	9:50	10:25	10:45	11:35	12:10	12:55	1:35	2:15
Ends	9:45	10:25	10:40	11:30	12:10	12:50	1:30	2:10	2:55
Duration (minutes)	35	35	15	45	35	40	35	35	40

This is the schedule for all second semester Mondays.

DISTRICT

Superintendent faces questions

Panucci reveals her views regarding her role in the district and its future

by Michael Krishnan and Ramesh Srinivasan

Despite serving as district superintendent for only three weeks, Mary Panucci has already formulated a set of visions and goals for the district.

Replacing the retired Betty Pacheco, who served for eight years, Panucci inherits the several month old teacher contract dispute.

Relations between teachers and district officials at one point fueled a request by teachers for a state of impasse to be declared (see page 2). It was denied. Negotiations between teachers and management have recently improved. Panucci remains optimistic about resolving the matter quickly. "We are committed to interest-based bargaining. Our long-term interests are the same. I expect that they will resolve the contract soon."

One of Panucci's greatest strengths lies in her ability to effectively head a district, said Marilyn Wells, president of the California Teachers Association chapter in Red Bluff, where Panucci was formerly superintendent. "I can't say enough about her. She's outstanding and a good listener."

In an exclusive interview with the Epitaph, Panucci talked about her views ranging from her own philosophies to the district's future.

Panucci

Do you like being an educator and, if so, why? I think, especially for a woman, it's being a mother. I think to an extent it is innate to want to help, guide, support and make our world a better place.

What is the district's greatest strength? The people here make me feel like I have been here all of my life. It comes from the accepting atmosphere. I think that is extraordinary.

What are your aspirations for the district? I think our young people need to be better prepared and focused while they are in high school. . I think (students) need to look beyond college to the rest of their lives. I think we can do more.

How do you view the district's future? I see that the district is going to continue to be on the leading edge. There are a lot of things happening in this country....and no matter what happens, the programs are going to be superior. The community is changing, growing, responding and getting better.

As a leader, what are your strengths? I can set a good example. I can share a sense of urgency and importance of what were about: education.

What is your opinion of Homestead's current redesign process? I think it's wonderful. Principal David Payne is a wonderful human being and extraordinary leader.

LEGISLATION

District adopts state's new transfer policy

Students now can attend other district schools

by Ramesh Srinivasan

Responding to a recently passed state policy, the Board of Education gave students the privilege of transferring to other schools in the district for the 1994-95 school year.

But district students will not be allowed to transfer to Homestead or Monta Vista High School because both schools have reached capacity enrollment. According to Trustee Homer Tong, students also will not be allowed to transfer in the case that a school's ethnic balance will be disrupted.

Giving parents the freedom to choose the district school their child attends, was the principal motivation behind the state policy, Tong said. "After the defeat of the voucher initiative, the state wanted to give parents some school choice."

Another advantage of the policy, Tong said, is it allows students to maximize their abilities. "We want students to develop their maximum potential. We want an environment where every student can excel. Conceptually, I'm a hundred percent in favor of this policy."

Parent Sarah Broadbent said she thinks she may use the new policy for the benefit of her younger children. "I am so dissatisfied with this school. I would definitely be interested in this policy."

On the whole, Principal David Payne said that the school will not be affected by the policy. " I don't think Homestead will be affected since we're at capacity. Students who would be crazy enough to leave the school can now do it."

Reprinted with permission from The Epitaph, *Homestead High School, Cupertino, Calif.*

◢FACTORS INFLUENCING NEWS

A story that would be high on the budget today might not have been news if it had happened yesterday, and it might not make the news if it happens tomorrow. How can the same story be news one day and not another day? What is considered news on any one day depends on a number of factors not directly related to any single story.

Size of the News Hole

news hole
>the amount of space in the newspaper or time in a newscast available for news

The **news hole** is the space or time available for news after the ads or commercials are run. Broadcast media are strictly limited by the amount of time available for news. In a 30-minute television news program, approximately 22 minutes are news, and eight minutes are advertising. Stations divide those 22 minutes among news, weather and sports. The news slot is subdivided among international, national and local news. Some stories will be given more time than others because of their importance, and some will be left out for lack of time.

In the newspaper, the news hole is the space left on the pages after the advertisements are placed. The amount of advertising sold determines the number of pages the paper can print. If fewer advertisers purchase ads for Monday's paper than for Wednesday's paper, there will be fewer pages available Monday and more available Wednesday. The news hole, therefore, will be smaller on Monday, and fewer stories will be printed. Some stories that have strong characteristics of news may not run because of the limited number of pages.

Sunday papers have many more pages and sections than do daily papers. Advertisers like to buy ads in Sunday papers because people spend more time reading the paper on Sunday, and more people buy the Sunday paper than the daily paper. Grocery stores usually advertise their weekly specials on Tuesday or Wednesday, so there is a larger paper, and a larger news hole, that day.

Your staff may be able to sell more advertising for an issue close to a special event, such as homecoming or prom, when students are spending money for flowers and special clothes. More ads and more income mean your staff can print extra pages and have a larger news hole in that issue.

News Flow

news flow
>the number of news stories available to run at any one time

cut
>removed from the budget. A cut occurs when a story that is planned gets set aside because a more significant story appears before the paper is printed or the newscast is run

The **news flow** is the number of stories available at any time. The news flow determines a story's importance or newsworthiness, because newsworthiness is relative. News that happens at the same time may make any story more or less newsworthy. The top story suddenly may no longer be the top story if something more important happens. Consequently, stories will be rearranged, and one or more stories may be **cut**, or omitted, from the budget to make room for the new story.

For example, 12 firefighters in Colorado die when they are trapped by a wall of fire. The planned top story, a piece about the cease-fire agreement reached in the Middle East yesterday, suddenly becomes of less interest to most American readers and is replaced by the story of the firefighters' deaths.

You discover that your school must forfeit three hard-fought games because of a rules violation, but you had planned a front-page story about the groundbreaking for a new sports complex. You decide your readers are more interested in knowing the details of the forfeitures just announced than in knowing more about the groundbreaking for a building that has been planned for a long time. Thus, you shorten the groundbreaking news to a picture in order to make room for the new story. Compared with the breaking story, the planned one loses significance.

Sometimes there is just nothing happening. The news flow is slow. On those days more human interest and timeless stories become news.

Medium

Some formats work better than others for some messages. Fires, for instance, often receive more coverage on television than in the newspaper. Television reporters can show the firefighters in action. Viewers can see the firefighters in bright yellow slickers streaked with soot as they tug heavy hoses to reach the flames with streams of water that arch and fall into the blazing inferno. They can hear the roar of the fire and the screams of the emergency sirens. The newspaper is limited to one or two still photos and a written account. It has the advantage of being able to give more information and detail, but it lacks the gripping emotional appeal of the television coverage.

Radio is limited to very short stories listeners can comprehend without visual images, but it has the advantage of being able to put news on the air very quickly. News may change more often in radio, where newscasts are heard frequently throughout the day. But the short time allotted to each newscast limits the number of stories put on the air and the amount of detail that can be given about each one.

The difference in the coverage of any one story in the broadcast versus the print media says more about the basic differences between the television and the newspaper than about the importance of the story.

Deadlines

The **deadline** is the time at which all stories must be ready to print or to be broadcast. Radio and television can break into their programming and put a news bulletin on the air on a few moments' notice. These media have very short deadlines. The newspaper staff must gather the facts, perhaps go to the scene and take pictures, write the story, place it on a page in the next edition, wait for that edition to be printed, deliver it to the doorstep or rack and wait for the reader to read it. Several hours elapse between the time a story is written and the time a reader reads it.

Television stations have several news programs each day. The average daily newspaper prints one edition; larger papers print more.

deadline
> the latest time a story can be finished in order to be printed in that paper or shown on that newscast

THIS JUST IN: *Portrait of a Young Journalist*
Noah Kotch, editor, The Proconian

"We're a real paper. We write about school politics, school policy. . . . We're using the power of the press like real newspapers do," said Noah Kotch, 18, editor of the newspaper at Chapel Hill High School in North Carolina.

The mission of *The Proconian* throughout its nearly 70 years of publication has been to present the pros and cons of the school. Kotch, whose model for *The Proconian* is a paper he reads daily, the *New York Times,* has taken that role seriously.

When he became editor, Kotch set an aggressive editorial policy as he tried to live up to the traditional press role of watchdog. He emphasized hard news and cut out club news and awards listings, labeling them as "fluff." He doubled the length of the paper and added an op-ed page and a column based on the popular TV show *Beverly Hills 90210.*

The staff of *The Proconian* writes about multiculturalism, sexual harassment and condoms in the schools. The paper exposed a grade gap between black and white students. The report led to a school system panel to study the issue. Investigative stories reported on students who rejected nomination to the National Honor Society, and placed the criteria for membership under scrutiny. Other stories investigated what the staff saw as unnecessary secrecy and delay in the search for a new administrator.

Not everyone agrees with Kotch's editorial philosophy. The principal often calls him in to talk about stories that concern her, and the adviser wonders whether the paper is as representative of the student body as it might be. The staff overruled Kotch when he wanted to endorse political candidates.

Students also disagree about the role of the paper. Wendy Nichols, 17, said, "I always read it. A lot of people say *The Proconian* is too focused on the bad parts of school, on negative things, on anything controversial. But I think that's really good."

According to Quana Mitchell, 16, "They need to stop printing that thing. It's just a waste of paper. They tell you if a white person is playing hockey. They don't tell you if a black person can sing. They need to put in stuff black people do for a change."

Todd Mesibov, 17, co-sports editor, says, "I think we've totally missed the mark on the mission of a regular high school paper. . . . We're so fixated on becoming a 'real' newspaper and trying to expose 'real' issues that we've completely alienated the student body from our news pages."

Amy Evans, 18, staff writer, said, "The news puts me to sleep. It's journalism, but I personally think the newspaper has not done the school a service."

Kotch defends *The Proconian*'s stance: "We're doing what real newspapers do. Real newspapers in many ways push agendas and push ideas and have an editorial policy that's somewhat reflected in the articles."

Source: Adapted with permission from Gelareh Asayesh, "Revisiting a High School Newspaper," in Death by Cheeseburger, Freedom Forum.

Evening papers have deadlines before noon, so stories that happen after noon won't appear in that evening's edition. Morning papers have deadlines before midnight. Weekly papers have once-a-week deadlines. Even though desktop publishing has shortened production schedules for school newspapers, deadlines may be weeks apart. Anything that happens after the deadline has to wait for the next edition.

Newspaper deadlines dictate that a newspaper story must be treated differently than a broadcast story. The morning headlines scream, "Plane Explodes over the Atlantic." But you knew that shortly after it happened at 8:30 the night before. The newspaper must focus on other points of view and on giving more detail than the broadcast news can.

Editorial Philosophy

Publishers and station owners set editorial policies for their newspapers and broadcast stations that guide reporters in knowing what is news for their paper or program. Some newspapers, for instance, do not print the names of rape victims or the cause of death in obituaries to protect the privacy of the persons involved. Pictures and stories about little girls being crowned Miss Tot USA or Young Miss American Beauty are no longer carried by many papers because their editors believe that many of the contests exploit the children and their families. The gardener who raises a 15-pound tomato or a 100-pound pumpkin may be disappointed to find that the newspaper does not want a picture of the amazing produce. Many newspapers have concluded that these natural wonders, usually produced with chemical help, are too common today to be news.

Since the 1700s the press has assumed the role of government watchdog. Newspapers have reported on the workings of government, and editors have offered their interpretation of issues through their editorials. Each newspaper has a political agenda, conservative or liberal, that it supports. The editors may endorse or denounce political candidates on their editorial pages, and they regularly express opinions about proposed laws or expenditures by governmental bodies.

Until recently, the Federal Communications Commission prohibited licensed broadcast stations from taking political stands, because there were a limited number of stations available to listeners in any area. The FCC has changed the policy, but most broadcast stations still refrain from taking political sides or expressing editorial positions.

The editorial policies of the scholastic press have become more professional. Most school publications staffs would say they aren't involved in politics, but they do determine editorial policies by what they choose to include or to leave out of their publications. When your newspaper staff chooses to print a feature on multiculturalism, gender issues or sex education in schools in place of the "Heap of the Month" feature about someone's dilapidated car, you have established an editorial policy. When the yearbook staff phases out large color pictures of seniors to make room for a section on world news, it is saying something important about its responsibility to its readers. The topics your staff chooses for editorials and those your columnists write about become the publication's image and reflect its editorial policy.

Choices like these reflect the way publications staffs view their roles as media in the school community. For a sample editorial policy, see the Editor's Handbook at the end of this book.

column inch

> a method of measuring space on a newspaper, yearbook or magazine page. The number of columns multiplied by the number of vertical inches in the columns equals the total number of column inches. Advertising is often sold by the column inch

Business

Newspapers and broadcast stations are businesses. Owners expect them to show a profit. Salaries and bills have to be paid.

Advertising sales are the largest source of income for broadcast stations and newspapers. Subscriptions, newspapers sold at news stands or from racks on street corners, and special printing and video production jobs pay for the rest. Advertising rates are based on the number of subscribers or viewers a medium has.

To stay competitive and pay expenses, the paper or station has to control expenditures. Fewer advertising dollars coming in may mean having fewer employees or printing fewer pages each week.

1. Compare network television and newspaper news coverage as follows. Listen to an evening network news broadcast. Make a list of the stories on the news. Look at a newspaper for the same day. Are the same stories there? Where? Are they all front-page stories, or even on the front page of sections such as national news, local news or sports? Count the stories in the paper. How many of them were on the broadcast? What percentage of the stories in the paper were on the news broadcast? Were there stories on the broadcast news that did not appear in the paper? Why do you think those stories were not in the paper? Now compare the network television news broadcast to one-half hour of a 24-hour news channel. Are the same stories covered? Why or why not?

2. Newspaper pages are measured in **column inches.** One column wide by one inch deep equals one column inch. Measure the column inches of news and of advertising in an edition of your local newspaper. Calculate the percentage of news to advertising. (*Hint:* Divide the class into groups, and have each group measure a section.) To compare the variation from day to day and calculate an average percentage, measure editions from several days.

3. Get a copy of a local newspaper or broadcast station's publications policy, including the advertising policy. Analyze it. Why do you think each statement or exception was made? What changes should be made in the policy? If no policy exists, draft one that represents the publication or station as it is or as you think it should be.

DATELINE

UNITED STATES, 1970s—From transistor to silicon chip to microcomputer to time base corrector, the television industry downsized its equipment until, by the 1970s, reporters could cover on-the-spot news with portable cameras and send pictures directly back to the station via microwave or satellite relay.

The development of inexpensive magnetic recording tape also helped revolutionize television news production. News could be recorded directly to the tape, wound on two reels inside a plastic case, and played back immediately or edited from the tape.

One or two reporters could go to the scene of a story in a car or helicopter and have pictures on the air in minutes, whereas before it would have taken a crew of several technicians and a semi-trailer full of equipment traveling to the scene.

The system is called electronic news gathering (ENG). When satellite transmission from a remote site is involved, it is called satellite news gathering (SNG).

◢FINDING NEWS

Now you know how journalists recognize news. But how do they find all those stories?

News Judgment

An experienced journalist is sometimes said to have a "nose for news." This cliché might make people think reporters look like Snoopy when he dons his reporter's hat and goes in search of a story. His round black nose almost glows at the thought of sniffing out the news. The cliché actually refers to the fact that with practice, journalists develop a sense, called **news judgment,** for which events and stories make news in their communities. They ask questions, jot down ideas and look at everything they see or hear as potential news.

Journalists use sources such as wire services, letters, and calls and tips from people to develop ideas for news stories. Editors and producers also expect each reporter to find two or three story ideas each week.

news judgment
> a sense that experienced journalists develop about what events will make good news stories

Beats

Beats are another way journalists find news. Reporters are assigned beats, or sources to contact regularly, from which ideas for stories may come. On a city newspaper or radio or television station, a staff reporter may be assigned the police beat, the education beat, the city government beat or a beat made up of any group of sources with whom the producer or editor wants to make regular contact. From these sources, the reporter expects to gather information that will lead to news stories. The beat reporter checks with these sources frequently so that no news is missed between publications or newscasts.

School editors and producers assign reporters to beats such as the administration beat, the science and math beat, the board of education beat, the organizations beat and the athletic department beat. Prior to each staff meeting, reporters visit with the sources on their beats. They find out what has happened recently and what is being planned. In the staff meeting, each reporter then shares the information from the beat sources.

beat
> a regular assignment given to reporters; a place reporters go regularly to get information, such as the courthouse, schools, the police department or the city council

Professional Sources

Journalists also use their competitors as sources. Broadcasters read the newspaper to get ideas, and newspaper reporters watch the television news to see what stories are news today. Newspapers trade subscriptions with other newspapers, and broadcasters watch other newscasts to get story ideas. Journalists attend professional meetings where they hear presentations and compare their work with that of their colleagues.

As a high school journalist, you can do the same things. Read the school bulletin. Ask for copies of other school publications, such as the

local angle

a fact or person that connects a story which originates in another location to the local audience

localize

to find someone or something in your community that has a tie to a story from somewhere else and then to report it in order to make the story more interesting to local readers

futures file

a list or file containing ideas for stories and dates of upcoming events for future issues of a publication or a later newscast

administrator's newsletter to school patrons or the parent-teacher organization's newsletter. Exchange subscriptions or tapes with other schools. Attend meetings of your state scholastic press association, and enter competitions. Join a national high school journalism organization such as the American Scholastic Press Association, the National Scholastic Press Association, Columbia Scholastic Press Association or the Journalism Education Association.

Localizing News

Journalists find stories in news that originates in other places. A story written in Africa or Malaysia can become news in your community if journalists find a **local angle,** a fact or person that connects the story to the local audience. This is called **localizing** a story. When the president sends troops to a foreign location, it is news because the United States is involved. If, however, one of the soldiers is a resident of your community, perhaps even a graduate of your school, that individual's role gives the story special meaning to local residents. Interviews with the soldier's family and classmates generate quotations that interest your audience and give the story a local perspective.

Futures Files

Editors and reporters keep **futures files** of ideas, too. Whenever they hear, see or think of something that might be the subject for a story, or someone gives them the date of an upcoming event, they put it in the file or on a calendar. Before making assignments, they check the futures file so they won't miss a good idea or a story that will be happening soon.

1. Find a story in the news that could be localized for your school newspaper. Explain to the class why you chose the story and what you would need to do to make the story specifically of interest to your readers.
2. Analyze the audience for your school newspaper or newscast. Make a list of the groups represented who have different interests. If some groups presently are being overlooked, suggest ways in which they might be included in your news coverage.
3. Listen for news. Carry a notebook just for recording tips. A small one that fits in your pocket is best. Each time you hear people talking, write down the topic. The topics students are discussing in the cafeteria or in the halls before school are the things they are interested in. It may be an assignment for a class

that sounds interesting, a movie or show they've watched, a competition that's coming up or is just completed, the kind of cars they like or their jobs after school. Teachers, school announcements, television shows, homework assignments and parents may be sources of ideas, too. Bring your notebook to class and share your ideas.

4. As a class, establish a futures file for your school newspaper, broadcast station or yearbook. Put in a calendar with future issue or broadcast dates. Put notes and clippings for story ideas for future issues in the file. Keep the file where everyone can add ideas. Check the file before making assignments for the next issue or newscast. Some assignments that will take more time to research and write may be made several issues ahead.

CHAPTER REVIEW

KEY TERMS

Show that you know the meanings of the following key terms by correctly using them in complete sentences. Write your answers on a separate sheet of paper.

news	human interest	deadline
gatekeeper	wire service	column inch
timeliness	tip	news judgment
run	budget	beat
prominence	top story	local angle
proximity	news hole	localize
conflict	news flow	futures file
impact	cut	

OPEN FORUM

1. As a class, brainstorm ideas for a regular issue of your school newspaper or a regular broadcast of your school radio or television station. If your staff could print a special edition of your paper or produce a special broadcast for an event or to highlight a topic of importance to your audience, what event or topic would you choose to highlight? Why? Brainstorm ideas for the articles or segments you'd include so that there would be something of interest to everyone in your audience.

2. Who selects the newspapers, magazines and materials for your school media center? What criteria do they use for making their selections? What other publications or materials do you think should be included? Who would use them? Who, if anyone, would object to them?

    Write a letter to the person or persons in charge of selecting materials for your school media center. In the letter recommend a change in policy or something you think should be added to the school's collection. Be sure to explain why you think your recommendation is worthwhile and should be considered.

3. Check the Internet for newspapers and magazines. How does the content of electronic publications differ from that of traditional publications? Is news the same for Internet users as it is for readers? Who is the audience for Internet publications?

4. Information has been considered a valuable commodity made available at no individual cost to people in the United States through such means as public libraries and public broadcast stations. How does having information available on the Internet, or online, affect the availability of information to everyone in the United States? What about cable television and satellite dishes—have they had, or will they have, any effect? What would you suggest should be done to ensure that information remains available at no cost to individuals?

CHAPTER REVIEW, *continued*

FINDING THE FLAW

Who is the little boy in this photo? Is he the same little boy being described in the story? During the time that "Baby Richard" was news because of the court case regarding his custody, his name was carefully kept secret to protect him and his family. In this follow-up story one year later, his name is not revealed. The boy in the photo, however, is identified by name. Because of the layout with a box surrounding the story and the picture, the reader assumes that the picture and the story belong together. But do they?

The issue may be more complicated than simply changing the name in the story or in the sentence under the photo. If Baby Richard could not be identified by name one year ago, what has changed? Should the paper have used his name now? Is Danny Kirchner really Baby Richard? Did the paper use the wrong picture with the story? How can the reader tell?

Danny Kirchner holds his sister, Sharon in this recent photo.

Baby Richard's legacy

By MIKE ROBINSON
Associated Press Writer

CHICAGO — One year after a weeping Baby Richard reached for his adoptive mother while his biological father carried him to a car, the 5-year-old boy is "happy and well-adjusted," a psychologist says.

The youngster with the tousled mop of blond hair is happy living with his birth parents, smiles readily and shows a special fondness for Batman, Nintendo and Chicken McNuggets, say those who work closely with him.

"There are no signs of trauma, no eating or sleeping problems, no withdrawal, no angry outbursts, no asking for the other family," says Karen Moriarty, a clinical psychologist.

But the custody switch that followed a 3½-year court battle has had an unsettling aftermath all the same.

Couples are more wary of domestic adoptions, fearing U.S. courts may return children to their birth families, experts say. And the couple that took care of Baby Richard for the first four years of his life will mark today's anniversary by beginning a nationwide crusade to expand the rights of adoptive families.

Source: Reprinted with permission from Associated Press, from Mike Robinson, "Baby Richard's Legacy," *Hastings (Nebraska) Tribune.*

MEDIA WATCH

1. Invite professional journalists to your class to talk about how they define news for their newspapers or broadcast stations, who their readers or viewers are, how they're trying to meet the demands of their audiences, and what editorial policies they have established.

2. As a class, design a survey to measure the media habits of your community. Each member of the class will survey 10 people about their news media habits using the questions the class has developed. Include at least five adults, such as your parents, grandparents, teachers or neighbors. Find out what media the interviewees use most, how often they use it for news, and what parts of the news they listen to or read first or most often. As a class, compile the results of your survey. What did you learn about the news and media habits of your community? What predictions can you make about the future of the news media in your community?

3. As a class, examine one issue of a local newspaper and one issue of *USA Today* section by section. What kind of news is in each section? Who might read each section? In what ways are your local paper and *USA Today* alike? How are they different? Why do you think the similarities or differences exist?

String Book

You may use any newspapers for this activity, including school newspapers. Clip the page header with the name and date of the newspaper for each article; keep it with the example.

1. Search until you find six examples—one to represent each of the six characteristics of news. For example, the timeliness story should be news mostly because it happened today. The human interest story should be news only because it is about people in emotional situations. The proximity story should be about something that is news only in your community and would not be news somewhere else because no one there would care. Label each story with its characteristic, and write a short explanation to help you remember what the characteristic means.

2. Begin a futures file for yourself. In it, put notes and clippings that give you ideas for stories you'd like to write someday. Check the file whenever you need a story idea for your news staff or for an assignment.

Gathering the News

Chapter 4
Searching for Sources

AUTHOR

"It was long ago in my life as a simple reporter that I decided that facts must never get in the way of truth."
—James Cameron, British writer

KEY TERMS

In this chapter, you will learn the meaning of these terms:

scooped
physical source
morgue
Freedom of Information Act
human source
sponsorship
anonymous source
on-the-record information
not for attribution
background information
deep background
    information
database

LEARNING OBJECTIVES

After completing this chapter, you will be able to:

◆ cover beats, such as school board meetings, student council meetings and school organization activities,

◆ collect written information and incorporate it into a news story,

◆ verify and protect human sources for a news story.

◆

*T*hink about the most recent story you wrote for your school newspaper. Maybe it was a news article about the new weight room being added to the gym or a feature story on a foreign language teacher who spent a year abroad teaching in Japan. How did you approach the story? What kind of sources did you use, and how did you get them? Chances are you interviewed the persons involved. This process would have included the coaches and students who train in the weight room or the teacher who taught in a Japanese classroom.

Interviewing is an excellent way to get information, but there are other ways to search for and gather sources. Think of your completed story as a sculpture and the sources as the clay. As you collect more information, your masterpiece will gradually take shape. Just as a sculptor experiments with clay, a journalist must also experiment before deciding what sources to incorporate into a story.

In this chapter, you will learn how to cover beats in your school, how to collect information for a story and how to protect the human sources you use in researching that story.

◢ BEAT REPORTING

A reporter may be asked to cover a specific area, called a beat. A beat reporter is assigned to check the same news source for each issue of the paper. The beat may be a topic or a geographic area. It may include places such as the police station or city hall. The use of beat reporting helps reporters keep a step ahead of the competition so as not to be **scooped,** or in a situation in which they find out that someone else has obtained the story first. The media together have often been compared to a shark and the public, to the shark's prey. Every branch of the media, however, also feeds off the other branches in getting ideas for stories. Newspapers, magazines, television networks and radio stations are constantly watching one another for story ideas. Because several reporters cover the same beat, they may have the same idea at the same time.

In beat reporting, you must be careful to cover stories because they are interesting to readers, not because your media outlet wants to get an important story before its competition does. For example, imagine that your beat is the women's track team. You receive a tip that there may be steroid use among some of the athletes. As a well-informed

scooped

in a situation in which another reporter has obtained a story first

CALVIN and HOBBES reprinted by permission of Universal Press Syndicate.

journalist, you know that other schools in your area that compete with the track team may be aware of this drug use and could also be involved. Therefore, other school newspapers may be covering the story. However, that is not a good enough reason to pursue the story. It must also interest your readers. In this case, you know the story would interest not only the student body but also the administration, coaches and school board.

You need to establish a relationship of trust with the sources on your beat. Talk to everyone—athletes, student managers and coaches, as well as others in charge of practices and meets. People are usually happy to chat with reporters, and it's a good way to develop sources. However, make no promises that you cannot fulfill or that interfere with your responsibilities as a reporter.

There may be times when interviewing someone in a one-on-one situation doesn't provide enough information. You may have to spend time, for example, in the locker room, attend several practices and talk to a variety of people in order to break a story for the women's track team beat. If you cover your beat thoroughly, most events or activities that the public should be aware of will surface. Author Melvin Mencher suggests applying the following techniques to the area you are covering:

1. Get started fast; get out of the office. Don't waste time. Not many stories are found in newsrooms.
2. Build sources. There is no substitute for regular, perhaps even daily, contact.
3. Ask the sweeping questions; ask the "dumb" questions. The only dumb question is the one you fail to ask.
4. Listen carefully; watch carefully. As former Yankee baseball catcher and manager Yogi Berra once said, "A great deal of observing can be done simply by watching."
5. Look at the record. When covering a beat, go for the original source.
6. Set up calls. Check and double check your sources. Phone calls are a supplement, not a substitute, for direct contact. (Adapted with permission from Melvin Mencher, *News Reporting and Writing*, 7th Edition, Brown & Benchmark, Dubuque, Iowa 1997, p. 374.)

Select a beat—for example, activity sponsors, athletic coaches, heads of departments, administrators or student council—that you think would be interesting to cover for your high school newspaper. List five specific sources you would contact for a story on your beat.

PHYSICAL SOURCES

In a study conducted about Washington, D.C., reporters, Stephen Hess found that the journalists he interviewed used no library research in over half of their stories. "When newspaper and television reporters are given more time to do stories, they simply do more interviews," says Hess. A heavy reliance on interviews may lead to stories that reflect only the subjective judgments of the interviewees.

physical source

> these research tools are records, documents, reference works, newspaper clippings and direct observations

This problem can easily be overcome. **Physical sources** are records, documents, reference works, newspaper clippings and direct observations to which journalists have access. Journalists gather information for stories the same way you would if you were writing a research paper.

Let's say that your topic is the violence portrayed in gangsta rap lyrics. Where would you start your search for information? You could begin by listening to the various artists who have been targeted for censure in order to narrow your subject down. Let's say you chose PUBLIC ENEMY as the focus of your paper. After hearing the group's CDs, you decide the next step is to find some record reviews that give a cross-section of opinions and open more doors. Although you find several reviews in *Rolling Stone, Entertainment Weekly* and *Spin,* you aren't convinced you have enough information to start writing. Now you must turn to other kinds of physical sources.

Kinds of Physical Sources

If you've ever written a research paper, prepared for a debate or planned a speech, you know that the extent of physical sources is vast. The only limit to physical sources is the reporter's knowledge of their existence. The only way a reporter is going to uncover these sources is to dig. Almost any reference is available to the public. References can be found in libraries, local and state agencies, and other places. And keep in mind that other information might be just as useful in a story, although it might be more difficult to locate.

morgue

> reference library that stores clippings of published articles

Clippings.   Stories are recycled from newspaper to newspaper all over the country. Most stories that have been published can be found in **morgues,** or reference libraries that store clippings of stories that have been published in newspapers.

Employees of the Seaside Post News Sentinel *in Oakland, California, use the newspaper's reference room-museum in this 1976 photo. Many newspapers have historical displays and allow the public to utilize their morgues.*

Clippings can save you a good deal of time in your search for information. For example, they can provide background information on a person you will interview. Furthermore, clippings can provide one way of verifying the answers of the interviewee.

Encyclopedias. Encyclopedias may seem like an elementary way to find information, but they are a good place to start. Encyclopedias provide cross-references, maps, charts and illustrations. If you were assigned a story about the increase in eating disorders among high school girls, for example, you could use an encyclopedia to look up a variety of topics, such as anorexia or bulimia.

Telephone Directories. The white and yellow pages of telephone directories can be very useful to a reporter. For example, you might be doing a story on area day care centers for teen moms. A reasonable starting place in the process of setting up interviews is the yellow pages. Telephone directories provide more than just telephone numbers. They include postal zip codes, street indexes, city maps, and information about city and county government.

Cross-Directories. Cross-directories list residents of a community three ways: by name, address and telephone number. Suppose you have the address of a teacher who lives in a neighborhood where several houses have been broken into. You want to get comments from the residents. How can you get this information if you don't know the neighbors' names? If you can look in a cross-directory under the address you have, you will find neighboring homes listed nearby according to street address, with names and telephone numbers beside the addresses. If you have only a phone number and not a name, the section for phone numbers can give you the name of the person with that phone number.

City Directories.   City directories are published by private firms. They alphabetically list the names, addresses and telephone numbers of residents. Other information includes street address guides; telephone number directories; zip codes; elementary school districts; and information on such things as population, average income per household, news media, tax bases, airlines, buses, railroads and industrial sites.

State Directories.   Also called blue books, state directories include information on the executive, legislative and judicial branches of state government. These volumes also have information on state schools and colleges, election returns and miscellaneous statistics.

Facts on File World News Digest.   *Facts on File World News Digest* is a weekly publication that summarizes, records and indexes the news. National and foreign news events are included. Also included is information on deaths, science, sports, medicine, education, religion, crime, books, plays, films and people in the news. The index also includes subjects and names of people, organizations and countries.

Libraries.   Your high school, local and college libraries hold numerous sources to help you search for background about a story. Some of these sources include newspaper indexes published in bound volumes, almanacs and atlases. Libraries also have the *Reader's Guide to Periodical Literature, Business Periodicals Index,* and *Social Sciences Index.*

Other References.   *Editorials on File* contains editorial reprints from more than 130 American newspapers (and some foreign newspapers), with 20 to 30 editorials on each subject covered. For example, if you wanted to write an editorial on the issue of corporal punishment in schools but you weren't familiar with the important arguments on the topic, you could use this source to learn the opinions of journalists around the country.

The Dictionary of American Slang is a jim-dandy resource that can help you find definitions of catchphrases from the past five centuries. You may be a greenie to the art of research, and you may think that only schleps or sickniks get wigged out by reading a blat, but you will be a yo-yo, a schlemiel or a kluck if you try to fake it. As times change, so does the language.

Famous First Facts is a staple of reference collections that is useful when researching the first incidence of anything. More than 9,000 facts in American history are listed alphabetically by subject in this book.

BYLINE

ELLIE MCGRATH
ON HER FIRST YEAR AS A JOURNALIST

Ellie McGrath is a senior editor at *Self.* She spent 10 years at *Time,* principally as a writer covering national politics and education. Her first job after college was as a researcher for Time-Life Books. She remembers her time there in the following excerpt.

When I first started at Time-Life Books in July, my first job was to check the accuracy of the text for its Emergence of Man series. The Emergence of Man was an anthropology series, so I was checking for accuracy against academic sources. My first assignment was on *The Israelites.* I would spend all day long reading the Bible. Some afternoons I would start weeping quietly while I read, because the work was too academic, too much like being in school. I wanted to be a journalist, not a junior librarian.

Assignments got better after I finished with *The Israelites.* I got to work on *The Celts* and found it rewarding to take a subject I had stud-ied in depth [McGrath's senior thesis was on the 1916 Easter Rebellion in Ireland] and apply what I knew. It gave me a feeling of mastery. While on the American Wilderness series, I worked with environmentalists and naturalists. For a picture essay on sea turtles, I would be on the phone every day with an expert from the University of Florida. I researched a volcano picture essay for a book called *Central American Jungles,* which led to a long-standing fascination with volcanic eruptions and earth-quakes.

When Time-Life Books announced at the end of my second year that it was relocating out of New York City, I immediately contacted *Time* and was offered a job as a reporter-researcher. Although it helps to have talent, timing can make all the difference. I had been fortunate to get my foot in the door when I did.

Source: Dianne Selditch, ed., My First Year as a Journalist *(New York: Walker and Co.).*

Bartlett's Familiar Quotations contains "passages, phrases and proverbs traced to their sources in ancient and modern literature." It even includes the following quotation of Ralph Waldo Emerson: "I hate quotations. Tell me what you know." The book includes an author index and an index of key words.

Finally, the *Guinness Book of World Records* is an invaluable resource for adding color to your writing. The man who can smoke 38 pipes simultaneously, the single largest serving of mashed potatoes and the world record for worm charming—they are all listed in seemingly endless categories.

Using Records and Documents

As we have said, to develop true in-depth or investigative stories, high school journalists must do more than merely talk to a few sources. They must use documents in their reporting.

American society is based on paperwork. Every person, every day, leaves behind a paper trail. When you are born, the paper trail begins. When you enter or leave a hospital, write a check, use a charge card, enter the military service, marry, divorce, buy or sell land, have children, drive a car or do so many other things in your day-to-day life, you leave a paper trail. Even your high school yearbook picture is part of that trail. And much of the paper you leave in your wake is a part of the public record.

Gaining Access to Public Records.   One way to learn about the public record is to take a trip to city hall or the county courthouse. There, a clerk can explain, for example, how to trace the ownership of a piece of property. You might begin by looking up your parents' property. Chances are that you will be surprised at how much you can learn—for example, the sales price, mortgage terms and tax payments. Clerks also can show you how to look up somebody's voter registration, how to find out whether someone is involved in litigation (the court system), and how to check someone's driving record to see if it is free of tickets and accidents.

What good is all this knowledge? Documents are an important part of in-depth reporting. They can provide the basis for an investigative story or back up what your sources have told you. A reporter who can follow the paper trail gets stories that the less enterprising journalist misses.

For example, a student reporter might attend a board of education meeting at which the board approves the purchase of a piece of land for $200,000. A savvy reporter could investigate that piece of property. Maybe the search will show that everything is aboveboard. But maybe it will show something else—for example, that the school board president owns the property and that its assessed value is $100,000. That could mean the board has lined the pockets of a public official at the taxpayers' expense.

One resource that will lead you down the paper trail is the *Reporter's Handbook,* an invaluable guide for reporters at all levels. The handbook explains where to find public records such as criminal complaints, building inspections and campaign contributions. If you're investigating a specific individual, for example, you can find out if the person has a clean driving record, whether he or she owes people money, and if the person is being sued. The book also tells reporters how to investigate whether a business has unpaid taxes, if the local police department is using excessive force during arrests, and whether a hospital has a high death rate. Furthermore, the book devotes a chapter to education records and story suggestions.

Reporters for the *Morning Advocate* in Baton Rouge, Louisiana, used public records for a story about school bus drivers. After a number of accidents involving school buses, the reporters checked police and court records on each bus driver in the school system. They found that more than a third of the drivers had infractions, including drunken driving convictions, on their driving records.

FIGURE 4.1
SAMPLE FREEDOM OF INFORMATION ACT REQUEST

Date

Name of Agency Official

Title
Name of Agency
Address
City, State, Zip

Dear

    Under the provisions of the Freedom of Information Act, 5 U.S.C. 552, I am requesting access to... (identify the records clearly and specifically as possible).

    (Optional: I am requesting this information because...state the reason for your request if you think it will assist you in obtaining the information.)

    If there are any fees for searching for, or copying, the records I have requested, please inform me before you fill the request. (Or...please supply the records without informing me if the fees do not exceed $_____.)

    As you know, the Act permits you to reduce or waive the fees when release of information is considered as "primarily benefiting the public." I believe that this request fits that category and I therefore ask that you waive any fees.

    If any or all of this request is denied, please cite the specific exemption(s) which you think justifies your refusal to release the information and inform me of your agency's administrative appeal procedures available to me under the law.

    I would appreciate your handling this request as quickly as possible, and I look forward to hearing from you within 10 working days, as the law stipulates.

Sincerely,

(Signature)
Name
Address
City, State, Zip

Source: Reported with permission from Reporter's Handbook: An Investigator's Guide to Documents & Techniques. *3rd edition. Steve Weinberg. St. Martin's Press.*

State and Federal Records.   State and federal laws allow many types of records to be inspected by the public. Reporters should get a copy of their state's open records act, along with the federal Freedom of Information Act. The **Freedom of Information Act** is a law enacted in 1966 requiring government records except those relating to national security, confidential financial data, and law enforcement be made available to the public on request.

Open records laws are based on the presumption that everything is public unless it is specifically exempted. Open records acts commonly exempt student records and medical files. Your state attorney general's office can help you determine if the records you need are available to the public.

Many states require citizens simply to ask to examine and copy records during the appropriate agency's regular business hours. Some states and the federal government occasionally require written requests to inspect documents. (See Figure 4.1 for a sample Freedom of Information Act request.) When making a written request, ask for the

Freedom of Information Act
a law enacted in 1966 requiring government records except those relating to national security, confidential financial data, and law enforcement be made available to the public on request

specific information you want to receive. The agency must then respond within a certain time period. Federal agencies can take from one to three months to respond because of backlogs of requests and understaffing, according to the *Reporter's Handbook.*

The book cautions reporters to make requests only when absolutely necessary. After all, you can often get the information more quickly in other ways. Furthermore, you usually have to pay for copies of the records. Some states will even charge you for the time it takes the government employee to find the information. Under the federal law and some state laws, you can ask that the fees be waived if your request will directly benefit the public.

If the agency turns down your request, it must state under which exemption it is withholding the information. If your request is denied, you can appeal to a higher official in the agency or to a court.

YOUR BEAT

Write a Freedom of Information Act request for information from a federal agency that funds a program in your school or community.

For example, you might request information about salaries for coaches paid by public institutions. This information would be useful in preparing a story about gender equity since the implementation of Title IX guidelines.

USING HUMAN SOURCES

In an article on sources in *AP World,* Arthur L. Gavshon, a reporter for the Associated Press (AP), says, "To me anyone on the inside of any given news situation is a potential source. But they only turn into real sources when they come up with a bit, or a lot, of relevant information."

Think of some of the major stories that have happened in the world—the assassination of President Kennedy, the *Challenger* explosion and the TWA Flight 800 crash, for example. Now think of all the people who witnessed these events. They were human sources. **Human sources** are persons involved in events. Although all people who witness something are potential sources for a story, many turn out to be unreliable either because they have interests to protect or because they just can't provide the information the reporter is looking for.

human source

a person who was directly involved in an event

The important thing to remember when using human sources is to find the person or persons with authority on the subject. If a calculus teacher was fired because she altered several student athletes' test scores so the students would be eligible to play basketball, you would want the source with the most dependable information to use in the story. You need, therefore, to interview both the person who did the firing and the calculus teacher. First, though, you would have to know how to keep these people as sources once you found them.

Building a Relationship with Your Source

Because a reporter depends on a source so heavily, it's a good idea to establish your credibility as a reporter as soon as possible. When you speak to a source for the first time, introduce yourself right away. Tell the person who you are and what you are doing. Then move on to the questions. That way, if you want to use the source again in the future, the source will already trust you. Having good rapport with your sources is essential to getting the information you need.

Some sources, however, may be reluctant to talk. Mark Potter, an investigative reporter for the ABC television network, was working on a story about Haitian refugees in Miami. Many were unwilling to talk to him because they were illegal aliens. Potter said the refugees thought he was an immigration official looking to deport them. Instead of abandoning the story, however, Potter turned to a technique called **sponsorship**—getting someone who knows and trusts you, and who the source knows and trusts, to recommend you to the source. Sponsorship can also be used when you set up an interview or meet a source for the first time. For example, you might say, "Dr. Anna Rodriguez suggested I talk to you" or "Dr. Anna Rodriguez gave me your name." Then explain why you are calling.

Tips

Sometimes the reporter doesn't find the source. Rather, the source finds the reporter. This happens through tips, or information passed on to a reporter that usually requires additional research. Sometimes the source has read or heard something he or she thinks might be of interest to the reporter. However, tips often come from individuals who are angry at officials or employers. Reporters have to be careful to check and double-check tips for accuracy.

For example, let's say you receive a tip from a student who says the choral instructor refused to cast him in the role of Captain von Trapp in the production of *The Sound of Music* because he was Asian. You decide to investigate further and discover not only that the role is being played by another Asian student but also that the person who gave you the tip hadn't even auditioned for the part. In such instances, it pays to investigate further. That way, you avoid not only false information but also embarrassment.

Reliability

Have you ever met someone who tells a story to several people, and at every telling the story becomes a little more dramatic and a little more exaggerated? Sources can do just that in talking to reporters, even though they may not mean to stretch the truth. Frequently, people provide inaccurate information not on purpose but because it's what they think reporters want to hear. An observer who says she saw a boy "throw the first punch" during a fight in the parking lot may not be

OUT TAKE

The High Cost of News

Throughout the history of journalism, sources have been paid for providing information. For example, in the 19th century, a speaker of the House earned a hundred dollars a week by charging reporters for interviews. The *New York Times* footed the bills for Robert E. Peary's expedition to the North Pole in exchange for the exclusive rights to his story. Later they paid Charles Lindbergh $5,000 for the story of his historic flight. *Life* bought the rights to the Zapruder film of President John F. Kennedy's assassination ($150,000), the rights to Lee Harvey Oswald's diaries ($20,000), and the rights to the stories of the *Mercury* astronauts (about a half-million dollars).
Source: Stephen Bates, If No News, Send Rumors *(New York: Henry Holt), p. 183.*

sponsorship
a technique for getting recommended to a source

telling what really happened but rather what she has read in books or seen in the movies.

How can you tell if a source is reliable or not? Ask yourself these questions as you decide whether to use a source's information:

1. Did the person actually witness the event?
2. Is the person an expert on the subject of the story? The basketball coach is more likely to be knowledgeable about free throw misses in the fourth quarter than is an irate fan.
3. Can the information provided by the witness be corroborated (confirmed)?

Anonymity

anonymous source

an unnamed source

on-the-record information

information that can be used and whose source can be identified

not for attribution

a description of information that may be used as background but whose source may not be identified

background information

information that may be used but that can't be attributed (a source can't be given) except in a general way

deep background information

information that may be used, but only without a source indication (even an indication of a general source)

Perhaps the most famous **anonymous source** is Deep Throat, the source who gave *Washington Post* reporters Carl Bernstein and Bob Woodward information about Richard Nixon's involvement in Watergate. The use of anonymous or unnamed sources is controversial. Some reporters believe that confidential sources are essential to getting and keeping a story, whereas others think anonymous sources decrease the credibility of newspapers. *USA Today* is one newspaper that won't use anonymous sources. Its policy states that "unidentified sources are not acceptable at *USA Today.*" The *Wall Street Journal,* in contrast, says that an anonymous source is someone whose name will not be used in the story by agreement "but whose identity we may later need to disclose—in the event of a libel suit, for example—in order to show we had good reason for using the information."

Imagine that a student teacher told you that his first-period class had been instructed by the teacher to observe a moment of silence before taking a test. Although he is not sure, the student teacher thinks the teacher is encouraging prayer, a practice not allowed by the school. As a reporter, you know this needs to be further investigated. You think the student teacher is a reliable source, but he has requested that you not mention him if the story is printed. In other words, the student teacher wishes to be anonymous. What should you do?

You can handle information from sources in several ways. **On-the-record information** may be used, and the source may be identified. Off-the-record information may not be used at all. Information that is **not for attribution** may be used as background, but the source may not be identified. **Background information** is similar to information that is not for attribution. You may use background information, but you may not attribute it (give its source) except in a general attribution, such as "a janitor said." Finally, **deep background information** may be used, but no source should be indicated. Not even a general phrase such as "school board member said" should be used.

Many newspapers have policies against the use of pseudonyms such as John Smith (not his real name). This trend began after Janet Cooke, a former reporter for the *Washington Post,* won the 1981 Pulitzer Prize for a story called "Jimmy's World," about an 8-year-old heroin addict. When Cooke discussed the story with her editors before writing it, she said she had found Jimmy's mother, but she was reluctant to talk. The editors told Cooke she could keep the mother's name anonymous. After Cooke won the Pulitzer Prize and was featured in several newspapers, questions were raised about her credibility. Cooke finally admitted that she had made up the story; Jimmy didn't exist. Cooke resigned from the *Post* and had to return her award.

Remember that a source who wishes to be anonymous may or may not be supplying accurate information. Clearly, a reporter should confirm information from sources both named and unnamed before using it.

Mark Potter, an investigative reporter for ABC, keeps a source book that he calls his "bible." According to author Carole Rich, this source book, a 7-by-9-inch address book, is so worn that it's held together by strips of packing tape. Inside it are the names, occupations and locations of each source. Start your own source book, and keep track of the people you interview.

THE COMPUTER SEARCH

Think about the last time you used a computer. What did you use it for? Perhaps you typed a reaction paper to a book discussed in English class. You may have sent e-mail to a friend who is studying abroad in Wales or conducted a search on endangered species for a report in biology class. No matter what the purpose, the computer enabled you to do these things more quickly. You no longer have to spend countless hours copying information from an encyclopedia; a computer can cross-reference it and print it out. We are still uncovering the computer's potential as a machine for retrieving, processing and delivering information.

Knowing how to obtain information by using the traditional references already described is important, but computer searches greatly extend your resources. Computer searches are too time consuming for writers of daily news stories, but they are very useful in researching background for in-depth stories.

A **database** is a collection of information stored in a computer. Thomas L. Jacobson, a professor at the State University of New York at Buffalo, and John Ullmann, assistant managing editor of the *Star Tribune*, conducted research on the value and use of databases. In the *Newspaper Research Journal* they said, "It seems fair to say that data bases can be used to support most beats, including the vast majority of kind of stories covered on these beats. Data bases are thought to improve

database
 a collection of information
 stored in a computer

DILBERT reprinted by permission of United Feature Syndicate, Inc.

reporting by substantially adding depth, perspective, wider geographical coverage and better command of relevant facts."

As a high school journalist, you probably won't need to conduct in-depth computer searches for stories. However, imagine that your newspaper is featuring a series of articles on alcohol-related stories to promote Alcohol Awareness Week. If you were assigned a story about the drinking habits of minors, a database check might be helpful. Typically, information in databases is classified according to key words and concepts. Thus, you might begin your search under the term *alcohol* and then continue searching the subcategories that are listed. Because some databases are designed for general users, most get their information from newspapers, magazines, government reports and books.

A trip to the library, you will soon learn, is a crucial step in preparing any piece of writing. As a student, however, the process of finding an answer is significantly more important than the answer itself. Once you have mastered that process, you can find out almost anything you want to know. And that is what this chapter is really about. As the writer Stephen King said, "What scares me are the people who don't use the library."

Choose a topic for an in-depth story about an issue concerning your school. Ask your librarian to help you conduct a database search.

Note that a search through databases is limited by what a particular database includes and by how well you choose "key words," those words that best describe the desired information. For example, in researching a story on the disintegration of the nuclear family, you might begin a subject search by typing the key word *divorce* into the computer. Some other key words you might try include *single parents* and *child care.*

CHAPTER REVIEW

KEY TERMS

Show that you know the meanings of the following key terms by correctly using them in complete sentences. Write your answers on a separate sheet of paper.

scooped	human source	not for attribution
physical source	sponsorship	background information
morgue	anonymous source	deep background
Freedom of	on-the-record	information
Information Act	information	database

OPEN FORUM

1. In the book *The Journalist and the Murder,* author Janet Malcolm dissects the betrayal that lies at the heart of the relationship between a journalist and a source. This betrayal raises some troubling questions. For example, syndicated columnist Matthew Miller asks us to imagine how history or literature would have differed if television had been around: "Cut to Barbara Walters walking across a village green with a sad-looking woman in tow. The camera comes in close. 'Hester Prynne,' says Walters, 'just between us, did you ever think you'd really end up with that Scarlet A?'" How should journalists avoid betraying their sources and still make certain that their readers get the complete story?

2. According to *News Reporting and Writing,* by Melvin Mencher, reporter Gail Roberts of the *Sun-Bulletin* in Binghamton, New York, had heard stories about young people making their homes on streets, in basements and in parks. Rather than relying on city officials to describe the situation, she sought out the street people themselves. They told her they managed to survive by selling sex, fencing stolen items and asking for handouts. Although Roberts was covering a beat, do you think she should have used information in addition to her own observations and conversations with the people? Would using other sources have made her story more or less credible?

3. Suppose you are writing a story about a 17-year-old girl who is recovering from a cocaine addiction. During an interview, the girl admits to selling cocaine to other students who attend your school. You agree to keep the girl's identity anonymous. However, after the story is published in the newspaper, several members of the community call and demand to know who the girl is. Although you are pressured by the administration and school board members to reveal your source, you refuse. As a result, you are expelled from school. What would you do in this situation? Should anonymous sources be protected if the reporter, the newspaper or both are put in jeopardy?

4. Why do you think newspapers are not licensed by the government, whereas radio and television stations are?

CHAPTER REVIEW, continued

FINDING THE FLAW

Harry Romanoff, a police reporter on the *Chicago Herald-Examiner,* was called "the Heifetz of the telephone" for his masquerades. Author Stephen Bates describes how Romanoff gathered information on the 1966 murders of eight student nurses. First, he called a policeman and identified himself as the Cook County coroner. Next, he called the mother of the principal suspect, Richard Speck, and identified himself as Speck's attorney. On other occasions, Romanoff pretended to be the chief of police, a member of the State Department, a White House official, a reporter for a rival newspaper, the governor of Illinois and a bishop. After his retirement in 1969, Romanoff explained his masquerades: "Once in a while, you have to shade things to protect the public's right to know." What, if anything, is wrong with Romanoff's explanation?

 MEDIA WATCH

1. Read the prize-winning story "Jimmy's World," by former *Washington Post* reporter Janet Cooke. What made it so convincing? What actions do you think should have been taken?
2. According to the author Richard Saul Wurman, "Information Anxiety is produced by the ever-widening gap between what we understand and what we think we should understand. It is the black hole between data and knowledge." Discuss what the media might do to reduce this gap.

String Book

1. Cover a beat in your high school for three weeks. Then write a story based on your own observations, as well as the observations of people you talk to.
2. Using information from a database, write an in-depth story on a topic of your choice.

Chapter 5
Interviewing

"Skillful interviewing is the basis for all good reporting and writing."
—Kris Gilger, *New Orleans Times-Picayune*

KEY TERMS

In this chapter, you will learn the meaning of these terms:

interview
human element
primary source
secondary source
5 Ws and an H
open-ended question
yes-no question
note-taking language
follow-up question
rapport
third person question
person-on-the-street
    interview
news conference

LEARNING OBJECTIVES

After completing this chapter, you will be able to:

◆ plan and set up an interview,

◆ research background information about the interview subject,

◆ write appropriate questions for interviews,

◆ take notes efficiently,

◆ conduct an interview,

◆ participate in news conferences and other special interviews.

◆

---

interview

a formal conversation between a reporter and a source for the purpose of gathering information and opinion

human element

the quotations and personal interpretations gathered in an interview that make stories interesting to readers and viewers

---

H ow important is the skill of interviewing to a reporter?

"Fundamental," according to ABC *Nightline* host Ted Koppel.

"Critical," according to Joel Brinkley of the *New York Times.* He added, "There are no star reporters in America who are not good interviewers. If you don't acquire a skillful technique, you're going to be in trouble from your first day as a reporter."

Los Angeles Times reporter Bill Endicott said interviewing is crucial. "It's probably the most important thing reporters do. What we do is essentially dependent on talking to other people."

Why did these journalists say these things about interviewing? Someone interviewed each of them. Someone asked Koppel, Brinkley and Endicott, "How important do you think the skill of interviewing is to a journalist?"

Interviewing is the heart and soul of reporting. An **interview** is a formal conversation between a reporter and a source. If a reporter cannot interview effectively, the finished product lacks the **human element,** the quotations and personal interpretations that bring news stories and features alive in readers' or viewers' minds. People like to hear and read what authorities have to say, and they like to know people's reactions to issues and situations. Reporters get information from authorities and learn people's reactions by interviewing.

Without interviews, a reporter's only sources would be physical sources such as books, maps, surveys and news releases. News needs a human element, a real-life perspective achieved by using quotes from people acting as sources of information.

In this chapter we will begin to practice the fundamental skill every reporter needs, the skill of interviewing. From suggestions for doing background research and formulating the best questions to tips for taking shorthand during the interview, this chapter will help you become an expert interviewer.

PLANNING FOR AN INTERVIEW

Reporters who plan their interviews carefully get the most information and the best quotations. Some interviews are more structured than others, but every time you ask a question, you are practicing your interviewing skills.

Asking the principal's secretary when the principal will be available for an interview is a mini-interview in itself. Asking the librarian what time the school library opens in the morning is gathering information. Asking the librarian what he or she thinks about censorship of library materials is interviewing for opinion or interpretation. In an interview, reporters both gather information and solicit opinion.

You are already performing informal interviews every day. Moving into interviewing to gather information and interpretation for news stories is an easy transition.

Primary and Secondary Sources

The editor of the school newspaper, eager to help you make that transition in interviewing skills, gives you your first story assignment: write a story about the new student council president, Joan Smiley. The editor asks for a story that describes the president's aspirations and goals for the year and that has comments from student council members who will serve with her.

To get this information, you will have to interview Smiley. She will be a **primary source,** a person who has information that is essential to the story. Every story will have at least one primary source, and some will have several. Without the primary source or sources, there is no story. **Secondary sources** are people or documents that add information, perspective and interpretation to a story but are not vital to its existence. Primary and secondary sources may be people or they may be physical. Books, surveys, budgets, minutes of meetings, and data gathered from the internet are physical sources.

The reporter's first job is to find out who or what the primary sources for a story are. For a profile feature story such as the student council president assignment, the choice is easy. Smiley is a primary source. Members of the student council are secondary sources. Other secondary sources might be the student council adviser, who could talk about the election, or minutes of meetings that record the recent activities of the group.

A story on the next school play would use the director, the actors and perhaps the script as primary sources. A story on the school board's decision to buy new band uniforms would center on information from the band director and school board members. A story about next year's budget would require the reporter to review the budget and to interview the school officials who set the budget. Secondary sources for the budget story might be students who won't have new textbooks next year because of budget cuts or a teacher whose request for new computers has been approved as part of the budget.

Los Angeles Laker and NBA All-Star Kobe Bryant is interviewed by Jessica Kerns, a young high school reporter from California.

primary source
> a person or document essential to the meaning of a story

secondary source
> a person or document that adds information and interest to a story but that is not essential to the story

DATELINE DATELINE DATELINE

BOSTON, March 10, 1876— Alexander Graham Bell successfully demonstrated his unique system for transmitting voices over wire by sending for his assistant, Thomas A. Watson, who was in the next room of their Boston laboratory. Bell had accidentally spilled a jar of acid and called for Watson's assistance.

The first message transmitted by telephone was a call for help: "Mr. Watson, come here. I want you."

By the next year, Bell was demonstrating his invention by sending messages over 18 miles of long-distance wires from Salem, Mass. to Boston.

Bell patented the key part necessary to construct a telephone in 1876. The key to the telephone is a transducer, a modulating device that converts complex sound energy from air to electric current that can be carried over wire.

Bell could not afford to develop his invention, and the patents were eventually sold to a company known today as AT&T.

Coast-to-coast telephone service was possible by 1919, less than 50 years later.

Researching for an Interview

After you have made a list of sources for the story, it is time to research your topic. Being prepared for an interview is very important to a reporter's success. Being unprepared makes the reporter and the newspaper look bad. It may make sources hesitant to talk with you or your colleagues in the future.

Before calling for an interview, gather the facts about your topic. Information gathered about a person or subject before an interview is called background information. Background information helps the reporter prepare for the interview. It is not intended to be used as primary material for the story itself. For the Smiley story, for example, background information would include the issues of the student council race and what Smiley has said about them. Knowing that information, you will be able to ask informed questions.

If you had no background information, your interview with Smiley might go something like this:

Reporter: I'm supposed to ask you about your plans for student council.

Smiley: Okay.

Reporter: What can you tell me about your plans?

Smiley: Well, big things will be happening.

Reporter: How do you plan to implement those things?

Smiley: The student council will work very hard to make the changes.

How would you prepare for an interview with someone as famous as Alexander Graham Bell shown here with one of his inventions in his laboratory about 1915?

No pertinent or usable information has been exchanged in this conversation. You had no idea what to expect from the source, because you knew nothing of Smiley's background. By looking at past issues of the newspaper or contacting secondary sources, you could have prepared more informed and focused questions in order to control the interview and get precise information.

The last issue of the newspaper reported that Smiley has promised to work toward more student input in school board policies, to fight against all decisions to suspend or expel a student, and to try to reintroduce prayer into all school ceremonies and classes. An interview with the past president of the student council reveals that some of Smiley's goals aren't new. They have been discussed by the council during the past year, and some actions have already been taken. The student council adviser explains the operations of the council and its accomplishments over the last three years.

With that background information in mind, you can expect better responses to your well-prepared questions:

> **Reporter:** Joan, how do you plan to fight against student suspensions and expulsions, as you promised in your campaign?
>
> **Smiley:** Actually, that will be tough at first. More important is my promise to have more student input in school board policies. With that input, we can work toward stopping the suspensions.
>
> **Reporter:** I believe the council tried two years ago to get more student input in board decisions and failed. How do you propose to become more involved in the decision-making process now?
>
> **Smiley:** Well, I've already met with the superintendent and the school board president to create a student liaison position on the policies committee.
>
> **Reporter:** What was their reaction?

You are much happier with the results of this interview, but you remember that the editor wants comments from other members of the student council, too. More research provides the names of the student council members. Because you know the issues from your research on Smiley, you can contact student council members to get their thoughts on the upcoming year.

Making the Most of Sources

By doing some simple research before an interview, a reporter can have enough background information to formulate questions that will elicit valuable information and usable quotations from appropriate sources. For a school story assignment, try to interview people you don't know. Readers at school know your friends and can figure out whether you did the necessary background research for a story or whether you waited until the last minute to ask your friends a few questions.

Experienced reporters will sometimes ask questions to which they already know the answers. This tactic can help verify or update information and establish the credibility of the source. It is a good way to make sure you and your source have the same information and a mutual understanding of your topic when you begin the interview.

If sources give answers that do not agree with information you have, you will need to check further to see which information is correct. Even when information seems to agree, a good reporter verifies it with a third source.

Sometimes, however, the only way to get information is from the primary source. No amount of research yields any background information. When that is the case, don't despair. Although sources like to talk with a knowledgeable interviewer, they also understand that a reporter cannot know everything. Most sources will be happy to help clarify information for reporters. Because a reporter's task is to convey information accurately and clearly to an audience, ask your sources to repeat explanations until you are confident you understand.

One interview is not usually enough for a complete story. The number of sources needed for a story depends on the type of story being written. A good news story that covers all sides of an issue will likely require five to 10 sources. A feature about one person will focus on that person but should include quotes from several other people about the subject. A story about an athletic competition ideally has quotes from the coaches, key players, and fans or observers.

Some sources interviewed for a story may not be quoted in the story but can still provide background information that helps the reporter understand the story or verify the information. The number of interviews is not as important as the reporter's thorough understanding of the information. It is better to have more information and sources than are necessary than to miss a key point.

1. Look at a recent issue of a local newspaper. Read the stories on the front page and decide who you think the reporter interviewed for each story. What are the other sources in the story? Why do you think these sources were used? Who else might you have included to interview? Why?

2. Select someone who is known by everyone in the class, such as a school official or local celebrity. Brainstorm to create a list of primary and secondary sources you could use to find background information on that person. Assign groups to check those sources and report their findings to the class.

3. Make a list of the primary sources in your school for each organization and activity. Make another list of general information sources, such as the administrators, the media services coordinator and the secretaries. Include telephone and e-mail addresses for each source. As a group, compare lists to be sure they are complete. Compile a master list, and distribute copies to all class or staff members.

◢PREPARING THE QUESTIONS

The next step in preparing for an interview is compiling a list of questions. In the previous section you saw how background information is useful in helping you come up with questions. After you have researched the background of your sources, a good place to move on to is the standard news cues known as the **5 Ws and an H:** who, what, when, where, why and how.

Using News Cue Questions

Answers to questions beginning with the standard news cues provide information for the lead of the story, as we'll see in Chapter 6. For the Smiley story, for instance, six standard news cue questions could be as follows:

+ *What* are your aspirations as student council president?
+ *Who* in the political world would you compare yourself to and why?
+ *When* do you hope to have your goals accomplished?
+ *Where* do you expect support to come from for your proposals?
+ *Why* did you choose these goals as your priorities?
+ *How* do you plan to accomplish all this?

More than six questions will be necessary to get enough information for a story, and some of the six news cues may not be appropriate for a particular story. To make an interview productive, a reporter must go into it knowing what questions need to be answered to make the story interesting and to meet the requirements of the editor's assignment.

Multiple *who* and *what* questions can be formulated for most stories. Asking "Why?" or "Why do you say that?" is a good follow-up response to a source's answer if you want to keep a source talking or have the source clarify a point:

Reporter: Who do you expect to support your recommendations?

Smiley: I expect Principal Zulkoski and Coach Zavala to support my recommendation not to expel or suspend students in the future.

Reporter: Why do you say that?

Smiley: They have both argued against the suspension policy in the past.

It's much easier to write from an abundance of information, so prepare more questions than you think are necessary to get the story. Sometimes a source will answer several questions in responding to one. A good reporter always has another question ready.

Open-Ended and Yes-No Questions

Some questions work better than others. **Open-ended questions** are questions that ask for an opinion or interpretation from the source.

5 Ws and an H
news cues based on the classic news questions: Who? What? When? Where? Why? and How? These cues help reporters organize questions for an interview

open-ended question
a question worded to encourage the source to give an opinion or interpretation, or to expand on basic information

yes-no question

a question worded to generate a response of yes or no

They are more likely to provide good quotations than are **yes-no questions.** Yes-no questions are questions worded in such a way that the source may easily answer yes or no. When sources begin to answer questions with yes or no, reporters should revise their questions. Answers of yes or no not only make interviews boring but also make the final story very hard to write, because the reporter has too little information with which to work.

To avoid responses of yes or no, try rephrasing the questions. For example, "Do you think it will rain?" can be changed to "When do you think it will rain?" or "What makes you think it will rain?" (Note the use of the standard news cues.) The following list shows more examples of how questions can be rephrased to avoid answers of yes or no:

Yes-No Question	**Open-Ended Question**
Did you sign the petition?	Why did you sign the petition?
Do you floss regularly?	What are your views on flossing?
Does your computer do calculus?	What is your computer capable of doing?

Notice that the yes-no questions limit responses, whereas the open-ended ones ask for more detailed information. Each of the open-ended questions will get the same basic information as the yes-no questions, but they will also elicit extra information.

A direct yes-no question is sometimes useful. It can be a follow-up when the reporter wants to verify information or to clarify a source's response:

> **Reporter:** Why did you sign the petition to put the minimum wage question on the ballot?
>
> **Source:** Who says I signed the petition? Besides, I don't think the government should be telling employers what to pay people.
>
> **Reporter:** Did you sign the petition?
>
> **Source:** Yes.

How would Smiley handle yes-no questions? Let's see:

> **Reporter:** Do you have goals for the student council?
>
> **Smiley:** Yes.
>
> **Reporter:** Are you going to accomplish these goals?
>
> **Smiley:** Yes.
>
> **Reporter:** Do you have a time line to accomplish your goals?
>
> **Smiley:** No.

The reporter is getting the basic information, but the explanations—the interesting parts—are being left out. Replies of yes or no answer the questions, but they do not explain anything, nor do they bring the same human element into the story that a colorful, enthusiastic quotation would.

Avoiding one-word answers from Smiley would be easy. Questions that begin with *how, what* or *why* elicit explanations. If the reporter had asked, "*What* are your goals for the student council?" Smiley might have answered with a list of goals. "*How* are you going to accomplish these goals?" or "*What* is your time line for accomplishing these goals?" are other open-ended questions that would prompt Smiley to give specific, informative responses.

Phrasing Clear Questions

Asking questions that get good responses is important. Asking for too much information at one time, however, may confuse the source and make it difficult for the person to answer.

David Letterman is a popular talk show host who has interviewed countless people. But if reporters modeled their journalistic interviews after Letterman's, they might confuse their subjects. Letterman often asks two or three questions at a time. Interview subjects should not be expected to answer more than one question at a time.

A typical Letterman question might sound like this: "Are you married? For how long? What do you do in your spare time?" The information Letterman is fishing for may be important, but by the time he is finished asking the questions, the person being interviewed has probably forgotten all but the last part. Because a reporter's job is to get all the information, asking one question at a time works better.

A question that asks for more than one response is difficult to answer:

> Principal Zulkoski, what is your opinion of the present school policy on the suspension and expulsion of students who get caught violating too many school rules, what do you think should be done to those students instead, or do you have a better plan for rehabilitating them so they can stay in school and graduate?

Explaining the background before you ask a question seems to create a long question that could confuse the source. However, it helps the source to know why you're asking the question and that you have some knowledge of the subject:

> Principal Zulkoski, Joan Smiley told the *Hometown High Herald* last month that one of her goals as president of the student council would be to try to get the suspension and expulsion policies at Hometown High changed so students would no longer be suspended or expelled. Instead, she would like to see them rehabilitated so they could return to the classroom. She said she expected to have your support for her plan. What is your opinion of the present policy?

1. Rewrite these questions as open-ended questions:
   ◆ Do you have plans for the weekend?
   ◆ Will you be involved in the Spring Fling concert and dance?
   ◆ Should the president be reelected?
   ◆ Do you like the new class scheduling system?
   ◆ Do you plan to go on to college after graduation?

2. Reporters write out key questions before they go to interviews. It is helpful for beginners to start with the standard news cue questions: Who? What? Where? When? Why? How?

   Your teacher or editor will assign you an interview for a story. Write at least 10 questions you will ask, including those based on the 5 Ws and an H. Check your list for yes-no questions. If you find any, rewrite them as open-ended questions.

CONDUCTING INDIVIDUAL INTERVIEWS

Most interviews a reporter does are one-on-one with a source. Common courtesy and common sense are the best tools a reporter can use when working with individuals in person, on the telephone or in front of a camera. This section provides some general guidelines that will help you get a good interview that you can turn into a great story.

Before the Interview

When you have completed your research for an interview and have carefully planned your questions, contact the source to make an appointment. Be straightforward. If the source is someone you know, such as Smiley, you can catch up with her in the hall at school and tell her your newspaper wants to run a story about her election and her plans for the student council. If you do not know the source, it may be easier to telephone at a time when you will be able to explain in detail who you are and what you want. Chances are the source will be happy to talk to you if you are friendly and polite.

Always identify yourself as a reporter when you contact a source for an appointment. That way the source will know you are acting in your official capacity as a reporter and not just being nosy.

Arrange a time to do the interview. Because you are asking for some of the interviewee's time, try to be flexible and work around his or her schedule. Thank the person for agreeing to speak with you. Be prepared to do the interview when the source is available. Many sources will be ready and willing to talk at the time you call, so have questions prepared before you call. Reporters do telephone interviews regularly, but try to conduct as many interviews as possible in person while you are practicing your interviewing skills. You'll have more time to ask questions, and you'll get an impression of the person by interacting one on one.

In addition to setting a time that is convenient for the source, try to meet the source on his or her territory, such as in an office where the person works. Next best is to meet the source on neutral ground, such as in a restaurant or the school library. Always arrive on time for the interview.

Taking Notes

If all it took to be an effective interviewer was asking questions, almost anybody could do it. What sets a good interviewer apart from a person who just asks good questions is the ability to interact with, listen to, and observe the subject and the surroundings to gather a complete picture.

This sounds easier than it is. The interviewer has to be able to ask questions, listen carefully to responses, write down answers, comprehend what is being said and prepare for the next question, all in a short amount of time. Practice and experience are the best teachers of interviewing skills.

The first skill to master is a personal shorthand for taking notes. Writing down every word would slow the interview and interrupt the flow of the conversation. Time might run out before you asked all your questions or before the source said everything he or she wanted to say. At the same time, it is very important to record the facts and quotations accurately.

With practice, reporters devise their own **note-taking language.** This is a set of symbols and abbreviations reporters develop to help them take notes quickly. No two people use exactly the same note-taking code. With a little time and practice, you'll figure out what is easiest for you. Here are some suggestions to get you started:

- *ppl* for *people*
- *ev* for *every*
- *w/* for *with*
- *<* and *>* for *greater than* and *lesser than,* or similar meanings
- Δ for *therefore*
- *diff* for *different*
- *2* for *to, too* or *two; 4* for *for, four* or *fore,* as in *4head*
- *2B* for *to be; B4* for *before*
- initials of people in a group to distinguish which one is speaking

It isn't necessary to write down every single word a speaker says. The *ums* and *ya knows* should be left out, of course, but also try leaving out the little words like *a, an, the, and, but* and *or* and reinserting them later.

Say a basketball coach reels off the following words to you after a basketball game: "We stood around flat-footed and waited for something to happen, and nothing ever did. And we couldn't press, because we weren't scoring. We can't have quarters like the first and third. We need to play consistent and get good shots."

Your notes may look something like this:

stood ard. f-footed waited 4
sthing 2 happen, nothing ever
did. couldnt press, wrnt
scoring. Cant have 1st & 3rd
play   ,get good shots.

Jot a question mark in the margin by anything that needs to be clarified before the interview ends. Write the speaker's name and phone number in the notes to make it convenient if you need to contact the source.

DATELINE DATELINE DATELINE

LONDON, Jan. 26, 1926—The first instantaneous moving picture transmission was accomplished by John Logie Baird.

The Scottish engineer used a method called mechanical television to send pictures from one room to another. His television scanner used a perforated, rotating disc that produced a 30-line image that was repeated 30 times per second.

Witnesses said that the black-and-white pictures, although blurry, were clear enough to be seen on a screen only a few inches square.

In 1928, Baird sent a televised image from London to Hartsdale, New York, using a shortwave band. He also sent a televised woman's image to her fiancé on a ship 1,000 miles out at sea, but the sailor admitted he had trouble recognizing the image as that of his fiancée.

In 1932, Baird demonstrated the capabilities of his television system to more than 1,000 people, who watched televised pictures of the English derby live on a movie screen in London.

Baird manufactured video-disc receivers, which were sold at Selfridge's department store in London for several years.

The British Broadcasting Company used Baird's mechanical system until the mid-1930s, when it adopted the electronic transmission system.

Write out the questions you want to ask before you interview a source. Preparing questions ahead of time will assure that you remember to ask for all the important information, and it will allow you to relax and enjoy the interview.

Asking Follow-Up Questions

follow-up question

a question that follows a source's response to another question, intended to get the source to add to or continue with an answer or explanation. Follow-up questions usually begin with *why, how* or *what*. They cannot be planned ahead of time, as they relate to the source's statements

Reporters who are good listeners pick out confusing concepts from a source's answers and ask questions that will help clarify the information, even if those questions were not on their original lists. These **follow-up questions** enable the reporter to be flexible enough to move in a different direction if the interview shifts away from the planned topic.

A source's answer to a prepared question may bring another question to mind, or you may not completely understand the source's answer. You need to ask another question—a follow-up question that you haven't prepared—to help you write the best possible story. Ask follow-up questions as often as you need to, but be sure to steer the source back to your prepared questions so you get all the information you need to write your story.

A follow-up question may also be sparked by something the source says that you didn't know about ahead of time. If you aren't listening closely and don't follow up a source's lead, you may miss the most important information the source wants to share.

Listening is important. If you go into an interview, ask the 10 questions you prepared and leave, you probably won't get a full story. Even with the 10 best questions in the world, a lack of follow-up questions to clarify information or pursue other possibilities will leave the completed story sounding unfinished.

Listening during an interview is more than just being a bystander. As a reporter, you must look interested in your source and the information he or she is sharing. A nod at appropriate times or a well-placed "I see" or "Uh-huh" will encourage the source to keep talking. Feedback, or a verbal or nonverbal sign from you—a nod, a glance or a smile—lets the source know you are listening and keeping up with the information. Extreme silence or a bored look on your face will tell the source that you would rather be somewhere else. The source may stop talking or end the interview before you get all the information you need.

Observing and Recording Details

A good interviewer is also a good observer. Before, during and after the interview, an interviewer must pick up visual clues that will help add detail or human interest, especially if the assignment is a feature story. A room can reveal a lot about its occupant. A clean desk can mean that the person is efficient in getting work completed. Pictures of wildlife on the wall can point to the person's love of nature. Titles of books on the person's bookshelf will give the interviewer a glimpse at the subject's interests and areas of expertise.

Be careful not to stereotype individuals by their surroundings, however. A clean desk may just mean the boss is coming to visit or the janitorial staff has cleaned recently. A good approach is to ask the subject about your observation. For example, you might say, "Your office is certainly neat. How would you describe your organization style?"

Write your observations in your notes right along with the answers from the interview. Use some observations as a basis for follow-up questions: "I see you like to read books about travel. What's the most exotic place you've been?" or "You appear to be very happy about the announcement of the grant for the new computers for the school. What does it mean to you personally?"

A tape recorder helps a reporter get details during an interview. Taping an interview is a good idea, if you do it carefully. On the positive side, tape recordings capture every word of the interview and thus give the reporter more accurate and interesting quotations to put in the story. Recording the interview in addition to taking notes frees the reporter from some of the concentration on note taking and allows a more conversational tone to develop between the reporter and the source. The source may almost forget he or she is being interviewed.

On the negative side, tape recordings are not always reliable. Batteries die. Tapes stop and interrupt the flow of the interview. Many sources don't like to be recorded. Ask permission from a source before recording an interview, and place the recorder where everyone can see it. Tuck a new set of batteries in your pocket. Always take notes, even though the recorder is running. If the recorder stops in the middle of the interview and you didn't write anything down, you're left with nothing.

Listening to a recording and finding the quotations you want slows down the writing time, too. However, if a quotation is essential to a story on a sensitive issue, it will certainly be worthwhile to have it on tape.

When you are just beginning to practice your interviewing techniques, it is best to leave the tape recorder at home and work on your note taking, listening and observing skills. These skills will take you further than a recording ever will.

Broadcast reporters have no choice. They must be able to get their information on tape or on camera because all the interviews they record are potentially for broadcast. Broadcast reporters take notes, too. Their notes give them information for the parts of the story they must write. The notes also remind them of what is on their tapes so they can find the parts they want later.

One Key to Interviewing

Mireza Navarro knows how to get that tough interview. After getting her journalism degree in 1979 from George Washington University, Navarro was hired by the *San Francisco Examiner,* where one of her first assignments was to find and interview a woman who had been arrested for stealing.

The woman was a mother, lived in a middle-class neighborhood and had no criminal record. Her defense for stealing was that she suffered from multiple personalities. Navarro found her at home, but when she tried to get the woman to talk, she just kept repeating: "My lawyer told me not to talk to a reporter."

Navarro went to her car and deliberately locked the keys inside. Then she returned to the house and asked to use the phone. The woman overheard the conversation and offered Navarro a ride.

Navarro recalls: "During the ride she started talking. I couldn't take notes because that would make her nervous. But I agreed that I would check with her attorney and would leave out anything he thought would hurt her case. I listened intently and etched a few things in my mind. She just talked and talked and talked . . . I made a point of remembering three direct quotes." The next day Navarro had a front-page story no one else had.

Source: Adapted from Dianne Selditch, ed., My First Year as a Journalist *(New York: Walker and Company.).*

THIS JUST IN: Portrait of a Young Journalist
Phil Scott, freelance writer

If Paola, Kan., had had tracks, I would have been growing up on the wrong side. Beneath my layers of working-class, teenage attitude, though, I had always longed to become a journalist. My first step, before heading off to college J-school, would be to sign up for my high-school newspaper class at the earliest possible moment, the beginning of my junior year.

"You can't type and your grades are too low," said the counselor. While I protested, he signed me up for a drama class, figuring that since my father worked in a lumberyard, I could probably handle building scenery.

I gave up the idea of college.

After one semester, I got kicked out of drama for continually disrupting class and found myself back in the counselor's office after hours.

"Just let me in the newspaper class," I demanded. He reluctantly allowed that he would let me in if I could get the adviser's approval. So I strode off to the classroom, and found the adviser, Kevin Gray, a short, young, yellow-haired teacher fresh out of college, sitting at his desk in the empty room, looking exhausted.

"Hi. I want to be on the newspaper staff," I said to him.

"What class are you in now?"

"Drama. They wouldn't let me in here 'cause my grades are too low," I said. "But all I ever wanted to do was to write."

"Okay," he said after a moment, "you're in." He filled out a form and gave it to me.

"You won't be sorry," was all I could think to say.

He probably was, though, at first. Joining the class at the halfway point, I didn't fit in right away to the existing power structure, and so I didn't always show up to do work—or even show up. But then over the summer break, I decided I was going to try for a fresh start. Mr. Gray had taken a chance on me, and I wanted to show him how much I appreciated it and respected him for it. Starting that fall, I started pitching story ideas, took every writing assignment and wrote reams of terrifically bad stuff. But I also waded in and virtually took over running the newspaper.

Gray (who had identified with me from the start, since—I found out later—he had been somewhat of a rebel himself), rewarded my involvement by making me the managing editor that year. It's a title I've had a hard time shaking. Two years after graduating from the University of Kansas with degrees in journalism and English, I became the managing editor of *Flying* magazine, then *Omni,* both based in New York City. Now, however, I am a full-time freelance writer for such magazines as *Self* and *Air & Space/Smithsonian,* and I have just finished my first book, *The Shoulders of Giants, a history of human flight to 1919.*

The day I finished writing it, I sent Kevin a post card (he's still teaching journalism at the high school), thanking him once again for just giving me that chance, half my lifetime— another lifetime—ago.

Source: 'All I ever wanted to do was write,' by Phil Scott. Adviser Update, *The Dow Jones Newspaper Fund.*

Sources tend to speak more formally and professionally when the camera or tape recorder is running, because they know they are going to be seen or heard by the audience. They will give the same information, but the atmosphere becomes more energized when a source is speaking in front of a camera. The more time the source spends in front of a camera or microphone, the more at ease he or she will become.

Establishing Rapport

Whether it's in front of a camera, in a source's office or on the telephone, establishing an agreeable, harmonious relationship between you and your source will help you get good information and encourage the source to be open. A friendly greeting, a handshake, or an exchange of comments about the weather or people you both know helps build the desired harmony, or **rapport,** you want before you begin the formal interview.

Consider the interview with Joan Smiley. Now that you've arrived on time for the interview, you must establish a rapport with her. If you go rushing up to her and start asking questions without any preliminary interaction, she will be less likely to give you any information. She doesn't yet know what kind of person you are or whether she should trust you.

How might she react? See for yourself:

Reporter: Hi, Joan. Tell me your goals for the year.

Smiley: Who are you?

Reporter: I'm the reporter for the school paper. So, what are your goals?

Smiley: Didn't you read them in the last paper?

Reporter: Of course I did, but I wanted to make sure they were still the same.

You two were not ready for an interview. You did not take the time to get acquainted or to establish a comfortable rapport before beginning the serious questioning.

If this is your first face-to-face meeting with Smiley, introduce yourself, shake hands and chat for a while. This will let Smiley know that you are a comfortable person to talk to. Your credibility and professionalism are on the line during this most important part of the interview, so be businesslike but friendly.

Many sources have a negative image of what reporters want, so they are hesitant about opening up to a reporter. A good first impression will help break the ice and set a positive tone for the interview.

Sources will usually decide when they are ready to be interviewed. At that point, the source may say, "So, what can I do for you?" or something similar. Or you may sense when the source is relaxed and open the interview yourself.

Briefly describe the purpose of the interview once again, and begin with some routine questions such as "How do you spell your name?" and "What is your title?" Then you can move through other questions that will give information to provide a well-rounded story.

Avoid asking confrontational questions—those that put the source on the defensive. For example, asking "Did you punch the principal in the face?" will cast you in the role of bad guy. The source will avoid giving you information. A reporter is supposed to be a neutral bystander who gets facts on all sides of an issue. If the reporter asks a confrontational question, the source will feel like the reporter is siding with the opposition and may answer accordingly. That doesn't mean the ques-

rapport

a harmonious, agreeable relationship between a source and a reporter established by friendly greetings and casual conversation preceding the formal interview

tion shouldn't be asked. It means the question should be asked more diplomatically.

One way to accomplish this diplomacy is by attributing the question to someone else. For example, the question could be worded, "How do you reply to allegations that you punched the principal in the face?" or "Many students are worried about allegations that you punched the principal. What is your response to them?"

By phrasing the question in the impersonal, general terms of *many students* or *people,* the reporter is giving the source a chance to explain the action so that his or her side of the story is presented fairly to the public. The use of a question that seems to come from unnamed others, a **third person question,** is a simple way of getting sensitive information without seeming to pry for personal gain. Asking the same question in the first person—"I understand you punched the principal . . ."—would make the reporter sound gossipy or intrusive. Asking it in the third person gives the question more power, because the source is answering to more than just the reporter.

third person question

a question phrased in an impersonal manner as though someone other than the reporter were asking for the information; usually begins with a phrase such as "People say that . . ." or "What do you tell people when. . . ."

Concluding the Interview

Before you close an interview, quickly review your notes. Ask the source to clarify any points you are uncertain about and answer any questions you may have overlooked.

In just about every interview, the last question should be the same: "Is there anything you'd like to add?" or "Is there anything we haven't talked about that we should have?" No matter how many questions the reporter has asked or how many anecdotes the source has related, this is an important question with which to end an interview. Many a story has begun or ended with information garnered from such an open-ended question.

The question allows the source to summarize or restate points made earlier or to introduce topics the reporter may have missed. It also serves as a very good conclusion to the interview, because it lets the source know that the reporter has the basic information.

Using the 5 Ws and an H is another way to conclude an interview and be sure basic information has been covered. A checklist of questions to ask might include the following:

◆ *How* do you spell your name?
◆ *What* is your title?
◆ *Where* may I reach you if I have questions?
◆ *When* is a good time to call?
◆ *Who* else do you suggest I talk to about this subject?
◆ *Why* would that person be a good source?

Reporters know they may need the same sources for future stories, so they try to end interviews with the same positive rapport they created at the beginning. Before thanking the source and saying goodbye, a courteous reporter opens the door to further contact. "Would you mind if I checked back if I have more questions?" and "Is there a telephone number where I might reach you if I need more information?" are good questions to let the source know the reporter cares enough to double-check information when writing the story.

Writing Up the Interview

Read your notes as soon as possible after the interview. Highlight quotes or points you think are especially significant. Add notes about your impression of the person, mannerisms or actions that will help you remember how the words were spoken or how the person reacted to a question. Fill in the missing words, write out abbreviated words, and rewrite or type the notes. Don't wait a day or two and then try to read what you've written. You may not be able to decipher your note-taking language if you wait too long. Contact the source to ask for any information that is missing or unclear.

Date your notes, and keep them on file. You will need them if the editor has questions or wants you to add to your story. The notes may also be handy for future stories on the same topic or for recalling sources' names if you want to call on them again. Your notes are also your defense if you're ever challenged by a source.

BYLINE

JOHN BRADY
FORMER EDITOR OF *WRITER'S DIGEST* AND *BOSTON*

A few years ago, I was working on a book of interviews with major screen writers. With great difficulty, I landed an interview with the giant of them all, William Goldman, who wrote such classics as "All the President's Men" and "Butch Cassidy and the Sundance Kid." Goldman was reluctant to give me any time, but he finally agreed to squeeze me in between 10 and 11 a.m. on a Thursday.

I knew, even as I accepted that, that I needed at least six hours to do the job. And I knew that I had to prove at the start that I was worth more of his time.

I began, as usual, with extensive research. I learned about Goldman's early life, his schooling, his career. I learned that he'd started as a paperback writer, and I happened to learn that in the early '60s he'd published a novel written under the pseudonym Harry Longbaugh.

I continued with research on the screenplays he'd written, including "Butch Cassidy and the Sundance Kid," which was particularly important because it made Goldman's name and earned him an Academy Award. And in poring over old issues of *Variety*, I discovered that the real name of the Sundance Kid, an Old West outlaw, was Harry Longbaugh.

The next Thursday, at 10 a.m. exactly, I looked William Goldman in the eye. I started the tape recorder. And I asked, "Why were you using the Sundance Kid's name on your own novel seven years before you wrote the screenplay about him?"

He looked at me and said, "Harry Longbaugh. Isn't that a wonderful name? When I was a kid, I thought the Sundance Kid was a make-believe hero. But there was a Sundance Kid, Harry Longbaugh, and he was the fastest gun in the West."

One hour turned into two and spilled over into lunch and then to the next day. When I finally left New York, I had eight or nine hours on tape.

The moral of this story: Don't waste the first question. Get your subjects' attention. Tell them you're not just another interview in off the street to do the usual canned interview. If you show that you've worked, they're going to work. They'll give you a little bit more of their time, a little more honesty, and a better story in the end.

Source: from "Smooth Talk," by John Brady, published in Case Currents.

1. Devise your own system of abbreviations and symbols. Have someone read aloud a paragraph from a book. (It's not fair to ask to have it repeated!) After you take notes on the passage that was read, see how closely you can reproduce the entire paragraph. What did you miss? How can you prevent that from happening again?

2. Compare your note-taking techniques with those of your classmates. Share your favorite abbreviations and symbols with your classmates.

3. Choose a partner to do a role-playing interview. One person will be the reporter, and the other will be a new teacher at your school. Compile a list of questions, and then interview the teacher as if you were doing an introductory story on him or her. Switch roles and choose a person for the reporter to interview. After the exercise, discuss with the others in your class what obstacles you encountered and how you might overcome them.

4. Interview a friend or relative outside of class. Make sure you have an original list of questions that you want answered. During the interview, write down observations about the person's gestures and mannerisms, as well as about the setting. Also write down the follow-up questions you ask. Relate your findings to the class, and explain how you would incorporate them into a story.

▲INTERVIEWING GROUPS

So far all the explanations and examples in this chapter have been about interviewing only one source at a time. One-on-one interaction is best for interviews. Interviewing a group, especially a close-knit one, or trying to interview a single person in a group situation, can detract from individual responses and change the atmosphere of the entire interview.

As a student reporter, you should avoid doing one-on-one interviews where students congregate, such as the local arcade, the cafeteria or the stands at an athletic event, where sources are surrounded by their friends. In these settings the sources will be tempted to give the answers their friends expect rather than the thoughtful responses they might give in a one-on-one interview.

As with many other situations, however, there are exceptions. Sometimes a reporter may want to get a sense of the camaraderie or the feeling of accomplishment among the sources—members of a championship athletic team or organizers of a successful fund-raiser, for instance—by interviewing them as a group.

Getting quotations from **person-on-the-street interviews** is another exception. These interviews are conducted in places where people gather or move around. The reporter asks individuals to respond to one or two specific questions and records their answers. Again, interviewees are more likely to treat the reporter's questions seriously if they are alone than if they are with a group.

Person-on-the-street interviews produce a random sampling of opinions on specific, high-profile issues and provide good student com-

person-on-the-street interview
brief interviews with people passing by a location or locations the reporter chooses; usually used to gather a sampling of opinion about an issue or topic in the news

ments for stories and opinion pages. To fairly represent the groups within a school or community, a reporter should interview people at several locations.

News conferences are group interviews planned to convey information simultaneously from one source to many reporters. The news conferences people see most often today are televised and usually focus on the president or a spokesperson for a special interest group. After the source delivers a prepared statement, reporters are allowed to ask questions.

The source, not the reporter, is in control at a news conference. The source, place, time and number of reporters present all affect the opportunity for one reporter to ask questions. Each reporter, therefore, must decide what questions are most important to the story, because he or she may get only one chance to ask them. Often there are so many reporters that not every reporter gets to ask a question. Reporters must listen carefully to the questions being asked by others and record that information so they don't waste time by asking similar questions.

Practice is the best way to learn to get information from news conferences. Each news conference, like each individual interview, is slightly different. With patience and experience, a reporter learns to get the needed information in almost any interview.

news conference

a group interview planned to convey information simultaneously from one source to many reporters representing all media

Hartford Connecticut City Manager Sandra Kee Borges answers a question from a reporter during a news conference at City Hall.

YOUR BEAT

1. Invite a school administrator or school board member to hold a news conference for your class. Ask your guest to speak for a few minutes about a current issue or upcoming event at the school. Prepare a list of questions you would like to ask about that topic and other topics about which the guest would have information. Ask as many questions as you can. Compare your questions to those asked by others. What other information would you need to write a story? How could you get that information?

2. Plan a person-on-the-street interview to get student opinion on an issue such as a new school policy or an election. As a class, select a topic and write the question. Assign each person to go to a different place (an exit or a hallway, for example) at the same time (such as right after school) and ask 10 people to answer the question. Each reporter should keep track of the class and gender of each respondent. Compare results. How can you know if the quotes the class solicited fairly represent the student body? What one location would best represent the student body? Why?

LONDON, 1896—Italian inventor Guglielmo Marconi, 22, registered a patent in London for instruments to send and receive messages by transmitting bursts of electromagnetic waves through the air. Marconi's method was called wireless telegraphy because it used Morse Code and sending and receiving equipment similar to that of the existing wire telegraph system. The wireless enabled Marconi to transmit messages through the air from point to point over land and water.

His wireless system was the basis for forming the first commercial wireless company, Wireless Telegraph and Signal Company, Ltd., in London in 1897. Marconi received one-half of the company's stock and 15,000 British pounds for his invention.

On Dec. 12, 1901, Marconi received the signal "S," the first message successfully transmitted by airwaves across the Atlantic Ocean (from England to Newfoundland). The wireless made ship-to-shore communications possible. Within a decade, transatlantic transmission service was in place.

A Marconi Wireless employee, who would become the founder of RCA and NBC, David Sarnoff, was the first to pick up distress signals from the sinking *Titanic* in April 1912. He remained at his post for 72 hours in order to relay communications between ships in the area and families and reporters in New York.

American businesspeople, intrigued by the potential of Marconi's invention, invested $10 million to form American Marconi in 1899.

▲ PUTTING IT TOGETHER

Now let's try to put together all the guidelines that this chapter suggests by doing one great interview with Joan Smiley:

Reporter: Hi, I'm the reporter from the school paper.

Smiley: Hi, I'm Joan Smiley, your student council president.

Reporter: It's nice to meet you. Thanks a lot for fitting me into your busy schedule.

Smiley: Any time. Your paper is going to be very important in getting information out about what we plan on doing.

Reporter: How are your plans going so far?

Smiley: Well, they are just plans right now, but we are hoping to have finalized versions soon.

Reporter: Which issues are you placing high on your priority list?

Smiley: I'm hoping to get students to have more input on the school board decisions that affect them, and I want to fight against suspensions and expulsions.

Reporter: Why are these issues so important to you?

Smiley: Well, the school board makes many decisions that will affect how we are treated, how we learn, how many vacation days we get. We should be able to put in our two cents' worth before the final decision is made.

Reporter: What about the suspensions and expulsions?

Smiley: I've always been taught that the student's proper place is in the classroom learning. We can't do that if they won't allow us to come to school.

Reporter: Some people would say that the expulsions help create a better learning environment for the students who want to be here, though. What do you say to them?

Smiley: I've heard that argument, but I believe all students should be allowed to come to school and get the same education as everyone else. I want to ensure that they get that chance, even if it is a second chance.

Reporter: Your campaign for president also promised the introduction of prayer into all school ceremonies and classes, didn't it?

Smiley: Yes, it did. Thanks for remembering.

Reporter: Is that issue on your list of priorities?

Smiley: No.

Reporter: Why not?

Smiley: Well, it is something I feel strongly about, but I don't see how it can be incorporated when the ACLU threatens to sue any school that tries to do it. There's a big cloud over that issue that would take all my time away from the other issues that are just as important.

Reporter: I can see how that would be tough. Now, I want to change gears a little. To whom, politically, would you compare yourself, and why?

Smiley: I've never really thought about it, but I would have to say probably Hillary Clinton. I mean, I don't agree with all of her views, but I have the same passion for issues that she does. Once I attach myself to a cause, I hold on until I have accomplished what I set out to do or until finally there is no hope of its getting done.

Reporter: Speaking of "getting done," I have to get this story done by the end of the school day tomorrow. I think I have what I need. Is there anything we didn't talk about that you wanted to discuss?

Smiley: I think we covered everything in a nutshell. Oh, but we are having a forum open to all students next Monday so I can incorporate some of their ideas into my presentation to the school board on Wednesday. You are welcome to come and cover it for the paper.

Reporter: Thanks. We'll do that. If I find I'm missing any information for this story, may I call you tonight?

Smiley: Sure, that would be fine.

Reporter: Thanks again for your time, and have a good day.

Figure 5.1, "An Interview Checklist," will help you prepare for a successful interview assignment.

FIGURE 5.1
AN INTERVIEW CHECKLIST

BEFORE an interview, do the following:

✓ Know exactly what the purpose of the interview is.
✓ Research the subject and the source for background material.
✓ Write more questions than you think you'll need.
✓ Sharpen two pencils. They're better than pens which can run out of ink or won't write in the rain.

✓ Get a notebook.
✓ Take two pencils because one might break.
✓ If you're using a camera, tape recorder or microphone, have extra film, tapes or batteries in your bag.
✓ Make an appointment.

Follow these procedures DURING an interview:

✓ Arrive ahead of time.
✓ Introduce yourself and shake hands.
✓ Thank the source for giving the interview.
✓ Be friendly.
✓ Take a few minutes to establish a rapport with the source.
✓ Ask permission if you plan to use a tape recorder.
✓ Arrange the recorder or microphone to avoid wind or crowd noise.
✓ Begin with easy questions.
✓ Ask follow-up questions.
✓ Take notes.
✓ Look interested.

✓ Encourage the source with smiles, nods, and comments such as "I see" and "Uh-huh."
✓ Observe the surroundings and body language of the source.
✓ Double-check name spellings and titles.
✓ Say thank-you.
✓ Review your notes for missing or confusing information and ask for clarification.
✓ Say thank-you.
✓ Write the name and phone number of the source in your notes.
✓ Say thank-you.

AFTER the interview, be sure to take these steps:

✓ Review your notes immediately.
✓ Write out abbreviations, and fill in missing words.
✓ Rewrite or type your notes.

✓ Be sure the date is written on the notes.
✓ Call the source if you need more information.
✓ File the notes in a safe place.

If you were writing a story following your final interview with Joan Smiley, what other questions would you want to ask? Who else would you want to interview? (*Hint:* Review the editor's assignment.)

CHAPTER REVIEW

KEY TERMS

journalism \ˈjər-nə-ˌli-zem\ n (1833) **1 a :** the collection and editing of news for presentation through... b : the public press c : an academic study concerned with the colle...

Show that you know the meanings of the following key terms by correctly using them in complete sentences. Write your answers on a separate sheet of paper.

interview	note-taking language
human element	follow-up question
primary source	rapport
secondary source	third person question
5 Ws and an H	person-on-the-street interview
open-ended question	news conference
yes-no question	

OPEN FORUM

1. Brainstorm to create a list of personal qualities and skills a reporter needs to conduct a successful interview. Explain why each quality or skill is important.
2. How many sources or interviews does it take to make a good story? Role-play a discussion between an editor and a reporter in which the reporter contends that one interview is sufficient for a story on a vote by the school board, whereas the editor believes that more than one interview is necessary.
3. It has been said that there are no embarrassing questions, only embarrassing answers. Are there questions a reporter should not ask? Why or why not? At what point does the individual's right to privacy end and the public's right to know begin?
4. Stage a news conference for the class. Invite a guest speaker, perhaps a school counselor or the student council president, to deliver a prepared statement. Members of the class may ask questions, but limit time so not all questions get answered. Discuss how you would write the story based on the information gathered during the news conference. Is information missing? Are there questions you would want to follow up on in order to write a complete story? What problems did you experience as a reporter attending a news conference? How would you overcome these problems next time?

FINDING THE FLAW

Did the interviewer forget to ask a key question? Find the flaw in this story.

Name that whale: The winner's from . . . Melville!

NEW YORK—Drumroll, please: It's time for Name That Whale!

Two rare baby belugas received their names Friday and met the humans—picked from a litter of 10,000 entries—who won the New York Aquarium's Moby-moniker contest.

Are you ready? One winner's maiden name was Whalen and she's from Melville. (However, historians say the Long Island hamlet apparently was not named for "Moby Dick" author Herman Melville.)

The newly named whales are the longest-surviving belugas born in captivity.

The name contest began Nov. 27. Entries included Percy, "short for persevere," and Raffi, after the children's entertainer famous for "Baby Beluga."

"We had a lot of Borises, a lot of Coneys (as in Island, the aquarium's home), Nathan (of hot dog fame), Brighton (Beach), Brooklyn, a few Dodgers," said spokesman Rick Miller.

And the winning names are . . .

. . . Like any contest worth its sea salt, you'll have to wait.

The whales have different moms, but the same dad, Newfy.

Natasha's son, born Aug. 7, is about 5 feet long; Kathi's son, born Aug. 14, is around 6 feet.

The beluga boys, accompanied by Moms, shyly greeted the women who named them: Kim Pestour of Melville and Pia Proios of Queens.

"We feel like we're the godmothers to the whales," said Proios.

The winners' prizes include scuba lessons (though not in the whale tank) and a whale tongue-petting session.

A what?

"It's a very pleasant tactile sensation for them, like a person getting their shoulders massaged," said Miller. (And who discovered that whales liked this? Jonah?)

"It was so neat touching the baby in the mouth, it was so soft," said Pestour. "One time I stopped touching him, he spurted a little water to get our attention. My fingers still smell like fish."

Aquarium staff, practically herniated by the mail, sent the judges 50 or 60 entries that "were representative of something: where the whales came from, or Brooklyn, or something marine related or scientific," said Miller.

Source: Reprinted with permission from Associated Press, from Kiley Armstrong, "Name That Whale: The Winner's from . . . Melville!" Hastings (Nebraska) Tribune.

MEDIA WATCH

1. Invite a newspaper reporter and a television reporter to speak to the class about interviewing. Compare the similarities, the differences, and the difficulties of interviewing for different media.
2. Watch a televised or videotaped news conference. Discuss the problems you think the reporters might have had getting information at the news conference. In what ways is getting information at a news conference better for newspaper and magazine reporters? In what ways is it better for radio and television reporters? How is it more difficult for each group?
3. Watch television news for person-in-the-street interviews. From a viewer's perspective, what are the advantages of using person-in-the-street interviews to tell news stories? What are the problems?
4. Clip articles from newspapers or magazines written in the question-and-answer format. After reading each article, write a list of questions that the interviewer had to ask in order to write the article but that are not printed as part of the article.

String Book

You may use any newspapers for this activity, including school newspapers. Clip the page header with the name and date of the newspaper for each article; keep it with the example.

1. Clip three news and three feature stories that you think demonstrate the results of good interviewing skills. Affix each to a piece of paper that leaves room for you to write comments. Highlight the quotes and information you think were elicited through interviews. Beside each highlight, write the question that might have been asked. Keep the articles in your stringbook to remind you of questions to ask when you do interviews.
2. Interview a classmate, and write up your notes in a question-and-answer format. Put the finished notes in your stringbook.
3. Make a key for your note-taking shorthand. Leave room to add to the key as you develop more shortcuts.

Writing the News

Chapter 6
Writing a News Story

"Accuracy! Accuracy! Accuracy!"
Joseph Pulitzer, editor, *New York World*, 1883 to 1890

LEARNING OBJECTIVES

After completing this chapter, you will be able to:

◆ identify the types of news leads and their elements,

◆ write news leads,

◆ organize news stories,

◆ be accurate and objective,

◆ use third person point of view,

◆ use sentence length and structure that are appropriate for journalistic writing,

◆ use transitions.

◆

KEY TERMS

In this chapter, you will learn the meaning of these terms:
lead
direct news lead
hard news story
soft news story
5 Ws and an H lead
summary lead
indirect lead
delayed lead
feature lead
storytelling lead
nut graf
inverted pyramid
crop test
crop
storytelling pattern
clincher
third person point of view
transition
editing

*Y*ou have a story assignment. You have researched the topic, talked to some people and written pages of notes.

You have a hodgepodge of facts and information.

You have a deadline that is rapidly approaching.

And you have questions: Where do I begin? How do I know what to put first? How can I tell this story so my readers will want to read it and will understand what I'm trying to say?

No simple answers exist. However, there are some guidelines for writing news that help reporters determine the most important facts and organize them into readable stories. In this chapter, you will discover some of those guidelines and learn how to make them work for you as you begin to write news.

WRITING THE LEAD

Which of the following introductory paragraphs interest you? Why? Which ones make you want to read the rest of the story?

Michael Jordan, John Lennon, Malcolm X, Gary Coleman? It seems that no one is immune from being a young man's hero. (*Shakerite,* Shaker Heights High School, Shaker Heights, Ohio)

Lights shine and sirens roar. It's midnight and the police are scanning the streets searching for youth out past curfew. (*Bruin News,* Twin Falls High School, Twin Falls, Idaho)

Three students await their expulsion hearing in front of the Board of Trustees after violating school and district policies in the last two months. (*Epitaph,* Homestead High School, Cupertino, Calif.)

As the clock strikes midnight, a procrastinating student sits down to work on a composition which is due tomorrow. (*Crier,* Munster High School, Munster, Ind.)

lead

the beginning of a news story; conveys the main idea in a few words to several paragraphs

direct news lead

the first paragraph or two of a hard news story. The direct news lead gives the most important facts, the 5 Ws and an H, about the story

hard news story

a story about timely, breaking news; must run the day the event occurs or have new information added each time it appears in the news

soft news story

a story about individuals or lifestyle issues; less timely than a hard news story; can run anytime and still be interesting to readers

The **lead** is the beginning of a news story. It is the most important part of the story because it conveys the main idea.

All of the leads just given will interest readers. Each individual reader, however, will be more interested in some than others. If you don't recognize any of the names in the first lead, you are not likely to read the story. If you have ever procrastinated in doing your homework, you probably will be intrigued enough to read the fourth story to find out how someone else has resolved the procrastination dilemma.

Readers scan leads to gather information quickly and to help them decide which stories to read. No reader has time to read every story in the paper every day, and no single reader is interested in all the stories offered. By reading the leads of several stories, readers quickly gain key information about a number of topics and get an overview of the day's most important news events. Scanning a number of leads also helps readers prioritize the stories according to their own interests so they can decide which ones they want to read.

Readers decide in the first seven to 14 words whether or not to read a story. The lead must grab the readers' attention and arouse their curiosity. If the lead doesn't get the readers' attention, all the rest of the reporter's hard work on the story will be wasted, because readers won't read it.

Direct news leads are used on **hard news stories**—stories about timely, breaking news. The first one or two paragraphs, the lead, give the most important facts about the story.

Leads on **soft news stories,** the less timely feature stories about individuals or about lifestyle issues, are often several paragraphs long. Soft news leads use anecdotes or set up scenarios that capture readers' imaginations. These indirect leads may run as many as six to 10 paragraphs before the reader discovers the subject of the story. But whether a lead is one paragraph or half a dozen, it must be dynamic enough to make the reader want to know more.

Direct News Leads

Direct news leads, the staple of front page stories in daily newspapers, are not used as often in school newspapers, magazines or yearbooks. These publications contain stories about events that happened days, weeks or months ago. These stories lend themselves better to leads that summarize the event, set the scene or explain why the story is news in today's publication.

5 Ws and an H lead

a direct news lead, so named because it answers most or all of the questions readers ask—Who? What? Where? When? Why? and How?—in the first paragraph or two

Direct news leads are also called **5 Ws and an H leads,** because they answer most or all of the main questions readers will ask: Who? What? Where? When? Why? and How? The answers to these questions, given in the first paragraph or two, make up the lead. The following is an example:

> Choir members mixed business and pleasure at a recent national contest in New Orleans April 14–18 where the choirs reached first place all around. (*Rampage,* John Marshall High School, San Antonio, Texas)

FAMILY CIRCUS reprinted by permission of King Features Syndicate.

Try analyzing this direct news lead according to the 5 Ws and an H:

- Who: choir members
- What: mixed business and pleasure
- Where: in New Orleans
- When: April 14 to18
- Why: a national contest
- How: by winning first place

Now try analyzing this lead:

Positive feedback from last year's "Choices for Youth" program has allowed Overland's Human Relations Committee, Youth Advisory Board and IMPACT Team to bring back the program again the week of May 2–6. (*Overland Scout*, Overland High School, Aurora, CO)

- Who: Human Relations Committee, Youth Advisory Board and IMPACT Team
- What: bring back program
- Where: Overland
- When: May 2 to 6
- Why: positive feedback
- How: "Choices for Youth" program

Prioritizing Information for the Direct News Lead.

The direct news lead puts the most important information at the top of the story. An easy way to write a direct news lead is to begin with one of the 5 Ws and an H of the story. Here are five direct news leads for the same story about a school budget issue. Each begins with a different one of the 5 Ws and an H.

- *Who:* District school officials said Monday that preliminary budget cuts for the school year have been reduced from $1.2 million to approximately $450,000 because of an unanticipated grant from the state.

CHARLESTON, S.C., Jan. 4, 1737—Elizabeth Timothy became the first female publisher in the colonies when her husband, Louis Timothy, was accidentally killed.

The weekly *(Charleston) South Carolina Gazette* was founded in 1732 with the assistance of Benjamin Franklin, to whom Louis Timothy had been apprenticed. The paper was to go to Timothy's son, Peter, but Timothy died when Peter was only 13.

Elizabeth published her first edition on Jan. 4, 1737, under her son's name. Franklin retained his one-third interest until 1746, when Elizabeth bought his share and turned the business over to her son.

Because colonial printers always signed their work, it is easy to identify the early female printers. Most early female printers were the wives, widows, mothers or sisters of printers. Print shops were family businesses, which often operated out of homes. Women were often thrust into leadership roles by changes in family situations.

The physical skills of setting type and inking the presses were easy for the women to learn. However, as editors, they were mostly responsible for writing the material that went into the papers, too. In an era when women were not routinely given formal education, the women who became printers were those who had been taught to read and write.

♦ *What:* A reduction in preliminary budget cuts from $1.2 million to $450,000 is the result of an unanticipated grant from the state, according to district school officials.

♦ *Where:* The local school district budget will have to be cut only $450,000 instead of $1.2 million because of an unexpected grant from the state, district school officials announced Monday.

♦ *When:* Monday, district school officials said preliminary budget cuts for the school year have been reduced from $1.2 million to $450,000 because of an unanticipated grant from the state.

♦ *Why/How:* Because of an unanticipated grant from the state, preliminary budget cuts for the school year have been reduced from $1.2 million to $450,000, according to district school officials.

Deciding which fact to use to begin the lead is extremely important. Remember, the reader is going to make a decision about the story in the first 14 words. Leads that tell who, what and why are popular because readers recognize prominent names, and they want to know what is happening and what it means to them.

When something happened is seldom the most important or interesting part of a story, so it is not often used as the lead word. Readers don't care which day an event happened as much as they care who was involved or what the result was.

A good strategy is to use the values that make a story news: timeliness, prominence, proximity, conflict, impact and human interest. Which value or values make this story news to the audience? Who will be reading this story? What will they be most interested in reading about?

If a reporter is not sure which of the 5 Ws and an H will interest readers most, assigning a number value to each word or phrase may help. Using a scale of one to 10, with 10 being the highest interest and one the lowest, assign each key word or phrase a number value. Values for the above lead might look like this:

♦ Who: district school officials—3
♦ What: reduced preliminary budget cuts from $1.2 million to $450,000—9
♦ Where: in the district—4
♦ When: Monday—1
♦ Why/How: unanticipated grant from the state—7

Based on the numbers, the lead should begin with the dollar figures or the unanticipated grant from the state. The day of the week and the district school officials have the least reader interest. Readers don't care which day it happened as much as they care about the money that will be saved. The nameless officials are simply the source of the information.

Creating the direct news lead helps writers organize their stories by forcing them to identify the basic elements before they begin to write. It's a good idea for beginning reporters to write down six one-word questions—Who? What? Where? When? Why? How?—and the key words that answer each question before starting to write a lead. With the answers to these basic questions, the reporter will be able to organize and write a lead that includes all the most important information.

Summary Leads.   Direct news leads sometimes begin with a paragraph that summarizes the story and then add specific details, such as names, ages, dates and locations, in the second paragraph. These direct news leads are called **summary leads.**

The opening statements of summary leads are similar to the previews of movies. Readers get an idea of what the story is about, but they can't really tell how the story will evolve until they have more information. Or, like a synopsis of a short story, the summary lead outlines the plot but leaves out all the descriptive narrative. Summary leads help readers determine whether or not they want to read the story based on a brief preview of the content.

Either the first or second paragraph of the following story about an accident could have been the lead, depending upon the reporter's preference and the newspaper's style. The first paragraph is a summary lead that says the story is about an accident involving some local youths:

> One teen died and three others were injured in an accident in Adams County over the weekend.

The second paragraph gives detailed information for readers who are interested in knowing more about the accident and those involved:

> Travis J. Vapp, 17, died at 12:20 a.m. Sunday when the car he was driving went off a dead end at the T-intersection of Highway 14 and the KICS Road. Three passengers, Tom B. Hansen, 17, Amy M. Hayes, 17, and Ryan M. Conroy, 16, were injured in the crash.

Here's another summary lead for a news story:

> An auto mechanic has been arrested after he bit off the ear of a dog to collect a $100 bet, according to police.

In the second paragraph of that story, readers find out the mechanic's name and more about the bet.

summary lead

a direct news lead that begins with a paragraph summarizing the story; the second paragraph presents specific details, such as names, ages, dates and locations

Write a summary lead for what you think happened to cause this accident.

Leads that summarize the story before giving specific information are variations of direct news leads, because they give all the information necessary for the reader to know what the story is about in the first paragraph. The summary is a carrot to tempt the reader into reading the story. It is also a quick way for the reader to look at the stories on the page and choose which ones to read. The summary lead adds one or more sentences to the 5 Ws and an H lead. By the end of the second paragraph, the reader should know the basic facts.

School papers use summary leads for news stories because they work well for hard news stories that are not published immediately after the event. The following is an example:

> Bodiless heads are not usually the mainstream definition of beautiful art, but for one TFHS class, they have become both a creative outlet and a teaching tool.
>
> Art teacher Shelly Christensen's Studio Art class has recently been learning about sculpture and the human body through the molding of heads and torsos. (*Bruin News*, Twin Falls High School, Twin Falls, Idaho)

In this story, the second paragraph could have been the lead. However, the writer chose to summarize the activity before getting into the details of which class and why bodiless heads.

Indirect Leads

Indirect leads are leads that set a scene or begin a story before revealing the topic of the article. Indirect leads entice readers to read the article by introducing a person or situation that arouses readers' curiosity or invites them to feel some emotion or relationship to the person or subject of the story. They are also referred to as **delayed leads, feature leads** and **storytelling leads** because they are usually longer than direct leads and they most often introduce soft news stories. Indirect leads have been popular for use in lifestyle and feature stories for a long time. Today they are being used for hard news stories, too, as the trend in newswriting moves toward making news more reader friendly.

Today's reader is also today's television viewer and computer user who is surrounded by visual images. Indirect leads tell stories and create images that help the reader visualize the story. Some indirect leads appear on news stories, and some lead into feature stories. They may be several paragraphs or just one sentence long:

> WASHINGTON (AP)—There's a way to tell people about your missing pet beyond tacking signs on telephone poles.
>
> The U.S. Agriculture Department's Animal and Plant Health Inspection service has made its new Animal Care site on the World Wide Web available to people who want to advertise missing or found cats and dogs.

> DAVENPORT, Iowa (AP)—Once upon a time, in toy factories far, far away, "Star Wars" toys were churned out by the thousands. And now, a millennium—well, 20 years, anyway—later, the search for "Star Wars" collectibles continues, with aficionados vying for A-Wing Fighters, Yoda shampoo bottles and R2D2 action figures.

indirect lead
a lead that sets a scene or introduces a character before letting the reader know the topic of the story

delayed lead
an indirect lead in which the nut graf is placed after the first anecdote or main point. Can be used on hard or soft news stories

feature lead
an indirect lead; usually an anecdote or description that draws the reader into the scene before revealing the topic, introduces a feature story

storytelling lead
an indirect lead; another label for feature leads that begin by telling a story

The much-touted February release of the "Star Wars" movie trilogy back to the big screen complete with new footage, has helped launch '90s versions of the toys that also are becoming collectors' items, some as soon as they leave the shelves.

Collectors, in the hopes that the Collectibility Force will be with them, are joining the hobby-avocation that is worldwide in its scope. (*Omaha World Herald,* Omaha, NE, Oct. 1996)

Staggering to her Chevy Nova, the drunk senior girl flounders through her leather purse for her keys.

A few minutes later she is in her car, swerving down an empty road in her quiet neighborhood. After observing the movements of the car typical of drunken driving, a police officer decides to pull the driver over for questioning.

With the festivities of Prom approaching, some teens will attempt to drive to and from their post-dance destinations after drinking alcohol. (*Crier,* Munster High School, Munster, Ind.)

Can it.

The recycling program at Westside, headed by instructor Harley Hardison, has been successful this year. (*Lance,* Westside High School, Omaha, Nebr.)

Most indirect leads are longer than the last example. Typically, they vary from one to six or seven short paragraphs, but there is no rule. The **nut graf,** the paragraph that tells exactly what the story is about, concludes the indirect lead. In the "Can it" lead, the second paragraph is the nut graf, because it tells the reader that the story is going to be about the success of Westside's recycling program. In a direct news lead, the first paragraph is the nut graf.

In the following seven-paragraph lead, the reader sees the classroom and feels the lack of interest being displayed by the students. The reader becomes part of the scene and has empathy for the students, because the reader has experienced similar circumstances. Suddenly, both students and reader are jarred awake by the teacher's words.

nut graf
a paragraph in a lead that tells exactly what the story is about

Your eyes are drooping closed and your mind is far from the classroom, and you doodle drawings on your paper just trying to keep awake.

"Today we're going to learn about birth control, class."

Suddenly, your attention shifts to the teacher rather than to the squirrel prancing across the telephone wire in the distance.

"Who can tell me what I mean by abstinence?"

A few people giggle and others turn red. What you thought would be another boring day may turn out to be interesting after all.

Abstinence, particularly in high school, is the most effective form of birth control. However, abstinence is only as effective as the percent of people who use it.

The school, therefore, teaches contraceptives as part of the health curriculum to keep the students protected if they will not abstain, according to health teacher Christy Matta. (*Shakerite,* Shaker Heights High School, Shaker Heights, Ohio)

BYLINE

RUSSELL BAKER

In his short autobiography *Good Times*, acclaimed journalist Russell Baker writes about his early days as a police reporter in Baltimore, where he learned what makes a "good" murder:

Phoning the desk, I might say, "I've got a little murder." To which the rewrite man might say, "Just give me enough for a couple of paragraphs. We've got a six-alarm fire on the harbor taking up most of the page."

Saying "I've got a good murder," however, got the editor's attention. It meant a story worth prominent play even on a busy night. Any number of things could elevate a "little murder" into a "good murder." Was the victim "a prominent Baltimorean" or "a member of an old Maryland family"? Could the rewrite man justifiably describe the victim as "statuesque," the universally understood code word meaning "big breasts"? If so, it was a "good murder," especially if the murderer was still unknown and the cops could be persuaded to hint at sexual motives behind the crime. Multiple murders were "good." So were murders of children.

The "terrific murder" was one so uniquely gory, so sex-drenched, so mysterious, or so diabolical as to be irresistible even to the *Sun's* stodgy readership. Such murders featured dismembered corpses, "statuesque" women found dead in full nudity, and similar elements beloved by connoisseurs of barbershop magazines like *The Police Gazette* and *True Detective*. The "terrific murder" was so rare that as a police reporter I never had the pleasure of covering one.

Source: Russell Baker, Good Times *(Morrow, William & Co. New York, NY).*

This indirect lead works because it invites readers personally into a setting with which they have some familiarity. They may not have been in this particular class, but they have all been in classrooms when they would rather have been somewhere else, when it was difficult to concentrate on what was being said, when it was warm and they were sleepy. They remember how they felt in those situations, so they have some empathy for the person in the scenario.

The interest level of this lead is also strengthened by the writer's use of the pronoun *you* to include each reader individually in the scene. While the word *you* would not be appropriate in a direct news lead or in the body of a hard news story, it is occasionally effective in an indirect lead that invites the reader to become part of the story.

The topic of this story is hinted at through the quotations from the teacher. These contain words that have high interest for members of the specific reading audience: young adults. When the topic is made clear in the nut graf—"The school, therefore, teaches contraceptives as part of the health curriculum . . ."—the reader is already interested and eager to know more. The story goes on to explain the school's health curriculum and to present several points of view on the subject.

Indirect leads like this one are often used in timeless stories and in feature stories where the subject is more significant than the timeliness.

This story could appear in any issue of the newspaper and be as appropriate and timely as if it appeared in any other issue.

The lead could have been this:

> Health teacher Christy Matta talked about abstinence and other methods of birth control in health class today in accordance with the school's health curriculum.

A direct lead like this one would work for a story about the school's health curriculum, but the indirect lead is much more appealing to readers.

A story about a speaker's appearance at a school might take either a direct or an indirect lead. The speech might be a timely news event if the story appeared very soon after the event. In that case, a direct news lead would be appropriate. For a school newspaper, however, the indirect lead might be more appropriate. Readers would want to know what the speaker said more than they would need to know the day and place of an appearance that happened sometime in the past.

A direct news lead about the story could read as follows:

> Pulitzer Prize winner N. Scott Momaday was the first national speaker for the Artist Lecture Series, which began Friday in Perkins Auditorium.

An indirect lead for the same story might be as follows:

> "Your lives will never be the same after hearing the story," N. Scott Momaday said as he began one of several stories he would share in the next hour.
>
> Professor of English at the University of Arizona in Tucson and a Pulitzer Prize winner, Momaday was the speaker at the first Artist Lecture Series event, which began Friday morning in Perkins Auditorium.

Here is a longer indirect lead for the same story:

> "A boy chased his seven sisters pretending to be a bear. Suddenly he was a bear. Terrified, the girls ran. They came upon a tree stump. The stump spoke and bade them to climb upon it. The girls did so, and immediately the stump began to rise in the air. The girls, just beyond the bear's reach, were saved. The seven sisters were borne into the sky, and they became the stars of the Big Dipper."
>
> A middle-aged Native American man shares this story and others that were passed down to him as a child.
>
> Friday morning in Perkins Auditorium, author N. Scott Momaday read from his work and talked about his prose and poetry.

Which lead would be most likely to get you to read the story? Why? None of the leads is correct or incorrect. Each works for some readers. The judgment the reporter has to make is which kind of lead will work best for most readers. A reader who knows N. Scott Momaday's work will likely read on after seeing his name in the lead. Readers who don't recognize Momaday's name will be more attracted to the lead that draws them in through a quotation that promises to tell a story that will change their lives, or a lead that simply starts telling them an intriguing story to which they'll want to know the ending.

YOUR BEAT •

1. Identify the 5 Ws and the H in each of the following leads:

The only incumbent up for re-election on the Board of Education won her bid Tuesday as three new members joined the board. *(Hastings [Nebraska] Tribune)*

The Knowledge Master Senior and Junior teams met on April 18 in the Teachers' Library. *(Buffalo Chip,* Chappell High School, Chappell, Nebr.)

In their first competition of the year, the mock trial team took first place at the seventh annual San Joaquin County Mock Trial competition. *(Scholar and Athlete,* Tracy Joint Union High School, Tracy, Calif.)

There'll be no smoking in the Marlboro College Library. Majority ruled. (AP, *Denver Post)*

2. As a class, try the interest rating test with the following facts. After the group assigns a value from one to 10 to each item in the 5 Ws and an H, write a lead for each story.

◆ Who: members of the student council
◆ What: will eat banana splits
◆ Where: at their meeting in Room 202
◆ When: last meeting of the year, 7:30 p.m. Tuesday
◆ Why: treat from officers for the hard work the council has done
◆ How: each person will assemble his or her treat from ingredients provided by the officers

◆ Who: student athletes
◆ What: will receive rehabilitation through personal programs prescribed by Dr. Andrew Tucker, school doctor and fully licensed trainer
◆ Where: training room outside south gym
◆ When: every day after school.
◆ Why: injured in practice or a game
◆ How: lift weights, ride exercise bike, exercise routines

3. Identify a news event that has happened in your school recently. List the 5 Ws and an H for that event. As a class, decide the value of each item based on the interest scale of 1 to 10. Write a lead for the story about the event based on the interest scale.

4. Write a direct news lead for each of the following stories.

a. The Student Council met.
It heard a proposal from some music students.
The council was asked to donate money toward a new sound system for the auditorium.
It voted to donate $500.
It voted to postpone the next meeting one week because of the district volleyball tournament.
It voted to sell candy after school as a fund-raiser.
The meeting was adjourned.

b. The Environmental Club, Youth Serving Youth and the Distributive Education Clubs of America chapter are working together.
They are sponsoring a community service project.
They will go door-to-door collecting canned and non-perishable food items for the local food pantry.
This will be done in November in time for the pantry to distribute the food for Thanksgiving dinners.
Before they collect the food, the club members will go door-to-door to distribute brochures telling about the food drive and asking residents to put their donations in bags, also distributed by the club members. Residents will be asked to place the bags on their front porches on the designated date.
"The students volunteered this project as their community service for the year," Barry Tushaus, DECA club sponsor, said. "I think they really want to help those who don't have the good homes they have."
"We expect to collect about 2,500 pounds of foodstuffs over the two Saturdays of the drive," Kathleen Good, Environmental Club sponsor, said.

5. Write a summary lead for each of the stories in Item 4. Include the second paragraph with the specific information, the nut graf, for each story.

6. Identify the nut graf in each of the N. Scott Momaday leads in the chapter. (See page 121.)

◀ORGANIZING THE NEWS STORY

You have identified the 5 Ws and an H. You have written an appropriate lead. Now what?

Inverted Pyramid

The organization of a news story is very important. It gives the reader information that explains the lead. It tells the story in a logical sequence. The sequence in which information is presented in most news stories is called the **inverted pyramid.**

The inverted pyramid organizes information from most important to least important. The majority of news stories are written in inverted pyramid style. Readers are comfortable with it. They can extract information quickly from a story organized in inverted pyramid style. The style makes it easy for editors who must place the stories on the pages to shorten them to fit smaller spaces. It is also a logical thinking pattern for reporters.

Inverted pyramid structure looks like a pyramid turned upside down. The top-heavy inverted pyramid implies that the heavy information, the foundation, is at the top of the story. Figure 6.1 graphically shows the inverted pyramid.

inverted pyramid

the organizational pattern in which information is presented in most news stories. Information is organized from the most important to the least important.

FIGURE 6.1
THE INVERTED PYRAMID ORGANIZATION PATTERN

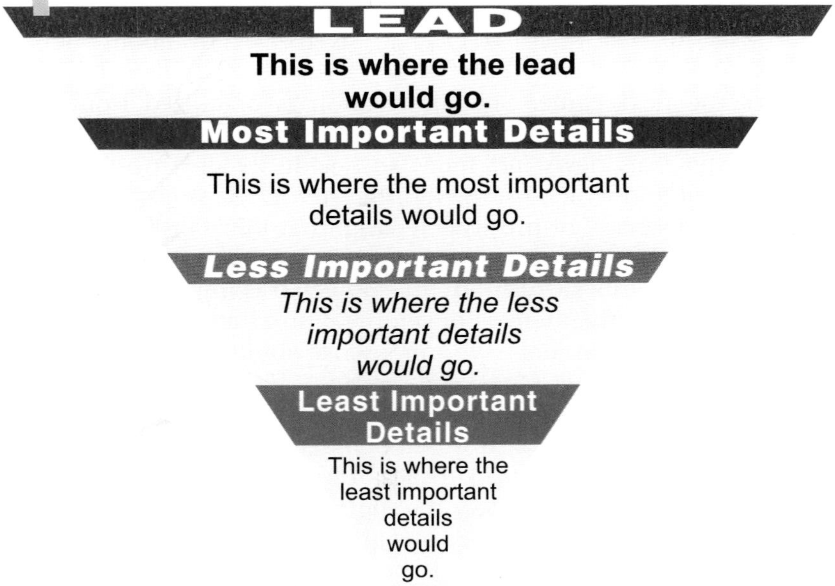

LEAD
This is where the lead would go.

Most Important Details
This is where the most important details would go.

Less Important Details
This is where the less important details would go.

Least Important Details
This is where the least important details would go.

UNITED STATES, 1907—The word *television* was first used in a 1907 article in the magazine *Scientific American*. In just three decades it would become a household word.

In 1938, RCA displayed television sets in department stores. Within a year more than a dozen manufacturers were offering the sets. Sets had screens from three to 12 inches across and sold for $125 to $600.

NBC debuted regular television broadcasting at the New York World's Fair on April 30, 1939. The first televised sports event, a baseball game between Princeton and Columbia uniersities, was carried May 17, 1939, on NBC.

The Federal Communications Commission (FCC) approved licenses for 18 commercial stations on July 1, 1941. The first two, New York stations WNBT (NBC) and WCBW (CBS), went on the air that day.

Within a year, 10 stations were serving viewers on 10,000 to 20,000 home sets in New York, Chicago, Los Angeles and Philadelphia.

The stations were allowed to broadcast 15 hours of programming per week.

News came to television in a vivid way on Dec. 7, 1941, when WCBW brought to an audience of a few thousand viewers the latest bulletins on the attack on Pearl Harbor.

Twelve million sets were in use by 1951, up from 6,000 in 1946. Coast-to-coast television broadcasting was accomplished through the use of coaxial cable and a series of microwave relays.

Figure 6.2 illustrates an inverted pyramid story about a new attendance policy. The direct news lead is the first paragraph of this story. Readers could stop after the first sentence and know that there's a new attendance policy in effect. Those who stopped reading at this point would know the essence of the story.

After the lead, the story is logically organized into blocks of detail that explain the lead. The second paragraph details the essential change in the attendance policy, and the third explains the reason for making the change. The rest of the story is feedback from those affected by the policy.

Another example of inverted pyramid organization is a sports story. What do readers want to know about any sports event? They want to know who won and what the score was. When do those watching the event know who won? Not until the end of the event. Does that mean the writer should tell the story in chronological order and put the name of the winner and the score in the last paragraph? Of course not. The winner's name and the score belong in the lead.

After learning the score, what do readers want to know? They're interested in key plays, records set, exceptional achievements by individual players, injuries, coaches' comments, statistics and information about the next game.

The order in which the reporter presents this information depends upon the significance of each item. If a key player was injured, readers might want to know the seriousness of the injury more than they want to know the game statistics. If a touchdown in the last 20 seconds or a long kickoff return was the key play or the turning point of the game, readers would want to know about that first.

Newspapers sometimes have to cover sports with summary stories that include more than one game. Even sports summary stories can follow the inverted pyramid pattern. In the short sports story shown in Figure 6.3 on page 126, the first paragraph brings the reader up to date on the soccer team's season. The next two paragraphs give details about the two games that have been played since the last paper. The last paragraph announces the next game. The information is organized from most important to least important as it relates to the two most recent games.

The reporter uses news judgment to decide which information is most important and which can be left for later in the story. News judgment is a "sixth sense," or intuitive feeling, that journalists have about what stories and issues are newsworthy and what their readers will want to know first in a story about an event that is important to them. A journalist's news judgment is developed and strengthened through practice, but even beginners have some sense about what their readers will want to know first.

If you heard that there was a fire at your school, what would you ask first? Was anyone injured? How much damage was done? Which parts of the building were affected? Will school be closed? What caused the fire? What is being done to repair the damage?

Readers will ask the same questions about the fire, and they probably will ask the questions in much the same order. The order reflects people's concern and curiosity. First, people care about people who may have been injured in the fire. Next, they'll be concerned about the

FIGURE 6.2
STORY IN INVERTED PYRAMID STYLE

LEAD

This year, due to new state standards, the administration has adopted an attendance policy requiring parental consent for absences.

Most Important Details

As Jane Rose, dean of students, explained, "Basically we've reverted to the excused/unexcused system, where parents are asked to call in or send a note explaining the student's absence." Rose clarified that last year's policy, which was considered most comparable to that of the "real world," was not ineffective. "Our percentage rates stayed right about the same," she said. but a change in state statute requires all schools to use the excused/unexcused system."

Less Important Details

Administration realizes that there is no sure way to get or keep kids in class. "There isn't a magic number at which point students are removed from class. If a student begins a negative pattern of attendance, we'll go through conferences and, if necessary denial of credit," Rose said.

Least Important Details

According to Rose, the policy hasn't provoked much feedback from students or faculty. "Most everyone is more comfortable with these set of guidelines. It is much clearer in terms of make-up work," she said. "I don't think it will be effective any more than last year's," Ethan Zlomke, senior, said. "I figure if kids are going to skip, they'll skip. A different policy won't change their minds." Brooke Oakland, sophomore, agreed. "(Though) I think this system will be easier for the teachers, I don't think it will affect a student's decision to ditch. It's still easy for them to lie and get out of class," she said.

Source: Reprinted with permission from Trojan News, *Longmont High School, Longmont, Colo.*

EXHIBIT 6.3
USE OF INVERTED PYRAMIDSPORTS STORY

LEAD

Coming off a 3–0 loss to Richard Montgomery, the junior varsity soccer team improved their record to 6–2–1, with two victories in their last two games.

Most Important Details

The Cougars crushed High Point 7–0 on Oct. 19. Scoring for the team were freshmen Kirk Myers who had four goals, and juniors Rudy Gomez, Andy Topez and Jose Ayala.

Less Important Details

In the game against Gaithersburg played Oct. 16, the Cougars won 1–0, and the goal was scored by freshman Jason Golden.

Least Important Details

The Junior varsity team looks towards Churchhill in their last home game of the season which will be played on Oct. 25.

Source: Reprinted with permission from Quince Orchard Prowler, *Quince Orchard High School, Gaithersburg, Md.*

amount of damage done and how that damage will affect them. Students and teachers will want to know if the damage is serious enough to prevent school from being held. Taxpayers will want to know if the damage can be repaired and how much it will cost. When they have the answers to these questions, readers will be curious about the cause of the fire and what those at the scene had to say about it. Then they might be interested in knowing if there have been previous fires at the school or fires at other schools in the area.

Look at the organization of this news story about a fire on school property.

A late night blaze on March 5 left the LHS paper recycling trailer nothing but pieces of mangled aluminum and charred paper. A sign attached to the remains of the trailer reads, "Because of obvious reasons, please do not drop off paper."

The fire caused an estimated $2,300 in damages. The roof and most of the sides of the trailer were destroyed, which left the paper within unsalvageable.

Volunteers cleared away the remains of the damaged trailer and replaced it with another one.

"I'm sorry there are anti-social types that exploit other people for their own sick minds," Stan Roth, biology teacher said. "It is fortunate that most people grow out of that immature state and become worthy contributors to society."

The Lawrence Fire Department investigated the incident and has information that could incriminate several LHS students. Fire Marshal Rich Barr said the department was turning the information over to the district attorney. If prosecuted, the students would face felony charges for arson.

"We want to get the word out that this is serious. When something like this happens, we are going to push it as far as the law will provide," Barr said.

The LHS recycling project began in 1975 as an environmental awareness project. Because of increased awareness in recycling, income has gone down because student volunteers were getting more paper than they could handle. Despite the overflow, the project continues as a service to the community.

This year, the money from recycling will go toward the CP Biology trip to Florida in April. The trip is still on, but because of the fire, the students raised less money than expected. (*Budget*, Lawrence High School, Lawrence, Kan.)

How Many Words Do You Remember?

Source	Number of Words
Declaration of Independence	300 words
Ten Commandments	297 words
Gettysburg Address	276 words
Lord's Prayer	56 words
First Article of the Bill of Rights: Freedom of the Press	44 words
Pledge of Allegiance	31 words
The legal marriage vow	2 words
General McAuliffe at the Battle of the Bulge: "Nuts"	1 word

The information in this story is organized from most important and most recent to least important. The lead tells the following:

- What: blaze
- Where: LHS paper trailer
- When: March 5

Then the story answers the secondary questions readers will ask:

- How much damage did it do? Estimated $2,300
- Who or what caused it? The fire department has information about possible suspects
- What is being done? The trailer has been replaced

Within five paragraphs, readers have all the information about the fire. The last three paragraphs add background information through quotations, history and explanation.

No exact order is prescribed for placing the facts in every story, but the inverted pyramid provides a framework that helps writers arrange the facts of any story in a reader-friendly order. The facts about the fire could have been given in a different order and still have told the story.

Some information is not as relevant to understanding the fire itself, but it helps readers place the story's significance in relationship to other things. The story says that because of this fire, students won't have as much help with their trip. It says that this project has been going on for over 20 years, and it is a valuable service to the community. This information is placed after the information about the immediate event, the fire.

Testing the Inverted Pyramid

Stories can be tested to see if they are organized in inverted pyramid style. Journalists call this test a **crop test. Crop** means to cut or to shorten. To use the crop test, start at the end of the story. Read each paragraph and decide whether it contains information that is absolutely necessary to the understanding of the story. If the information in the paragraph is not crucial to the story, it can be cropped without damaging the reader's understanding of the basic story. If several paragraphs can be cropped from the story without losing important information, it is written in inverted pyramid style.

In the fire story, the last paragraph tells about a trip that will be paid for in part by funds from newspaper recycling. This is interesting, but it is not necessary to the reader's understanding of the fire. It can be cropped. The next-to-last paragraph tells the history of the recycling project. Again, this information is not necessary to understanding the fire, so it can be cropped. This story can be cropped up to the paragraph that tells about students being suspected of arson. Who was responsible or how the fire was started is crucial to the story. The story is written in inverted pyramid style, because the editor can easily crop three paragraphs from the bottom of the story without losing important information. Some stories can be cropped all the way to the first paragraph.

The Storytelling Pattern

More and more news stories are being written in an organizational pattern called the **storytelling pattern.** The storytelling pattern invites the reader in with an indirect lead. The body of the article gives the facts and information necessary in any news story. The ending is usually a **clincher,** a statement that returns the reader to the scene introduced in the opening paragraphs, or that reaches a conclusion necessary for complete understanding of the event or story. The end of the story ties back to the lead and is a necessary part of the story. It cannot be cropped without diminishing the meaning of the story.

The story of this frustrated driver could have been told in inverted pyramid form, but the reporter chose to give it an indirect lead and a clincher:

TUSTIN, Calif. (AP)—A motorist who got stuck behind a slow-moving pickup truck apparently forgot her license plate read "Peace '95."

Lisa Lind pulled alongside the pickup, swatted at it with a baseball bat, then threw a can of air freshener at it as she passed, said Peros Doumas, the California Highway Patrol officer who arrested her.

"She said she was in a hurry and was getting frustrated," Doumas said.

Ms. Lind, 26, who had been tailgating the truck on a two-lane canyon road, was never able to make contact with it using her aluminum bat because it was too windy. She ended up denting her own car with the can, investigators said.

crop test

a test by which journalists determine whether a story is organized in inverted pyramid style. The journalist begins at the end of the story and decides, on a paragraph-by-paragraph basis, whether paragraphs can be cropped off without losing essential information

crop

to cut or shorten a story by cropping paragraphs from the end

storytelling pattern

an organizational pattern that invites the reader in with an indirect lead, goes on to give the pertinent facts and information, and ends with a clincher

clincher

a statement in a news story that returns the reader to the opening paragraph or that reaches a conclusion necessary for complete understanding of the event or story

Doumas said he couldn't help but ask Ms. Lind about the license plate message. "She told me she got it because she thought there was too much violence going on in today's society," he said. (AP, *Omaha World Herald,* Omaha, NE, September, 1996.)

The quotation in the last paragraph refers to the description of the driver's license plate given in the lead. If the crop test were applied to this story, it would immediately show that the last paragraph is a clincher that explains the lead and is vital to the story as a whole.

Instead of giving facts in the inverted pyramid style, from most important to least important, the storytelling organization tells the story in a circular fashion. The end of the story refers back to the beginning, completing the circle of facts that make up the story (see Figure 6.4).

The following Associated Press story is an example of a news story written in the storytelling pattern. The same ideas appear in the lead and in the closing paragraphs, the clincher, completing the circle. The paragraphs between the lead and the clincher tell the story in inverted pyramid order:

FIGURE 6.4
STORYTELLING ORGANIZATION

> LAS VEGAS—David Hacker found $25,000 in the back of his cab, tracked down the man who lost the cash and gave it back. His reward: a share of the loot and a taste of the high life.
>
> Hacker spotted the bulging alligator-skin wallet—containing a year's salary for the cab driver—lying in his taxi's back seat at the end of a 10-hour shift.
>
> It contained three $5,000 packs of $100 bills, a sports betting slip worth another $10,000 and numerous gold credit cards imprinted with the name Lance Dykes.
>
> Hacker, 45, remembered the man was staying at Bally's. He raced to the hotel-casino on Feb. 11 and found Dykes at the roulette table.
>
> The 38-year-old Georgia businessman had figured the wallet was long gone.
>
> "I was almost speechless," Dykes said Tuesday.
>
> To thank Hacker, Dykes peeled off 20 $100 bills and handed them to the cabbie. He also told Hacker to take the week off and spend it at the hotel as his guest.
>
> Hacker dined on lobster tails in an expensive suite and gambled with the high rollers. (AP, *Hastings* (Nebraska) *Tribune,* Hastings, Nebr., Feb. 19, 1997.)

Choosing an Organizational Pattern

All leads and stories can be organized in more than one way. No one organizational pattern is right for every story. Sometimes a blend—putting a storytelling lead on an inverted pyramid story—works better than either inverted pyramid or storytelling organization.

The reporter determines the organization in the planning stages of the story. Hard news stories—such as those about accidents, fires and meetings—are most often written with direct leads and inverted pyramid organization. Features and timeless stories most often lend themselves to indirect leads and storytelling organization. Human interest news stories may fall into either category.

Some stories organize themselves easily and logically into one pattern. If there's a disaster or an accident that claims lives, the loss of life is always more important than the dollar value of the damage done. Deaths and dollars become the most important facts, and explanation and background about them should follow in inverted pyramid order.

Other stories can be organized in either basic pattern or a combination of the two. If the oldest building in a community burned and no one was injured, the lead would probably focus on the sentimental significance of the loss to the community rather than on the dollar damage done. An indirect lead that places the reader at the dedication of the building or in one of the rooms for a special event might tell the story better than a direct news lead. The rest of the story could be in either inverted pyramid or storytelling organizational style.

1. Find five examples of stories written in inverted pyramid form. Cut out each story, and affix it to a piece of paper. Write an explanation of why you think each story is in inverted pyramid form.

2. Apply the crop test to each story you chose for Item 1. Draw a line between paragraphs where you think the story could be cut without losing vital information.

3. Find five examples of stories written in storytelling form. Cut out each story, and affix it to a piece of paper. Mark the lead, and draw a line where you think the lead ends. Draw an arrow back to the lead from each paragraph that refers directly to it. (*Hint:* Examine the ending carefully for references to the lead.)

4. Using the following facts, write a story in inverted pyramid style.

   He is in fair condition at the hospital in Springfield.
   Cassville is about 50 miles southwest of Springfield.

   He has Down's syndrome.

Hundreds of volunteers have been looking for him.

Two stray dogs apparently kept him alive by curling up with him and keeping him warm. The temperature was 2 degrees overnight.

He had been lost for three days.

One of the dogs chased the ambulance as it drove away with Josh, but then the dog ran off. Neither dog has been found since the rescue.

His name is Josh Carlisle.

A 10-year-old boy has been found.

The dogs' barking got the attention of a searcher on horseback.

Josh was found about one and one-half miles from his home.

He was lost in the woods near his home in Cassville, Missouri.

Josh has frostbitten toes.

5. Using the same facts as in Item 4, write a story in the storytelling pattern.

WRITING THE NEWS STORY

Once you have decided what kind of lead your story calls for, what will go in your lead, and what organizational pattern you will use to write your story, the easy part is done. Now begins the challenging part of writing the story—the writing itself.

Accuracy

Above all, as *New York World* editor Joseph Pulitzer said, what a reporter writes must be accurate. The facts must be checked and double-checked. The spelling of the names and the identification of the people must be checked and rechecked. Failure to double-check, or verify, information, may result in stories like this one:

> ROCKFORD, Ill. (AP)—Paula Ann Moore was home watching television when a local newscast flashed her photograph on the screen and reported that she had been murdered.
>
> A Paula Ann Moore had indeed been killed the previous day. She was from Rockford, 18 years old and black. Two local television stations illustrated the story by using the ninth-grade school photograph of the Paula Ann Moore who was alive, from Rockford, 18—and white.
>
> "I knew that a Paula Ann Moore had been killed," Ms. Moore said. "But then the news showed my picture. I didn't know what to do. All I could think was that everybody, my friends and relatives, would think I was dead."
>
> The real victim was found dead in a small storage shed behind a Rockford home. Rennie Jones, described by police as an acquaintance of the victim, turned himself in and has been charged with first-degree murder. (AP, *Omaha World Herald*, Omaha, Nebr., Oct. 13, 1988.)

The following story tells how an impostor duped the reporting staff at ABC in 1990:

> LOS ANGELES (AP)—A producer responsible for an interview with a Buckwheat impostor on ABC's "20/20" has resigned, the network said.
>
> Lynn Murray resigned in a "mutual decision" with ABC after last week's segment, "Whatever happened to 'Our Gang'?" said "20/20" spokeswoman Maurie Perl.
>
> The news magazine aired an interview with a man who said he played Buckwheat in the "Our Gang" comedies of the 1930s and '40s and was working as a grocery bagger in Tempe, Ariz.
>
> William Thomas, who portrayed Buckwheat, died in 1980. (AP, *Omaha World Herald*, Omaha, Nebr.)

Errors like these can be prevented by careful reporting. A quick check of the police report would have given the reporter a physical description of the Paula Ann Moore who was murdered. Double-checking with the person who provided the photo to be sure that it was of the Paula Ann Moore who lived at the victim's address would have raised doubt.

DATELINE DATELINE DATELINE

NEW YORK, 1928—A new show, called *Newscasting*, was introduced by radio station WOR. The 10-minute news program ran during the dinner hour. *Newscasting* was the brainchild of Fred Smith, the originator of *Musical News* on Cincinnati radio station WLW in 1925.

On *Musical News*, each news story was followed by organ music. The combination proved very popular with the station's listeners.

Newscasting, according to Smith, combined the concepts of *news* and *broadcasting* for the first time in one show. *Newscasting*, and its successor *NewsActing*, led to a syndicated program called *The March of Time*. That show was carried by more than 100 stations.

The March of Time, which ran until 1945, brought listeners dramatic reenactments of the week's news events.

The William Thomas impostor could have been unmasked by a simple scan through ABC's files on people in the news, by a database search on Thomas, or by consulting a biography of Thomas or the history of *Our Gang.*

Checking facts with more than one source is a good habit to develop. Journalists recommend verifying information with at least three sources to be certain that it is accurate. If three sources do not agree, the information needs to be checked until the reporter is certain that it is correct. Any information that cannot be verified should not be used.

Objectivity

Reporters report facts. They must be careful to maintain objectivity—that is, to report only facts, not their own opinions. The reporter's job is to look at news from a distance and from all sides. In a news story, whether it is hard news or soft news, the reporter must present only the facts about an issue or event and let readers draw their own conclusions. The reporter's personal views and values should not be part of a news story.

In this story about a budget hearing, the reporter's feelings show in the choice of descriptive words used:

> The student association held its budget meeting in Room 215 Wednesday night. *They got off to a rocky start* as the student representatives found out they had to trim $5,000 off the budget. Voluntary budget cuts were made first. Then they went through the entire budget for a *grueling* two hours looking for anything else to cut out.
>
> *Tensions were made worse* by heat in excess of 90 degrees caused by *a lot of* people crammed into the room that had no air-conditioning.

Reporters regularly cover city council meetings and interview public officials.

By carefully choosing just verifiable facts, the reporter could have written an objective lead for the story:

> The student association trimmed $5,000 from the budget in a two-hour meeting Wednesday night.
>
> Approximately 70 people gathered in unair-conditioned Room 215, where the temperature rose above 90 degrees by the end of the session.

Adjectives and adverbs describe things and events, but some of them imply opinion. Be careful of words such as *definitely, largely, quickly, eagerly, unfortunately, especially, really, wonderful, just, tragic, greatly, finally* and *only*. Words like these imply emotion or judgment that must be proven by the facts. Seventy people might be "a lot of people" in a small room but "a few people" in a stadium. Unless the reader understands the number in relationship to the size of the room, "a lot of people" is the reporter's judgment. That the heat made tension worse is judgment. That the temperature rose to more than 90 degrees is a fact. That the session was grueling is opinion; that it lasted two hours is fact.

The following sentences from school newspapers show how one or two words can imply the writer's opinion and add judgment or emotion to the facts:

> In an *especially* competitive race, originally including seven candidates and several write-ins, junior Benjamin Boye edged out Tonia Gell by just *a few* votes.

> Coronado was the only band to be awarded a Division 1 rating by all three judges. *More important,* they also reached their twenty-fifth consecutive year of receiving the superior rating at UIL contest.

> *Unfortunately,* not all students are ready to admit they need help.

> After four scrimmages and more than two weeks of practice, the varsity baseball team *finally* claimed an 11–1 victory in the season opener.

In the first example, readers will want to know how many votes make an *especially* close race. They will also wonder how many votes make "a few."

In the second example, readers will ask why one fact is more important than the other and why the reporter didn't simply state both facts and let the readers decide which they think is more significant. By placing one fact before the other, the reporter has already told the reader which fact, in the reporter's opinion, should come first.

In the third example, readers will want to know the source—the name of a counselor or other authority—who believes it is *unfortunate* that students are not ready to ask for help.

In the last example, readers will have trouble understanding how *finally* describes what happened in the first game of the season. Two weeks of practice doesn't seem a long enough time to merit the word *finally*. A score of 11–1 doesn't tell the reader that it was a game that kept fans on the edges of their seats until the last pitch that meant the hard-fought game was *finally* over.

In each of these examples, the judgmental or vague word could be omitted without changing the meaning of the story. Stronger, more factual statements would result. In some examples, like the one about

DATELINE DATELINE DATELINE

NEW YORK, 1885–1900—Richard Outcault's cartoon character the "Yellow Kid" gave a journalistic style practiced in the last decades of the 1800s its name: yellow journalism.

New York City newspapers, always in competition for the same readers, continually looked for ways to boost circulation. The two strongest competitors in the late 1800s were the *New York World,* edited by Joseph Pulitzer, and the *New York Journal,* edited by William Randolph Hearst.

Pulitzer, who would eventually be called the leading American editor of modern times, believed it was a good day if the paper featured a big exclusive story or a crusade. His editorial pages were strong and devoted to fighting injustice and corruption. They also promoted welfare reform and fair treatment for the common people.

Pulitzer's definition of news was "that which is apt to be talked about." At the same time that he admonished his reporters to dig until they got to the bottom of issues, his papers featured sensationalized stories readers would talk about.

One of the most publicized stunts the *World* promoted was sending Nellie Bly (reporter Elizabeth Cochrane) around the world to see if she could beat the record 80 days suggested by fiction writer Jules Verne. The paper chronicled her adventures via ship, horse and special train. It also ran a contest for readers to guess how long her trip would take.

the election, a number could be inserted to add a fact. Here are objective versions of the leads:

> In a race originally including seven candidates and several write-ins, junior Benjamin Boye edged out Tonia Gell by four votes, 124–120.
>
> Coronado was the only band to be awarded a Division 1 rating by all three judges. They also reached their twenty-fifth consecutive year of receiving the superior rating at the UIL contest.
>
> Not all students are ready to admit they need help.
>
> After four scrimmages and more than two weeks of practice, the varsity baseball team claimed an 11–1 victory in the season opener.

Rewriting the band award lead to make the two elements equally important would remove the need for judgment of which fact is more important.

> Coronado reached its twenty-fifth consecutive superior rating at the UIL contest by earning a Division 1 rating from all three judges in the most recent competition.

Reporters who write news for publications that appear less often than daily write most of their news stories in news feature style. Descriptive words appear more often in features and in news stories with indirect leads than in timely news stories. Reporters can use descriptive words and still be objective if the descriptive words add detail rather than opinion to the picture being created for readers. Note the following example from the *Rampage,* the newspaper at John Marshall High School in San Antonio (Vol. 39, #6):

> Abdul Tabhat and his *fellow cab driver* wife immigrated to America with their family from Yemen *five* years ago and now have *nine* children. At first glance, Tabhat appears to be a *small, unworldly* man. However, his *dark, weary* eyes paint a *different* picture.
>
> Tabhat can remember moments that he thought would be his last. *Less than one* year ago, a passenger entered his cab and demanded money. When Tabhat refused, the man fired a shot which *narrowly* missed him.

To be more objective than they might be if they described a person or a scene themselves, reporters can quote someone describing the person or scene:

> "It was a snowy day, so we built a ramp on a hill at a golf course near my house," sophomore David Kush said. "We poured water on the ramp and the path to make it icy. When I went over the jump, I fell off my sled and kept sliding. Unfortunately, there was a creek on the other side of the ramp. Luckily, it was frozen over or I would have been trapped in an icy tomb." (*Lance,* Westside High School, Omaha, Nebr., Vol. 38, #11, p. 8.)

The reader can see the terrain, watch as water is poured and ice forms, and feel the bumps as Kush slides toward the creek. *Unfortunately* and *luckily,* when used in a direct quotation, tell how the speaker felt about an event, not how the reporter felt.

Reporters sometimes feel so strongly about an issue that they are tempted to put their opinions into their stories. After carefully crafting a story about date and acquaintance rape, this reporter could not resist adding personal opinion:

> These are just a few of the myths that our society has about date or acquaintance rape. The truth is, there are no circumstances that make it OK to rape someone. No one ever deserves to be raped!

Reporters cannot make statements like this no matter how strongly they feel about an issue. Reporters may quote sources who respond emotionally to facts in the story, but reporters must not reveal their personal feelings in writing news.

Point of View

Reporters also demonstrate objectivity through point of view. News should be written from a **third person point of view** with no first or second person pronouns such as I, we or you. A story with third person point of view is written as though the writer were standing back, watching people in action and writing a description of their activities. Third person writing allows the reader to view the story from the same watching-the-action-from-a-distance perspective.

If the reporter writes that "air-conditioning has been installed in part of the school and *we're* really cool now," he or she is using first person point of view. Those readers who are in the air-conditioned rooms will agree that "we" are cool, but those readers who are not in the air-conditioned part of the building will say, "Oh, no, *we* are not!" They will react negatively and may stop reading. If the reporter had used the third person point of view and written that "air-conditioning has been installed in part of the school, and some students can now attend class in cool rooms," all readers would be able to visualize some students in cool rooms and some sweltering in the heat in other rooms. Student readers would see themselves in the appropriate rooms and read on to get more facts.

The second person pronoun *you* can be a problem for news writers. *You* gives a command. It tells the reader how to think and what to do. Although it is implied in editorials and reviews, *you* should not be used in straight news stories. Even when giving information for individuals to use, such as phone numbers to call for information, a reporter should avoid the word *you*. The following statement gives explicit instructions by using the word *you*.

> For more information on date/acquaintance rape and assault, you may contact a member of the CARE organization, you may talk to a counselor at the health center, or you may call the SASA hotline.

Instead of giving directions to "you," it is better to tell readers where the information is available:

> More information on date/acquaintance rape and assault is available from members of the CARE organization, counselors in the health center and the SASA hotline.

The word *you* is occasionally used in an indirect lead to entice the reader to become personally involved in the story, especially if it is a

third person point of view
writing that uses *he, she* and *they* as subjects. Third person writing allows the writer to stand back and watch people in action, then write about their activities from a non-participating point of view

feature story. This story about bumper stickers uses *you* in the lead to place the reader in a familiar setting.

> Ya know the feeling. You're driving along completely bored and oblivious to anything going on around you. You come to a red light and accept the fact that you're going to have to sit there doing nothing for at least 15 seconds. But wait? You peer a little closer at the car in front of you. It's plastered all over with bumper stickers. Oh yah, you've got entertainment for at least one short pause in your life. (*The Axe,* South Eugene High School, Eugene, Ore.)

After the lead, the story should change to third person. The bumper sticker story continues:

> People decorate and plaster their cars with bumper stickers for a variety of reasons. Some people are trying to express their political views or share something about what's important to them. Others are just trying to make people laugh.

"You" is also acceptable in a direct quotation in a story, because it is being said by someone other than the reporter. Look at these examples:

> "When you're picking out music for festivals, you have to go with the strengths of your band, just like you go with the strengths of a basketball team," Dierolf said. "If you've got a great center, then you're going to the middle with the ball all the time. It's the same way with jazz band. You have to create around your personnel." (*The Rampage,* John Marshall High School, San Antonio)

> "All you're doing is cheating yourself," psychology teacher Bob Jama said. (*Coronado Crest,* Coronado High School, Lubbock, Tex.)

Quotations are used in news stories to give readers information from sources. Quotes are also used to interpret information introduced by the reporters in news stories.

Readability

Newspaper readers don't want to work hard at reading and understanding when they read the paper. One of the reasons for the popularity of *USA Today* is that readers say they find its short stories and short paragraphs inviting to read. They find it easier to grasp the meaning of a two- or three-line paragraph and then another two- or three-line paragraph than to comprehend one four- or six-line paragraph.

Because most newspaper readers want to be able to read and understand the news quickly, reporters write in ways that make news easy to read. Short sentences and short paragraphs make news appear inviting and easy to read.

Standard reading material appropriate for a newspaper audience averages 17 words per sentence (see Figure 6.5). Some sentences will be longer; some will be shorter. Variety in sentence length makes reading interesting. However, by keeping the average number of words per sentence close to 17, reporters are able to write stories that can be read quickly and be understood by most of their readers.

FIGURE 6.5
HOW SENTENCE LENGTH AFFECTS READABILITY

Average Sentence Length	Readability
8 or fewer words	Very easy to read
11 words	Easy to read
14 words	Fairly easy to read
17 words	Standard
21 words	Really difficult to read
25 words	Difficult to read

Sentence structure also affects readability. The subject-verb-object order is preferred for quick, easy reading (see Figure 6.6). Even a sentence in S-V-O order can be difficult to read and comprehend if too much information is included. Compound and complex sentences can quickly become long:

> Neal Green is the manager of the food service operation at the school, and his job is to make sure a variety of healthy, well-balanced and inexpensive meals are served twice a day to the school community.

When a sentence begins with a phrase or clause, it becomes more difficult to read and understand:

> Although Green admits to some problems with the system and the food itself, he likes to look at the positive aspects of the improvements that have given students more choices and shortened lines for people waiting to get into the cafeteria.

Not every sentence should be a simple S-V-O sentence. However, if the majority of sentences in a story follow this pattern, the story will be easier to read.

Transitions

Transitions are the threads and glue that hold a story together. Transitions are key words, phrases and even entire paragraphs that link the sentences and paragraphs together while letting the reader know when a story moves from one idea, place or time to another. Transitions also may help the reader remember who is speaking. Sometimes they set up contrasts or comparisons.

transition

a key word, phrase, theme or paragraph that links together the sentences and paragraphs of a story

FIGURE 6.6
SUBJECT-VERB-OBJECT SENTENCE STRUCTURE

```
          S      V      O
Neal Green's job requires him to be sure a variety of healthy, well-balanced
          S     V       O
meals are served. Green is the manager of the school cafeteria.
```

THIS JUST IN: *Portrait of a Young Journalist*
Lori Wiechman, Reporter

It's amazing how one experience could jolt my mind back to high school in Naperville, Ill., and to *The Central Times,* my school's student newspaper.

I was sitting in the White House and had just finished asking President Clinton a question during a press conference less than two years ago when my experience as a high school journalist came flooding back to me.

As the editor-in-chief of the University of Georgia's daily independent student newspaper, I was in Washington, D.C., for a college media day, when 200 college students had the opportunity to interview top government officials. The day ended with a short question-answer session with the president. I managed to get a seat near the front middle row and nervously raised my hand, hoping he would choose me. Once he pointed at me, I calmly asked my question, shocked to be speaking to President Clinton as a young reporter.

That's when I remembered what I had told my journalism teacher, Linda Kane, my peers and other newspaper reporters when I was a senior in high school: *One day I would be asking the president a question.*

Having questions is what journalism is all about, though, whether they're directed to a public official or a local newsmaker. My desire to ask questions, find the answers and create a story was stirred during my high school experience.

My school didn't have a newspaper until my junior year, when two teachers decided to start one and asked for applications. I didn't hesitate. I loved reading the newspaper and knew I wanted to be a journalist since my days in elementary school. I viewed the student newspaper as a way to make sure I wanted a career in journalism and to gain some valuable experience. More than 50 students applied for the staff, and I made the final cut of 25 students.

We started the tough work immediately of deciding a name, planning issues and learning the production process. Many friends and classmates quit. But a small group of 10 students put out the first edition, which I still have. We eventually began to publish once a month, making mistakes, writing great and horrible stories and learning about teamwork along the way.

The Central Times won many awards in its first two years, but I've forgotten which stories and issues were the best. I do remember the burst of energy I got by developing story ideas, following through on the stages of production (which amazed me to think that professional journalists could do in a day what we did in a month) and being part of a team of students dedicated to journalism.

Since then, I've progressed from writing stories read monthly by 800 high school students and teachers to the same duties in college, where my stories and editing were in the hands of 18,000 people five days a week. Now, I'm writing news articles, entertainment stories and features for teenagers at *The Augusta Chronicle,* a daily newspaper read by nearly 80,000 people in the Georgia/South Carolina area.

And hopefully one day I'll interview another president. That experience will again bring me back to my days as a *Central Times* staffer, and the time when I asked President Clinton, "Looking back on your college years, what advice would you give to college students today who hope to make a career in politics?"

His answer, in a capsule, was to get experience and to listen to others' opinions. Now, those are at least two things politics and journalism have in common.

Source: Reprinted with permission from Lori Wiechman, 'One day I'll be asking the president a question,' Scholastic Adviser, (Princeton, New Jersey: Dow Jones Newspaper Fund).

Common types of transitions are key words, ideas, or themes; pronouns; transitional terms; paragraphs; and quotations. We'll look at these types of transitions separately. However, more than one type of transition is usually present in every story.

Key words, ideas or themes. Most stories have one or two key ideas, and they are identified in the lead. The same words, ideas or themes appear throughout the story to remind the reader that the story is still about the same subject.

In the following story, the key words are *Reiger* and *Disney*. The key theme is Disney, so all things that refer to Disney relate to the theme and help tie the paragraphs in the story together. *Disneyland, 101 Dalmatians, Peter Pan* and *"The Jungle Book"* all reinforce the Disney theme.

> ANAHEIM, Calif. (AP)—Heads are turning and George *Reiger* is loving it, sucking in the attention like oxygen, like a drug, like his flesh was an epidermal sponge.
>
> This is what he lives for, what he craves: to strut through *Disneyland,* as he did Tuesday, and feel the bug-eyed recognition of people gaping at his full-body collection of *Disney* tattoos.
>
> From his shoulders to his shins, *Reiger* is *Disney* on parade.
>
> *Peter Pan* flies across his right shoulder. *Beauty and the Beast* grace his left shoulder. Characters from *"The Jungle Book"* and *"Song of the South"* spill down his right arm.
>
> He has all *101 Dalmatians* on his back and the genie from *"Aladdin"* on his chest.
>
> "I have 303," said *Reiger,* 40, a maintenance worker for the U.S. Postal Service in Easton, Pa.
>
> "I'll have 350 by Christmas and 400 by the end of next year. My goal is 500. Once I have that I'll be happy."
>
> *Reiger* says he has visited *Disneyland* 54 times, *Walt Disney World* in Florida 75 times, and *Euro Disneyland* near Paris and *Tokyo Disneyland* twice each. (From the *Orange County Register,* reprinted in the *Omaha World Herald,* Omaha, Nebr.)

Pronouns. Using a pronoun to refer to a person named in an earlier sentence or paragraph simplifies the writing. In the Disneyland story, *he* refers to Reiger. "This is what *he* lives for, what *he* craves" ties the second paragraph to George Reiger in the first paragraph. "*He* has all 101 Dalmatians on his back" ties a new paragraph to the one before by continuing to give information about Reiger.

This story has only one source, Reiger, so all the personal pronouns clearly refer to him. If a story has more than one subject or source, pronouns must have clear antecedents to avoid confusion.

Transitional terms. All kinds of words serve as connectors. To understand how transitional terms work, picture an outline:

I. Transitions
  A. Glue that holds story together
  B. Help reader understand story

    II. Types of transitions
       A. Key words
         1. Definition
         2. Example
       B. Pronouns
       C. Transitional terms
       D. Quotations and paragraphs

Each entry in the outline is preceded by a roman numeral, a letter or number. Each time a new topic is introduced or a fact that explains that topic is added, a new letter or number is added to the outline. The letter or number before the new information is a transition. It indicates that another thought is being added, a different topic is being introduced or a new time period is being entered. Transitional terms in news stories serve the same function as the letters and numbers in an outline.

The following are common types of transitional terms:

- *Conjunctions: and, but, or.* Conjunctions usually connect ideas that go together, such as two halves of a compound sentence, or they set up contrasts that tell the reader that there is another side to the story.

- *Additives: also, in addition, again, further, moreover, finally, in conclusion, next, so, thus.* Additives help the writer move on to the next piece of information.

- *Contrasts and comparisons: but, however, on the other hand, yet, instead, likewise, similarly.* Words like these tell readers that there is another side to the story or issue and that now the reporter is going to tell them about that other side.

- *Place indicators: near, here, there, adjacent to, across, by, alongside, opposite.* Any word that tells the reader that the scene is changing or adds information that enlarges or adds detail to the picture in the reader's mind may be a transition. These words say, "We've been here; now we are moving over there."

- *Time indicators: later, that evening, after, meanwhile, soon, next, finally.* A word or phrase that moves a story forward or backward in time helps the reader keep track of the sequence of events. Time indicator transitions help the reader organize the information chronologically.

Here's an example of how transitional terms help the reader follow a story:

> RICHMOND, Va. (AP)—When Rosa A. Dickson answered her telephone, the caller requested an ambulance.
>
> *It took only a moment* to figure out that the caller had dialed 911 and got Ms. Dickson instead.
>
> "*When* I realized what happened, I dialed 911 and couldn't get 911," she said *Monday.*
>
> *For one half-hour last Wednesday,* Ms. Dickson tried to help 911 callers as best she could by passing them on to police. She received two calls for rescue crews and one for police between about 5 a.m. and 5:30 a.m.

The first thing she did was alert police that there was a phone problem.

Gene Scott, account manager for Bell Atlantic, said the phone system was upgraded in July and the mix-up occurred during maintenance. He said a company computer mistranslated some of the phone numbers and routed the 911 calls to Ms. Dickson, whose number doesn't include a nine or a one.

"We've done this 100 times and never had a problem. It's not going to happen again," Scott said.

Paragraphs and quotations. A paragraph or a quotation can be the transition that moves a story from one idea to another. Paragraphs are used as transitions in the examples we analyzed for key words, ideas or themes. "From his shoulders to his shins, Reiger is Disney on parade" is a transition paragraph that shifts the reader's attention from Reiger's walking through Disneyland attracting attention to a description of his tattoos. In the 911 story, "The first thing she did was alert police that there was a phone problem" takes the focus of the story away from the incident itself and introduces the phone company spokesperson to respond to the situation. For more on quotations as transitions, see Chapter 7, "Writing with Quotations."

1. Count the number of words in each of 10 sentences in five news stories in your local newspaper. Calculate the average number of words per sentence. Using Exhibit 6.5, determine the readability of the stories. Do the same with *USA Today,* the *New York Times,* or another national or regional newspaper. Now do it with your school newspaper. Compare the results.

2. Using a story you have written, count the number of words in each sentence. Calculate the average. Use Exhibit 6.5 to find the readability of your writing.

3. Identify key words, themes and transitional terms in the following story.

    ### Patent Office Picks Up the Scent

    WASHINGTON, (AP)—The Patent and Trademark Office on Monday recognized an aroma as a subject for trademark registration for the first time. It granted a trademark to the scent of a line of embroidery yarns and threads.

    The office approved registration of a scent described by its developer, Celia Clarke of Goleta, Calif., as "a high-impact, fresh floral fragrance reminiscent of plumeria blossoms."

    Ms. Clarke's application was initially turned down on grounds the product's fragrance did not qualify for a trademark. The ruling was overturned Sept. 19 by the Trademark Trial and Appeal Board.

    "This marks the first time in the history of trademarks that a fragrance has been approved for registration," said Jeffrey M. Samuels, assistant commissioner for trademarks. "We are all familiar with what trademarks look like. Now we'll see what they smell like."

    In an earlier case, the color pink was recognized as a trademark for a type of fiberglass insulation. The trademark was granted in the mid-1980s to the Owens-Corning Corp., whose Fiberglas product is pink. (AP, *Omaha World Herald,* Omaha, Nebr., Dec. 4, 1990, p. 7.)

4. Select a news story in a recent issue of your school newspaper and a feature story from the yearbook. Identify the transitions used in the stories.

Part of editing is choosing the appropriate photo.

EDITING THE NEWS STORY

editing

checking writing for accuracy, organization and writing style

Every reporter is an editor. Writers and editors continuously check stories for accuracy, organization and writing style. This checking process is called **editing.**

Editing is a continual process. It begins as soon as the reporter receives an assignment and ends when the story appears in print. Each decision the reporter makes about which sources to consult, which facts to include and which quotes to use is part of the editing process. Each time the reporter chooses one organizational pattern or lead instead of another for a story, that reporter is editing.

Stories should also be carefully reread and edited for accuracy, objectivity and readability. After stories are placed on the page, they should be checked to be sure that vital information has not been deleted or errors introduced into the story during the placement process.

Editing is a team effort. Everyone who writes, reads or places a story as it moves through the newsroom is responsible for editing it. The team's goal is to make every story as accurate and well-written as possible. Each member of the team should check the facts in the story to be sure they're accurate. Each person should question every fact or word that doesn't seem right, every word or name that might be misspelled, and all writing that may not conform to the publication's style or to standard rules of grammar. Getting this feedback from others helps the reporter identify and correct errors in the writing or gaps in information before the story goes out to the readers.

In Chapter 8, "Writing in Journalistic Style," you'll have a chance to practice your editing skills using the correct journalistic style and symbols.

1. Here are some facts and bystanders' observations about a news event. Write an accurate, objective story using these facts:

    ◆ A definitely unusual event happened in the parking lot of the best supermarket in town in the middle of the night. A workman, who was probably tired from working all night, was reportedly using some kind of high-pressure power spray painting tool to apply yellow stripes to the parking lot.

    ◆ Shortly before 3:30 a.m., witnesses said, a crazy, scatterbrained 21-year-old woman drove wildly into the lot and screeched to a halt half in and half out of a parking place. They said she must have been in a hurry, because she jumped out of her car and over the rope around where the guy was working. She stepped on a freshly painted stripe and tracked yellow paint across the lot. It made the man's paint job look real sloppy, according to the people standing around when the police arrived. The police report said it was "minor damage" to the paint job.

    ◆ After the wild woman walked in the paint, the painter yelled at her. Apparently she ignored him and kept going toward the door.

    ◆ The painter ran after the weird woman and caught up with her near the entrance. He was still yelling things like "You dumb woman! Didn't you see that wet paint? I been workin' on this all night, and you just put your fat feet right in that paint and made tracks all over the place! Why, I oughta beat some sense into you right here!"

    ◆ The woman just looked him in the eye and tried to spit on him.

    ◆ The painter got mad when she spit at him, and he shot her with the paint sprayer. She was a real mess!

    ◆ "He took the power sprayer and painted her yellow," said police Sergeant Elgin Kuhlman.

    ◆ According to a police report, officers arrested the 42-year-old workman in the parking lot of the local 24-hour supermarket this morning.

    ◆ Police have charged the man with two misdemeanor criminal citations: one for assault and the other for vandalism (for the yellow paint the man applied to the woman's clothing).

2. Circle the transitions you used in the story. Draw a line back to the word each transition refers to if it has an antecedent.

CHAPTER REVIEW

KEY TERMS

Show that you know the meanings of the following key terms by correctly using them in complete sentences. Write your answers on a separate sheet of paper.

lead	nut graf
direct news lead	inverted pyramid
hard news story	crop test
soft news story	crop
5 Ws and an H lead	storytelling pattern
summary lead	clincher
indirect lead	third person point of view
delayed lead	transition
feature lead	editing
storytelling lead	

OPEN FORUM

1. Analyze the leads on the front page of your daily newspaper. Are they direct or indirect? Now analyze the lifestyle section. What kind of leads are in this section? Is there a difference in the percentage of direct and indirect leads between the front page and the lifestyle section? If there a difference, why do you think it exists? If not, why not? Now try the sports section. Analyze the leads. Are the sports leads more like those in the news or in the lifestyle section? Why?

2. Divide the class into groups of five or six. Each group is the editorial staff for the school newspaper. The following are the stories available for the next issue:

   ◆ A student has been arrested for shooting a gun in a science lab, an action that broke some equipment and wounded a janitor.

   ◆ The woman's basketball team has won the state championship.

   ◆ The principal has announced his retirement after this year.

   ◆ A student has revealed that he has AIDS as a result of a transfusion to treat his rare blood disease.

   ◆ The board of education is working on a proposal to split school into two shifts next year: 7:30 a.m. to noon and 12:30 p.m. to 5 p.m. to accommodate increased enrollment.

   ◆ An English teacher has been challenged for teaching a book that a parent finds objectionable. After three months of discussion, the parent filed suit against the teacher and the school yesterday.

   You have room on the front page for three or maybe four news stories with direct news leads. The others may go on an inside page with indirect leads or be used as editorial subjects. Which stories will you choose for the front page? How will you cover the others? Explain your reasons for each choice.

3. Divide the class into groups of five or six. Each group is the editorial staff for the school newspaper. The paper comes out once a month. The most recent issue came out last Friday, and the next issue is due out three weeks from today. The story ideas for the next issue follow:

   ◆ Two music students have won individual honors in a district music competition, one for playing the saxophone and one for composing and arranging a song. They will compete in state contests next month.

   ◆ The school board is considering cutting back on extracurricular activities because of a recently imposed state spending lid. The first thing on its list of programs to cut is the school newspaper. There is no word on when the board will make a decision.

   ◆ The annual school play opens this weekend.

◆ The women's soccer team completed its first season today with a 5–4 record.

◆ The homecoming royalty were crowned during the fall festival dance last Saturday night.

◆ The principal has said that he'd like to see a story about the faculty's $600 contribution to the local United Way campaign, which wraps up soon.

◆ Viruses have infected the school computer lab, and student disks brought from home are being blamed. A decision will be made next week on whether to close the lab to outside users. This action would affect the newspaper staff, whose members bring disks into the lab from the newsroom to print the paper.

Which stories will you make news stories with direct leads? Which will be news stories with indirect leads? Which stories will work best as inverted pyramid stories? As storytelling stories? If you have room for only five stories when it comes time to lay out the paper, which two will you discard or leave for the next issue?

4. Try the activity in Item 2 again, but this time the staff may choose only three stories to cover. The rest will have to wait for the next issue, which will come out two weeks from now. Which stories can wait? Which stories must run now? Is it possible to change any of the direct news stories into storytelling stories that could run any time? If so, which ones?

FINDING THE FLAW

Find the flaw in each of the following examples. As a reporter, how would you find the correct or missing information?

1. The following example is from a news story about a concert honoring the birthday of Johann Sebastian Bach:

> Bach was born in 1683 and lived until 1680. He was orphaned at a young age and lived with an older brother, with whom he studied music. At the turn of the century, he served as chorister in the Church of Saint Michael in Luneburg.

2. The following are the headline and lead for a sports story:

Women's soccer defeats Northwestern 4–2

With a 2–0 victory over conference opponent Northwestern, the women's soccer team improved to 4–2 on the season.

The game was not in doubt for the women who dominated the game by outshooting Northwestern 32–7.

◆ FINDING THE FLAW, continued

3. The following recipe appeared in a food section feature story:

    Baked Fogs in Phyllo Dough

    8 tablespoons butter
    1/2 cup finely ground almonds
    1/2 cup sugar
    1 egg
    12 sheets phyllo dough
    2 tablespoons melted butter
    12 figs, quartered

4. This example is from a news story on new dress code guidelines:

    Big baggy pants and long oversized shirts are the new styles today, but it is one style that will not be seen in the halls of Grand Senior High.

    The new guideline for the dress code states that if a teacher or administrator cannot tell if a student is sagging his or her pants because the shirt goes beyond the midlevel of the biceps muscle in the leg, then that teacher has the right to ask that student to pull up his pants and tuck in the shirt. This is stated on pages 26 and 27 of the Student Handbook under Dress and Grooming.

5. The following is from a front-page story:

    New furniture was received in the library thanks to the reconstruction fund established last year.

    The Reconstruction Fund was given to Lakeside High by the state in order to remodel the school.

    "Lakeview High was old enough to qualify for this special fund offered by the state to the older schools," said Nathan Rutt, librarian. "In order to qualify, Lakeview had to apply for the fund and meet the minimum age requirement."

    The library could not use the $12,600 spent on furniture for new books.

    "The fund was set up to purchase furniture only," said Rutt. "The Library has had the same furniture for more than 20 years, and it was time for something new."

    The new furniture was picked for its durability and comfort.

    "The Purchasing Agent, Lynn Horne, Principal Dr. James Franco, and I picked out furniture we thought would last awhile," Rutt said.

    The old furniture was sent to various rooms on campus.

◆

MEDIA WATCH

1. Invite one newspaper reporter and one broadcast reporter to your class on the same day to tell how they write stories for their media. Ask them to explain how their jobs are similar and how they are different from both a coverage and a writing perspective. Ask how each identifies the lead for a story. If possible, have the two compare how they planned the way they would report on a recent event that both covered.
2. Identify one story that is news in *USA Today,* another national or regional paper, and your local paper (or use three area papers, if national papers are not available). Compare the leads. Did all the papers use the same type of lead? If not, why do you think the leads are different? Did all the papers organize the story the same way? Why or why not? Did all report the same information? Did all the papers place the story on the same page or in the same section? Why or why not?

String Book

You may use any newspapers for this activity, including school newspapers. Clip the page header with the name and date of the newspaper for each article; keep it with the example.

1. Clip three good examples of direct news leads and three good examples of indirect leads. Label each lead.
2. Clip an example of an inverted pyramid story. Draw an inverted pyramid to illustrate the points at which the story could logically be cut.
3. Clip an example of a story written in the storytelling pattern of organization. Explain why you chose this story to demonstrate the storytelling pattern.
4. Clip examples of each category of transition. Label at least one example of each type.

Chapter 7
Writing with Quotations

"I like the journalism road more every day, even with all its bumps and potholes of low revenue, computer problems, hard work and low pay."

—Areeya Chumsai, college student

LEARNING OBJECTIVES

After completing this chapter, you will be able to:

◆ recognize and use different types of quotations,

◆ choose and place meaningful quotations,

◆ correctly punctuate quotations,

◆ use quotations in graphics,

◆ define and use appropriate attribution,

◆ use attributive verbs.

◆

KEY TERMS

In this chapter, you will learn the meaning of these terms:

quotation
balance
direct quotation
attribution
paraphrase
partial quotation
fragmentary quotation
sound bite
transition paragraph
pulled quotation
lead-in
attributive verb

*I*magine sitting down to watch the evening news, weather and sports. Visualize yourself turning on the television, watching the anchor, viewing news stories, hearing people speak, seeing colorful graphics and reviewing game highlights.

Now imagine turning on the television and seeing nothing but the anchor staring straight into the camera and reading the news to you— no pictures of the storm damage, no Doppler radar, no slam dunks, no cuts to scenes where reporters are interviewing participants who tell stories in their own words. All you see is someone sitting in front of a camera telling you what happened. It's pretty boring, isn't it?

The same comparison can be made between stories with quotations and stories without quotations in your newspaper. A 15-inch story about a championship football game that had no quotations in it would be a long and tiresome collection of statistics and play-by-play accounts. But a story of the same length with comments by the head coaches or reactions from the players to give it a personal dimension would be interesting for the reader. In this chapter, you'll learn how to use quotations to make news stories interesting to read or hear.

USING QUOTATIONS

Quotations are the exact words spoken by a source. The words are placed in quotation marks, and the name of the source is given with the quotation.

Quotations can be used to provide the reader with descriptive accounts or explanations of what happened, as in a news story about an airplane exploding in flight or in a summary of a basketball game. Quotations are also used to pull the reader deeper into a story, to capture the reader's feelings and emotions. The best examples of this kind of quotations are found in feature stories on individuals and their special talents, hobbies or backgrounds. Quotations in these stories give insights into a person's character and personality by revealing his or her thoughts and opinions.

quotation

the exact words spoken by a source and cited as such in a media story

By using quotations, reporters are able to remain neutral while they let readers and viewers know what the sources are thinking. For example, as the writer of a story on nutrition in school cafeterias, you can't say that the food served in your school cafeteria doesn't taste like home cooking. However, a quotation from a student with her thoughts on yesterday's main course would be acceptable:

> "I thought yesterday's lunch was the worst thing I've tasted in years," sophomore Susan Smith said. "Our school really needs to re-evaluate its lunch program."

You, the reporter, can't say that in the news story, but you can say that Susan said it. Be careful to quote Susan's exact words and to tell her that she will be quoted in the paper. Reporters always need to ask permission from sources to use their words and their names in the newspaper or on the air.

When you use direct quotations to introduce or explain a point of view, use quotations that present all sides of the issues. For example, if you used the above quotation in an article on improving your school's lunch program, you should also have tried to get quotations showing a different opinion on the subject:

> "The lunches at this school have improved dramatically since I've been here," senior Tyler Jones said. "The cafeteria personnel should be commended for what they've done in the past four years."

Quotations from the primary sources for a story are the most important. The cafeteria story would not be complete without input from the food service personnel:

> "We try to provide food that students like that also has the nutrients they need. That's not easy when most of them prefer junk food or burgers and fries for every meal," food service worker Alberta Bruning said.

This is an example of how quotations can be used to **balance** a story—to represent all sides of an issue fairly.

Journalists also use quotations to do these things:

- ✦ enhance the content of stories,
- ✦ give stories the human element that makes them interesting to the audience,
- ✦ provide thoughts and opinions from sources,
- ✦ break up the monotony of long stories.

balance

to represent all sides of an issue fairly

Information or Quotation?

Reporters use quotations to put people's interpretations and opinions into their stories. Statements of fact or general, common knowledge can be made without using quotations—for example, July 4 is Independence Day, there are seven days in a week and George Washington was the first president of the United States. Any fact that the average person would know or any data that could be easily verified, like the data in the following quote, do not need to be enclosed in quotation marks:

"Our school is open seven days a week and until 11 at night," the superintendent said.

The information contained in this quotation could be verified by school authorities, so it is unnecessary to attribute it to one source. The reporter may simply state the information:

The school building is open seven days a week from 6 a.m. until 11 p.m.

There's a simple guideline to help determine whether a quotation is necessary. If a source expresses opinion, use a quotation. If the source recites facts, simply state the facts.

Types of Quotations

Just as there are several reasons why reporters use quotations, there are also different kinds of quotations and different ways to use them. Among the types of quotations used are direct quotations, paraphrases, partial quotations, and fragmentary quotations.

Direct Quotations. A **direct quotation** is an exact, word-for-word account of what a person said, enclosed in quotation marks and credited to the source. For example, the following is a direct quotation:

"It's not going to change our strategy," coach Jim Smith said. "It's one of those things where you just try to put together your best plan of attack. Then you cross your fingers."

Crediting a source is called **attribution.** Whether it is a direct quote that is attributed to the source, *Smith said,* or information cited from a physical source, *according to the San Francisco Examiner,* all specific information must be attributed to the source.

direct quotation

the exact, word-for-word account of what a source said, enclosed in quotation marks and attributed to source

attribution

the crediting of the source of information. The source may be human or physical

DATELINE
DATELINE
DATELINE

LONDON, Aug. 16, 1858—
"Glory to God in the highest, on earth peace, good will toward men" was the first message sent over the transatlantic cable connecting London and the United States.

Another cable linked London with India and the Orient, making international communications possible in minutes rather than days.

It was almost a century before the first transatlantic telephone cable linked London and the United States in 1956 with 50 compressed voice circuits.

Less than 40 years later, fiber optics made 85,000 simultaneous connections possible over the same distance—a 170,000 percent increase.

Fiber has replaced copper wire as the communications carrier of choice because of its speed. More than one gigabyte of information—approximately the equivalent of the *Encyclopedia Britannica*—can be transmitted in less than one second by fiber optics technology.

This quotation displays the speaker's feelings by relating them in his own words. But be careful. As a reporter, you are responsible for making sure that the speaker's words are not changed or twisted around. If you change something, you are misquoting the speaker, even if you forget only a single word or somehow add a single word. Although a single word—or a single letter—may seem harmless, you could be changing the entire meaning of what the speaker said.

Consider the difference between these two quotations:

> "It is ever our intention to serve healthful, colorful, tasty food in the school cafeteria," food service manager Tanisha Jones said.

> "It is never our intention to serve healthful, colorful, tasty food in the school cafeteria," food service manager Tanisha Jones said.

See how the meaning of the quotation was changed by adding or subtracting just one letter? The two quotations have opposite meanings and could cause unnecessary confusion for readers.

Misquoting sources upsets them. If it's done often enough, or to the point of embarrassing them too much, they may refuse to talk to you again. Your credibility as a reporter depends upon your ability to get and use accurate quotations.

Occasionally the person you're interviewing will use incorrect grammar or profanity. It is acceptable to edit out profanity and words or expressions such as *uh* and *you know* that the speaker uses habitually but that do not add information to the quote. It is also acceptable to correct minor errors in grammar or fact if not doing so makes the speaker sound foolish or uneducated.

A reporter can change the words of a source from "I feel good today," to the correct "I feel well today" without changing the meaning of the source's comment. An administrator who says "A student who parks their car in the no loading zone can expect to have it towed" would appreciate reading in the paper that the admonition was "Students who park their cars in the no loading zone can expect to have them towed."

Sometimes you will want to leave in colorful expressions or grammatically incorrect sentences to show a personality. If the coach's highest praise after an especially good play is the phrase "Ya' done good, kid!" and everyone on the team and in the audience knows that it's intentional and the highest compliment the coach gives, then it should be left that way. Telling a story about the coach and leaving out the quote or, worse yet, correcting the grammar would be like telling someone else's story.

Your publication may choose to follow a policy that allows profanity or one that prohibits it. Either way, having a policy will make it easy for you to decide what to do about quotations that contain words your publication considers potentially objectionable. Policies established by a news service such as the Associated Press or by local newspapers may provide guidelines for you to use. According to AP policy, for example, profanity should be used only in direct quotations when there is a compelling reason to do so, and a profane word should not be replaced by a euphemism. For example, AP policy would not change *damn it* to *darn it* and would leave intact the words of the police officer who said

FOR BETTER OR FOR WORSE reprinted by permission of United Feature Syndicate.

"We're not so naive to think that we have knocked the hell out of narcotics here" if the officer used the profanity to punch home a point that would not be made as forcefully without it. For more about AP and writing in journalistic style, see chapter 8, "Writing in Journalistic Style."

Paraphrases.   A **paraphrase** summarizes what the speaker said without using the source's exact words and without using quotation marks. In a paraphrase, a reporter rewords the thoughts and ideas of the source without changing the meaning of what the source said. The reporter lets the reader know the source of the information in the paraphrase.

Paraphrasing is done to condense a speaker's comments from several sentences to several words or to convey information that is fact rather than opinion. For instance, the school counselor tells reporters:

> "It's been a tough year. We've had so many problems we never used to have. Gambling, for instance. Never used to be a problem. Now the number-crunchers tell me we've had more cases of student athletes throwing big money away on games, horses, dogs, you name it, in the last year than we had in the whole five years before that."

The reporter condenses the information and leaves out the extra words. When the story appears in the paper, the counselor's rambling statement looks like this:

> More students were involved in gambling in the past year than in the previous five years, school counselor Elaine Hoover said.

The reporter could have printed some or all of the counselor's comments as a direct quotation, but doing so wouldn't have added anything to the reader's understanding. If the counselor had offered an opinion about the impact of gambling on attendance or on student performance, that opinion might have been added as a quotation:

> "It's sad, really sad. Students have a hard enough time making it in school without adding the pressure of gambling their security away," Hoover said.

paraphrase

> a summary of what the speaker said reworded by the reporter. A paraphrase does not use quotation marks but is attributed to the source

partial quotation

a combination of a direct quotation and a paraphrase, attributed to the source

Partial Quotations. The combination of a direct quotation with a paraphrase, attributed to the source, is called a **partial quotation.** Partial quotations are used when the source has expressed an opinion or used words the reporter feels must come directly from the source, but those words are a part of a quotation or speech that is too long to be printed in its entirety. The reporter paraphrases the source's point and includes the key words in quotation marks:

> Jones said he was displeased with the proposed plan because it was "excruciatingly long, drawn out and expensive."

Excruciatingly, drawn out and *expensive* are opinion words. Reporters can't express their own opinions in their writing, but they can and do report the opinions of their sources through quotations. Sometimes it saves time and space to paraphrase the speaker's point and add the opinion words in quotation marks.

Be careful of pronouns in partial quotations. It's easy to forget to use the first person pronoun in a partial quotation when the quote follows a third person paraphrase:

> **Incorrect:** Johnson said he was feeling much better but that he was "the sorest that *he* had ever felt after a game."

> **Correct:** Johnson said he was feeling much better but that "this is the sorest *I* have ever felt after a game."

Johnson wouldn't have referred to himself as *he,* and the reporter shouldn't have used *he* in the direct quotation.

Fragmentary Quotations. Individual words or phrases a person says can be singled out and placed in quotation marks within a sentence. These are known as **fragmentary quotations.** They are always attributed to a source.

Fragmentary quotations are permissible when a reporter needs to quote a word the source said in a sentence that has been paraphrased:

> Slingsby said the movie was "awesome," that the sound effects were "cool" and that anyone who missed the show is "stupid" and would "regret it for the rest of his life."

> Martin, who witnessed the airplane crash, said the noise was "earth shattering."

The reporter shouldn't use the terms *awesome, cool, stupid* or *earth shattering,* because they express opinion. The terms were those of the sources, not of the reporter, and they should be placed in quotation marks.

fragmentary quotation

a single word or short phrase used by a source that is included in a paraphrase, enclosed in quotation marks and attributed to the source

This reporter is taping her interview with the soccer coach. The taped interview will be an invaluable reference when she needs to paraphrase as she writes her piece.

BYLINE

JOHN HOCKENBERRY
TWO-TIME WINNER OF THE PEABODY AWARD

John Hockenberry, two-time winner of the Peabody Award for excellence in broadcast news, spent more than a decade with National Public Radio as a general assignment reporter, Middle East correspondent and program host. He has also worked in television for ABC, for which he won an Emmy, NBC, and MSNBC. "Hockenberry has been a wheelchair user since age 19, when an auto accident left him with paraplegia (paralysis of the lower half of the body).

"Finding and telling stories was easy, getting the nerve to go up and talk to total strangers was not. It was more than bashfulness: I was afraid of irritating people. I was afraid of their ignoring me.

I was afraid of getting a flat tire. I was afraid of running over someone's feet. I was afraid of stairs. I was afraid to succeed. They would think I had escaped from the hospital, that my tape recorder was a toy with no batteries in it. They would think I was panhandling for spare change.

I was down here, they were up there. But most of all, I was afraid to come back without a story: the 'guy in the wheelchair who tried but couldn't do it.' I was trapped between twin stereotypes, theirs and mine."

Source: Reprinted from John Hockenberry, Moving Violations: War Zones, Wheelchairs and Declaration of Independence *(Hyperion: New York), pp. 164–165.*

Using Quotations in Broadcast

Sound bites are taped quotations used by radio and television stations for the same reasons newspapers use quotations. They are portions of the source's message that the listener or viewer can hear or see. Actually hearing or seeing the source brings a broadcast to life.

Many of the same guidelines that apply to quotations in print apply to sound bites in broadcast. For example, reporters need to ask permission from sources to audiotape or videotape interviews. All reporters need to clarify with interviewees that they may be quoted in the media and get permission to use their names.

Paraphrasing in broadcasting is used much the same way it is in print. When partial quotations are used on the air, the newscaster reads the lead to the story, pauses briefly or says "quote," and then reads the exact words of the source. When the quotation had ended, it is not necessary to say "end of quote." Another brief pause between the end of the quotation and the beginning of the next sentence will signal the listener or viewer that the quotation has ended.

Listening to partial quotations in a news broadcast can confuse listeners. It is better for the newscaster to use a sound bite of the speaker's voice than to repeat what the speaker said word for word.

sound bite
a taped quotation from a source used by radio and television stations in their newscasts

YOUR BEAT

1. Decide whether each of the following quotations should be printed as quotations or as paraphrases. Rewrite those you think should be paraphrases.
   a. "The population has grown from 100,000 to almost 250,000 in just 10 years," the mayor said.
   b. "This year's team is the best tennis team that this school has ever seen, and I think we have what it takes to win at state," junior Andrea Wood said.
   c. "The boys team has six returning lettermen, including three seniors," Coach Quentin Kidd said.
   d. Superintendent Joe Johnson said, "We will observe the birthday of Martin Luther King, Jr., on Jan. 16 with a special assembly at 2 p.m."

2. Some words and phrases should be punctuated as partial quotations. Decide which, if any, words in each of the following sentences should be quoted, and punctuate them correctly.
   a. Jose Williams said he is in perfect shape and will without a doubt be among the top 40 in the nation this year.
   b. Roode said she feels some regret about leaving the English department, because it is the best one in the city.
   c. Though Hirsch loves the physical aspect of kendo, he admits the sport was easier for him because of previous experience in other sports.
   d. Relations between the teachers and the school board have deteriorated considerably, and tempers have escalated as salary negotiations enter the sixth month, according to Elaine Booth, chairperson of the negotiating team.

3. If you were the editor, would you use the following quotations as they are? Why or why not? If not, would you omit them or alter them? What other options are available? Write your reason for altering or not altering each quote. Rewrite those you would alter.
   a. "Our ancestors lived here long before Columbus landed on Manhattan Island in 1742," Patricia Longbottom, a spokesperson for the Native American Alliance, said in a speech before a congressional committee Wednesday. "We deserve to be reimbursed for the land his followers stole from us."
   b. "What we needed to do—what we all, uh, thought was necessary—was, like, together, uh, show that we had solidarity on the issue," student council president Keisha Johnson said.
   c. "Our house has five televisions, and there's always one going someplace," she said.
   d. "If the brotha' was cheatin' me, he's gonna get hit." (from an interview with a student for an article on cheating in school)
   e. "Me 'n Old Red here, we been together for nearly as long as I can remember," Pete Davis said, pointing to his prized Texas Longhorn. (from an interview for a feature story about Davis)

◄CHOOSING APPROPRIATE QUOTATIONS

Choosing quotations that are significant is very important. If reporters just insert quotations here and there without putting any thought into what the quotations add to the story, they may diminish the impact of good stories.

For example, if you were a chef cooking the main course of a dinner for a group of people you had never met, you wouldn't suddenly toss in a couple of ingredients that weren't in the original recipe. Similarly, you shouldn't choose quotations that don't belong or that say nothing at all. Quotations are an integral part of a story. They should be chosen carefully and placed with caution.

When to Use Direct Quotations

Use direct quotations to display thoughts and opinions. The following is an example of a comment from a source that must be used as a direct quotation:

> "This letter is monstrous," Manhattan City Councilwoman Kathryn Freed told *Newsday*. "It really is like, 'Merry Christmas, and kill your dogs.'" (Story from AP on a letter from a New York housing authority official who ordered tenants to get rid of their dogs.)

This quotation can't be paraphrased by the reporter. It contains specific words the speaker used to express a feeling on a particular subject. The quotation shows emotion and gets the speaker's point across.

Placing Quotations

To catch the readers' attention, use quotations early in a story. Many stories begin with the lead, add a paragraph expanding on information presented in the lead, and follow up with a quotation from a primary source:

> An open enrollment policy that became state law at the beginning of the year will not take effect until the 1995–96 school year and will not drastically affect the Tracy School District system.
>
> According to the law, parents and students would have a choice of which school they want their child to attend, granted there is space available at the chosen school.
>
> "The law is in effect, meaning it has been passed, but not implemented yet," interim Assistant Superintendent Rebecca Frame said. "There will be a board policy adopted early next school year." (*Scholar and Athlete*, Tracy Joint High School, Tracy, Calif. Vol. 67, #10, April 29, 1994.)

Other stories may go directly to a quotation in the paragraph following the lead:

> With two state championships already under their belts, the softball team is playing well enough to win their third state championship in a row.
>
> "We definitely have a chance of winning the state championship," Coach Ed McQuade said. "I can't say for sure, but we are one of the top four or five teams in the state." (*Demon Dispatch*, Greenway High School, Phoenix, Ariz.)

Beginning a story with a quotation is usually not recommended, because it is difficult to sum up a story with the content of one quotation. In some cases, however, a direct quotation that teases readers into the story may work as a lead:

> "I've always looked at college as the chance to step away from the family, to step away from home and to start my own life," GHHS senior Kit Heinritz said.
>
> "It's the beginning of my life as an individual."

Power Words

Direct quotes pack power no writer could make up.

A United Press International story about a British explorer returning from a 14-month trip around the poles included the man's words upon seeing his wife: "How do you do? Are you my wife?"

A mother who was ejected from a restaurant for breastfeeding her baby in public responded, "You wouldn't want to eat your dinner in the restroom. Why should my baby have to?"

During the Revolutionary War, colonial officer William Prescott ordered his troops at Bunker Hill to withhold their gunfire until they could clearly see the British troops. A direct quote has kept the command alive for more than two centuries: "Don't fire until you see the whites of their eyes."

When asked if his troops would surrender at the Battle of the Bulge during World War II, General Anthony C. McAuliffe responded, "Nuts!"

> Life seems to almost begin again as many graduating seniors take their first steps into the "real world" of college. (*Buc's Blade,* Grand Haven High School, Grand Haven, Mich.)

The key to placing direct quotations effectively is to spread them throughout a story. Place a quotation early in the story. Then place another one every few paragraphs to hold the reader's attention.

Paragraphs that begin with quotations attract more readers than do paragraphs in which the quotations are buried within text. If a direct quotation is placed in a paragraph after two lines of text, it loses some of its ability to attract readers' attention to the quotation.

Connect a series of quotations by different speakers or quotations on different topics with **transition paragraphs.** Transition paragraphs link quotations by providing additional information or indicating a change of topic. They avoid readers feeling bombarded by too many quotations. Stories that are nothing but quotations strung together are just as boring and tiresome to read as stories with no quotations.

Note how the transition paragraphs in this excerpt from a story on teens and smoking introduce new topics and lead into the quotations:

transition paragraph

an information paragraph that links quotations from more than one source or about more than one topic

> At a time when a favorite fad seems to be declining among adults, teenagers are picking up the habit at an alarming rate. What is it that attracts millions of people every year?
>
> Smoking.
>
> Today, about three million teenagers are addicted. *So why do teens smoke?*
>
> "People think that is it cool. Peer pressure," guidance counselor Suzanne Marzonie said.
>
> To some extent this is true, *like the case of senior Laura Gustin.*
>
> "It started off as a social thing, but eventually I got hooked," Gustin said.
>
> For others it is a little different. Many teenagers start smoking because they see their peers doing it. *Still others like the flavor that cigarettes provide.*
>
> "I enjoy the taste," senior Jason Jecker said.
>
> Another senior, who wishes to remain anonymous because of "labels" put on smokers, has *his own reasons for smoking.*
>
> "Why does someone collect stamps or go shopping or do whatever?" he said. "Because it is a hobby. I also enjoy the taste. I don't smoke to be 'cool,' I smoke because I enjoy it." (*Seahawk's Eye,* Cape Coral High School, Cape Coral, Fla.)

Sometimes it is necessary to divide a direct quotation into more than one paragraph. A transition paragraph is not necessary as long as the speaker is talking about the same subject:

> "I'll need the help of fellow officers and students," President Sueann Ramella said. "The main thing we want to do is raise funds so that our Senior Ball tickets will be inexpensive.

What Price Words?

Imagine for a moment the nightly news of the future. Tom Brokaw appears on your television screen as the theme song plays and the words *Dateline-NBC* emerge. Under them the figure $1,000,500.25 flashes across the screen.

"What is this number?" you wonder. It is the amount the network paid the interviewee for performing. The laws of the future require that the broadcasters divulge the amount they pay for interviews.

According to Walter Cronkite, a former CBS news anchor, the viewer has the right to know how much the interviewee was paid so that the viewer can judge the value of the interviewee's testimony: the higher the price, the greater the possibility of bribery. According to Cronkite, the integrity of news programs is compromised when networks pay interviewees to tell their stories. Yet, he says, the practice is so common that there is no turning back.

Bill O'Reilly, host of the *O'Reilly Factor* on Fox News, agrees. He says the ethics of checkbook journalism can be debated forever, but the practice is not going to go away.

According to O'Reilly, "Big money has changed the news and information industry just as it's changed professional sports. Few journalists like it, but there's nothing we can do about it."

Source: New York Times, *various articles by Bill O'Reilly and Walter Cronkite.*

"It will take teamwork to accomplish our goals. I hope we can also become even better friends along the way," she added. (*Viking Vanguard,* Puyallup High School, Puyallup, Wash.)

Notice that when a quotation continues into a second paragraph, no closing quotation marks are used at the end of the first paragraph. This indicates that the same speaker is speaking in the next paragraph. Quotation marks are used at the beginning of every paragraph, however, so that readers know the paragraph is a quotation and not the reporter's comments.

Choosing the Right Sound Bite

Like direct quotations in print, sound bites also need to get the attention of the listener or viewer. Sound bites that quote general information are worthless. Choose sound bites that give the audience insights into the sources' thoughts or opinions.

Keep sound bites short—no more than 10 to 15 seconds. Just as a newspaper story with nothing but paragraphs of direct quotations becomes dull, a radio or television story packed with several minutes of sound bites becomes tedious for listeners.

Punctuating Quotations

Correctly punctuating quotations can prevent confusion for readers. This section will give you guidelines to follow when in doubt about how to punctuate a quotation with attribution.

1. Place a comma between the end of a direct quotation and its attribution:

Incorrect: "The idea is extremely ludicrous" he said.

Incorrect: "The idea is extremely ludicrous." he said.

Correct: "The idea is extremely ludicrous," he said.

2. When the attribution comes first, place a comma between the verb and the direct quotation:

Incorrect: He said "The idea is extremely ludicrous."

Correct: He said, "The idea is extremely ludicrous."

3. When ending an indirect quotation with the attribution, place a comma directly before the attribution.

Incorrect: The crowd was the biggest one in years Smith said.

Correct: The crowd was the biggest one in years, Smith said.

4. When beginning an indirect quotation with the attribution, no comma is needed:

Incorrect: Smith said, the crowd was the biggest one in years.

Correct: Smith said the crowd was the biggest one in years.

5. Always place punctuation marks inside the closing quotation marks:

Incorrect: "The situation is getting out of hand", she said.

Correct: "The situation is getting out of hand," she said.

Incorrect: "What was I supposed to do"? he asked.

Correct: "What was I supposed to do?" he asked.

6. Use only one punctuation mark at the end of a direct quotation:

Incorrect: "What was I supposed to do,?" he asked.

Correct: "What was I supposed to do?" he asked.

7. When using a punctuation mark that relates to a direct quotation (as in a question mark or exclamation point), place it at the end of the quotation, not at the end of the sentence:

Incorrect: "What was I supposed to do," he asked?

Correct: "What was I supposed to do?" he asked.

8. When using a quotation mark that relates to the sentence and not the quotation, place it at the end of the sentence:

Incorrect: Wasn't it Shakespeare who wrote the line "To be or not to be, that is the question?"

Correct: Wasn't it Shakespeare who wrote the line "To be or not to be, that is the question"?

Again, only one terminal punctuation mark is necessary at the end of the sentence:

Incorrect: Wasn't it Shakespeare who wrote "to be or not to be, that is the question."?

Correct: Wasn't it Shakespeare who wrote "to be or not to be, that is the question"?

9. Use single quotation marks to offset a quotation within a quotation:

Incorrect: "It really is like, "Merry Christmas, and kill your dogs," " she said.

Incorrect: "It really is like, 'Merry Christmas, and kill your dogs," she said.

Correct: "It really is like, 'Merry Christmas, and kill your dogs,' " she said.

10. Closing quotation marks are not used at the end of a paragraph if the same speaker is continuing in the next paragraph:

Incorrect: "I'll need the help of fellow officers and students," President Sueann Ramella said. "The main thing we want to do is raise funds so that our Senior Ball tickets will be inexpensive."

"It will take teamwork to accomplish our goals. I hope we can also become even better friends along the way," she added.

Correct: "I'll need the help of fellow officers and students," President Sueann Ramella said. "The main thing we want to do is raise funds so that our Senior Ball tickets will be inexpensive.

"It will take teamwork to accomplish our goals. I hope we can also become even better friends along the way," she added.

"Teamwork pays off!" could easily be the quotation for this photo.

1. Rewrite these quotations punctuating them correctly.
   a. "Thursday is my birthday, and I'm going to party from breakfast until bedtime", senior Hannalore Genaidy said.
   b. "We felt the need to speak out rather than lose our open campus privileges, he said.
   c. Principal Bill Clancey said "We're going to take some time and analyze this. We won't have immediate answers.
   d. "What was I supposed to do." he asked?
   e. She said my goal is to graduate and get a good job.
   f. "That's ridiculous" he said.
   g. Mayor Marcos Martino said, the city is having its best year ever.
   h. "We're going to play a Beatles medley that includes "Yellow Submarine," the jazz band director said.
   i. The crowd at the annual Turkey Supper and Band Concert was the biggest one in years band director Ron Troester said.

2. Indicate which of these statements you think must be quotations and which you think could be paraphrased. Explain your choices.
   a. "We're still operating at a high level," state game director Tom Ash said. "We won't set a record every year." (in reference to the number of individual entries in the state games)
   b. "We were three weeks later in starting registration this year, because for the first time we had Winter Games. Also, we had a cruddy spring and people were slower in starting to work out," Ash said.
   c. "We scientists have known for 70 years that if you feed laboratory mice less food, they age slower, they live longer and get diseases less frequently," researcher George Rothwell said.
   d. "It was so cool skiing cross country. It's really quiet out there and occasionally a bunny hops by or a pheasant flies out of a field," first-time skier Barbara Krapff said.

FIGURE 7.1
PULLED QUOTATION WITHIN AN ARTICLE, QUOTATION AND ATTRIBUTION APPEAR IN DIFFERENT TYPE STYLES

Committees form to improve school environment

Sarah Wolf '95

STAFF WRITER

The Student Concerns Committee (SCC) and the Parent Advisory Board are subcommittees formed with the goal of raising the self-esteem of students, teachers and parents. Both committees aim to raise the self-esteem for the best possible environment in the school and at home. "If you improve the students', parents' and faculty members' self-esteem, they work together and impact the students' chance of success. Being successful is what it's all about," said Larry Smith, member of the district wide Self-Esteem Board and coordinator of the Parent Advisory Board.

The SCC developed the Chemic Dialogue Day, when students filled out the Chemic Pride Survey. Jim Samocki, counseling department head and member of the district-wide Self-Esteem committee, said the Chemic Dialogue Day was a positive experience. Students were given the opportunity to voice opinions on how the school environment needs to be changed to raise the esteem of the students.

"The Chemic Dialogue Day was a very positive day; it helped us realize the problems in the school and the need to deal with them," Trish Foley, SCC member, said.

The results of the Chemic Pride survey were given to another self-esteem based committee called the Parent Advisory Board. Chairperson of the Parent Advisory Board at MHS, Laura LaLonde, said that the survey helped with the goals of the Parent Advisory Board. "The Chemic Pride survey shows us what the kids wanted. It is a good guideline for us."

The Parent Advisory Board hopes to institute small projects aiming to boost an individual's self-esteem. For instance, they plan to create a bulletin board featuring a student. It's a way to reward someone who is doing something outside of school for the community, Lalonde said.

"It's nice to acknowledge people; it helps their self-esteem. It's nice to be recognized," junior Jessica Sumner said.

The board would also like to begin a program encouraging higher attendance at school events like athletics, drama, band and orchestra. "We want to reward the student who is supportive of their friends in athletics etc. because they may not be involved in extracurricular activities," Lalonde said.

Foley agrees that students need to be noticed. "Some students show personal pride in competing in business and math competitions, mock trial and drama. These groups of students don't receive the acknowledgements and it's important for them to be recognized," she said. Junior Dan Verlinde also said that certain sports

> It has got to go beyond the pay check or report card. All of us need positive strokes along the way to know we're doing a good job."
>
> *Laura La Londe*
> *Parent Advisory Board*
> *Chairperson*

don't receive the recognition that others do.

The SCC has developed a Self Esteem Survey that eventually all students will take. It combines 50 questions and/or statements asking about the students' feelings toward themselves and the school. "We will determine from the data how the students feel about themselves as a whole and then can see what we need to work on to improve the self confidence in students," Foley said.

Self-esteem is important for the students to have in order to accomplish the challenges that they face, Samocki said.

"Everybody does better with higher self-esteem," Lalonde said. "Teachers get paid and students get report cards. It has to go beyond the pay check or report card. All of us need positive strokes along the way to know that we are doing a good job; we need to nurture each other."

Source: Reprinted with permission from Sarah Wolf. "Committees form to improve school environment," Focus, Midland High School, Midland, Mich.

◄Other Uses for Quotations

Direct quotations aren't reserved only for use within text. The size of their type may be enlarged so they can be used as a focal point to a story. They also may be used in graphics form, as in an opinion poll on the editorial page.

One example is a **pulled quotation,** a direct quotation taken from the story, enlarged and placed in a way that draws attention to the story. Pulled quotations should be placed in a box or separated from the text in some visual way. Styles for pulled quotations vary from publication to publication, but most pulled quotations are boldfaced, italicized or both, with the name and title of the speaker printed in a different typeface. Figure 7.1 is an example from the *Focus,* the newspaper at Midland High School in Midland, Mich.

Pulled quotations are used as art in place of pictures or graphics to break up text on a page (see Figures 7.2 and 7.3). Pulled quotations should use only quotations that say something meaningful. Choose

pulled quotation

a direct quotation taken from a story and treated as a graphic to draw attention to the text

Figure 7.2
Pulled Quotation with an Article

By Shauna Knobloch
Staff Writer

A child of survivors struggled to communicate the horrors of the holocaust to instructor Pam Cool's novel students earlier this month.

"I would prefer to run away from this," Dr. Murray Haar, a professor at Augustana College, said. Dr. Haar stood behind the podium anyway and spoke of an event that happened over 50 years ago. The holocaust involved the killing of 6 million Jews and millions of others.

In 1939, rumors of Adolf Hitler spread throughout Europe.

"Who could believe people were just killing, just killing for no reason?" Dr. Haar asked.

Hitler thought anyone with defects was inferior. "They weren't really human," Haar said. "They needed to be cut out."

Haar's father was a survivor of Auschwitz. Over 3.5 million people died there.

"Auschwitz was a place of nonsense," Haar said.

Dr. Murray Haar

 I think the hope is that if you hear what happened back then and you see the hatred again, you will stand up.

It was a place without limits, he said. The Nazi doctors had the chance to try any medical experiment on the prisoners, and they did.

"These killers were human beings like us," Haar said. "We have that capacity inside ourselves."

The holocaust cannot be expressed in any language. The facts can be passed on

but not the horror, he said.

The professor has hopes for the younger generations, though.

"I think the hope is that if you hear what happened back then and you see the hatred again, you will stand up," Haar said. "Wherever there is hatred, you can stand up and say, 'No, we are not haters. This is not right.'"

Source: Reprinted with permission from Shauna Knobloch, "The Holocaust: Child of Survivors Speaks about Horror," Brandon Valley Echo, Brandon Valley High School, Brandon, SD.

Figure 7.3
Pulled Quotation with Photograph, Graphics

School's future looks to enhance technology

Andy Kulas
Front Page Editor

Munster High School

As the clock strokes midnight, a procrastinating student sits down to work on a composition which is due tomorrow.

Although he has left his disk at school, he is not worried. He merely networks his computer at home to the writing lab at school and continues from where he left off during third period.

This sort of occurrence may be in the school's not-so-distant future, according to Mr. Greg Kovich, technical director. The changes might happen within the next five years, according to Mr. Kovich.

Mr. Kovich, along with the School Board's technical committee, has a definite idea of what is in store for the school's and community's future with computers. "I have a vision of Munster becoming a global community," Mr. Kovich said. "If you're at home doing homework, why should that stop you from accessing the information you need to get going?"

Community networking is not the only change in store for the future, according to Mr. Kovich. Classrooms throughout Munster schools may be connected, along with the possible installation of new computer labs in the high school.

The emphasis of all the technological improvements is on access to the technology. "All these buildings were paid for with tax money," Mr. Kovich explained. "How can we deny people access to their buildings, just because the school day is over?"

Other changes in the future include installing electronic mail (E-mail). "E-

"I have a vision of Munster becoming a global community. If you're at home doing homework, why should that stop you from accessing the information you need to get going?"
Mr. Greg Kovich, technical director

Source: Reprinted with permission from Andy Kulas, "School's Future Looks to Enhance Technology," Crier, Munster High School, Munster, Ind.

quotations that summarize the story or say something so persuasive or intriguing that the reader will want to learn more.

Direct quotations may also be used in opinion features. Many high school publications use them on their opinion or editorial pages to show students' views on selected subjects for each issue (see Figure 7.4).

To get quotations for an opinion feature, an editor or reporter may conduct a person-on-the-street survey. This type of survey asks a number of students a question—for example, "What do you think the school should use the old gymnasium for?" Answers such as "Open it up as a community center," "Remodel it into additional classrooms" and "Use it as a secondary gym for basketball practices" might be given. Then the editor can construct these into a sidebar or an information graphic for an editorial on uses for the old gymnasium. The graphic should include the question that was asked and the speakers' responses. Each speaker should be identified.

Because the speaker is a person-on-the-street source—someone selected at random—a title may not be necessary. In the case of students, the speaker's year in school is often given: *Mary Smith, junior.* Figure 7.5 is a good example of quotations used in the graphics form just described.

During elections, many newspapers use a similar format to ask candidates issue-oriented questions. This format may involve more questions and answers than a person-on-the-street interview does, but it serves as a good addition to a newspaper when carefully planned. (See Figure 7.6 for an example.)

FIGURE 7.4
QUOTATIONS USED AS
SIDEBARS WITH FEATURE
ARTICLE

"Now a days the people who stand out as role models are the celebrities in the spotlight. They don't have a deep philosophy or an idea that they're trying to portray."

Ted Jensen, Ashman Court Hotel

you don't have any group that's saying we are one people, let's get together instead of separating into political orientation, sexual preference, etc."

Szok said, "If you're thinking of heroes who are very interested in the welfare of society, than I don't think kids have so much of that, it's artificial."

As a child, Szok looked up to a number of figures. "I considered a lot of saints heroes, since I was thinking about doing missionary work. Like Saint Francis of Assissi, he was kind and charitable to people in need. He protested the hypocrisy in society."

He also was impressed by some boys from his old neighborhood who were a bit on the "rough side". "They were so kind, good and gentle on the inside, though. They weren't pretentious like some people who seem 'nice,'" he said.

No matter what their status, heroes have always been important in shaping the generations that they influence.

"Heroes are living examples of what you would like to incorporate into your own life," Szok said.

Why do you think a hero is important?

"I like to have someone to remember when I think times are tough. I think about how she would handle it."

"It gives you someone to look up to, to believe in despite the disappointments caused by others."

Why don't you have a hero?

"Everybody has flaws, so I concentrated on fixing my flaws instead of trying to replace them with another's good points."

How has your hero changed as you've grown older?

"From super-powered people to down-to-earth heroes."

"From complete admiration to respect."

Source: Reprinted with permission from Jessica Heritier, "Past Role Models Strived for Change," Focus, Midland High School, Midland, Mich.

FIGURE 7.5
PERSON-ON-THE-STREET INTERVIEWS ADD QUOTATIONS TO OPINION PAGES

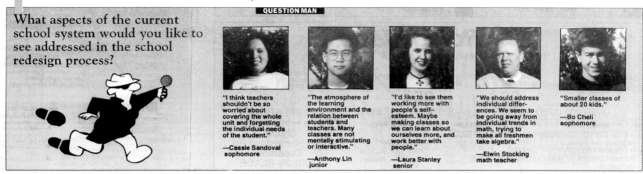

Source: Reprinted with permission from "A Vision of the Future," The Epitaph, Homestead High School, Cupertino, Calif.

FIGURE 7.6
STUDENT OPINIONS PERSONALIZE ELECTION STORIES

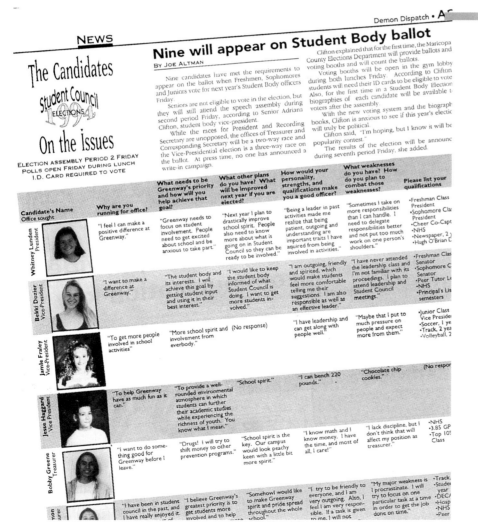

Source: Reprinted with permission from Joe Altman, "The Candidates on the Issues," Demon Dispatch, Greenway High School, Phoenix, Ariz.

Your newspaper's style is to use only one pulled quotation per story. Decide which quotation from each of the following pairs you would put in the story if you were on the editorial staff. Explain your choice.

1. For an article on overcrowding:

   "The class size isn't what bothers me. The halls are just too crowded. Getting through the halls is like walking through wet cement when you're short."—Megumi Yano, senior

   "There is a dramatic increase in the sheer number of people in the halls. Enrollment has increased, and we don't have as many teachers as I'd like to patrol the halls."—John Harness, principal

2. For a feature page on drinking and driving:

   "I wouldn't even think of driving drunk, or even getting into that kind of situation. I have enough trouble getting the car."—Amy Cornelius, junior

   "Even when I am a little drunk, I can still drive fine. Some people argue that it impairs driving, but I think it is blown way out of proportion."—a junior girl

3. For a story on the possibility of a third state championship.

   "We definitely have a chance of winning the state championship."—Vince Zavala, varsity softball coach

   "The team is coming together real well right now. The girls are finding out what their roles are and are playing their roles real well. We are getting hits and big plays from the people we expect the big plays from."—Vince Zavala, varsity softball coach

4. For a story on a proposed curfew:

   "Children belong inside their house after 11 p.m. or midnight. We are not babysitting. The more officers we have, the more individuals we can keep off of the streets and the more we can help eliminate the number of crimes committed past curfew."—Bill Bunner, school resource officer

   "By stalking teenage drivers, police officers are not only harassing the innocent people, they are not eliminating the real problem on the streets."—SuLynn Dalvitt, senior

   "We need to stop those cruisers. The more people in their houses, the less crime there is."—Oleg Kalinski, junior

ATTRIBUTION

Attribution is giving credit to the source of the information. In news writing it is important to let the reader or viewer know the human or physical source from which information came. This helps the consumer judge the credibility of the information.

A direct quote is always attributed to the speaker:

"In the same way you can see what's in your morning cereal, you can now see what's in cigarettes," Dr. Jack Henningfield, a panel member of the National Institutes of Health, said.

Not only do reporters need to identify their sources; they also need to credit each source, or give the source a title, so the reader knows why the source is being used for the story. In the above quotation, *Dr., panel member,* and *of the National Institutes of Health* are examples of credits. Without these, the reader would know only that the speaker was Jack Henningfield and would be wondering whether or not to believe anything he says. But if the reader knows Henningfield is a doctor, a panel member or a member of a national institution, then the reader is more likely to conclude that Henningfield is a credible source.

What to Attribute

Attribution involves more than just identifying sources of quotations. Information that would not be commonly known by the consumer, whether it is used in quotation form or not, should be attributed. This kind of attribution can involve anything from dollar estimates to reports of what happened at an accident.

The following sentences need attribution, because they contain information that the reader didn't know before reading them and couldn't find in a common source such as an encyclopedia:

> The fire caused an estimated $5,000 in damage.
>
> Jones has been asked to resign as school board president.
>
> Both students were charged with felonies.

By not attributing the information, reporters would be failing to let consumers know where the information came from, and they would be setting themselves up for possible lawsuits. The sentences should be attributed as follows:

> The fire caused an estimated $5,000 in damage, according to Captain Dale Murphy.
>
> According to John Woods, school principal, Jones has been asked to resign as school board president.
>
> Police Chief Joe Robinson said that both students were charged with felonies.

In contrast, information that is general knowledge doesn't need attribution. In some cases, attribution would even be awkward:

> The first snow of the season fell last night, according to reports from the weather service.

DATELINE DATELINE DATELINE

MENLO PARK, N.J., 1877— "Mary had a little lamb. . . ." Thomas Alva Edison shouted the familiar nursery rhyme against the recording diaphragm of a model phonograph his assistant had constructed from Edison's sketch. Both report being amazed when the recorded words played back to them.

The phonograph was one of 1,053 inventions patented by Edison. Others were the electric light, and parts for the motion picture camera, the telephone and the typewriter.

One of his less well known contributions was to the world of radio. The first radio patent ever issued was to Edison in 1885 for an induction system that used antennae to transmit signals above the curvature of the Earth.

Primary sources give credibility to your reporting. The owner may say "My car is a total wreck," but the estimator who works for the body shop, and whose job it is to estimate damages and the cost of repairs, would be a more accurate and reliable source to interview.

Placing Attribution in Print

The following are some guidelines for using attribution most effectively in newspaper, magazine and yearbook stories.

1. Attribution is placed after the quotation or the information given if the information is more interesting or prominent than the source. Most readers are interested in the potential of an asteroid's hitting Earth, but few would recognize the name of the astronomer who observed the asteroid if it were used in this *Washington Post* quotation:

> An asteroid about the size of a small school bus narrowly missed striking Earth Friday, a University of Arizona astronomer said.

Teens from all over the United States were quoted in a *Parade* article headlined "How Teenagers See Things." Because most of *Parade's* readers didn't know the teens personally, what the teens had to say was more interesting to readers than their names:

> "My goal is definitely happiness," says Eric Arsenault, 18, of Chesterfield, Mich. "What would give me that? I don't know yet. But a lot of people in the 1980s made money and weren't very happy. I want more. My main reason for seeking further education is self-enrichment."

> "A lot of us look at teens who are doing drugs or getting into trouble as examples of what we do not want to follow," says Stephanie Shields, 18, of Starkville, Miss., who credits religion with shaping her values. "I don't go out drinking and smoking: number one, because it's unhealthy; and, number two, because it doesn't please God. It's important to have standards to live up to."

2. If the source or speaker is more important or will get the attention of more readers than will the information, the attribution is placed first. For example, everyone has a birthday every year, but the *New York Times* recognizes only a few:

> Bill Clinton, the nation's highest profile baby-boomer, is not going quietly into that sixth decade that he says signifies he "has more yesterdays than tomorrows."

3. When a direct quotation is longer than one sentence, the attribution is normally placed between the first and second sentence. An example is the quotations from the teens that illustrate the first guidelines. The following quotation by an educational analyst appeared in the same *Parade* article. The quotation is divided the same way, because few readers will recognize her name but most are interested in what she has to say:

> "The emphasis on family values has definitely increased from the 1980s to the 1990s," says Janis Cromer, an educational analyst based in Washington, D.C., who wrote and analyzed surveys on the mood of America's youth that were conducted in 1974 and 1983. "In the 1970s, kids were challenging parents and authority. In the 1980s, their attitude was, 'I'm out to get mine,' and the top priority

was making money. Today's kids want to have successful careers, but they know that, without family and love, they wouldn't be satisfied." Source: reprinted with permission from Dianne Hales, "How Teenagers See Things," *Parade,* August 18, 1996, p. 4.

4. The attribution should not separate a subject and verb or divide parts of a complete thought. Incorrect and correct examples follow.

Incorrect: Another improvement, according to food service coordinator Neal Green, is the later opening time for the cafeteria.

Correct: Another improvement is the later opening time for the cafeteria, according to food service coordinator Neal Green.

Incorrect: "I don't think working with any attorney has influenced my judgment," he said, "because I am not easily influenced."

Correct: "I don't think working with any attorney has influenced my judgment, because I'm not easily influenced," he said.

5. One attribution per paragraph is sufficient. More than one attribution in a paragraph is redundant:

"At that point, I didn't think we were any good either," Coach Tony Hermann said. "We're not playing as a team. As individuals, we're great. We have the best talent in the state," Hermann said.

6. When a direct quotation is longer than one paragraph, attribute as often as necessary to make it clear who is speaking. Each paragraph may need attribution, or attribution every other paragraph may be enough. Personal pronouns may be substituted for the name after the first attribution. The source in the following excerpt from "Kids and ATVs Don't Mix," an article in the *Hastings (Nebraska) Tribune,* is Bob Wolfe, owner of a store that sells ATVs:

Wolfe Cycle Sports has seen steady sales of the vehicles the last several years, Wolfe said.

"Anything with a spark plug needs to be used with precaution and safety in mind," he said. "For us, that means not selling the vehicles to anybody under age 16.

"We have very few buyers who haven't ridden before. If we feel they don't have the experience, we'll spend whatever time is necessary to get them comfortable on the machine."

Bill Nielsen, a local farmer, said he has used three-wheelers on his farm for 10 years. He also teaches safety sessions to kids.

"Kids shouldn't be on ATVs," he said. "We demonstrate how heavy a three-wheeler is, for example, how they wouldn't be able to move if it flipped on top of them. How they can't reach the handle, how they can't reach the brake lever without moving and how their legs don't fit right.

"They (ATVs) weren't physically designed to handle people their size." (*Hastings Tribune,* Hastings, Neb.)

7. When an additional speaker is introduced, name the speaker before the quotation: In the previous example, when the speaker changes from Bob Wolfe to Bill Nielsen, Nielsen is named before he speaks. In the following quotations from a sports story, the reader is led to believe that a source is continuing to speak, when in reality, another speaker has been introduced:

> "Our goal is to win the league championship, but we have some very tough opponents this year," senior Matt Van Hoesen said.
>
> "Tough is not the word to describe our league. It's more like a death march," Coach Lynn Harrod said.
>
> "We have a talented pitching staff, as good as any we have had before," senior Jason Thoren said.

8. When multiple sources are quoted or the story is moving to a different topic, a transition paragraph is needed. The transition paragraphs are highlighted in the following continuation of the baseball story:

> *Experience, however, will be on the Lions' side: they have 10 seniors and six juniors on their roster.*
>
> "Our distribution is really good, it will allow the seniors to work with the juniors and help improve their abilities," Harrod said.
>
> *"Teamwork already appears to be one of the strengths of the squad.*
>
> "The team has shown a lot of unity, and it is only the beginning of the season," junior Jim Ward said.
>
> *The coach agrees.*
>
> "I haven't seen pitching this tough in all the years I have been coaching," Harrod said.

Some transition paragraphs, such as the last one in the example, are used only to let the reader know the speaker or topic has changed. Although the transition paragraphs in these examples are short and don't provide a great deal of additional information, they are still necessary. Go back and try to read the excerpt above without the highlighted transition paragraphs. See if you can keep track of which source is speaking.

Attribution in Broadcasting

lead-in

information read by a newscaster to introduce a sound bite

Many of the same rules for attributing sources in print apply to attributing sources in radio and television. The **lead-in,** or the last sentence read by the newscaster before a sound bite, commonly contains the words *said* or *according to:*

> **Newscaster:** The mayor said work on the downtown freeway will begin soon.
>
> **Mayor** (on tape): Construction on the Kennedy Freeway through downtown should start next week. . . .

Attribution in broadcast is placed before the information so that listeners can judge the information based on a known source:

> A White House spokesperson said the president's hotline rang early this morning.

"See you on the radio . . ."

Criticized in a letter from a listener for signing off his weekly radio show with the phrase "See you on the radio," CBS newscaster Charles Osgood responded in his inimitable poetic style:

"Dear Sir," I then wrote back to him, and this was my reply:

I do believe that you are wrong, and let me tell you why.

I've worked some years in radio, and television, too.

And though it's paradoxical it nonetheless is true

That radio is visual, much more so than TV.

And there's plenty of good reason why that paradox should be.

You insist that on the radio there are no pictures there.

You say it's only for the ear . . . but I say "au contraire."

There are fascinating pictures on the radio you see.

That are far more picturesque than any pictures on TV.

No television set that's made, no screen that you can find,

Can compare with that of radio: the theatre of the mind.

Source: Reprinted with permission from Charles Osgood, CBS radio network, in a speech at the National Broadcasters Convention.

Transitions need to be used between sound bites of two different speakers or between sound bites on different subjects from the same speaker. These transitions are always read by the reporter or newscaster. The following is an example:

Newscaster: The red telephone that no one wants to hear ring rang last night at the White House. A White House spokesperson said the president's hotline rang early this morning.

Tape: The hotline in the president's bedroom rang about two o'clock. It was answered by security personnel, who said it was a wrong number. The caller was attempting to reach a veterinary clinic in Virginia.

Newscaster: The hotline is reserved for national emergencies. According to White House officials, faulty wiring is to blame for the wrong number.

Tape: The telephone was tested last week after the phone jacks were relocated during the remodeling of the family living quarters on the third floor. The telephone company has been working on the problem this morning.

Newscaster: The president and his family have been staying at Camp David during the remodeling.

Source: Adapted from Melvin Mencher, *Workbook for News Reporting and Writing*, "Hot Line," p. 17. (New York: Brown and Benchmark) 1997.

Attributive Verbs

attributive verb

a verb used with the name of the source in an attribution

Attributive verbs are the verbs used in attributing information to a source. The most common attributive verb is *said.* There are numerous words available to indicate the tone or volume in which someone says something, but the word *said* is the only one that does not add to the impact of the quotation by implying the manner in which the words were spoken.

If a reporter writes that the school board president *exclaimed, stated* or *emphasized* something during a meeting, the attributive verb implies an emphasis or an emotion that may not have been intended by the speaker. The reporter should let the president's words speak for themselves and not add interpretation or emphasis through the attributive verb.

Consider these examples of incorrect, overused verbs of attribution:

"This was by far the best game we've played all year," he *exclaimed.*

"We'll consider their proposal at the upcoming meeting," she *maintained.*

"It's a tough thing, and I understand what they're trying to do," *she cried.*

"The safety of our students always comes first," he *stressed.*

The solution is to consistently use one neutral verb—*said*—for attributing quotations. *Said* conveys no emotion, tone of voice or physical activity. It leaves everything to be interpreted by the reader:

"This was by far the best game we've played all year," he *said.*

"We'll consider their proposal at the upcoming meeting," she *said.*

"It's a tough thing, and I understand what they're trying to do," she *said.*

"The safety of our students always comes first," he *said.*

Beginning reporters often object to using *said* repeatedly in a story. They're afraid it will bore readers because it will become repetitious. Readers, however, do not object. The attribution is inserted in the story only to keep the reader informed as to the source of the information. Frequently the source changes from paragraph to paragraph, and the reader needs to know who is speaking in each paragraph.

Readers tend to skip over the attributive verbs. The only reason a reader actually concentrates on the attribution is to learn who or what the source is and to know when it changes. An attributive verb other than *said* is like a red flag to the reader. It causes reading to stop and reaction to begin. That should not happen in a news story. The information may cause the reader to stop and react, but the attributive verb should not.

Occasionally another neutral verb of attribution is acceptable if it reflects the manner in which the words were delivered and not the emotion with which the source delivered them. A question is *asked.* A speaker may *tell* or *add* words:

He *told* reporters that he will not run for re-election.

"How can our school be satisfied with the views of the student council?" she *asked*.

The phrase *according to* also is frequently used to attribute information when a direct quotation is not used:

The fire caused an estimated $5,000 in damage, *according to* the fire marshal's report.

Verbs of attribution are used in reference to speech, not in reference to action. For example, someone can't "smile" a statement or "frown" an opinion. Laughs and smiles cannot be spoken; they are actions of the face muscles. Write *said with a laugh,* or *said with a grin* if it is necessary to show the speaker's action. The following examples are incorrect:

"This was the best game we've played all year," he *smiled*.

"It's a tough thing, and I'm not sure I understand what they're going to accomplish," she *frowned*.

Try adding a prepositional phrase to indicate an action:

"This was the best game we've played all year," he said *with a grin*.

"It's a tough thing, and I'm not sure I understand what they're trying to accomplish," she said, *as frown lines creased her forehead*.

Prepositional phrases indicating emotion or expression are used more often in stories about people than in hard news stories. Readers want to know how people live, feel and think, but they want to interpret facts and events for themselves.

An example of a prepositional phrase added to show how a comment was spoken comes from a story in the *Omaha World-Herald*. The story described the thoughts of University of Nebraska's head football coach Tom Osborne on security at Miami's Orange Bowl:

"Well, I was scared," Osborne said in a deadpan delivery that drew a big laugh. Again mixing sarcasm and humor, he added: "If the whole Miami police department can't protect you, we thought about taking the National Guard down there."

Putting Attribution to Work

Now that you are more familiar with attribution, let's take a look at a story that carefully attributes information and uses partial and fragmentary quotations to convey specific words used by sources. Notice how important attribution is in this story—even when there are no direct quotes to be attributed:

Two people found dead in their burning home Saturday were the victims of a double homicide, *police investigators said*.

Firefighters called to 6814 S. 41st St. at 5:52 a.m. discovered the bodies of Susan A. Anglim, 37, and her daughter, Michelle Marie, 12.

DATELINE

MOON, July 20, 1969—"That's one small step for man, one giant leap for mankind," astronaut Neil A. Armstrong said as he stepped from the *Eagle* spacecraft onto the surface of the moon.

Radio signals carried these first words spoken from the moon to an estimated one billion radio listeners and television viewers on Earth. A television camera set up by the astronauts sent pictures of the historic event to the spellbound audience.

President Richard Nixon used the telephone to speak to the men on the moon from the White House. His voice was carried via radio signal from Mission Control in Houston to Armstrong and Edwin E. "Buzz" Aldrin, Jr., as they stood on the dusty surface of the Sea of Tranquillity.

The astronauts used radio headsets to talk to each other from inside their globe-like space helmets.

Later in the mission, the astronauts gave television viewers a tour of their spacecraft. *Newsweek* reported that the picture was "startlingly clear . . . so good the setting on the craft's control panel could be read, and when the sun slanted through the windows, dust particles could be seen swirling about the cabin."

The television camera even caught the astronauts littering the lunar surface. Before leaving, they dumped from the spacecraft their boots and other gear that might have been contaminated.

Less than one decade earlier, on April 12, 1961, Soviet space officials held the first radio talks with a human being in space when cosmonaut Yuri Gagarin circled the Earth for one hour and 48 minutes.

The bodies were found by firefighters extinguishing a small fire in the neatly maintained split-level house, *said Lt. Larry Roberts of the police homicide unit.*

Roberts would not say whether the two were dead before the fire, but *said* foul play was suspected in both deaths.

Firefighters noticed something "that was not normal" about the bodies and notified police after arriving at the scene, *Roberts said. He described* the fire as "suspicious."

Damage to the house was moderate, *according to Assistant Fire Chief Michael Dineen.* It is suspected a "flammable accelerant" was used in the fire, *he said.*

Roberts said no arrests had been made.

He would not say where in the house the bodies were found or whether a weapon was found or how Mrs. Anglim and her daughter died.

Roberts said the fire was reported by a neighbor who saw smoke and flames coming from the frame house.

Window screens were knocked out of two windows on the north side of the home and charred wood was visible on the frames.

About 10 family members and friends gathered outside the house where Red Cross workers comforted them and offered blankets and coffee.

World-Herald records indicate Mrs. Anglim was granted a divorce from her husband, Michael, in 1964.

The City Directory lists Mrs. Anglim as an employee of Taylor's Flower Shop and Greenhouse, 5414 S. 36th St. *A woman answering the phone at the business* would not confirm that Mrs. Anglim worked there.

Source: Reprinted with permission from John Melingagio, *Omaha World-Herald,* Omaha, Neb.

Both people and print sources are attributed in this story, so the readers know where the reporter learned the information. The statements about the windows being knocked out and the Red Cross's providing blankets and coffee for family members are not attributed. The reporter saw these things at the scene. What a reporter witnesses is first-hand observation and does not have to be attributed.

1. Rewrite the attribution for these phrases condensing each to one or two words:

    she went on to say
    she told the audience that
    she concluded by saying that
    she said that, in her opinion

    he also made mention of
    he also pointed out
    he revealed the fact that
    the author made the remark that

2. Rewrite the following sentences correcting the frequency, placement, punctuation and verbs used in the attribution:

    a. "The British" Paul Revere shouted "are coming"!
    b. "Nice guys" Leo Durocher said "finish last."
    c. "I like it. I feel more kids go to school, and those kids should be rewarded," said junior class president Ian Lane.
    d. "I'm gonna die someday anyway! Might as well get my kicks out of life now! I'm young, and I still

have my health. When I'm old and don't have my health then I'll have to quit," says Jay Jecker.

e. "Smoking can only be stopped," Welton said, with the cooperation of the student body. Students are hurting themselves and others".

f. Said Gen. William Tecumseh Sherman: "War is hell".

g. "It should be based on grades", Principal Goldman said, "not attendance."

h. Jennings announced his resignation yesterday. He is quitting because he is tired of the red tape in the administrative office. He wants to go back to teaching.

i. Companies frequently give Jeanette Hunt samples of handwriting along with job descriptions to screen future employees. Hunt said this use of graphology (handwriting analysis) should be used more often because of the traits it can reveal, Hunt said.

j. According to Brad Sahy, a counselor at Good Samaritan Hospital, "It seems to me that there are a lot more people gambling than there were before," he said.

Sahy said he was hired two years ago to work with people who suffer from addictive behaviors. He said the recent upswing in the number of addicted gamblers is, in his opinion, due in large part to the introduction of lottery games in the city.

3. These sentences were written for newspapers. Rewrite the sentences for broadcast style.

a. The highway death toll soared to 500 over the holiday weekend, according to a highway safety official.

b. The new program should help students meet requirements for college entrance, school officials said.

c. *The Bronco* will not offer price cut incentives for students who purchase the yearbook early this year, according to Principal Phil Dudley.

d. Student Council voted Feb. 18 to prohibit seniors from voting in student body elections, but logistic problems have kept Student Council from making the change final, according to senior Andy Egan,

student body vice-president.

e. Worried that some freshmen go home during free periods and lunch to smoke marijuana or engage in sexual relations, faculty members have discussed requiring students to remain in school all day as a way to better monitor students' free time.

4. You have the following quotations on tape. You are preparing a radio broadcast of this week's news for your school. Indicate how you would edit these quotes for the radio broadcast. Write a lead-in for each.

a. Principal Bert Dent: "Ah, students, what they won't think of! A flagpole sitter. No, no decision has been made on disciplinary action yet, but it was scary watching, I tell you. I hate to think what would have happened if she'd fallen."

b. Truck driver Bob Augustine: "Yeah, I was right behind them when they crashed. It was just like a big explosion on my front bumper. Frightening? I guess my heart must have sunk all the way to my toes and helped me get stopped so I didn't run over them, too. No, I don't know what caused it. I'm not even gonna' guess. I can't believe anyone got out of those cars alive."

c. Emily Wagner, student government president: "It's going to be a real exciting year. We're going to get action big time. Our plan is to start with getting the policy on closed campus changed so we can all go someplace else for lunch, and when we get that through we're going to go for a smoking lounge for students like the one the teachers have. I have a couple of personal gripes that I'd like to get taken care of, too, like that rule about not putting posters in your lockers and having assigned parking places. I think seniors should get the front row even if the freshmen get in to sign up first, the little scumbags."

5. You are using the quotations in the previous question in stories for the school paper that will come out in about two weeks. Rewrite the sentences to make them more effective for print. You may use direct quotes, paraphrases, or partial quotes. If you divide the quotations into more than one paragraph, write a transition paragraph.

CHAPTER REVIEW

KEY TERMS

Show that you know the meanings of the following key terms by correctly using them in complete sentences. Write your answers on a separate sheet of paper.

quotation	paraphrase	transition paragraph
balance	partial quotation	pulled quotation
direct quotation	fragmentary quotation	lead-in
attribution	sound bite	attributive verb

OPEN FORUM

1. You interview the principal and tape the interview for the school radio station. In the sound bite you'd really like to use, the principal says, "I seen the fight start on the south side of the parking lot just after halftime. Archway has always been a big rival, but we've never had out-and-out violence before. Those hot-headed intruders from across town had no damned business here anyway." Will you use the quote as is? Why or why not? Would you use an edited version? Would you paraphrase the quotation and include it as part of the story to be read by the newscaster? Write the quotation as you would use it in the story.

2. Based on the same interview, you write an article for the school paper. Will you use the quote? Will you edit it? Why or why not? How else might you handle it in print?

3. A reporter for your school paper turns in a pre-prom story about how students plan to celebrate the event. It includes these paragraphs:

    One senior said that he plans to use alcohol and drugs on prom night if they are available. It makes the whole experience more fun and memorable. He added that he expects his date to drink and use drugs during the course of the evening. If she opts not to, the senior plans to leave his date in search of more fun people.

    "I'm not going to allow my evening to be ruined by a stuck-up brat," he said.

    Will you run the paragraphs as they are? With changes in punctuation to indicate partial quotes? With the name of the senior? Explain your answers. Rewrite this to make it acceptable copy for your school paper.

4. Add punctuation to the story in Question 3 to properly separate the opinions of the speaker from the reporter's writing. What criteria did you use for determining which words or sentences to quote?

5. Assign members of the class to read the following sentences aloud, with each person reading the sentence as though one of the attribu-

◆ Open Forum, continued

tive verbs were accompanying it. Listen and try to guess which of the attributive verbs is appropriate for the reader's expression.

"I never said you stole my red bandanna."

accused	indicated	whined	exclaimed
screamed	cajoled	stressed	explained
whispered	stated	cried	said

What differences did you hear? How would readers feel about the speaker if the attributive verb were *accused? Whined? Cajoled? Cried? Stated?* What difference does it make to you as a reader? A reporter's job is to present facts objectively. Can reporters influence readers' thinking—and lose their objectivity—through their choice of attributive verbs? Is that practice ethical? Why or why not?

FINDING THE FLAW

This column uses quotations to tell a story. Readers enjoy feeling that they are sitting in the coffee shop listening to the farmers' conversation and sharing in their perplexing situation. Check this column carefully for punctuation, grammar and use of quotations. Rewrite sentences which contain errors correcting the punctuation, grammar and attribution.

Mystery of missing calf solved
by Denise Allen

"I've got a cow I'm pretty worried about," Alvin muttered the other day. "She should have calved two weeks ago and I still haven't seen a calf. I think I'd better call the vet."

I thought Alvin was done calving for the year.

"Normally, I am but this year I had four cows that weren't bred right away and came up late," he explained. "All the rest have had theirs now, which is why I'm worried."

The other guys in the coffee shop murmured in agreement and we all thought about our own worry in a similar situation.

"Wait a minute," Carl said. "is that the cow you have off by itself in that small north pasture?"

It was, Alvin replied. He put her there so he could keep an eye on her.

"Well, she's already calved," Carl said. "I saw a black calf standing right next to her last evening."

"Last evening,?" Alvin asked, scratching his head. "I was out there last evening before dark and I didn't see a calf."

I nodded.

"You know I saw a calf in with her about a week ago when I was coming to town early in the morning."

"You did,?" Alvin asked. "You're sure?"

I was.

Alvin was puzzled.

"I walked that entire pasture three days ago and hunted all over for a calf because I thought the cow looked like she had calved, but I couldn't find anything out there.

~~CHAPTER REVIEW,~~ continued

◆ FINDING THE FLAW, continued

You're sure you saw a calf?"
I still was.
Alvin scratched his head.
"And you're sure you saw a calf?" he asked Carl.
Carl also was sure. That cow's definitely had a calf.
Alvin was grumbling when he left the coffee shop, but he was determined to go and find that calf.
He straggled into the coffee shop the next morning, looking as if he had been awake all night.
"I was," he said after that comment was made. "I decided to find that calf so I set up a surveillance operation."

His surveillance included a set of binoculars and a seat in his pickup.
"I spent all afternoon and all evening watching that cow and I still never saw a calf," Alvin said. "Before it got dark I went out and searched again and still didn't find one."
He was determined, though, and spent all night watching by light of the moon.
Finally, about 5:30 a.m., just as it was getting light, the calf appeared, just out of nowhere.
"I don't know where it was but I got it rounded up," he said. "And, I named it Houdini."

Source: Reprinted with permission from Denise Allen, "Mystery of Missing Calf Solved," Hastings (Nebraska) Tribune.

◆

 MEDIA WATCH

1. Critique the quotations used in the following story. Are there enough quotations used so the students, not the reporter, are telling the story. Are the quotations meaningful? Do they add to the story? Are the quotations attributed correctly? Are the quotations punctuated correctly? Is the fragmentary quotation used effectively?

German culture celebrated at KU
By Brooke Wilson

Students from 26 Kansas high schools competed Feb. 26 in the third annual Schulerkongress. Students recited poetry, read stories, practiced conversing and competed in a German spelling bee and a geography quiz.

"It was a good experience. I got to talk with a lot of German-speaking people, and I learned a lot," Joanne Bjorge, junior, said.

Throughout the day, students had the chance to speak with Bergwanders, German-speaking people, and receive Geld, or fake German money, for participation and conversation. Students "bought" German books and games with the money.

Sophomore Erik Lundsgaarde took first place in all three competitions he entered: prose reading, a culture quiz and a spelling bee.

◆ MEDIA WATCH, CONTINUED

"It was an interesting experience. I was surprised I really did that well," Lundsgaarde said.

"The words themselves (in the spelling bee) weren't that hard. The hard part was saying the letters."

Those who placed among the semifinalists in the events were juniors Joanne Bjorge, Cassie Hays, Davis McElwain and Jennie Roberts, and sophomores Rebecca Hamburg, Bernice Lee, Jean Lin and Margaret Zeddies.

"I don't do it for pressure, just to have a fun day and get some German experience," Hannelore Hess, German teacher, said.

Jon Tramba, junior, said, "It was a good experience because you take everything you've learned in the classroom and use it in a fun way."

Source: The Budget, *Lawrence High School, Lawrence, Kans.*

String Book

You may use any newspapers for this activity, including school newspapers. Clip the page header with the name and date of the newspaper for each article; keep it with the example.

1. Clip three examples of news stories you think demonstrate good use of quotations and paraphrases.
2. Clip a feature about a person in which the quotations are used to give the reader insights into the individual's personality.
3. Clip examples of different ways in which quotations are used. Look for the following:
   ◆ a quotation followed by an attribution
   ◆ a quotation following the name of the source
   ◆ a quotation with the attribution in the middle
   ◆ a fragmentary or partial quotation
   ◆ a quotation that continues through more than one paragraph
   ◆ a quotation with the punctuation outside the closing quotation marks
   ◆ pulled quotations
   ◆ quotations in headlines
   ◆ other uses of quotations

Chapter 8
Writing in Journalistic Style

"The difference between the right word and the almost right word is the difference between lightning and the lightning bug."

—Mark Twain, journalist and author

After completing this chapter, you will be able to:

◆ understand style and use stylebooks,

◆ edit copy for journalistic style,

◆ choose bias-free language,

◆ format copy,

◆ use copyediting symbols.

◆

*H*ow should I write this number? What title should I use for this person—or should I use a title at all? Can I say this, or will it show bias or offend readers? Should there be a comma here? Is *homecoming* capitalized?

You've probably asked some of these questions or at least thought about them as you gathered information and wrote down the quotations you wanted to put in a story. For journalists there are easy answers and one quick source for finding them—a stylebook.

The best way to learn journalistic style is to study the rules in the stylebook and to question every word, phrase and sentence you write until you are in the habit of using correct style. This chapter will introduce you to basic style rules and to the copy editing symbols that you will use to correct errors or make changes in the copy you prepare. It will also explain some of the special situations that will confront you in journalistic writing such as the use of bias-free language and the use of courtesy titles.

STYLEBOOKS AND STYLE

A **stylebook** is a handbook for writers and editors. All newspapers and magazines and all radio and television stations have individual sets of rules and guidelines their employees use in writing and scripting news stories. These rules and guidelines are like a constitution; they are the governing principles for the **style,** or the way in which writing is to be crafted, in that newsroom.

Stylebooks specify the way in which dates, numbers, titles and other variable things should be written by the publication or station. These guidelines keep the writing or speaking style consistent within a publication or broadcast.

Consistent style is one way to create and maintain the overall image of a publication or station. Readers and viewers like consistency. They pick up the same newspaper every day because they like being able to turn to the same page or section to find the world news or the sports. They tune to the same station because they know the weather map will

stylebook

a handbook for writers that contains rules and guidelines for writing in a particular style and in the style appropriate for a particular publication or newsroom; a manual of operations for writers

style

the way in which writing is to be crafted to be consistent within a publication or broadcast; the general ways in which journalists format their writing

THEBES, Egypt, 500 B.C.—Egyptians made papyrus, a form of paper, from the stems of the papyrus plant.

Papyrus was first made in long, rectangular sheets that were rolled and tied like scrolls. Later, sheets were shorter and were bound together into books.

The Egyptians used papyrus to carry their messages, including advertising. For the first time, information in a written form became easily transportable and could be shared with a larger community.

The Egyptian ads, recovered from the ruins at Thebes, are all for the return of runaway slaves.

Among the first ads in American newspapers as well were those for the return of runaway slaves or for the sale of slaves.

have the same symbols they saw yesterday, and they'll be able to glance at the map and know if it's going to be cool and cloudy or hot and dry.

If readers found a different writing style every time they picked up the latest edition of the newspaper or magazine, they would have to work a little harder in reading it. If viewers found different maps and symbols being used every time they tuned to the weather, they would be confused.

Readers and viewers may not be able to identify specific style rules being used, but they become accustomed to the overall style of a publication or station and quickly recognize when something is different. You want them to choose your publication or station regularly, so you must create and maintain a style.

Reporters, too, like consistency. If there is a rule for the way a person should be addressed in a story, for example, the reporter doesn't have to waste time researching how to write each name.

Unfortunately for reporters, there are no rules to answer some of the questions that arise in writing news. In those cases, the publication or station should decide on one solution to the problem and handle it the same way each time it occurs.

Most large news organizations, such as the *Washington Post, Newsweek* and CNN, have published complete style guides that their reporters and producers use. Smaller organizations have style sheets for special terms and usages that occur in their newsrooms, but for general guidelines they rely on a standard stylebook such as the *Associated Press Stylebook and Libel Manual*. Schools may choose to use a scholastic stylebook, such as the *Columbia Scholastic Press Association Stylebook*, as their general reference manual.

Standard Style and Special Situations

Some style rules are almost universal for newspapers and can be considered standard style. For example, at most newspapers, numbers are written as words up through nine, and numbers 10 and over (all multiple-digit numbers) are written as numerals: one vote, 10 days, 250 people. But be careful. Most stylebooks make exceptions for numbers in time, dates, ages, amounts of money and measurements. In these cases, single- and multiple-digit numbers are written as numerals: 6' 10"; 5-year-old child; $15; Jan. 1, 1999.

Other guidelines vary from stylebook to stylebook. One example is the rules for how individuals are addressed. In some publications, courtesy titles (Mr., Mrs., Miss, Ms.) always appear before names. In other publications, the person's first and last names are used without a courtesy title the first time the person is identified, and a courtesy title is used for women's names thereafter. The trend is to omit courtesy titles altogether. Almost all stylebooks recommend the use of professional titles the first time a person is named: *Dr.* Jinshi Tsao, *Rev.* C. J. Willis, *Gov.* Christie Whitman.

Most stylebooks agree that the first time someone is identified, the person's first and last names should be given, and that whenever the person is named again just the last name is used. People like Cher, Madonna and Prince, who use only one name and no courtesy title, are addressed according to their preferences.

THIS JUST IN: *Portrait of a Young Journalist*
Steven R. Lincoln, editor

Kids called him "the newspaper guy." Adults counted on him as a source for news. He was constantly on the job, as evidenced by the 35-millimeter camera he wore slung across his left shoulder.

In his first job out of college, Steven R. Lincoln, 21, was the managing editor of the *Goodland Daily News,* in Goodland, Kansas (population 4,500). Former editor of the weekly newspaper at Hastings College, Lincoln got his editorial position three months after graduation and kept it until he became an editor at *Inside Flyer* magazine two and one-half years later.

He said it took some time to adjust to operating a "real" newspaper in an unfamiliar community. "The first month I was editor, we printed a letter to the editor which turned out not to have been written by the person whose signature was on it. That was learning the hard way," Lincoln said.

"I didn't have a clue about Goodland," he said. "I relied solely on input from my pub-lisher and other co-workers. It took time, but I slowly started meeting key people, such as the city manager, the city clerk and the superintendent of schools. I also wrote an editorial introducing myself to the community and asking for help in finding information."

As editor, Lincoln said he got story ideas by "digging deeper" into stories and by getting more involved. "'If you're not involved in anything, it is very difficult to keep up with what is going on around you. You have to look for news."

Specializing in one area is tough for a small-town journalist, according to Lincoln. He wore the hats of managing editor, layout editor and reporter— and he became handy with a camera, too, taking pictures at a moment's notice. With its staff of eight, the *Daily News* lacked the hierarchy of editors, writers and production staff usually found in a newsroom. Lincoln came up with the news story ideas, assigned them to himself, wrote them, edited them and using the newspaper's computer pagination program, layed out the pages. Then he proofread the pages a couple of times.

Whatever the duty, Lincoln said, it is important to be orga-nized. He said that students in high school and college need to develop organizational skills and that courses in management would also be helpful for a young editor.

Lincoln had received mainly positive feedback from the community. He said he feels he improved the consistency of the paper. He kept improving on the design and getting more local coverage.

"When I was working on the newspaper in college, I kept thinking that if all of us on the staff worked hard enough, we could produce a perfect paper. Now I know that will never happen. There will always be a typographical error or a misspelled word somewhere. The challenge is to keep trying to improve."

Readers look to the *Daily News* for information they can't get in any other newspaper. Local sports, local people and local activities are the paper's top priorities. State and national news come second with most readers.

Lincoln said striving to meet readers' expectations can be a day-to-day struggle. But that's the life of a small-town newspaper editor.

Rules differ from print style to broadcast style, too. In broadcast, where each word takes time to say in a news show with a limited number of minutes, some titles and words are more abbreviated than they are in print where the space available is more flexible. For instance, print style generally uses middle initials, but broadcast style uses middle initials only when the person commonly includes them (Michael J. Fox and Tom T. Hall). Middle names, when commonly used by the individual, are used in both print and broadcast style (Dr. Martin Luther King, Jr.).

Styles vary from newsroom to newsroom. Therefore, it is important that reporters learn the style preferred in their own newsrooms.

Scholastic Style

Each school publication or station has special situations that call for style decisions. The style guidelines for school media, for instance, often call for the use of courtesy and professional titles: Miss Garcia, Mr. Beck, Professor Kosloski. This keeps the school media consistent with the environment in which teachers are addressed by title as a matter of respect.

Titles may precede or follow a name, or both sometimes. However, if two titles are used, make sure they do not say the same thing. For example, *Dr. McGahan, Ph.D.*, literally says *Dr. McGahan, doctor.* It is redundant. Also avoid multiple titles or job descriptions before names, as they can be awkward:

> chair of the chemistry department and women's soccer coach Dr. James McGahan

> art teacher and business club sponsor Mrs. Martinez

To eliminate such awkward constructions, place the professional title before the name and the job descriptions after the name:

> Dr. James McGahan, chair of the chemistry department and women's soccer coach

If a job description is a form of address and takes the place of a courtesy or professional title, it may be placed before the name:

> Coach James McGahan

The use of job descriptions should be specified in the stylebook, especially for school media in which individuals are commonly addressed by job description:

> Superintendent Toczek, Coach Romo

If the information is used as a job description rather than a title, it should be placed after the name:

> Dr. James McGahan, women's soccer coach
> Mr. Joe Toczek, superintendent
> Mr. Jorge Romo, coach

The stylebook should indicate which title should be used in specific references or whether all titles are to be used in every story. If the story is about Dr. McGahan's addressing the school board with a request for a new chemistry lab, it would be more important to know he is chair of the chemistry department than that he coaches soccer. Thus, he

While you might address the principal of your school as "Coach K" on the softball field, you will have to identify her as "Dr. Konstantin Karos, principal of Wilson School" in a story on the new school computer lab.

would be referred to as *Dr. James McGahan, chair of the chemistry department.* If the story is about the soccer team's winning the district tournament, it is more important to know he is the coach. He then should be referred to as *Dr. James McGahan, women's soccer coach.* In either case, one job title could be omitted. Professional titles should be used the first time individuals are named except when they are replaced by another title more appropriate to the story. For example, *Coach James McGahan* could replace *Dr. James McGahan* in a story about soccer. Consistency is the key. It is not as important which style for titles is used as it is that the selected style be used consistently.

Another style rule school media need to specify is the use of acronyms for the names of school organizations. The staffs should decide whether they will use the full names of school organizations or use acronyms. An acronym may always replace the name of the school, or the name may be written out the first time and the acronym used thereafter: *Thompson Valley High School, TVHS.* The stylebook should also specify whether periods are to be used in acronyms.

Capitalization can be another tricky style area for school staffs. Many stylebooks capitalize proper nouns and the names of legal holidays, but the school newspaper may need a style rule about which school activities will be considered holidays. The staff may decide that Homecoming, May Fete, Prom and other special celebrations are the school's equivalent of legal holidays and should be capitalized in its publications.

Style guidelines chosen by the staff should be written out and distributed as a part of the publications manual or as a style sheet. Every member of the staff should have a copy for easy reference. Everyone should use the guidelines in writing and editing stories.

A condensed version of the *Associated Press Stylebook and Libel Manual* adapted for the scholastic press appears following Chapter 20 of this book.

1. Using the stylebook following Chapter 20, find and write out the rule for each of the following. Write two examples of each rule as the examples might appear in your school or community publications.
    a. writing time
    b. writing a date when the month, day and year are used
    c. writing ages
    d. writing an address in which a number appears with a street name, including the street, avenue, boulevard or road
    e. writing the title of a newspaper
    f. writing the temperature this morning
    g. writing about money: cents, dollars and millions of dollars
    h. writing fractions
    i. writing percentages
    j. writing state names and abbreviations when used with a city

2. Rewrite these sentences correcting the style errors. Use the stylebook following Chapter 20.
    a. Lunch will be served at 12 a.m.
    b. The meeting is scheduled for September 28, 1996.
    c. Please address this letter to Miss Taunya Mallory at 101 West California Street, Minneapolis, Minnesota.
    d. School begins on August 15th next year and is out June 3rd.
    e. The construction project proposed by the school district has a price tag of $2,293,467.23.
    f. School is in session 1/2 day on Fri., Dec. 9.
    g. He jumped 18 feet and three and three-eighths inches for a school record.
    h. The band tour will stop in Dallas, Texas, Baton Rouge, La., and Tallahassee, FL.
    i. Classes are dismissed at 3:48 PM and athletic practices begin at 4:10 p.m.
    j. "It was 101 the day we started school, and ten below the day we got out for Christmas vacation." she said.
    k. I read USA Today and The Wall Street Journal every day last year, and I watched the tv news magazine shows 48 Hours and Dateline every week.
    l. The Multicultural Student Union has members who are Native American, Chinese, Black and White.

WORKING WITH WORDS

Words are the tools a writer uses to tell a story. Chosen carefully and used creatively, words are powerful tools. Even though television adds colorful moving pictures and radio uses sound effects and speakers' voices to interpret their stories, these media depend on words to tell the facts. Print journalists may have the luxury of using more words than broadcast journalists to tell their stories, but all must choose their words carefully to achieve the most interesting and understandable stories.

The words a writer chooses do more than tell the story. In journalism, the words can establish the writer's reputation as a credible reporter who cares enough to get all the facts and report them accurately and fairly, or they can give the writer the reputation of being a careless reporter who doesn't do the job that the employer and the audience have a right to expect. A few misspelled words or inaccurate presentations of facts can destroy a reporter's reputation and damage the image of the publication or station.

Check Spellings

Misspelled words are the first thing a reader notices in a newspaper, yearbook or magazine, and they are the greatest liability to a reporter's reputation. Editors hold correct spelling in such high esteem that they often give spelling tests as part of job interviews for reporters.

Editors and readers equate spelling skills with good reporting and think a reporter who misspells a word may not check facts either. They begin to mistrust everything the reporter writes.

Word processing programs with spell-checking capabilities have made it easier to find and correct spelling errors. Writers using computers should make it a habit to spell-check every document before considering it complete.

The spell-checking feature may give writers a false sense of security, however. Words may be spelled correctly and still be misused. Common among these are the homonyms *their/there/they're, to/too/two* and *whose/who's.* The spell-checker won't detect incorrect homonyms, because the word may be spelled correctly but be misused. The following are two examples:

> Mary Walley, *whose* competed in 12 All Star Golf tournaments, said the tournament has blossomed since it began in 1984.

> The artists will be displaying *there* work in the park.

Typographical errors, such as transposing the *o* and the *n* in *on* or *no,* result in correctly spelled words but nonsensical sentences. So does substituting an *r* for an *f,* creating *or* rather than *of:*

> The teacher placed the book *of* the desk.

> The teacher placed the book *no* the desk.

Leaving out a letter can create a correctly spelled word—and spell disaster:

> AMES, Iowa (AP)—An error in the Iowa State University yearbook has made geeks out of Greeks.

> The title page of a section on fraternities and sororities refers to "geek houses." Yearbook officials were printing up 200 correction stickers to be placed over the misspelled word. Those books will go to Greek houses. (*Omaha World Herald*)

Using spell-checking programs does not take the place of using a good dictionary. A dictionary is a vital resource for checking spellings and exact word meanings.

DATELINE DATELINE DATELINE

NEW YORK, 1895—William Randolph Hearst, son of a wealthy California entrepreneur and the editor of the *San Francisco Examiner*, bought the *New York Journal* in 1895. His purchase signaled the beginning of an era and a style of news writing known as yellow journalism.

Hearst's philosophy of news was that it was whatever appealed to the "Gee-Whiz" emotion. He set out to make the *Journal* a paper readers would buy for the emotional appeal of its content. Its pages were filled with stories of stunts, crusades and drama-drenched events.

By the time he bought the *Journal*, Hearst was recognized as an editor not afraid to spend money to get the personnel he wanted or to stage extravagant promotional events to attract readers. Hearst also experimented with type, color and design styles until he achieved a distinctive look that was imitated by many papers.

Hearst's competition was the *New York World*, owned and edited by Joseph Pulitzer. The *World* by this time had added a full Sunday edition, a regular comic section, and color, including a daub of bright yellow on the outfit worn by the main character in the cartoon known as *The Yellow Kid*.

By 1900, about one-third of American newspapers were practicing what had come to be known as yellow journalism, a highly emotional, exaggerated style of news that emphasized crime, sex and violence. It took another decade for the influence of yellow journalism to fade from the pages of American newspapers.

Choose the Correct Word

Using the correct word is as important as getting the facts straight or spelling the word correctly. One incorrectly used word may distort the meaning of the whole story. Look at the following example:

> After a four-hour public hearing, the city planning commission passed the resolution with one descending vote.

Descending means "to go down." The reporter should have used *dissenting*, which means "to vote against." Now consider this example:

> The Commission on Presidential Scholars is a group of imminent private citizens appointed by the President.

Imminent means "impending" and is usually used with words like *danger* or *evil*. *Eminent*, which means "of respected position or character," is the correct word.

Homonyms like *fowl* and *foul* and *red* and *read* create amusing pictures—and major mistakes—as the reporters who wrote these sentences discovered:

> The police said they suspect fowl play.

> Sophomores red more books than juniors and seniors combined in the reading contest.

Sometimes words that are not homonyms but that have similar pronunciations are mistaken for each other:

> The judge ordered the courtroom clothes to cameras.

> She folded her arms and looked on in discuss.

Choose the Concise Word

Choosing the correct word also means using the most concise word that conveys the correct meaning. In general, if there is a simpler or shorter word that means the same thing, use it. If there is a shorter way to say it, do so. Look at the examples in Figure 8.1.

FIGURE 8.1
CHOOSING THE CONCISE WORD

TERM	MORE CONCISE WORD
activate	start, begin
terminate	end, stop
fabricate	lie
adhere	stick
fracture	break
incinerate	burn
demonstrate	show
transformation	change

BYLINE

WRITING IT RIGHT
ADVICE FROM THE EXPERTS

"Writing is a matter of exercise . . . if you write for an hour and a half a day for ten years you're gonna turn into a good writer."
—*Stephen King, author*

"A powerful agent is the right word. Whenever we come upon one of those intensely right words . . . the resulting effect is physical as well as spiritual, and electrically prompt."
—*Mark Twain, journalist and author*

"The writer's only responsibility is his art."
—*William Faulkner*

"Good writers, especially those in news writing, must master first the basics of accuracy, clarity, conciseness and completeness, then look toward developing a graceful style of writing."
—*John C. Quinn, deputy chairman,*
Freedom Forum

"I can't write five words but what I change seven."
—*Dorothy Parker*

"Modern English, especially written English, is full of bad habits that spread by imitation and that can be avoided if one is willing to take the necessary trouble."
—*George Orwell*

Proper use of the English language requires great diligence, but the effort is necessary to good newspapering. Otherwise, readers may pay more attention to the infractions than to the information."
—*John C. Quinn*

"Men of few words are the best men."
—*William Shakespeare*

"Don't use three or four words when one will do; don't use an empty word when none will do."
—*David A. Fryxell, nonfiction writer*

Readers will not feel insulted if writers use simple words and simple sentences. Instead, they will be grateful that they can read a story quickly and understand precisely what happened. Choose the simpler word if it works, but keep the more sophisticated word if the shorter word changes the intended meaning. For example, *immediately* could be changed to *soon, now* or *as soon as possible. Frequently* could become *regularly* or *often*. However, none of the simpler substitutes implies the same urgency as *immediately*. Something that occurs frequently may not occur at regular intervals, but it may occur more regularly than *often* implies. If a word is necessary to the meaning, use it.

Specific words paint complete pictures and give clearly defined facts: *45 percent, rollerblading* and *opera*. Weasel words are vague and generic. They're called weasel words because they weasel out of saying anything meaningful, for example: *some, fun, a lot,* and *music*. Look at these examples:

"I had *a lot* of *fun,*" she said.

The freshman had an *unusual* look on his face.

There are *many various* organizations for students to join.

"I'm going to *do stuff* with my friends."

Based on the size of your school and community, you might call this a large crowd or a small one. Use precise modifiers in your stories.

How much is *a lot?* What is *fun?* How does *unusual* look? How many are *many?* Is *many* different from *various?* What is *stuff?* Even in quotations, these words don't tell the reader anything. The reader's definition of *fun* or *doing stuff* might be very different from the speaker's definition.

Readers want to know more specifically what the speaker or writer means. If someone you are interviewing says, *"I had a lot of fun,"* ask that person, *"What made it fun?"* or *"Can you give me an example of fun?"* Quotations can just as easily give information that will help readers understand the speaker's intent. Here are some quotes with genuine substance:

> "I enjoyed meeting the 18 other candidates and hearing about their experiences as participants in the Harvest of Harmony parade," Central High School candidate Angie Vaga said.

> Students may choose from over a dozen organizations, including FHA, DECA, Spirit Squad, National Honor Society, VICA and Science Club.

> "I'm going to Creation Station, which is an indoor skateboard park with hip-hop concerts. I'm going to spend four days with my best friend."

Each word a writer chooses must be the precise word that conveys the intended meaning. If a word doesn't do the job, such as *fun, stuff,* or *many,* the careful writer throws it out and finds a better word or a more descriptive quote.

Place Modifiers Carefully

Choosing the best word also means using the word correctly and placing it properly in the sentence. Misplacing or omitting a modifier can alter the meaning of a sentence and affect the accuracy of a story.

Incorrect: A feature story on eyeglasses mentioned *"a German-made frame for men with snakeskin-covered temples."*

Correct: A feature story on eyeglasses mentioned *"a men's German-made frame with snakeskin-covered temples."*

Incorrect: Dr. Laura Marvel told how *one woman escaped from slavery during her review of the book.*

Correct: *In the book review, Dr. Laura Marvel told* how one woman escaped from slavery.

Incorrect: She neared, I offered up a winning smile and a cordial hello, then turned back to *an absorbing article about a demonic elephant in* Reader's Digest.

Correct: She neared, I offered up a winning smile and a cordial hello, then turned back to *an absorbing* Reader's Digest *article about a demonic elephant.*

Incorrect: Anderson will discuss his experiences *as a hostage at the University of Northern Colorado* on Friday night.

Correct: Anderson will discuss his experiences *as a hostage in Iran* at the University of Northern Colorado on Friday night.

Incorrect: *As the daughter of country music legend Mel Tillis, one* might think making it to the top would be easy for Pam Tillis.

Correct: *As the daughter of country music legend Mel Tillis, singer Pam Tillis* might have had an easy time making it to the top of the country music charts.

Incorrect: Because of their conduct, Sun Valley Stages *is not allowing the pep band the use of their busses.*

Correct: *Because of their conduct, pep band students* will no longer be allowed to use busses from Sun Valley Stages.

Headline Headaches

Word choice is even more noticeable in headlines than in stories. Here are actual headlines sent to the Iowa Press Association:

◆ Something Went Wrong in Jet Crash, Expert Says
◆ Police Begin Campaign to Run Down Jaywalkers
◆ Farmer Bill Dies in House
◆ Eye Drops Off Shelf
◆ Teacher Strikes Idle Kids
◆ Squad Helps Dog Bite Victim
◆ Shot Off Woman's Leg Helps Nicklaus to 66
◆ Miners Refuse to Work After Death
◆ Juvenile Court to Try Shooting Defendant
◆ Two Soviet Ships Collide, One Dies
◆ Checkout Counter Killer Sentenced to Die for Second Time in 10 Years

Source: Reprinted with permission from Iowa Press Bulletin.

Use Action Verbs

Verbs pack power. Choose vigorous, descriptive verbs in the present tense that help the reader or listener see the action as it happens. Verbs that describe an action precisely such as *slide, seize, amble, roar* and *slam* give a clear impression of the activity.

Sportswriter Mitch Albom of the *Detroit Free Press* captured Detroit Tigers baseball player Cecil Fielder's 50th home run this way:

He *swung* the bat and he heard that smack! and the ball *screamed* into the dark blue sky, higher, higher, until it *threatened* to bring down a few stars with it. His teammates knew; they *leaped* off the bench. The fans knew; they *roared* like animals.

DATELINE DATELINE DATELINE

BRANT ROCK, Mass., Dec. 24, 1906—Radio operators on ships in the Atlantic were surprised to hear voices and music coming through their wireless telegraph receivers on Christmas Eve.

Up until this time, the only sounds they had heard had been the long and short staccato taps of Morse code messages, which were sent by telegraph operators tapping out coded messages using mechanical keys.

Using the same continuous waves Guglielmo Marconi had used to transmit messages, Canadian Reginald Fessenden broadcast the first music and voices to distant receivers not connected by wires.

Fessenden began his broadcast with the traditional Morse code call to anyone listening: "CQ, CQ." He then recited Christmas scripture, played a violin solo of "O Holy Night" and a phonograph recording of Handel's *Largo*, and wished his listeners a merry Christmas.

The broadcast was repeated on New Year's Eve, when it was heard by ships as far away as the West Indies.

Fessenden, a researcher in wireless communication, had taught electrical engineering and had worked for Thomas Edison, the Westinghouse Company, and the Weather Bureau of Agriculture before receiving special funding in 1905 to study wireless transmission.

Fessenden manufactured simple units he called crystal detectors on which people could receive the radio waves. Within a few years, however, he was bankrupt, and his patents were acquired by Westinghouse.

Fielder may have *run* the bases, or he may have *skipped, walked, strolled, ambled, danced, shuffled, trudged,* or *strutted.* Each of these verbs shows a distinctly different action. The tone of the story and the reader's understanding of the action is different for each verb.

Active verbs pump up scholastic sportswriters' writing, too. Feel the action in this lead from the *U-High Midway,* University High School, Chicago:

> *Digging* his cleat into the ground and *staring* down the pitcher with his big greenish-brown eyes, senior Ben Browning easily *cracks* a baseball against his aluminum bat, *knocking* the ball deep into right field.

Sportswriting lends itself to emotion-packed action, but news verbs express action, too. Bombs *explode,* causing airplanes to *plummet* from the sky *gutting* buildings and sending mobs *surging* through streets.

Here's an active front-page lead from the *Bruin News,* Twin Falls, Idaho:

> Next Friday and Saturday, some of the best high school track athletes in the nation will *hurdle* themselves toward Holt Arena in Pocatello, Idaho.

The exception to the suggestion that writers use colorful verbs is *said.* Using substitutes for *said* when attributing a quote implies emotion or emphasis on the part of the speaker, as in *exclaimed, stated, explained, chided, mused* or *barked.* The writer's job is to relay the speaker's words to the reader or listener and let that person interpret how the words were said. Stick with *said* for attribution.

Use Active Sentences

Sentences which begin with the name of the person or thing doing the action are active sentences. Sentences which begin with the object or with a substitute for the subject, such as *there* or *it,* followed by a verb such as *is, are* or *was,* are passive sentences. The action is delayed because the reader has to figure out what the subject really is and what the subject is doing. Passive sentences lack the straightforward power of active sentences. For example, the following sentence is passive:

> **Passive:** There were $4,850 worth of scholarships given out at the Future Farmers of America banquet May 16.

You could easily rewrite to form an active sentence:

> **Active:** Future Farmers of America members collected $4,850 in scholarships at the banquet May 16.

Sentences which begin with the object are also passive. Who gave the awards in this sentence?

> **Passive:** Twenty-six proficiency awards were also given for student projects.

This sentence would be active if rewritten this way:

> **Active:** Twenty-six student projects earned proficiency awards.

Watch out for weasel leads like this one:

> **Passive:** There are not going to be Associated Student Body elections. Interest in the offices was low. There was enough for one candidate in each position.

An active sentence would give this lead more interest:

> **Active:** Associated Student Body elections died for lack of interest, but one candidate volunteered for each office.

The elections and the students who volunteered are the important factors in this lead. Make them do the actions.

Let the person or thing doing the action be the subject of the sentence, even if that person or thing is not the most important part of the story. A fire is bigger news than firefighters doing their jobs, but there's more power in a sentence that shows the firefighters in action:

> **Passive:** The fire was put out by the firefighters.

> **Active:** Firefighters put out the fire.

The names of persons readers know are more important than is the fact that they traveled to the tournament. Put them first:

> **Passive:** Traveling to the tournament were the debaters, seniors Jeff Dierkson, William Langford, and John Fitzhugh, and junior Cassidy Wall.

> **Active:** The debaters, seniors Jeff Dierkson, William Langford, and John Fitzhugh, and junior Cassidy Wall, traveled to the tournament.

Eliminate Redundancies

Redundancy is repeating what's been said or using unnecessary words. We may recognize obvious redundancies, such as *10 a.m. in the morning* and *two twins*. There are also many subtle redundancies, such as *both tied, blue in color* and *small in size,* that sneak into reporters' writing and waste space and readers' time.

Watch for unnecessary words in terms such as *lift it up, a dead body, invited guests* and *went on to say*. By definition, *lift* implies *up,* just as *drop* implies *down*. A *body* is dead, or it would be a person. *Guests* are invited, unless they are specified as uninvited. *Went on to say* can be shortened to *said*.

The following is a list of some of the most common redundancies:

absolutely necessary	honest truth
ask the question	necessary requirements
call up	other alternatives
canceled out	pay out
continue on	refer back
end up	small in size
fall down	totally destroyed
fatally killed	totally unnecessary
first annual	true facts

The name of the school, the name of the school mascot and the words *this year* are redundant in school media. The news is this year's, unless the reporter specifies otherwise. It is about this school or team if it is news in this school's media. A Hyannis High School publication or broadcast might report the following:

> **Redundant:** This year's Hyannis High School Bronco football team won the district championship.

> **Correct:** The football team won the district championship.

redundancy
repeating what's been said; usually subtle, for example 9 a.m. in the morning

To compare the team's current performance with that of another year, the reporter would use *the team versus last year's team.*

This reporter wanted to be sure readers knew which yearbook was being distributed:

> Distribution of this year's 2000 yearbook will occur on June 3, the Friday before the last week of school.

This year's 2000 yearbook is redundant and meaningless. Specify *the 2000 yearbook,* or *the yearbook.*

Rewrite Clichés

Clichés are weasel phrases. They are sayings that have become part of our shared language through time. They've also become meaningless through overuse. Like weasel words, clichés don't say anything new or specific and should be replaced with information or omitted. The following are examples of clichés:

> When the crowning ceremonies were over and the audience was gone, students *danced the night away.*

> After starting its Midwestern League season by winning its first two matches, the women's varsity tennis team is *on a roll.*

The students might have *danced to the music of Middle Earth* or *danced until 1 a.m.* Do two games put the team *on a roll?* If so, it is unnecessary to include the phrase at all.

Use Journalistic Punctuation and Sentence Style

The guideline for punctuation in journalistic writing is to keep it to a minimum. Period-sized dots and commas are hard to see and to tell apart in the fine print on newspaper pages. Writing short, simple subject-verb-object sentences helps simplify punctuation and makes the story easier for readers and listeners to understand.

Comma use follows English punctuation rules with one exception. Journalistic style does not place a comma after the last item in a series unless it is a long, complicated series or would confuse readers if the comma were not there:

> The new band uniforms are red, white and blue.

> Journalistic-style sentences are written in subject-verb-object style, use active verbs and contain little punctuation.

Colons and semicolons are used sparingly because they create more complex sentence structures:

> Journalistic-style sentences are written in subject-verb-object order; use colorful, action verbs; and do not use symbols for percent, cents or degrees.

The dollar sign is the only sign used in print stories. *Percent, cents, degree* and the numbers in fractions are written as words. In broadcast scripts, all words—even the word *dollars*—are written out to make it easier for the newscaster to read aloud.

Headlines have special style and punctuation rules. You'll find them in Chapter 16.

Do the following exercises on a separate sheet of paper.

1. Write more specific, descriptive terms for these weasel words:

some	few
many	soon
various	sometime
different	fun
around (time)	a lot

2. Write a simpler way to express each of the following:

for this reason	accomplished
at regular intervals	in addition to
a majority of	all of a sudden
a sufficient number of	encounter
detailed information	transmit
taking into consideration	cooperation
when asked he said	evacuate

3. Rewrite these phrases eliminating the redundancies. Be sure you do not lose any meaning.

a bald-headed man	in a dying condition
Christmas day	repeat again
enrolled students	a rich widow woman
two complimentary passes	a complete monopoly
his final conclusion	from both students
reason was because of	and teachers
new bride	old traditions
free pass	first began
the month of February	the state of Alabama

4. Rewrite these sentences changing them to active sentences.

    a. Political correctness was the intention of the students.

    b. Raising enough money for a trip to Disneyland was the goal of band members.

    c. The family was forced to flee by the flooding Ohio River.

    d. It was revealed last week that bills could no longer be paid by Orange County.

    e. Five hundred yearbooks have been recalled by Greenwood High School administrators after they discovered that several photos of her rivals were allegedly defaced by one of last year's editors.

5. Rewrite these sentences into clearer, more concise sentences. You may choose to divide each example into more than one sentence.

    a. The focus on school life beyond academic concerns Principal Larry Smith brought to U-High will continue after he leaves, students and teachers hope.

    b. Hawthorne High seniors can sit back and relax now that this year is almost ancient history.

    c. After high school when people no longer have these goals to work toward their motivation falls and high school becomes the best year of their lives because they were acknowledged for their success through competition.

    d. By the end of the month of May, the administrator should have a team of experts; and throughout the summer months, and the first three months of the next school year, community input will be gathered.

    e. After the 1992 games in Alberville, France, the winter Olympics circus now moves to the small Norwegian town of Lillehammer, only two years after the last, not the normal four years, due to a change by International Olympics Committee.

    f. The first offense is a punishment of ten hours of community service and the second time a person is caught without a parental note giving permission to be out after curfew because of school functions, community events, the exercise of First Amendment rights, emergencies, and jobs, s/he will be sent to the city court system according to a recent *Times* article.

    g. There are many different organizations that arrange foreign exchanges, and, depending on the organization, there are several different requirements that an applicant must meet.

    h. The conference opens Friday night with the keynote address by Dr. Ferenc Szasz, professor of history, who will speak about "The Day the Sun Rose Twice" in the French Memorial Chapel at 7:30 p.m.

▲AVOIDING BIAS IN LANGUAGE

Are you a knowledge-base nonpossessor? Not if you've made it this far into this book, you're not! A knowledge-base nonpossessor is a person, especially a student, who knows nothing about a given subject, according to *The Official Politically Correct Dictionary and Handbook*. People would rather be called *knowledge-base nonpossessors* than *ignorant*, even though the dictionary defines *ignorant* as "lacking knowledge." *Knowledge-base nonpossessor* sounds less offensive than *ignorant*.

In today's multiculturally sensitive world, reporters must use **bias-free language** that does not offend individuals or groups. This inclusive language treats individuals of different genders, races, cultures and abilities equally. It avoids offending or alienating members of the audience.

Bias-free language has become the norm since women's rights supporters raised the issue in the 1960s and 1970s. People agreed that men and women have the right to be addressed in equal terms, yet members of both genders recognized that the language itself prevented that in many cases. In response, the media revised style rules that treated people differently. They began with the question of what to do about courtesy titles. Traditionally, men had been identified by first and last name, and married women had been identified by their husbands' names: *Jerry Wall, Mrs. Jerry Wall, Mr. and Mrs. Jerry Wall*. Single women were identified as *Miss: Miss Anna V. Jennings*.

Some publications and newsrooms solved the dilemma by eliminating courtesy titles and using first names for both men and women: Jerry and Tammie Wall. Others offered *Ms.* as an optional courtesy title for women: Ms. Anna V. Jennings. This avoided courtesy titles that declared a woman's marital status, making a statement which many felt was discriminatory.

Other problems created by the desire to eliminate bias in language are more difficult to solve with a style rule. Prior to the women's movement of the 1960s and 1970s, masculine pronouns and masculine-based nouns like *mankind* were accepted as normal in references to groups of people that included members of both sexes. But how can this bias be avoided?

Substituting *humankind* for *mankind* and *mail carrier* for *mailman* helps. However, the problem of gender-based pronouns like *he* and *she* remains. For instance, the following sentence implies that all the students are male:

> The student should bring his book to class.

Using *her* instead of *his* would not solve the problem. Using both—*his or her* or *s/he*—is awkward and takes up extra space. A better solution is to change the subject to the plural—in this case, *students*. Then the pronoun becomes *their*, which is plural, in spite of common usage today. *Their* should not be used with a singular antecedent:

> **Incorrect:** The student should bring their book to class.

> **Correct:** Students should bring their books to class.

Changing a noun or pronoun to plural may make it necessary to change other words in the sentence from singular to plural:

---

bias-free language

inclusive language that treats individuals of different genders, races, cultures and abilities equally and that is not offensive to individuals or groups

Incorrect: Playing in an athletic competition such as football not only frees a student's mind from the stress of life but can also get the student a full-ride scholarship to a college of their choice.

Correct: Playing in athletic *competitions* such as football games not only frees *students' minds* from the stresses of life but can also get *students* full-ride *scholarships* to the *colleges they* choose.

Try to avoid sexist language by eliminating unnecessary descriptions. For example, saying *female lawyer* or *blonde surgeon* shows bias. The person's job performance has nothing to do with gender or hair color. Also make sure you use parallel adjectives. The female counterpart to the *men's* basketball team is the *women's* basketball team, not the *girl's* basketball team. Avoid the term *coed*. It has negative overtones for women.

Using concise language is another way to avoid bias. Someone who is *disabled* has a condition that interferes with that person's ability to do certain things independently. That does not mean the person is *handicapped. Handicapped* is vague; *disabled* is preferred. The *Associated Press Stylebook and Libel Manual* suggests avoiding either term unless it is clearly pertinent to the story. However, if it is necessary in the context of the story to include the fact that someone has a disability, then state clearly what the physical impairment is and how much it affects the person's performance. *Blind,* for instance, means that a person has complete loss of sight. *Partially blind* is the correct term for those individuals who have some ability to see. *Dumb* as in *deaf and dumb* is imprecise and derogatory. Use *speech-impaired* to be more accurate. Check a dictionary or stylebook for the correct use of terms to describe persons with disabilities.

Terms referring to nationalities and races have changed with the movement toward bias-free language, too. *African American* is preferred to *black* or *Negro,* and *Native American* has replaced *American Indian.* Check the most recent edition of your stylebook for the preferred terminology for nationalities and races. Also watch for hidden bias. A *Los Angeles Times* book of identification guidelines issued in the mid-1990s, for example, instructs reporters to avoid such culturally biased terms as *Welsher* and *Dutch treat.*

Identifying persons by race is as inappropriate as referring to them by hair color unless it is important to the story. Identifying a person's race is acceptable in stories that involve individuals' exceptional feats or achievements or when the identification provides insight into conflicting emotions that may have been the cause of conflict.

In a story about Rosa Parks, the African-American woman who started the civil rights movement in the United States by refusing to give up her seat on a bus, it would be important to know her race. It would not be as important to know she was an African American if the story were about the thousands of people who ride buses to work every day:

Unnecessary identification by race: Rosa Parks, an African American, rides a bus to work.

Appropriate identification by race: Rosa Parks, the African-American woman credited with starting the movement toward racial equality in the United States when she refused to give up her seat on a bus, rides a bus to work.

Politically Correct

Dean Kagan, distinguished faculty, parents, friends, graduating seniors, Secret Service agents, class agents, people of class, people of color, colorful people, people of height, the vertically constrained, people of hair, the differently coifed, the optically challenged, the temporarily sighted, the insightful, the out of sight, the out-of-towners, the Eurocentrics, the Afrocentrics, the Afrocentrics with Eurail passes, the eccentrically inclined, the sexually disinclined, people of sex, sexy people, sexist pigs, animal companions, friends of the earth, friends of the boss, the temporarily employed, the differently employed, the differently optioned, people with options, people with stock options, the divestiturists, the deconstructionists, the home constructionists, the home boys, the homeless, the temporarily housed at home, and God save us, the permanently housed at home.

Source: Reprinted from the introduction to a speech by Doonesbury cartoonist Gary Trudeau at a Yale University Class Day.

1. Rewrite these sentences to make them bias free and grammatically correct.
   a. The ninth grade students sent the letters to the school in each town telling about his school, community and himself.
   b. The ordinance will demand more manpower and more resources and require a heavier workload for policemen.
   c. The ladies of the Spirit Squad were greeted by the visiting cheerleaders.
   d. The school offers counseling services to blind and crippled students who seek them out.
   e. Companies work hard to get kids to get their own credit card.
   f. Overjoyed with excitement, the player jumps up and down to show the satisfaction with themselves and then removes the helmet from the sweaty head under it. Long blonde hair tumbles out. Yes, you guessed right. It is a girl.

2. Analyze this headline from the point of view of language bias:

   13% of coeds need remedial courses

   The article accompanying the headline refers to "undergraduates" and to "all college students." It breaks the 13 percent down by racial minorities but does not give numbers for men and women.

WORKING WITH COPY

copy
> the written form in which a story, headline, caption or advertisement is prepared

Copy is the journalistic term for the written form in which a story, headline, caption or advertisement is prepared. Whether written with a pencil and paper, typed on a typewriter or composed on a computer screen, the resulting words and paragraphs are called copy.

Computers and word processors have made formatting copy easy. Staffs using completely computerized production systems may edit stories and pages on the computer screen and may never work with **hard copy,** or paper copy. Other staffs may prefer to edit from the printed page even though the copy is prepared on the computer.

hard copy
> copy appearing on paper, as opposed to copy on a computer screen

Formatting Copy

If a computer pagination program is used to place stories directly on the page, the margins, indentations, and appearance of the copy are determined by the pagination program. The look of the type, the size of the type, the margins and the spacing are preset in the computer. Editors check the hard copy for factual and grammatical errors in the story and ignore indentations and spacing.

If your staff, teacher or technology requires stories formatted in the style traditionally used in newsrooms, follow these guidelines:

byline
> the name of the person who wrote a story, usually printed along with the story

- type the copy using a typewriter or a computer
- double-space the copy
- leave wide margins, at least 1¼ inches on all sides
- type the **byline** (the name of the person who wrote the story—in this case, your name) in the upper left corner of the page

+ type the date and a **slug** (a word or words identifying the story, which will not be printed), below your name. For example,

Jesse Dimas
Jan. 10
Semester Tests

+ begin the story just above the middle of the first page
+ mark the bottom of each page with an end mark; if additional pages follow, write MORE. Mark the last page with END, -30-, ###, or -0-.
+ in the upper left corner of subsequent pages, put your name, the date, the story slug and page number.

A **dateline** may be typed before the beginning of a story to indicate where it was written. Datelines do not appear on stories written in the city in which the paper is printed. Therefore, unless the staff reprints a story from another newspaper or a reporter covers a game or school activity that takes place in another town, there are usually no datelines in school papers.

If used, a dateline includes the name of the city or place where the story originated written in all capital letters followed by a comma, the state's abbreviation (if the city is not well known) in capital and lowercase letters, and a dash: FRANKFORT, Ky.—.

slug

words that identify a story from the time it is assigned to the reporter until it is placed on the page

dateline

the place a story was written; appears at the beginning of stories that are not written locally

Editing

Each time the reporter chooses one word instead of another, editing is taking place. Each time the reporter rewrites a sentence or a lead, substitutes a more specific word for a weasel word, or checks the pronunciation or spelling of a word, editing is taking place. Reporters edit as they write. They edit as they proofread stories before submitting them to the editor.

Technology has changed the way editing takes place in most newsrooms. When stories were written on typewriters and edited before being given to someone else to set in type, the editing was done with a pencil on the typed copy. Newspapers had copy editors who read all the stories for factual accuracy and for spelling, grammar and punctuation errors. Editors and reporters used standardized symbols, called **copyediting symbols,** to communicate the changes they wanted made on the final copy. (See Figure 8.2 on page 200 for a key to copyediting symbols.)

Today many newspapers assign page editors the responsibility of editing the stories on their pages. The page editors edit the stories on the computer screen, and neither the reporter nor the editor handles hard copy.

However, reporters and copy editors sometimes prefer to proofread from hard copy rather than on the computer screen. The copyediting symbols still provide a common language through which those journalists communicate desired changes and corrections. Journalists should become familiar with the copyediting symbols and use them when working with hard copy.

copyediting symbol

a standard symbol used to make a correction or change on hard copy; a symbolic language used by reporters and editors working with hard copy

Figure 8.2
Copyediting Symbols with Example of Edited Story

Function	Description of Symbol	Example
Abbreviate	Circle word to be abbreviated	(Doctor) Smith
Boldface	Squiggly line under	Set this in boldface type.
Capitalize	Three lines under	1600 pennsylvania ave.
Change letter	Carats above and below, letter above	advi_e
Change word	Line through, new word in bracket above	She left [today] ~~yesterday~~
Close up space between words	Line through space, bridge space	The car was totally ⌣destroyed.
Close up space within word	Bridge space	Neil Arms⌣trong walked on the Moon.
Continued on next page	More, circled	(More)
Delete letter	Line through letter, bridge space	The do_g barked lo_udly.
Delete phrase	Line through phrase, bridge space	Don't use redundant ~~or~~ ~~repetitious~~ words or phrases.
Delete punctuation	Line through punctuation, bridge space	I said, it was acceptable
End of story	# # #, or –30–, or –0–, or END (all circled)	(# # #) (–30–) (–0–) (END)
Ignore correction	Stet, circled	Do ~~not~~ change this. (stet)
Insert apostrophe or quotation marks	Carat with mark above line of type	"It's acceptable to use contractions."
Insert comma, colon, or exclamation mark	Carat with punctuation mark below line of type	Add punctuation: comma, colon or exclamation mark.
Insert dash, hyphen	Carat above and below line, hyphen symbol above	The 3 year old child
Insert letter	Carat above and below, letter above	The student failed te class.

Function	Description of Symbol	Example
Insert period	Period or X, circled	Michael J.Fox was here.
Insert word	New word in bracket above line, carat below line	Add my name here.
Italics	Solid line below	Please print this.
Lowercase	Slash through	The Mayor spoke.
No new paragraph, bring copy together	Line connecting	The mayor spoke to the crowd at the airport. He had just returned from Japan.
Separate words	Straight line, pound sign (optional)	Journalists are writers.
Spell out	Circle word or number to be spelled out	Jan., Feb., 5 days
Start new paragraph	Indent (⌐) sign, ¶ sign	President Abraham Lincoln spoke … ¶ "Four score and seven years ago …
Transpose letters or words	Transposition sign	journalits, Lincon Four score and seven ago years...

Function	Edited Story	Correct Format
spell out	Officers from the OPD recsued a	Oakland Police Department
capitalize letter	german shepherd from a burning	German shepherd
abbreviate	home at 1001 Main Street about	Main St.
lowercase letter	1 P.M. Saturday.	1 p.m.
indent	Battalion Chief Joe Schissler said	Battalion Chief ...
	neighbors reported the fire and	
insert letter, close space	tht three children might be in side.	that, inside
	Schissler said officers searched for	
bring copy together	the children	the children but found only ...
add period	but found only the cowering dog	dog.
add a space	Schissler said the fire started on	Schissler said
insert punctuation	a bed in the basement apparently	the basement, apparently
transpose	from smoking materials.	materials.
change word	Schissler said a mother and three	woman
delete letter	childreen live in the house, but	children
restore marked out letters	authorities did not have her name.	not, her name.
end of story	# # #	

1. Use the stylebook following Chapter 20 to identify the errors in style in these sentences. Rewrite the sentences, and use copyediting symbols to correct the errors.

   a. The game was played on October 25, 1999, at 2 p.m.
   b. Jerome R Walford Junior was arested after he bit off a dog' ear.
   c. She si the number one stude nt in her clss.
   d. The United States Army cancelled all all maneauvers until further notice.
   e. The Hurricane, which hit Texas on monday and LA on tu3esday, left at least 9 dead.
   f. He said he had recieved over 40% of the money as of 12 p.m.
   g. She lives at number 5 Shamrock road.
   h. A 5 year old boy was hit by a car at the intersection of Pine and elm Streets.
   i. 10,000 People attended last nights game at Wrigley Field.
   j. Five people survived the accident in New York, New York on Easter Sunday.

2. Test your spelling skills. One word in each line is misspelled. Identify the misspelled word, and write it correctly. Try to do this without consulting a dictionary. Then check your work with the dictionary.

   a. interpret, manifest, leutenant, occur
   b. receipt, clothes, cemetery, oblidged
   c. accomodate, acceptable, heart, yield
   d. judgment, campaign, conscience, beverege
   e. goverment, exception, character, weird
   f. cafeteria, maintanance, connection, flier
   g. chasity, heir, invoice, memorial
   h. milage, shiny, quite, receipt
   i. library, Feburary, contrary, luxury
   j. tentative, procede, precede, privilege

3. Find the word or words in each of the following examples that are used incorrectly. Rewrite the sentences using the correct words.

   a. Any high school science teacher knows that showing students a formula for oxidation is likely to illicit blank stares, grimaces and even a yawn or two.
   b. "I'm not a member of any sect or cliché," he said.
   c. It was only after the touch of her shower spicket shocked her arm into numbness that she became fearful.
   d. Robert Wagner had his hair curled and died for his role in *Beneath the Twelve-Mile Reef.*
   e. The school principal caused an electrical ark when he put a piece of medal in the microwave oven.

4. Write a simpler way to express each of the following:

   at that time
   a small number of
   any one of the two
   told his listeners that
   once in a great while
   tendered his resignation
   not any one of the two
   is of the opinion that
   united in holy matrimony
   on one occasion
   in the near future

   at the present time
   all of a sudden
   during the time that
   taken to jail and locked up
   was able to make his escape
   uniform in both size and shape
   gave birth to a little baby boy

5. Write these expressions eliminating unnecessary words.

   returned back home
   set a new record
   throughout the entire day
   his other alternative
   in the year 2000
   owns a private yacht
   during the course of the day
   wore a white goatee on his chin
   throughout the length and breadth of the entire nation

   past history shows
   wearing a happy smile on her face
   assembled crowd of people
   red-colored cloth
   was circular in shape
   in the city of Los Angeles
   is in the process of negotiating with
   is located next to the bank

CHAPTER REVIEW

KEY TERMS

Show that you know the meanings of the following key terms by correctly using them in complete sentences. Write your answers on a separate sheet of paper.

stylebook	copy	dateline
style	hard copy	copyediting symbol
redundancy	byline	
bias-free language	slug	

OPEN FORUM

1. Analyze your local newspaper's style for using courtesy titles. What does the policy seem to be? Are there exceptions or inconsistencies? If so, where do they occur? (*Hint:* Style sometimes varies from section to section.) Why do you think the newspaper has chosen the style it is using?

2. After you think you know what the newspaper's style for courtesy titles is, call the editor and ask for a copy of the style guide for that newspaper. Also ask the editor to explain any special style choices the newspaper has adopted.

3. Discuss your school media's policies on bias-free language. If there is no policy, write one. Don't forget to include features such as student surveys and photos or graphics that may be offensive or hurtful to individuals or groups in your audience.

4. Critique your school media stylebooks. Are there things you would change, include or exclude? Why or why not? Write your suggestions, with an explanation for each, and submit them to the staffs.

5. Obtain stylebooks from the media staffs at other schools. Make a list of policies and style rules included in these stylebooks that are not in your school's stylebooks. With the staff, discuss whether similar rules should be in your school stylebooks. If the group decides that some rules should be included, draft the copy.

FINDING THE FLAW

The Associated Press distributes stories worldwide to member newspapers. Each newspaper chooses stories to reprint according to the size of the news hole that day. Many papers will print the same story, but each paper may edit the story to match the style of the paper and to fit the amount of space available.

Here is an AP story as it was reprinted in two newspapers. Identify the differences in the two stories. Why do you think there are differences? Are the differences in style? Grammar? Content? In those places where the stories are different, is one correct and the other incorrect? Why or why not?

Nation's Oldest Mayor A Man for '90s in His 90s

MCCALL, Idaho (AP)—Some men make mountains. Others make excuses.

John Allen makes a martini and watches the world go by.

"I haven't got any worries now," he says. "I've lived too long."

At 91, Allen is said to be the oldest mayor in the United States. His only competition for that title was 90-year-old Andrew Gowans, who recently quit as mayor of Weir, Kan., to serve on the city council.

These are heady times for McCall. Shops in this sleepy mountain town at the tip of central Idaho's Long Valley are bustling. And retailers say a proposed year-round resort to the north could double—even triple—business. Others worry that growth will spoil the town's appeal.

But Allen is in no hurry. He meets with City Administrator Bud Schmidt at City Hall several times a week "so I know pretty much what's going on."

He signs the city's checks and raps the gavel at council meetings. He cajoles neighbors to serve on thankless committees. They rarely refuse.

And while Allen plays down his role, others insist that he's the right man at the right time for McCall, a man for the '90s in his 90s.

"I told him this is no time to retire just because you're 91," says Schmidt, 47. "Compared to him, I'm a mere child. He's seen how the circle comes around, that there's some projects you don't push, that they'll happen in their own time.

Allen, the son of a judge, graduated from the University of California in law and won his first political race at 23—a 1922 school board election in Oakland, Calif. After serving in the South Pacific during World War II, he was elected to Congress in 1946.

He lost his seat in 1958, but was quickly named undersecretary of commerce for the final two years of the Eisenhower administration.

Allen confounds expectations.

He is the last Republican to represent Oakland and Berkeley, home of the free-speech movement and the Black Panthers.

"He's always had exceptional tolerance for diversity and been open-minded," said his daughter Sally Ann Hess of Riverside, Calif. "I know he's a conservative Republican and all, but he's always enjoyed learning about new ways to do things."

Allen and his first wife, Carol, had two daughters. When she died

♦ **FINDING THE FLAW, continued**

of a heart attack in 1957, he remarried a year later to Sally Clement, a watercolor painter who is 24 years younger than him. They had three more daughters.

After retiring from his Oakland law practice in 1969, Allen and his family moved to McCall, where he immediately was asked to join the senior citizens center. Allen, then 70, said, "You know, I have a first-grader at home. I think I better wait."

When townspeople asked him to run for mayor four years ago, he relented and won by a 2-to-1 margin. "We're not looking at him as just an old fossil," said Tom Grote, publisher of the Central Idaho Star-News, "but as a source of knowledge and expertise."

Allen's term expires at the end of the year, and some in town are anxious to see him run again. Allen has decided only one thing.

"Last time I stood for election. This time I'll probably sit."

Source: Reprinted with permission from Associated Press, from Cliff Hadley, "Nation's Oldest Mayor, A Man for '90s in his 90s,"—*Omaha World Herald*.

Oldest mayor, 91, ponders next step

MCCALL, Idaho—Some men make mountains. Others make excuses.

John Allen makes a martini and watches the world go by.

"I haven't got any worries now," he says. "I've lived too long."

At 91, Allen is said to be the oldest mayor in the United States. His only competition for that title was a kid in Kansas, 90-year-old Andrew Gowans, who quit as mayor of Weir recently to serve on the city council.

These are heady times for McCall. Shops in this sleepy little town at the tip of central Idaho's Long Valley are bustling. And retailers say a proposed Valbois year-round resort to the north could double—even triple—business. Others worry that growth will spoil the town's appeal.

But Allen is in no hurry. He meets with City Administrator Bud Schmidt at City Hall several times a week "so I know pretty much what's going on."

He signs the city's checks and raps the gavel at council meetings. He cajoles neighbors to serve on thankless committees. They rarely refuse.

And while Allen plays down his role, others insist he's the right man at the right time for McCall, a man for the '90s in his 90s.

"I told him this is no time to retire just because you're 91," says Schmidt, 47. "Compared to him, I'm a mere child. He's seen how the circle comes around, that there's some projects you don't push, that they'll happen in their own time."

Allen, the son of a judge, graduated from the University of California in law and won his first political race at 23—a 1922 school board election in Oakland, Calif. After serving in the South Pacific during World War II, he was elected to Congress in 1946.

A fellow freshman Republican in the California delegation gave his photo to Allen. "It's signed, 'To the noblest statesman of them all—Dick Nixon.'"

Allen lost his seat in 1958, but was quickly appointed under secretary of commerce for transportation for the final two years of the Eisenhower administration.

Allen confounds expectations.

He is the last Republican to represent Oakland and Berkeley, home

◆ **FINDING THE FLAW,** continued

of the free-speech movement and the Black Panthers.

"He's always had exceptional tolerance for diversity and been open-minded," says daughter Sally Ann Hess of Riverside, Calif. "I know he's a conservative Republican and all, but he's always enjoyed learning about new ways to do things."

Allen and his first wife, Carol, had a pair of daughters. When she died of a heart attack in 1957, he remarried a year later to Sally Clement, a watercolor painter who is 24 years younger. They had three more daughters.

After retiring from his Oakland law practice in 1969, he and his family moved to McCall, where he immediately was asked to join the senior citizens center. Allen, then 70, said, "You know, I have a first grader at home. I think I better wait."

When townspeople begged him to run for mayor four years ago, he relented and won by a 2-to-1 margin.

His term is up at the end of the year, and some in town are anxious to see him run again. Allen has decided only one thing.

"Last time I stood for election. This time I'll probably sit."

Source: Reprinted with permission from Associated Press, from Cliff Hadley, "Oldest mayor, 91, ponders next step,"—*Grand Island (Nebraska) Independent.*

 MEDIA WATCH

1. Find examples of as many of these style rules as possible in one newspaper or news magazine:
   ◆ time: *a.m., p.m., noon, midnight*
   ◆ dates when written with month, day and year
   ◆ ages used with names and used to describe unnamed persons (for example, *a 5-year-old*)
   ◆ addresses that include street names and numbers
   ◆ temperatures written in weather reports (not charts)
   ◆ money in cents, dollars and millions of dollars
   ◆ state names when used with a city and when used alone

   Is the publication following AP style or another style? Look through the publication for more examples. Is the publication consistent with the rules? Find examples of these style rules in another publication. Are these rules consistent with AP style? With that of the first publication? If the second publication appears to be using AP style, why do you think the staff has chosen it? If it does not use AP style, why not?

2. Listen to a newscast. What style is the station using for courtesy titles? Try to identify other style rules in use by the station (you may include weather or sports). Compare the style used by a local station on a local newscast with the style used by a national news

◆ MEDIA WATCH, CONTINUED

channel or network newscast. What differences do you hear in style? Why do you think the style is the same—or different, if that's the case—for the local and national news broadcasters?

3. Look at the newspaper or watch television news for examples of incorrect use of words like *their* and other grammatical problems created by the attempts to be free of bias. Make a list of the errors you find. Write corrections.

4. Senior citizens can be referred to as *older Americans* to avoid the negative connotations of terms like *the elderly* or *the aged*. However, some publications go to extremes in their attempts to avoid bias and come up with such terms as *the chronologically gifted*. Nudists have even been said to be practicing *clothing optional recreation*. Look through your newspaper or a news magazine for other currently popular terms used in an attempt to avoid bias. With the staffs of your school media, discuss which terms you think your school media should or should not use.

String Book

You may use any newspapers for this activity, including school newspapers. Clip the page header with the name and date of the newspaper for each article; keep it with the example.

1. Clip examples of what you believe is well-written news copy. Make notes about each example that point out the characteristics that make it well written, such as active verbs, no weasel words, correct style, correct spelling and concise word choice.

2. Clip examples of "how not to do it." Include examples of the following:
    ◆ wordy phrases, sentences or paragraphs
    ◆ redundant phrases
    ◆ clichés
    ◆ style or editing problems or inconsistencies
    ◆ inaccuracies in fact (*Hint:* look for corrections the newspaper runs)
    ◆ misspellings
    ◆ misplaced modifiers
    ◆ bias in language
    ◆ typographical or computer-generated errors

3. Create a sample of the correct way to format news copy to be used as an example in your publication's stylebook. Put a copy in your stringbook.

Chapter 9
In-Depth Reporting

"Journalism gives its greatest respect and its highest honors to those who dig the deepest."

Melvin Mencher, journalism professor, Columbia University

LEARNING OBJECTIVES

After completing this chapter, you will be able to:

◆ find ideas for in-depth and investigative stories,

◆ expand and enhance your interviewing and news-gathering techniques,

◆ build longer stories using a variety of methods other than the inverted pyramid.

◆

KEY TERMS

In this chapter, you will learn the meaning of these terms:

in-depth reporting
investigative reporting
anecdote
point of view

*R*eporters strive to uncover hidden truths or seek out answers to difficult and complicated questions. Under the right circumstances (a promising story or a supportive editor, for example), their efforts can result in long stories called *in-depth reports*. Sometimes those efforts lead to investigative stories that expose wrongdoing or poor decision making.

In any event, creating these in-depth stories involves the skills you've learned in previous chapters—sound interviewing and research, plus careful and accurate writing. But it also requires some special storytelling techniques and plenty of patience.

Some high schools do not make in-depth journalism a significant part of their campus coverage, but many do, as you will see in this chapter. The chapter examines how reporters find in-depth subjects, how they adapt their reporting techniques to fit longer and more challenging stories, and how they go beyond the traditional inverted pyramid structure to create suspense and interest for the reader.

◢TACKLING THE IN-DEPTH STORY

Covering meetings, press conferences and other news events is the most basic responsibility of the journalist. But the news media would be dull if reporters never ventured beyond those obvious stories. Fortunately, most news organizations devote a portion of their resources to **in-depth reporting.** In-depth stories present a thorough examination of an issue or event, drawing on many different sources of information including both people and documents. Reporters dig below the surface to find special or unusual stories that a superficial glance might miss. Such stories require strong reporting skills, initiative and creativity.

In-depth reporting requires many of the same techniques used in daily reporting. But in-depth stories take more time, effort and energy than usual. Such stories provide a deeper understanding of a person, issue or event. They can expose an injustice or celebrate the remarkable; they can make people laugh or move them to tears.

in-depth reporting

reporting and writing in which reporters dig beneath the surface to provide a deeper understanding of a person, issue or event. In-depth reports present a thorough examination of an issue or event, drawing on many different sources of information

Finding Stories to Cover

Ideas for in-depth stories are everywhere. Look around. Observe your friends and classmates. Do they feel unsafe on campus or elsewhere in the community? If so, examine the rise in youth violence. Are your classrooms overcrowded? Explore how student-teacher ratios can affect your school's quality of education.

Staffs that produce the best publications stay in touch with national events and trends to find subjects for their stories, according to Nick Ferentinos, past president of the Columbia Scholastic Press Association. They find a local angle to keep their readers aware of what is happening in the world.

You can localize state or national stories by exploring how a large issue might affect your community. For example, teen pregnancy has become a national concern, with everyone from local health officials to members of Congress searching for solutions. You might examine teen pregnancy in your community. Are the numbers of pregnant teens growing? What are teenagers' attitudes toward having children? What are local schools, health officials and parents doing to address the issue?

Following current events in the news media can be a great way to develop in-depth story ideas. Look at the headlines for key words such as *teen, teenage, youth* or *students*. Look for subjects such as education, health, the environment or technology. Think about how the following topics in the national media could be turned into excellent in-depth stories:

- The *New York Times* reported that teens with school days that begin very early are likely to be sleep deprived. Teens need more sleep than adults, the article asserted, yet in many communities schools start early in order to leave time for extracurricular programs. Thus, millions of high school students arrive droopy-eyed and less than alert. Talk to local experts, including physicians and psychologists who specialize in sleep disorders, to find out how those in your community view the problem.

Are these students bored, tired or just not listening?

✦ Another article in the *Times* reported a dress-code fight in Massachusetts over a "Coed Naked" T-shirt. Meanwhile, many public figures and school officials are saying they support the idea of uniforms in schools. Explore your school's policy on student dress. Find out what parents, teachers and administrators say about uniforms. Compare those findings with what students tell you about their feelings on the issue.

✦ "You've got jail." A New Jersey programmer pleaded guilty to creating the "Melissa" computer virus and spreading it through cyberspace where it did more than $80 million damage. Students are often avid computer users and news stories involving many kinds of computer issues should be high interest items.

Another way to find good ideas for in-depth reports is to talk frequently with those in authority or those who are well-informed about their communities. School employees and officials can be important sources for good ideas. Cultivate relations with people who seem to be in touch with what is going on, and talk to them regularly about story ideas.

School programs provide interesting stories as well. Investigate your school's new bilingual classes, its drug prevention efforts or its sex education program. What's working, what isn't and why?

A patient, dedicated reporter can also find good stories in school budgets and other financial records. Many reporters, intimidated and confused by financial documents, avoid such material. Don't be one of them. All student reporters should know how their school districts spend their money. Such information reveals your school district's priorities in a clear and undeniable way.

Check your school's teacher salaries, and compare them with state or national figures. Compare funds for athletic programs with money budgeted for other school programs. Find out how much your school district spends per student on instruction, and compare that with spending in other school districts. Other financial records may also be worth checking. Expense forms, for example, show what school teachers and administrators spend on travel and training.

Not long ago the *Chicago Sun-Times* reported that the Chicago public school system spent more than $4 million for travel, convention and dining expenses over two years. That occurred even though the school system was in a severe financial crisis. As a result of the two-part series, the school board cut the system's travel budget and adopted a new travel policy.

Let Your Fingers Do the Walking

It's surprising how many times reporters overlook the telephone book in trying to conduct research. You can use it, for example, to check the spelling of a name or find an address. Most phone books have city maps, street directories and lists of government agencies, as well as information on local attractions, parks, playgrounds, recreation areas and recycling sites.

Many large cities have reverse phone books, which list telephone numbers by address. You can use this kind of directory to obtain a phone number if you have only an individual's address. You can also use it to verify an address or find other phone numbers for the same address.

Many urban areas also have a *Polk's City Directory* or social directory ("blue book") that lists an individual's occupation and home or business ownership. Taken as a group, these resources give the reporter another way to answer questions. Any information you can find through public documents means one fewer question you have to ask of a source and thus frees up time during an interview for more interesting questions.

What Some Schools Are Doing

In-depth stories can take many different forms. A full-page story in the *U-High Midway* on school security offered a sweeping portrayal of the problems violence was bringing to the school and its students. Reporters interviewed dozens of sources, including the mayor, parents,

DATELINE
DATELINE
DATELINE

UNITED STATES, 1893–1912—
A few magazines became instigators for social reform in the
early years of the 20th century.
Their style of investigative
reporting was labeled "muckraking" by President Theodore
Roosevelt. Roosevelt said the
reporters were like the Man with
the Muckrake in *Pilgrim's Progress*.
Instead of looking up to the
heavens, the man continued to
dredge up the dirt as he raked
through the muck. Although
intended as an insult, Roosevelt's
remark became a badge of honor
with those writers whose work
exposed the unethical practices
of big business and unscrupulous
politicians.

McClure's, started in 1893 in
New York as an illustrated
monthly magazine, became the
leader in the muckraking efforts.
It published exposés on the
Standard Oil Company by Ida
M. Tarbell, on municipal corruption in St. Louis and other major
midwestern cities and on unethical practices by labor unions
and railroads.

Tarbell was the only woman
in her class at Pennsylvania's
Allegheny College. She had
worked as a freelance writer in
Paris, submitting articles to
McClure's and several newspapers. In 1894 she joined the staff
of *McClure's* as an associate editor. The 19-part series on
Standard Oil, which cemented
her reputation as a muckraker,
began running in 1904. The
Supreme Court verified Tarbell's
work in 1911, when it declared
Standard Oil a monopoly and
ordered it broken up.

law enforcement officials, school administrators and the students of
several nearby schools to develop a comprehensive look at both the
threat of violence and the security measures designed to defuse such
threats.

The *Little Hawk*, at City High School in Iowa City, Iowa, devoted an
entire front page to the nationwide debate over gun control. The main
story had quotations from a local gun store owner, police officers and
a candidate for U.S. marshall. It also had a brief recap of federal legislation, including the Brady Bill. A sidebar on the bottom third of the
page presented a fascinating interview with a witness to a gruesome
shooting spree in a classroom at the University of Iowa.

In-depth stories often appear in the centerfold rather than on the
front page. In that way schools can devote two full pages to the stories.
Frequently, the topic is broken down into several different stories.
"Family Ties" was an in-depth project in the *Crier*, the newspaper at
Munster High School in Munster, Indiana. The project offered a feature
story on sibling rivalry, a clever sidebar on birth order ("Older children
tend to be higher achievers"), a gripping story on coping with divorce
and a chart on family values.

At Hastings High School in Hastings, Nebraska, the *Tiger Cub*
devoted two pages to a teenager's love affair with the telephone. Stories
in the two-page spread included a look at new phone technology, a
humorous investigation of 1-900 numbers, a feature on psychic lines,
an up-to-the-minute account of modems and on-line computer services, and a lively photo-opinion box headed by the question, "What
would your life be like if you didn't have a phone?"

Sharpening the Focus

Be flexible. Your search for information may lead to a story you
never expected to find. But once you have settled on an idea, tighten
your focus. What do you want the story to explore? What main point
do you want to convey? Focus on a small piece of a broad issue. A story
about violence in school, for example, could be narrowed to an exploration of gangs, disciplinary procedures or police resource officers.

Start small, and move on to more difficult projects as you gain confidence. A complex story could drain your energy and enthusiasm. A
story that overwhelms you will also overwhelm your readers.

Often team efforts work best. Three or four heads are almost always
better than one when it comes to in-depth reporting. Many schools
have found that assigning one or two reporters, a photographer and a
page designer to an in-depth project works well. A team of ten students
at Peninsula High School in Gig Harbor, Washington, won sweepstakes
honors in in-depth reporting for the Quill and Scroll Society with a
two-page spread on the realities of crime committed by teenagers. The
stories, which focused on the punishment that results from teenage
crime, were described by one judge as "insightful—and chilling."

Developing an In-Depth Report: An Example

Let's examine how one staff developed an important and challenging in-depth report. In Cape Coral, Florida, the staff of the *Seahawk's Eye* decided to devote two pages of the paper to a brave and uncompromising look at cancer. The idea may have been motivated by the battles two teachers in the school were waging against the disease, but the staff members also knew that every one of their classmates had someone in their lives—friend, relative or neighbor—who was fighting cancer.

The two-page spread contains three major stories, some student-designed artwork, a poll, two fact boxes and special headlines. In addition, the spread features an overview in the top left corner—an introduction to the spread set in larger-than-normal type. The overview reads in part:

> Cancer is a disease in which cells reproduce abnormally, destroying healthy tissue and endangering the life of that person. Cancer can affect people of all ages but especially middle-aged or elderly people.
>
> Cancer patients today have about a one out of three chance of recovering completely. Most patients, due to new technology, live much longer with proper treatment.

The overview sets the scene for what follows. To the right of the overview are two fact boxes. One covers the warning signs of cancer, and the other describes the main methods for curing cancer. Below those items is the wrenching personal account of a business teacher who survived cancer. That story contains strongly emotional passages; the following is an example:

> Business teacher Julie Hale knows first hand how cancer affects a person. Diagnosed in May 1992 with breast cancer, she had her last chemotherapy treatment in November of that same year. In that time she not only had chemo, but she also had a mastectomy, a painful process. Those seven months, she says, were, "pure Hell."

The article on the top righthand side of the spread offers a panoramic view of the national impact of cancer. The reporter cites statistics from the American Cancer Society and the *Surgeon General's Report on Nutrition and Health,* as well as several personal interviews. Below that is an extensive student poll that reveals that many students are concerned about cancer but few are aware of the causes, treatments and possible preventive measures.

Finally, the spread ends with the unusual story of a teacher who is fighting cancer with unorthodox and even illegal means. TV production teacher Ken Case discovered a sore spot under his tongue that was eventually diagnosed as cancer. But Case decided to bypass normal medical procedures:

> "I believe the cancer industry wants to restrict cancer therapy to costly chemotherapy surgery and radiation only," he says. "I think that is not the only answer, especially seeing how damaging those methods are to one's body. Chemotherapy and radiation are both known to cause cancer, and they both ruin your immune system."

The article follows Case's trip to Germany for special treatment and his self-prescribed diet of health foods and vitamins. This story on a nontraditional alternative therapy helps balance the entire spread and probably creates more reader interest. Taken as a whole, the spread is an impressive example of what in-depth reporting can accomplish.

YOUR BEAT •

1. Follow a daily newspaper for one week, cutting out articles that you think could be localized for your school community. Share and discuss the possibilities you find with other students.

2. Find a good example of an in-depth story in the local media, and make a list of all the sources mentioned in the story. Reconstruct the process the reporter might have used to research the story.

SPECIALIZED REPORTING TECHNIQUES

In-depth reporters get close to their stories by immersing themselves in the lives of their subjects. They interview many people with varied points of view and observe them in their environments. The setting can reveal information about a person's life and character, as well as what role he or she plays in the issue you're investigating. Careful observation is the key to getting a fully rounded story.

Concentrating on Details

When conducting in-depth interviews, you must often gain the confidence of the people on whom you are focusing before you can capture a picture as warm as this one. Read the story of Joe Starita's experience with Native Americans on the next page.

Reporter John Gregory Dunne once wrote that he hates to ask questions and doesn't trust the answers: "What I do is hang around. Become part of the furniture. [Be] an end table in someone's life." Dunne's quiet and unobtrusive observations often yield important insights. "What matters is that the subject bites his nails," he said. "What matters is that he wears brown shoes with a blue shirt, what matters is the egg stain on his tie, the *Reader's Digest Condensed Books* on the shelves, the copy of *Playboy* with the centerfold torn out."

Such details make a story real. Greta Tilley used details to great effect in a story she wrote about a teen suicide for the *Greensboro News and Record*. Her simple description of the teenager's room sparks emotions in the reader:

> Seven weeks have passed, yet the dim lavender room with the striped window curtains has been kept as Tonia left it.
>
> Haphazardly positioned on top of the white French provincial-style dresser are staples of teenage life: Sure deodorant, Enjoli cologne, an electric curling wand.

A white jewelry box opens to a ballerina dancing before a mirror. Inside, among watches and bracelets, is a gold Dudley High School ring with a softball player etched into one side and a Panther on the other. Also inside is a mimeographed reminder that a $9 balance must be paid in Mrs. Johnson's room for the yearbook. The deadline was Jan. 15.

In-Depth Interviews

In-depth reporting requires consistent and untiring efforts. That's what Joe Starita, a former *Miami Herald* reporter and New York bureau chief, found when he set out to write about his favorite subject—cowboys and Indians.

Starita's interest in Native Americans had been aroused by the Academy Award–winning movie *Dances with Wolves.* When he left his crime and vice beat to write a book, he knew what he wanted to do. Starita's idea was to find a Native-American family whose lives spanned the history of the West. To do so, he drove to the Pine Ridge Reservation in South Dakota and met with skeptical tribal officials. He tried to convince them to give him the names of families with interesting histories. "I think just by sheer dint of effort they became convinced I was going to do exactly what I said I was going to do," Starita says. "That was basically allowing this family to tell its story, that I would essentially be the vessel or the instrument that history passed through."

Tribal officials provided Starita with a list of about 10 families scattered across the huge reservation. Starita went door to door asking questions and seeking out the right family. On his fourth or fifth try, he found the Dull Knifes.

> Within 30 minutes of listening to the broad outline of their story, the bells and alarms started going off. It was just a wondrous thing to hear unfold for the first time.
>
> Here was a man, Guy Dull Knife Sr., whose closest neighbor was in the Battle of the Little Big Horn where Custer fell. You start hearing things like this and, if you're a writer, these are the things that get your attention.

It took a great deal of persistence on Starita's part to pry the story loose:

> It took weeks and weeks and months and months of very patient, very diligent effort to get this family to trust me. You've got to remember that the American government made 371 treaties with the Indians and broke every one.
>
> It took a long time before they would let down their guard and open up.

Eventually, the Dull Knifes drew Starita into their family circle and related the astounding story he has now shaped into several articles and a book. Starita said he filled 37 legal-sized notebooks with material he gathered from hundreds of hours of interviews.

FOIA: Four Letters That Mean Trouble for Shady Operations

"Unconstitutional and unworkable" was how President Gerald Ford described the legislation to strengthen the Freedom of Information Act (FOIA) when he vetoed it in 1974. But Congress overrode his resistance and justified the bill's passage by saying that the law "is based upon the presumption that the government and the information of government belong to the people."

Today, the FOIA is beginning to fulfill Congress's intention that the burden must be on the federal government to justify secrecy rather than on the citizen to prove why information should be available. Routinely, reporters now use the law to gather information on such matters as the effectiveness of drugs, the safety and efficiency of cars, consumer complaints, faulty products, the harmful effects of pesticides, pollution control programs and occupational safety.

investigative reporting

reporting that seeks to uncover something hidden. Investigative reporting requires that reporters learn the innermost details about how things work

DATELINE DATELINE DATELINE

NEW YORK, 1923—"When the demonstration was over and the group was departing, I saw that my boss was not really happy. I asked him what was wrong . . . he finally said, 'Good work but you should be doing something more practical.'" That, at any rate, is how Vladimir Zworykin recalled the first demonstration of his new invention, television.

The man who would earn the reputation of "Father of Television," Vladimir K. Zworykin, immigrated to the United States from Russia in 1919 at age 20. Four years later, working as an engineer for Westinghouse, Zworykin patented the first electronic camera pickup tube. The electronic tube, called an iconoscope, was the key to the television system that was adopted universally by the late 1930s.

Zworykin, one of two major U.S. inventors of electronic television, patented a color tube in 1925. He then patented the kinescope, a cathode-ray tube that functioned as the core of the receiving unit, in 1926. In 1930 he became head of a research team at RCA that spent almost a decade refining television from a 60-line picture to a 441-line picture and improving image size and brightness.

Investigative Reporting

A special variety of in-depth reporting, the kind often associated with Watergate and other government scandals, is called **investigative reporting.** Investigative reporters seek to uncover something hidden, either because no one was interested before or because someone wanted the information hidden.

The investigative reporter relies on techniques that are in the repertoire of all good journalists. Such techniques include finding sources, conducting interviews and locating relevant documents. This is why some reporters say all good reporting is investigative. But the use of these techniques in investigative reporting frequently involves an unusual dose of dedication and determination.

Investigative reporting requires that reporters learn the innermost details about how things work. Investigative reporters are shoe-leather journalists; in other words, they might wear out their shoes tracking down facts and sources. Reporters learn to find useful sources—documents, records, transcripts and so on—by learning how offices, bureaus and departments work.

At your school, all reporters, and investigative reporters in particular, should know how the school and school district are governed. They should be able to answer these questions:

+ Who makes policy decisions?
+ Who is empowered to carry out policy decisions?
+ Who are the current school board members?
+ What power does the faculty have?
+ What rights do students have?
+ Who runs student government?

The investigative reporter wants to know where power lies and needs to know the channels through which money flows. "Follow the buck" might be the motto of an investigative reporter, because money often reveals the priorities a school is setting. By analyzing a school budget, for example, some persistent reporters have learned of attempts to phase out some programs and build up others.

Vast areas of official records are open to students. All states, for example, have sunshine laws, which give the public access to an array of hearings, sessions and documents. Journalists took officials at North Carolina universities to court when they refused to allow the contracts of athletic officials to be examined. The state court ruled in favor of the journalists. Eventually, thanks to this decision, journalists in North Carolina and elsewhere found that football coaches at 26 state universities make more money than their state's governor.

Multistory Reports

"Divide and conquer" might make a good motto for in-depth reporters. When *Lincoln (Nebraska) Journal-Star* editors became increasingly concerned about a rise in gang activity, they turned to Joe Starita, then a freelance writer, to prepare an in-depth report. Starita's report eventually took the form of 10 different news stories that ran in the paper over a period of three days.

The *Journal-Star* began Starita's report in its Sunday edition with a front-page overview of local gang activity and three stories on an inside page:

- a close-up look at Asian American gangs,
- a historical look at gangs in the United States, and
- a close-up story based on interviews with two former gang members now in prison.

On Monday, day two of the report, the paper ran three more stories:

- a look at how gangs affect schools,
- a focus on a parent who has fought back by forming a chapter of MAD DAD (an organization dedicated to fighting the use of alcohol by teens), and
- an examination of why gang membership seems so alluring to some teens.

Monday's edition also featured an informational chart for parents on the warning signs of gang membership.

The report concluded on Tuesday with three stories:

- how the community is responding to increased gang activity,
- how one minister and churches in general are responding, and
- what other cities are doing.

The informational chart in this issue gave numbers and addresses to show parents where to find help.

In all, Starita contributed at least four full newspaper pages of material. He conducted more than two dozen interviews with teachers, counselors, psychologists, law enforcement officials, clergy, parents and teens. He also checked numerous local, state and national studies on the subject. Starita took the better part of two months to complete his work.

Sometimes an in-depth report covers so much ground and takes up so much space that it would be unwise to present it all as a single story. When a publication has an unusually long story, it might be best to break the story into several smaller, "bite-sized" stories that might be more reader-friendly.

1. Gathering details that reveal a person's character can be difficult. Practice observing people—your friends, your family, students you pass in the hallway and shoppers you see at the mall. How would you describe them to someone who had never met them?

2. Sometimes magazines run the full text of an interview with a question-and-answer format that enables the reader to see both the questions and the responses. Try to find an example of such an interview, and analyze it. Watch carefully for unscripted follow-up questions the reporter may have asked.

3. Find out how much your school's budget has increased or decreased as a percentage over the past five years. Compare this to the rate of inflation. What conclusions can you draw?

▲STRUCTURING LONGER STORIES

In-depth stories can take almost any form as long as the way they are organized doesn't confuse the reader. The writer of an in-depth story usually avoids the inverted pyramid style, in which readers can stop as soon as they're satisfied. The in-depth writer wants to pull the reader through the story to the end. The story should make the reader want to find out what happens next. The writer can make a story do that by using the elements of good storytelling.

A normal news story begins with a lead. But an in-depth story takes a different approach. Rather than blurt the news out in a sentence or two, the in-depth writer wants to create intrigue and suspense, to whet the reader's appetite for more. Most in-depth reports begin by raising questions rather than by stating answers.

Using Creative Beginnings

The ancient Greeks knew how to create suspense. Homer's *Odyssey* begins with the hero's return, very near the end of the story. Before completing the epic, however, Homer backtracks with a series of flashbacks. By beginning near the end, Homer aroused a strong desire on the listener's part to know how the characters had gotten in such a predicament. Christopher Scanlan, a national correspondent for Knight-Ridder, explained a similar technique he uses for in-depth stories in this way:

> I like to write what you might call "story stories"—they have a beginning, a middle and an end. In particular, each story needs to have a "spine," something to drag the reader along to the end. I know that the question I want to set up immediately in the reader's mind is the one that keeps every storyteller going: What next?
>
> I've also learned that stories should start as near the end as possible. I ask myself what was the moment where the story could have gone either way. I make that my lead, since I figure readers would want to know what was going to happen, and I could make them read until the end to find out. (Lecture, National Writers Workshop, Poynter Institute)

anecdote

a short account of some interesting or humorous incident

One of the most common beginnings for an in-depth story is an **anecdote,** a very short story with a point. This story by Robert Tomsho, a reporter for the *Wall St. Journal*, begins with an anecdote about a bass fishing class:

> Lansing, Mich.—Danny Joe Humphrey flicks a rubber night crawler into the front row of the crowded college auditorium. Then he tosses another, then another—slick wigglers the color of bubble gum, motor oil and lemon sherbet. Husky men in ball caps jump and jostle for them like bridesmaids after bouquets.
>
> "When I'm teaching," Mr. Humphrey chortles, "y'all should sit down front."

BYLINE

CHRISTOPHER SCANLAN
NATIONAL CORRESPONDENT FOR KNIGHT-RIDDER

Like many reporters and editors, I'm interested in stories about people's daily lives. I once did a story on loneliness and how a women's center in the neighborhood tried to help women with it. Another time I did a story on the courtship and wedding of a young couple. In late summer once I wrote a story on the first day of school from the point of view of the mother who must let go.

Sometimes I found some resistance in the newsroom when these stories began to run—the "Is this news?" debate that always seems to arise when a story has no obvious news angle. About that time a friend handed me a piece of paper with a quote on it from philosopher Will Durant:

"Civilization is a stream with banks. The stream is sometimes filled with blood from people killing, stealing, shouting and doing the things historians usually record; while on the banks, unnoticed, people build homes, make love, raise children, sing songs, write poetry and even whittle statues. The story of civilization is the story of what happened on the banks. Historians are pessimists because they ignore the banks for the river."

So do journalists, I decided, and stopped worrying about the criticism.

Source: How I Wrote the Story, *Providence Journal Co., Providence, R.I.*

Having captured the reader's attention, Tomsho then adds a nut graf, a paragraph that summarizes what the reader knows so far and provides an overview of the rest of the story:

> So begins another session of one of the hottest classes on American campuses: the Bass Fishing Techniques Institute. The roving seminars are hosted by various colleges around the country for an intensive weekend of classes or for shorter sessions spread out over several weeks. The instructors are bass tournament pros and television fishing-show hosts who are mobbed like rock stars (*Wall St. Journal*)

Roy Peter Clark, associate director of the Poynter Institute, a Florida-based organization devoted to media studies, says writers should fill their stories with "gold coins." He explains that if he finds a coin while walking in a forest, he will pick up the coin and put it in his pocket. When he comes across another coin, he will pick that one up, too. The coins make him want to keep walking. Writers should do the same with their stories. Clark said a gold coin can be an anecdote, a quotation that says something special or a startling piece of information. Search your material for gold coins, and scatter them throughout your story.

Writing in Scenes

Christopher Scanlan, a news wire reporter, says newspapers contain too many articles and not enough stories. Like a novel or a short story, he suggests, a newspaper story should have a sense of people, place,

Winning a football game was probably not what the framers of the Freedom of Information Act had in mind, but that was exactly what the graduate of a rival school was up to when he tried to get a look at the Texas Longhorns' playbook.

Michael Kelley, a 1989 graduate of Texas A&M, sent a letter to University of Texas President Robert Berdahl, requesting photocopies of offensive plays the Longhorns might use during the season and a copy of their playbook. His request was made under the Texas Public Information Act, the state law that defines what records of state government are open to the public.

"I'm personally a football fan and I'm just interested in the ability to get information," Kelley said.

Whether football, which some feel is almost a religion in Texas, is on equal footing with state government records remains to be seen. However, one suspects that the president sent Kelley a three-word reply: "Hook 'em Horns."

time and drama. It should have a beginning that grabs the reader's attention, a middle that keeps the reader engaged and an ending that lingers in the reader's mind.

What Scanlan describes is a narrative, the most typical structure for an in-depth story. Such stories have the same form as fiction—a beginning, middle and end. The beginning draws the reader into the story slowly. The middle continues the suspense, making the reader want to know what will happen next. The story builds to a climax and a resolution. In a narrative, the ending is even more important than the beginning.

Scanlan once wrote a story about a woman who nearly lost her baby after a frantic race to the hospital. He tells the story through a series of scenes, almost as if he were writing a play: the day the woman discovered she was pregnant, the night she began to hemorrhage, the drive to the hospital, the emergency delivery and the moment the woman holds her newborn daughter.

Scanlan begins the story with a hospital scene that takes place shortly before the baby will be born:

> In the labor room at Kent County Memorial Hospital, Jackie Rushton rose from the stretcher, her face pale and smeared with tears. A nurse pressed the fetal pulse detector against her abdomen, a taut mound stretched by seven months of pregnancy. The detector was blue, the size and shape of a pocket flashlight with earphones attached, and Jackie Rushton's eyes fixed on the nurse who strained to hear the bird-like beating of her baby's heart (*How I Wrote the Story,* Providence Journal Co., Providence, R.I.)

Later scenes in the story flash back to a desperate race through town to reach the hospital, complications with the baby's delivery and, finally, a successful birth. Thorough reporting helped Scanlan write a vivid, dramatic story. He interviewed Rushton, her husband and her best friend about the incident, asking what each had said and thought at the time. He visited the hospital so he could describe details, such as the color of the emergency room's walls and the types of lights in the hallways. He even drove the route the Rushtons took to the hospital, noting what stores and houses they drove by.

Reporter Erin Hoover of the *Oregonian* in Portland used a similar method to tell the story of a tragic shooting. Instead of writing, "A 22-year-old Portland man was shot to death yesterday, . . ." Hoover dramatizes the story by showing how other people reacted to the death:

> Nathan stands alone near the yellow police tape, his hands shoved into the pockets of his black Raiders jacket, hood pulled over his short braids. The 17-year-old stares at the body.
>
> It is a young man he knew. Not very well. But well enough.
>
> He met him a couple of months ago while hanging out with friends. Nathan can still see the guy laughing at a joke they'd made. He had a nice laugh. Earlier this week, he had pedaled by Nathan's house on his bike. Nathan waved. The man smiled and nodded hello.
>
> Leshon Denail Brown, better known as Corey Taylor, 22, was on that same bike Friday when he was gunned down on Northeast

Beech Street just west of Cleveland Avenue. It was 2:20 p.m. Broad daylight.

The police don't know why it happened. They don't know who did it. They only know that a group of youths were there, scattering when the shots were fired.

Hoover then describes other people at the crime scene, who talk one by one about the death and how their neighborhood has changed. Hoover ends the story by returning to Nathan:

Nathan, who didn't want to give his full name, stands alone trying to understand.

He was hanging out with some friends a few blocks away when a girl ran up and told him the news. It took a minute. But then he remembered Taylor.

"I flew down here," said Nathan, his face tense, his eyes moist. "I just kept looking [at his body]. Then tears started coming down my eyes a little bit."

Nathan's tone changes. He talks with determination about his own life. He says he's stayed close to God, but many of the boys he grew up with have gone astray. He says he dropped out of school but now plans to go to Portland Community College.

He wishes he could change his world.

"I want us to wake up," he said, looking at Taylor's body. "How many more people have to get killed?"

Tell your in-depth story in narrative scenes that keep the reader wondering what might happen next.

Creating a Sense of Place

William Zinsser, in his book *On Writing Well,* noted that nonfiction writers must know how to write about places as well as people. "Every human event happens somewhere," he says, "and the reader wants to know what that somewhere was like." Zinsser suggests that writers practice this skill by visiting a local park, mall or bowling alley to observe the details that make it special. Note the sights, sounds and smells. Describe the people who inhabit the place and how they dress, act and talk. Whatever place you write about, though, says Zinsser, "Go there often enough to isolate the qualities that make it special."

Truman Capote began his famous investigative book *In Cold Blood* with a description of Holcomb, Kansas, the town where a family was murdered. The book, considered a masterpiece of reporting and nonfiction writing, first appeared as a four-part story in the *New Yorker.* The story begins as follows:

The village of Holcomb stands on the high wheat plains of western Kansas, a lonesome area that other Kansans call "out there." Some 70 miles east of the Colorado border, the countryside, with its hard blue skies and desert-clear air, has an atmosphere that is rather more Far Western than Middle West. The local accent is barbed with

DATELINE DATELINE DATELINE

MURRAY HILL, N.J., June 1948—Three Bell Laboratory engineers, John Bardeen, Walter Brattain and William Shockley, demonstrated the transistor. This tiny, solid crystal block would replace the fragile, bulky tube construction in radios and televisions. With its compact construction, cooler operation and more economical use of electricity, the solid-state transistor revolutionized the broadcasting industry and won the 1956 Nobel Prize in physics for its inventors.

Transistors allowed the construction of much smaller, more easily portable radios, which went on the market in 1954. The radios did not become popular until the 1960s, when costs began to drop. By the 1970s the public could buy transistor radios for as little as $5. In addition, the perfection of the transistor opened the door for the development of the computer.

a prairie twang, a ranch-hand nasalness, and the men, many of them, wear narrow frontier trousers, Stetsons, and high-heeled boots with pointed toes. The land is flat, and the views are awesomely extensive; horses, herds of cattle, a white cluster of grain elevators rising as gracefully as Greek temples are visible long before a traveler reaches them.

A breezier descriptive style was appropriate in a *Boston Globe* story about a new Canadian territory, to be created when the gigantic Northwest Territories split into two new geographic areas:

Ah, the great Canadian northwest, where the mighty Mackenzie River rumbles to the frigid Beaufort Sea. Land of the Mounties, land of the Inuit. Land of peat bog, permafrost and polar bear.

A land soon, perhaps, to be known forever as Bob.

Bob was one of the most popular candidates for a new name for the western half of the old Northwest Territories.

Consider the places you write about as being just as important as the characters in them. A longer story offers room for significant descriptive sections, so take advantage of this extra space.

Point of View

Feature and in-depth writers sometimes step away from the objective tone of traditional third person reporting to adopt a more personal point of view. **Point of view** refers to the vantage point from which the reader sees the action. Most newspaper stories are told in the third person, using the pronouns *he, she* and *they*. The stories are told from the point of view of an objective, unbiased narrator.

On rare occasions, however, writers use first- or second-person points of view to create different effects. These stories can use the pronouns *I, me* and *you*. A story about school overcrowding, for example, could be written in the first person, from an individual student's perspective. The narrator could describe the hassles of sharing a cramped locker with other students and the lack of attention he or she gets in bulging classrooms.

Occasionally, a reporter has such an unusual experience that a first-person account is really the only way to do it justice. Here, the challenge is to keep the readers' interests at heart and yet still convey a rich personal insight. Lisa White, a writer for the *Focus* at Midland High School in Midland, Michigan, worked toward those goals in an account of her battle with anorexia, a severe eating disorder. Here is an excerpt:

I've always been small and thin, even when I was a baby. Throughout the years, all of my friends have joked about my size. It never really bothered me until around May last year. I started dieting to fit into my Prom dress, which actually fit fine. Prom came and went. My next excuse to diet was swimsuit season. That's when I started taking diet pills and making myself purge. When school started, I weighed 88 pounds.

I knew it wasn't normal and it wasn't healthy. I was so terrified I'd get fat. I was controlled by food. When I started dieting, I was so proud of myself because I had self-control over food. I don't know when that all changed, but in the end it was the other way around.

Save your first person experiments for special stories. Almost all the stories you write will seem more credible if told in an objective voice. But if you are an eyewitness to an unusual event or have a truly unique experience, consider creating a story from a first person point of view.

THIS JUST IN: *Portrait of a Young Journalist*

Broadcaster ?
Journalist ?
Sports Writer ?
Designer ?
Editor ?
Columnist ?
Anchor ?
Reporter ?
Photographer ?

Merry Hayes, reporter, Skagit Valley Herald, *Mount Vernon, Washington*

Reporter Merry Hayes isn't always content to observe the action of a story. Sometimes she wants to experience it. A reporter at the *Skagit Valley Herald* in Mount Vernon, Washington, Hayes has written a series of first-person stories about topics such as handguns, hang gliding and hydroplane racing. Hayes says she spent the first few years of her career comfortably telling stories in the objective third-person point of view.

"I was afraid to write from my perspective," she said. "I didn't think my opinions would matter to my readers." But Hayes realized she could use the first person in special cases to write about her thoughts, actions and emotions and thus reveal the excitement of trying something new.

Hayes wrote a story, for example, about the increasing number of women buying hand-guns for protection. To give the story a personal touch, she took a handgun safety class. In a sidebar to the main story, Hayes described the power she felt when shooting a gun for the first time, seeing the flash of light from the gun's muzzle and smelling the acrid smell of gunpowder.

Hayes also flew in a hang glider despite her fear of heights. "Pilots told me that hang gliding was quiet and peaceful," Hayes said. "But, being afraid of heights, I found that hard to believe. To write a good story about the sport, I knew I had to try it." Hayes flew as a passenger with pilot James Fieser. In the story, she says her excitement turned to fear once she reached the launch site on a mountain overlooking the San Juan Islands:

Hooked to the glider, we walked to the wooden launching ramp. I looked down at the islands and water as we waited for a gust of wind. My legs began to shake.

"Are you sure you want to do this?" Fieser asked.

It was a question he asks all his passengers before launch.

"Yes," I said softly.

"Are you ready to run? Let's go!" he said.

We ran a few steps and the glider lifted us into the air. We floated.

"Oh my God," I said, gripping Fieser's harness and looking down in amazement. I couldn't believe I was flying. (*Skagit Valley Herald*)

Hayes says first-person stories aren't appropriate in most cases. But she says they are a good way to get close to a subject. Through such stories, Hayes learned the importance of detail and emotion in telling a story that people will enjoy reading. "They helped me become a better reporter," she said. "I realized that you have to ask a lot of specific questions to get a real sense of what an experience was like for another person."

YOUR BEAT

1. Write an amusing or touching anecdote about each of three people you know well. Keep the anecdotes to one or two paragraphs. Could this anecdote be used effectively as the beginning of a long story?

2. Find a partner, and make a complete chronology of events for his or her most recent weekend. Then make your own chronology for the same time. (A chronology is a list of events in the order in which they took place.) Can you see any patterns? Do these chronologies suggest any interesting story ideas?

3. Go to a public place for an hour, and take notes on what you observe. Who comes and who goes? What do people seem to be concerned about? Follow William Zinsser's advice: try to find some special quality about that place. Turn your notes into a story for the school paper.

CHAPTER REVIEW

KEY TERMS

Show that you know the meanings of the following key terms by correctly using them in complete sentences. Write your answers on a separate sheet of paper.

in-depth reporting

investigative reporting

anecdote

point of view

OPEN FORUM

1. Suppose that a new group has asked the student council for recognition as an official organization. The group calls itself La Raza Club, and group leaders say its purpose is to increase awareness about minority issues. In particular, the group wants to provide support for Hispanic American students and promote what it calls "brown pride." The members of your newspaper staff see this as an opportunity to devote a two-page spread to your school's Hispanic American students—focusing on their cultural heritage, as well as the obstacles some of those students may have found in the community. How would you organize your coverage? What stories would you try to tell?

2. "I would be dead if I hadn't been taken out of my home," explains a senior at your school. "But I have always felt left out, like people

◆ **Open Forum, continued**

haven't accepted me." In answer to further questioning, you learn that this student has lived in 33 foster homes over the past 10 years. You also learn that there are over 40 families in your county foster care program. How could you organize coverage of an in-depth story on foster families? What sources would you try to tap?

FINDING THE FLAW

Study the following story on abusive relationships. Although the story represents a good effort, it has several flaws. Look for information that needs more support or attribution. Is the story structured in such a way that it holds your interest? If not, how could it be reorganized? Has the reporter remained objective, or have her opinions drifted into the story? How would you handle confidentiality issues and the identity of the two abused females mentioned in the story?

Abusive Relationships: How do you know when enough is enough?

"When the [abuse] occurred there were no serious injuries; for example, no broken bones, but there were bumps and bruises, inside and out. For two days I laid on a couch not being able to do anything. My [boyfriend] sat by me the whole time," said *Lisa*, an upper school student who was beaten by her boyfriend. *Lisa* said that she didn't report this incident because, "I didn't feel that it was serious enough, and because I love him and I couldn't stand not being able to be with him."

In a study conducted by researchers at California State University, Sacramento, 27 percent of the 256 seventeen and eighteen-year-olds questioned said they were involved in violent relationships. Many of them even considered such violence an act of love. *Lisa* said that she thought the reason for the abuse was because, "I told [my boyfriend] that I had cheated on him with my ex-boyfriend, two

months after [the cheating] had happened."

In reality, her boyfriend could have chosen to storm out and slam the door. Instead, he chose to hit her. "There really wasn't a time when I was afraid of him. A few days after [the assault] I was a bit nervous."

Lisa said that "this was the first and last time" that she had been or will be hit by her boyfriend. "Although I do admit that sometimes even today, over a year later, when he moves his arm a certain way I get a little scared because I have flashbacks."

Julie, another upper school student, was also involved in an abusive relationship. However, in this case the abuse occurred more than once. *Julie*, just like *Lisa*, didn't report the abuse because she said, "I didn't think that anything was wrong with it. I thought that it happened to everyone." After one night of an extreme attack by her boyfriend, *Julie* decided to breakup

CHAPTER REVIEW, continued

◆ FINDING THE FLAW, continued

with him. She knows now that the abuse cannot happen again.

"Getting out of an abusive relationship is hard to do on your own. You need to talk to someone that you trust," said Marcia Halperin, WFS school psychologist.

Halperin said that there are three stages of a typical abusive relationship. First, tension builds: "There are verbal threats of physical abuse," she said. "Then there is an explosion. That is where the abuse starts. Finally, the abuser feels horrible for what he did, and then apologizes."

Julie noticed a pattern with her boyfriend. After he hit her, instead of saying he was sorry, *Julie* said that "he would buy me things." She also added, "He mainly [abused me] when he was frustrated. School frustrated him a lot so he would take it out on me."

Halperin commented that "abusive relationships can happen to anyone," but "statistics indicate that many abusers were once abused themselves."

[**Note:** The real names of the abused females (Lisa and Julie) have been changed to protect their identities.]

Source: Reprinted with permission from Jen Gatenby, "Abusive Relationships: How Do You Know When Enough Is Enough?" Whittier Miscellany. Wilmington Friends School, Wilmington, Delaware.

 MEDIA WATCH

1. Watch a TV news program such as *60 Minutes, 48 Hours* or *Nightline* that specializes in in-depth reporting. Discuss the strengths and weaknesses of each story presented. If possible, find a story on a similar subject in a newspaper. How does in-depth coverage compare, depending on the media involved?

2. Watch an in-depth interview program such as *Charley Rose* on PBS. What differences do you find in the interviews on these shows compared with the interviews you see on regular news programs? How might the interviewers' preparations differ?

String Book

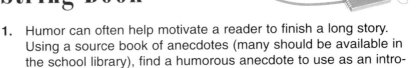

1. Humor can often help motivate a reader to finish a long story. Using a source book of anecdotes (many should be available in the school library), find a humorous anecdote to use as an introduction for an in-depth story on a subject of your choice.

2. Write an in-depth story on a topic of your choice. Here are a few suggestions: family history, war veterans in your community, the fast-food industry, the popularity of team logos on sportswear and the minimum wage.

Beyond Page One

Chapter 10
Writing Features

"You've got to understand a lot to write even a little bit."
—John McPhee

LEARNING OBJECTIVES

After completing this chapter, you will be able to:

◆ describe the special characteristics of a feature story,

◆ list ideas that could be developed into feature stories,

◆ explain the importance of organization in the writing process,

◆ write a polished feature story for publication or production.

◆

KEY TERMS

In this chapter, you will learn the meaning of these terms:

feature
sidebar
news peg
profile
hook
focusing
structure
persona
tone

A fter an Olympic athlete sets a new world record, you may hear one of your friends proclaim, "Records were made to be broken!" Your friend's interest is warranted. Being the best in the world in an Olympic sport is, after all, an important news story.

Perhaps you wondered at the time, are there some records not made to be broken? If you then had researched and written a story on the 10 most unbreakable records, you would have produced a feature. That story, however, has already been written—many times. Why? Because people always seem to be fascinated by lists of the ultimate in anything. Fortunately, though, no ultimate list of feature ideas is possible. To the talented journalist, the world is a storehouse of story ideas.

In this chapter, you will learn how to find ideas for feature stories, how to write a feature story and how to refine that story for publication. You will soon discover that in high school journalism, the length of time between publication dates does not allow for immediacy of reporting; it requires that most straight news stories be treated as features. It is not surprising, then, that features dominate school magazines, television shows and yearbooks.

WHAT IS FEATURE WRITING?

If you haven't already, you will soon discover that defining **feature** is as difficult as explaining *news*. As Richard Cheverton, an editor at the *Orange County Register* says, "You can nail down a news, or sports, or business story—but grabbing the essence of a feature is like wrestling a squid; it'll soon depart in a cloud of ink."

But there is a way to get a firm hold on what is required of a feature writer. Perhaps you should think of a feature as a news story written like a piece of short fiction. You, as a writer, must combine the rigors of factual reporting in news writing with the creative freedom of short-story writing. Therefore, the feature story's form must be more fluid than that of a news story; the inverted pyramid style must be sacrificed so that the story can have a distinct beginning, middle and end. The readers won't be able to scan a few paragraphs; they will have to read the entire story to understand it.

feature

a prominent news story written like a short piece of fiction. The story is usually not related to a current event

Teen volunteers could be an interesting news peg to a major story about a hospital building expansion.

Feature stories place a greater emphasis on facts that have human interest. As author Donald Murray says, "Features put people in the story; they make the reader think and care." You can write a feature about anyone if you can find an unusual angle that captures the interest of your readers. In fact, some feature writers, by picking a name at random from the telephone book and then producing a story on the person selected, have proved that you can, indeed, write an interesting feature about anyone.

Generally, feature stories are of two types: news features and timeless stories. A news feature is usually written as a follow-up or a sidebar story that is linked to a breaking news event. A **sidebar** is an article that accompanies and appears beside the main news story. Additionally, many features are developed around what is called a news peg. A **news peg** merely means the relationship of a feature to, or how it is pegged on, something else in the news. For example, a story on the safety of football equipment might be pegged on the fact that your school's quarterback recently suffered a head injury in a game. That feature, of course, should run during the football season.

A timeless story, in contrast, does not have to be used immediately. The information in the story will be just as relevant in the next edition of the paper as it is in this one. A feature on how to make a good impression or on the funny things people do in bathrooms is not time bound.

In either type of feature—news features or timeless stories—good reporting is at the center of what you do. You collect details as many as possible. You describe people, settings and feelings: the elements of storytelling. When all the details are added together, the reader is placed in the scene you are describing. But how do you find a story worth telling?

sidebar

> an article that accompanies and appears beside the main news story

news peg

> the relationship of a feature to, or how a feature is pegged on, something else in the news

Choose a story from your school paper, and draw a geometric diagram of that story that reflects its structure. Discuss with your classmates the differences between your drawings of features and the inverted pyramid structure of a straight news story. Although your geometric diagrams will vary, do they suggest a changing pattern of importance for the facts in a feature story?

▲FINDING FEATURE IDEAS

Author E. B. White's advice to young writers who want to get ahead without delay was, "Don't write about man, write about a man." Perhaps the best way to follow this advice is to localize and personalize your stories. Tell your stories through the experiences of individuals in your school community. The more your readers are affected, the more importance they will place on a story. Furthermore, a story that takes place close to your readers will have more appeal. Reading a story about a classmate's volunteering time at a local soup kitchen will engage your audience more than a story about a new soup kitchen's opening in a neighboring community.

Although feature stories can be about things, the strongest features are almost always about people. Would you rather read a story about a baseball card collection or a story about a certain collector and the lengths she went to obtain that Mickey Mantle rookie card?

BYLINE

CHARLES KURALT
THE ROAD MOSEYED

Charles Kuralt, who died in 1997, was a folksy CBS newsman whose reports from the small towns and back roads of America endeared him to millions. He was without question the master of the television feature story.

Balding and pudgy, but gifted with the ability to see poetry where others saw prose, Kuralt logged up to 50,000 miles a year in a motor home with a three-man crew, searching for what some called "the little people." Kuralt delighted in what made them unique. He did pieces on a school for unicyclists, horse-trading and a gas station/poetry factory. He interviewed professional wrestlers, lumberjacks, whittlers and farmers. "He just touched something that audiences responded to," said CBS colleague Charles Osgood.

"You were humbled to be around him, to watch him in operation," said CBS newsman Harry Smith. "There wasn't a real person on the planet who wouldn't talk to Charles Kuralt. He was prideful of his work, but there was no ego. So much of the things that this business grows, he would have none of. He cared about telling stories."

Kuralt's soothing style and personal observations made him one of television's most beloved journalists. He once admitted that against all rules of journalism, he became friends with some of the subjects of his features: for example, Eddie Lovett, a man with a third-grade education who built a great library in the piney woods of Arkansas so that his children would become well educated.

"He brought tears to my eyes," Kuralt remembers, "with the—with the intensity of his desire to learn; his studying Shakespeare. He used to sit up on the barn roof at night and study astronomy with a flashlight and an astronomy book."

In his *On the Road* series, Kuralt reassured us "that the whole country is not in flames and that everything going on in America is not represented by those big black headlines on Page One."

profile

a short, vivid character sketch

Finding Subjects That Matter

In feature writing there are no restrictions on subject matter. You are limited only by your imagination. Often, a feature is nothing more than a simple story about a common person in an uncommon circumstance. The feature writer's job is to find a fresh angle—to find the story behind the person. Consider the following topics that deal with the ordinary:

foreign exchange students,
eating disorders,
part-time jobs,
unusual hobbies,
teacher features,
favorite movies,
favorite celebrities,
fast-food restaurants,
fashion trends,
top ten lists (like this one).

In contrast, author Roy Peter Clark suggests that a writer can cultivate an eye for the unusual, offbeat topic: "A waitress takes an order, not on a pad, but on a hand-held computer. A small public school is established at a large GE plant. Little kids are collecting baseball cards not for fun, but for investment. Suddenly a grain of narrative appears before the author's eyes."

The following feature story topics deal with the offbeat:

talk radio,
guerrilla kindness,
weirdest craving,
the truth about goat cheese,
the best books *not* to read,
crazy answering machine messages,
beepers,
coincidences,
psychotherapy,
the irony of individualism.

Profiles

One of the more popular types of feature story is the profile. A **profile** is a short, vivid character sketch. Unfortunately, too many profiles turn into a tedious recounting of biographical facts: "She was born near Red Cloud and attended high school in Superior. . . ." Other unsuccessful profiles are merely a few unrelated anecdotes sandwiched between quotations.

A good profile includes impressions, explanations and points of view. A writer should make sure that the subject of the profile lives on the page by providing dramatic tension and telling details. Begin with an unusual insight or noteworthy detail. Then emphasize what is unique about the person. Peter Jacobi, a professor of journalism at Indiana University, recommends organizing the material by "using flashbacks" or "highlighting the individual's many roles."

• •

Ideas for feature stories can be found almost anywhere. Seeds for your next story may be gathered in books such as Daniel Evan Weiss's *100% American* or Tom Heymann's *On an Average Day.* Using one of these books or a similar reference work, create three unusual ideas for feature stories. List at least two related facts for each idea. The following are examples:
Idea: The value of celebrity.

Facts: On an average day in the United States, the president earns $547.95. The estate of Elvis Presley earns $41,095.89 (from *On an Average Day*).
Idea: The overemphasis on beauty in our culture.
Facts: Eye makeup is used by 97 percent of American teenage girls. Of American women, 99 percent would change something about their looks if they could (from *100% American*).

GETTING THE STORY DOWN

You are a reporter, then a writer. This means that before your fingers ever hit the keys, you get to experience the thrill of the hunt, the giddy feeling that comes when the facts all fit together and you have something important to say. However, after you have had the fun of getting the story, you still have the painstaking work of getting the story right. The advice in this section should assist you in this process.

Thinking about Beginnings

The beginning of a story must pull the reader in. The first sentence must make the reader want to continue to the second sentence. That does not mean that the beginning—the lead—has to be extraordinarily clever. Instead, it should be honest to the story first and compelling second.

Being honest or compelling is not always easy. "The problem with the concept of a *lead,*" according to feature writer Leonard Witt, "is that it is most often seen as a separate entity." The lead, however, does not need to be viewed in terms of a gimmick or a hook. (A **hook,** you'll learn from the Funky Winkerbean cartoon in this chapter, is "something in a story that captures the reader's attention enough to cause him to move on to the next paragraph.") You must think of making the whole story compelling rather than merely focusing on a clever beginning.

What follows are five categories of leads that may be useful to you as you put together the beginning of your next feature story. You will note that some of the leads listed overlap into two or more categories.

hook
   a detail that draws in the reader's attention

The Summary.   Using a summary paragraph as a lead is similar to the use of the lead in a news story. The introductory paragraphs indicate the direction the entire article will take. Often, the summary paragraph answers the questions of who, what, when, where, why and how.

FUNKY WINKERBEAN reprinted by permission King Features Syndicate.

The following are two good leads that take the form of a summary:

> Warner Bros. recently started an educational campaign using Sylvester and Tweety to relay the message of the three R's. Not reading, 'riting and 'rithmetic, but the three recycling R's: reuse, reduce and recycle. On a world-wide scale the environment has become a top priority, but has never topped Marshall's list, until now.
>
> A new club has surfaced and is not promoting spirit or leadership, but environmental issues. The environmental club was the idea of one freshman who had been brought up by her parents to respect the world around her, especially the environment. (Leslie Voigt, *Rampage,* John Marshall High School, San Antonio)

> It is the thing your parents make you do. It is the place where you first fall in love. It is the way you learn the disturbing truth that many people's work is tedious. It is what you will be nostalgic about—but not for many, many years. It is the last time you will have to know how to make a lanyard.
>
> It is the Summer Job, that moderately distorted Introduction to Adulthood—accurate to the extent that it introduces kids to paychecks, taxes and getting up early, false to the extent that come Labor Day it is over. (Elizabeth Kastor, *Washington Post*)

The Striking Statement. A striking statement used as a lead shocks or surprises the reader. The reader, astounded by some fact or idea, is promised the details later in the article:

> I have a confession to make, a revelation that may tarnish my reputation as a politically correct woman of the 90's—I laughed at Rush Limbaugh. This has been such a traumatic experience for me that I have repressed any memory of what was said by a man whom I usually insult every chance I get. (Tiffany Hartgen, *Bruin News,* Twin Falls, Idaho)

> The 137th Ohio State Fair still had more than two weeks to run when the fat man died. The sideshow workers took down the sign advertising 529-pound Big Billy Pork Chop, and with considerable effort the mortal remains of Big Billy were removed too.

But the show—one of America's largest and longest-running state fairs—must go on and so, a good fat man being hard to find, Zoma the Deranged from South America was brought in to replace Mr. Pork Chop. (Christopher Corbett, *Washington Post*)

The Descriptive Lead. The descriptive lead is constructed with concrete, vivid details. The writer paints a clear picture of the scene, the individuals and their emotional states. The following are two examples:

> You might find them staring at the stars, or you may see them building telescopes. But wherever you spot them, planetarium director Gene Zajac and librarian Kelly Jons are "out-of-this-world."
>
> Jons and Zajac have a starlit history together in astronomy they said. They have star-gazed, built telescopes and constructed a mirror-grinding machine that rubs two glass surfaces against a coarse surface to make a concave and convex lens. (Debbie Libman, *Shakerite*, Shaker Heights High School, Shaker Heights, Ohio)

> Things are ugly right now.
>
> They are also exhausted, fatalistic, sterile, beleaguered and loud, but what you notice is the ugly.
>
> For instance, you decide to catch a matinee of "Total Recall."
>
> On the way to the theater in Dupont Circle you see: four half-shaved heads, a guy urinating in a stairwell and an utter-obscenity T-shirt printed in colors that make you think of a nerve gas factory blowing up. You hear a car a block away erupting with rap music, a sort of grand mal seizure of sound . . . You see a man with five day's growth of beard and a pair of fluorescent plastic reflecting sun-glasses that make him look like a mutant 1950's starlet. You see a woman with orange hair. "Hey, look at me!" a guy yells at her. He keeps yelling it: "Look at me! Look at me!"
>
> Ugly. (Henry Allen, *Washington Post*)

Do the clothes and hair of this couple say "Look at Me!"? Would their appearance help you write a descriptive lead about them?

DATELINE
DATELINE
*DATELINE*LINE

NEW YORK CITY, Nov. 15, 1926—The first of the national television networks, the National Broadcasting Company (NBC) went on the air with a program of music and comedy that lasted 4 1/2 hours. The program originated from the Waldorf Astoria Hotel.

NBC was established as a subsidiary of the Radio Corporation of America (RCA), a company that helped develop both radio and television communication.

The second national network, the Columbia Broadcasting System (CBS), began broadcasting on Sept. 18, 1927, with a music variety show frequently interrupted by advertising. Two years later CBS was purchased by the cigar-manufacturing Paley family. William S. Paley, 26, took control of the company, a position he would hold for more than 50 years.

CBS began televising sporadic news reports shortly after the United States entered World War II in 1941. The first regularly scheduled network news was broadcast on NBC in 1945.

The third television giant, the American Broadcasting Company (ABC), was organized in 1945 when Edward J. Noble, head of the company that produced Life Savers candy, purchased part of NBC for $8 million and renamed it.

ABC was slow to enter the broadcast market, however, because it did not yet have a New York flagship station. Finally, in August 1948, ABC got its own New York station and began network service on a regular basis. By the 1950s it was airing popular programs such as the *Mickey Mouse Club.*

The Narrative.   The narrative lead is probably the most popular. Narrative leads recount stories in which things happen. They often incorporate incidents or anecdotes. Dialogue can be used to draw the reader into the narrative. Action is the key:

> The beat rhythmically transforms the dancers. Competing rhythms challenge everyone's ability. The rain that had been competing for attention stops and so does the music. The dancers are told, "Do it again. But with more feeling this time. Get over being self-conscious. You'll never grow as a dancer if you're so concerned with what everyone else thinks." The music starts again and the dancers attempt perfection one more time. (Chelsea Bushnell, *Axe,* South Eugene High School, Eugene, Ore.)

> He is the movies' new $7 million man, the year's surprise star, but Jim Carrey still approaches an interview as if he were auditioning for the roles of all three stooges and a couple of minor Marx Brothers (Zippo and Gonzo?). On a high balcony of Los Angeles' Ma Maison hotel, the star exhausts successive teams of reporters and photographers with his giddy verve. He not only entertains them, he outmans them, peopling the place with dozens of nutsy, improvised characters.
>
> "O.K.," the current photographer suggests, "now just be yourself. Show me who you are."
>
> Carrey pauses, scans the floor, shrugs and says, "Who knows?" (Richard Corliss, *Time*)

Quotations and Questions.   Leads that use quotations or questions generally are ineffective choices for inexperienced writers. Most quotations need explanation to be understood. As for questions, you, the reporter, are supposed to answer them, not ask them. There are exceptions, of course, that make for strong beginnings. Here are some examples:

> ". . . an entire civilized people followed a buffoon whose figure today inspires laughter, and yet Adolf Hitler was obeyed and his praises were sung right up to the catastrophe," Holocaust survivor Primo Levi wrote. "It happened, therefore it can happen again: this is the core of what we (holocaust survivors) have to say."
>
> Large numbers of Holocaust survivors give testimonies similar to the one above, yet many people believe the Holocaust may never have happened. (Kaela Davis, *Omaha Westside High Lance,* Omaha, Nebr.)

> They call it Prom Fever. Temporary insanity is more like it. How else to explain this seasonal mania? (Roxanne Roberts, *Washington Post*)

> It's your worst nightmare: you've been expelled from school. What happens now? Can you ever go back?
>
> Expulsion is mandatory when a student commits a category III offense such as possession or use of a weapon, or possession of drugs or alcohol on school premises. According to Principal Thomas Hensley, the administration has no control over such situations; the student is immediately expelled if found guilty of the charge. (Abby Flower, *Griffin,* Dulaney High School, Timonium, Md.)

THIS JUST IN: *Portrait of a Young Journalist*
Molly Falconer Ackerman, reporter

Before she could even speak, Molly Falconer Ackerman wanted to be a journalist. "The earliest film my parents have of me," Ackerman explains, "is, as a baby, shoving a toy microphone at a squirrel and then returning the microphone to my mouth."

Ackerman began preparing for her career in journalism while she was a high school student at Milton Academy. She served as editor-in-chief of the *Milton Paper.* "Since the school did not sanction the paper," Ackerman remembers, "we had to raise all of our own funds. We found out a lot about the business end of things."

Following graduation from Harvard University, Ackerman got a job as an assistant to the executive producer of ABC's *Turning Point.* Making telephone calls and researching feature stories filled most of Ackerman's days. She recalls, however, standing in for Peter Jennings while they "checked lights" and "walked through the marks" for the first broadcast of *Turning Point.* Ackerman attributes the self-confidence that she felt—in spite of the pressure of having Jennings watch her every move—to her years of speech training in high school. "In fact, I learned more from competitive speech about writing, speaking, and thinking, than I did from my four years at Harvard."

Today she interviews people—"some of them squirrelly"—for a living. Ackerman left her network position to take on other challenges—to get more experience as a journalist. Now she is in front of the camera as a reporter for New England Cable News in Boston and is working hard to become a "thinking head not a talking head."

Thinking about Endings

Sometimes writing the beginning of a story is not as great a challenge as writing an effective ending. You want those final lines to leave a lasting impression. Readers, after all, remember best what they read last.

The feature writer has many ways to end any story—many ways to create a vivid impression. One type of ending is the circle, in which the ending is related back to the beginning. Another popular approach is the summary ending, in which the story is quickly summarized at the close. The anecdotal ending can be effective, especially the split-anecdote technique. In this approach, the writer begins telling the anecdote early in the story and concludes it at the end. Or you might experiment with the add-on closing by making a point at the end that was never made in the story.

No matter which ending you choose, make sure that it is a logical extension of what you have already said in the story. The reader should feel that the story has run its natural course and that the subject has been covered.

GROVER'S MILLS, N.J., Oct. 30, 1938—A radio program broadcast as a Halloween joke has become one of the single most famous radio broadcasts in history.

The H. G. Wells novel *War of The Worlds* was adapted as a radio drama by Orson Welles, director of Mercury Theater of the Air. Welles changed the location to New Jersey and the time to the present.

The drama included a simulated remote band pickup interrupted by simulated news bulletins announcing that aliens, presumably Martians, had landed near Grover's Mills, New Jersey, and were invading the countryside.

Even though announcements preceding and during the program assured listeners that it was fictitious, large numbers of people became convinced that a Martian invasion was actually taking place, and they panicked.

Police received thousands of calls. Many residents fled their homes, taking furniture and valuables with them. Some were even treated for shock at local hospitals.

Checking Your References

Chapter 4 discussed how to search sources for information. However, the importance to the feature writer of careful research cannot be overemphasized. As a high school journalist, you are ultimately responsible for the accuracy of everything you write. You do not have the luxury of a staff of professional fact checkers to save you from an embarrassing misstatement.

The magazine *Vanity Fair* has a research editor and five research associates who must verify that every single fact in each issue is correct. Nothing is too trivial. According to *SPR Student Press Review*, "They look for the misspelled name of a photographer on the credits page, for the inaccurate title of a *Vanity Fair* employee on the masthead, for the suspiciously dwindling age of a celebrity, and for the real price of John Gotti's silk suits."

Until you have the commitment to the truth of those fact checkers, you can't expect to gain the trust of your readers. Little can do more damage to your reputation as a journalist than having someone you interviewed say he or she was misquoted in your feature. To avoid this all-too-common occurrence, use a tape recorder, and take notes. However, tape recorders malfunction, and memory fades. Therefore, ask a potentially provocative question twice—in slightly different words and at different points—during the interview. Be meticulous. Be right.

Organizing Your Material

In her first job as a reporter, Jane Harrigan, now the director of the journalism program at the University of New Hampshire, learned that writing is a process made of distinct steps. Harrigan diagrams that process as it applied to her as a beginning feature writer as follows:

report—write—curse & eat cookies—rewrite

Years of experience led her to revise the process:

report—ORGANIZE—write—curse & eat cookies—rewrite

Today, Harrigan suggests asking yourself four vital questions as a way to improve the organization of your feature stories:

1. What's your subject?
2. What are you trying to say?
3. How will you say it?
4. Have you said it well enough?

What's Your Subject?   As you gather and organize the details for a story, you must begin a selection process that will separate the wheat from the chaff, the telling detail from the one that will go thud on the page. To help you in this selection process, discuss the story idea with your teacher or a friend. Take note of which details interest him or her and the direction the story takes as you retell it. Furthermore, using another person as a sounding board may force you to articulate your ideas more clearly. Once you have a clear focus for the story, you are less likely to waste time in false starts. An unfocused feature wastes your time, the editor's time and the reader's time.

Focusing means narrowing—reducing a large quantity of material to a usable amount. For example, when you write a term paper for history class, you don't choose an overly broad topic such as "the history of the United States." Instead, you focus on a topic such as "the role of Malcolm X in the rise of black power." Similarly, as a feature writer, you would avoid choosing an idea such as "school life" in favor of a narrower topic such as "detention: the newest vacation spot." See Figure 10.1 for the results of a survey about the most popular topics in high school newspapers.

What Are You Trying to Say?   You can decide what you are trying to say by translating the focus of your story into a summary sentence. Try writing this summary sentence as if it were a headline, a phrase that includes both a specific subject and an active verb (for example, "New math curriculum multiplies headaches for teachers" or "Student council president embezzles funds").

Another useful strategy for some feature writers is to plan the ending of the story first. To organize their thoughts effectively, these writers find it helpful to know where they are going to arrive. This strategy of writing an ending first may or may not work for you. In any case, you should experiment with several leads before deciding on the direction for the rest of the story. The right lead not only pushes you forward into the story but also provides a map to keep you going.

focusing

narrowing; in journalism, reducing a large quantity of material to a usable amount

FIGURE 10.1
CONTENT OF HIGH SCHOOL NEWSPAPERS

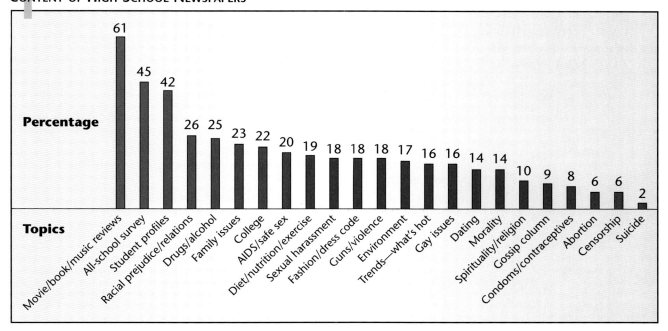

Bizarro by Dan Piraro reprinted by permission of Universal Press Syndicate.

structure

the organizational pattern a writer uses to establish relationships between rele-veat pieces of information

How Will You Say It?   After you have written the lead (and possibly the ending to the story), you need a structure in which to place the rest of your information. A **structure** is an organizational pattern the writer uses to synthesize—that is, to establish relationships between—relevant pieces of information. Some common structures are the hour-glass, the spatial story, the story in scenes and parallel narratives.

The hourglass structure begins as an inverted pyramid, arranging information in descending order of importance. Below the "waist" of the hourglass, the information is introduced in chronological order. This structure works well with day-in-the-life features.

The spatial story uses physical space rather than logical sequence to determine order. For example, you could describe the new wing at your school by moving from room to room. You could follow a maintenance person from task to task, and geography would become the focus of your feature.

Writing the story in scenes can be an effective approach to a profile. By using some typographical device (for example, bullets) to separate scenes, you can show the subject of your story reacting differently in different situations. Another advantage of this structure is that it allows the reader to view what you are describing through the eyes of many different people. For example, you might want to present a cross-section of opinion if you were writing a feature on a controversial assembly. Keep in mind that a good scene-by-scene structure has a seamless narrative.

One of the best examples of the use of parallel narratives may be in Truman Capote's chilling novel *In Cold Blood.* At the beginning of the story, the reader follows the separate courses of the killers and the victims and waits for the inevitable grisly murders. You might want to experiment with parallel narratives. Imagine and describe two debate teams from different schools as they prepare to meet in the state finals, or a boy and a girl as they nervously await a blind date.

No matter which structure you choose, the key is to provide the reader with logical connections. Each paragraph must be connected to the previous paragraph. Harrigan advises you to "think of each idea in your story as an island. Your task is to write bridges between the islands to keep your readers from drowning."

Have You Said It Well Enough? Most writing will benefit from being seen with a fresh eye. Try to walk away from your story for a while and then come back and refine the writing. Stories that flop usually suffer from poor organization. You can literally take scissors to paper and cut the text into paragraphs. Then reassemble the pile of paragraphs until you have an organization that pleases you. This reassembling process often suggests an entirely new approach that eliminates the structural weaknesses of your rough draft. Of course, you may learn that the problem is not your method of arranging the materials at all; sometimes you simply may have a bad idea for a feature. Bad ideas happen to even the best of writers.

In the next section of this chapter, however, you will learn about the good times: how to polish a feature story that is worth saving.

In *The Complete Book of Feature Writing,* Leonard Witt offers this example from the first two paragraphs of an avalanche story by Claire Martin of the *Denver Post.* The asterisks indicate facts that had to be gathered and checked:

> At about 20 minutes past 11* on a warm Sunday morning* in early February,* 6-year-old* Taylor Huddleston* and his cousins, Erwin Effler,* 6*, and Michael Effler,* 4,* were playing* in the snow.*
>
> Below them,* in the driveway of the Mountain Sunrise Condominiums,* the Effler's father, Erwin,* was helping load luggage* in an airport limousine van* as the families got ready to leave Mount Crested Butte.* They had expected to leave a couple days earlier,* on Friday,* Feb. 3,* but a heavy snowstorm had closed the airport* in nearby Gunnison* for two days,* extending the Efflers' and Huddlestons' skiing vacation.*

Pretend you are a fact checker. Use a feature story from your local newspaper. Count how many obviously gathered facts, bits of information and quotes are involved in the reporting.

REFINING THE STORY

Ernest Hemingway's advice is still true: if you want to be a writer, you have to write. And for the aspiring feature writer, let us add, you have to rewrite. In fact, satisfying your editor, and yourself, is often a Sisyphean task. You start to revise the story . . . you falter . . . you start again . . . you falter again. The techniques that follow should help you push the computer mouse up that forbidding hill of information and put the finishing touches on your next feature.

Finding the Right Voice

You have many voices. You speak to your friends differently than you do to your parents or your teachers. If you have a part-time job, chances are you have a different voice for your boss. And in every story you write, you, as the narrator, take on a **persona,** or character. That doesn't mean that you always have to write in first person singular, but it does suggest that you must choose a voice that best imparts the information in the story.

persona

the character taken on by a writer

The choice you make becomes the tone of the story. The tone may be ironic if you are discussing the hypocrisy of a flawed grading system. It may be childlike if you are describing a mentoring program for elementary school children through the eyes of one child. The **tone,** or mood of the story, should always match the content. After all, you wouldn't describe a tragic car accident in a light or humorous tone. Remember, the possibilities for different voices and different points of view are limitless. What you must do is listen to your voices and trust them.

tone

the mood of a story

Using Description Effectively

Vivid description in a feature can take the reader on a journey of the senses. The details you choose should appeal to taste, sight, smell, hearing and feeling. Consider how the following descriptive passage from Kim Ode, a feature writer at the *Star Tribune* in Minneapolis, takes our senses to the Badlands in South Dakota:

> The sun drops like a coin into a slot on the horizon, triggering a jukebox of coyotes. The full moon rises so huge and fast, you unconsciously brace yourself against the rotation of the Earth. Stars burst into view. You wouldn't be anywhere else. There is nowhere else.

How can you create such vivid description? Your notebook should be filled not only with facts but also with your observations of anything out of the ordinary. These observations put meat on the factual bones. In a straight news story you may refer to the boys' basketball coach as the basketball coach or, if it is more accurate, the winningest basketball coach in school history. In a feature story, however, the coach can become a paunchy, balding, Coke-chugging workaholic.

As you are sorting through the details you have collected, eliminate those observations that are unnecessary or that do not contribute to the reader's understanding. Pulitzer Prize finalist Bob Ehlert reminds us,

"Never describe the gun above the mantel unless you're going to use it. In other words, don't describe people or things that won't play into the theme of your story."

Rounding Out a Profile

As suggested earlier in this chapter, a profile must be more than a simple recounting of biographical facts. A profile is only as good as the characterization of the subject. You create memorable characters by showing, rather than telling. That means that you provide telling details, concrete bits of information that allow the reader to "see" the subject.

If journalist Rita Kempley says in a profile of actor Jack Nicholson that he smokes Camels; dresses in made-for-strutting loafers, Appaloosa hide and dandified; looks like the Nutri-System poster child; and is free with four-letter words like a kid who's just learned to curse, then we have a vivid image of this man once described as the Big Bad Wolf. The feature writer has succeeded in showing us the man; he lives on the page.

Furthermore, the subject of the profile needs to have a story. The anecdotes must demonstrate specific attributes of the subject. Do the attributes in the Kempley profile, for example, show Nicholson as a romantic or a rascal? Avoid anecdotes that don't directly contribute to the describing of those attributes you have selected to highlight.

Impertinent Facts

Research associate Simon Brennan, *Vanity Fair*'s Hollywood expert, has actually experienced "fact checking nightmares." Brennan said, "I dreamed I had to research a detailed story about torture. Because we weren't sure about the facts, I was sent to Africa to be tortured. I dreamed that I was suspended, with my hands tied, above a ditch with snakes, spiders and rats. They dipped me into it again and again. The worst part is, while this was going on, I was trying to scribble notes with my hands tied, recording all pertinent facts."
Source: Adapted from SPR Student Press Review.

Could a simple biographical sketch capture the man once described as the Big Bad Wolf?

Humoring the Reader

Humor, when appropriate, can breathe life into a story. It can keep the reader who is in a hurry from putting the story down. Develop an eye for humorous details.

In a feature story on the college application process, Jennifer Wyatt gives a tongue-in-cheek account of what happened after she indicated on the PSAT form that she wanted her scores made available to colleges around the country. Wyatt writes:

> If only they had printed a warning: "DANGER! Answering YES will result in more mail coming to your house than was postmarked within the borders of Labrador during the previous year."
>
> This is not to say I don't relish mail. It's just that college brochures are like cheese factories and martial-arts films—if you've seen one, you've seen them all.

The humor in Wyatt's feature story is effective because many students can relate to the absurdity of the college selection process. In short, the details chosen have universal appeal.

When you are choosing amusing details for a story, always exercise good judgment. Your humor should never be at the expense of others. Sensitivity to people's feelings far outweighs any desire you might have to get a few laughs.

Listen to the voices of many writers—for example, Ernest Hemingway, Mark Twain, Maya Angelou, Molly Ivins or Russell Baker. Choose one you like. Then, as Andy Merton, a journalism professor at the University of New Hampshire, suggests, "Get the writer's voice inside your head. The sound, the rhythm, the sensibility."

Now experiment with that voice in writing your material. Rewrite your most recent feature story by imitating the style of the author you chose. You will be imitating the author not to plagiarize but to learn the possibilities for variations in style. Soon your own voice will emerge in the process, a little wiser and a little more seasoned. Besides, you'll have fun.

CHAPTER REVIEW

KEY TERMS

Show that you know the meanings of the following key terms by correctly using them in complete sentences. Write your answers on a separate sheet of paper.

feature	profile	structure
sidebar	hook	persona
news peg	focusing	tone

OPEN FORUM

1. Cyberspace offers opinionated people a forum that they might not have otherwise. Moments after the arrest of O. J. Simpson, computer bulletin boards, special interest forums and real-time conferences were buzzing. *Dallas Morning News* reporter Todd Copilevitz said, "Anyone with a question can drop in on a law enforcement group or lawyers conference, or grill top editors at a national magazine in the online world." In what ways might a feature writer take advantage of the ability to travel through cyberspace?
2. A rule many feature writers follow has been attributed to editor Byron Dobell: "A story should be a verb, not a noun." What do you think Dobell meant by this rule? Can you think of examples of "noun" stories that should have been "verbs"?

FINDING THE FLAW

In reviews of Joe McGinniss's book on Ted Kennedy, McGinniss was accused of making up many of Kennedy's thoughts and feelings, as if Kennedy were a fictional character in a novel. "It's true that most biographers don't make up quotes and thoughts," McGinniss explained. "But I'm not just a biographer. I'm a ruminator. We ruminators go for inner truths that transcend journalism."

Or so says author John Leo in a satirical feature about McGinniss. Leo points out that on Page 231 of McGinniss's book, he has Kennedy thinking that Pierre Salinger was a more evolved species. "Is it really ethical to insert a thought like that into a living brain?" asks Leo.

Can you think of situations where a writer would be justified in imagining a character's thoughts?

MEDIA WATCH

1. It has been said that the tabloids increase circulation by dipping into society's cesspool. These papers are associated with rumor-mongering reporters, checkbook journalism and scandal. To compete, network news organizations frequently do more timid versions of the stories covered more boldly by the tabloids. This competition to entertain the public has a price. What does it cost us when all news is entertainment?

2. Musician Frank Zappa complained, "Most rock journalism is people who can't write interviewing people who can't talk for people who can't read." Do you agree or disagree? Why? Find examples of rock journalism that prove or disprove Zappa's assertion.

3. In the "Dateline" feature on page 238, you read about the Orson Welles 1939 radio drama *War of the Worlds.* Obtain a recording of the original broadcast with help from your teacher and listen to it. In your opinion, what makes the recording so real? Can you understand how some listeners may have been fooled into believing that Martians were actually invading our planet? Make a list of the techniques that Welles used to create a sense of realism.

4. Watch a local TV newscast for one week. Make a list of all of the news stories covered each evening and keep track of the amount of time spent on each story. At the end of the week, review your list and place each story into one of the following three categories—international, national, and local news. How much time did your local news station devote to local versus national news? Local versus international news? You might also take the same data and rate the stories as either news or entertainment. What other ways could you categorize the information you have gathered to make additional observations?

String Book

You may use any newspapers for this activity, including school newspapers. Clip the page header with the name and date of the newspaper for each article; keep it with the example.

1. Start an idea file. Spend a week collecting as many ideas for feature stories as you can. Record all thoughts in your notebook or computer. To generate ideas, refer to the suggestions included in this chapter. At the end of the week, go back over your ideas, choose the best ones and present them to the class as possible feature stories to discuss and develop.

2. Choose one of the following feature story assignments to write as if you expected it to be published.
    a. Station yourself for one hour in a public place with lots of traffic. Observe what happens. Write about who comes and goes, as well as what conclusions you can draw about the people who frequent that particular place.
    b. Interview a local newsmaker (a state senator, city official, public servant or celebrity). First research your subject thoroughly.
    c. Explain how to do something. Use the advice and opinions of both experts and amateurs. Try out your directions yourself.

3. Each year the yearbook covers homecoming activities. Write a feature story that makes this year's coverage unique.

4. Using a camcorder, produce a video feature story on "A Day in the Life of Your Pet" from the point of view of the animal (or your friend's pet, if you don't have one).

Chapter 11
Editorials

"Modern editors spend the bulk of their days attending mandatory workshops on how to halt the decline in newspaper readership: this leaves them very little time to read what they put in the actual newspaper."
—Dave Barry

LEARNING OBJECTIVES

After completing this chapter, you will be able to:

◆ explain the importance of editorials in contributing to community conversation,

◆ write editorials that explain, evaluate or persuade,

◆ understand the role of editorial cartoons.

◆

KEY TERMS

In this chapter, you will learn the meaning of these terms:

editorial
editorial page
masthead
op-ed page
editorial board
brainstorming
editorial that explains
editorial that evaluates
editorial that persuades

"*W*ho cares what you write in editorials? Nobody reads them anyway." Have you ever heard your newspaper staff say something like that? Although journalists express concern that newspaper readers increasingly avoid editorial pages, the editorial does not have to become the last dinosaur. After all, Americans hunger for opinion and analysis. Radio and television talk shows flourish. The challenge for the high school editorial writer is to create a community conversation that will not be bland or boring.

It is unlikely that as a high school editor, you will have ten shots fired at you, as did Edward Taylor, publisher of the *Pulaski Enterprise* in Mound City, Illinois, after he wrote editorials against slot machines. In fact, editorial topics like cafeteria food and school spirit—which appear regularly in high school newspapers—seldom raise an eyebrow, let alone a voice. But you can make a difference by discussing important issues.

In this chapter, you will learn how editorials can play a vital role in your school community. Your news, sports and feature coverage mirror your school and community. Editorials and other opinion articles show the way your school and community could be. In this chapter, you will also learn how to write different types of editorials, how to involve your readers in a dialogue on important issues, and how to select cartoons to reinforce editorial messages.

DRABBLE reprinted by permission of United Feature Syndicate.

WEIGHING OPINIONS

Pulitzer Prize–winning editorial writer Vermont C. Royster advises that "the editorial page of the paper should begin where the rest of the paper leaves off." What Royster means is that on the editorial page, the reader should find ideas about the things reported elsewhere in the paper. The key word here is *ideas*. An **editorial** is an article that states the newspaper's ideas on an issue. These ideas are presented as opinions.

You probably haven't given much thought to who writes the anonymous opinions that appear as editorials in your local paper. Some of the writers may be fairly described as opinion leaders, and others are accurately called "publisher's mouthpieces." Today, however, most editorial writers are hired not for their willingness to parrot the views of the paper's owner but for their education and experience. These writers try to make sense out of complex, and sometimes controversial, issues.

The **editorial page**—typically, the second page of a four-page high school newspaper—includes editorials, columns, opinion articles, reviews and cartoons. The newspaper's **masthead**—a statement providing the details of publication—appears on this page as well. Newspapers of six or eight pages often offer what is known as an **op-ed page**—literally, the page opposite the editorial page. The op-ed page contains more of the same features you will find on the editorial page.

High school newspaper editorials today offer opinions on a broad range of issues. Student editors weigh opinions on topics that were once rarely discussed, from school tardiness policies to sexually transmitted diseases. Popular editorial topics such as date rape and drug abuse reflect the reality of growing up in the United States in the 1990s.

Because editorials state the newspaper's position on controversial issues, many high school newspapers have an **editorial board.** The editorial board, which usually consists of top editors, decides on a plan for each editorial. One student is then selected to research and write the actual article. Editorials are usually unsigned, because they represent the newspaper's opinion, not the writer's.

Of course, the process of deciding the newspaper's positions on controversial matters can include long and heated debates. Larger staffs schedule periodic conferences during which the staff members discuss what is to be written about, decide the newspaper's position on various topics, and make assignments. One useful strategy in these conferences is brainstorming. **Brainstorming,** as you remember from Chapter 6, is a technique in which participants suspend critical judgment as they generate as many ideas as possible. Brainstorming, or free association, often helps individuals engaged in group participation to be more creative than they would be as individuals. The process is thus useful in helping people generate ideas for editorials and in suggesting approaches to specific topics.

The primary source of material for editorials, though, is the daily lives of students in your school. Students interact with the faculty, the administration and one another in many ways. That interaction affects academic pursuits, extracurricular activities, vocational training and

editorial
> an article that states a newspaper's ideas on a particular issue

editorial page
> the page in a newspaper that includes editorials, columns, opinion articles, reviews, cartoons and the masthead

masthead
> a statement in a newspaper that provides the details of publication

op-ed page
> the page opposite the editorial page in a newspaper

editorial board
> the group of people (usually the top editors) who decide on a plan for each editorial that will appear in a newspaper

brainstorming
> a technique in which participants suspend critical judgment as they generate as many ideas as possible; also called *free association*

FIGURE 11.1
SAMPLE EDITORIAL POLICY

I. GOALS
A. To inform, educate and entertain the readers.
B. To provide a forum for the High School community to express their attitudes and opinions.
C. To provide an educational opportunity for both the students who produce the newspaper and those who read it.
D. To provide a medium for commercial messages.

II. BACKGROUND
A. Funding: The newspaper receives school district funds, although a majority of its income comes through the sale of advertising space at the basic rate of $_____ per column inch.
B. Distribution: The newspaper is published ___ times per year. It is distributed to students and faculty free of charge. Subscriptions are available for $_____ per year. Issues are mailed to subscribers. The newspaper also participates in exchange programs with numerous schools throughout the nation.

III. CONTENT
A. General
1. The Editorial Board (consisting of the Executive Editor, Managing Editor, Opinion Editor, News Editor, Sports Editor, Culture Editor, Special Report Editor, Photography Editor, Business Manager and the adviser, (a non-voting member), retains the right to choose the newspaper's content and to determine story priority.
2. Work on the newspaper is not limited strictly to its staff members.
3. All material—writing, photography or art work—appearing in the newspaper will receive credit, with the method of credit being at the discretion of the Editorial Board.
B. Writing
1. Commentary
a. The Editorial Board will select editorial topics.
b. Editorials will be signed and will reflect the opinion of the majority of the Board. The Board will take full responsibility for all editorials.
c. Commentaries will be signed, and they reflect the views of the writer. They may or may not reflect the views of the Editorial Board.
2. Letters to the Editor
a. Any person with an interest in the community who has an opinion to be voiced is encouraged to submit letters.
b. All letters must be signed but anonymity may be requested. It will be granted only if deemed necessary by the Editorial Board. Each request will be reviewed on a case by case basis.
c. Letters may be submitted to a designated box in the library, brought to Room ___ or mailed to the school.
d. Letters should be less than 250 words.
e. The newspaper reserves the right to edit any letter for grammatical errors, libelous content or space limitations.
f. Each letter's author will be verified.
C. Photography
1. Misleading photos will be avoided and no person will be ridiculed by the use of a demeaning photo.
2. Students not of legal age appearing in photos for advertising must have their parents sign a model release form.
D. Art work
1. Editorial art work represents the view of the artist. It may or may not represent the views of the Editorial Board.
2. No person shall be ridiculed by the use of demeaning art.

IV ETHICS
A. The newspaper will strive to present information in a fair, impartial, accurate and truthful manner.
B. The newspaper will function in accord with all applicable laws, both in regard to the rights and the restrictions of journalism.
C. The newspaper will accept the Canons of Journalism of the American Society of Newspaper Editors as the basis for good journalistic ethics.
D. The newspaper reserves the right to refuse any advertising not found to be within the publication's standards.

V. CORRECTIONS
In the event of error (omission, misidentification, etc.) the Editorial Board will attempt to mitigate the damage. Every reasonable precaution is made in avoiding errors but some amount of error is inevitable. Each case will be evaluated on its own merit.

Knowing When to Duck

Columnist Dave Barry once wrote about his experiences as the editor of a West Chester, Pennsylvania, newspaper called the *Daily Local News*. Barry claims that he is not proud of his time as an editor. Perhaps this excerpt from his column in the Miami Herald will help you understand why:

So one spring day I made the editorial decision to put a photograph of some local ducks on the front page. At least I thought they were ducks, and that's what I called them in the caption. But it turns out that they were geese. I know this because a WHOLE lot of irate members of the public called to tell me so. They never called about, say, the quality of the schools, but they were RABID about the duck-vs.-goose issue. It was almost as bad as when we left out the horoscope.

I tried explaining to the callers that, hey, basically a goose is just a big duck, but this did not placate them. Some of them demanded that we publish a correction (For whom? The geese?), and by the end of the day I was convinced that the public consisted entirely of raging idiots. (This is the fundamental underlying principle of journalism.)

the lives of the students outside school. Furthermore, national and international issues are of concern to the well-informed student. Figure 11.1 provides an example of a high school newspaper editorial policy.

Remember, the newspaper is the voice of the community, and editorials are the voice of the newspaper. This voice can inform readers, stimulate thinking, mold opinion and occasionally move people to action. Ask yourself, Would I write an editorial if it were only read and believed by one person? What if that one person were the principal of the school?

As Vermont C. Royster suggested at the beginning of this section, editorials present ideas about topics found elsewhere in the paper. Choose a news story or feature from a past issue of your school paper, and brainstorm with the rest of the class to create possible approaches for an editorial about it. Finally, discuss potential negative reactions of readers to the different approaches generated by the brainstorming session.

WRITING EDITORIALS

To be worthy of print space or broadcast time, an editorial needs to tell the reader something that would not be discussed in a straight news story. Like a news story, though, an editorial requires careful research. The newspaper or broadcast station's reputation is staked on the accuracy of the supporting material in each editorial.

Generally, you should organize an editorial in four steps:

1. State the subject and your position on the subject in the introduction.
2. Discuss opposing points of view.
3. Prove your position with supporting details.
4. Draw a conclusion.

These four parts do not have a set order. The editorial, for example, may begin with the conclusion. Often the steps are woven together. No matter how the steps are taken, the key is to make the editorial both logical and compelling.

Editorials can have many purposes—from defending actions to praising people to simply entertaining readers. Three of the most common purposes are explaining, evaluating and persuading. Of course, any editorial can serve more than one purpose.

Editorials That Explain

editorial that explains

an editorial that attempts to interpret or inform rather than to argue a point of view

Editorials that explain are somewhat like expository essays. They attempt to interpret or inform rather than to argue a point of view. The only expression of opinion comes in the interpretation of the facts. These editorials explain topics such as the elimination of an intramural program, a change in the grading system or the sudden departure of a faculty member. Editorials that explain are most effective when they describe what has taken place, give a detailed explanation of the causes, and highlight the importance of the topic.

The following excerpt, taken from the *Scout* at Overland High School in Aurora, Colorado, is part of a guest editorial written by police officer Steve Cox. In this editorial, Cox explains why the police bust parties:

Have you ever wondered why the police show up at your party and break it up? Have you ever been at a party with alcohol or drugs? How about a party where you have 100–200 people there? Have you ever had to pay a "door" charge to get into a party?

As high school students, most of you can personally relate to one of the above questions. Those of you who don't have first-hand experience probably know someone that has. In fact, some of you may have been charged with liquor possession, disorderly conduct, trespassing, disturbing the peace, or a DUI.

Why do police worry about this? Nine times out of ten, the police respond to a party because someone in the neighborhood or community has called in a complaint. Very seldom do we just drive by and see a party.

Editorials That Evaluate

Editorials that evaluate focus on actions or situations that the editors view as being wrong or in need of improvement. The criticism in these editorials should always be constructive, though. In writing these editorials, be sure to emphasize anything positive about what you are criticizing, or your readers will no longer trust you. Furthermore, you have a responsibility to offer alternative solutions or courses of action.

editorial that evaluates
an editorial that focuses on actions or situations that the editors view as being wrong or in need of improvement

The following excerpt, from an editorial in the *Crest* (the paper at Coronado High School in Lubbock, Texas), comments on the state of school restrooms:

> **It grabs you.**
> **It permeates your clothes.**
> **It stinks.**
> The problem?
>
> School restrooms. Stench hangs heavy in the air and seeps from cracks and crevices where brown and black slime have a heyday.
>
> Take a close look. Some areas of the floor are constantly wet. Slow leaks from the fixtures provide a soggy, sticky film that coats the corners and seeps on the floors where the caulking is cracked.
>
> Oh sure, the restrooms are swept daily, their trash emptied. This procedure, timed several days within the past month, took an average of 2 minutes and 4 seconds each, start to finish. But a quick sweep won't cut it; this is a serious job screaming for Mr. Clean.
>
> So wake up and smell the restrooms. (You can't miss 'em.)

Editorials That Persuade

Generally, **editorials that persuade** offer specific solutions to a perceived problem. Unlike editorials that evaluate, they expect immediate action rather than the achievement of a general or long-term objective. A persuasive editorial can provide leadership in bringing about changes in school policy or in student behavior. Furthermore, when the school community is embroiled in controversy, editorials that persuade offer the opportunity to suggest compromise solutions.

editorial that persuades
an editorial that offers specific solutions to a perceived problem

This excerpt is from an editorial in the *Lance,* the paper at Westside High School in Omaha, Nebraska. The writer argues that the school candy store should be re-opened:

If a student is hungry enough, he will buy food . . . even from a vending machine. This year, students are able to purchase various products from the vending machines located in the cafeteria. Many people hoped the machines would reduce stress caused by clubs using the candy store. However, the *Lance* believes the candy store should be utilized again because too many problems are created due to the vending machines and to the questions raised by the new distribution system. . . .

The administration closed the candy store due to congestion and uncleanliness. . . .

This year, numerous cafeteria messes from the vending machines have resulted in punishment for the entire school. When a select few cause problems, it is unfair to punish everyone. No one can buy anything if the machines are turned off, and clubs won't receive money when the food is not sold.

The clubs which used the candy store last year are to be given the same monetary amount from the vending machines' proceeds. Profits from the past three years were averaged for each organization. This average is the amount to be given to the group. Some organizations that didn't sell candy last year have received money, and as a result reduced the funds which were allocated to other clubs. . .

The candy store allows students to take responsibility for themselves and organizations. Individuals must sacrifice their open mods and work for the funds. Students' efforts result in visible rewards. They can see the money their club is accumulating and take an active role in the process. . . .

Although complications existed when the store was used, the *Lance* believes the candy stores should be re-opened. The vending machines have not solved any problems; actually they have only produced additional negative situations. Uncleanliness and punishment have replaced school spirit and club cooperation. That's definitely not a fair trade.

YOUR BEAT

Imagine that you have just learned that your school is going to require uniforms for all students. Consider the following statements. The principal explains, "What we want is a learning environment, not a fashion show." The police chief comments, "These school uniforms will reduce violence on campus." A parent notes, "The social pressure to have designer clothes was too much." And a student says, "I dress to please myself, not to please others."

Write a brief, 200-word editorial in which you support or criticize the new school policy.

◢ INVOLVING READERS

As was explained earlier in this chapter, a newspaper editorial staff has the responsibility to create community conversation. In order for readers to have their turn to speak, newspapers provide space for dialogue on current topics of concern. Readers are given their voices in two ways: in letters to the editor and in opinion features.

Letters to the Editor

Most readers like reading letters to the editor, but they must be encouraged to write. If you want to strengthen this part of the editorial pages, you have to ask readers to respond. Furthermore, you must be willing to print critical, as well as complimentary, letters. Finally, to receive vital, well-written letters, you must publish vital, well-written editorials. Most editors have discovered sometimes to their dismay, that there is a correlation between the quality of the letters to the editor and the quality of the columns that appear on the editorial pages.

Editors have a tremendous incentive to solicit responses for their opinion pages. Carefully crafted letters from readers can stimulate worthwhile dialogues on important topics. In an issue of the *Griffin* (the paper at Dulaney High School in Timonium, Maryland), for example, letters were printed in response to an advertisement the newspaper had run for the Island Dreams Surf Station. The girls who wrote the letters were concerned that the ad portrayed women as possessions. In the ad, women were referred to as "chicks" who could be surfers' "scores."

In the following issue of the *Griffin*, two opposing "Viewpoint" columns argued the legitimacy of the points raised by the concerned girls. Accompanying letters to the editor included these comments:

> Island Dreams is a surf shop that sells *bathing suits*. That ad was simply trying to market their products. It's called advertising! Seeing a cartoon of a female in a bikini is not going to cause or affect anyone's ideas or beliefs of women in society. (Ashley Door)

> The advertisement wasn't promoting sex, drugs, or violence: therefore, I feel their comments were absurd. I agree that female discrimination is an important issue, but the ad was clearly not what you made it out to be. (Melissa Hajimihatis)

> What they failed to realize is that the man is portrayed as a scruffy, ugly, stupid caveman. This portrayal would seem to discredit any complaints about stereotypes. (Nitin Goel)

You may not agree with the opinions stated in these letters, or about ads but you probably agree that the editorial pages of the *Griffin* offered readers a useful sounding board for ideas and a safety valve for emotions. In short, the letters to the editor provided an open forum for community conversation.

One Letter Fits All . . .

National Public Radio's humorist Ian Shoales suggests that if you really want to know what people in the United States are thinking about, you should read the letters to the editor in your local paper. Furthermore, if you want to write a letter yourself but don't have the time, Shoales will do it for you. What follows is an excerpt from one such letter that will please anyone regardless of political bent.

> I realize this won't get printed in your so-called newspaper. The (Leftist, Conservative) slant is a disgrace to all (real Americans, taxpayers, our unborn children). Still I must urge everyone to (register to vote, write your Congressman, vote No on Prop 17) or we might not have (another four years, streetlights, a tomorrow).
>
> As a (taxpayer, life-long Democrat, homeowner) I (view with alarm, am frightened by, am angered by) our (foreign policy, domestic policy, bleeding-heart environmentalists). Are we living in (a welfare state, Nazi Germany, a fool's paradise)?

Source: Ian Shoales, I Gotta Go: The Commentary of Ian Shoales *(New York: Putman Publishing).*

Here are seven suggestions for generating more letters to the editor:

1. Set up rules, and follow them.
2. Focus on school issues.
3. Identify letter writers.
4. Encourage serious discussion.
5. Verify all information.
6. Run letters promptly.
7. Run as many letters as possible.

Opinion Features

In its first editorial in 1982, *USA Today* wrote of its challenge to provide a daily forum for the free exchange of opinions. The editorial stated: "Our goal: to offer an opinion page where people with diverse points of view can help establish, amid the chaos of personal agendas, a national agenda for America. For those who listen only to what they already believe speak only to themselves." In its attempt to reach that goal, *USA Today* includes a "Voices" feature on its opinion pages. Many college and high school papers have borrowed the idea and typically present five responses to a question. Figure 11.2 was taken from the January 27, 2000 issue of *The Eagle* (Chadron State College, Nebr.).

FIGURE 11.2
COLLEGE NEWSPAPER
OPINION FEATURE

Voices: What are your weekly expenses and where do you spend most of your money?

■ Most students live on a limited budget and don't realize where their money is going. Organization of your finances is the key to a healthy financial future and it begins with noticing where the money you spend is going.

Zach Even, sophomore
"All I've spent money on lately is school, my deer-damaged truck and a fishing license."

Mary Tewahade, freshman
"Tuition and books are killing me so I hope I will get a scholarship."

Heidi Todd freshman
"Food, gas and Wal-Mart."

Jon Schwaderer sophomore
"Gwen, Gwen, Gwen! Enough said."

Jenifer Reisner junior
"Where I spend my money is on apartment bills, but it is well worth it."

Many high school newspapers have created their own versions of *USA Today's* "Voices" feature. The example in Figure 11.3 appeared in the *Advocate,* the newspaper at Albuquerque Academy in Albuquerque, New Mexico.

FIGURE 11.3
HIGH SCHOOL NEWSPAPER OPINION FEATURE

CHARGERTALK

Question:
Does academic pressure affect your awareness of World Issues?

"Yes and no. Yes because certain classes make me more aware of current world events such as history and English and even in some other classes, but the academic pressure forces me to spend more time with schoolwork and be less concerned with world events."
(photo of Scott Butterfield by Barbara Lilie)

"Yes, but in a good way. In P.E. today a conversation that began about real estate turned into a discussion about politics, and I realized that only at Academy would this be set in a locker room."

Malcolm Alonzo

(photo by Barbara Lilie)

"Yeah, if I had less homework I'd be able to watch the news and stuff like that." *(photo of Caryn Thesing by Barbara Lilie)*

Source: Reprinted with permission from Advocate.

After studying the opinion features in this section, create your own "Voices" feature. Select several of your classmates to interview on a question that you believe is important to your school community. Now choose the three answers that best represent a cross-section of the opinions gathered. Edit those answers to an appropriate length for the feature.

THIS JUST IN: *Portrait of a Young Journalist*
Kelly Lewis, Intern to an Editor

The speeding SunTran No. 7 Candelaria-University bus has to screech to stop when its driver realizes I'm standing at the bus stop on Camino de la Sierra and that I actually want to get on and ride.

Maybe the driver has passed by a few other passengers today—it's 7:10 on a Thursday morning and the bus is empty. Or maybe the passengers have passed by the bus—for good—with their economy cars, time-slotted lives and Western independence.

This feature story lead would hardly surprise anyone who knows Kelly Lewis, the author. After all Lewis rarely misses anything. During her senior year at Sandia High School in Albuquerque, Lewis entered an apprenticeship program with Tim Gallagher, editor of the *Albuquerque Tribune.* For five hours a week, Lewis shadowed Gallagher. The remainder of her work time was spent as editor of her high school newspaper.

From this experience, Lewis learned that she faced the same situations in her school setting as did the editor of a daily paper, only on a smaller scale. According to Gallagher, "Kelly struggled with the Trib as we put together a budget. . . . She heard our thorniest personnel debates. She shared our joy on the day we won a Pulitzer Prize. She wrote. She was edited. She shot pictures. She was edited. She designed pages. She was edited."

Lewis now plans to use what she has learned by pursuing a career in journalism. Following four years at Northwestern University, she hopes to work at an inner-city newspaper in Chicago, Or maybe make photodocumentaries. When asked if she ever dreamed of a Pulitzer Prize for herself, Lewis admits, "I want one but that's not why I got into journalism. I got into journalism because I love words."

◢Choosing Cartoons

Cartoons can do more than enrich popular culture and make us laugh. Editorial cartoonist Thomas Nast, who invented the Democratic donkey, the Republican elephant and the modern image of Santa Claus, helped bring down New York City's corrupt political boss William Marcy Tweed. Tweed didn't worry much about newspaper stories because, as he quipped, most of his constituents couldn't read anyway. He did worry, though, about his constituents' understanding Nast's razor-sharp cartoons.

Editorial cartoons can be a powerful form of expression. They can grab the attention of readers in a single glance. Unfortunately, however, they are not always understood. One study reported in *Journalism Quarterly* revealed an overwhelming failure of nationally syndicated cartoons to get their message across. Most interpretations offered by readers were not at all what the cartoonist had intended. Therefore, your goal in drawing or selecting editorial cartoons is to make sure that your readers get the intended message. An effective way to achieve this goal is to have a cartoon reinforce a message that is contained in an accompanying editorial.

An editorial cartoon that appeared in the *Axe* at South Eugene High School in Eugene, Oregon reinforced the theme of the editorial page. Both the cartoon and the text dealt with the ways male and female high school students are treated inside and outside the classroom (Figure 11.4).

In addition to reinforcing editorial messages, cartoons should also be timely and well drawn. Jeff Stahler, of the *Cincinnati Post,* based a cartoon on the fact that as businesses across the country continued to trim workers, college and high school graduates were finding jobs scarce (Figure 11.5).

FIGURE 11.4
CARTOON REINFORCED BY EDITORIAL PAGE

Reprinted by permission of the Cincinnati Post.

FIGURE 11.5
CARTOON REINFORCING TIMELINESS OF ISSUES

Reprinted by permission of the Cincinnati Post.

Choose an editorial from a past issue of your school or local newspaper. Now draw an editorial cartoon that could be used to illustrate an important point in the editorial. If you prefer not to draw, describe in a brief essay what you might have drawn.

BYLINE

JIM MORIN
EDITORIAL CARTOONIST

Jim Morin, editorial cartoonist for the *Miami Herald,* has made a career of targeting the hypocrisy of politicians and the absurdities of modern life. No subject is spared his often biting commentary—depicted through his signature short, stumpy figures. Long regarded as one of the nation's finest and sharpest cartoonists, he won the 1996 Pulitzer Prize for editorial cartoons.

Morin spends the bulk of his days closeted in a small office with a drawing board. His desk is cluttered with tools of the trade, and the floors are strewn with drawings, books and newspapers. The walls are plastered with memorabilia: cartoons by people who have influenced him; letters from fans and some "hate mail" from foes; photos of famous people, including the Beatles and President Clinton; a framed picture of his treasured guitar; and photos of his kids, Elizabeth and Spencer.

A Pulitzer finalist twice before, Morin likened winning journalism's highest honor to being thrust into another dimension. "My voicemail box is full, my in-box is filled with letters, and I've used the hold button on my phone for the first time," he laughed.

Although enjoying the limelight, the unassuming, bespectacled satirist remains pragmatic. "It's been 20 years of really hard work, and this is a culmination of sorts," he said. "It's a pat on the back, saying 'Nice job.' And you wake up the next day and go back to work."

For Morin, that means going back to looking at the world in his own special way. "Cartoonists are observers in the same way that newspaper columnists are," he said. "The difference is that I visualize what I see. And, the more succinctly the point is stated, the better the cartoon is."

Source: Adapted with permission from Knight-Ridder News.

CHAPTER REVIEW

KEY TERMS

Show that you know the meanings of the following key terms by correctly using them in complete sentences. Write your answers on a separate sheet of paper.

editorial
editorial page
masthead
op-ed page
editorial board

brainstorming
editorial that explains
editorial that evaluates
editorial that persuades

OPEN FORUM

1. According to the *New Yorker,* in a world of 500 channels, where viewers can program for themselves, where databases or facts can be summoned to the screen without the newspaper package in which they originally appeared, the editorial challenge to the *New York Times* is to be the one unassailable source of information. Clearly, when several hundred "voices" fight to be heard, the competition may distort the news process. How important is it, do you think, for people to have one institution that speaks with the same editorial voice every day?

2. Most editorial writers rely on reading as their primary source for ideas and information. Pulitzer Prize–winning editorial writer Paul Greenberg says that he reads a 2-day-old *New York Times.* He does not, however, subscribe to *Newsweek* or *Time,* because he would prefer to get his news "unpremasticated and not at the discount store." Chew on Greenberg's preferences for a moment. Do you agree? Why or why not?

3. When a newspaper prints the ideas of readers in an opinion feature, do you believe it risks creating opinion rather than defining opinion?

FINDING THE FLAW

National Public Radio humorist Ian Shoales tells the story of a San Francisco radio talk show host who conducted an unusual poll. Shoales says, "Apparently, the host gave his listeners a number, asked for a response without giving them anything to respond to, and got a response anyway. He got 281 responses, in fact, of which 35 percent were yes, 33 percent no, and 32 percent undecided. That's a good spread, demographically, considering that he didn't ask a question."

Do you think that polls ever accurately reflect public opinion? What are some of the reasons why so many polls are flawed?

 ## MEDIA WATCH

1. According to author Harry W. Stonecipher, most of the resources of newspapers and the news staffs of broadcast stations are devoted to the communication of information, not persuasive communication. The typical newspaper in the United States devotes about

CHAPTER REVIEW, continued

◆ MEDIA WATCH, CONTINUED

4 percent of its nonadvertising space to editorial comment. Another 12 percent is devoted to various kinds of columns, some dealing with politics and public affairs. The typical national television network is likely to devote about 16 percent of its evening newscast to commentary. Local television stations, however, rarely include editorial comment. Find an example of editorial comment on your local television station. What was the topic? Why do you think the station chose to editorialize on the particular subject?

2. Write a letter to your local paper. It it prints the letter, note any changes made by the editor. If you believe the meaning of your letter was altered, call the editor of the editorial page for an explanation. If your letter is not published, call the editor to ask why.

String Book

1. Some high school newspapers write what are called *mini-torials.* The *Little Hawk,* the paper at Iowa City High School, for example, includes mini-torials in a "thumbs-up, thumbs-down" format. Study the following mini-torials:

    Thumbs-up

    To the varsity football team for being ranked number one in the state.

    To Fred, the janitor. Are you satisfied now?

    To winter and the next exciting bowling season.

    Thumbs-down

    To the windows being bricked up, providing us with one less escape route.

    To the military tactics used by the Hall Monitor and the Library Aides.

    Create three thumbs-up and three thumbs-down mini-torials.

2. Review the three kinds of editorials. Make a list of possible topics for each type. Then write a summary sentence that describes each topic. With your teacher's help, select the best topic to develop. Write the editorial.

Chapter 12
Column Writing and Reviewing

"The truth is, I write for myself, which is the act of arrogance that powers the work of most columnists."

—Anna Quindlen

KEY TERMS

In this chapter, you will learn the meaning of these terms:

column
syndicated
review
specialized column
jargon

After completing this chapter, you will be able to:

◆ describe the different types of columns, including the various features of columns,

◆ review a current school production, film, video, book or album,

◆ create ideas that could be used in a column,

◆ write a column for publication.

◆

*O*n your way to school, you notice a homeless man who is standing on the street corner and holding a tattered piece of cardboard with the message "Will work for food" scrawled on it. This isn't the first time you've seen this man. You wonder how long he has been homeless, where he stays at night and if he has a family.

Although these are questions any person may ask, it is a columnist's job to do something with them. Some people may notice the man and simply shake their heads. You may do the same and then write about the failing economy, or about the increasing number of homeless people in the United States. Writing a column allows you to share very personal feelings with your readers. It also gives you the freedom to write about any topic you wish. These are two luxuries that news reporting doesn't permit.

In this chapter, you will learn how to polish a column for publication, what the different types of columns are and where to search for column ideas. Although most newspapers allot more space and less attention to columns than anything else on the editorial page, columns continue to capture the attention of readers.

▲BUILDING A COLUMN

column

an article with a byline that expresses an opinion about something and that shows individuality. Columns usually have between 450 and 1,000 words

A **column** is a bylined article, usually between 450 and 1,000 words, that expresses an opinion about something. A column's subject matter is unrestricted and varies widely. The distinguishing feature that separates column writing from news reporting is individuality. From colonial times to today, newspaper readers have shown interest in columns because columns give readers the opportunity to peek into someone else's life and discover the writer's thoughts on an event or subject.

The objectivity that rules news reporting does not apply to column writing. Each columnist is expected to take a unique approach when addressing issues. Each columnist must develop a unique voice. The personal touch is often the key to a column's success. *New York Times* columnist William Safire advises column writers to forget what they learned in journalism school. For example, columnists should never put the story in the lead. They should keep the reader off balance and guessing. "Let 'em have a hot shot of ambiguity right between the eyes," says Safire.

So when you stare at that blank screen, think of an unusual angle on which to focus—your own angle. If you have a fresh outlook on a subject, your column will be successful, no matter how much the topic has been discussed.

There is no specific formula for writing columns. However, the various parts are much like those of a short story: beginning, middle and conclusion.

The Beginning

"Writing is not hard," wrote Canadian humorist Stephen Leacock. "Just get paper and pencil, sit down, and write as it occurs to you. The writing is easy—it's the occurring that's hard." To write an effective introduction for your column, what "occurs" to you should grab the reader's attention. This can be achieved in a number of ways. You might include a current news item exclusive to the column, an anecdote or even a joke. Study these examples:

> I've done everything to avoid facing up to the geography crisis. It's not that I haven't seen the evidence. Every week I seem to read about the results of yet another study confirming a shocking level of geographical ninnyism among the young. Apparently, if you asked the average American high school student where, say, Alabama is, he might identify it as the capital of Chicago, which he thinks of as a large country somewhere in the Middle East. A high school student who lives in Montgomery or Birmingham or Huntsville wouldn't say that about Alabama, of course; he'd say it was a football team. (Calvin Trillin, *If You Can't Say Something Nice,* Random House NY, p. 149.)

> While visiting my grandmother over spring break, she asked if I had any friends from California. I told her I didn't think so, and asked why.
>
> "Well, because you say 'like' a lot," was her response. (Tres Kryfko, *Advocate,* Albuquerque Academy, Albuquerque, N.M.)

The Middle

Whether you are presenting an argument about why marijuana should be legalized in the United States or telling readers about your most recent trip to the dentist, you must be able to present it in an appealing way that doesn't bombard your audience with boring statistics and a jumble of words. It's very important to back up your opinions, so the details you include should contribute real meaning to your column. You can include colorful descriptions or factual evidence, which can be found in numerous sources (see Chapter 4).

Magazines, newspapers and television can be useful sources of information for columns. Think of all the times random quotations have

SHOE reprinted by permission of Tribune Media Services.

caught your attention or television programs have struck a nerve. Incorporating these quotations or information from television programs into your columns is a good way to support your points and present outside information to which others can relate.

Another technique writers use to boost the appeal of their columns is the use of description. However, be careful not to overdo it. Description should be subtle. It should add color and detail to the column. It should highlight the message intended by the writer rather than cloud it through unnecessary explanations. The following examples illustrate how well-chosen details can increase the effectiveness of a column's message:

> Studies have shown that television coverage can contribute to an increase in teen suicides. A researcher in New York found that suicide rates were higher within the two weeks following a program that has dealt with suicide. (Jennifer Levine, *Overland Scout*, Overland High School, Colo.)

> I soon found myself face-to-face with the zoo's star polar bear, Binky, who in terms of size is basically a Winnebago motor home with teeth. Binky became a major news story in Alaska last year when, on separate occasions a few weeks apart, he attempted to eat two people. The victims, both of whom survived, had climbed over two fences to get close to Binky's cage. One of them was an Australian tourist, who said she climbed the fences because she wanted to take a close-up photograph; she wound up with her leg in Binky's mouth. (Dave Barry, *Miami Herald*)

The Conclusion

Always conclude a column in a way that will satisfy readers. Three common types of conclusions are the circle ending, the rhetorical-question conclusion and the summary ending.

Do you remember the circle ending that was discussed in Chapter 10? The circle ending is a good way to end a column, because it relates the reader back to the beginning and ties up the loose ends. For example, assume that you are writing a column about the nudity portrayed in Calvin Klein magazine ads. You choose to focus on an Obsession ad in which the model is draped seductively over a couch. You might begin your column by describing the ad, how it made you feel and what you think it means. Perhaps you think it exploits women, or perhaps you believe it is a beautiful, original way to sell products. As you discuss your ideas throughout your column, you can hold the readers' attention by repeatedly coming back to the original example. Avoid bringing in anything completely new or unrelated at the end.

Another type of ending is the rhetorical-question conclusion. This type of column ending leaves the readers with a question to mull over. For example, let's say you are writing about the reaction of the crowd at a state execution. You stayed up late watching the news reports and were startled to see masses of people carrying signs that were mocking the man who was about to be put to death. "Take a seat and get the shock of your life," reads one. "Strike a match, light a fire and pull up a chair to the state BBQ," says another. Seeing these things on television has confused you. Although you understand that the man committed a terrible crime, you are not sure the death penalty is justified. In your column you talk about what you saw and how you reacted. You also include an explanation of what the criminal did to receive the death penalty. Rather than end the column by drawing a conclusion, though, you pose a question that allows the readers to reach their own conclusions. For example, you might ask, "Whose life is it anyway?"

The most popular conclusion is the summary ending, which can wrap up a column in whatever way the writer chooses. Like any story, news article, review or broadcast, though, be certain the ending is effective, has a certain amount of closure and makes sense so the reader feels satisfied.

Column Characteristics

Most columnists try to incorporate three characteristics in their columns: humanity, wit and freedom of approach. These characteristics give the columns individuality and variety, the spices that flavor a column.

A column reflects humanity if the columnist is people oriented and focuses more on human interest than on exciting or breaking news. A column is the only place in a newspaper where writers are allowed to write about human-interest topics or even about themselves. The majority of columnists take advantage of this opportunity.

Many columnists include the element of humanity in a serious way. They often discuss topics close to their hearts, as in the following example:

> She had known, ever since she first read about the Vietnam Veterans Memorial, that she would go there someday. Sometime she would be in Washington and would go and see his name and leave again.

So silly, all that fuss about the memorial. Whatever else Vietnam was, it was not the kind of war that calls for some "Raising the Flag at Iwo Jima" kind of statue. She was not prepared, though, for the impact of the memorial. To walk down into it in the pale winter sunshine was like the war itself, like going into a dark valley and damned if there ever was any light at the end of the tunnel. Just death. When you get closer to the two walls, the number of names start to stun you. It is terrible, there in the peace and the pale sunshine.

The names are listed by date of death. There has never been a time, day or night, drunk or sober, for 13 years she could not have told you the date. He was killed on Aug. 13, 1969. It is near the middle of the left wall. She went toward it as though she had known beforehand where it would be. His name is near the bottom. She had to kneel to find it. Stupid cliches. His name leaped out at her. It was like being hit. (Molly Ivins, *Dallas Times Herald*)

A column does not have to paint a portrait of a particular person. It can discuss something as simple as the bond young children have with their first pet. It can bring up a controversy, such as genetic engineering:

Whoever thought that someday we will be capable of genetically engineering our children? Would it be like buying a car? Do you pick the options and features you want?

"Can I get one with brown hair please?"

"Ma'am, we're all out of those. I could put one on special order from the plant if you'd like." (Griffin Creech, *Rampage,* John Marshall High School, Tex.)

Another characteristic that tends to mark the work of a columnist is wit. Wit does not necessarily mean humor, but instead how well writers express themselves. A witty columnist writes in an imaginative, insightful way and has the ability to communicate his or her thoughts and ideas originally. Wit also includes the columnist's ability to change tone, subject and style.

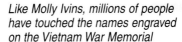

Like Molly Ivins, millions of people have touched the names engraved on the Vietnam War Memorial

Some communities and schools have provided spaces where the same elements—spray paint and chalk—that taggers can use can be turned into artistic murals. Is there any "artistic" graffiti in your community?

The following example is set up like a story. Told in third person, the column tells about the encounters of a San Francisco bus driver with gang violence:

Put your ear to the street and listen.

"Too much freedom here," he told me—the Bay area bus driver who'd fled his homeland, China, for no other reason but to revel in the same freedom he now called excess.

Dreams die hard in the city. His faded like the green grass he sought on the other side of the world.

Freedom. An ideal denied to him by the abuses of others. . . .

The debt of freedom was painted on the walls.

Sprawling webs of graffiti cloaked the interior from my seat to the ceiling to the other side, then all the way back, back past the second door. And even on the second door.

Aerosol-armed bandits, known as taggers, had covered virtually every inch of what used to be paneled ads and white plastic. . . .

He told me everything was worse at night.

He told me of the SFPD [San Francisco Police Department] and their disease of lethargy. . . .

He told me about guns—not the ones in Communist China—the guns in the city, on his line, in his bus.

The guns pulled on him, on and off the job.

Prepared for whatever unsettling answer he might provide, I asked an all encompassing, "Why?"

He shook his head, groaned and locked his eyes on the graffiti-stained bus stop we'd just approached.

"Too much freedom here," he told me.

"Yeah," I agreed, "this is a pretty liberal town."

"No, not San Francisco," he said, looking out the streaked window and down the rolling hills.

"America." (Corey Takahashi, *Bucs' Blade,* Grand Haven High School, Grand Haven, Mich.)

The characteristic of freedom of approach means that a columnist may do just about anything on paper. For a change of pace, some columnists have been known to abandon straight column writing altogether and instead write verse or imaginative prose. The following is an example of a column written as poetry:

My grandfather speaks to me still
His voice inside my head, sometimes
escapes
through my mouth, or worse yet, I will
walk
with his legs, let his hands do my work. Or
I am
wearing his hat, the black felt one with the narrow brim,
and I
hear sermons, feel my hair thinning under
their weight
so when I swear to visit his grave, he knows,
as he lives
inside me, I am lying again, that I am more than
like him
that before I would taste the dirt or feel my fingernails
grow
I would be back on the road from town, headed east
toward
the grove of trees, dangling my feet in the stream,
and he is there,
cutting back the willows, saying this is where it began, as he has
    said
every time I am alone with her, every time I am in love, not leav-
    ing, me
even in the private moment, not letting me forget this miracle,
this flesh. (Ted Genoways, *CornerStone*, Nebraska Wesleyan
    University, Lincoln, NE)

The amount of freedom of approach given to columnists differs from newspaper to newspaper. Problems can arise when an editor thinks that a columnist is being inaccurate or biased. Some editors argue that all columns should be published as written—that writers or columns must take responsibility for what they say. Other editors don't want to present readers with material that could mislead or misinform them (Figure 12.1).

Using the three characteristics for column writing outlined in the chapter, write a column about a situation close to you—something "straight from the heart." Keeping in mind that you have freedom of approach, try to address the topic from an innovative point of view. Be sure to include vivid description.

FIGURE 12.1
DO'S AND DON'TS FOR COLUMNISTS

DO

DO vary your subject matter.

DO look for oddities and the unusual to spark interest in your readers. Say your class took a field trip to the state penitentiary, and after you were shown a cell in solitary confinement you wondered how anyone could endure such isolation. In order to understand what it might be like, you spend a certain amount of time in a place similar to "the hole." Your column would then discuss the effects that isolation had on you.

DO use a style that is usually offbeat—use the personal flavor and touch. Be yourself. To be a successful columnist you must have confidence in what you're saying and how you are saying it.

DO keep it short and to the point. A column is a reasonably short piece of writing so try not to give your readers too much of a good thing.

DO admit it when you make a mistake. Even if it's something as simple as a misspelled name or as wrong as a misquote, keep in mind that some readers take everything they see in print seriously. Swallow your pride and make a note of it in your next column, apologizing to those you may have misrepresented.

DO have a genuine interest in your readers; write for them instead of yourself. It's easy to get caught up in your own ideas, opinions and frustrations. Just remember—your readers will more than likely have these same ideas, so present them in a way they can relate to. For example, if a food fight broke out in the school cafeteria, most of the student body either witnessed or heard about it. Try to approach the subject in a fresh way by projecting your thoughts on the situation into the minds of your readers.

DON'T

DON'T embarrass anyone without real reason. Have respect for yourself and for others. Readers get ideas about your personality from your writing, so be alert to people's feelings.

DON'T assume that you always know best—that you have all the answers. Part of your credibility as a columnist comes from the knowledge you have about the topic, but that doesn't mean your ideas are correct. Someone will always be around to challenge them.

DON'T claim all the credit. Although your ideas and words are your own, don't overlook those who may have helped put those thoughts in order. Remember to cite outside sources.

DON'T overwork the pronoun I. Having your own column is, in some respects, an expression of ego. Everyone likes to see their name in print, but don't let your 15 minutes of fame go to your head.

DON'T think that your own experiences and ideas are always fascinating to others. Telling the story about the time you saw someone fall into the lake at a class reunion might be hilarious to you, but others might not think it's so funny since they weren't there to see it.

DON'T overwork your family. Columns about your family can be touching. Columnist Robert Haggart once wrote about the death of his father and how his dad's failing health had brought them closer. This is fine to an extent, but remember that not everyone is interested in your family.

DON'T hesitate to give both sides of the story. Columnists are not required to be unbiased as reporters are, but they don't always have to present just one side of the issue, either. Joint editorials are a good way to cover this.

Source: Adapted with permission from Kenneth R. Byerly, "Community Journalism," Chilton Company, New York, NY.

▲TYPES OF COLUMNS

If you look through any newspaper, you'll find that almost every section carries a column. But because columnists draw from a variety of literary styles and subject matter, classifying columns into types can be difficult.

As we said in the previous section, some columns are humorous, some are serious, some discuss news events and some tell stories. Most columns fit into one of the following classifications: syndicated columns, humor columns, editorials, gossip columns, entertainment page coverage and reviews, and specialized columns.

Syndicated Columns

syndicated

published through a syndicate, an association that acquires such things as columns, stories, articles and cartoons for simultaneous publication in numerous newspapers and periodicals

When a column is **syndicated,** it is published through an association (a syndicate) that acquires such things as columns, stories, articles and cartoons for simultaneous publication in numerous newspapers and periodicals. A handful of today's nationally syndicated columnists have become household names—Dave Barry, Molly Ivins, William F. Buckley, Jr., and Ann Landers, for example. Topics they discuss range from "Magnolias and Moonshine" to "Shopping in the Chromosome Mall." You can learn much from studying their columns.

Humor Columns

The purpose of humor columns is to amuse and entertain readers. The success of a humorist, much like that of any other columnist, depends on the writer's point of view and his or her ability to shape opinions into words that will entertain readers. For example, Dave Barry and Art Buchwald are humor columnists whose work has been widely syndicated. Many newspapers also have their own humor columnists.

Humorists have been compared to cartoonists, because they are expected to exaggerate to make a point. Stepping outside the boundaries of normal column writing is not unusual for these journalists. Columnist Sam G. Riley once took a storybook approach in a column about *Skylab*. He wrote about it in the form of a children's tale—specifically, the story of Henny Penny, the talking chicken who ran to tell the king that the sky was falling. Riley's version began, "Once upon a time, Henny Penny went over the hill in search of nuts. Since she was on Capitol Hill, she didn't have to look far." This approach—rewriting a children's story—is a creative way to make a political point.

Editorials

You learned how to write an editorial in Chapter 11. When you are writing an editorial, remember to take a direct stand on a specific issue. An editorial should stir up action among your readers. It should make people think. The examples that follow illustrate the strong commitment that editorial writers have to their topics.

Columnists may choose an issue to write about that they can relate back to their own lives:

> I really didn't want to do it. But since the national media have made such a to-do about it—and as an American Indian journalist—I feel it is necessary to get my two cents into the hype.
>
> *People* magazine displayed its special brand of ignorance with a cutline under the photo of Pocahontas that read: "Pocahontas: the squaw that stirs the drink; at last, a heroine who knows the ways of nature and the art of belting out show tunes."
>
> There is not an American Indian woman alive who is not immediately repulsed by the word "squaw". . . .
>
> The theme music repeatedly refers to Indians as savages. Savage is a name Indians have had to live with from the day the first book was written about them. (Tim Giago, *Indian County Today,* Rapid City, S.D.)

Community totem raising in Tsimshian, Alaska, offers a positive image on which to make editorial comment, unlike the problem columnist Tim Giago outlines above.

Sometimes two staff members write with opposing viewpoints on the same issue, and they are printed side by side. This gives the readers a more balanced coverage of a particular subject. The following two columns appeared in the same issue of *Crossfire,* the newspaper at Crossroads School in Santa Monica, California:

It seems that many students were either asleep or absent when the "integrity experiment" was announced at convocations last month. This proposal was not intended to stop cheating, and its creators are not under the impression that dishonesty on campus will cease upon its institution.

The statement, "This work represents my own honest effort," must be signed at the bottom of a test or essay in order for the work to be accepted by the teacher.

Many feel that the administration is presuming dishonesty in asking them to sign this statement. Do these same students feel that their integrity is challenged when they are asked to sign their names on college application essays claiming that this is in fact their own work?

Sometimes, the limitations that a rule places on individual freedoms must be weighed against the positive impact that it will have on the group. Signing one's name is not that great of a sacrifice to make in order to bring cheating on campus down from its all-time high. (Maura Pally)

It seems harmless enough. How hard can it be to simply write a little statement in the defense of our integrity, and then sign it?

But however the student-faculty council chose to label their "integrity experiment;" essentially, we are all being asked to defend our integrity. The mere fact that teachers are required not to accept the major assignments from their students unless they have been signed in such a manner, proves that we are all suspected of cheating until we sign that sworn statement.

It is insulting that we must prove our honesty because other people have decided to be dishonest. If our integrity has not previously been in question, why should it now? Until there is evidence to the contrary, administration and faculty should consider honesty and integrity to be self-evident. Is it now assumed that if a few scattered people are caught cheating that everyone must be cheating? If one person decides to jump off a cliff, will the rest of the student body be forced to sign medical release forms in the event that they decide to follow suit? (Seth Rosenson)

Gossip Columns

Gossip is something in which almost everyone is interested. But things like who is seeing whom and who was cruising Main Street Friday night do not need to be reported in the school newspaper. Gossip columns generally take little creativity to produce. They are supposed to be entertaining, but too often they do little more than repeat rumors.

Futhermore, gossip columns are subject to the same libel laws as the rest of the paper. Libel is a published false statement that damages a person's reputation. The most famous case of libel related to a false rumor was the 1981 libel suit brought by actress and comedian Carol Burnett against the *Enquirer,* a tabloid known for its sensational stories about celebrities.

Fear of lawsuits is not the only reason to avoid gossip columns, however. They often give a negative impression not only of the newspaper but of the rest of the school as well. Although gossip columns are popular in the commercial press, it's best for you to avoid them.

Entertainment Page Coverage and Reviews

Much of the space on your school entertainment page will be devoted to either reviews or coverage of school performances (plays, music concerts and so forth). **Reviews** are columns that typically comment on movies, recordings, books, television programs, concerts, plays and even restaurants. A review is more than just an opinion, however. It is an argument with a heavy emphasis on judgment. The

review

a column that typically comments on movies, recordings, books, television programs, concerts, plays or restaurants

BYLINE

WALTER WINCHELL
THE WINCHELLIZATION OF CULTURE

To his enemies, Walter Winchell was a journalistic Attila the Hun, invading the once well-defended realm of privacy, looting, polluting, leaving behind scattered bricks and bones where solid reputations once stood. Today he's almost forgotten, but the raucous, staccato melody of his style lingers on.

Winchell turned his Broadway gossip column of the 1920s into a nationally syndicated institution and could have taken out a patent on the celebrity culture. In *Winchell: Gossip, Power and the Culture of Celebrity*, Neal Gabler tells us that by the late '30s, 50 million Americans either read Winchell's column or heard his weekly radio broadcast. FDR invited him to the White House for consultations. J. Edgar Hoover exchanged secrets with him (Gabler has an acute section on their prying, paranoid affinity). In time, Winchell became arguably the most influential American journalist of the century. Not bad for an uneducated former minor-league vaudeville hoofer born into a poor New York Russian-Jewish family.

Gabler does a good job of mapping the confluence of popular culture and social history, though the detail can be pedantic. The tabloids, he explains, attracted a mass audience by turning news into entertainment, casting real people as headliners in soap operas, melodramas, and murder mysteries. Winchell, the archetypal tabloid journalist, began at New York's grotesque *Evening Graphic* and moved to the *Daily Mirror*. He soon began deploying his gift of innuendo, distortion, needling, and sentimentalizing to politics, first on behalf of FDR, then in a Red-baiting alliance with Sen. Joseph McCarthy. He had become an anachronism well before his death in 1972, but by then, America, mesmerized by new celebrities and scandals, was thoroughly Winchellized.

Source: Reprinted with permission from L. S. Klepp, "It Didn't Begin with O. J." Entertainment Weekly, p. 54.

reviewer or critic is attempting to persuade or influence readers. A review may try to persuade you to go see the latest *Star Wars* release or not to bother reading John Grisham's newest novel.

There is a trend in reviews toward rating such things as movies or restaurants with stars or other tag lines (repeated phrases identified with specific individuals). Many journalists contend that such devices do not persuade or argue. They simply label, and labels do not offer sufficient discussion of the merits of a performance, text or restaurant. For example, Ian Shoales in his article "Deep Personal Beliefs Are Like Bagel Crumbs," wrote that the influence of theater critics Roger Ebert and the late Gene Siskel had grown to almost absurd proportions:

> [It] has become kind of scary. They can no longer praise a movie with a simple "Two thumbs up." No their power has grown. Now I see in promotional blurbs: "Two thumbs up. Way up!"
>
> We're going to destroy the thumbs of Siskel and Ebert with our senseless devotion! Before you know it, it will be "Two thumbs way up so far they're orbiting Earth!"

What gives critics the right to critique? The job must have some requirements, or anyone could do it. Drama critics, for example, need three things. They need to have seen a lot of theater productions. They must have thought about the theater and read about it. And they should be able to discuss their thoughts in a meaningful way.

A reviewer, then, really isn't much different from a columnist writing about a subject. To be a critic or reviewer, you must be knowledgeable. In other words, you must actually have attended the play, read the book or viewed the television program. And you must remain open to

Use your investigative skills and research where "thumbs up/thumbs down" as a way of expressing approval or disapproval originated. Hint: people used this sign long before Siskel and Ebert.

new ideas and influences, because not everyone will think *Beverly Hills 90210* is the hottest zip code on the planet or realize that Hootie and the Blowfish is a rock group, not a seafood platter at Red Lobster.

When reviewing, keep in mind that your column should be brief and thorough. Include what you liked and disliked about your topic, and why you felt that way. Be sure to support your opinions with proof. Cite concrete examples that you considered in reaching your conclusions. Your purpose is to give readers specific reasons why they should or should not spend their time and money on the attraction about which you are writing.

Look at the following examples. See if what these students wrote would persuade you to experience the various forms of entertainment they describe:

> 'Twas "The Nightmare Before Christmas," and all through the hall, sat a swarm of children—even worse than the mall.
>
> Popcorn was balanced on their laps with care, in hopes that entertainment soon would be there.
>
> Its sets were so bizarre and its music so groovy—I settled to watch the short Disney movie.
>
> But instead of toy trucks and dolls and cheer, Santa's bringing decapitated heads this year. . . .
>
> Wait a minute—that's not Santa Claus! It's Jack Skellington, the gaunt leader of Halloweentown who has taken over for Saint Nick.
>
> "Nightmare" is only the latest of films inspired by the creative genius of Tim Burton. Also responsible for "Beetlejuice," "Batman," and "Edward Scissorhands," Burton employs the painstaking process of stop-motion animation to bring his ghouls to life. . . .
>
> While Jack delivers Christmas tree-eating pythons and random body parts to little boys and girls, the real Santa faces off with Oogie Boogie, the sinister, theatrical potato bag who runs the local dungeon. . . .
>
> Like most animated films, "Nightmare" suffers from a predictable ending. Despite its dingy plot, the film is saved by sensational animation, soulful vocals, and Burton's subtle but biting satire. (Matt Winters, *Epitaph,* Homestead High School, Cupertino, Calif.)

Michael Crichton, author of *Jurassic Park* and *Rising Sun,* has come out with yet another fantastic work, *Disclosure.*

Disclosure is a suspenseful book which holds the reader's attention. Crichton does a good job of wrapping up the complex story in a mere four days.

He forgets about subplots and unnecessary descriptions in order to concentrate on what is really important, the plot. . . .

The novel examines harassment for what it is really about, power. It makes some thoughtful criticisms and raises some good questions, while acknowledging that most sexual harassment cases are filed by women.

Most of the writing is conversational, so the book, though complex in idea, is not very hard to read. (Brett Bennett, *Fourth Estate,* Bartlesville High School, Bartlesville, Okla.)

Reviews "R" Us

May a school principal remove movie reviews from the student newspaper merely because the films in question were rated R? The New Jersey Supreme Court, agreeing with two lower courts, said no.

The case of *Desilets v. Clearview Regional Board of Education* concerned reviews of the movies "Mississippi Burning" and "Rain Man" submitted in 1989 to the student paper at Clearview Junior High School in Gloucester County. They were written by Brien Desilets, who was then an 8th grader.

The principal pulled the reviews solely because the films were rated R, for restricted, by the Motion Picture Association of America.

Patricia Desilets sued on behalf of her son, claiming the principal's action violated his First Amendment free press rights. *Source: Reprinted with permission from "Student Newspaper's Right to Review R-Rated Movies Upheld,"* Education Week.

For the first time in two years Southeast alumnus Matthew Sweet returned to play at the one year anniversary for radio station 104.1 The Planet.

The most impressive thing about the show was the way Sweet took the acoustic guitar parts of songs and replaced them with electric. "Winona," a song from Sweet's third release "Girlfriend," is normally a soft, sweet, tear-jerking song about a man desperately in love with a girl he barely knows. The live performance made it sound like a gut-wrenching rock ballad about a man desperately stalking a movie star.

He ended the show with the song that the entire crowd had been calling for, "Girlfriend." The song managed to show off the talents of every member of Sweet's band. Lead guitarist Richard Lloyd's guitar solo was close enough to add extra flavor to the song. Bassist Tony Marsico's solo toward the end of the song was twice as long as normal, and made every bassist in the crowd drop his jaw. (A. Fritz Gibson, *Clarion*, Lincoln Southeast High School, Lincoln, Nebraska)

Reviewing school performances is a controversial issue. Many school newspapers include only information on when a school performance is scheduled and the cost of tickets. They don't believe student journalists should publicly criticize their peers.

A negative review of the school performance of the musical *Cabaret* appeared in the *Westlake PI,* the paper at Westlake School in Los Angeles. The review created a controversy over whether or not it is appropriate to review school productions. "I think that criticizing one's peers in black and white in the paper only lowers their self-esteem; it does more harm than good," said Westlake School choral director Jayne Campbell.

Dan Sullivan, theater critic for the Los Angeles *Times,* however, feels that high school papers definitely should review school shows. "It's part of the community," he said. According to Sullivan, the main purpose of a review is to "inform the reader as to what happened, who was in it, and to state your opinion of it." He also said that the purpose of a review is not to discourage people from seeing a show or to encourage them to see it. Rather, based on the reviewer's opinion, readers should be allowed to make up their own minds.

When writing a review, think about the possible effects of your opinions on others. Although student performers are not professional actors or musicians, they are subject to criticism because they are a part of a public performance. However, as a high school journalist, you are not a professional, either. Be careful not to embarrass your peers or yourself through your reviews.

specialized column

a column that appears in a specific area of the newspaper, such as a sports column, travel column or politics column

Specialized Columns

Columns that appear in specific areas of the newspaper, such as on the sports, travel or politics pages, are called **specialized columns.** Columnists who write these types of columns usually know their readers. They speak the language of the people for whom they are writing. If you read about a baseball game on the sports page of your school newspaper, no doubt your eye will catch terms such as *no-hitter, squeeze, hit-and-run* and *turn a double play.* Specialized words that are used exclusively by people in a particular group or activity are called **jargon.**

Using jargon in a specialized column is good to an extent, because it proves you know your subject. However, too much jargon can throw a column off balance. You want your readers to understand what happened during a game, for example, but not have to ask for a translation to be printed beside the column.

Like opinion columns, specialized columns can cover many different events and issues. The writer is not restricted simply to detailing what occurred at a swim meet or during the homecoming game. Perhaps when you heard about the liver transplant of Yankee baseball player Mickey Mantle, you were upset that he did not have to wait as long as other patients needing the operation. This could lead to a column on favoritism for celebrities.

Maybe it upsets you that professional athletes are often in the news for criminal acts. You could write a column on what it means to be a role model. To give your column a community context, include observations about the leadership roles played by athletes in your own school.

Although sports columns are only one type of specialized column, they are probably the kind featured most often in high school newspapers because of their community appeal. The sports column that follows discusses the widespread practice of trash-talking.

> When tempers flared during Grand Haven's Homecoming and a few scuffles broke out, people again easily assumed the Bucs were a bunch of trash-talking no-gooders who love to fight. . . .
>
> The trash-talking, for those who don't understand it, by definition: the winner is determined by who can get in the most mama jokes in a short period of time. This uncontrollable urge to intimidate the opposition with words is shunned upon and usually banned by coaches. But, it still exists and always will.
>
> High school athletes dedicate their summers, winters and all free time so they can succeed and be better than their opposition. They try to succeed more than anything else, and sometimes during competition an athlete's pride is broken. In desperation, he/she tries to gain this back and sometimes this results in dirty play, fights and penalties. Not because that athlete is a bad kid, he or she just wants to succeed. It happens in all sports. (Matt Smith, *Buc's Blade,* Grand Haven High School, Grand Haven, Mich.)

jargon

specialized words that are used exclusively by people in a particular group or activity

YOUR BEAT •

1. Clip five columns from student newspapers of other schools, and write brief critiques of each one.

2. Find a book that collects the writings of a syndicated columnist. Evaluate the columnist's work in terms of content, style and appeal.

CALVIN AND HOBBES reprinted by permission of Universal Press Syndicate.

◢ Searching for Ideas

You know the routine. It's midnight, and you are sitting at your desk with only the blue glow of the computer providing light. An empty pizza box, Twinkie wrappers and empty soda cans litter the floor. You stare blankly at the screen, with the blinking cursor becoming a big blur as you try desperately to think of something to write about in your column. Does this sound familiar? The hardest thing about writing a column is coming up with an idea.

In her book *Talking Out Loud,* columnist Anna Quindlen addresses this issue:

There are three questions people always ask about writing a column:

Q. Where do you get your ideas?

A. The same places that you do.

Q. How long does it take to write a column?

A. As long as I've got.

Q. How far ahead do you have columns stockpiled?

A. Say what?

Sometimes columns come out of an unusual area of expertise or personal exposure. Sometimes they are crafted over days of thinking about a subject. Sometimes they are written and then left in computer storage until an opportunity presents itself for their use. Most of the time newspaper columnists work exactly the same way they did when they were reporters—on the news, on deadline.

Every writer experiences dry spells, when there doesn't seem to be anything to write about. When it happens to you, take a look again at what is happening in your life, at your school or in the world. Chances are you will discover something worth writing about. According to Quindlen, the best way to know what to write about is "when you hear it from people at dinner, hear it discussed on the street, or hear it in your mind's ear."

If readers are familiar with your work as a columnist, they will probably expect you to write about whatever hot topic is circulating. If open campus privileges are suddenly taken away because a group of seniors decided at lunch to skip the rest of the school day, most of the student body will want to know your perspective on the issue. If the basketball team wins its first state championship in 10 years following a half-court shot made in the last three seconds of the game, people will want to hear about it. "Your best columns will be about something you feel very keenly and know thoroughly," wrote Robert K. Beck of the *Centerville Iowegian and Citizen* in *Publisher's Auxiliary.* You are a student first and then a writer. Keep your eyes and ears open. Listen, and then write.

YOUR BEAT

1. Create a list of 10 column ideas. Try to find a unique approach or unusual angle to make familiar topics fresh.

2. Invite a columnist from your local newspaper to speak to your class about the challenge of finding topics to cover.

CHAPTER REVIEW

KEY TERMS

Show that you know the meanings of the following key terms by correctly using them in complete sentences. Write your answers on a separate sheet of paper.

column	review	jargon
syndicated	specialized column	

OPEN FORUM

1. Although it's important to use outside sources in columns to support your points, it's even more important to cite this information and give credit where credit is due. If a columnist misquotes someone or fails to cite a particular fact, what should the columnist do? Is it the responsibility of the columnist or the newspaper to supply the correct quotation or the missing fact?

CHAPTER REVIEW, continued

◆ OPEN FORUM, CONTINUED

2. Anyone can stand in line at the grocery store and read the headlines in the tabloids: "Woman Gives Birth to Two-Headed Alien Baby," "Loch Ness Monster Nabbed by Tourists," or "Elvis Presley Seen in Taco Bell Restaurant—Again." As far-fetched as these stories are, some people actually believe everything they read. Often the tabloids increase their readership by gossiping about celebrities. Do you think high school newspapers should include gossip columns? Why or why not?

3. Dave Barry once quipped, "If you're not part of the solution, you're a newspaper columnist." Do you think there is any truth to Barry's observation?

FINDING THE FLAW

More than 50 irate calls to Abraham Lincoln High School in Council Bluffs, Nebraska, were made as a result of a column written by student Ryan Heuwinkel in the school newspaper. Heuwinkel's column, "Attitude Adjustment," was published in the Feb. 28, 1994, issue of *Echoes.* The column, which was titled "Confession of a Telephone Swindler," gave step-by-step instructions on how to get free food from a Taco Bell restaurant by phoning in false complaints of items missing from a takeout order. Heuwinkel's column also gave instructions on how to phone in false complaints to food companies to receive replacement products or cash refunds, as well as a tip on how to cheat phone companies out of pay-telephone charges.

According to Heuwinkel, he got the idea for the column when he "heard people were doing this, and it seemed totally nutty that companies would do this [provide products or money] just to please the customers."

Besides being distributed to students at Abraham Lincoln High, *Echoes* was also inserted in copies of the *Daily Nonpariel,* a Council Bluffs area newspaper that was delivered in the school attendance area. According to Linda Smoley, the school's journalism teacher, many advertisers threatened to withdraw their services. As a result, Heuwinkel wrote a letter of apology that was specially printed and circulated the following Monday and was paid out of the *Echoes*'s advertising fund. In his letter, Heuwinkel said the object of the column was to make people laugh. Adapted with permission from Gary Newman, "School Paper's Column Prompts Howls of Protest," *Council Bluffs Bureau.*)

Discuss Heuwinkel's rationale for writing a column. How do you decide if a column is worth laughing at?

 **MEDIA WATCH**

1. Study the syndicated columns in your local newspapers. Do the ideas presented in these columns reflect the editorial policies of each newspaper? Are the local newspapers providing a variety of opinions on controversial issues?

2. Compare two different reviews of the same movie. Do you believe that either reviewer chose to dumb down his writing for increased readership? If so, give examples. Can a one-paragraph-long review or a thumbs-up rating on television ever be more than a label or a tag line? What should the media do to offer more meaningful reviews?

String Book

1. Write one of the following types of columns: humor, editorial or specialized.

2. Attend a theatrical performance outside of school, and write a review of it. Include observations about costumes, lighting and sets, as well as about the acting.

Chapter 13
Sports Writing

"He's intercepted the ball at the forty-five-yard line. He's broken away, ten, thirty, forty-five yards for a touchdown. He's really earned his twelve point five million today."

—John Madden

284

LEARNING OBJECTIVES

After completing this chapter, you will be able to:

◆ understand the importance of backgrounding to a sportswriter,

◆ list the essential facts to include in an advance,

◆ explain a sportswriter's responsibilities in covering a game,

◆ write a sports story without jargon or clichés.

◆

KEY TERMS

In this chapter, you will learn the meaning of these terms:

backgrounding
advance
press row
press box
homer
clichés

*w*hat was the biggest news story of 1994? Not Whitewater. Not Haiti. Not even the Republican's takeover of Congress. No, like a running back breaking away from the pack, the top news story of 1994 and one of the most widely covered stories of the century, was without a doubt the O. J. Simpson murder case.

As the late *Chicago Tribune* columnist Mike Royko put it, "Simpson was the most famous American to be accused of murder since Aaron Burr, the vice-president of the United States, killed Alexander Hamilton, his political rival, in a pistol duel in 1804." What made Simpson such an important celebrity? Sports. Had Simpson not been a great football player, he certainly wouldn't have gained the fame he subsequently received in broadcasting and the movies. Had he not been a celebrity because of his success in sports, no one would have cared about his much-celebrated trial. The Simpson case is just one of the many ways sports and news overlap. You've probably read quite a few sports stories on the front page of your local—or even your high school—newspaper.

After all, sports combines the best of all elements of journalism. It provides readers with news, features, celebrity stories, columns and, of course, the myriad statistics the true fan craves. Furthermore, sports brings together people who otherwise would be worlds apart. As the character Phil in the movie *City Slickers,* Daniel Stern hints at the power of sports: "When I was about 18 and my dad and I couldn't communicate about anything at all, we could still talk about baseball. Now that was real."

Sportswriters give people something "real" to talk about. This chapter will give you the tools to write stories that will be discussed in the hallways and on the street corners of everyday America. First, you need to be prepared.

▲PREPARATION FOR SPORTS WRITING

Robin Cook pores over the latest statistics. She looks at the starting lineup. She examines the key matchups. It sounds like a coach preparing for a game. But that's not the case. Cook is a sportswriter, not a

backgrounding
finding out information about the sport, team, coaches, events and issues that will be covered in sportswriting

Irrational Pastimes

"Trash sports," exclaims John Cherwa, associate sports editor at the *Los Angeles Times*. "That's our official name for them. Because they're not traditional and, in many cases, they're not real. Supposedly, in Atlanta, they have a thing called cat chasing. They throw a cat out of an airplane and then different parachutists try to chase and catch the cat. I don't know if it's true, but I've heard of it."

Most people acknowledge that America is a nation of sports nuts. Humorist Margo Kaufman would argue that the sports, too, get nuttier and nuttier. From motorcycle racing on ice to rattlesnake rodeos, each weekend finds fans turning out for another "dubious sport." Kaufman says she can't believe what passes for sports these days. While watching a Battle of the Monster Trucks and Mud Racing Spectacular, she remembers her jaw dropping "as a giant truck with immense tractor tires drove over ten cars and squashed them like soda cans."

Kaufman's husband, Duke, offered an explanation for why people watch truckers plowing through mud bogs: "It's riveting in its awfulness."
Source: Adapted from Funny Times.

coach. However, just like a coach, she's concerned with all aspects of the next contest.

Athletes will tell you that games are won or lost in practice. Sportswriters will tell you that the great stories are either noticed or overlooked during their research before the game. As a sportswriter, though, you probably won't have as much time to devote to the next game as a coach does. However, you should gather at least some basic background. In sports writing, **backgrounding** is finding out information about the sport, the team, the coaches, the events and the issues you'll be covering.

Preparing to cover a game or to conduct an interview is usually quite enjoyable. "Backgrounding," sportswriter Steve Sipple says, "is the one time when I don't have to worry about writing or asking the right question. It's the one time when I'm able to relax and have fun while I familiarize myself with an athlete or an issue."

How can you best prepare to write your sports article? First, read all the articles you can, from those in *Sports Illustrated* to those in your rival school's newspaper. In so doing you will pick up on how others

Bizarro by Dan Piraro reprinted by permission of Universal Press Syndicate.

cover sports. Additionally you'll learn to spot the styles of certain writers. In studying the different styles, you'll learn approaches to material that you can use.

Second, get to know the rules of the sport and the vital statistics of the team before you get to know the coaches and the players. This knowledge will not only impress your interviewees but also will give you something to talk about during interviews.

Finally, get to know the coaches and players you'll be covering. You probably have friends or acquaintances on most teams at your school. Try not to let friendships keep you from doing your job, which is to provide fair and accurate coverage. Furthermore, try to establish a good working relationship with the athletes and coaches you don't already know. These people should feel comfortable coming to you with their story ideas. In turn, they should be confident that you will come to them when you are planning a story.

Once you've made contact with coaches and athletes, you'll need to conduct interviews, especially at the beginning of each season. Many student journalists are intimidated by the interview process. The key to overcoming your fears is careful preparation. Robert Scheer, a *Los Angeles Times* national correspondent, is considered one of journalism's best interviewers. He has interviewed world leaders from Jimmy Carter to Bill Clinton, from Fidel Castro to Mikhail Gorbachev. Scheer says that none of his interviews would have produced a single good quotation, had he not done his homework. He suggests that by the time you go to an interview, you know your questions by heart.

It's crucial that you prepare well for interviews with sports figures. Athletes and coaches are often too ready, willing and able to respond to questions with pat answers. How often have you heard a coach say, "It was a really big win for us" or "We are playing the games one at a time"? This information is of little use to you or your readers. You must be prepared to ask as many questions as necessary until you get the information you need to write your story.

Instead of focusing on obtaining a great quotation, many writers attempt to get anecdotes, or colorful stories, from athletes and coaches. When you ask questions about athletes' most or least memorable moment, best or worst game, biggest dream or worst nightmare, you may find that they open up to you. And the stories often paint a portrait of the athlete that your community rarely sees.

DATELINE DATELINE DATELINE

LONDON, Nov. 2, 1936— The British Broadcasting Company (BBC) went on the air today with the world's first open-circuit television broadcasts. About 2,000 viewers saw the first program and praised the high quality of the picture.

The BBC was the first television station in the world to offer regular programming. It was on the air two hours a day, six days a week. Among the first programs was a demonstration of self-defense techniques.

YOUR BEAT

1. You're assigned to interview the student manager for the football team. You have to write a story on his background and his contribution to the team's success. List five questions that you believe will produce meaningful answers.

2. The biggest game of the season is this weekend. You have a few days before you have to broadcast the story. What is your game plan?

FUNKY WINKERBEAN reprinted by permission of King Features Syndicate.

▲ Pregame Stories: Advances

advance

> a preview of an upcoming game that compares teams and players, discusses team records and gives lineups

A preview of an upcoming game that compares teams and players, discusses team records and gives lineups is known as an **advance.** Mark Derowitsch, a sportswriter for the *Lincoln Journal-Star,* once quipped, "You could train a chimpanzee to write an advance." Indeed, professional sportswriters sometimes seem to be monkeying around, because their previews of upcoming games are often painfully predictable. The lazy sportswriter merely throws in the time and place of the game, mixes it with the teams' records and statistics, and adds a few quotations from the coaches. This formula produces the same stale story week in and week out.

Your advances, however, shouldn't serve as sedatives for your readers. In fact, they should have exactly the opposite effect. Think about the anticipation your classmates share for the upcoming game. Typically, the next game is the most-talked-about topic at school—not only among the players but also among the general student population and even the faculty.

In some ways, your advance should match the emotions of your school community. Your story should not be mistaken for a pep talk or a cheer. However, your advance should capture the anticipation and significance (or lack thereof) of the matchup. If you simply churn out the time, location and statistics of an upcoming game in a formulaic story, the readers will not be cheering either. Remember, as a high school sportswriter, your advance probably will stir up more emotion than will your story about the game itself. After all, the game will be old news by the time the story about it gets into print.

How can you add flavor to your advances? Find an angle that the student body might not know about. For instance, if your starting fullback has a number of friends on the opposing team, talk to him about how that situation will affect his playing during the game.

Put simply, try to spice up or featurize your advance stories to keep them from sounding the same. Interviews, historical features or short human interest stories can add to your advances and create a far more interesting sports page. Of course, don't forget to include the basic information about the game. If you can't find this basic information about the matchup through microfilmed copies of your city newspaper at your local library, a call to the opposing coach or the sports editor of the opposing school can produce the essential facts for any advance.

BYLINE

THOMAS BOSWELL
ON SPORTS: NOW AND THEN

Sports writing offered little status, less respectability, and $90 a week when I chose it with half my heart 25 years ago as the job I disliked least.

Within newspapers, sports was a niche for some of us who, while perhaps not lost, were seldom entirely found. We had everything from alienated artists to cheerful goof-offs. Sports writing promised us a modestly paid but entertaining escape from the slavery of a career. I was home.

Back then, nobody called sports writing a profession. It was just a job. One with well-defined minimum standards. Get the facts straight. Work hard when hard work is needed. Don't blow deadlines. Beyond this it was pretty loose, even at a paper like the *Washington Post,* which had a high opinion of itself.

Nobody wore a tie unless an assignment required it. Nobody thought sports writing was a stepping stone toward a TV career, a six-figure talk radio gig or a big book contract. Nobody was going anywhere too special, and few worried about it. If you were in a rush, you were in the wrong racket.

If somebody tried to throw a boomerang around the Washington Monument, or hold a golf tournament in the dark at midnight with phosphorescent balls, we were there. Certainly none of us had an agent. None of us could *name* an agent.

Then it all changed. Sometime between the late sixties and the mid-seventies, sports depart-

ments became a kind of cultural guerilla battleground all across the country. The old guard cared about who the new backfield coach might be at State U. The insurrectionists wanted to "blow out the page" with a brainy feature on a ballet dancer plus a mammoth photo—even if it ate 70-inches out of the day's pinched news hole.

The reason, of course, was the astronomical growth of sports on TV. The whole country watched the same games and then wanted to read and talk about them the next day.

So, we became respectable. These days, the *Post* sports department is bigger than an airport. More and more sports writers resemble dentists or stockbrokers. They tend to have brains, ambition, organization, dedication, degrees from good colleges, straightforward writing styles, and upright private lives. Some of us, who never aspired to such traits, have acquired them out of self-defense so as not to be trampled.

There's peer pressure to be nice. And productive. And responsible. And politically correct. Some of my colleagues write 300 or 400 stories in a year. I thought I was killing myself at 200. As a group, they're easy to like. Then can even spell. But, sometimes, I don't feel so at home any more.

Source: Reprinted with permission from The Best American Sportswriting.

Perhaps girls' volleyball is a new sport at your school. A feature story on the players and the coach could help launch it successfully.

The following should be included in each advance you write:

◆ The significance of the matchup. Will this game decide who goes on to the playoffs? Will one team finally win its first game of the year?

◆ Both teams' records, background of the rivalry and last year's score.

◆ Key players, injuries and starting lineups.

◆ Styles of play.

Furthermore, try to involve the entire community by including advances and features on the so-called minor sports. The tennis, golf and wrestling teams might not attract the crowds that the football and basketball teams do, but they are putting forth as much effort—and often have as much at stake—as the teams that are more visible. Make sure that sports activities of both males and females are reported. Promote pep rallies and halftime shows to increase a sense of community in your school. Remember, any activity can draw more fans only if it's given more coverage.

1. Your star basketball player's best friend is the star on the opposing team. What are some creative approaches you could use when writing an advance for the game between these two teams?

2. At last year's homecoming game, a bench-clearing fight broke out. Your running back, now a senior, started the fight last year. Would you make note of the incident in your advance for this year's homecoming game? If so, how? If not, why not?

COVERAGE: ON-THE-SCENE REPORTING

Bob Uecker, an announcer for the Milwaukee Brewers and a former major league catcher, made the statement "I must be in the front row" a standard (although overused) one at stadiums across the country in the 1980s. As you may remember, in a television commercial that made the quotation famous, Uecker ended up nowhere near the front row. He had to settle for the upper deck. But sportswriters can't afford to take a back seat to fans at games.

Indeed, as a sportswriter, you sometimes must be in the front row. At least you must be on **press row** (a row of seats reserved for the press, usually at courtside), in the **press box** (a group of seats that usually provide a good view of the entire field) or on the sidelines. Your job depends on your ability to see all of the action with minimal distractions.

Lee Barfknecht, the Nebraska football and basketball beat writer for the *Omaha World-Herald,* described a sportswriter's duties: "My job is to take fans where they normally can't go—the sidelines, the field, the practices, the locker rooms. And I have the opportunity to interview the athletes and coaches they don't get a chance to talk to. You have to know how to use the amount of access that you're given."

With the access, though, comes responsibility. Fans depend on you to provide insight into the bad news (why the coach called a particular play in the fourth quarter, the cause of the crucial fumble, or the reason the star volleyball player was benched), as well as the good news (why the athletes were so inspired, why they outlasted the opposing team, or the reasons they came back and won). Your job is not to be a cheerleader for your school but to report objectively what happened. Sportswriters who become partisan in their reporting are sometimes called **homers.**

However, don't put undue pressure on yourself. Most likely, if you're curious about something, your readers will be curious, too. Almost anything that commands fans' attention at a game deserves at least a brief description or explanation in your game story.

The key plays may call for more elaboration. How, then, should you decide which plays are more crucial than others? The first step is taking detailed game notes that highlight the momentum swings, the big plays, the bad plays and the key performances. A professional sportswriter depends on clear notes to finish a story by deadline—usually only a few hours after the game ends.

Figure 13.1 on the next page shows the notes taken by Roger Angell, of the *New Yorker,* at a baseball game at Yankee Stadium. David Gray, a 12-year-old aspiring sportswriter, wrote Angell to ask for one page of the notes Angell had taken during a baseball game. Some of these are reproduced here. Note that Angell marked certain passages that he thought might be useful later.

When the game ends, a writer on deadline needs to get good quotations quickly. To get these quotations, the writer must ask good questions. A good question isn't always a question that a coach or player

press row

a row of seats at an athletic event that are reserved for the press, usually at courtside

press box

a group of seats at an athletic event that usually provide a good view of the entire field

homer

a sportswriter who becomes partisan (favors the home team) in his or her reporting

FIGURE 13.1
REPORTER'S NOTES FOR A SPORTS STORY

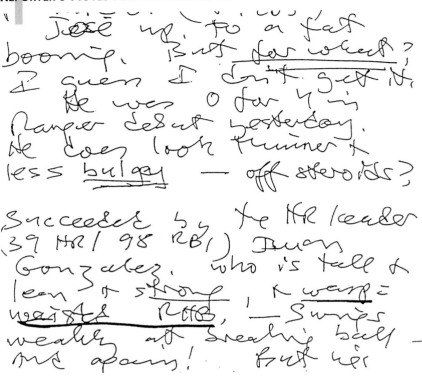

likes. In fact, a coach or player won't like many of the questions that need answers. Don't be afraid to ask a tough question, however. Sometimes you won't get an answer. Sometimes you'll get an angry response from a coach who is frustrated by a loss. Generally, though, if a question is legitimate, the coaches and players will be willing to cooperate.

YOUR BEAT

1. You are assigned to cover a swim meet. Many of your readers are unfamiliar with what is involved in swimming competition. What can you do to give this "minor" sport its due?

2. After a basketball game, you witness a fight between two teammates in the parking lot. Each was apparently frustrated with the other's performance—and their team's performance—during that night's loss. What kind of story could evolve from this fight?

POSTGAME HEROICS: WRITING THE STORY

Dick Enberg, a sports commentator for NBC, once said that "the beauty of all sports is how grown adults can act like little kids." Indeed, sports can bring out the same emotions in 8-year-old softball players and 30-year-old professional baseball players. Sportswriting is about reporting those emotions. Whether it's a blowout or a nail-biter, every sports contest produces at least one prevailing emotion. Agony. Heartache. Frustration. Relief. Jubilation.

Capture that emotion in your story. Develop it. Support it with descriptions and quotations. Make that emotion the theme of your entire story. Describe the pure drama of the contest. You'll rarely find a sporting event that doesn't produce some sort of drama you can write about.

How do you evoke that emotion on paper? How do you make the action come alive? In addressing that issue, Daryl Moen, a journalism professor at the University of Missouri, often tells his students the story of a blind newspaper publisher. The publisher would ask his reporters to come into his office and tell him about their stories. Often, they would just tell him the facts—the who, what, where, when, how and why of the story. Then he'd ask the reporters about the physical characteristics of the event. He'd ask about the emotions that were evident on the faces of the people. He'd leave each reporter with one piece of advice: "Make me see. Make me see your story."

Don't just make your readers see, however. Make them *hear* the crack of the bat, the rip of the basketball net and the roar of the crowd. Make them *smell* the locker room after two-a-day practices. Make them *feel* the volleyball slam against the hardwood floor. Make them *taste* the bitterness of defeat. In other words, use all your senses—sight, sound, touch, smell and even taste. But don't overdo it. Make sure you support your descriptions. For example, it's not good writing to say that the volleyball players were "down in the dumps" after losing the title game. Unless you're a volleyball player, you don't know how they feel. Instead of offering your opinion on how they must feel, ask the players about their disappointment. Describe their distraught faces and the tears streaming down their cheeks. As in any good writing, show rather than tell.

When you use all your senses, you're on your way to developing your own style—your own voice. As you work on your own style, it helps to analyze the styles of the great sportswriters. *Sports Illustrated's* writers are considered by many to be the best in the business at using short, punchy words and sentences to create elaborate, detailed descriptions of an event, athlete or issue. Rick Reilly, a writer for *Sports Illustrated,* has risen to the top of his field by using this concise style. Study, for example, his description of how close a golf shot came to costing Fred Couples the Masters Championship: "One less drop of rain. One more run of the mower. A cup less of fertilizer last fall. One more breath from a nearby butterfly. A blade of grass with weak knees. An eyelash less luck. Any of these things could have cost Fred Couples the Masters. But somehow, some way, Couples' golf ball hugged the steep slope at Augusta National's 12th hole, clung to it the way a sock clings to a towel fresh out of a hot dryer. The ball steadfastly refused to fall into the water."

If Reilly can make a golf shot, of all things, come alive, just think how dramatic a story about an athlete, coach, event or issue in his style could be. Effective sportswriters use crisp, lively words—especially verbs—to describe the action. They try to combine a wealth of vivid details in an imaginative style. Consider how Yaniv Salzberg, sports editor of the *Union Street Journal* at Cherry Creek High School in Cherry Creek, Colorado, enlivens the lead to a story on rugby: "Rugby is a straight-forward, simple game. The game isn't about who has more deceptive plays or gadgets; it's simply about who's better. The stronger, faster team wins. At first the game just seems like 30 men in collared shirts running around and tackling each other, but soon one can see the order of the sport."

Beginning sportswriters too often rely on jargon and clichés. Jargon is highly specialized language developed for use by a particular group, as Chapter 12 described. If you use *maplemen* instead of *basketball players* or *grid mentor* instead of *football coach,* you are using jargon. Your story may be unclear to some of your readers and seem silly to others. **Clichés** are trite, overused words or expressions. When you use expressions such as *split the uprights* and *scoreless deadlock,* you are merely echoing other inexperienced writers. Avoiding clichés will help your stories be fresh and lively rather than worn-out and stale.

cliché

a trite, overused word or expression

Grantland Rice, who has been called the "Matthew, Mark, Luke and John of American sport," often combined the best of a short, punchy prose style and a longer, more eloquent style. You can see the contrast in style in the following passage, considered by many to be the best lead in the history of sportswriting: "Outlined against a blue-gray October sky, the Four Horsemen rode again. In dramatic lore they are known as Famine, Pestilence, Destruction and Death. These are only aliases. Their real names are Stuhldreher, Miller, Crowley, and Layden. They formed the crest of the South Bend Cyclone before which another fighting Army football team was swept over the precipice at the Polo Grounds yesterday afternoon as 55,000 spectators peered down on the bewildering panorama spread on the green plain below." Note that Rice started the paragraph with a short, vivid description of Notre Dame's Four Horsemen. He ended with an eloquent—and, some would say, overdone—description of Notre Dame's defeating Army.

That type of lead is not used today. People now don't make the time or have the patience to read dense prose about a game that they've often already seen. But they will spend the time to read good, lively writing, as exemplified by the first four sentences of Rice's lead.

Many people criticized Rice's writing for being too dramatic. At times it was. But few writers have ever had more enthusiasm for sports than Rice. That spirit was reflected in the more than 67 million words—an average of 10 to 15 typed pages a day for 53 years—that he wrote on the pages of newspapers and magazines.

Carl Session Stepp, a journalism professor at the University of Maryland's College of Journalism, understood Rice's dedication: "[His] writing might not have been clinically executed, but it had heart and soul. What set him apart seems to have been his true love of the game, his devotion to fair play, his sense of wonder, and his thrill at the chance to write about it all." If you share that spirit, you may have the makings of a legend.

THIS JUST IN: *Portrait of a Young Journalist*
Todd Cooper, Sports Reporter

Todd Cooper couldn't believe his ears. Cooper, a sports reporter for the *Daily Nebraskan,* heard the unthinkable while covering a press conference called by former Cornhusker tight end Johnny Mitchell. Everyone—especially Cooper—assumed that Mitchell was going to announce his intention to enter the National Football League (NFL) draft. After all, Cooper thought, why else would the standout sophomore tight end call a press conference just a week before the draft? Cooper waited for the inevitable when Mitchell stepped up to the microphone.

"People" who are wondering and asking me every day," Mitchell said, seemingly waiting for a drum roll, "I'm going to stay in school."

"What?" Cooper thought. "Come again. I must have misunderstood him. Why would someone call a press conference to announce that he was staying in school? Isn't it sort of taken for granted that if the person simply keeps going to class that he, in fact, is staying in school?"

"It was unbelievable," Cooper said. "I couldn't believe that someone would gather every major media outlet in the state to announce that he was going to stay in school—which everyone expected anyway. Usually, college underclassmen only call press conferences before the draft when they indeed are going pro. But Johnny, I guess, felt the need to feed his ego—and waste our time."

However, Cooper said, the press conference didn't turn out to be a complete waste of time. The next day, Cooper wrote a column announcing that he—like Mitchell—also wasn't going to turn pro. Mitchell didn't find Cooper's column amusing. In fact, the 6-foot-five-inch, 250-pound tight-end confronted Cooper at the Cornhusker's next practice. Cooper said that he escaped bodily harm, but that Mitchell's action taught him a few things about the profession he was entering.

First, Cooper said, be careful when criticizing 250-pound, NFL-bound athletes. Second, don't take athletes and their egos too seriously. Third, always have fun. And most important, he said, make the most of every opportunity.

After covering the University of Nebraska athletic programs for three years—and earning national and regional awards for his writing—Cooper decided to switch to writing news. "I felt like I needed to develop some hard-edge investigative skills," he said. Cooper wrote news stories for a year and a half at the *Lincoln (Nebraska) Star.* While he was there, the Associated Press selected one of his articles as the state's top spot news story of 1993. (The story described a gunman's attempted assault on 20 University of Nebraska students.

In January 1995, Cooper joined the *St. Cloud (Minnesota) Times* as a regional reporter. Three weeks after his arrival, he wrote an in-depth piece on racism at city hall. But Cooper said he hopes to return to sports soon. He's learned much from writing news, he said, but he's anxious to transfer those tools to sportswriting. And he should have some good tools. He's covered not only a gunman's attack on a classroom but also a soldier's struggle to restore hope in Somalia and a formerly paralyzed man's battled to walk again.

However, Cooper said, sports offers the most dramatic stories around. "That's why everyone loves to talk about sports," he said. "It's a source of heroic—and sometimes heartbreaking—stories for people everywhere."

1. During a game that you're covering, the school's star player scores 20 points but goes down with a season-ending injury. Her replacement, however, comes in and leads the team to victory. What would you focus on while writing the story?

2. You're assigned to do a feature on the football team's 6-foot-3-inch, 270-pound lineman. He doesn't talk much, but he works hard, lifts weights and gets good grades. Try as you might, you get virtually no interesting comments from him during your interview. What else could you do in preparing to write a good, detailed feature story?

CHAPTER REVIEW

KEY TERMS

Show that you know the meanings of the following key terms by correctly using them in complete sentences. Write your answers on a separate sheet of paper.

backgrounding   press row   homer
advance   press box   clichés

1. You find out from a friend that the basketball team's star player is failing four courses. Exposing the player's academic situation would make him ineligible to play for the rest of the season. You approach the coach, and he confirms your suspicions. However, he urges you not to report the player's academic standing. If you do, he says, it will ruin the team's chances for the championship. What should you do?

2. One of your high school coaches is accused of playing only his favorite athletes. Some of the team's reserves are complaining to you about unfair treatment. They say the coach has taken some of the starters out to dinner. And, they say, he has held meetings with a select few players without notifying the rest of the team. The reserves say they'll quit unless the coach is fired. They've aired their complaints to the school's athletic director. The coach contends that those players haven't played because they simply haven't progressed as far as the others. Furthermore, he says, those so-called private meetings were only informal talks. How would you pursue this

◆ **OPEN FORUM, CONTINUED**

story? Whose side do you believe? And how would you find the facts to back up any suspicions you might have about the coach?

3. On Sept. 11, 1987, Dan Rather stormed off the set of CBS's *Evening News.* Rather's action came after a tennis match threatened to cut short his broadcast. However, the final game ended sooner than expected, and more than 100 stations had to fill an unprecedented six minutes of dead airtime. Responding to criticism, Rather issued a statement of explanation, but he never apologized. Walter Cronkite told a reporter, "I would have fired him." Do you agree with Cronkite? Why or why not?

FINDING THE FLAW

Which Side of the Field Are You On?

The following are examples of how two newspapers cover the same football game. Discuss the differences between the two stories. What might account for these differences?

Home Crowd Gives East Added Boost

If the Los Angeles Dodgers call it their "tenth" man, then Lincoln East can call the home crowd their "12th man."

Because it took a strong Spartan defensive stand, pepped by a raucous crowd of 3,041 fans, of which all but 700 were from Lincoln, that rattled Fremont's effort to overcome a one-point deficit with less than four minutes to play. . . .

With third down and one on the East seven, Fremont quarterback Tim Meier had to ask for the crowd to quiet down twice, and finally when the ball was put in play, the Tigers were tagged with an illegal procedure penalty.

"The crowd was really enthusiastic, but it was our defense that blocked the kick," said East coach Lee Zentic.

Fremont coach Gerry Gdowski disagreed.

"Our kids simply couldn't hear the quarterback's signals" he said, "and we got the procedure penalty that we might have gotten anyway, but it would have been interesting to see if the circumstances and crowd noise had been normal." *(Lincoln (Nebraska) Journal)*

Crowd Helps Lincoln East Beat Fremont

Fremont High School caused Lincoln East to sweat a little more but when it was all over Saturday night the Spartans emerged with another victory over the Tigers. . . .

The partisan East crowd joined in to urge the East defense (when the Tigers were on the seven-yard-line) and a Fremont lineman jumped before the snap.

~~CHAPTER REVIEW,~~ continued

◆ FINDING THE FLAW, continued

Gdowski said that first the Lincoln East band was playing while Fremont was trying to run a play. The officials stopped the band and then the crowd "went crazy. They (officials) stopped play and tried to calm the crowd down but then they told Tim (quarterback Meier) to snap the ball."

"Whether it was the noise that caused us to jump, I don't know," Gdowski said. "It would have been nice if the kids had been able to hear the signals. The kids said they could hardly hear anything and the backs said they couldn't hear Tim's signals at all."

But despite that one sour taste, Gdowski said the Tigers played well against the tough odds presented in Lincoln's Seacrest Field. *(Fremont Tribune)*

MEDIA WATCH

1. The swimming coach has been complaining about the school newspaper's lack of coverage of her swimmers' accomplishments. She says the football team gets all the ink. That week, the all-academic teams are announced. Twenty-five football players make the academic all-district team. Likewise, six volleyball players, four cross-country runners, two gymnasts and 25 swimmers make the list. How would you report the accomplishments? After you decide, make a survey of local media to determine if other sportswriters balance their coverage of different sports. If they do strike a balance, how do they do so?

2. Sportswriter Red Smith once said, "Any sportswriter who thinks the world is no bigger than the outfield fence is not only a bad citizen of the world but also a lousy sportswriter, because he has no sense of proportion. He should be involved in the world in which he lives." Find three examples of sports coverage that demonstrate a sense of proportion (that is, an understanding of the world in which we live).

String Book

You may use any newspapers for this activity, including school newspapers. Clip the page header with the name and date of the newspaper for each article; keep it with the example.

1. If you are a print writer, follow a professional sportswriter on the job for a day. Most sportswriters will be extremely accommodating (they know how it feels to be rejected for an interview). Take notes on how the sportswriter establishes contacts with the athletes and coaches, asks questions, and gathers and selects information. Before reading the finished story that you watched the professional sportswriter prepare, write one of your own. Compare the two efforts. Summarize the results for your portfolio.

2. If you are a yearbook writer, pay close attention to how magazines cover sports. Notice that they don't settle for simple statistical summaries of a season. Neither should you. Learn to write about the character and personality of a team, as well as the emotions of the season. Include anecdotes that will create long-lasting memories for players, fans and coaches. Collect three such anecdotes about your favorite sport.

3. If you are a broadcaster, find coverage of your favorite sport on network or cable television. Carefully listen to how the professional announcers describe the action. Then turn down the sound and try to supply the play-by-play coverage yourself. You may be surprised at how difficult it is to keep up with fast-paced sports such as bastketball. Practice, practice, practice. Then tape-record yourself doing play-by-play coverage, and include it in your portfolio.

Producing the News

Chapter 14
Photojournalism

"Photography is a medium of formidable contradictions. It is ridiculously easy and almost impossibly difficult."
—Edward Steichen, photographer

In this chapter, you will learn the meaning of these terms:

photojournalist
composition
lens
film
aperture
shutter
exposure
time exposure
f-stop
film speed
depth of field
telephoto lens
wide-angle lens
zoom lens
sizing
stand-alone

photojournalist
a news photographer

LEARNING OBJECTIVES

After completing this chapter, you will be able to:

◆ compose a photograph for maximum impact,

◆ adjust a camera's shutter speed and aperture to take a correctly exposed photograph,

◆ crop and size a photograph,

◆ write a cutline.

A photograph of an apple in a bowl of fruit on a kitchen table: that's photography. A photograph of an apple floating in a barrel of water and bobbing away from the outstretched mouth of a teenager on Halloween: that's photojournalism. The difference is simple, but important. Photojournalism is a special branch of photography in which a photographer uses all the techniques available to create a picture that tells a story—usually a news story.

Many excellent **photojournalists,** or news photographers, are in high schools across the country. Journalists know that it's not enough to tell a story through words; they need to show the story, too. That's where photojournalists come in. They are the people brazen enough to march to the front of a room, or a concert or a game, carrying packs full of lenses on their backs and wearing cameras dangling on straps around their necks.

In this chapter, you will learn why some photographs are better than others. You will see that photographers do most of their work before they ever put a finger on the shutter button. You will learn which lenses are best for which shots, along with other camera-handling techniques. You will also learn what to do with a photograph to prepare it for publication, including how to write a cutline. Information about developing film and enlarging negatives is available in the Teacher's Edition.

MAKING GREAT PHOTOS: THE ART OF COMPOSITION

"If I won the lottery, my life would not change in the slightest," explains photographer Julia Dean. "I love what I do so much that it sort of takes over my life."

That sort of love affair is not unusual for many photographers, who find that they would rather leave home without shoes or socks than without their cameras. Dean has taken her camera to India, Malaysia and Thailand, among other places. She has taken photographs for the Associated Press and magazines as diverse as *Bicycling* and *National*

Geographic World. She also took her camera to tiny Monhegan Island off the coast of Maine, where she lived, off and on, for a year, taking photos of the 75 year-round residents. Those photographs were eventually gathered into a children's book that captures an unusual, almost-vanished style of life.

Photos are, indeed, the stuff of life. Everyone knows that photographs are basic to all yearbook spreads and form the center of interest for most newspaper pages. Photos are the first elements that viewers see and maybe the reason that many students buy a yearbook or read the newspaper.

A photojournalist, or news photographer, enables us to see people, things and places that, for various reasons, we cannot see for ourselves. In the same way that a reporter tells readers what is going on in the world, a photojournalist shows them. A photojournalist needs an inquiring mind, a wide range of general knowledge and an appreciation of the issues that interest readers. The job of snapping photos is not a nine-to-five routine for a professional photojournalist. News can happen at any time of the day or night, and it does not stop after a 40-hour week.

Sometimes the job is emotionally wrenching. No one enjoys calling on the relatives of people who have died to see if they have a photograph the paper can print the next day. Sometimes there are disappointments. Not every photo makes it into the paper. But on good days, a photojournalist has a ringside seat for the pageant of life.

Composition Rules

An old joke holds that the most important piece of equipment in a car is the nut behind the wheel. Similarly, the most important element in photography is the person holding the camera. Think of making, not taking, photos. Don't just aim. Start with an idea.

"A good photo is like a well-written story," says Tim Harrower, design specialist for the *Portland Oregonian.* "It's easy to read. It presents information that's free of clutter and distractions." To do that, the photo must be sharply focused and cleanly composed, so that its most important elements stand out instantly.

Composition essentially means the arrangement of the elements in the photograph (subject, foreground, background and so forth). Experienced photographers keep the subject area simple. They check for distracting backgrounds in the viewfinder. They move up close to the subject or use a telephoto lens to get a tight shot where the subject fills the picture area. And they follow the rules of composition. "A photograph is not an accident—it is a concept," said Ansel Adams, one of the finest U.S. photographers. The following sections explain some of the best composition rules.

Fill the Frame. Photographs in newspapers and magazines have to compete with other items on the page for the reader's attention. Few photographs are printed as large as the photographer would like, and some of the detail in the original may be lost in the printing process. Photographs must therefore be bold and simple.

composition
the pleasing selection and arrangement of the elements in a photograph, including the subject, foreground and background

Make sure the subject fills the frame, or picture area. Don't leave empty space in or around the center of interest. The easiest way to accomplish this is simply to move closer to the subject until it fills the frame.

Watch the Background. Sometimes the background is an essential part of the photograph and can be used to place the person being photographed in context. At other times, the background is distracting (poles or trees, for instance) and needs to be eliminated.

Photojournalism is based on spontaneity. Moving people around sometimes makes the resulting photo seem staged. Therefore, as the photographer, try to move yourself in such a way as to minimize the background. Avoid asking the subject to move. Use the largest aperture possible. This shrinks your depth of field and fuzzes the background out of focus. (You will find out more about apertures and depth of field later in the chapter.)

Observe the Rule of Thirds. Imagine drawing a tic-tac-toe grid over your viewfinder. Many professional photographers do this by dividing the image area into thirds, both vertically and horizontally, with imaginary lines. Then they try to position the subject at the intersection of any two of those lines (see Figure 14.1). This method gets the subject out of the center of the photograph and creates dynamic tension. A perfectly symmetrical picture is monotonous and usually bores the viewer. Moving the subject out of the center, however, creates visual tension, or a sense of motion, because a large area is either in front of or behind the subject.

The rule of thirds is especially useful when the horizon is visible in your photograph. Put the horizon one-third or two-thirds of the way down from the top of the photograph. Putting the horizon in the middle of a photograph indelibly marks it as an amateur snapshot.

Use Leading Lines. The human eye tends to follow a line wherever it leads. That's why experienced photographers use lines to help compose a photo. The lines might be streets, fences or any kind of diagonal lines. These leading lines draw the viewer's eye into the photograph.

Frame the Photograph. You can give your photos a three-dimensional feel by framing the photograph with a branch, a tree or any other object in the foreground. Place one of these objects in the corner of the photo. It won't call attention to itself, but it will help put a photographic frame around the true subject.

Developing an Eye for Photos

Composition isn't the whole story. You must also learn to recognize the photographic potential in your immediate environment. "You cannot claim to have really seen something," said the writer Emile Zola, "until you have photographed it." Here are a few tips to help cultivate a photographic eye:

FIGURE 14.1
RULE OF THIRDS

Divide the viewing area into thirds with imaginary vertical and horizontal lines. Try to locate the main point of interest at one of the four places where those lines intersect.

- *Look at everything you see as if you were planning to take a photograph.* Watch movies and videos, look at photography books in the library and visit photographic displays to analyze why certain photographs have more impact than others.
- *Learn from others.* Although it is wrong to copy another's work, it makes sense to find inspiration in the work of real professionals. Try a technique you saw in a famous picture or painting. If you saw a subject holding a pet in a certain way, for example, you could try a similar composition.
- *Become a people watcher.* Watch students in lines at school, at plays on the stage or in the audience. Go to concerts, the cafeteria, club meetings and parties to observe the emotions and reactions on people's faces. The more you can observe, the easier it will be to capture moods on film.
- *Study photographs to avoid photographic clichés.* Using the ever-popular "armpit shot" in basketball as an example, Dick Johns, director of Quill and Scroll, an organization that recognizes and rewards outstanding high school journalism, said he sees the same pictures year after year in sports coverage. Johns said staffs should strive instead for something special, "not the kinds of shots that you

DATELINE DATELINE DATELINE

WASHINGTON, D.C., 1923—President Warren G. Harding's face was immortalized through wireless transmissions in 1923, when Charles Francis Jenkins sent a likeness of Harding from Philadelphia to Washington, D.C., by wireless transmission.

Jenkins began experimentation with what would become television as early as 1894.

By 1925 he was transmitting moving silhouettes and then pictures that moved, similar to cartoons, over radio waves. By 1928 he was showing regular "radiomovies" in Washington.

Jenkins invented the phantascope, one of the earliest motion picture projectors. His company, Jenkins Television Company, manufactured and sold mechanical television receivers and began regular programming in 1930.

The business failed during the Great Depression and was eventually bought by RCA.

see year in, year out, in thousands of yearbooks across the country." In sports photography, sideline situations are among those that deserve more attention, according to Johns. He suggests that games be covered by two photographers—one for the action and one for the coaches, bench and crowd.

◆ *Look for emotions.* In addition to capturing the main event as it happens, move your camera position around and zoom in on the expression of a spectator. The photograph may be worth those famous thousand words.

All too often, the only things that change in school photos from year to year are the faces. The events on a school calendar remain fairly constant from one year to the next. Therefore, the photo assignments are basically the same. Such photographs don't have much chance of touching readers unless the photographer takes the time to get a new angle.

If you are a sports photographer, emphasize the players rather than the game. Focus on the swimmer nervously biting a towel, a runner wearing mascot earmuffs, a player being hugged by the coach or a teammate contorted by stretching exercises. Instead of the match itself, photograph the wide grin of a wrestler on the victory stand. Rather than a sea of helmets on the football field, show an exhausted lineman pouring water over his head, or the pain on the face of an injured halfback.

A Strategy for Taking Quality Photos

How can photographers produce quality photos every time they cover an event? Part of the answer lies in developing a useful strategy. The strategy consists of adopting the proper attitude, being organized and having a method for finding photographs.

Having the Proper Attitude. The photographer's attitude makes or breaks the photos. The high school photographer must assume responsibility for the pictorial content of the yearbook or newspaper. Accepting this responsibility involves the following:

◆ Know the times, dates and purposes of each photographic assignment.
◆ Always carry enough film and equipment to complete the task.
◆ Shoot photos of popular and not-so-popular students. Shoot one shots (photographs with one person), as well as two, three, five and 10 shots.
◆ Take a variety of photographs from different angles and at varying distances from the subject.

A photographer must cover an event from beginning to end. Avoid the impulse to shoot and run. Cover the whole story, which includes

BYLINE

KENNETH KOBRE
PHOTOJOURNALIST

One of the most enjoyable aspects of photojournalism is meeting different kinds of people. Conversations with subjects often loosen them up. During a shooting session, the talk usually turns to why the person is in the news. When they become engrossed in explaining their involvement, they forget about the camera.

Sometimes photographers should research their subject. To photograph President Carter upon his arrival in Washington, D.C., George Tames of the *New York Times* read Carter's book, *Why Not the Best*. Tames tried to know enough about his subject for a preconceived notion of "what I was going to get before I got there." Tames would calm his subjects down with "strokes." He massaged their egos—who can resist that? Tames would put subjects at ease because they would sense he was their friend. "I have never deliberately made a bad picture of anyone," he once said. His media-conscious subjects knew Tames' reputation for honesty.

Tames also never shot a roll to the end because he found that as soon as he put his camera down, the conversation would liven up. He used those last frames to catch the subject—uninhibited and animated.

Source: Adapted from Photojournalism *by Kenneth Kobre (Focal Press, Boston), p. 90.*

preliminaries (practices, rehearsals or meetings) as well as endings (striking the set or riding the bus home). What the photographer captures on film is what shapes the memories of the high school experience.

Organizing for Success.   Press photographers ought to adopt the Scout motto "Be prepared." Good organizational skills are crucial to success. Equipment should always be ready for use. Once a job is over, the exposed film should be removed and a new roll put in the camera. A camera without film is dangerous. You may forget to reload it before the next assignment.

Once a week, use a can of compressed air to clean the dust and dirt from inside the camera. However, don't shoot the air directly onto the delicate shutter curtain, and take care not to touch the mirror. Lenses should be protected by a filter at all times.

On the job, always bracket your shots. In other words, take the same shot three times, each with a different exposure. This way you can be confident of getting a usable print (this will be discussed later in the chapter). Change your perspective by getting down and shooting up, or by getting up and shooting down. Also vary the distance between you and your subject. Finally, after completing the roll and rewinding the film, label the cassette. Write the name of the event and the film speed on the film container. This will help you to develop it properly later.

Finding Photographs.   Although the picture editor tells most staff photographers which assignments they are to cover, those who can find their own ideas for photographs, especially when the news lacks obvious drama, will rapidly become valued members of the staff. Good photojournalists show readers something they have not seen before. On duty, off duty or just between jobs, a photographer should always keep an eye open for the changes that reflect the time of year. A photograph of city workers moving beach huts onto the shore, for example, tells readers that it's the start of summer. The same workers testing the lights on the Christmas tree outside city hall might provide a photograph in December.

A photographer needs good contacts. These come with time. They are the people you meet on jobs and with whom you cultivate working friendships. They may be keepers at the local zoo, a police sergeant, a city council member, a farmer, a football manager or the fire chief. Sometimes a contact may call you with an idea or tell you that something newsworthy is occurring. At other times, you may call contacts and ask if they have any ideas for photographs.

Don't ignore your own paper or that of a rival school as a source of ideas for photographs. Reporters may not recognize the photographic potential of a story they're writing, but you can. Scan the small ads and the personal columns. There might be a good photographic idea lurking there.

Ethical Concerns.   If a news event occurs on public property, photographers have a legal right to cover the event so long as they do not interfere with police or the free flow of traffic. Police and fire officials, however, have the right to restrict any photographer who might interfere. Photographers who disregard police orders can be arrested for disorderly conduct.

Thus, photographers are free to take pictures in public places and on public property. You can take pictures on the street, on the sidewalk, in public parks and in the zoo. You can also take pictures in the airport, as well as in public schools and universities. However, you must first seek permission to take pictures of a class in session.

Photographers need permission to take photos in

- courtrooms,
- prisons,
- legislative chambers or
- medical facilities (hospitals, ambulances, doctor's offices or clinics). They can, however, shoot in the following places if no one objects:
- hotel lobbies,
- restaurants,
- movie theaters and
- business offices.

Certain restrictions may apply to taking photographs in

- government buildings and
- museums.

Having permission to take a photograph, however, does not relieve a photographer of the need to exercise good news judgment and good taste. Many newspapers, for instance, ran a graphic photo of a teenager impaled on an iron spike atop a six-foot fence. The teen had slipped as he climbed over the wrought iron fence, and a sharp spike about an inch in diameter had entered his neck and come out his mouth—just missing his jugular vein. Rescuers spent 20 minutes freeing the young man by cutting the spike with an electric hacksaw. During that time a photographer from the Associated Press had plenty of time to snap a dramatic photo.

Newspaper editors had no legal worries about running the picture, as the incident happened in a public park. However, they were faced with ethical concerns about showing a victim in extreme distress. The fact that the young man had no major or permanent injuries no doubt played a role in the decision of many editors to run the picture. Most newspapers avoid using photographs of the bodies of dead victims. They rely instead on photographs of the scene; for example, a wrecked car for an accident story.

Good taste is not the only consideration editors take into account when estimating the value of a photograph, but it should be an important one. The yearbook editor at the University of Southwestern Louisiana, Jeff Gremillion, lost his job when he published two offensive photos in the yearbook—one of a topless woman feeding a student spaghetti and the other of a bulldog sitting on an American flag. The news value of a photograph in school publications must be weighed against whether the photo will offend readers. Sometimes the decision to run or not to run a photograph can be difficult and controversial.

1. Analyze the photos in a recent issue of a newspaper or magazine. Look for examples of good composition. Can you find any photos that represent the rules listed in this chapter? Can you discover other rules of your own?

2. Make a list of 10 photographs you could take to illustrate a brochure promoting your community. Compare your list with the lists compiled by your classmates. Now assume that you have space for only two or three photos. Prioritize your list to make sure that you would have the most effective photos possible in the brochure.

3. Examine a family vacation photo. What specific differences can you find between a snapshot and true photojournalism?

4. What would your decision have been if you had been forced to decide whether or not to use the photo discussed above, of the boy injured on the wrought iron fence? Write a rational statement explaining your philosophy with regard to publishing photos of seriously injured or deceased victims.

5. Survey your local newspaper and one of the national tabloids for a period of one week, looking for photos that you personally consider offensive. Did either publication contain offensive photos? If so, describe (don't bring to class) the most offensive photo(s) in your opinion, and identify photos that would be relevant, appropriate replacements.

THIS JUST IN: *Portrait of a Young Journalist*
Julia Dean, Photojournalist and Photo Agency

From first grade on, by her own account, Julia Dean's life has been a version of show-and-tell. By fifth grade, she had all the makings of a photojournalist. At that age, she said, she was taking "zillions of photos" with her Instamatic camera and dreaming of travel to places far from home.

After college, Dean did travel the world, taking photos for the Associated Press and a number of magazines. She built a solid portfolio, gained a world of contacts and experience, and accumulated only what would fit in the trunk of her compact car.

Now she is in the process of realizing a long-time dream.

She has formed Julia Dean and Associates, a company that links photojournalists working primarily in Third World countries with magazines and social service organizations. Agencies that could not afford to launch a photographic jaunt to East Africa, for example, can afford photos from a professional photographer who is already there working on assignments for several clients. "It piggybacks the needs of everyone," she said.

"Her agency is amazing," said Joel Sartore, a photographer for *National Geographic.* "It's the only one of its kind, dedicated solely to humanitarian concerns. Most are out to make a buck. Julia's is out to save the world."

Dean said she honed her interest in photography when she became an apprentice to master photographer Berenice Abbott, who photographed, among other things, the Paris literary and art scene of the 1920s. Dean moved in with Abbott, who was 80, living in New York and no longer shooting photographs. "I worked for free," Dean said, "getting room and board, and borrowing $100 a month from my mom for the first six months I was there."

During her yearlong stay with the master, she learned photographic printmaking as she filled orders for the popular Abbott photographs. The women remained friends until Abbott's death in 1991, at which time Dean began to develop her idea for a new kind of photo agency. (Adapted from *Omaha World-Herald*).

CAMERA-HANDLING TECHNIQUES

Photojournalism is undergoing a technological revolution. Cameras are lighter, film quality has improved and specialized lenses are better than ever. Processing methods have also advanced. Most large newspapers now have automated film processing, which relieves the photographer of hours of work with chemicals. Beyond that, many newspapers have switched to digital photography. Editors at these papers never see photographs as paper prints but only as electronic images on a computer screen where the images can be brightened, cropped and sized. (These concepts will be discussed in the section "Photo Editing.")

No matter how much the technology changes, however, a photojournalist still should know the fundamental principles behind photography. This section examines a few technical aspects of photography, including achieving correctly exposed pictures and using a wide variety of lenses.

How a Camera Works

A camera has often been compared to the human eye. Both contain a small opening that allows light to enter the dark chamber within and then pass through a lens. Both have a light-sensitive area behind the lens, where the image can be processed and interpreted. The **lens** in both the camera and the eye serves the same function: to gather the rays of light from the scene and transmit them, in an expanding cone, back to a light-sensitive area. In the eye, this light-sensitive area is called the retina; in a camera, it is the **film.** Film is a plastic strip coated with silver particles that turn black when exposed to light.

Both the eye and the camera work best when there is a moderate amount of light. If there is too little light, the details cannot be seen; too much light is blinding. In both the camera and the eye, a device in the lens controls the amount of light transmitted. In the eye, this device is a muscle called the iris. In the camera, the device is called the **aperture.**

The one big difference, however, between an eye and a camera is that a camera has no intelligence of its own—it has no brain to control it. Camera manufacturers try to make cameras easier to use by installing electronic systems that automatically focus the image and adjust for changing light levels. Yet no camera, no matter how new or expensive, can see for you. The camera serves the photographer; it is not the master.

Parts of a Camera

All cameras share at least seven basic parts:
- a light-tight box or body,
- a lens to sharpen the image,
- a lens opening to control the amount of light that reaches the film,
- a **shutter** to control the length of time the film is exposed to light,
- a mechanism to release the shutter,
- a lever to move the film through the camera and
- a viewfinder to frame the photograph.

If all cameras share these basic features, why are there so many different kinds of cameras? Simply, different cameras are used for different purposes and for different conditions. The best choice for most photojournalists is the adjustable camera—a camera that allows the photographer to take photographs under a variety of different conditions.

The kind of adjustable camera most school publication staffs use is a single-lens reflex camera. This camera lets the photographer view the subject right through the lens (with the help of several mirrors). That feature is especially important when it's necessary to change lenses, as you'll see later in this section.

lens

the part of a camera that gathers the rays of light from the scene and transmits them to form a sharp image on the film

film

a thin piece of plastic coated with an emulsion containing light-sensitive silver halide particles. The film can record an image as a result of exposure in a camera

aperture

the lens opening that admits controlled amounts of light into a camera. Its size is regulated by an iris diaphragm and expressed as an f-stop

shutter

a dark curtain that slides back and forth across the back of the camera (across the lens) at a predetermined speed, thus controlling the length of time that light falls on the film

FIGURE 14.2
THE PARTS OF A CAMERA

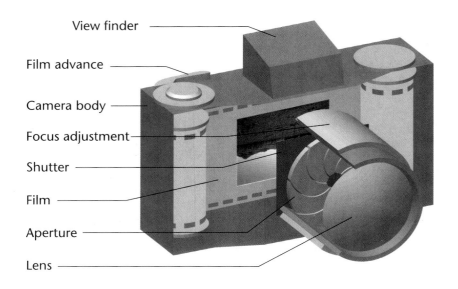

View finder

Film advance

Camera body

Focus adjustment

Shutter

Film

Aperture

Lens

Achieving the Correct Exposure

The word *photography* comes from two Greek words that mean "light drawing." Light is the heart of photography, from the initial exposure of the photograph to the final developing and printing. **Exposure** refers to the amount of light that reaches the film. A correct exposure is the amount of light needed to produce a usable image on film. Overexposure results when too much light has been allowed to reach the film, causing dark or black negatives. Underexposure occurs when too little light comes through the lens, producing light or clear negatives.

Exposure is controlled by three variables: the shutter speed (how long the lens is open), the aperture (how large the opening is) and the film speed. Think of achieving the correct exposure as if you were filling a bucket with water. The length of time you have the faucet turned on compares to the camera's shutter speed. How far you open the faucet (how much water comes out each second) compares to the aperture opening. Together, the time the faucet is turned on and how hard the water pours out determine when the bucket will be full—in other words, when the correct exposure will be achieved.

Shutter Speeds.   The shutter is a dark curtain that slides back and forth across the back of the camera. The shutter moves across the lens opening at a predetermined speed, thus controlling the length of time that light falls on the film. This type of shutter is called a focal plane shutter, because it is located in the back of the camera where the light rays are focused. The shutter speed is usually set by turning a dial at the top or front of the camera.

Most photographic film is extremely sensitive to light. Because of this, a precise amount of time is needed to produce a correctly exposed negative. For this reason, shutter speeds are usually measured in fractions of a second. The shutter speeds typically found on modern cameras are expressed as 1,000, 500, 250, 125, 60, 30, 15, 8, 4, 2, 1 and B.

exposure

the amount of light that reaches the film in a camera. Exposure can be controlled by shutter speed, aperture and film speed

Each number represents a fraction. For example, a shutter speed of 2 indicates a time of ½ second; a speed of 250 indicates ½₅₀ of a second. This system can be confusing at first, but remember that the numbers are fractions. The higher the number, the less time light will have to reach the film.

Each speed produces about half (or twice, depending on which way you're going) as much light as the previous speed. A setting of 250 is half as fast as 500 and thus allows about twice as much light to enter. B is the exception; it enables you to set the speed for whatever time you wish. When the dial controlling the shutter speed is set at the B (for "bulb") position, the shutter remains open as long as the shutter-release button is pushed. This position is often used for long exposures (called **time exposures** when the shutter is open for more than a second or two), such as would be necessary when photographing a comet at night.

If you want to take a photograph of a lightning bolt, you could leave the lens open by choosing B, aiming the camera, pushing the shutter button and releasing it only when you actually see the lightning. The light flashes too quickly to get the photo any other way. Under normal conditions, a shutter speed slower than ⅟₃₀ is a poor choice, because it's impossible to hold the camera steady enough by hand to avoid blurring. if you must use a slow shutter speed, find a rigid support, such as a tripod, to hold the camera steady. Many photographers like to use a cable release for both long exposures and tripod shooting. A cable release is a long wire attached to the shutter. It has a bulb that the photographer squeezes by hand, allowing the photographer to snap a picture while standing a few feet away from the camera without the slight jarring that usually occurs with hand-held shots.

F-Stops. In addition to controlling shutter speed, another way to control light in a camera is by regulating the opening in the aperture. The aperture setting, which is called the **f-stop,** controls the amount of light passing through the shutter. The aperture works very much like the iris that controls the size of the pupil of the eye; it gets larger or smaller as light strikes it. You can see how the aperture works with a simple experiment. Ask a partner to close his or her eyes for 30 seconds. During this time, your partner's iris will grow larger to admit more light. When your partner opens his or her eyes, you can see the iris shrink rapidly.

Some cameras have an electronic exposure system that adjusts the opening automatically as the brightness of the light grows or diminishes. On an adjustable camera, however, the f-stop must be set by the photographer. This setting is made with the f-stop ring, which is usually located on the lens of the camera.

Typically, an adjustable camera lens has six or seven f-stop positions, each indicating a different-sized opening. Some common f-stop numbers (going from smallest to largest) are 16, 11, 8, 5.6, 4, 2.8 and 2. The largest number produces the smallest opening. The numbers used for f-stops, like those used for shutter speeds, are actually fractions. They express the ratio between the diameter of the lens and the focal length. (Focal length is the distance from the lens to the focal point; image size

time exposure
> a long exposure, often necessary in conditions of low light. Usually longer than one second

f-stop
> the setting that controls the amount of light passing through a camera's shutter. Each lens is capable of a series of aperture settings

FIGURE 14.3
F-STOPS
The smaller the opening of the aperture, the larger your field of focus. This size is measured in units called f-stops. The relationship between the f-stop and the size of the opening is shown in this illustration.

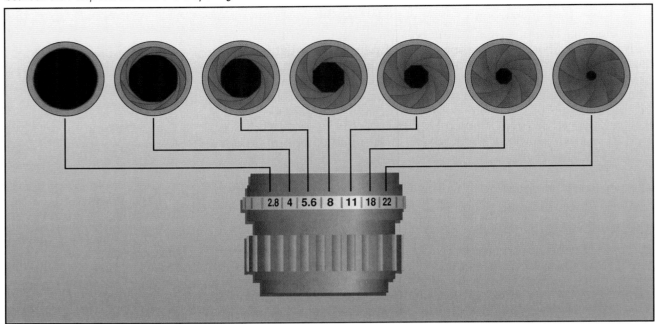

increases with focal length.) Each f-stop allows the camera to admit twice as much light as the next setting. Thus, an f/2 setting allows twice as much light as f/2.8, and so on. By opening the lens two stops (a *stop* is photographic jargon for f-stop), four times the amount of light will reach the film.

An automatic camera will select the correct f-stop for the photographer. You may want to override that choice under certain circumstances, however. Be sure, for example, to stop down by closing the lens one or two stops when you're shooting in an extremely bright situation, such as new-fallen snow or mid-day sun.

Shutter speeds and lens openings work together to determine exposure. Exposure must always be expressed in terms of both shutter speed and f-stop. Invariably, the photographer must choose which variable is more important. If the photographer is shooting a sports event, for example, a fast shutter speed is needed to freeze the action. In contrast, the photographer may need a large depth of field, as when keeping focus down the length of a banquet table. In this case a smaller aperture will be needed—and, consequently, a slower shutter speed.

film speed

> a measure of a film's sensitivity to light, measured on a scale set by the American Standards Association (ASA)

Film Speed. A third factor in determining exposure is film speed. **Film speed** is a measure of the film's sensitivity to light. Film speed is measured on a scale set by the American Standards Association (ASA). The higher the speed, or ASA number, the more sensitive the film is to light. For example, film rated at ASA 400 is more sensitive to light than that of ASA 200. Therefore, photographers say 400-speed film is faster than 200-speed film, because it requires less light, or shorter exposure time, for a properly exposed negative.

Choose film speeds according to what you want to shoot. If you're taking outdoor photographs on a bright, sunny day, you can choose a low film speed (say, 64 or 100), because a great deal of light will be available. If you're trying to shoot on a dark day or perhaps take an indoor photo without a flash, use a faster speed, such as 400. For some fast-moving sports, such as basketball or hockey played indoors, photographers routinely use film speeds rated at 1600 or even 3200. The only problem with such fast film is that it can cause graininess in the final print where the smooth texture of the image appears to break into small grains of light and dark. Most schools buy film in bulk to save money. A good film speed to use in most cases is ASA 400.

A Soloist with a Leica

No one who knew Alfred Eisenstaedt can ever forget his eyes. During seven decades spent wandering the world in pursuit of the revealing moment, his camera recorded more than a million photographs—an enormous, jumbled mosaic that is both a chronicle of the century and a masterpiece of graphic art.

He was present at the creation of photojournalism, and from the first he was a force that shaped the new medium. At 31, having survived a severe wound in World War I—and a seven-year stint as a button salesman—he burned his bridges and prepared to starve as a photographer. Instead, this son of a German merchant became famous. Liberated from the studio by fast film and the new lightweight cameras, he chased all over Europe capturing candid views of the high and mighty: Hitler and Mussolini, for example, smirking warily at their first meeting.

In 1935, convinced that a Jew had no future in the new Germany, Eisenstaedt left for the U.S. Soon after, he was hired by *Life* as one of its four original photojournalists. Tiny, precise and elegant in his bow tie and beret, Eisenstaedt shot more than 2,500 stories for *Life,* including 86 cover photos.

Eisenstaedt was a virtuoso of the camera. He almost always worked alone, without assistants, without batteries of lights, without sacks of film to squander on insurance shots. A soloist with a Leica, he would run off a roll or two in the natural light he loved, and always bring home a winner. He was fearless. He once rode out a hurricane lashed to the flying bridge of the ocean liner Queen Elizabeth, snapping pictures of 80-foot billows as they broke over the bow—and sometimes over his head. And he was tireless. He would go anywhere, shoot anything. He once got into a cage with a 500-pound gorilla because he was fascinated by its face.

Photography was Eisenstaedt's obsession. Asked what he did at night in Paris, he replied, "A thirtieth at f/2."

Source: Adapted from "The Death and Life of A Soloist with a Leica," by Brad Darrach, Life, p. 105.

Using Different Lenses

Your eyes are constantly focusing and refocusing as they look at a subject. Focus means to sharpen an image until it reaches a point of maximum clarity. An automatic camera uses an automatic focusing system; adjustable cameras, on the other hand, enable you to focus manually. Essentially, you rotate the lens until the image comes into focus. Lenses refract or bend light rays so that they converge to form an image. A number of different focusing systems are available to help you get the sharpest image possible.

One of the biggest considerations when focusing a camera is **depth of field.** Depth of field is the amount of space that is in focus both in front of and behind the exact point at which the camera lens is focused. The larger the lens opening, the shallower the depth of field. The smaller the lens opening, the greater the depth of field. For example, if you need to shoot a subject in front of a busy background, a very small depth of field is desirable. It will keep the subject in tight focus while everything else goes blurry. To the viewer, it will seem as if the image jumps out of the background. Sports photographers like this effect if they need to shoot a basketball player in front of an excited crowd.

The purpose of a lens is to gather and direct light, and there are many ways to do that. Photographers have a large variety of lenses at their disposal—including telephoto, wide-angle and zoom lenses—to help them get just the image they seek. The more you know about how lenses work, the better your chances are of taking a great photograph.

Many cameras can accept interchangeable lenses. They allow you to change the lens you're using when you want to get a different kind of photograph. A so-called normal lens (a 50-millimeter lens) "sees" objects in just about the same size and proportion as the human eye does. In other words, when you shoot a photograph with a normal lens, the photo will look very much like the image you would see if you weren't looking through the camera. The 50mm (millimeter) lens is the most common lens in use today, but other kinds of lenses are useful in special circumstances.

Telephoto Lenses.   Sometimes your subject is too far away to be photographed with the kind of detail or impact you'd like. Sometimes you don't want the subject to know you are taking a photograph (for example, a moose munching reeds at the edge of a pond). A **telephoto lens,** like a telescope, magnifies the subject so that it appears closer than it really is.

Telephoto lenses are generally divided into three categories: short, medium and long. Short telephoto lenses are between 85 and 105 millimeters. Many photographers use a short telephoto lens for portrait work, because the camera can be placed farther from the subject's face, allowing for a more relaxed, natural pose.

Medium telephoto lenses are in the range of 135 to 200 millimeters. These lenses are widely used for sports events and candid photographs

depth of field

the area in front of and behind the subject which appears acceptably sharp

telephoto lens

a camera lens that magnifies the subject so that it appears closer than it really is. Such a lens has the capability to produce a clear and large image of subjects relatively distant from the camera

of people. A 200-millimeter lens will magnify the image four times compared with a normal lens.

Any lens longer than 200 millimeters is considered a long telephoto. These are used when the photographer must shoot from a great distance—at a football game or ski run, for instance. They are also quite useful for photographing animals in their natural habitats. Long telephoto lenses are heavy and awkward, however. They often require a special tripod to support them. They are rather slow (few have apertures larger than f/5.4), and they're usually expensive.

When using any lens, remember that the longer the focal length, the shorter the depth of field. Thus, a lens with a long focal length, such as a telephoto, would have a very shallow depth of field. If you zero in on the quarterback's face, for example, the image had better be in focus, because you don't have much room for error. Even the smallest focusing mistake would bring something else on the field into focus instead of the quarterback. Shallow depth of field focuses the attention on the primary action in the photograph.

Wide-Angle Lenses. Depth of field is greatest with a lens of short focal length, such as a wide-angle lens. **Wide-angle lenses** are the opposite of telephoto lenses. They allow the photographer to record more of the total area of a scene without moving the camera back. For example, if you had to be 20 feet away to photograph an object with a normal lens, using a wide-angle lens would enable you to shoot the same area from only 10 feet away.

Many schools make frequent use of wide-angle lenses. Some even use them as their standard lens. The slightly wider angle produces a more pleasing image. Because the wide-angle lens covers more area, however, objects close to the camera can appear unusually large. Shooting a person's face up close with a wide-angle lens might cause the subject's nose to look like an eggplant.

wide-angle lens
a camera lens with a wider angle of view than a standard lens and, in addition, greater depth of field.

Zoom Lenses. A **zoom lens** allows the photographer to vary the focal length. For example, one popular zoom lens has a range from 85 to 205 millimeters. This lens allows a focal length of anywhere from 85 to 205 millimeters. Thus, it is a short, medium and long telephoto lens all in one. Some zooms combine the features of both telephoto and wide-angle lenses, such as a lens with a range from 35 to 70 millimeters.

zoom lens
a camera lens that allows the photographer to vary the focal length

FIGURE 14.4
TYPICAL LENSES

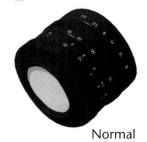

Normal

Wide angle

Zoom

Photos from the Hubbell Space Telescope are received digitally. Notice the pixels (squares) in this "false color" image of Comet Hale-Bopp.

Digital Photography

Hand-held digital cameras convert images into electronic data. Digital cameras are continually improving. Some are now fast enough to catch a running back going for a touchdown, sensitive enough to get detail in deep shadow or bright sunlight, and compact enough to allow the photographer to shoot in tight situations.

Digital photography offers a host of intriguing advantages. The new technology virtually eliminates the cost of darkroom supplies and the mess of darkroom processing. Pictures can be viewed quickly to make sure they are what was wanted. However, the start-up costs for digital cameras and related software are high. Furthermore, photo quality may suffer to varying degrees, depending on the school's desktop publishing system.

Digital photography allows photographers and editors to make a virtually unlimited number of changes in photographs without the viewer's or subject's knowledge. This power raises a number of ethical concerns. In response, the National Press Photographers Association (NPPA) has recommended the following guidelines:

- Certain technical changes that do not affect a photo's content, such as lightening football players' faces, are acceptable. Photographers may also correct defects in a photo, such as dust spots.
- Photos that offend community standards may in some cases be altered. For example, gruesome pictures or those showing overwhelming grief and distress can be electronically changed.
- Every photo that has been altered should be labeled as a photo illustration. The NPPA also encourages photojournalists to include in the cutline (caption) an explanation of any special effect used in the creation of the photo illustration in order to eliminate the reader's perception of any intent to deceive.

1. The simplest kind of homemade camera does not even have a lens. Even so, it uses the basic principles of the camera—light entering a dark chamber to produce an image. This device is called a pinhole camera.

   Make a pinhole camera. To do so, find a box that can be made lightproof when closed. Shoe boxes or cylindrical oatmeal boxes usually work well. Be sure your box has a tight-fitting lid and will hold a four-by-five-inch sheet of photo paper. Next, make the pinhole, which will serve as the aperture. Take a smooth piece of aluminum foil about an inch square. Lay it on a flat, hard surface. Press the point of a needle down through the foil. The hole should be too small for the entire pin to fit through.

   Paint the inside of the box a flat black. If the inside remains a light color, it will reflect or bounce the light passing through the pinhole in all directions and fog your paper. Now make a one-inch-square hole in the center of one side of the box (or the lid of the oatmeal box). Tape the aluminum foil with the pinhole securely over the larger hole, using an opaque tape

(such as black electrical tape) to fasten it. Make sure the pinhole is in the center. Then use another piece of tape to cover the pinhole. This piece of tape will act as the shutter of the camera.

You must load the pinhole camera with photo paper under darkroom conditions, that is, in an area where no light can reach the paper. Cut an unexposed sheet of photo paper into four-by-five-inch rectangles. Tape one of the rectangles to the side of the box opposite the pinhole. Replace the lid on the box, and you are ready to take a photograph.

To take a photograph with a pinhole camera, place it on a firm support, such as a table or chair. This is important, because any movement during the exposure will cause your photograph to blur. Open the tape that covers the pinhole. Expose the photograph for two minutes if it's sunny outside or eight minutes if it's cloudy. Then develop the photo paper in the darkroom. The resulting image will be a negative.

2. Bring a camera from home to class. Compare it with your classmates' cameras. Perhaps someone has a disposable or a panoramic camera, or maybe a Polaroid camera. How do the cameras compare in terms of shutter speed, aperture and focusing systems?

◢ PHOTO EDITING

Even after a photograph has been shot, developed and printed, the photographer still has a great deal of work to do to prepare the photograph for publication. Some of these tasks may be shared with others on a publication staff, but the photographer should know how to do each of them. The tasks include cropping, sizing and writing cutlines.

Cropping

Cropping a photograph means choosing the best areas of the photograph to keep and discarding everything else. Cropping a photograph actually starts when the photographer frames the picture in the view finder, continues in the darkroom when the print is made, and finishes when the design editor lays out the page. How a photograph is cropped also determines its proportions when it appears on the page.

Suppose you have an eight-by-10-inch print to work with, and the photo editor has told you to crop it to fit in a five-by-six-inch news hole. First, look carefully at the photograph to assess its most important elements. One handy way to evaluate a print for cropping involves cutting out two L shapes from a piece of paper or cardboard. By laying the L shapes in various configurations on the photograph, a rectangle of any size can be formed to isolate the desired portion of the image.

When you decide how you want to crop the photo, mark straight lines on the border of the photo to line up with the edges of the cropping. The printer will then know what portion of the photograph to use. You may also make your cropping marks directly on the photo with a grease pencil.

How can you decide what to crop? Here are a few tips:

- Cars, trains and football players need space to move into a photograph. A motorcyclist racing from left to right should not be cropped with the front wheel of the bike tight up against the right side of the photograph. Be sure to give a baseball hitter room to hit the ball, a soccer player room to run and so on.
- Take notice of the direction in which the people in your photographs are facing. Are they looking to the right or to the left? Generally, you can crop a photograph much closer to the subject from behind than in front of the subject. If a subject is looking toward the left, say, you can more easily crop the photograph behind the subject's head and shoulders on the right.
- Be especially careful to crop out any distracting background images. Often overhead lights, people in the background (who are not part of the story but are nevertheless still mugging for the camera), and trees or poles can be cropped out to create a much stronger image.
- Cropping seems more natural at some places on the body than on others. Crop below the subject's feet or at the waist, neck or chin. Avoid cutting off hands and feet, wrists, ankles or fingers. A simple rule of thumb is never to crop at a joint.

Sizing

sizing
calculating what the new dimensions (height and width) of a photograph will be after it has been enlarged or reduced

Before a photo will fit on a newspaper or yearbook page, you may need to rescale it. That is, you may have to calculate what its dimensions will be (height and width) after it's been enlarged or reduced. This process, called **sizing,** usually requires the use of a proportion wheel.

Imagine that you have a nice eight-by-10-inch photo that is cropped perfectly. You bring the photo to the layout editor, who says, "That's great, but I only have a three-column-wide place to put it." You know that a three-column space is six inches wide. Therefore, the photograph as it will be printed in the paper will be six inches wide. The question you must answer is how tall the photograph will be when it is reduced to fit. You could recrop the photo, but you decide to resize it instead.

FIGURE 14.6

Cropping can eliminate distracting influences and strengthen the art's impact. The dashed lines show a few of the many ways this photograph might be cropped.

To determine the new height, find the original width (eight inches) on the inner wheel of a proportion wheel. Then turn the wheel so that the 8 (the old height) lines up with the 6 (the new height) on the outer wheel. The inner wheel represents the original size; the outer wheel is the reproduction size. Now, without turning the wheel, find the original height (ten inches) on the inner wheel. You discover that it's lined up with 7.5 on the outer wheel. That means the new height of your reproduction will be 7.5 inches. Some printers may prefer that you tell them the percentage of enlargement or reduction. If so, look in the small window near the center of the proportion wheel for that figure. In this case, you'll reduce the photograph to 75 percent of its original size.

Creating Cutlines

The photographer's job is not finished until the cutline is written. Cutlines, or captions, are sentences that describe the photographs in a publication. They should add information, such as the names of those photographed, that the reader can't know by looking at the photograph. Part of the photographer's responsibility is to record the names of the subjects when the photographs are taken and to write down any other pertinent information at the scene.

Cutlines may be several paragraphs long or as short as three or four words. No matter who writes the caption, it is the photographer's duty to provide the necessary information accurately. An error in a caption undermines the credibility of the whole paper.

Try writing a caption for this photo. It doesn't look as though these three are "'chuting into the face of fear," does it?

Recording the Information. Cutline information should be recorded in a small notebook. The names of people in the photograph should be spelled correctly. Check the spelling with the subject. It's easy to confuse Ann with Anne and John with Jon.

Other relevant information may include the person's age and a street or city address. After all, there may be several John Smiths in your immediate vicinity. How will readers know which one you mean? You may also want to record telephone numbers at which people can be reached in, say, two hours' or two days' time, when you're back at school and an editor has a question about the photograph.

When there are several people in a photograph, the photographer must devise a way to identify each of them, usually by recording their position from left to right. Be careful not to mix up names because people sometimes move between the time the photograph was taken and the time the cutline information was recorded. In some cases, it may help to write down a description of a person or his clothes (for example, "John Smith—wire-rim glasses and sports jacket").

Writing the Cutline. When you're back at school or in the publication office, you can start to write your cutline. The first few words of a cutline function as the headline of a story does—they have to arouse the interest of the reader. They should form a link between the photograph and the rest of the cutline. Depending on the publication's style, the introductory word or phrase may be set in bold type or all capitals and possibly be separated from what follows by a colon, dash or a thin dark line.

Suppose you have a photograph of a person who is ready to skydive for the first time. The cutline might begin as follows:

'CHUTING INTO THE FACE OF FEAR

These words make a good link between the photograph and the rest of the cutline. Then you can add information:

'CHUTING INTO THE FACE OF FEAR
Al Laukaitis hangs on for dear life to the strut of a Cessna 182 flying over the Weeping Water area at about 3,500 feet.

However, this doesn't tell us much more than can be seen in the photograph. Try adding more of the facts that you might have gathered when speaking to Laukaitis. That approach might lead to the second sentence of the cutline:

'CHUTING INTO THE FACE OF FEAR
Al Laukaitis hangs on for dear life to the strut of a Cessna 182 flying over the Weeping Water area at about 3,500 feet. Seconds later he let go, and a static line opened his chute as he approached a velocity of 90 m.p.h. (*Lincoln Journal-Star,* Lincoln, Nebraska)

The cutline should not state the obvious, such as "Mr. Smith smiles for the camera while Mr. Jones looks on." Why is Mr. Smith smiling? Why is Mr. Jones there? The cutline should provide answers to those questions.

Good cutlines, like good leads, answer the 5 Ws and an H in describing the photo: "Workers begin building South's new science wing, which is expected to be ready by the next school year. The project is being paid for by a district-wide bond measure" (*Axe,* South Eugene High School, Eugene, Ore.)

As illustrated in the previous example, cutlines should be written in the present tense. The action in the photograph is, after all, frozen in time. Using the past tense tends to reduce the immediacy of the photograph. Sometimes, however, the second sentence of a cutline, or the cutline for a sporting event that has already been played, is written in past tense: "Steve Carlino attempts to pin down his Kenwood opponent on Jan. 6. Carlino compiled a score of 13–2 during his first season at Dulaney as a transfer student" (*Griffin,* Dulaney High School, Timonium, Md.).

Each person in a formal group photo should be identified by name. Casual photos of groups may be identified by naming the group: "Yearbook and newspaper staff members enjoy a stop at the Hard Rock Cafe on their way to the FSPA state convention in Orlando" (*Seahawk's Eye,* Cape Coral high School, Cape Coral, Fla.). As a rule of thumb, name everyone in a group of five or fewer. When naming people in photos, always list them in order from left to right. Because that's standard, you don't need to say "left to right." You will have to explain your method, however, if you identify people some other way. Sometimes people aren't arranged in neat rows, and you will need to indicate who's who:

> Camped out inside the school after being scooted from Jackman Field, seniors pitched tents in the third-floor lounge around 7 a.m. From top are Matt Shirrell, Silvana Marzullo, Joanna Sharp, Parathima Neerukonda and Sari Siegel. (*U-High Midway,* University High School, Chicago, Ill.)

> Class officers are (clockwise) president Sueann Ramella, secretary Audra Hammond, yell leader Heather Mickelson and treasurer Jess Qunell. (*Viking Vanguard,* Puyallup High School, Puyallup, Wash.)

Sports cutlines should include the final score and the names of the players photographed, even those on opposing teams: "Kate Fowler, senior, drives a ball past two Thompson Valley players, Chris Baker and Donna Williamson. The volleyball team beat the Eagles in two games, 15–3, 15–7" (*Trojan News,* Longmont High School, Longmont, Colo.).

Finally, photos sometimes run as **stand-alones.** That is, they run without a story. The cutlines for stand-alones must provide all the information the reader needs to know. Note the following example from the *Arrow,* the paper at Clearwater High School in Clearwater, Kansas: "The six Homecoming candidates, Katie Chicester, Jeb Becker, Angie Pauly, Casey Gerberding, Ashleigh Self and Chad Pike, battle fierce winds at the game last Friday against Kingman. Angie and Casey were crowned as queen and king. After the game, students gathered in the gym to dance and watch the school video on the largest screen in CHS history. Proceeds from the dance went to Stu-Co."

stand-alone

a photograph with no accompanying story

· ·

1. Practice resizing photographs with a proportion wheel. How high would an eight-by-10-inch photo be, for example, if it were reduced to 3.5 inches wide? What if it were enlarged to 11 inches wide?

2. Bring three family photos from home, and write cutlines for each. Use the first sentence of each cutline to identify the people and activities in the photo. Use the second sentence to provide background information.

CHAPTER REVIEW

KEY TERMS

Journalism \\\\ ⁀ \\ ĕm\ n (1833) **1 a :** the collection and editing of news for presentation through the public press **c :** an academic study concerned with the colle

Show that you know the meanings of the following key terms by correctly using them in complete sentences. Write your answers on a separate sheet of paper.

photojournalist	time exposure	wide-angle lens
composition	f-stop	zoom lens
lens	exposure	sizing
film	film speed	stand-alone
aperture	depth of field	
shutter	telephoto lens	

OPEN FORUM

1. Suppose a staff photographer rushes in with what he claims is a "stop-the-presses" photo. It turns out he was listening to a police scanner and heard about an accident near his home. Upon arriving at the scene, he discovered rescue workers retrieving the body of a teenage boy from electric power lines about 25 feet off the ground. The boy had apparently climbed the electric pole to snatch a small glass globe covering one of the power connections. (Some people like to collect these globes.) He inadvertently touched a power line and was electrocuted. The photographer says the photograph shows the boy's body but not his face, because his parka had fallen over his head. Should you run the photograph to alert other teens to the dangers of this hobby? Or, should you respect the privacy of the boy's family and destroy the photograph?

2. One of the school administrators learns that for a yearbook assignment, you took photographs at a recent party. The administrator believes that several of the school's athletes were at the party and, according to a few rumors, were seen drinking alcohol. The administrator wants to see your negatives to find out whether there's any

◆ OPEN FORUM, CONTINUED

truth to those rumors. You recognize that you were using a camera borrowed from school, shooting school film and working on a school assignment. However, you also want to protect the reputations of your friends. What should you tell the administrator? What support would you have for your position?

3. One of the yearbook photographers wants to get a shot of a student at your school who is finally coming home after a long stay at a hospital following a ski accident. The photographer decides to wait for the student on the lawn at the family's home. Irritated with the photographer's behavior, the student's mother comes out of her house and orders the photographer to leave. The photographer doesn't want to be obnoxious but doesn't want to miss the photo, either. Where would you advise the photographer to stand—on the lawn, in the street or on the sidewalk on the opposite side of the street? Or would you tell the photographer to forget this photograph and to take one when the student comes back to school?

FINDING THE FLAW

1. What is wrong with the following cutline (see the photo)?
    These four Davenport students won first place in the Reading Classics competition held March 22 in Hebron. In the back row (from left) are Sara Nippert, Reese Pearson, Gurayn Sylte and Shandi Schoming. In front are Tony Fehr and Brett Walburn.

◆ **FINDING THE FLAW,** continued

2. What is wrong with this photo?

MEDIA WATCH

1. Ask your teacher to invite a professional photographer to class to talk about learning to "see" good photos. What strategies does this person use to get fresh, interesting shots?

2. Check out some back issues of *Life* or *Look* from your school library. These magazines were justly famous for their outstanding photographs. Pick three favorite photos, and explain to your classmates what you admire about each one.

String Book

1. Put together a portfolio of your best photographic work. A solid portfolio should contain 10 to 12 of your best photographs, including at least one of each of these kinds of photographs: portrait (close-up of one person), still life (an object such as a bowl of fruit), landscape (a natural scene), breaking news (a fire or an accident, for example) and reaction (faces in the crowd or cheerleaders at a big game). Also include examples that show you know how to use different lenses.

2. Begin a collection of your favorite photos. Clip good photos from newspapers, magazines and other sources. Jot a few notes beside or below each photograph that explain what young photographers can learn from the photograph. Collect the photographs in a notebook.

Chapter 15
Newspaper Design

KEY TERMS

In this chapter, you will learn the meaning of these terms:

art
rule
deck
gutter
tabloid
broadsheet
entry point
modular design
infographics
story package
teaser
flag
initial cap
internal margin
mug shot
standing head
cutline
index
jump line
refer
folio
subhead
photo credit
white space
pica
point
leg
boldface
italic
design
paste-up
dummy
identity system
grid
dominant photo
tombstoning
bastard measure

LEARNING OBJECTIVES

After completing this chapter, you will be able to:

◆ use the correct terminology for design techniques,

◆ draw a dummy for a newspaper page,

◆ modify stories by stretching and shrinking them to fit.

◆

Most people read their newspapers in a poorly lit kitchen with the radio or television turned on and someone else in the room. Most students read their papers in the cafeteria or during the last few minutes of class amid a world of distractions. The challenge for page designers is to somehow arrest and hold people's attention long enough to engage them in the important and significant stories contained in the paper. But doing so is a considerable task.

What do people like to look at? Television commercials, CD covers or tortilla chip packages? The key to good design is analyzing what you see, recognizing what works and deciding how to apply that to your own work. If your paper looks like it did five years ago, you're in big trouble. Readers are not where they were five years ago, and your paper should not be there, either. Writers have to learn to think visually, because design should be part of the initial planning stage for any story. Newspaper layout—the process of designing the way a newspaper page looks—requires skill and creativity, as well as plenty of elbow grease.

In this chapter you'll learn how to blend the basic elements of print journalism—stories, headlines, photographs and cutlines—into exciting and professional-looking combinations. You'll learn why some pages look better than others and how to stretch or shrink stories to fit the space available. You'll also get some tips on how to take advantage of desktop publishing technology to produce great-looking publications.

◤DESIGNING FOR THE MODERN READER

Do you resemble your parents or grandparents? You almost certainly do. But do you like the same things they do? Probably not. Your taste in food, clothing and entertainment reflects the relentless pace of change that sweeps all of us along. And those changes cause us to have different opinions than previous generations about what is appealing or appetizing.

Your grandparents, for example, probably used to read newspapers that were heavy on content and light on visual appeal. Those papers contained long, gray columns of type that looked like pillars in front of a bank. Today, we're different. We have color TVs, home computers, portable CD players and glossy magazines. We collect information in a dazzling variety of ways. For the most part, we don't care for long, gray columns of type anymore. Instead, we want something different. We want newspapers that are snappy, inviting, easy to grasp and instantly informative.

That's where you come in. If you can design a newspaper that's inviting, informative and easy to read, you can successfully compete for your readers' attention. You can help keep your school paper a vital part of the campus scene.

There's no getting around it: for many students, newspapers are dinosaurs. They're big, clumsy and slow. Although they've endured for ages, it's possible that newspapers will either become extinct or evolve into a new species. (Imagine a video newspaper that lets you tune in to sports highlights, scan some comics and then view the hottest fashions on sale at the local mall.)

For some, that evolution has already taken place. Many college papers, for instance, have already gone online; that is, students can access the newspapers through their personal computers. In fact, if you can get on any large computer network, you can probably pull up many national and international papers on your computer screen.

But it's just as likely that traditional newspapers will stick around for a long time to come. That means we need to do our best with what we have: black ink; white paper; and lots of lines, dots, letters and numbers. A good designer can put all those things together quickly and smoothly so that today's news feels both familiar and new.

A Brief History of Newspaper Design

America's earliest newspapers actually looked more like pamphlets than what we would recognize as the newspaper of today. The first paper in colonial America, *Public Occurrences* (printed in Boston in 1690), was only seven inches wide. This four-page paper had just three pages of news—the last page was blank. The paper ran news items one after another in deep, wide columns of text.

Other colonial papers were similar. There were no headlines and very little **art** (photos, drawings, or other kinds of illustration). A young Ben Franklin printed America's first newspaper cartoon in 1754.

After the Revolutionary War, papers began to appear more often; many became dailies instead of weeklies. They also introduced several new design elements: thinner columns; primitive headlines (one-line labels such as PROCLAMATION); and an increasing number of ads, many of them placed along the bottom of the front page.

Throughout the first half of the 19th century, the appearance of most papers changed very little. Copy (stories or articles) was hung like wallpaper, in long strips, between thin, black, vertical or horizontal lines, called **rules.** Maps or engravings were sometimes used as art, but there were no photographs.

During the Civil War, papers scrambled to satisfy readers eager to hear news from the battle front. Designers began devoting more space to headlines by stacking layers of headlines, or **decks,** on top of one another. The largest headline would be on the top, and smaller, secondary headlines would follow as the reader read down through the

Even The New York Times, *generally considered a graphically conservative newspaper, has become more visually oriented than this type intensive 1974 edition announcing President Nixon's resignation.*

art

photos, drawings or other kinds of illustrations in a newspaper or other publication

rule

a thin horizontal or vertical black line in a newspaper or other publication, notably between columns of text

deck

a layer in a grouping of headlines

FIGURE 15.1
DECKS

> **MURDER**
> of
> **PRESIDENT LINCOLN**
>
> His Assassination Last
> Night While at Ford's
> Theatre in Washington!
>
> **J. WILKES BOOTH THE
> SUPPOSED MURDERER**
>
> **THE PISTOL BALL
> ENTERS HIS BRAIN**
>
> **THE ASSASSIN IN HIS
> PRIVATE BOX**
>
> The Murderer leaps upon
> the stage and escapes!

gutter
> a narrow strip of white space between columns of text

tabloid
> a half-sized newspaper

broadsheet
> what today is considered a full-sized newspaper

entry point
> a visual element that draws a reader into the page or story. Examples include pictures, headlines, art, subheads, maps, boxes and other graphic devices

decks. The *Chicago Tribune,* for example, used 15 decks to present its report on the great fire of 1871. Figure 15.1 shows how the *Philadelphia Inquirer* reported the assassination of President Abraham Lincoln in 1865.

By about 1900, newspapers began taking on a more modern appearance. Headlines grew bigger, bolder and wider. The deep stacks of decks were gradually dropped to save space. The news began to be compartmentalized as topics of special interest—crime, foreign news and sports, for example—occupied their own sections or pages.

Many of the trends that influence newspaper design today came into being in the 1960s. Those trends included more and bigger photos, simplified headlines, a shift to a standard six-column page and the use of **gutters** (narrow strips of white space) instead of rules between columns of text.

As printing presses improved, newspapers also began to use more and more full-color photos, as well as more exciting graphic treatments. Perhaps some of these features have already found their way into your school paper.

Many school newspapers are printed as **tabloids** (half-sized papers such as the *National Enquirer* and some local newspapers). Other schools use a **broadsheet** format (about 13 by 22 inches) similar in size to *USA Today.* Some schools publish their papers as a supplement to the regular town or community paper and follow the format that paper uses. But no matter what format you use, the design principles we will cover in this chapter apply equally well.

Today's Look

Perhaps you have noticed that the vending machines for *USA Today* look like miniature TV sets. That's no accident. Modern newspapers and magazines find themselves competing for attention in an extremely visual market. As a result, print publications have changed their designs to be as visually appealing as possible. Professional newspaper editors and designers realize that most people judge a product by its package. Your readers simply won't respect a newspaper that looks hopelessly old-fashioned.

How does a paper look up-to-date? For starters, a modern newspaper uses entry points, modular design, infographics, story packages and color.

◆ *Entry points.* **Entry points** are visual elements that draw a reader into the page. They are paths that lead readers into stories. Entry points include such obvious attention-grabbing elements as pictures, headlines and art work. They also include subheads, maps, charts, graphs, icons, bylines, boxes, screens and many more graphic devices. A typical *USA Today* front page may have as many as 40 different entry points.

BYLINE

MARIO GARCIA
NEWSPAPER DESIGN CONSULTANT

How would readers define "good design?" If I could distill my conversations with the thousands of readers of the more than 80 newspapers I have consulted with around the world, their answers might read like this:

◆ Get me in and out of the page quickly.
◆ Show me how to get where I want to be.
◆ I'm going to look at those big photographs anyway; use them to guide me around the page.

◆ Make the headlines big so I can find topics I'm interested in and make them say something so I know if the story is worth my time.
◆ Surprise me! I like chocolate after a meal and spice in my soup, so don't be afraid to tempt me with some exciting treats.

Source: Adapted from Contemporary Newspaper Design *by Mario R. Garcia (Englewood Cliffs, N.J.: Prentice-Hall), p. 2–4.*

◆ *Modular design.* In a **modular design,** all stories are neatly arranged in rectangular shapes. Everything that belongs to a story—its headline, the copy, and related photos or art work—is printed as a mod (short for *module*). A mod is a rectangle—either horizontal, vertical or square. When a newspaper page consists of a number of different mods, it's easy for readers to find all of a story that they are particularly interested in reading.

◆ *Informational graphics.* **Infographics** is short for informational graphics. Papers don't just report the news anymore, they illustrate it with infographics—charts, maps, and diagrams, quotations and factual sidebars that make information visual and easy to grasp.

◆ *Story packages.* Everyone on a newspaper staff should think visually. Stories should be planned with visuals in mind from the beginning. The copy and its visual treatment is called a **story package**. For example, a reporter, photographer and graphic artist might work together as a team to create a story package consisting of a story with several subheads and a pulled quotation, photos, and a special headline treatment (designed by the graphic artist). More and more, design is becoming a team effort.

◆ *Color.* Nothing makes a newspaper look more modern than color. If your newspaper has a large budget, you may already be publishing full-color photos on the front page. Papers with smaller budgets can sometimes afford single-color treatments in lines, bars and graphs. But even the smallest budget can achieve the same effects by using a variety of grays. Computer software makes it easy to print screens and tints.

modular design
a design in which stories are arranged in rectangular shapes, or modules

infographics
design elements that illustrate a story, such as a chart, map, diagram, quotation or sidebar; short for *informational graphics*

story package
the copy for a story and related photos or infographics

teaser

a brief preview that high-lights the best stories inside the newspaper

flag

the newspaper's name, especially as it appears on Page 1

initial cap

a large capital letter set into the opening paragraph of a story to help draw the reader's attention to the beginning of the story

internal margin

a margin that keeps a consistent distance between all elements of a page, usually one or two picas

mug shot

a small photograph of the face of someone mentioned in a story

standing head

a label used to identify special items such as news briefs or columns

cutline

information about a photo or illustration

index

a listing of the paper's contents

jump line

a line telling the reader on what page the story continues

Design Terms

To be successful as a publication designer, you'll need to speak the language of design. In a typical newsroom, for instance, you'll find slugs, bugs and dummies, not to mention a widow in the gutter. Not all publication staffs use the same jargon, but the most common terms are almost universal. Here are some design terms (graphically illustrated in Figure 15.2) you should know.

- ◆ *Teaser.* A **teaser** is a brief preview that highlights the best stories inside the paper.
- ◆ *Flag.* The newspaper's name, especially as it appears on Page 1 of each issue, is the **flag.**
- ◆ *Headline.* The headline is a story's title, usually shown in large type above or beside the story.
- ◆ *Byline.* The writer's name, often accompanied by the writer's position (for example, sports editor or feature reporter), is the byline.
- ◆ *Infographics.* Diagrams, maps or charts are infographics.
- ◆ *Initial cap.* A large capital letter set into the opening paragraph of a story is an **initial cap.** The letter helps draw the reader's attention to the beginning of the story.
- ◆ *Internal margin.* Spacing that keep a consistent distance between all elements of a page—usually one or two picas—is called **internal margins.** This consistency helps hold the design together.
- ◆ *Deck.* A smaller headline added below the main headline is a deck.
- ◆ *Mug shot.* A **mug shot** is a small photograph of the face of someone mentioned in the story.
- ◆ *Standing head.* A label used to identify special items such as news briefs or columns is called a **standing head.**
- ◆ *Cutline.* Information about a photo or illustration is a **cutline.** Nonjournalists frequently call this a *caption.*
- ◆ *Index.* An **index** is a listing of the paper's contents.
- ◆ *Jump line.* A **jump line** is a line telling the reader on what page the story continues.
- ◆ *Masthead.* Sometimes called the *staff box,* the masthead is a block of information that identifies the staff members of the paper and tells readers where to send their letters and comments.
- ◆ *Refer.* **Refers** (pronounced "reefers") send the reader to another related article or item in the same issue of the paper.
- ◆ *Folio.* A **folio** is a line showing the page number, date and name of the paper.
- ◆ *Pulled quotation.* A quotation from the story that is given special emphasis by a larger size and special display treatment is a pulled quotation.
- ◆ *Subhead.* A **subhead** is a line of type set apart from the rest of the story to break up the text and create more visual interest.

FIGURE 15.2
DESIGN TERMS

TEASERS
These promote other stories inside the paper. (Also called *promos* or *skyboxes*)

FLAG
The newspaper's name (also called the nameplate)

HEADLINE
The story's title or summary, in large type above or beside the story

BYLINE
The writer's name, often followed by other credentials

REVERSE HEAD
A white headline set against a dark background

INFOGRAPHIC
A diagram, chart or map conveying information pictorially

DISPLAY HEAD
A fancy headline adding graphic impact to special stories

DECK
A smaller headline added below the main head (shown here is a summary deck, which gives a brief outline of the article)

HEADER
A label used for packaging special items (graphics, teasers, briefs, columns, etc.)

INDEX
A content guide

JUMP LINE
A line telling the reader the page on which the story continues

MUG SHOT
A small photograph (usually just the face) of someone in the story

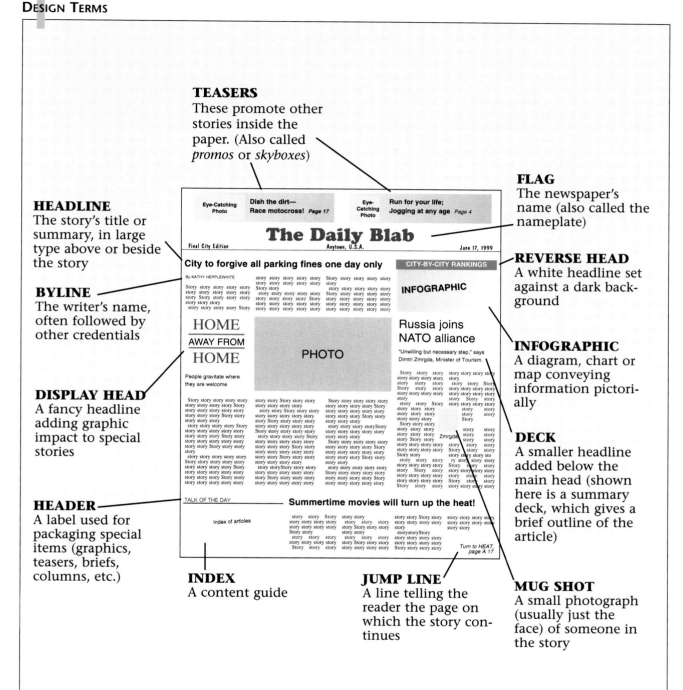

refer

> a line that sends readers to a related article or item in the same issue of the paper; pronounced "reefer"

folio

> a line showing the page number, date and name of the paper

subhead

> a line of type set apart from the rest of the story to break up the text and create more visual interest

photo credit

> a line giving the photographer's name

white space

> an area without ink, frequently used by designers as a graphic element to define stories and give special emphasis

pica

> a unit of measure. There are six picas to an inch

point

> a unit of measure. There are 12 points in a pica, or 72 points to the inch

◆ *Gutter.* The white space running vertically between elements on a page, especially between columns of text, is the **gutter.**

◆ *Photo credit.* A **photo credit** is a line giving the photographer's name.

◆ *White space.* Far from being simply emptiness, **white space,** or an area without ink, is frequently used by designers as a graphic element to define stories and give special emphasis.

Measuring Systems

In addition to knowing the terms of design, you must also know a special measuring system. That system includes three different kinds of measures: picas, points and inches.

If you're trying to measure something very short or very thin, measurement in inches is clumsy and involves too many fractions. So designers generally use picas and points for precise measurements. There are six **picas** in an inch and 12 **points** in a pica, or 72 points to the inch. These small increments eliminate the need to fuss with fractions.

Points are used to measure the size of headlines (a large headline, for example, might be 48 points). Points are also used to measure the thickness of lines that make up bars or boxes, as well as the space between each line of a story. Picas are used to measure the width of stories and photos. Inches are used to measure story length (a 12-inch story, for example) and the depth of ads. An ad, for example, might measure two columns wide by six inches deep.

Electronic Publishing

Although almost every design strategy could be accomplished with traditional cut-and-paste methods, we assume that your school is using a computer to create your school publications. The major design programs such as Aldus Pagemaker and QuarkXpress (the industry standard) give you almost complete creative and technical control over your publications. These programs allow you to control every aspect of lettering—from size to style—as well as other visual elements such as lines, bars, boxes and screens. The major graphic arts programs such as FreeHand and Adobe Illustrator give you the capability to create infographics, drawings and other illustrations that rival the best that can be found in the professional media.

Emerging technology will take us even further. Image scanners, for example, enable student designers to digitize photographs. Once digitized, the photographs can be reduced, enlarged or even modified. Adobe Photoshop is a software program that enables students to combine photos, distort images and create all kinds of unusual effects. Not long ago, a Pulitzer Prize–winning photo caused considerable controversy when judges discovered that the photographer had electronically removed a Coca-Cola can from the photograph. That controversy stirred up discussion about a whole new area of journalistic ethics—and the controversy is far from settled.

No matter how powerful your desktop computer may be, however, it still can't tell the difference between good designs and poor ones. The computer remains a tool at your beck and call; you still call the shots.

THIS JUST IN: *Portrait of a Young Journalist*

Craig Pursley, assistant art director, Orange County Register

Broadcaster ?
Journalist ?
Sports Writer ?
Designer ?
Editor ?
Columnist ?
Anchor ?
Reporter ?
Photographer ?

"I was a day away from becoming a shoe salesman." That's how Craig Pursley, now assistant art director at the *Orange County Register,* one of the world's most visually appealing newspapers, describes his job search in Southern California.

Pursley had given up a career as an art teacher in Wyoming and moved to Los Angeles, hoping to follow his dream of becoming a professional artist. That dream came true when he found a position at the *Register* and later began doing freelance work for the California Angels and many other professional sports teams. One of Pursley's favorite projects was a poster depicting Wayne Gretzsky, one of hockey's all-time greats.

Pursley is responsible for graphics and illustrations for the *Register,* which he says can include anything from a traffic map to a bar chart. Occasionally, Pursley gets to indulge his creative side. He created

"Dreamscapes," a project in which the paper publishes a whimsical picture and invites readers to send in stories that might account for the strange picture. Among Pursley's "Dreamscapes" (which run monthly) are pictures of a boy liquefying from the knees down and a mother and daughter looking out the window at a landscape that eerily resembles a calendar picture inside the home. Pursley has won several awards of merit from the Society of Newspaper Design, as well as a number of other awards and recognitions.

He got his start as an illustrator in an unlikely way. As a college student, he was in the habit of reading the newspaper and noticed, one slow afternoon, that a police composite drawing of a criminal was poorly done. "I could do that," he thought to himself. He called the local sheriff and offered his services the next time police wanted to create a picture of a criminal from the statements of witnesses. The sheriff seemed to shrug off the suggestion. But a few weeks later, Pursley got a call at 3 a.m. "Der

Weinerschnitzel, a local fast food place, had been held up, and they wanted me to come down to talk to the clerk," he recalls. Pursley shook the sleep out of his eyes, went down to the store, and drew a picture that quickly led to the robber's capture.

Over the next few years, Pursley's fame as a police artist spread. Soon he was drawing composites for 12 different law enforcement agencies, including the Federal Bureau of Investigation. He estimated he did nearly 400 sketches of both suspected criminals and victims.

"Once the police found a body dumped on the side of the road. Because there was no identification, they asked me to draw the victim's face. I had to do it while the autopsy was going on," Pursley remembers. "I approached it like a frog dissection. I couldn't think of her as a person."

Pursley also worked for the Forest Service, making maps and charts. Eventually, his skills drew him toward journalism, where thousands now enjoy his work on a daily basis.

1. Investigate whether online newspapers already exist in your community. What can you find out about computer networks, such as the Internet and America Online in terms of online papers? How do these online editions differ, designwise, from their non-electronic versions?

2. Imagine that you found the following headline—written in the deck style of 1865—in a current newspaper. Rewrite it in modern form.

More Americans using home health tests
Parents can check kids for drug usage
More than $1 billion spent on home health tests last year
*People check for high cholesterol, colon cancer
or even AIDS*
Federal government has no policy regarding the accuracy of such tests

THE ELEMENTS OF DESIGN

A puzzle is an apt metaphor for the challenge that faces a newspaper designer. As a designer, you have a variety of pieces to fit within a rectangular border, but your puzzle is more complicated than most. For one thing, your pieces come in an endless number of sizes and shapes. Also, they can fit together in any number of different ways. How well you fit the pieces of a publication together determines how successful you'll be as a designer.

Although page design may look complicated at first, you'll find that four key elements—four kinds of puzzle pieces, if you will—do most of the work. Because these four elements are used over and over, they take up nearly all the space you have to work with, not counting advertisements. Once you master these four basic building blocks, you're well on your way to achieving good page design. The four elements are headlines, copy, photographs and cutlines.

Headlines

+ Baby born in middle of 70-car smashup
+ Accused master spy was really a henpecked wimp
+ Steven Seagal: How I brought a dead dog back to life

These headlines probably won't appear on the front page of your school paper any time soon, but if you saw them in huge 100-point type on the cover of a tabloid newspaper, they would surely grab your attention. Headlines can be very powerful. In fact, they're often the strongest weapon in your design arsenal. No matter how beautifully a story has been written or how vivid a photo might be, it can't be spotted from 10 feet away, as a great headline can. You'll find an explanation of how to write and design headlines in Chapter 16. For now, remember that designers pay a great deal of attention to the size and placement of headlines.

Copy

Copy is the major building block of publication design. It's the gray matter that communicates with that other gray matter inside the reader's head. Yet copy is visually dull. It takes all a designer's skill and imagination to make copy look interesting, especially when it comes in the form of a long, long story.

The first step in using copy is to measure the length of a story. Remember that newspaper designers measure stories in inches. A short filler on caps and gowns, for example, might be just 2 inches, whereas an investigative report on the senior ski trip might be 20 inches. To keep page design consistent, designers generally use a standard width for most stories. That standard helps them plan and organize pages more efficiently.

Having established a standard column width, the designer can calculate the area each story will cover. The vertical dimension of a story, its depth, is called a **leg.** If a 12-inch story, for example, were divided evenly into two 6-inch columns, it would be said to have two 6-inch legs. By varying the number and depth of a story's legs, designers can create variety and visual interest. The examples in Figure 15.3 indicate five possible shapes for a 12-inch story.

leg
the vertical dimension of a story (its depth)

Photographs

Nothing gives a page more visual interest than a great photograph. Strong photography lies at the very heart of newspaper design.

Your readers are probably so spoiled by television and magazines that they expect photos to accompany every story they read. Few staffs,

Figure 15.3
POSSIBLE SHAPES FOR A 12-INCH STORY

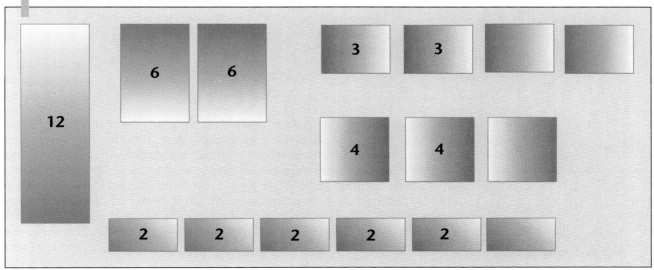

FIGURE 15.4

THREE BASIC SHAPES FOR PHOTOGRAPHS

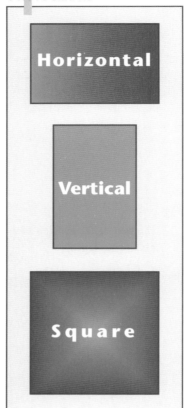

however, have enough photographers to shoot a photo for each story (and few could afford the space anyway). But you should try to take as much advantage as possible of the photos you do have. Without them, you simply can't create an appealing publication.

The best way to show off a good photo is use a large version of it. Remember that a photo is a prime entry point for most readers—it's what draws them to the page. Running a photo large—that is, a third to half the width of the page—gives you the best chance to lure readers in. For some reason, beginning designers are often reluctant to run a photo as large as they could. They can keep this tip in mind: give the page the dollar bill test. You should not be able to lay a dollar bill anywhere on the page (the front page in particular) without having it touch a photo or other image. If the dollar bill covers only copy, you need to do some redesigning.

Photos come in three basic shapes: horizontal, vertical and square (Figure 15.4). Each shape has its own strengths and weaknesses.

- *Horizontal.* The most common shape for photos is the horizontal rectangle, probably because it seems closest to the way we see the world through our own eyes. Most scenes (classroom activities, pep rallies, sports contests and so on) can be pictured best in a horizontal rectangle. Some subjects, such as basketball players and space shuttle launches, however, may need a vertical approach.
- *Vertical.* Vertical rectangles are usually considered more interesting or dynamic than horizontal shapes, because they're more unusual. That six foot six freshman is indeed unusual, and his picture won't fit well in a two-inch horizontal space. But verticals can be tricky to use in page design. Because they're so deep, they sometimes look as if they might belong with any one of several different stories running alongside them.
- *Square.* Squares are usually considered the dullest of the three shapes for photographs. In fact, some page designers avoid squares altogether. But the content of a photo is more important than its shape. Try to accept each photo on its own terms, and design the page with the photo's natural shape in mind.

Cutlines

boldface
> extra dark or heavy type

italic
> type in a style that resembles cursive handwriting

Every picture tells a story. But it's the cutline's job to tell the story behind every picture: who's involved, what's happening, when and where the event took place. A well-written cutline makes the photo instantly understandable and tells readers why the photo is important.

To set cutlines apart from stories, most newspapers use a different typeface than that used for the copy itself. Some use **boldface** type (extra dark or heavy print) so that cutlines pop out as readers scan the page. Some use **italic** (a style that resembles cursive handwriting) for a more elegant look. Others set the first word or two in capital letters to give the cutline a sort of miniheadline.

1. Jay Leno, host of the *Tonight Show*, has published several books of funny headlines sent in by alert readers. Get a copy from a local library, and find out how the style of headline writing (brevity carried to the extreme, almost as if the journalist were writing a telegram) can sometimes lead to unintended humor.

2. Discover what photo shapes the editors of your local paper prefer. Take a complete issue of the paper, and count the number of photos that fall into each shape category: horizontal, vertical and square. Do your findings agree with our recommendation that the majority of photos should be horizontal?

3. Take several old photographs from journalism class or a yearbook, and practice writing cutlines. Compare your efforts with the original cutlines.

4. Create a style book for staff members that explains your design specifications. Include guidelines for identity items (flag, bylines, icons and so forth) and photos.

◣ DESIGN PRINCIPLES THAT WORK

Now that we know the pieces of our newspaper design puzzle, it's time to put them all together. This section explores the basic principles of page design. We'll examine ways you can place rectangular mods (photo-story packages) together to create attractive, well-balanced pages. Once you understand how these principles work, you can adapt them to any pages you design.

Completing the puzzle requires two key steps: **design** (the planning stage; also called *layout*) and **paste-up** (the physical process of assembling the page, either on a computer screen or with glue or wax on a full-size paste-up board). As with many other activities in journalism, wise workers plan ahead. Accomplishing good page design begins with a blueprint. You'll work more efficiently if you draw a detailed page diagram in advance—a **dummy**—before you try to assemble the real thing.

design
the planning, or layout, stage in creating a newspaper page

paste-up
the physical process of assembling the newspaper page, either on a computer screen or with glue or wax on a full-size paste-up board

dummy
a detailed page diagram drawn in advance

Drawing a Dummy

Dummies are generally about half the size of actual pages. Artists use the same principle when they make a thumbnail sketch before attempting a large painting or piece of sculpture. Drawing a dummy isn't an exact science. Stories don't always fit the way you want them to. And even when you're certain you've measured everything perfectly, you inevitably find yourself fudging here and there once you start putting the actual stories and pictures in place. However, that doesn't mean a dummy isn't a terrific time-saver.

Computer users can draw a dummy on the computer and then print it on a single 8½-by-11-inch piece of paper by telling the printer to print the page at 60 percent of normal size. This assumes that you are designing a tabloid-size paper. If your paper is a broadsheet (the size of most daily papers), 40 percent should work.

LONDON, 1814—The steam-driven press, invented in 1811 in Germany, was first used by the *London Times* in 1814. It could print 1,100 sheets an hour.

Americans advanced the printing industry rapidly in the last half of the 19th century, beginning with the invention of the rotary press by Richard Hoe in 1846. It was first used to print a newspaper, the *Philadelphia Public Ledger*, in 1847. Hoe's press printed from a revolving surface, similar to the drum on today's web presses. It could produce 8,000 one-sided sheets an hour.

William Budlock's perfection of the process of printing paper from a continuous roll in 1865 enabled printers to use high-speed rotary presses. When Ottmar Mergenthaler's rapid typesetting machine, known as the linotype, came on the scene in 1884, it completed the steps necessary to produce newspapers in quantity in just minutes.

Newsboys appeared on street corners hawking the latest editions, and even the poorest wage earner could afford the inexpensive mass-produced papers. The improved printing processes made newspapers the common denominator for communication within the growing cities of the industrialized United States. Combined with inventions that made news gathering much faster, such as the telegraph, the new printing methods put world news on the front porches of Americans almost overnight.

Here is one method for creating a dummy:

1. Start with the photos. Draw a box on your dummy the size you want the photo to be, and give the photo a short label. Most designers put a big *X* over their photo boxes. The *X* indicates that this is a photo, not an ad (which gets a single diagonal line) or a boxed story (which gets a single vertical line).
2. Next draw the cutline. Allow a little space (a pica or two) under the photo, and then scribble wiggly lines where the cutline will go.
3. Now sketch in the headline. Many designers imitate the feel of the headline by drawing either a row of *X*s or a squiggley horizontal wave. Some like to write in words to suggest the headline—real or imaginary words do equally well.
4. Finally, indicate where the story goes. Some designers use straight lines, some use wavy lines and some just leave blank space. We recommend a line with a directional arrow. Write the name (or slug) of the story where the text begins. Under it, draw a line down the center of the leg. When you reach the bottom of the leg, jog the line up to the top of the next leg. This will trace the path of the text. Draw an arrow in the direction the reader would read the story at several points along the line.

Every newspaper has its own system for drawing dummies. Some, for example, use pens of different colors for each design element (boxes, photos, copy and so on). Many create their dummies right on the computer. Whatever the system, make your dummies as complete and legible as you can. Figure 15.5 shows a completed dummy page.

Creating Emphasis Areas

Readers don't spend a long time with newspapers. Research shows that the average reader might spend as much as 20 minutes looking at a paper, but not much more. That means that designers must prioritize. They have no time or newsprint to waste. Readers are asking, "So what?" The paper must answer quickly. The page design should show at a glance what's essential, what's important and what may be worth only a passing glance.

Thus, one basic idea in design is to be both louder and softer. The problem with many page designs is that everything on the page looks the same. The stories are the same size, the headlines are the same size and the photos are the same size. Avoid the monotony of sameness by running a very large headline or a very large photo. Vary the size and emphasis given each item so that the reader can tell what is most important, somewhat important and not too important.

FIGURE 15.5
A COMPLETED DUMMY PAGE

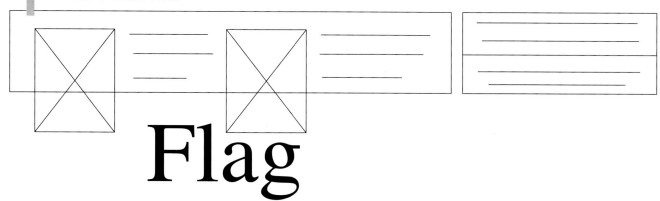

Flag

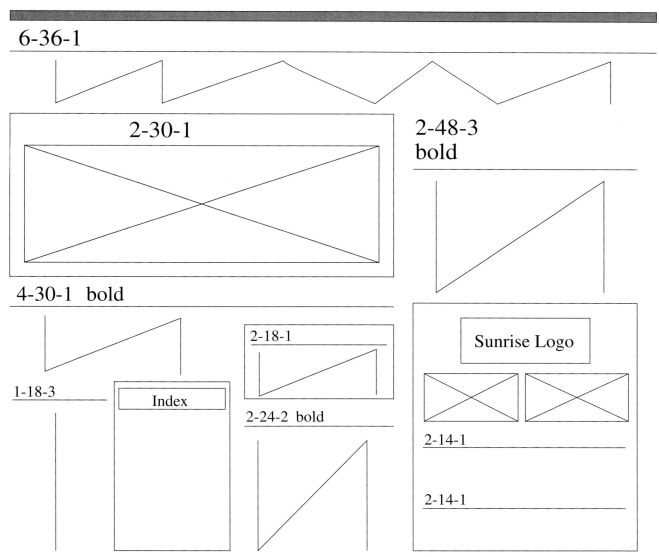

6-36-1

2-30-1

2-48-3
bold

4-30-1 bold

1-18-3

Index

2-18-1

2-24-2 bold

Sunrise Logo

2-14-1

2-14-1

FIGURE 15.6
USING LARGE TYPE FOR EMPHASIS

HELP
MY **CAT** *IS*
LOST

identity system

a newspaper's flag, labels and column heads, as well as other consistent graphic devices, that are used throughout to create a personality

FIGURE 15.7
TYPICAL RESPONSE BOX

What You Can Do:

❒ **Call**

❒ **Attend**

❒ **Write**

❒ **File**

❒ **Save**

The idea of being both louder and softer can be illustrated by the poster shown in Figure 15.6. A young girl lost her cat and decided to enlist the aid of neighbors in her search. She tacked up the poster on telephone poles around the neighborhood. Notice that the important words are in boldface, all capital letters and very large type. The less important words don't detract from the major message. Giving important items great emphasis often requires dramatic contrast.

The Front Page

The front page is so critical to the success of your paper that it deserves special attention. Many contemporary designers insist that the front page must be useful and, above all, user-friendly. Donn Poll, a design consultant, says that the number of stories on Page 1 is a good way to judge your paper. "Have you covered all of your reader groups?" he asks. Is there something on Page 1, for example, for readers interested in:

- school activities?
- student organizations?
- their classmates (freshmen, sophomores, juniors, or seniors)?
- financial issues?
- their teachers or administrators?

Some papers have moved to a single-story, magazine approach for their front page. The majority of school papers still prefer a menu-style Page 1, however, and that is the style we will focus on here.

The personality of your paper comes through most strongly on Page 1. You create that personality through an **identity system** consisting of the paper's flag, page labels (such as Features or Sports) and column heads, as well as any other consistent graphic devices—bylines, icons and pulled quotations, for example—that will be used throughout the paper. The identity system can also include all those items that serve the newspaper's listening function. Does your paper contain a line or box explaining how readers can respond to a story? What about relevant phone numbers? Meeting times and dates? These types of items make a paper more interactive and also help establish the paper's personality. Figure 15.7 shows a typical response box that invites reader input. The *Minneapolis Star Tribune,* for example, has a special telephone number where readers can hear a snippet of an album or concert that has been reviewed in the paper.

The paper's flag can be thought of as its face. The personality of the paper comes through in the flag's design and the type choices that go with it. Most papers try to make their flags typographically interesting. Many incorporate a logo—often some form of the school emblem.

Standardization

All this designing can take up a lot of time. Consequently, designers are always looking for shortcuts. As a designer, you can probably organize your time more effectively by standardizing some areas of the paper. You shouldn't spend the same amount of time on each page. Put the majority of your effort into key pages such as the front page, the sports page and perhaps the editorial page. Create a standard pattern for other pages, with consistent locations for news briefs, features, classified ads and so on.

Readers depend on you to provide both guidance and predictability. Design trends may come and go, but your goal is always to guide the readers to look where you want them to. If you know what you're doing, you can create a page that's logical, legible and fun to read by guiding the readers' eyes wherever you choose.

You Name It: How Some Student Publications Got Their Names

Have you ever wondered where your student newspaper's name came from? Many staff members don't know the history of their publication's name, yet those names often reveal interesting insights about the school and its history. Consider the following name derivations.

◆ *The A-Blast* (Annandale High School, Annandale, VA). Annandale High School opened in 1955, not too many years after World War II had ended. Nuclear power and nuclear weapons were considered positive themes. The atom became Annandale's theme, as reflected in the names of the school's athletic teams (the Atoms), literary magazine (*Filament)* and newspaper (*the A-Blast*).

◆ *The Struggle* (The Frisch School in Paramus, New Jersey,) Frisch has a demanding dual curriculum of Judaic and regular studies. High school students at Frisch must be in school between 7:45 a.m. and 5:10 p.m. every weekday. Their paper is called the *Struggle*. Said *Struggle* adviser J. Chertkoff, "High school at Frisch is a bit of a struggle, but we feel it's one well worth the effort."

◆ *The Hyphen* (Jeffersonville High School, Jeffersonville, IN). When Jeffersonville Junior-Senior High School was formed in 1933 there was quite a rift between the junior and senior high divisions of the school. In an attempt to promote unity, its newspaper was named after one thing the two divisions had in common—the hyphen between *Junior* and *Senior* in the school's name.

◆ *The Bayonet* (Cocoa Beach High School, Cocoa Beach, Florida). The newspaper's name comes from the school's mascot, the Minuteman. This choice of mascot was inspired by the school's telephone number, (407) 783-*1776*.

◆ *The Beak 'n Eye* (West High School, Davenport, IA) is a reference to the school's mascot, the falcon. The beak was chosen to represent the newspaper because the paper is the voice of the students. The eye was chosen because the newspaper is constantly watching what happens at West High School.

◆ *Phloem and Xylem* (Miami Valley School, Dayton, OH). The newspaper is *Phloem and Xylem*. The school's logo is a tree. Phloem and xylem are the systems that distribute nutrients and water within trees.

◆ *Excalibur,* (Nazareth Regional High School, Brooklyn, New York), was named by Thomas Malone, the winner of a school wide contest in 1966. He chose to name the newspaper after King Arthur's sword because the school's athletes are called the Kingsmen, after Kings County, where the school is located.

Using a Grid System

grid

a guide to layout planning. The designer divides the page vertically by columns and horizontally by inches (or picas) to make a pattern that can then be filled by stories and photos.

Before you design a page, you must have an underlying pattern or system of organization. The best way to do that is to adopt a **grid** plan (using the same principle as graph paper in algebra) You can create a grid by dividing the page vertically into columns and horizontally inch by inch. A page grid provides the structure that keeps stories and photos evenly aligned.

One of the most important decisions in creating a grid is selecting the number of columns your page will have. Here are a few guidelines:

- Two- and three-column grids are widely used by newsletters. These grid plans make layout easier but limit the options for photo and text widths.
- Four-column grids are often used in tabloid papers. These grid plans have more flexibility than does a three-column grid plan, and the text is comfortably wide. However, this format often leads to symmetrical design, something most experts discourage.
- The five-column grid pattern is probably the most widely used by high school papers.
- The six-column grid is the standard grid pattern for broadsheets (thus, for most professional papers). Advertising space is generally sold in standard six-column widths.

Designing Pages with Art

In a perfect newspaper, every story might have some sort of art: a photo, a chart, a map or—at the very least—a pulled quotation. Practically speaking, though, producing all those extras takes a colossal amount of work. A more practical rule of thumb is this: Make every page at least one-third art. In other words, when you add up all the photos, graphs, teasers and ads on a page, they should occupy at least one-third of the total.

Some special pages may use even more art than that (for example, sports, features or photo spreads), but on average, one-third is reasonable. On many inside pages, especially those that carry jumped stories (those that continue on another page) this goal may seem almost impossible. Don't forget, though, that ads can count as art, too.

When you add art to page designs, you usually enhance their appeal. Remember that most readers graze, scanning a page until they find something of interest. By adding photos, maps or charts, you catch the readers' interest by providing a variety of entry points. But you also increase the risk of clutter and confusion, so go slowly at first. Once you feel comfortable adding art to stories, keep adding. Always keep in mind these three crucial guidelines:

- Give each page a dominant photo.
- Balance and scatter your art.
- Make stories fit.

Dominant Photo and Balanced Art. Readers expect designers to make decisions for them: to decide which stories are the most important and which photos are the best. Readers want designers to help them know where to look first, not just to shovel everything onto the page in evenly sized heaps.

Equality, in short, can be boring. Therefore, make sure one photo is always dominant on a newspaper page. To be truly dominant, a photo must be substantially bigger than any competing photo. Many designers, for example, say the **dominant photo** should be at least twice as big as the next largest photo (and two and a half times as large, if possible).

A strong photograph can act as an anchor for a story—or for an entire page. Two evenly sized photos side by side, however, will fight each other for the reader's attention. Or worse, they'll just sit there in two big, boring lumps. Once in a while two equal-sized photos can work together (a before-and-after comparison, for example), but usually you will be wiser to make one photo dominant.

When you choose your dominant photo, consider these factors:

- ✦ Does one have better content?
- ✦ Does one have better quality (sharper focus, better exposure or better composition)?
- ✦ Does one have a better shape (Which shape best fits your design?)

Once you have chosen the dominant photo, you can make it the cornerstone and build the rest of the page around it.

Use a dominant photo to anchor your pages, but remember to balance and separate your art, too. When photos start stacking up and colliding, you get a page that is either confusing (when unrelated art intrudes into stories where it doesn't belong) or lopsided (when photos clump together in one area and copy does so in another).

dominant photo
a photo that is substantially larger than any other photograph on the page

STRASBOURG, Germany, 1438–Johannes Gutenberg began working on a method of printing using movable type.

Although Gutenberg is often credited with inventing printing, or the reproduction of text or other images on a surface, he was not the first person to develop the method of printing. Humans were drawing on the walls of caves in France as early as 25,000 B.C.

Paper and ink were developed by the Chinese about 100 A.D., but Europeans did not begin using paper until the 1300s. The Chinese had a crude wooden printing press by the 1200s and a copper press by 1445.

Printing in Europe was done by hand until Gutenberg devised his method of casting individual letters from a mixture of lead and other metals. The letters were then arranged in trays or forms and fitted into a press, which would transfer the images onto one sheet of paper at a time. The type was called movable because it could be removed from the trays and reset to form plates for more pages.

By 1450, Gutenberg had adapted a wine press to hold the new type and had printed several books.

The Gutenberg *Bible* is considered to be the first book printed by movable type. Forty-seven of the estimated 180 Bibles printed still exist.

Gutenberg's principle of movable type was the standard for nearly five centuries before offset printing was developed in the early 1900s. Even so, more technological advances in printing have been made since 1930 than in all the years since Gutenberg developed the process in the 1440s.

Making Stories Fit. No matter how carefully you plan, and no matter how goof-proof your page dummy seems, some stories will end up too short or too long when you actually paste-up the page. If you are following the rules of modular layout, you must still be sure that everything ends up as a rectangle. If a story doesn't quite fit, there are several options.

If a story is too long, try the following:

♦ *Trim the copy.* As a rule of thumb, stories can usually be cut by 10 percent. For instance, a 10-inch story can usually lose an inch off the bottom without serious damage.

♦ *Trim a photo.* Shave a few picas off the top or bottom, if the image allows. If necessary, re-size the photo or crop more tightly.

♦ *Trim an adjoining story.* If the story you're working with has already been trimmed as much as possible, try shortening the story above or below it.

♦ *Drop a line from the headline.* But be careful: short headlines that make no sense can doom an entire story.

♦ *Jump a portion* of the story onto another page.

If a story is too short, one of the following techniques might help:

♦ *Add more copy.* If words were trimmed from a story, add them back. If you have time, break out a small response box to highlight key information.

♦ *Enlarge a photo.* Crop it more loosely, or size it a column wider.

♦ *Add a mug shot.* Be sure it's a photo of someone relevant to the story, however.

♦ *Add a pulled quotation.* Use meaningful material that draws in readers.

♦ *Add another line* of headline. Better yet, add a deck to those long and medium-sized stories.

♦ *Add some air* between paragraphs. Add one to four points of extra leading between the final paragraphs of a story. If you overdo it, however, the paragraphs may begin to float apart.

♦ *Add some in-house advertising.* Create small promotional ads for your paper in a variety of sizes.

♦ *As a last resort,* keep a Poetry Corner in reserve. People love to see their poems in print.

Designing Pages without Art

Up to this point, we've looked at different ways of designing pages when photos, drawings or illustrations are easily available. But what if they aren't? Imagine a scenario in which a designer must make do with only headlines and copy. Are there any techniques to make such pages lively and interesting?

The most obvious way to build a page in such a situation is to place one horizontal story after another, moving from top to bottom. The result, as in the example in Figure 15.8, is a contemporary-looking page that works quite effectively. The design of this page is clean, but its impact on readers will probably be weak. Why? It's too gray and monotonous. There's nothing to catch the eye. The only contrast comes from the headlines. Nothing speaks louder or softer than anything else.

Consider some other possibilities. Instead of simply stacking stories in rows, you could add variety by using contrasting headlines, boxing stories, using bastard measures or grouping small items together.

Using Contrasting Headlines.   Years ago, most newspapers ran headlines side by side, separating them only by a thin vertical line in the gutter. When headlines are stacked alongside each other this way, they look like tombstones (hence the term **tombstoning,** a derogatory term for butting headlines against each other).

Today, however, most designers try to avoid headlines that bump. Bumping headlines can cause confusion:

Britney Spears meets	**Frisbee title-holder**
pope at Dover Beach	**to challenge record**
Chorus sings out	**Bungee jump**
over Christmas	**for fun and exercise**

Occasionally, though, you'll need to park two stories alongside each other in order to solve other, more important design problems. (Remember, we don't have any art to use.) When you must bump headlines, create some contrast to minimize the problem. For example, you can mix styles, fonts or sizes (see Chapter 16 for more details). If headlines must bump, make them as unlike each other as possible. For example, if one is boldfaced, set the other in regular or italic type. If one uses large lettering on a single line, make the other use small letters on three lines. See Figure 15.9 for an example.

FIGURE 15.8
FRONT PAGE WITHOUT ART

tombstoning
> stacking headlines alongside each other

FIGURE 15.9
SEPARATING HEADLINES THAT BUMP

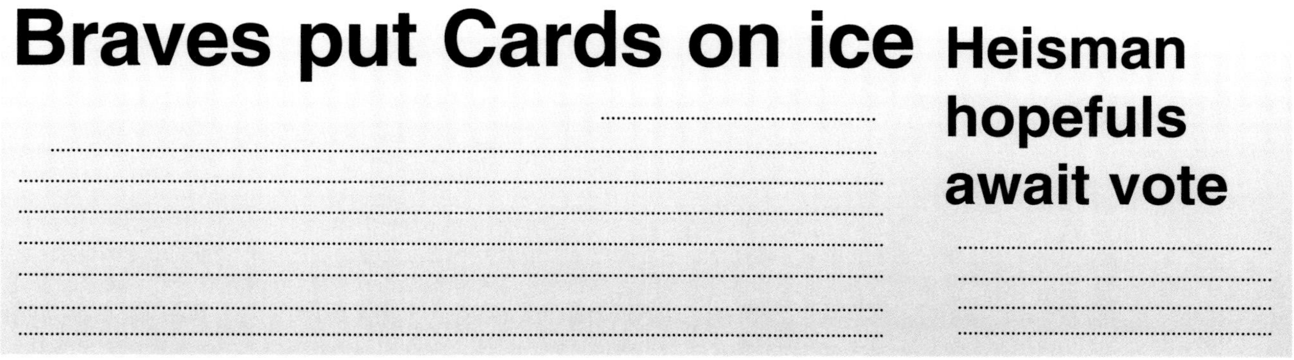

Braves put Cards on ice Heisman hopefuls await vote

Boxing Stories.   Another way to break up a monotonously gray page is to box a story. Putting a box around a story is a good way to help readers see your organizational scheme. Boxing a story also gives it some extra visual emphasis. It's a way of saying to the reader, "This story has something special."

Don't box a story just because you're bored with a page and want to snazz it up, however. Make your designs functional—your job is to communicate, not to decorate. Box a story with a related sidebar to show that they belong together, for example. Remember, too, that when you put text inside a box, you must also shrink the column width slightly to avoid having the story bump into the box itself.

Using Bastard Measures.   You can design an attractive publication without ever changing the width of your columns. Sometimes, however, you may decide to create more visual interest by stretching or shrinking the width of a column. **Bastard measures**—columns somewhat wider or narrower than the paper's normal column width—break up page monotony. Many papers use them for editorials as a visual signal to the reader that the article is something different. They can also be used on regular news pages.

Bastard measures add interest by freeing a story from the rigid page grid (see Figure 15.10). Changing column widths is a subtle but effective way to show readers that a story is special. Suppose you have a six-column page. You could run a story across the page in three columns by making the column twice as wide as usual (the computer will automatically adjust the spacing between columns). The result would be an attractive variation on the usual design.

Grouping Small Items Together.   Another design strategy involves packaging several short, related items into one text block. This technique doesn't add variety so much as it helps you organize the page. It offers several advantages.

- Instead of scattering news briefs or calendar listings throughout the paper, you can anchor them in one spot.

bastard measure

a column somewhat wider or narrower than the paper's normal column width

Figure 15.10
Bastard Measures

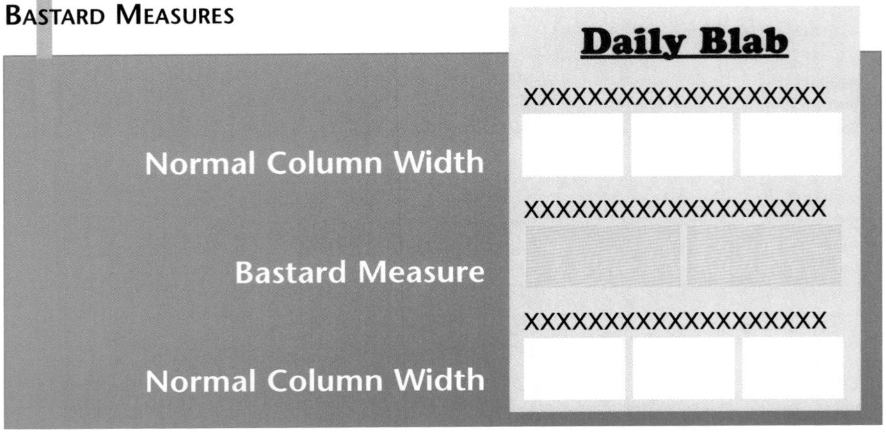

Daily Blab

XXXXXXXXXXXXXXXXXX

Normal Column Width

XXXXXXXXXXXXXXXXXX

Bastard Measure

XXXXXXXXXXXXXXXXXX

Normal Column Width

- You also create more impact for your main stories by keeping smaller ones out of their way.
- You appeal to readers' habits, because most readers prefer finding the same kinds of things (comics, for example) in the same spot every issue.

Short news briefs (say, club news or sports roundups) are ideal for packaging. So are person-in-the-street interviews where the paper runs a mug shot and a quotation responding to the hot question of the day.

Designing with Ads

News stories exist to inform readers. Ads exist to make money for publishers. In the publishing world, ads take precedence over news. Professional newspaper designers typically place the ads on a page first and then design the news in the remaining space.

The main difference between a front page and an inside page is that on inside pages, the news coexists with a loud, pushy heap of boxes—ads—stacked upward from the bottom of the page. Some stacks look better than others. But whatever format designers use, ad stacks are dummied onto pages before the news is. Thus, ads dictate the shape of the news hole.

Three formats for dummying ads are shown in Figure 15.11. The following formats work to varying degrees:

- *Stair-step (or pyramid format).* The traditional stair-step format makes sure that each ad touches a story, which is important to many advertisers. But for designers, it creates ugly news holes.
- *Well format.* As ads stack up on both sides of the page, a well forms in the middle—hence the name *well format.* Like stair-stepped ads, wells can be ugly.
- *Modular format.* Probably the best choice is the modular format. By stacking ads in modular blocks (rectangular

FIGURE 15.11
FORMATS FOR DUMMYING ADS

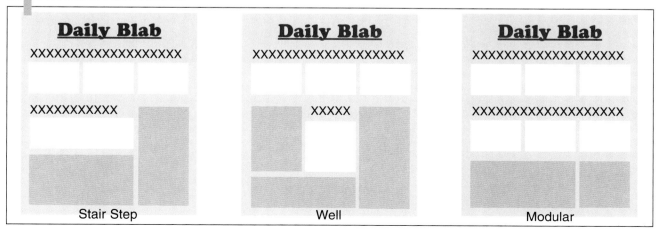

units), pages look more orderly and attractive. This solution is becoming more and more popular, especially with school newspaper staffs.

Some Final Guidelines

At this point you may be thinking, "Rules, rules rules. How can I remember them all?" It's true that there are a dizzying number of rules and requirements to remember when you design pages, but don't despair. You need to remember only a few important principles:

- Keep all story shapes rectangular. You've heard this before, but it's the key to good modular design. Use four-sided shapes instead of six-sided shapes.
- Vary the shapes and sizes of stories as well as art. Avoid falling into a rut where everything's square, vertical or horizontal. Give readers a variety of copy and photo shapes. Occasionally use a severe rectangle—an extremely tall or wide shape.
- Emphasize what's important. Play up the big stories and big photos. Place them where they count. Let placement reflect each story's significance as you guide the reader through the page.
- The grid gives you a solid starting point. The rules governing the grid are made to be broken, but don't break them until you understand them thoroughly.

YOUR BEAT

1. Look at a copy of your school paper or a local professional paper to analyze the use of art. What percentage of stories run with no art? What percentage of stories use one piece of art? What percentage of stories use more than one? Do these percentages change when you compare the front page to inside pages?

2. Find an example of a paper, newsletter or magazine for each of these formats: two-column, three-column, four-column, five-column and six-column. Can you find any publication that uses more than six columns per page?

3. Examine the photos in a recent issue of your school paper. Are there any dominant photos? Are there any good photos that could have been dominant but were not? Invite the paper's editors and designers to visit your class to discuss their design strategy (or they may already be in your class).

CHAPTER REVIEW

KEY TERMS

Show that you know the meanings of the following key terms by correctly using them in complete sentences. Write your answers on a separate sheet of paper.

art	internal margin	leg
rule	mug shot	boldface
deck	standing head	italic
gutter	cutline	design
tabloid	index	paste-up
broadsheet	jump line	dummy
entry point	refer	identity system
modular design	folio	grid
infographics	subhead	dominant photo
story package	photo credit	tombstoning
teaser	white space	bastard measure
flag	pica	
initial cap	point	

OPEN FORUM

1. Discuss future trends for newspaper design by conducting a debate. Choose two teams. One team will argue that newspapers have been rendered obsolete by new technology. The other team will argue that nothing can quite take the place of a real newspaper, printed on newsprint and delivered to homes and apartments every day.

2. Choose interesting examples of each of the following: movie posters, restaurant menus, soda pop cans, consumer packaging, community billboards and other public visuals as examples of design. Which examples seem to have the most appealing designs? Which have the least appealing designs? Why?

CHAPTER REVIEW, continued

FINDING THE FLAW

Find five significant flaws in the newspaper page shown below. Offer a suggestion for fixing each flaw.

SAS ELECTIONS ARE TODAY . . .
Get out, vote, and make a difference

ENTERTAINMENT
The Griswolds return to the big screen! This time, everyone's favorite family from Chicago in "Vegas Vacation."

the Cornerstone
The Student Voice of Washington High School

Volume 109, Number 12   Friday, February 31, 1997

Cloud of Complaints lingers over Centennial smokers

By Ken McQueen
Staff Reporter

Centennial is the only residence hall with a smoking pod. However, a survey done last October revealed that 77% of Centennial residents said they wanted a smoke-free living area. According to Darby Vannier, RHA President, "Residents and RA's have complained about cigarette smell in their rooms and pods."

In compliance with the Nebraska Clean Air Act, on November 2, 1992, the Administrative Council of Nebraska Wesleyan voted to ban smoking in all buildings except the Residence Halls. Again on April 24, 1995, the issue was brought before SAS. The Senate resolved that all Residence Halls except Centennial would be smoke free. Each of Centennial's pods would individually decide the smoking issue.

The issue is that smoke is getting into rooms and pods where non-smokers don't want it. Bob Snook, Wesleyan's HVAC Technician, says that "the pods have return-air and are ventilated. The air recirculates only within the pod areas, not in the rooms.

Washington sees enrollment increase

Student enrollment at Washington High School is currently on the rise. The increase comes after two years of declining enrollment.

The initial enrollment for the 1997–98 academic year is already expected to be at 1,550. This is as increase of around sixty students. The figure for fall 1996 showed that there were 1,488 enrolled.

Washington High has

Geoff Jamieson, Centennial Hall resident, enjoys a "fat" cigar in his room.

Campus forum set

Minority Advisor/counselor Traci Howard announced that March 6 will be Campus of Difference day. Approximately 60 Washington students, faculty and staff will participate in various cultural exploration exercises.

The program itself was developed by the Anti Defamation League, a civil rights organization committed to promoting positive cross cultural exchanges. The Campus of Difference program is modeled after their own World of Difference programs which are presented across the nation. ADL facilitators from Omaha will also be participating.

During the sessions, each participant will be given the opportunity to "share and relate information about themselves and explore the importance of identity. "They will also take part in cultural self-knowledge exercises so as to identify their own personal cultural gaps." explains Howard.

In explaining the motivation behind the day's activities, Howard em-

SOULS FOOD BEING SERVED. Traci Howard, Minority Advisor/Counselor is the sponsor of Wesleyan's annual Soul Good Dinner at the Marriott Cafeteria.

PLAY OF THE GAME. The Nebraska Wesleyan Plainesmen continue their drive towards an undefeated season with a smashing victory over Hastings.

Japanese exchange enjoys Midwest

If you could go to any school in America, what school would you choose? For Ai Yamaguchi and Yoko Iwaski, for-eign exchange students from Japan, the choice was fairly easy.

The two Japanese women decided on Nebraska Wesleyan University because as Yoko stated, "The faculty are more supportive because they are more understanding

Rainbow Club to sponsor Soul Food Night

"Someday we'll find it, the rainbow connection..." connection is? Think about it. All the different colors shining in unison. bow, the end product being a beautiful piece of natural art. Even though it is not composed of thousands of tiny water molecules The Rainbow Club is an organization made up of about 15 students, who

MEDIA WATCH

1. Gather a number of old issues of your local paper (or your school paper) that date as far back as possible. Often libraries keep copies of these issues or store them on microfilm. What changes can you find in the way the papers look over the years? Were these changes improvements? Why or why not?
2. Compare current copies of the *Wall Street Journal* and *USA Today*, the two papers with the highest national circulation. What differences do you detect in their designs? Why do these papers seem to take such a dramatically different approach to layout?

String Book

1. Draw a dummy recreating the front page of your school paper or a local professional paper.
2. Draw a dummy for the front page of an imaginary newspaper. Your flag runs the entire width of the page and is three inches deep. Your photos can be any size or shape you wish. Use the following elements:
   ◆ A 16-inch story with a photo on the death of a sophomore student in an automobile accident.
   ◆ An eight-inch story announcing tighter requirements for graduation.
   ◆ A nine-inch story announcing that members of the Chinese Embassy will be visiting your school. Assume that a staff artist has made a map of China you can use as an infographic.
   ◆ A seven-inch story about tryouts for the flag team, drill team and cheerleading squad.
   ◆ A six-inch story about the jazz band's winning a top rating at a festival held at a nearby college. A photo is available from the college.
   ◆ A calendar of upcoming school events, one column wide and eight inches deep.
   ◆ A 10-inch story about five students who recently attended a special program in Washington, D.C.
   Hint: You may jump one or two stories to inside pages, and of course, you don't have to use everything.
3. Design a new flag for your school paper. You may wish to look in the school library or check with the newspaper adviser to see what the paper's flag has looked like in the past.

Chapter 16
Typography, Headlines and Infographics

"Graphical excellence is that which gives to the viewer the greatest number of ideas in the shortest time with the least ink in the smallest space."
—Edward R. Tufte, professor of graphic design at Yale and president of Graphics Press

*I*t's one thing to visualize the big picture. It's quite another to sweat the details. In the previous chapter, you learned about page design, or combining large elements such as stories, headlines and photographs into a complete layout. In this chapter, you'll be asked to pull out your magnifying glass to see what's going on inside the design. In particular, you'll be introduced to the nuances of lettering styles and arrangements.

You'll learn about typography and printing specifications. You'll also learn how to write and design different kinds of headlines. You'll become familiar with one of the most interesting new features in journalism—the infographic. Along the way, you'll gain some valuable tips on how to take advantage of desktop publishing technology.

MAKING GOOD TYPOGRAPHIC CHOICES

Unless you're a musician, you probably don't analyze every note you hear; you simply settle back and listen. When you read a story, you probably don't scrutinize every letter, either. Like most readers, you surf across those waves of words, oblivious to typographic details. But those details, like notes to a musician, are critically important to the successful communication of a message.

Typography is the art of arranging letters in a pleasing and appropriate manner. Readers don't worry much about how the letters of the alphabet look, but designers do. They fret over the size, shape and spacing of their letters as they seek just the right look. Designers worry for a reason. Good typographic design makes the difference between attractive, readable type and type that looks like a ransom note from a kidnapper.

Typefaces and Fonts

Letters can have many different appearances. The letter *A*, for example, can look like A, A, A, A or *A*. Over the years, designers have produced thousands of different typefaces, which are sometimes even named after them—Bodoni or Zapf, for instance. **Typeface** refers to a distinctive set of letters, both uppercase and lowercase. The set is distinctive in the same sense that your handwriting is unique. No two sets of letters, or typefaces, are exactly alike.

typography

the art of choosing and arranging letters in a pleasing and appropriate manner

typeface

a distinctive set of letters (both uppercase and lowercase)

FIGURE 16.1
FONT FOR 14-POINT HELVETICA

A B C D E F G H I
J K L M N O P Q R
S T U V W X Y Z

a b c d e f g h i j k l
m n o p q r s t u v
w x y z

1 2 3 4 5 6 7 8 9 0

~ ! @ # $ % ^ & * (
) _ +
[{] } \ | ; : ' " , < . >
/ ?

font

a complete alphabet plus numbers and punctuation marks in a particular typeface and style such as bold, italic or bold italic

serif type

type with tiny strokes, or serifs, at the tips of each letter

sans serif type

type without tiny strokes, or serifs, at the tips of each letter

Designers often talk about typefaces as if they had personalities. Times, for example, is thought to be conservative, traditional and formal, while **Hobo** is funky, bizarre and unpredictable. Your computer is likely to have a good sampling of some of the more popular typefaces. These may include Times, Avant Garde, Helvetica and Palatino, to name just a few.

In a particular typeface and size, a complete alphabet plus numbers and punctuation marks is called a **font**. Figure 16.1 shows the font for 14-point Helvetica.

Most typefaces can be grouped into two main families: serif and sans serif. **Serif type** (serif means "with feet") has tiny strokes, or serifs, at the tips of each letter. Inspired by the letters chiseled in granite by the ancient Romans, type designers have used serif styles to create some of the world's most elegant type families, including Times and Palatino. Serif type tends to create a feeling of tradition and conservatism. It seems to say, "We've been here a long time; you can trust us." Most newspaper and magazine stories are set in serif styles.

Sans serif type ("type without feet"), on the other hand, has no serifs. These typefaces tend to have a more modern feel. They say to the reader, "Look at us: we're fresh and new." Helvetica is one of the most popular sans serif typefaces with school publication staffs. It is most often used in headlines, bylines and cutlines.

You won't have to look very long in magazines or newspapers to find an enormous number of typefaces. It's easy to see from that intimidating variety that typography can be a complex subject. Practically speaking, however, good design is a straightforward matter of judgment and taste. Your artistic intuition, combined with knowledge and skill, makes typography work. Like any other art or craft, you can master it through practice and trial and error.

Here is one tip, though, that may make your life as a designer less crazy. Stick to a few typefaces. Choose one for text (preferably a serif typeface) and one for headlines and cutlines (preferably a sans serif typeface). You can add a third typeface for the flag, standing heads, column titles and other special uses. By limiting your type choices to a reasonable few, you can spare yourself time for other design tasks and avoid creating a publication that looks like a circus.

Changing Type to Fit Your Needs

Using type right out of the computer is like wearing a shirt right out of the dryer—it won't look its best until you iron it a bit. By modifying type, you can adjust your letters to particular design needs and improve the readability of your publication in the process. As a designer, you have the option of changing type in two different dimensions: vertically and horizontally.

Changing Type Vertically. Changing the point size of a typeface changes the height of the letters. The greater the number of points, the taller the letters (see Figure 16.2). Small type sizes are used for copy. Many schools use 12-point type for stories, although 10- or 11-point

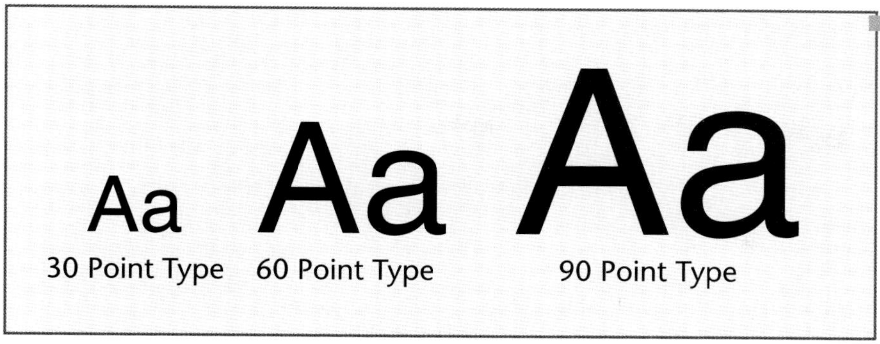

FIGURE 16.2
LETTER HEIGHT (POINTS)

type is also a reasonable choice. Headlines require larger sizes, ranging from 18 to 72 points or more, to achieve a dramatic look.

The space between two lines of type is called **leading** (pronounced "ledding"). The term comes from the days of hot-metal typesetting, when thin bands of metal, usually lead, separated the rows of type. Leading can greatly affect the readability of your publication.

Leading can be loosened by adding more space between lines or tightened until the letters nearly touch or even overlap. Tight leading saves space, but it also tends to make a page looked cramped and uninviting. Designers for *Raygun* and Nike ads have used overlapping type to suggest an attitude that breaks the rules. Note that leading, like type size, is measured in points.

The following example is 24-point type with 18 points of leading (it is tight):

leading
the space between two lines of type; pronounced "ledding"

Neck massage may zap pain of headaches

This is 24-point type with 26 points of leading, which is normal:

Neck massage may zap pain of headaches

Here is 24-point type with 42 points of leading (it is loose):

Neck massage may zap

pain of headaches

THIS JUST IN: *Portrait of a Young Journalist*
Dennis Ortiz-Lopez, Type Designer

"You have maybe two seconds for someone to see something that catches her eye and pick up the magazine." That's the challenge Dennis Ortiz-Lopez and other professional typographers face when they design special lettering for a magazine cover. Ortiz-Lopez has created special cover letters (often called *logotypes*) for many popular magazines, including *Parade, Premiere, Rolling Stone, Spy, Self, Texas Monthly* and *US*.

Most of his lettering styles are specially adapted for one-time use on a cover. As such, they are typically condensed and tightly kerned, although some can be adapted for use as a copy style inside the mag-

azine. Trained at Compton College and California State–Long Beach, Ortiz-Lopez left school early and joined Gould & Associates as a designer. In 1979, *Rolling Stone* hired him on staff for hand lettering. Two years later, he switched to full-time freelance work, specializing in magazine logos and custom fonts.

Ortiz-Lopez regards type as "an ornamented glyph that makes a thought into a graphic that other people can translate into a thought." He says he favors serif fonts and hates any gimmick that draws attention to the type itself rather than to the words. "Words on a page should flow smoothly into the mind of the reader, not stutter as barely decipherable knots passing for letters," he said.

Many of the older, elegant typefaces that fell out of use in the 1970s and 1980s have

come in for some retooling. Ortiz-Lopez has been producing computerized versions of these faces and then licensing them for sale. Rather than scanning and tracing the old characters, he often redraws the entire alphabet from scratch. In the process, he corrects type problems that have stymied other designers.

As a career-long perfectionist, Ortiz-Lopez has come to appreciate the precision of computerized design tools. But he also worries about the unprecedented typographic control they put in the hands of art directors. Ortiz-Lopez says he flinches when he sees type taboos broken or his own fonts handled in ways he never imagined. These are, he notes, "the best of times and the worst of times for type fanatics like me."

Source: Adapted from "Dennis Ortiz-Lopez" ALDUS MAGAZINE *March/April p. 28.*

---

tracking

adjusting the horizontal space between letters

Changing Type Horizontally. You can also adjust the horizontal spacing between letters. These adjustments are called **tracking.** Tracking enables you to squeeze copy to fit it into a single line or to stretch it out to cover a large area. Be sure to exercise caution, however. Even slight changes in tracking can affect the type's readability. Take this example of normal tracking, with no extra spacing between characters:

Grandmother of eight makes hole in one

Here is the same example with loose tracking:

G r a n d m o t h e r   o f   e i g h t   m a k e s   h o l e   i n   o n e

The following has tight tracking:

Grandmother of eight makes hole in one

Note that the example of normal tracking is easiest to read.

Tight tracking is often used when a designer needs to conserve space—for example, by making a six-line paragraph fit on five lines. Loose tracking is sometimes used to help cover some undesirable white space.

Designers use a special version of tracking called **kerning** when they want to bring a particular pair of letters together. This sometimes is necessary in headlines when an unsightly gap appears between certain pairs of letters (for example, *A* and *W*). If the two letters look like this:

A W

the designer could kern them (reduce the distance between them) to look like this:

AW

Kerning is not done on body copy, but it makes large headlines look much better.

A third way to control letter spacing is by controlling the **set width.** The set width control changes the width of the letters, stretching or squeezing them as though they're made of bubble gum. The set width control actually changes the shapes of the letters themselves. It is usually expressed as a percentage of the font's original width. For example, here is a headline with normal set width (100 percent of the font's original width):

Wind whips, strips, tips through town

Here is the same headline in a narrow set width (70 percent of normal):

Wind whips, strips, tips through town

The following shows the headline in a wide set width (130 percent of normal):

Wind whips, strips, tips through town

Set width control is most useful for headlines, especially unusual ones you might want to use for feature stories. Be advised, though, not to change one line of a headline without changing the others in that same headline.

Alignment

Let's turn our attention from letters, words and lines to larger chunks of copy. Copy in the hands of an unimaginative designer can be gray and dull, but it doesn't need to be. You can give your copy personality by the shapes and contours it fills on the page. For example, a designer can vary the sides of a story to create three different looks. The three types of alignments are:

- ✦ **Flush left.** Flush left type runs flush with the left edge of the column. It is also called *ragged right,* because the right edge of the column is uneven. Flush left alignment is typically used for headlines.
- ✦ **Justified.** Justified copy has straight margins on both the right and left edges. It is the usual alignment setting for most stories.
- ✦ **Flush right.** Flush right type runs flush with the right edge of the column. It's often used for photo credit lines.

kerning
a special kind of tracking that brings pairs of letters closer together to prevent unsightly gaps

set width
a means of scaling the width of letters. A line of type could be slightly condensed by choosing a set width of 95%

flush left
the alignment of type that runs flush with the left edge of the column; also called *ragged right*

justified
a description of copy with straight margins at both the right and left column edges

flush right
the alignment of type that runs flush with the right edge of the column

DATELINE DATELINE DATELINE

UNITED STATES, 1970–1990 —A revolution in newspaper production began when the computer began replacing typewriters in newsrooms in the 1970s.

The television-like screen sitting atop a keyboard allowed reporters to type, edit and store their stories in a central file. From another computer, the editor could retrieve the story, edit it and send it to the typesetter.

By the early 1980s, pagination programs and photocomposition machines made it possible to set copy in type on photographic film and send the negatives directly to the platemaker, thus eliminating the need to paste copy onto page layouts by hand.

Wire service stories could be called up, edited and placed directly on the page. By the mid-1980s, photos were being placed directly on the page either from the wire or from scanned photos. Color graphics soon followed.

Newsrooms today are completely computerized. From the time a story is composed at the keyboard until it comes off the press on the page, it is processed by computer. In addition to interviewing and writing skills, reporters must have editing and pagination skills. Editors must be able to solve computer problems as well as spot misspellings and grammatical errors. Photographers work with digital cameras, crop photos on screen and write cutlines at the keyboard.

widow

an unacceptably short line of type (often just one word) at the end of a paragraph

orphan

a partial line of type (the end of a paragraph) that appears at the top of a page or column

Alignment adjustments can help avoid two major design problems: widows and orphans. A **widow** is an unacceptably short line of type (often just a single word) at the end of a paragraph. The white space that follows the widow looks unplanned and unnecessary. Consequently, most designers try to eliminate widows. An **orphan** is a partial line (end of a paragraph) that appears at the top of a column or page. Both widows and orphans can be quickly eliminated by a little tracking or rewording, or even a slight bit of editing.

Some desktop publishing programs have their own built-in damage control. Damage in this case refers to widows and orphans. Aldus PageMaker, for example, has options for "Widow control" and "Orphan control" available from the Type menu under "Paragraph . . ."

Typographic Special Effects

Most desktop publishing programs provide a view on the screen that professionals call WYSISWG (pronounced "whizzi-wig"), or simply "What you see is what you get." In other words, these programs enable you to see on your computer screen exactly what your type is going to look like when it's printed. If your program has WYSISWG capabilities, special effects can be both fun and useful. They can be fun because you can see at a glance how they're going to look. They can be useful in solving design problems.

The simplest kinds of special effects are those that change the weight or appearance of the letters. In the last chapter we mentioned an effect called *boldface,* which adds weight (the letters look darker or thicker), and one called *italic* (the letters slant to suggest handwriting). Two other special effects available on most programs are **outline** and **shadow.** In outline, the inside areas of the letters become white or transparent:

Candidates compete for votes

In shadow, the letters appear to cast a shadow on the page:

Candidates compete for votes

Almost all these effects can be combined. For example, bold and italic can be combined as follows:

Candidates compete for votes

Outline and shadow also can make an effective combination:

Candidates compete for votes

As with all design effects, you might be wise to start slowly and use them sparingly.

Two other special effects are helpful when you wish to print words on top of a picture or shaded area. If the background is very dark or black, you can use a **reverse.** With this effect, the letters appear white.

This is a reverse.

If the background area is a light gray, you can use an **overburn.** Here the letters are printed in black on top of a colored or shaded background:

This is overburn.

Note that bold, sans serif letters work best for reverses. The thin serifs on some typefaces almost disappear when printed in white on a dark background. Any style reversed in a size smaller than 12 points is likely to be difficult to read.

outline
a special effect in some desktop publishing programs in which the insides of the letters become white or transparent

shadow
a special effect in some desktop publishing programs in which the letters appear to cast a shadow on the page

reverse
a special effect in some desktop publishing programs in which letters appear white (for use on a dark background)

overburn
a special effect in some desktop publishing programs in which letters are printed in black on top of a colored or shaded background

1. Conduct a "type search" through a recent magazine. Find three different kinds of serif type and three different kinds of sans serif type. Ads are a good place to look. Notice whether serif and sans serif typefaces are used to provide contrast with one another. Find three examples of special type effects.

2. Use a typeface guide to determine what typefaces in what sizes are used in your school yearbook and newspaper. (The company that prints your school paper or yearbook can probably provide one.)

3. Create a new typeface by designing all the letters of the alphabet in a special style all your own. You may find this assignment easier to do by hand rather than by computer, although a graphic arts software program might help. Compare your work with that of other students.

WRITING AND DESIGNING HEADLINES

In the days before computer technology, most newspaper headlines were quite narrow. That was partly because the printing presses used metal type locked into blocks. Type that was set too wide tended to come loose and fly off the cylinder as the presses spun around. Consequently, headlines were usually centered inside a single column. Often, headlines were printed with each word capitalized. Many were stacked in layers, with one deck on top of another.

Today's headlines, by comparison, are run as wide as possible, positioned flush left and usually capitalized in normal sentence form. This is called *down style* in newspaper parlance. The old-fashioned up style capitalized each word in a headline:

Attack Parrot Sends Thug Running for His Life

Here is the same headline in today's down style:

Attack parrot sends thug running for his life

In an ideal world, designers would never have to worry about the content of headlines. They could leave that to section editors or copy editors. But the truth is that designers are often left with the job of writing headlines, because they're the last people who work on the paper before it goes to the printer. For that reason, we'll digress briefly from the topic of design to discuss how headlines should be written.

Headlines Tell and Sell a Story

A savvy editor once gave a writer this advice: if you have 10 days to create a story, spend nine of them working on the headline. The editor meant that the headline is crucial, because it both summarizes and advertises the story. Too often, headline writers top a story with a "ho hum" headline, thus burying the story on the page instead of saying "Please read me!" The challenge becomes how to write a headline that both tells and sells the story.

Essentially, a headline is a short, telegraphic sentence giving the gist of the story. "Man jumps off building," reads the headline, not "A man has just jumped off the top of a building." The grammar of the sentence—its subject and verb—remains, but several words are missing. Headline writers use a sort of Western Union–style shorthand to trim away nonessential words. Headline writers also use present tense for past actions. That strategy gives headlines more punch and immediacy.

Good headlines help readers find what they want to read. Headlines should both catch the eye and guide the readers' attention to the main idea. For the headline writer, discovering the main idea shouldn't be a problem if the story is well written. The main idea should be located in the story's lead, which is where the headline writer, who won't have time to read the entire story anyway, should look to find out what's news.

Headlines can be creative and fun. Sometimes our favorite headlines are the ones that break the rules. But for beginners, it's probably best to start with a few standard guidelines. Here are some commonly accepted rules for headline writing:

- Give every headline an action verb: "Candidates *debate* issues"
- Use present tense for past events: "Club *chooses* president," not "Club chose president yesterday"
- Use an infinitive for future events: "Governor *to sign* bill"
- Use short, positive words: "*Some like it hot:* Spring Break hot spots"
- Use a comma for *and* and a semicolon for a period: "Learning moves out of school beyond U-High, across oceans" and "Soccerdogs beat Edison; host Lodi tomorrow"
- Use single quotation marks within a headline: "Critics say 'malice' rule puts public safety at risk"

Some rules warn writers about what not to do:

- Avoid forms of *to be:* "Teen boot camp—'strictly' a good idea," not "Teen boot camp is 'strictly' a good idea"
- Omit articles (*a, an* and *the*): "Habitat workers bring hope to homeless"
- Avoid the use of negatives (*no* and *not*): "Athletic department too lenient with drug offenders," instead of "Athletic department not harsh enough"
- Avoid excess abbreviation (one acronym per headline is probably plenty)
- Omit a period at the end of a headline
- Most important, don't use headlines to express the writer's opinion

Headlines should tell something specific and newsy. They should not be mere labels. Watch out, too, for generic headlines that could fit any of several stories: "Student meeting Wednesday," "Committee plans announced" or "Team seeks victory," for example. These headlines could be used over and over, but who would read those stories? Create a headline to fit one and only one story.

Finally, the headline should reflect the tone of a story. Use a serious tone for a serious story—for example,

Storm flattens fields, rips roof

For less somber stories, headline writers can enjoy using puns and plays on words:

Many possible ways to heal heel pain
Designer builds motorcycles wheely well or
It isn't easy being orange

banner

> a headline that runs across the entire width of a page

kicker

> a clever word or phrase that runs above the main headline; usually set in italics

slammer

> a two-part headline that uses a boldface word or phrase leading into the main headline

raw wrap

> a headline style in which the story wraps around the headline on two sides

hammer

> a headline that uses a big, bold phrase to catch the reader's eye and then adds a lengthier main headline below

tripod

> a three-part headline that includes a boldface word or phrase (often in all caps) with two smaller lines set alongside it

sidesaddle head

> a headline style that sets the headline beside the story

Headline Styles

The most popular and basic of modern headline styles is the **banner.** A banner runs across the entire width of a page. Banners are great for breaking news and big events, such as prom or awards night. A steady diet of banners, however, would soon become monotonous. Fortunately, designers have a number of other headline styles to choose from. These alternatives include:

A **kicker** is a clever word or phrase that runs above the main headline and is usually set in italics.

Slammer is a two-part headline that uses a boldface word or phrase to lead into the main headline.

A **raw wrap** lets the story wrap around the headline on two sides. Use this headline style sparingly.

A **hammer** head uses a big, bold phrase to catch the reader's eye and then adds a lengthier main headline below. It's like an upside-down kicker.

Tripods are headlines that come in three parts: a boldface word or phrase (often in all caps) with two smaller lines set alongside it.

The **sidesaddle head** style puts the headline beside the story. It's used to squeeze a story—preferably one that's boxed—into a shallow horizontal space. Figure 16.3 illustrates these six headline styles.

Headlines that are two or three lines deep can create a tricky problem—line breaks, or the place where one line ends and another begins. Line breaks can lead to miscommunication if a designer isn't careful. Avoid bad splits caused by dangling verbs, adjectives or prepositions. For example,

Instead of

Pet rooster pulls drowning child from icy pond

use

Pet rooster pulls drowning child from icy pond

Headline Sizes

Bigger stories usually get bigger headlines. The largest headlines range upward from 48 points on. Medium headlines range from 24 to 48 points. Small headlines range from 18 to 24 points. Designers generally put the larger headlines at the top of the page (sometimes in boldface) and then move down the page with smaller, lighter or italic headlines.

Designers communicate the kind of headline they want by using a special code. The code lists first the column width, next the point size

FIGURE 16.3
HEADLINE STYLES

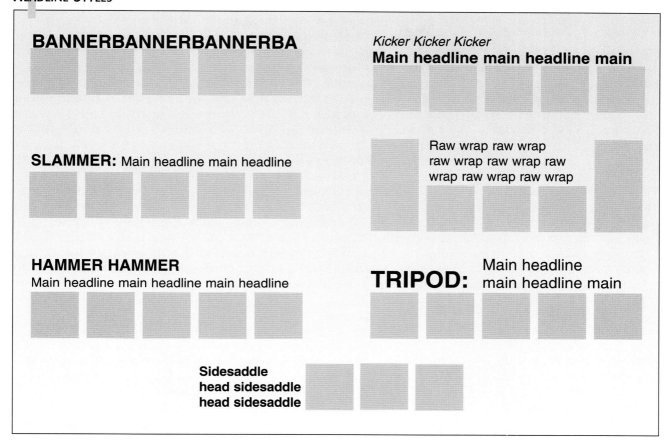

and finally the number of lines in the headline. Using that formula, a 3-24-1 headline would be a three-column, 24-point headline that runs on one line, like this:

Six ways to tell if he's really Mr. Right

If that headline needed to fit in a single, narrow column, it could be rewritten as a 1-18-3 headline (one column, 18-point type, three lines deep). It would look like this:

Six ways to tell if he's really Mr. Right

Designers often write each headline's code above the story it belongs with on the dummy. The person responsible for writing the headline—either the copy editor or the designer—then consults a chart showing how many letters will fit each column in various type sizes. This sounds complicated, but it simply means that different letters take up different amounts of space.

Computers have made it possible to adjust each headline to fit, but only at the expense of type consistency. If a headline written in 30-point type won't fit, for example, the computer can shrink the headline to 28 points with a single keystroke. But many designers prefer to work in regular increments of 18, 24, 36 and 48 points. If they stick to their plan, it is the writer and not the computer who must make the adjustment. For that reason, it's a good idea to at least understand why some headlines take more space than others.

Wide letters, such as *M* and *W*, take up more room than do skinny letters, such as *I* and *J*. Headline writers take these differences into account in calculating how much space a headline will take up by using a headline count chart. Most professional count charts are now digital and measure the width of letters to tenths or even hundredths of units. However, here's a simpler method you can use quite efficiently to determine a headline's length:

- Count all lowercase letters as one unit, except for five slender ones, *f, l, i, t* and *j* (think "flit-jay" as a memory device) and two wide ones, *m* and *w*. Count the slender letters as 0.5 units and the wide ones as 1.5 units.
- Count all uppercase letters as 1.5 units except for two slender ones, *I* and *J* (count these as one unit) and two wide ones, *M* and *W* (count these as two units).
- Count punctuation marks as 0.5 units except for the question mark, double quotation mark and dash (count each as one unit).
- Count each space as one unit.
- Count all numbers as one unit except for the number 1 (count it as 0.5 units).

If the headline count chart says you can fit 30 units in a 3-36-1 headline, then the following 29.5-unit headline would work:

Wild West town found on Venus

However, this 35-unit headline would not fit:

Scientists find Western town on Venus

Ideally, the copy editor creates headlines for your publication. But if you, as designer, have the job of writing headlines, you're now prepared to do it.

CREATING VISUAL NEWS: INFOGRAPHICS

A look at design trends suggests that most readers want specialized messages with lots of reader-friendly graphics. These readers are looking for shortcuts that give them the information they want without their having to read through long passages of text. They want lists, summaries, diagrams, bulleted information and quotations that provide the heart of the story. Recently, thanks to desktop publishing and the example of *USA Today,* an exciting new method to help tell a story has emerged—the infographic.

The infographic (short for *information graphic*) is a hybrid of typography, design and sheer imagination. Loosely defined, an infographic, as California yearbook adviser Jim Jordan puts it, "is any graphic presentation of statistical data." In other words, an infographic turns numbers into pictures.

An infographic can be used to supplement a written story or to tell a story all by itself. It can be as simple as a line drawing of a pizza slice (to illustrate favorite pizza toppings) or as complicated as a full-page diagram of the human eye (to show how laser surgery works). What all infographics have in common is their ability to communicate a message at a single glance.

Brainstorm, Research and Focus

Free-lance illustrator Dale Glasgow had never really thought about hurricanes until one hit his office. As a graphic artist, Glasgow was an

BYLINE

GEORGE RORICK
DIRECTOR OF GRAPHICS FOR KNIGHT-RIDDER

There was a time when the only map appearing in most newspapers was on the weather page. Graphs and charts were largely found in the financial pages. The rest of the information was presented through words or photographs. Today it is difficult to imagine how readers could have grasped such news events as the latest Shuttle mission, airplane hijacking or terrorist bombing without the use of infographics.

"Infographics are not simply pretty pictures to decorate pages," explained George Rorick, director of graphics for Knight-Ridder, one of the nation's largest newspaper chains. "And they are not type in a box. They are the careful and painstaking efforts of professional artists, illustrators, writers, editors, researchers, art directors and designers. That's commitment."

Source: Adapted from "Serving readers through infographics" by H. L. Hall, CJET.

expert in representing complex events as easy-to-see graphics. That's why a magazine editor commissioned him to create an illustration for an article on the formation of hurricanes.

The assignment set off a flurry of activity in Glasgow's Woodbridge, Virginia, studio as he struggled to understand the climatic forces that produce hurricanes. For days, his fax machine spouted a flood of background information sent to him by the magazine's writers. Ideas swirled in his head, and soon a storm began to brew on the screen of his Macintosh IIx.

Glasgow's challenge was to find a way to visualize the essence of a tumultuous, swirling, ever-changing hurricane. To do so, he worked his way through a checklist that every infographic artist would do well to consult:

+ *Research carefully.* You've got to be an expert on the subject, because your readers will be relying on your accuracy. Do your homework. Read the story, study photos and talk to experts.

+ *Focus tightly.* Pinpoint precisely what you need to explain before you begin. What's most essential? What's most interesting? Whatever you choose, the resulting image must be as clean and simple as possible.

+ *Design logically.* Let your central image give structure to the design. (In Glasgow's case, he chose an aerial view of farmland as his background and placed the hurricane in the foreground.) If you're using a sequence of images, find a perspective that lets you show the steps in the most logical order.

+ *Label clearly.* Make sure you can identify every detail in the infographic. Details are often identified with what are called *callouts* or *factoids,* that take the form of words with arrows, lines, or boxes.

Glasgow broke the hurricane down into several stages and then wrote a blurb (a brief description) for each stage. "I wrote how I thought a hurricane works based on the information I had researched," he explained. After Glasgow focused his thoughts and ideas, he moved quickly from a few rough sketches on paper to the computer. He decided to use Aldus FreeHand to create the clouds. Using a combination of drawing tools, he drew the shape of the cloud as a kind of squiggly line, added some depth and then placed arrows throughout the illustration to show wind direction.

The project was almost finished when hurricane experts spotted a technical error. Because of the direction of the trade winds over the Atlantic Ocean, Glasgow's hurricane was headed in the wrong direction. To solve the problem, Glasgow simply selected the reflection tool and flip-flopped his cloud, arrows and all.

Finally, Glasgow reversed the type in the darker areas so that words would be readable. "First and foremost," he said, "the information has to communicate to the reader what it is about. If they don't understand, or if they can't read the statistics on the piece of art, then I've failed." Figure 16.4 has three examples of infographics from *USA Today*.

FIGURE 16.4
INFOGRAPHICS

Copyright, USA TODAY,
Reprinted with permission

Brainstorming in teams might be a good way to come up with ideas for your publication's infographics.

Developing an Infographic for Your Publication

Many high school publications have started using infographics as a service to their readers. The *Ahlahasa* staff at Albert Lea High in Albert Lea, Minnesota, for example, used a list of facts about tobacco to create an infographic for a major story on smoking. The *Echo* staff at Glenbard East High School in Lombard, Illinois, included a table showing the procedure for a drug test. This infographic supported a front-page story on the random drug testing of high school athletes.

You might want to create an infographic for your school publication. Creating an infographic involves developing the concept, devising the question, gathering information and choosing the format.

Developing the Concept. A quick glance at exchange papers from across the country reveals a wide variety of topics used to develop infographics. These topics include the growth of youth violence; a comparison of school, state and national ACT results; and trends in safety, fashion and consumer purchases. Think of something you're genuinely curious about to investigate. Then envision an infographic that reflects the views of your readers on that topic.

Devising the Question. In a brainstorming session with other students, identify possible survey questions that could be distributed to students chosen at random. Short answer or multiple choice questions usually yield results most easily put in graphic form. The graphic artist can create a visual display of the answers to the questions you choose.

Gathering Information. You can gather information through surveys or polls. Surveys often take the form of person-on-the-street interviews. Reporters conduct person-on-the-street interviews by stationing themselves in a hallway and asking a single question of people as they pass by. Because of the limited number of participants (as few as 10 or 20), however, surveys give reporters and readers a sense for the story but have little true statistical value. Polls, in contrast, have a more substantial statistical base, so their results more accurately reflect a group's responses. A poll generally requires a sampling of no less than 10 percent of a group to get a representative sample. Furthermore, great care must be taken when tabulating the results to ensure accuracy.

Choosing the Best Format.   Once you or your team has developed a concept for an infographic and gathered statistics in investigating it, you're ready to choose the best format for your infographic. Designers usually choose from one of four main types: fever chart, pie graph, bar chart and table. The following examples will give you an idea of what each type looks like and what each does best.

A **fever chart** plots numbers recorded over time. It resembles a chart tracking the rising and falling temperatures of a person with a fever. The "fever line" is produced by plotting different points and then connecting the dots. The fever chart works well to illustrate questions about money or quantities that have changed over a period of months or years. A line that rises or falls dramatically will make a bigger impression on readers than one that barely shows a blip.

A **pie graph** divides a whole into its parts, usually by percentages. It looks like a circle with individual wedges, each representing a different component. (Imagine a pizza cut into six or eight slices.) As a rule of thumb, pie graphs should be divided into no more than eight segments. Beyond that, the slices are too thin. To create additional impact, you can make pie graphs from drawings or photos of the items being measured. You could slice a dollar bill into sections, for example, to show how the school district spends its money.

A **bar chart** consists of parallel, usually vertical, bars whose lengths represent different quantities. A bar chart is similar to a fever chart in that it represents quantities over time. Unlike a fever chart, however, which tends to focus on trends, a bar chart is used to make comparisons. A bar chart, for example, is a great way to show how many more three-point shots the basketball team made this year than last year. To add visual impact, the bars may be screened or shadowed.

A **table** displays a series of numbers or words. Tables may contain a good deal of text. For example, you could create a table showing holiday trends by superimposing words over a cartoon of Santa Claus. On the left, under a heading "What's OUT," you could list items such as "Price-no-object shopping," "Cashmere sweaters," "Nintendo" and "Oyster dressing." On the right, under a heading "What's IN," you could list "Backyard snowball fights," "Gift certificates to the local gas station," "Sweatshirts" and "Jeopardy home game."

Creating the Infographic.   No matter what the topic, each infographic must contain certain essential elements. George Rorick, director of the Knight-Ridder Graphics Network in Washington, D.C., says the following five items should appear in every infographic:

1. *Headline.* The headline is usually an easy-to-read label.
2. *Body.* The body of an infographic consists of the raw data or numbers.
3. *Credits.* The person or persons who created the infographic should be identified.

fever chart
a chart that plots numbers recorded over time

pie graph
a circle with individual wedges, each representing a different component. A pie graph divides a whole into its parts, usually by percentages

bar chart
a chart or graph that consists of parallel, usually vertical, bars whose lengths represent different quantities

table
a graphic element that displays a series of numbers or words

4. *Explainer.* A short sentence or paragraph should explain what the infographic is about and why it might be important to the reader.

5. *Source.* The origin of the information—who was polled, for example, or what book or magazine was used—should be identified.

Whatever type of infographic you choose, be sure to make it interesting. Adding a cartoon, character or drawing to your infographic is the final touch that will make it memorable. If you're not an artist, use an image scanner to capture an appropriate illustration. (Be careful about copyright laws.) For inspiration, look at *USA Today.* It runs a clever infographic every day at the front of each section.

1. Get a copy of an almanac from the library, and choose an information "nugget." An information nugget is a small group of facts that can be readily developed into an infographic. For example, rock concerts, at 120 decibels, rank among the most deafening experiences teen-agers may encounter. By determining the decibel level of a variety of noises, a student could create an infographic dramatizing the danger of long-term exposure to heavy metal music. Brainstorm to determine how this information might be presented as an infographic that supports a related story.

2. Create an infographic for either of the following information nuggets:

    a. Six of the longest-dating couples:
        1. Li'l Abner and Daisy May
        2. Archie and Veronica
        3. Clark Kent and Lois Lane
        4. Donald Duck and Daisy Duck
        5. Mickey Mouse and Minnie Mouse
        6. Popeye and Olive Oyl

    b. The cost of a U.S. passport, valid for 10 years, is now $60 (or $40 for persons 15 and under). Compare it with costs in other countries:

Country	Cost	Validity
France	$63	Good for 5 years
Japan	$59	Good for 5 years
Mexico	$51	Good for 5 years
Israel	$40	Good for 10 years
Great Britain	$27	Good for 10 years
India	$6	Good for 10 years
Russia	21¢	Good for life

Source: *Adapted with permission from "Passport, Please" U.S. News & World Report.*

CHAPTER REVIEW

KEY TERMS

Show that you know the meanings of the following key terms by correctly using them in complete sentences. Write your answers on a separate sheet of paper.

typography	justified	slammer
typeface	flush right	raw wrap
font	widow	hammer
serif type	orphan	tripod
sans serif type	outline	sidesaddle head
leading	shadow	fever chart
tracking	reverse	pie graph
kerning	overburn	bar chart
set width	banner	table
flush left	kicker	

OPEN FORUM

1. Sometimes editorial bias can creep into news headlines. At the conclusion of a capital punishment case, one so-called conservative newspaper ran this headline: "Smith dies for killing two." A so-called liberal paper ran this headline: "State executes Smith." Critics of the liberal paper said that its headline puts the blame on the state and thus reveals the paper's position against the death penalty, whereas the conservative newspaper's headline emphasizes the prisoner's responsibility for the crime. Do you agree? Can you detect any bias in the headlines in the latest issue of your local paper?

2. Lettering styles are very important in the way businesses present their trade names in advertising and on the products themselves (in other words, in the businesses' logos). Which logos are the most memorable? A logo is a representation of a company's name or emblem in a consistent and distinctive type style. What role do lettering styles play in making logos dramatic or visually appealing?

CHAPTER REVIEW, continued

FINDING THE FLAW

1. Correct the problem in each of the following headlines:
   a. Boy's choir competed in State Fair contest
   b. CHS Library Marks a Historic Milestone
   c. Smith and Jones tie for first
   d. Scientists seek Ebola in remote rain forest
   e. Disabled girl not allowed on cheerleading squad
2. Find an infographic in a newspaper or magazine, and discuss it with classmates. Has the information been successfully transformed into a visual message? How might the information have been presented if the designer had used a different format—a pie graph, say, or a table?

MEDIA WATCH

1. Look through newspapers and magazines to find an example of each of the seven kinds of headlines (banner, kicker, slammer, raw wrap, hammer, tripod and sidesaddle).
2. Consider movie posters, restaurant menus, soda pop cans, consumer packaging, community billboards and other public visuals as examples of typography. Which examples seem the most appealing? Which seem the least appealing? Why?

String Book

1. Some experts have called for the addition of new letters to our alphabet. If you could create a 27th letter for our alphabet, what would it be, and how would it be used? What would it look like?
2. Create a "concrete" poem, in which the words or letters themselves present a visual image. Several examples of "concrete" poems are on the opposite page.
3. Design a new flag for your school paper. You may wish to look in the school library or check with the newspaper adviser to see what the paper's flag has looked like in the past.

A Pencil Sharpener

Hungry Devourer,
Grinding away at defenseless victims,
Never giving up until
The problem comes
To a
P
O
I
N
T

Point Scored

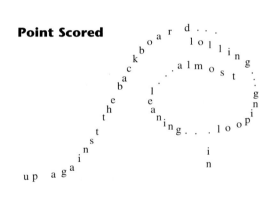

Death of a Little Man

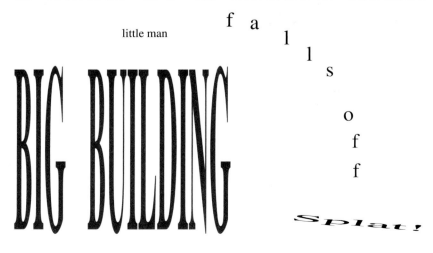

Chapter 17
Advertising

"Ads are the cave art of the 20th century."
—Marshall McLuhan
"Advertising is the second oldest profession in the world."
—Hugh Downs

*D*o you want a topic that is sure to start a conversation at your next party, family dinner, holiday gathering or study hall? Ask people to tell you about their favorite—or least favorite—advertisements. Everyone will have a story to tell. That's because ads—whether they're busy informing, entertaining, persuading or simply selling something—are hard to forget and impossible to ignore. And they work. In fact, U.S. teenage consumers spent $78 billion in a recent year.

Most student publications owe their existence, at least in part, to advertising sales. It makes sense, therefore, for everyone on a publication's staff, not just the business people, to spend some time learning about the complex world of advertising. Student journalists should have both a professional and a personal interest in learning about advertising. This chapter will focus on four elements of the trade: the message, the media, the makeup and the management.

◢ THE MESSAGE

Volney B. Palmer opened the first U.S. advertising agency in Philadelphia in 1841. Even if Palmer was a visionary, he could never have anticipated the $130 billion that U.S. advertisers spend each year. You may not realize it, but you are exposed to over 1,500 ads a day. By age 18, chances are you will have seen 350,000 commercials. Jean Kilbourne, an internationally known media critic, describes the power of ads: "They sell values, images, and concepts of success and worth, love and sexuality, popularity and normalcy. They tell us who we are and who we should be. Sometimes they sell addiction." Kilbourne may be right. According to the Center of Media Literacy, students can list more brands of beer than names of U.S. presidents.

The Power of the Message

Persuasion to buy is only one part of advertising, though. In fact, advertising performs a myriad of services that benefit both individuals and society. Advertising keeps down the cost of newspapers, magazines, radio and television, making them affordable and accessible to

DATELINE DATELINE DATELINE

LONDON, 1614—Decorative signs attached to buildings or swinging over doorways identified local inns and taverns. These signs were the forerunners of modern billboards. Because few people could read, the shopkeepers created logos, or artwork that represented the names of their establishments: The Three Squirrels, The Ape, A Hole in the Wall, Man in the Moon, a Hog In Armour and so on.

In 1614, England passed the first laws regulating advertising. One law prohibited signs from projecting more than eight feet out from a building. Another said signs must be high enough to allow a man wearing armor and riding a horse to pass beneath them.

more people. Ads help you make wise choices by presenting information about products, services and trends. Even the sale of a product or service ends up benefiting more than just the business. It promotes economic growth and improves the standard of living by encouraging spending, increasing mass production, creating jobs and, ultimately, leading to the manufacture of less expensive products and services.

Furthermore, advertising is influencing the direction of the "information superhighway." As other nations and cultures are exposed to more and more U.S. media and entertainment, our products and services, introduced through advertising, are finding growing markets outside this country.

Occasionally, a business's enthusiasm for these new markets, coupled with its commitment to U.S. advertising campaigns that have already proved successful, can add up to one big communications problem. According to author Robert W. Woodruff, when Coca-Cola brought its product to China, it had to make some last-minute changes. Originally, company officials had chosen the Chinese characters that most closely resemble the logo *Coca-Cola,* but those characters translated into "bite the wax tadpole." Instead, Coca-Cola officials finally settled on Chinese characters that mean "can mouth, can happy."

Kentucky Fried Chicken also had image problems in China, because its advertising campaign translated into Chinese, suggested "eat your fingers off." Of course, changing a company's image to please an international audience is only one of many challenges that face advertisers. Ads must reflect an audience's style, needs and desires. Those that do not are easy to spot because they seem so immediately out of place.

Similar miscommunication can affect your school newspaper. Sometimes businesses that clearly do not count teenagers among their consumers nonetheless advertise in a school publication. The ads, if noticed at all, may draw giggles or confused looks. They generally won't draw business, however. In the case of misplaced ads, the business usually has some personal connection to the school. Perhaps a staff member's uncle owns it, and the owner views the cost of the ad as more of a contribution to the publication than a wise investment.

In contrast, the *Encyclopedia of Bad Taste,* by Jane and Michael Stern, includes numerous references to products that succeeded by understanding the style of potential customers and creating a desire within these people for the products themselves. How else can we explain the relative, if sometimes short-lived, success of aerosol cheese, fish sticks, lava lamps, candied fruit sheets, pet clothing or TV dinners?

The Meaning of the Message

In a conversation in Lewis Carroll's *Alice's Adventures in Wonderland,* Humpty Dumpty told Alice, "When I use a word, it means just what I choose it to mean—nothing more or less." Indeed, determining the meaning of a message can be a highly personal matter. That's why it's so important for everyone, not only advertisers, to choose words carefully. After all, if you say "I love you" to a person, who subsequently

BYLINE

THE AD COUNCIL PAYS

Public service ads are similar to other ads or commercials except they do not sell products or services for money. Proving that public service messages do make a difference, the Ad Council has served as a sponsor and clearinghouse for public service announcements (PSAs) since World War II. Ad Council OSAs have helped the United Negro College Fund raise nearly $1 billion during the past two decades. These funds have enabled more than 150,000 students to graduate.

The council's Safety Belt Education campaign has been another smashing success. Since the campaign began in 1982, the percentage of Americans wearing safety belts has risen from 11 to 87 percent. More than 40,000 new teachers are working today thanks to the Ad Council's Recruiting New Teacher's campaign.

One of the Council's recent projects involves using real people and their real-life stories. The Organ and Tissue Donation campaign was launched in 1994 with a message that encourages willing donors to share their decisions with family members. That same year, more than 3,000 people died waiting for transplants. Meanwhile, more than 42,000 people are currently waiting for organ transplants.

By presenting several real-life scenarios, the PSAs convey the message that deciding whether to donate a loved one's organs and tissue at the time of death is extremely difficult if the issue has not been previously discussed. In one ad, for example, a husband contemplates whether or not donating his wife's organs was what she would have wanted. He explains that they had never discussed donation because they were young and "thought we had time." All the work to create the campaign was done without charge by media professionals.

---

misinterprets your intention, it can create an extremely uncomfortable situation. Of course, in the world of advertising there is little love ever lost. Language is used primarily to gain a strategic advantage over the competitor's products.

Advertising executive Rosser Reeves, in the book *Doublespeak,* points to the need for excellent writing to separate products that essentially are the same. "A client comes into my office and throws two newly minted half dollars onto my desk and says 'Mine is the one on the left. You prove it's better."

In 1972 a little-known tire company, B. F. Goodrich, had its own image problem. Potential customers kept confusing its name with that of another tire company, Goodyear. Instead of changing its name, though, B. F. Goodrich created an advertising campaign that acknowledged the confusion, even mentioning the competitor in the ads. The success of this campaign moved B. F. Goodrich from last in sales to second, behind Goodyear.

What is the lesson for you? Even if an advertiser, though research, has a complete understanding of its product, its audience and the temper of the times, without excellent writing other efforts mean little.

public service ads

Similar to other ads or commercials except they do not sell products or services for money. Support for ads come from non-profit organizations such as American Cancer Society or the Red Cross.

The Goals of the Message

In general, all good advertising must do certain things: attract attention, arouse interest, create a desire and incite action. At the heart of all ads, though, are the features and benefits of the product or service. Virtually every element of the ad should support and explain these features and benefits. Through concise but vivid writing, the members of the audience learn what the product or service offers and how it can improve their lives. Most consumers will make a purchase decision based on their understanding of these features and benefits.

Before the copy is written, however, the advertiser must decide what kind of appeal to use with the audience. An **advertising appeal** is an attempt to draw interest to the ad itself. The appeal should reflect the style of the business as well as the style of the intended audience. The most widely used appeals include the following:

advertising appeal

an attempt to draw interest to an ad. Among the most common are humor, emotion, sex, testimony, bandwagon, comparison, economy and prestige

- *Humor*—eliciting anything from a chuckle to a guffaw to attract attention to the ad.
- *Emotion*—tugging at the audience's heartstrings by including a moving story or illustration.
- *Sex*—using words or images of a suggestive nature.
- *Testimony*—promoting a product or service by including an account of how it changed an individual.
- *Bandwagon*—creating interest by telling the audience that everyone else is buying the product or service.
- *Comparison*—demonstrating that the features and benefits of one product are preferable to those of another.
- *Economy*—showing the opportunity to save money.
- *Prestige*—proudly proclaiming to be exclusive or the best.

The appeal should provide a framework for the advertisement. This framework will help the copywriter—the person who actually writes the words in the ad—to determine the style and content of the ad. Remember, though, that some ads are deliberately misleading or untruthful. Often these ads are nothing more than propaganda. **Propaganda** is the name given to any organized, widespread attempt to influence people's thinking or behavior. It may be good or bad, according to the purpose or intentions of its originator, the way it is used, or how it's received by an audience.

propaganda

the name given to any organized, widespread attempt to influence people's thinking behavior

YOUR BEAT •

1. Go through current magazines, and cut out representative examples of each of the eight advertising appeals described in the text.
2. Through research and interviewing, collect some of the most popular product slogans today. Quiz other class members to see what their "advertising IQ" is.
3. Find an advertisement that seems "at home" in your school's publication. Why is the school paper or yearbook the right place for this ad? Now find an example of an out-of-place ad, and explain its inappropriateness.

▲THE MEDIA

An excellent idea or product is not enough to guarantee sales. A business or individual must also consider the best way to introduce an idea or product to the public. That's where an advertising agency comes in. Advertising agencies determine how businesses should spend their advertising dollars. Agency representatives called **account executives** work with businesses to try to sell the agency's creative ideas to them.

After the idea or concept is sold, copywriters and artists begin their work. A **copywriter** is the person who writes the text for the ad. Throughout this process, they are guided and supervised by a creative director who is in charge of overseeing the development of the advertising campaign. The media buyer then determines the best way to get the product or message to the public. The media buyer is a specialist who selects which medium or combination of media (television, newspaper, radio, magazine, direct mail and so forth) would work best. Within each medium, the media buyer also decides such things as the time or place the ad will run, the frequency (number of times) the ad will run, and the possible reach of the ad (the average total number of homes or people exposed to it). A good copywriter and media buyer are crucial, because it is they who can get individuals in the audience to recall and act upon an ad.

account executive

a representative of an advertising agency who works with businesses to try to sell the agency's creative ideas to them

copywriter

a person at an advertising agency who writes the text for an ad

Television versus Radio

Increasingly, advertisers are turning to television as a means of reaching potential customers. There are some powerful reasons for this choice: television is considered by many to be the most influential, dominant and effective (if expensive) medium. Not only do TV ads in general cost more than radio or newspaper advertising, but the cost also fluctuates greatly within the medium itself, depending on when the ad runs, how often it runs, how many people may see it, what station carries it and how much production is required.

In terms of availability and access, radio easily beats television. In the United States alone, 500 million radios blare—almost two per per-

CALVIN AND HOBBES reprinted by permission of Universal Press Syndicate.

Instant Profits

Infomercials are a relatively new phenomenon that started in 1984 after the Federal Trade Commission lifted all restrictions on how much commercial time local TV stations could sell. Most of them run late at night, when entire hours can be bought cheap (and when bleary-eyed, lonely viewers are most susceptible to suggestions)—a slot known in the television trade as "remnant air time"—and although they cost little to produce, they can make fortunes. *Time* magazine reported that the thirty-minute Kitchenmate Mixer infomercial, which shows a lady turning skimmed milk into luxurious whipped cream, bread into bread crumbs, and oil into mayonnaise, was produced for $125,000 and generated $55 million in sales. Over twenty thousand different infomercials are broadcast on stations around the country; four out of five stations run them; and their total take is estimated at about a billion dollars a year. In 1991 the Home Shopping Network started a twenty-four hour-a-day infomercial-only channel.

"A sixty-second spot goes by so fast," said Nancy Langston of infomercial producer Media Arts International. "In a half-hour, we allow time to demonstrate and repeat and demonstrate and repeat. It's really an incredible way to sell a product." Some products, however, have defied successful infomercialization. According to Bernice Kanner, writing in *New York* magazine, these include back-pain cures, improve-your-garden products, and a videotape starring Walter Cronkite, Nancy Reagan, and Morgan Fairchild titled *How to Raise Drug-Free Kids.* Greg Renker explained, "Our audience wants instant, effortless success, fame, or beauty."
Source: Reprinted with permission from Jane Stern and Michael Stern, Encyclopedia of Pop Culture *(New York: HarperCollins).*

son. Chances are that you have two or three radios in your own house—one included in a stereo, another portable one and perhaps even a clock radio. Almost all cars come with radios as well. And because radios are so portable, almost anyone, anywhere—from the jogging path to the car to the workplace or department store elevator—can be listening to the radio.

In preparing ads for radio, it is important to remember that there is a difference between writing for the eye and writing for the ear. Although sound effects and music can go far in creating an image in the listener's head, the radio copywriter cannot dismiss the copy entirely. Because radio copy is unable to use visuals to increase the power of the words, it needs to be straightforward, concise and simple. Short, easily envisioned words should be chosen over complex, polysyllabic ones. Dialogue can work especially well in radio ads, because it tends to be conversational and readily understood.

Print Advertising

Eric Sevareid, a famous broadcast journalist, pointed to the strength and potential of newspapers when he said, "One good word is worth a thousand pictures." Newspapers can and do use photography and art as a means of telling or strengthening a story, but the print medium can't incorporate sound or movement as radio and television do. Still, the print medium continues to be a popular choice for advertisers for a number of reasons.

The most obvious reason is the fact that print is a tactile medium. The stories, photos, art and advertisements can be touched, cut out and referred to again and again. The print medium has a virtual monopoly on coupons, a highly valued advertising strategy to attract potential customers.

Another significant advantage of newspaper advertising over radio advertising has to do with competition. Most people have a number of choices when tuning in to the radio or television, because many towns and cities carry several stations. Fewer than 60 U.S. cities, though, have competing newspapers. That means that most people in a city or town who read the newspaper read the same newspaper. Thus, newspaper advertisements reach more local consumers than do radio or TV ads. This fact translates into more exposure per advertising dollar.

Like radio ads, newspaper ads take little time to create. This time savings allows advertisers to offer up-to-date information, something newspaper readers have come to expect from the paper's advertisements as well as its news.

Two common forms of print advertising are the classified and the display ad. The **classified ad** is an inexpensive, brief advertisement placed by individuals or businesses, classified by subject, and collected in one place in the newspaper. Examples might include puppies for sale, now hiring at the local burger barn, or baseball cards to trade. The **display ad,** on the other hand, is an advertisement with photos or images as well as headlines in large type that appear in various sizes and shapes throughout the paper.

classified ad

> an inexpensive, brief advertisement placed by individuals or businesses, classified by subject, and collected in one place in the newspaper

display ad

> advertisements with photos or images as well as headlines in large type. These appear in various sizes and shapes throughout the paper.

Not only are newspapers a bargain and a convenience, they can also save the consumer money through advertising and coupons.

YOUR BEAT

• •

1. Find print and broadcast commercial examples for the same product. Compare and contrast the way the message was delivered in each example.
2. Write and record a radio commercial that sells yourself as the student every teacher wants to have in class. Use music and sound effects to give the ad color.
3. Survey 10 people on their favorite and least favorite ads. Categorize them into print, radio and TV ads. Does there seem to be a favorite medium for these memorable ads?

THE MAKEUP

Most of you know when a new student enrolls in your class. There's a new face in the crowd, and like it or not, your first impression of that face will go far in determining how you will treat that person in the future. Teenagers, though, don't need a study to tell them how important it is to make a good first impression. Advertisers, too, know that good makeup or design can help create a positive first impression of their products.

Parts of an Ad

Most advertisements, like most people, start out with the same basic parts or elements. Whereas people usually have arms, legs, eyes, a mouth and hair, ads usually have a headline and **body copy** (which supports and expands on what the headline says). They usually include a photograph or illustration and a **logo** (an easily identifiable "flag" that can combine art and copy and that is associated with the product—McDonald's golden arches, for example). In addition, ads often use a **slogan** (a short, catchy phrase that helps the audience identify the product—Nike's "Just Do It," for example). How these elements are presented helps determine an ad's success or failure. An advertiser applies good design and layout concepts to these elements in order to make the ads memorable.

The parts or elements of an ad vary in importance. Recognizing this fact will aid the ad's designer in emphasizing the right things. Say there's a great sale at the local music store. The headline, which will mention the sale, should be highly ranked and given much space in the ad. If Chevrolet is introducing its newest Camaro, in contrast, a photograph of the car should receive top billing.

After deciding which elements are most important, the designer needs to consider the different ways to make an ad visually striking. A memorable ad, in addition to being simple and readable, often includes vivid photographs or artwork; wise use of white space; creative borders around the ad; and a bold, eye-catching headline. Even the ad size can make a difference in its effectiveness. Clearly, each of these design elements can pull a reader's eyes through the ad. How they are put together, though, is another decision that must be made.

Balancing the Elements

Just as different branches of the federal government have ways of balancing the powers of other branches, the individual elements of an advertisement can help balance one another as well. "Heavy" elements (large, bold type; dark colors; and strong, well-defined shapes) are softened and balanced by "lighter" elements (smaller type, subtle shading,

body copy

the text of an ad, which supports and expands what the headline says

logo

an easily identifiable "flag" in an advertisement that may combine art and copy and that is associated with the product

slogan

a short, catchy phrase that helps an ad's audience identify the product

© Sidney Harris. Reprinted by permission of S. Harris.

"...No, he can't really fly...no, the bad guys don't really have a ray gun...no, this cereal really isn't the best food in the whole world...no, it won't make you as strong as a giant..."

and smaller photographs or artwork). Light elements placed on the edge or in the corner of an ad tend to balance heavier elements that are placed near the center. An ad can also achieve balance by using two light elements with a single heavy element or by using a dark but small element above the center to offset a larger, lighter element placed below the center.

Regardless of how the balance is achieved, it's important to know that a balanced layout is not a mathematically centered one. More crucial than the geometric center is the optical center, which is slightly above and just to the left of the geometric one. This is the most noticed position in an ad, and it divides the layout into balanced segments.

This balancing act can create either a formal or informal feel, depending on the placement of the elements and the needs and style of the advertiser. A formal layout uses space on either side of the optical center in the same manner. In other words, similarly sized and weighted elements are positioned at equal distances from the optical center. As its name implies, a formal layout works well for a business that wants to portray a conservative, dignified and stable image. Though not particularly interesting to look at, the formal layout is easy to design.

Conversely, an informal layout uses different weighted elements to balance each other, one being placed farther from the optical center than the other. Informal layouts tend to work well for a business with a youthful, creative trendsetting image.

Self-Promotion

Starting in the late '60s, local TV newscasts became profitable and stations began competing fiercely for audience shares. In advertising the newscasts, some stations emphasized nonjournalistic elements:

◆ KGO in San Francisco ran full-page newspaper ads that showed its news staff dressed as cowboys sitting around a poker table. "Feel like you're getting a bad deal from poker-faced TV news reporters?" the ad asked. "Then let the Channel 7 Gang deal you in. They're not afraid to be friendly."

◆ KGO's competition, KRON, ran full-page ads showing its newscasters dressed up in dogs' heads. The copy: "The Bay Area's pet news team tracking down the news 24 hours a day. Watch the News-hounds of News-watch 4."

Source: Reprinted from Steven Bates, If No News, Send Rumors *(New York: Henry Holt and Co,), p. 17.*

picture-window format

a standard print advertising layout in which the illustration is the dominant element

copy-heavy format

a standard print advertising layout that emphasizes words rather than visuals

tool line

a black line that can vary in thickness and length from use to use in a print advertisement

type-specimen format

a standard print advertising layout that usually has little copy and wants to "shout" something to the reader. Its main elements are the headline and the subhead

circus format

a standard print advertising layout that is visually very busy and filled with headlines, small illustrations and copy blocks

multipanel format

a standard print advertising layout that has at least two dominant illustrations

Whichever style an advertiser chooses, a variety of standard layouts are available. *The Practical Guide to Better Newspaper Advertising* identifies and explains five of the most used print advertising layouts. (Figure 17.1 illustrates these layouts.) In the **picture-window format,** the illustration is the dominant element. This layout gets its name from department store display windows, in which the store presents samples of some of its best offerings.

A **copy-heavy format** emphasizes words rather than visuals. Because the copy is the dominant element, these ads seldom enjoy high readership. However, they may be the best choice for the advertiser when a good deal of detailed information must be given. In a copy-heavy format, the copy blocks often are broken up with initial caps (the first letter in a paragraph is made larger and bolder), **tool lines** (black lines of varying thickness and length), extra white space, bold type and subheadings (smaller headlines that expand on the main headline's message).

The **type-specimen format** usually has little copy and wants to "shout" something to the reader. The main elements in this format—the elements that give the ads a sense of immediacy and newsworthiness—are the headline and the subhead.

Another layout that seems to be shouting at the reader is the **circus format.** You may have seen this format used by a grocery store. Visually it is very busy, filled with headlines, small illustrations and copy blocks. The designer must consider weight, balance and eye focus, or the ad will push away potential readers. The often unorganized look of the circus format can give an impression of the business as being low in quality.

In the **multipanel format,** as in the picture-window format, the illustration is the key. The multipanel format, however, includes at least two dominant illustrations. It is a good approach for products that don't need much copy.

Now you know that ads share basic elements and that it's beneficial for designers to grade these elements by importance. You also know that there are formal and informal ad styles and that several standard layout formats can be used in each of these styles. You might not know where to begin, though, when the time comes for you to actually sit down and design an ad yourself. Fortunately, computers can be a great help in ad design.

Desktop Publishing

Practically every school has computers available to students. These computers have capabilities far beyond simple word processing. Check with your adviser, librarian or computer lab technician to find out if the school's computers have a page design program; they probably do.

Page Design. Regardless of which page design program your school's computers have, most recommend typing all of the copy except for the headline in a word-processing program and then exporting or placing it onto the page later. This approach is much easier and quicker than using the often clumsy and slow word processing available in the page design programs.

FIGURE 17.1
THE FIVE MOST USED PRINT ADVERTISING LAYOUTS

Q•R•O•K
87.3FM

We're
EVERYWHERE
YOU ARE

Picture Window

CIRCUS FORMAT
Advertising
usually **contains** many *different* typestyles

an ✎ array of ✈ small art ✄ and

*HEADLINES ALL IN
THE SAME ADVERTISEMENT !*

Circus

THE LEARNING CENTER

**SAT Prep Courses
IMPROVE YOUR
SCORES TODAY!**

OFFERS YOU 13 hours of direct
instruction by degreed professionals and
practice tests. All instructors are experienced and have multiple
degrees. Math and English are taught by specialists in each subject. Class size limited to ten *so everyone gets personal attention.
Stress management* classes are also included in the base price as
a bonus.

Classes begin October 12. Hours are 4:30-6:30 p.m. Tuesdays
and Thursdays. Practice Test will be administered on Saturday,
October 29.

Call <u>Today</u> 123-4567

Copy Heavy

Type Specimen Format

HEADLINE

TELLS YOU IMMEDIATELY
WHAT ADVERTISEMENT IS FOR

Type Sepcimen

**THIS ADVERTISING LAY-
OUT**

**BECAUSE IT IS BALANCED.
WORDS AND PICTURES
CREATE A SENSE OF
ORDER**

Formal

After typing and saving the copy, open up the page design program. Request a page size compatible with your publication's page size. Using the program's ruler or measuring stick to guide you, first draw a box that's the correct size of the ad. While the box is still highlighted, you can change its look and thickness simply by requesting another line choice. Experiment until you find a box that will work well with your ad.

Before bringing the text in from the word-processing program, it's important to adjust the page's columns or gutters (the vertical areas on the page that separate the columns of type and over which most copy should not run) until they are just inside the box's vertical lines. Placing the columns or gutters inside the box will prevent the copy from bumping into the box, making the copy hard to read. Now place or import your body copy into the box. After it has been placed, you might need to enlarge or shrink the typesize so that the ad fits in the box.

Type Fonts.   Experiment with the typeface or font (the actual design or look of the letters) to give different looks to the ad. Some fonts are very formal (Park Avenue, Tiffany and Chancery, for example), whereas others have a more casual and playful air (Freestyle Script, Kawasaki or Bedrock, for example). Two of the most used fonts in the world are Helvetica and Times-Roman, because they are clean and easy to read. Be sure, however, to employ a font that fits the style of the business being advertised and that serves the purpose of the ad itself. In general, try to avoid fonts named after cities or places. These are bitmapped fonts that will appear jagged when printed.

Here is an example of a bitmapped font:

This is Chicago. It may look OK on your screen but it will print broken on the page.

Artwork.   After you've chosen a font that is both stylish and appropriate, it's time to add the artwork. Use your computer, or print an incomplete version of your ad with a blank space where you will glue on the artwork yourself. If your school has a scanner, try scanning the business's logo or artwork, and then place it directly on the computer layout. This is less messy than the cut-and-paste technique. Is also gives you more flexibility in placement and sizing.

Sometimes the business will offer you the option of taking a photograph or using artwork. Whenever possible, choose photographs. Be sure to include students from the school in them. (You'll need a press release from each student. A press release grants you permission to use the photo for your publication.) Photos with familiar faces almost always do a better job of grabbing the reader's attention.

When you've completed the ad, save a copy of it on the computer. Make photocopies for the advertisers and yourself. Before sending the ad to the advertiser for approval, ask yourself if you've included all the necessary copy information, as well as the business's address, phone number and hours. Also ask yourself if you've included all the basic elements in the ad; if each element complements the others; and if the layout, font and artwork choices you've made attract the attention of the reader and reflect the style of the advertiser.

1. Using your school's newspaper or yearbook and your local newspaper, find good examples of each of the design formats discussed in this unit.

2. Go to the library, and search through magazines that clearly are aimed at different audiences (for example, YM and the *New Republic*). Do you see any patterns in which design styles and formats are used?

3. Find an advertisement that uses one design format. Sketch a new ad for the product, emphasizing another design format.

◢ THE MANAGEMENT

In a way, a school publication is like a professional baseball team—the management always seems to be changing. Every year, new faces fill each position. Unlike the baseball team, though, no one is making millions of dollars managing your school's newspaper, magazine or yearbook. Your staff, however, should act as if the decisions it makes are indeed million-dollar decisions. After all, unlike decisions made in most other classes, the decisions of a publications staff have an immediate effect upon the entire school. That's why it's worth your time to organize and manage your staff well.

The Advertising Staff

In producing a school newspaper, it's easy to forget about advertising. But that is a costly mistake. A professional newspaper, for example, hands over approximately 60 percent or more of its space to advertising every issue in order to make a profit and keep subscription rates low.

Why, then, do so many high school staffs complain when they have to make room for another Fred's Burger Barn ad? The answer is simple. More often than not, someone has forgotten to tell them about the crucial role of advertising. Perhaps your school's publication doesn't have an advertising manager or editor. Because the presence of an advertising editor's position suggests importance, the absence of such a position may send the staff the subtle message that advertising is not important.

Furthermore, many newspaper staff members resent being forced to sell ads. Writers who see themselves as the next Dave Barry or William Raspberry may object to the added burden of raising money to pay for the publication. They may argue that they didn't join the staff to sell ads. Fortunately, though, both apathy and resentment toward advertisements can be lessened by better organization.

The quickest and most certain remedy for these negative attitudes is to give the advertising people a prominent and powerful place on the newspaper staff. An excellent candidate for advertising editor must be sought with the same vigor that you seek an editor-in-chief. Ask your business teacher or DECA (Distributive Education Clubs of America) sponsor for the names of students who they enjoy and are competent at designing and selling advertising.

DATELINE

BABYLONIA (now in Iraq), 3000 B.C.—Clay, stone and wooden tablets were used by the residents of Babylonia to advertise their businesses.

The ads were crude insignia, or pictures, representing the merchants' wares. For example, a boot represented a shoemaker's shop, and a bush indicated a winery.

Give the advertising editor or manager a voice on your editorial board. Let him or her help determine advertising rates, sales goals, design decisions and staffing positions. Give the person a prominent place on the staff and the support needed to ensure that the publication succeeds financially.

Ideally, this person should have an advertising staff that will assist in contacting businesses and in designing and selling advertisements. If the small size of the staff makes it impossible to assign students to sell ads exclusively, don't eliminate the advertising editor's position. Instead, have this person carry out his or her goals by communicating them clearly and often to the staff as a whole.

You might also consider bringing in a professional sales representative to discuss with the entire staff the importance of selling advertisements, as well as some techniques that will help increase revenue. Another idea is to spend a day during the summer with the editorial boards of other schools. Find out how they manage their staffs, sell ads and raise money. Most staffs go away from such experiences with enlightenment, encouragement and enthusiasm.

Financial Considerations

After educating your staff on the importance of advertising, it's time to determine just what ads mean to your publication. How much does your publication rely on advertising? Some simple math will help you decide.

cost analysis
an itemized overview of all expenses

When you meet as an editorial board in the summer, take time to decide how often your newspaper or magazine will come out, how many pages will make up your paper or yearbook, and what special effects (color photographs, spot color and so on) you would like included. Review the expenses for last year's publication, and do a cost analysis. A **cost analysis** is an itemized overview of all expenses—production and printing costs, photography supplies and processing, staff activities and workshops, service charges, disks, supplies, and mailing and shipping costs—everything.

FUNKY WINKERBEAN reprinted by permission of King Features Syndicate.

Set priorities. Ask yourselves which expenses could be eliminated or reduced, which are necessary, which are the results of new technology, or which stem from the use of color or special effects. Also determine how many of these expenses are one-time charges (for the purchase of new equipment, for example). Setting priorities will make it possible for you to take control of your finances.

If more than one printer could publish your newspaper or yearbook, have the editorial board put together a proposal (including the decisions the board made in the summer about the frequency and quality of the publication), and submit it to the printers for bidding. Bidding will help you pick the best and most reasonably priced printer to use.

After you choose which printer will print your publication, you must decide how you will pay for it. Many publications receive some financial support, though the amount varies from a couple of hundred dollars to thousands a year. Consider meeting with your principal or school board when budgets are being debated. Remind the people in authority of the numerous services your publication carries out for the school and the district. Make them aware of the costs needed not only to maintain but also to upgrade your services.

Even if your publication receives additional support from the school, you probably will still need to sell ads. To project how many ads you must sell to break even or make a profit, figure out the expected costs of your publication this year. Subtract from that amount any funding you receive. The remaining amount is the amount of money your staff must raise. Divide this amount by the number of total pages you anticipate for the year to get a per-page cost of running your publication.

Call nearby schools to find out how much they charge for advertising (if you don't already know). Comparing your cost per page with your competitors' rates will help you decide how much to charge for ads and how many ads you'll need to sell. After discussing what your publication must have and what it can live without, and after studying your competitors' rates along with your own publication's financial situation, set ad rates that will be competitive and fiscally responsible.

Advertising Sales

Selling advertising space in a high school publication is useful for two reasons. First, it introduces students to an area of journalism they might not otherwise experience. Second, most publications need the additional funds to continue to exist. Three-fourths of all high school publications rely on advertising for survival. No matter how desperate a publication's financial situation is, though, a staff should never have to resort to begging in order to sell their product. That's because the dollars are already there for you to offer to savvy businesses. Remember, teenage consumers spend about $78 billion each year.

Your advertising staff should approach local businesses with the confidence that comes from having an excellent product to offer. After all, the potential customers are out there, they have money to spend, and you have a direct line to them. In fact, you have a more direct line than even the local newspaper does, and it charges much more for advertising. Still, confidence will never compensate for clumsy preparation.

DATELINE DATELINE DATELINE

NEW YORK, Aug. 16, 1922—Station WEAF went on the air on August 16, 1922, as the first truly commercial radio station.

AT&T built WEAF with the finest technical equipment available, but the company announced that it would not sponsor any programming.

The first paid commercial announcement, a 10-minute speech for a real estate business, ran one week later. It cost the sponsor $100 and was repeated for five days. The advertiser reported extremely successful results.

Called *commercials* after an AT&T accounting term, the paid advertisements earned WEAF and its licensed out-of-town stations $150,000 in profit in 1923. In six months WEAF had about two dozen paying advertisers.

Not everyone agreed with AT&T's approach. Commerce Department Secretary Herbert Hoover said, "It is inconceivable that we should allow so great a possibility for service to be drowned in advertising clutter."

Advertising on the radio grew rapidly, however. By 1928 it was the main source of revenue for broadcasting.

THIS JUST IN: *Portrait of a Young Journalist*
Emily Voth, director of client services, Metro Productions

Broadcaster ?
Journalist ?
Sports Writer ?
Designer ?
Editor ?
Columnist ?
Anchor ?
Reporter ?
Photographer ?

"The most fun is being weird with your co-workers," says Emily Voth, director of client services at Metro Productions in Kansas City. At this office, for example, the soundtrack to the film *Natural Born Killers* might be played over the intercom. After all, Metro Productions works with film, video and special effects. Voth explains, though, that the business of advertising is not as "goofy" as most people believe. Advertising is just as competitive as the corporate world, and, says Voth, "creativity often suffers from the pressure to compete."

A graduate of the University of Kansas, Voth majored in journalism and specialized in corporate television. Her first job after college was as a production coordinator for Sprint. Voth's degree in video helped her get "instant credibility" with the corporation. Voth then went on to produce the video *Hello, Hello,* which won for Sprint an Omni Award.

Today she finds satisfaction in watching the storyboards of clients turn into finished ads. The challenge is to keep up with the technological changes that are continually changing the industry. Occasionally, she performs before the camera. Voth has appeared in a regional Toyota ad and a spot for Topsy's Popcorn. She also has had a small role in a film with Paul Newman and Joanne Woodward.

Voth's advice to other beginning journalists is this: "Be hungry. If you get a position as an intern, knock yourself out. Always ask for more to do." Of course, that work ethic has already paid off for Voth. Her goal for her own career is to avoid the fate that awaits many creative people in the world of advertising. In other words, Voth says, "I don't want to be bitter."

One study showed that 80 percent of all sales made by professional sales representatives came after the fifth visit or contact with the potential customer. It is wise, then, for a high school advertising staff to be prepared for any and all visits.

Information on Local Businesses. At the beginning of the year, the staff should discuss the types of businesses or services that students use and the names of local businesses that offer these goods or services. These are the businesses that are most likely to place ads in your publication. Keep a file of these businesses, complete with mailing addresses, phone numbers and contact persons. Periodically update this information. Categorizing these businesses by the products or services they offer makes it easier to use your file. As prom or homecoming approaches, for example, you can then turn to your "flowers" or "tuxedos" section to create a list of businesses to contact for possible ad placement.

The Student Survey. Another worthwhile activity early in the school year is a survey of student spending habits. If you can, distribute it to all the students in your school. In the survey, ask students to list their gender, age, grade and any allowance they receive. Ask them if they work, where they work, how many hours a week they work and how much they earn from their jobs. Also include questions about their spending habits—on food, clothing, music, movies and entertainment, for example. Finally, include questions that focus on how and where they spend their time. Make sure the questions are clear, open-ended and nonleading (that is, they don't lead the respondent to a particular answer). You can compile the data and create a powerful tool to sell advertising—a detailed account of how students at your school spend their money and time.

The Sales Kit.   Once you've collected data about the types and names of local businesses and the spending habits of your student population, you should put together a sales kit. A sales kit is a package of information the members of the ad staff take with them when visiting local businesses. It may include an advertising rate sheet (how much you charge for advertising), a contract (see Figure 17.2), examples of your publication, the student spending survey, the school's size and mailing address, circulation information, and the names of your advertising staff members. The sales kit not only provides a business with a good deal of information but also sends the message that you take your publication and its advertisers seriously. It leaves a positive impression long after you've gone out the door.

ADVERTISING CONTRACT

BETWEEN *The Anytown High School Happenings*
and _____

All advertising will be billed at the rate of $ _____ per column inch per issue. The Happenings publishes _____ times per year.

Advertisements may be placed in single or multiple issues. Please indicate below the number of issues in which your ad will appear.

Run this ad _____ times.
Run this ad in the following specific issues:

_____
_____

Copy for this ad is
____ Attached   ____ Should be prepared by *The Happenings* staff
                                          for approval.

All advertising will be reviewed by the Publications Board before insertion. No known misleading photos or statements will be accepted. All students appearing in ads must have a model release on file with the Board.

The newspaper reserves the right to refuse any advertising not found to be within the publication's standards.

_____   _____
Advertiser   School Representative

SPECIMEN

FIGURE 17.2
AN ADVERTISING CONTRACT

DATELINE DATELINE DATELINE

BOSTON, 1704—The *Boston Newsletter* was the first American newspaper to carry advertising.

The first *Newsletter* ad offered a reward for the capture of a thief and the return of the stolen goods.

The early ads were similar to today's classified ads.

Newspaper advertising soon became so popular that some papers gave the entire front page to it. On Oct. 30, 1760, the *New York Gazette* ran 15 ads in three columns to fill the front page.

If you are going to sell advertising for either your school newspaper or yearbook, carefully consider your appearance before contacting potential advertisers. You should dress appropriately for the customer on whom you are calling.

The Advertising Policy.   One final and extremely important activity must be completed before the members of the ad staff go on their way. Your publication needs a written advertising policy. Check with your school district to see if it has an existing one for student publications. If so, read the policy over as a staff to be sure that everyone understands it. You might also consider adding to the policy if it seems incomplete.

An advertising policy is designed to guide your advertising staff's decisions. Certain businesses offer products whose use is illegal for the majority of your student population—alcohol and tobacco, for example. Clearly, the staff should not sell ads at these businesses. Will you, however, allow ads to run that include photographs of people smoking? Your advertising policy should cover such issues.

You must consider community standards as well. What is the prevailing attitude of your community on such issues as teenage pregnancy, AIDS, drug and alcohol abuse, and contraception? Several businesses promote messages and materials aimed at teenagers on these subjects. A carefully written advertising policy will guide you in deciding if ads from these businesses have a place in your publication.

Dealing with Advertisers.   By now you should feel confident that you know your readers' wants, needs and legal limitations. The next step is to take the time to know as much as possible about potential advertisers. If you can successfully anticipate their needs, you'll be better equipped to address those needs when you make your first contact with the businesses. For initial contacts, a phone call or form letter works best. After all, the purpose of the initial contact is not to sell an ad. It is to introduce yourself and your product (the publication), and to set up a time to meet with a representative in person.

Initial contact is vital in ad sales, but what you do after that determines whether you will succeed or fail. Follow-through is very important. Make sure that your second contact takes place in person and at the time you promised it would. Armed with an appointment, your sales kit and a friendly smile, you'll make it difficult for a business to dismiss you. It's always more difficult to say no to a face than to a voice on the phone.

During the meeting, offer to create a **mock-up ad** or **spec ad** for the business. This example of your advertising work uses information and artwork that is geared to the specific business. It is a "practice" ad intended to convince the business to run an actual ad in your publication. A well-done spec ad is an impressive sales tool.

mock-up ad; spec ad
> a dummy advertisement that uses information and artwork geared to a specific business made for the purpose of convincing the business to run an actual ad in a publication

When a business decides to run an ad in your publication, arrange a meeting with a company representative. During the meeting, you should complete a contract and have it signed. At this time you also can gather specific information, artwork and a logo. Let business representatives know your publication's deadlines, restrictions and charges before they sign the contract.

If the business prefers to have your staff design the ad, set the date at which you will show the ad for final approval. Be sure to get a signature that grants permission for the ad to run as designed. This permission signature may become useful if problems or questions arise after publication.

Finally, be prompt and accurate in billing your advertisers. Most advertisers prefer a **tearsheet,** or copy of the page on which the ad appeared. The tearsheet lets the business see the ad and proves that it ran as scheduled. Include the tearsheet with the billing statement. Keep accurate billing and payment records throughout the year. Rebill businesses with overdue payments on a monthly basis. Your goal is to collect all payments by the last day of the school year.

tearsheet
> a copy of the page on which an advertisement appeared

YOUR BEAT ●

1. Construct a survey that could be used to evaluate the spending habits of students in your school.

2. Contact three other schools in your area. Interview their publication editors about how they sell ads and manage their staffs.

3. Put together a sales kit for your school's publication.

CHAPTER REVIEW

KEY TERMS

Show that you know the meanings of the following key terms by correctly using them in complete sentences. Write your answers on a separate sheet of paper.

advertising appeal	slogan	circus format
account executive	picture-window format	multipanel format
copywriter	copy-heavy format	cost analysis
body copy	tool line	mock-up ad; spec ad
logo	type-specimen format	tearsheet

OPEN FORUM

1. Discuss the following scenario, which actually occurred at East High School in Lincoln, Nebraska. A local bookstore contacts your publication about buying an advertisement. The bookstore carries "new age" and alternative books and publications, including books about the occult and gay and lesbian lifestyles. The advertisement features the words *wiccan* (a religion whose followers, witches and warlocks, praise the earth) and *gay and lesbian.* A parent hears about the ad and offers to write a check to the publication for the amount the ad would have cost. The parent has threatened to organize an advertising boycott of your publication if the staff refuses the parent's check and decides to run the ad anyway. What should you do?

2. Remember the ad that showed eggs frying in a pan as the announcer warned, "This is your brain on drugs." A recent study of elementary schoolchildren showed an unexpected effect of this campaign: many of these children were afraid of eggs. Although this example is relatively harmless, do you believe that the media has a responsibility to consider the possible effects of all ads? If so, how would you balance that responsibility with an advertiser's freedom of speech?

FINDING THE FLAW

Each year columnist William Safire presents the Bloopie Awards. These awards "dishonor" advertising copywriters for playing fast and loose with the English language. Study some of the recent award winners listed here. Try to find the flaws.

"Tomorrow night, someone could win six million of dollars." (From an ad for the New York State lotto)

"When today's 30 year-olds retire, there will be less than two workers per beneficiary." (From an ad for

◆ FINDING THE FLAW, continued

Twentieth Century Mutual Funds)
"How to make a room smell like the windows are always open." (From an ad for Windex)

"Ever wish there was a team of you . . . ?" (From an ad for Whirlpool)

 MEDIA WATCH

1. At the time this book was written, one out of five young women in the United States had eating disorders. A survey of one group of fourth-grade girls revealed that 80 percent of them were on diets. Find examples of ads that encourage young women to "think thin." In light of the fact that the diet industry spends a fortune each year on advertising, what do you think high school journalists should do, if anything?

2. The editors of *Time* choose what they consider to be the best ads from each year. You may remember one of their favorites from 1995. The boy-chases-girl theme has a bearded twentysomething arrive in his car as a ferryboat is about to depart. His license plate reads *OHIO*. As he breathlessly runs up to a beautiful young woman in Lee jeans, he hands her a necklace. "Excuse me," he says, "you dropped this back there." She smiles and asks, "Where?" He responds, "Nebraska."

   Have each member of your class nominate one ad that warrants the honor of being named best ad for the current year.

String Book

1. Choose an everyday object or product (for example, a pen, toothpick, piece of paper or air). Write two print advertisements for it. Each ad should be aimed at a different audience (one for teens and one for older women, for example). Make sure you include each product's features and benefits, and choose an appropriate advertising appeal for each.

2. Interview or shadow a person who works in advertising. Find out how the person selected this career, how he or she prepared for it and what the career requires. Prepare a one- or two-page paper on your findings, and present it to the class. Also, send a copy of it to the person you interviewed.

3. As a class, come up with a list of local businesses that currently do not advertise in your publication but should. Each student should choose one of the businesses and create two mock-up or spec ads for the business. Be sure to pick appropriate design styles and formats, as well as good type fonts. One of these ads, if possible, should be computer generated.

Chapter 18
Yearbooks and Magazines

"High school is closer to the core of the American experience than anything else I can think of."

—Kurt Vonnegut, Jr.

KEY TERMS

In this chapter, you will learn the meaning of these terms:

title page
folio
table of contents
opening section
double-page spread
closing section
colophon
people pages
mug pages
panel pages
theme
logo
end sheets
division pages
ladder
signature
mini-mag
tip-in
magazine
literary magazine
creative arts magazine
general interest magazine
special interest magazine
zine
mosaic concept of design
column
elements of a spread
external margin
bleed
eyeline

LEARNING OBJECTIVES

After completing this chapter, you will be able to:

◆ create a yearbook theme and a magazine concept,

◆ adapt journalistic writing and design skills to yearbook and magazine publishing,

◆ plan, design and produce a yearbook or magazine.

◆

*e*ven the traditional yearbook has not escaped the technological revolution in high school publications. Schools are experimenting with alternative formats for the traditional yearbook. These new formats include monthly magazines, video yearbooks and yearbooks on computer disks. Desktop publishing and improved printing techniques have changed the look of the traditional yearbook, too. The stiff, formal record book has evolved into a contemporary book with more candid pictures and more color, graphic accents and infographics.

And the changes are just beginning. Undoubtedly someone will produce this year's book on CD-ROM so "readers" can pop it into any personal computer and watch the highlights of the school year flash across the monitor screen. Instead of signatures, there will be e-mail messages from classmates. Through digitizing, you will even be able to "age" the mug shots so you'll recognize your classmates when you come back in 25 years for your class reunion!

Similarly, many schools are experimenting with magazines, either as an alternative to traditional publications or, in some cases, as a substitute. Literary arts magazines that showcase student poetry, fiction and artwork have long been popular. Now it's also easy to find a wide range of other kinds of magazines that cover music, the cinema and many other special interests.

The design and layout techniques, the photography skills and the writing styles for newspapers that you have learned in this book apply to yearbook and magazine production as well. In this chapter you'll learn how to design and produce yearbooks and magazines by applying skills you already have to different kinds of publications with a variety of intended readers and purposes.

WHY A YEARBOOK?

No matter what format you choose, a yearbook is just what its name implies: a story about a year. One year. This year. It is also an historical record—probably the only permanent record of this year at your school. The story you capture in words and pictures will become the way in which people visualize your school now and the way in which they will remember it years from now.

A yearbook is all of the following:

+ a memory book
+ a history book
+ an inclusive publication
+ a reference book
+ a public relations publication
+ an educational experience.

A Memory Book

Aggieland, the Texas A&M University yearbook, is one of the most substantial yearbooks in the country. One recent edition contained 864 pages, was two and one-half inches thick, and weighed 12 pounds. Most are not that large, but all are valuable mementos to their owners.

No matter how many pages or pounds your yearbook is, it contains the pictures and words that affect the way students will remember this year. The pictures capture the culture of the year through the clothes and hairstyles people wear, the cars they drive and the events they plan. The copy tells the stories of the people and the things they thought were important. Did students dance to rock or country-and-western music? Did they wear flame red or camouflage? Did they snack on M&M's™ or animal crackers? Was it a cheese-in-the-crust pizza or a super soft-shell taco year?

The yearbook should cover the whole year, not just the school year. After all, it's a book about the lives of the people, and summer is one-fourth of their lives. Graduates will look back at the yearbook to recall which summer they went to music camp, when they built the float for the Fourth of July parade, or when the recreation park opened in town.

BORN LOSER reprinted by permission of United Feature Syndicate.

DATELINE DATELINE DATELINE

PHILADELPHIA, January 1741 —Printers Benjamin Franklin and Andrew Bradford raced to put the first American magazine into print.

Franklin's publication, *General Magazine and Historical Chronicle for all the British Plantations in America*, carried a cover date of January 1741. However, the 70-page magazine wasn't actually offered for sale until February 16.

Bradford was Franklin's chief competitor in the printing business. He also dated his magazine, *American Magazine, or A Monthly View of the Political State of the British Colonies*, January 1741. It appeared in print February 13.

Franklin produced six issues. Bradford produced three.

A few more magazines were published between the 1740s and the 1850s. However, production and circulation were limited due to the lack of easy publication and distribution methods.

Following the Civil War, a national transportation system was completed that made large-scale distribution accessible. Faster presses made mass printing possible. Free public education enabled everyone to read. Advertising became popular and began to help pay the costs of production.

National magazines did more than any previous publications to educate readers about social and cultural issues. They also successfully sold products ranging from cough syrup to farm equipment.

Among the national magazines that began publication before 1900 are some still in publication today, such as *National Geographic*, *Ladies' Home Journal*, *Popular Science Monthly* and the *Saturday Evening Post*.

A History Book

Did you know that Donald Trump was voted the Popularity Poll's Class of 1964 Ladies' Man at his high school?

That Madonna was in the Thespian Society?

That Sissy Spacek was homecoming queen?

That Ted Koppel's nickname was "Dumbo"?

It's all there—in their high school yearbooks. Thanks to their yearbook staffs.

Your yearbook will be the only history ever written of this year at this school with these people. Coaches keep statistics, but their records are eventually discarded. The office keeps a file on each student, but those are private records. Even the school newspaper may be lost if copies are not bound and saved. But students save their yearbooks.

As the historical record of the school, the yearbook must be factual, accurate and complete. The name of every person who is enrolled or works in the school should be recorded—and spelled correctly. Scores, dates of events, and special occasions such as anniversaries or charter meetings of organizations must be recorded for future reference. Because the yearbook is a record book, complete season records for each team are a necessity, as are the names of all members of organizations, classes and the faculty, whether they are pictured or not.

Important events in the national and local news should be included as part of the history of the year, along with things such as the most popular movies and books. Features on issues that concern students, are finding their way into the student life sections of more and more yearbooks. These features might cover subjects such as peer acceptance, dating, money, getting into college, teenage pregnancy, drinking, gangs, single-parent families, AIDS and suicide.

A history is not complete if it omits the news people don't like to hear. If the death of a classmate or faculty member occurs during the year, it should be noted in the yearbook. "In Memoriams" include dates, a brief biography of the person and quotes from friends. They usually feature a recent photo of the person.

Some topics may be controversial in your school or community and should be discussed by the staff before publication. Stating the cause of death in an obituary also should be discussed. Some fear, for instance, that a story on suicide or listing suicide as a cause of death will have a psychological impact on the family or the students. Others feel that it is better to be open and factual about the issue of suicide. Each staff must determine a policy based on the preferences of its school, the community and individual circumstances. The best solution is to have a policy before the need arises.

A Reference Book

People will turn to a yearbook to find information on an individual, an organization or an advertiser. Like other books to which people refer for information, your yearbook should be organized and have reference points.

Page 1, the **title page,** should contain the complete name and address of the school. It also should include the name of the book and the year it was published. The photo or illustration on the title page should be related to the theme of the book.

Each page should have a **folio,** or page number. The folio in a yearbook often contains a bit of art that reinforces the theme, as well as words that describe the contents of the page—for example, *Opening, Academics Division, Track* or *Freshmen.*

The **table of contents** should be at the front of the book, either on the front endsheet or following the title page. It should list each division, including the ads and the index sections, with a beginning page number.

The **opening section** should be the first two to four **double-page spreads,** depending upon the length of the book. A double-page spread is any two facing pages. The opening copy should introduce the theme of the yearbook and explain why it was chosen for this year. The layout for the **closing section**—the last double-page spread or two in the book—should be the same as that on the opening pages. The copy in the closing section should give examples of ways in which the theme applied to specific events throughout the year.

The index is a key reference tool that should be a part of every yearbook, no matter how large or small. The index should be placed immediately before the closing double-page spreads. It should contain the names of every person, organization, major activity and advertiser in the book, along with the page numbers on which they appear.

The **colophon** (pronounced "call-uh-fon") is a technical description of the book as a product. Colophons are references used by publication staffs and publishers to find out technical information about a book. If your staff likes the typeface used in another book, for instance, you can check the book's colophon to find the name of that type and the point sizes used. Information in the colophon should include the name and address of the printer; the number of copies printed; the special processes used to create the cover; the finish, weight and color of the paper; the typefaces and sizes used for headlines, body copy and captions; the graphic techniques used, such as spot color, screens, size of initial letters and tool lines; the computer system used; and the total cost, photography budget and selling price. For easy reference, the colophon is placed at the end of the index or on the back endsheet.

Acknowledgments should be given to everyone who assisted with the book. These people include students who provided information or photos, professional photographers, artists, secretaries, parents, administrators and yearbook representatives. Acknowledgments may appear with the colophon, but they should not be part of the closing double-page spreads.

A Public Relations Publication

Even though the yearbook is produced primarily for students, it has a larger audience. Parents, grandparents, friends from other schools and local businesses see or ask to purchase yearbooks. They are curious to see how the students view themselves and show their school to others.

title page
page 1 in a yearbook, which contains the school's name and address, the book's name and the publication year, and identifies or reinforces the theme

folio
in a yearbook, the folio is usually located at the bottom outside corner of each page and may include words describing the content of the page and/or graphic elements which reinforce the theme, in addition to a page number

table of contents
in a yearbook, a chart that lists each division with its beginning page number

opening section
in a yearbook, the first two to four double-page spreads which introduce the yearbook's theme and explain why it was chosen

double-page spread
any two facing pages in a publication

closing section
in a yearbook, the last double-page spread or two; reflects the opening and wraps up the theme

colophon
a technical description of a book as a product

Doctors, dentists, photographers and businesses like to purchase local yearbooks for their waiting rooms. Chambers of commerce and businesses such as real estate agencies like to have yearbooks to show people who are moving to the area and are looking for schools for their children. Police departments purchase yearbooks for identification purposes.

The image others see in the yearbook is the image they have of the school and of each student. The members of the staff determine the image the yearbook will have by the theme, colors, photos and words they choose to use and the care with which they edit the book.

Misspelled words, weak leads, poor-quality photos and inconsistent design give the impression that the staff doesn't care very much about the yearbook or how it makes them and their school look to others.

An Educational Experience

Schools provide an adviser and funds for yearbooks because they understand the importance of the historical record to the students and to the school. Schools also help make these books possible because the students on a yearbook staff learn writing and production skills.

Producing a yearbook, like working on the school newspaper, gives students hands-on experience practicing skills learned in English class, the computer lab and the darkroom. It also gives them credentials that might help when they apply to colleges or look for jobs.

Publishing is a major industry that offers career opportunities for creative artists and salespersons, editors and desktop designers, writers and photographers. Working on a yearbook gives students a chance to experience book publishing from the idea to the finished product. It lets them become the planners, producers, journalists, researchers, sales staff, marketers and distributors.

Everybody's Book

No matter what else it may be, the yearbook is everybody's book. It should reflect the school and each individual in the school, not just the staff or a few key people. It takes a concentrated effort to make sure the coverage includes every person. When planning the book, devise ways to be sure everyone is included at least once in addition to the individual photographs on the **people pages.** People pages are those on which the people associated with the school are recognized through photos and identified by name. They are also called **mug pages** or **panel pages** when they contain rows of head-and-shoulders photographs of individuals identified by name and class or job description such as *freshmen, seniors, faculty* and *staff.* People pages are more interesting if they contain some feature stories about individuals or a few candid photographs in addition to the individual portraits.

One staff made a master list of students' names and put a check beside the name each time a person was pictured. Its rule was that everyone would be pictured at least twice and no more than five times.

people pages

pages on which the persons who are members of the school community are featured through individual head-and-shoulders photographs and identified by name and class or job description; as a section, people pages may include candid photographs and feature stories about individuals

mug pages

the people pages which contain rows of individual head-and-shoulders photographs, also known as mug shots

panel pages

another name for mug pages, so-called because the rows of photographs resemble panels constructed by placing many small, even-sized pieces side by side

A computer database makes it easy to keep track of which individuals have been pictured or quoted; what percentage of those individuals represent each grade level; and how many pages represent student life, academics and so on. Quoting as many different individuals as possible in the copy and indexing the speakers' names also help ensure that everyone is represented in the book.

1. Analyze several of your school's yearbooks. List the specific ways in which each book fulfills the roles of a yearbook (a memory book, a history book, a reference book, a public relations publication, an educational experience and an inclusive publication).

2. As a class, brainstorm to come up with a list of the audiences for your yearbook. First, analyze the internal audience, or the groups and factions that form the audience within the school. Second, analyze the external audience, or the groups and factions outside the school that may see the yearbook. Save these lists to use when you begin planning a yearbook.

◢PLANNING THE YEARBOOK

With careful thought and planning, a yearbook staff can create a product that appeals to each segment of the audience and includes everyone in the school. Cover design and theme choice are ways to include everyone in the yearbook, too.

Cover

- ✦ "PINK? Why Pink?"
- ✦ "WOW!"
- ✦ "What does it mean?"
- ✦ "Hey! That's me!"
- ✦ "I don't get it."
- ✦ "This is cool!"

Students love, hate or ignore the yearbook at first sight as these reactions show. The cover makes the all-important first impression people have of the yearbook. Whether you choose a leather-look material, a shiny foil-stamped design or a colored photograph for your cover, you want people to respond positively to the book.

One of the services your yearbook representative provides is showing the staff all the materials available for covers and special effects. The staff's imagination—or the budget—is the limit. Good planning includes good budgeting, so always ask for cost estimates. Know the budget for extras before ordering anything that is not specified in your contract with the yearbook publisher. We'll discuss more about working with your yearbook representative at the end of this section.

theme

in a yearbook, a word or phrase that pulls all parts together in a relationship that reflects something special about this year at this school

logo

the graphic or visual element that represents the theme

endsheets

heavier paper pages immediately inside the front and back covers of a book; endsheets bind the cover and the pages of the book together

The design of the front cover should include the theme, the logo and the year of the book. For easy reference, the copy on the bound edge, or spine, of the yearbook should include the name of the school, the city, the traditional name of the yearbook (for example, *The Bronco* or *The Purple and Gold*), the year and the volume number.

Theme, Logo and Color

The **theme** of a yearbook is a word or phrase that pulls all parts of the book together in a relationship that reflects something special about this year at this school. The theme says something unique about the staff, the school and this one year. A yearbook's theme helps tell its story. Readers will notice the theme before they open the book. It will set the tone for their impression of what is inside. The theme influences the design and the colors the staff chooses for the cover.

The **logo** is the graphic that portrays the theme visually. The logo shows the theme through design or typography, sort of like a brand name identifies a wearer's choice of jeans or the stylized check mark identifies Nike products.

Themes are trendy. Like fashion, they change quickly. Sometimes a cliché can be adapted, or a current ad campaign, television show, popular song or movie triggers an idea. Sometimes a special event, such as an anniversary or a new addition to the school, can become theme material.

One school chose "Messin' with the Best" as its theme to talk about all the inconveniences caused by a major construction project at the school. Another school used "New and Improved" to show how an addition to the school added new classes and faculty, as well as bricks and boards, to the building. One staff used "XXX Rated" as its theme; the book's divisions were "eXtraordinary," "eXtra special," and "eXceptional."

Sometimes a cliché like "Just When You Least Expect It" will work for a year when the unexpected happens. It's also exciting to make a cliché unique by adding a twist such as "In One Year and Out the Other." Anniversaries beg for special themes: "Etched in Gold," "A Not So Traditional Year" or "This is What 40 Looks Like." The media, advertisements and package labels are good places to look for theme ideas. "Contents Under Pressure," "One Size Fits All," "After These Messages," "Behind the Scenes" and "Seasoned to Perfection" each became a unique yearbook theme.

Choose the theme as early in the year as possible. The organization of the book may depend on the theme. A theme focusing on the individuals in the school might call for placing the mug section at the front of the book with the student life section. A seasonal theme might organize events in time periods. A theme that emphasizes academics would encourage greater focus on that section.

The theme should be the central focus of the cover where it is identified through words, graphics, photos or illustrations, and color. Inside the book, the theme is established by a photo and caption on the title page. Theme reinforcement is carried throughout the book in words, graphics and colors. It may appear on the **endsheets,** the heavy paper

THIS JUST IN: *Portrait of a Young Journalist*
Marvin Jarrett, publisher, Raygun

Broadcaster ?
Journalist ?
Sports Writer ?
Designer ?
Editor ?
Columnist ?
Anchor ?
Reporter ?
Photographer ?

Once upon a time, Marvin Jarrett wanted to be a rock star. That dream didn't work out, but Jarrett has achieved the next best thing: he publishes magazines about rock stars. Jarrett is the originator and publisher of three magazines. *Raygun* is a free-form magazine that calls itself "the bible of music and style." *Bikini* is a bimonthly about cars, celebrities and nonteam sports. *huH* features music videos.

"There are a few perks" to owning a music magazine, admits Jarrett. "I get free CDs and whatever concert tickets I want, and I get to hang out with David Bowie."

Jarrett's publishing career began in an unlikely way. After graduation from Wolfson High School in Jacksonville, Florida, he began selling stereos through the Hi Fi Buys chain. After just a year on the job, he had become the retailer's number one salesperson. After a stint selling airtime for a Hawaiian radio station, Jarrett landed an ad sales job with the magazine *Creem.* "I went to work for a guy in his 60's who knew nothing about music or advertising," he remembered. "I realized that I should be running the thing."

Jarrett's freewheeling management style eventually cost him his job as editor of *Creem,* but within a few months he began *Raygun,* a magazine with a radical new look. "My strong suit is coming up with a title, a concept, an aesthetic for the magazine, and putting together a good team," Jarrett explained.

"It's almost like being a film producer."

Perhaps the most remarkable ingredient in *Raygun's* success has been its ability to appeal to people in their teens and twenties. "You have to remember," he says, "that this new generation gets its information from so many different media—TV, radio, online, CD-ROMs—so the magazines need to be as visually exciting as any of those other things." Jarrett said he remains as dedicated as ever to what he's doing. "If it came down to it, I would sooner get out the magazine than pay my rent."

Source: Adapted from "It's only Rock & Roll" by Michael Kaplan.

pages immediately inside the front and back covers which hold the cover and the pages of the book together. The endsheets may reinforce theme through color, graphics and content, possibly including the table of contents, printed on them. Theme reinforcement should appear in the table of contents in the subheads that describe each section by using variations on the main theme.

Opening and closing sections identify and explain the theme through copy, photos, graphics and layout design. The theme should be strongly represented on the **division pages,** the single page or double-page spread at the beginning of each section that introduces the content in the section through copy, photos, the logo, a theme-related label or headline, and perhaps color. The theme may also appear in the folio on each page if it includes a graphic or a theme word.

Seeing reminders of the theme as they look through the book gives readers a sense of continuity. They feel they're still reading the same book they started reading, no matter which section they may be viewing. A sense of continuity shows careful planning and consistent editing.

division pages

> pages that separate and identify sections within a yearbook

Color is the first thing people notice about a yearbook. Even from a distance, people can recognize the cover by its colors. Some schools traditionally use variations of their school colors on the cover, but the trend is to use currently popular colors. In choosing colors, a wise staff considers its audience, theme and budget. The audience is the people in the school, but within that audience are males and females, seniors and sophomores, country music lovers and classical music lovers, athletes and actors. Just as the theme encompasses the individual members of the audience, the colors must appeal to them, too.

Color makes a statement. School colors state that this is the book produced by the school represented by these colors. Every year there are "power" colors—colors that are trendy in clothes and decorating schemes. Using power colors in your yearbook says, "We know what's cool this year."

Colors represent emotions, too. Red can mean energy and love, or it can symbolize anger and hate. Green symbolizes life; yellow symbolizes happiness. Upbeat themes are best reinforced by warm colors like red, yellow and orange. Laid-back themes are better reinforced by cool colors—shades of blue, green and purple.

Ladder

ladder

a page-by-page plan of a yearbook that shows the proposed content of each page

The **ladder** is a page-by-page plan that shows the content of each page of the yearbook. As soon as the staff members know how many pages the book will contain, they can begin planning the ladder.

The ladder is designed to show which pages will be across from each other (see Figure 18.1). Books should be planned and designed in double-page spreads even if the subject matter on each page is different. Readers will see the pages as one unit when they open the book. Exceptions are the first page and the last page, which will be single pages.

FIGURE 18.1
SAMPLE LADDER

	1 Table of Contents/Title Page
Opening/Principal 2	*3 Opening From Principal*
Opening 4	*5 Opening*
Events Division 6	*7 Events Division*
New Student Days 8	*9 Parents Night*
homecoming 10	*11 Homecoming*
Mayfest 12	*13 Spring Fling*
Luau 14	*15 Festival*
GDD 16	*17 GDD*
Graduation 18	*19 Graduation*
Renaissance 20	*21 Renaissance*
Fall ALS 22	*23 Fall ALS*
Spring ALS 24	*25 Spring ALS*
SA Activities 26	*27 Blast Off*
Fine Arts Division 28	*29 Fine Arts Division*
Art 30	*31 Art*
Theater/Fall 32	

YEARBOOK SIZE	120 pages	240 pages	400 pages
NUMBER PAGES ALLOCATED TO SECTIONS			
Advertising:	12	32	50
Index:	6	8	12
Remainder:	102	200	338
Typical Allocations			
23% Student Life	24	46	78-80
12% Academics	12	24	40-42
25% People	26	50	84-86
15% Groups	16	30	50-52
18% Sports	18	36	60-62
Number Of Pages			
Staff Will Produce	96	185	312-322

FIGURE 18.2
SUGGESTED PAGE
ALLOCATIONS

Source: Adapted with permission from Scholastic Yearbook Fundamentals, *2nd edition,*
Columbia Scholastic Press Association, New York, N.Y.

The first page is always the title page. Other pages to set aside include the division pages at the beginning of each section, ad pages (if the staff sells advertising), opening and closing sections and the index. Add the number of pages needed for these sections, and subtract that figure from the total pages in the book to find the number of pages you have available to use as you choose.

Yearbooks are printed in 16-page sections called **signatures.** The ladder will show the signatures, but you can figure them out by counting 1–16, 17–32, 33–48 and so on. To get the best value, color pages should be planned in one or two signatures with early deadlines. Complete signatures should be sent to the printer together whenever possible.

Most yearbooks are organized in sections, such as student life, people, academics, sports, organizations and special events. Current or world events may be in a section by itself, be part of an opening or student life section or be in a mini-mag (see the next section). Ads and the index are also separate sections.

The staff can figure out how many pages will be needed for mug shots when they know how many people are in the school and how big they want each photo to be. To make the mug pages more interesting, many schools combine some student life stories with the people pages. To do this, add more pages on the ladder for the people section.

Another decision to be made is the order in which the sections appear. The theme, placement of color pages, individual school circumstances and staff preferences influence placement of the sections. The number of pages in each section, or the percentage of the book given to each topic, is determined by the staff. (See Figure 18.2 for the guidelines of the Columbia Scholastic Press Association.) The decision may vary based on the size of the yearbook, the number of students involved in each area, tradition and special events or circumstances. An athletic team that wins a state championship, an academic team that wins honors, a new program, or an unusual event such as an anniversary or an addition to the school building during the year may tip the ladder more heavily in favor of one section or another.

signature
a 16-page section of a yearbook printed on the same piece of paper during production; pages one through 16; 17–32, 33–48 and 49–60 are signatures

Special Additions

Mini-mags. tip-ins, cutouts, pop-ups, foldouts, specially designed covers and endsheets, postcards tucked in a pocket, individual photos affixed to the cover, holograms—whatever your staff can imagine and afford can probably be done. Before ordering special additions, however, get estimates from the yearbook representative and check your budget carefully.

Mini-mags are unique sections of yearbooks set aside for special topics or subject matter. They come in many forms. Some mini-mags are separate from the actual book and are stored in pockets inside the cover. Others are bound into the book but use paper of a different color, weight or finish for easy identification. Some are slightly smaller than the regular pages, which makes them easy to find. The content of a mini-mag may be devoted to student life, current events or special features. The design is usually similar to a news magazine, with lots of photos, graphics and sidebars. The results of student surveys often add a personal element to mini-mags.

Tip-ins are pages that are printed separately and attached to the book later with narrow double-stick tape. Tip-ins are used for special two- to four-page additions or for entire signatures. Books delivered in the spring use tip-ins to add the spring sports and graduation pages to books that are distributed before those events are completed. The tip-in section is mailed to graduates and distributed to returning students in the fall.

Pop-ups and multiple pages which fold out for viewing like the ones in children's books and greeting cards can be built into yearbooks. Because of the difficulty of construction, pop-ups and foldouts are produced as part of the book at the production plant. Individual photos, holograms and other special effects are often added by the staff after the book is delivered to save labor costs. Ask your yearbook representative about creating any of these special effects for your book.

mini-mag

a special section of a yearbook that is set aside for special topics or subject matter

tip-in

pages in a yearbook that are printed separately and attached to the book later with narrow double-stick tape

Working with the Yearbook Representative

The yearbook representative is your special consultant and emissary, the go-between for the staff and the yearbook company. It is the representative's job to make sure your school's book looks the way your staff wants it to when it arrives.

The representative will work with your staff to plan the book; offer cover, color and endsheet options; and help you create special effects. He or she will also help the staff set manageable deadlines and explain company policies and production schedules. The company or representative will provide all the supplies necessary to complete the book, from a blank ladder to layout sheets to computer software.

Yearbooks are the ultimate desktop publishing experience. Yearbook companies have developed software to allow staffs to design their own pages or to provide fill-in-the-blank templates. Each yearbook company has its own software, so ask the representative to demonstrate the special features available from the company.

Your staff may choose to submit layouts and copy on disc, or you may prefer to do the pasteup yourself. A new service allows schools to send in pictures, which are then recorded as images on compact discs. The discs are returned to the school, and the staff can then use the images to create completed pages on disc.

Don't be afraid to ask for help. The representative's service is part of what you're paying for. One call may save hours of time redoing layouts, may get the book done weeks earlier or may keep the staff within budget.

YOUR BEAT

1. Imagine students looking at their yearbooks for the first time (or recall the scene, if you've experienced it). What will the students say first? What will the males say? The females? What will the athletes say? What will the freshmen say? What will the members of the speech team say? What will the teachers say? Why will each group say something different?

2. Ask each member of the class to write down at least 10 things he or she remembers about last year at your school that should be recorded in the yearbook. Compare your lists. What are the similarities? What things appear on everyone's lists? On only a few lists? Make a composite list on the board so everyone can see all the items. (Keep a copy of this list for planning the ladder.) Why are the lists different? Would other classes write down the same events you did? Ask a few teachers if you can use five minutes of their class time to have students from different age and interest areas write lists of the top 10 things each remembers about last year's book. Compare these lists to your master list. Add things you have missed.

3. Brainstorm to come up with a theme for your yearbook. Begin by having each student write down the name of one music group that represents the whole school. List the groups on the board, and have each student explain the reason for his or her choice. Continue the discussion until you have a consensus on one group you believe is representative of the school as a whole. Try the same thing with food, colors and animals. Now that you have the idea of choosing *one* noun from a category best representing your school, try it with action words and phrases. Is your school *energetic? New and improved? On a roll? Breaking away from the crowd?* Have each student write three words or phrases that describe the school. Discuss how each one might fit the year. Select two or three you think might work. Use them to do Item 4.

4. Design logos to represent the themes you chose in Item 3. Add colors that go with each theme. Sketch a cover using the theme, logo and colors you like best.

5. Divide the class into groups of four or five. Give each group a ladder, and ask it to plan the yearbook using the list of contents from Item 2 and one of the themes chosen in Item 3 (or the theme for this year's book, if you have one). Compare ladders. What are the differences? Combine the ladders to create one that the class agrees works best with the theme. (Don't forget to allow for advertising and index sections, division pages, and opening and closing sections.)

UNITED STATES, 1972— Sony introduced the videocassette recorder (VCR) for educational and business uses in 1972, followed by a version for home use in 1975. The first home VCRs sold for $1300.

Sales boomed over the next decade while prices dropped to one-third the introductory cost. By 1988, about half of all American homes had VCRs, and basic models were selling for $300.

Television viewing habits changed as people recorded programs and duplicated tapes for their own use. As viewers experimented with "time shifting"—recording programs and viewing them at a later time— Hollywood realized it had a new market for movies. Video rental became the hottest new business in town.

Some businesses, such as HBO and other premium cable television services, saw declines as the VCR craze caught on. Inexpensive movie rentals and reasonable purchase prices for tapes of timely releases changed viewers' television-watching habits.

The VCR changed school media production, too. In the 1980s, many schools experimented with video yearbooks. Special events such as proms and graduations also were preserved in video packages.

By 1994, 94 million American homes had one or more television sets, and 74 million of those homes had at least one VCR.

◀ TELLING THE STORY IN A YEARBOOK

Writing yearbook copy is very much like writing feature stories for other publications, except the writer must wrap up all the important points about a whole season or an entire year in a few paragraphs. The writer must get the reader's attention, tell the story with facts and numbers, and use quotations to show the human element in each piece of copy.

Writing the Lead

Five words.

That's all you get, say the experts, to hook readers and interest them in reading a yearbook story.

Which of these leads would get you to read on? Why?

+ Another year of school brought many . . .
+ Number 1.
+ During the long, hot day of a track meet . . .
+ To those who were not interested . . .
+ There is an old saying that . . .
+ The schedule was from 8:20 a.m. to 3:26 p.m.
+ "Can you feel it?"
+ Leadership is the key to success.
+ "New hallway, No skipping" read the sign . . .
+ There once was a time when students . . .
+ A second consecutive berth in the championship tournament . . .
+ "Live from HHS" sparked crimson pride . . .
+ Dinosaurs, sandblasted millstones and neon lights . . .
+ Beginning the season with no seniors . . .
+ Despite the 5–7 season record . . .

Like news and feature story leads, yearbook leads are more reader-friendly if they contain high-interest words. "Number 1" and "Dinosaurs" are the top vote getters in this list. Leads that begin with *there, the, to* and *during* are at the top of the list of boring leads.

News Features with Style

Yearbook stories are basically news feature stories. Their job is to capture the essence of the year, season or event in a few paragraphs and include all the important facts readers will want to remember in 10, 20 or even 40 years. How do you write copy that will turn today's vote, party or game into those picture memories?

Use the "chill factor." Adviser Carole Wall says the copy should literally give readers chills all over. She suggests measuring the relative chill factor of each copy block by sight-and-sound writing, status details and specific details.

Sight-and-sound writing takes readers into the locker room, onto the bus, backstage at the rehearsal or cast party, or into the journalism room when the yearbook pages are being created. It describes the scene with specific details that help readers see the big picture. "Don't write about journalism students working hard on nights before a deadline. Tell me about the night Don Schmidt had 24 pages lined out on a table and accidentally spilled a bottle of India ink over all the pages," Wall said.

Status details are the difference between generic soda and Perrier. They are tools that make the distinction between blah and the United Colors of Benneton. For instance, you might write, "A new student came to class today wearing jeans, a T-shirt and a chain at his neck, and he was blond." Maybe that new student was wearing Levi 501s, a clean white T-shirt tucked into the jeans and a fine gold chain. His short, platinum blond hair was styled precisely. Or maybe that new student was wearing a black Harley-Davidson T-shirt over frayed plain-pocket jeans, as well as two or three heavy chains, including one with dog tags. His shoulder-length hair was blond at the roots but was obviously growing out from having been dyed black. Very different personalities can be revealed through status details.

Another way to take readers to the scene is to use the names of songs, movie titles, personalities and current events. Sidebars with Top 10 lists of the year's most popular movies, favorite actors and actresses, or most-listened-to CDs at your school can be created from student surveys.

Whether it's the lead, the status details or using *said* instead of descriptive verbs like *exclaimed* or *shouted* to show the way in which someone speaks, all the same guidelines that apply to news and feature writing apply to yearbook writing. The following guidelines also apply to yearbooks:

- Leads should not begin with a person's name or the name of the school. Also avoid beginning with "The goals of," "The purpose of," "This year" or a date.
- It is redundant to use both *this year* and to give the year. The cover identifies the year, and by its description a yearbook is the story of a year—*this* year. Report about this year. Don't rehash last year or make predictions about next year.
- Avoid words that imply opinion, such as *diligently, dedicated* or *hardworking*. Instead, show what makes a person or team dedicated (for example, "Practicing six hours a day for six weeks . . ."). Don't let subjective adjectives and adverbs sneak in. *A beautiful pass"* would be more objective as *a 75-yard touchdown pass*. "It was an awesome concert" could read "*Complete Music,* a five-piece band from New Meadows, played . . ."
- Weed out weasel words, such as *many, various, wide variety, numerous, some, a lot,* and *few.* Instead of "Many attended the musical," say "Over 400 attended the musical."
- Never use the name of the school or the school mascot to refer to students—for example, "The Vikings ate in a new cafeteria." Students know their yearbook is about their school. The name of the school, its initials or mas-

Leaving a Mark, Seven Times Over

Carol Jong wanted to leave an indelible mark on the University of Kansas. She did so, seven times.

The university's 1990 yearbook features photos of Jong in seven different looks—and in seven different places under seven different names.

There is Buffi J. Baker in business, Bertha Heffer in engineering and Violet Couleur in fine arts. Jong can also be found posing as Anne U. Rissom in allied health and Dorrie N. Collum in architecture, not to mention her own Carol Jong picture in liberal arts.

Jong's roommate tried to join in the prank by submitting fake photos, but all her fakes were caught and rejected by the *Jayhawker* staff.

"We wanted to leave our mark at KU," said Jong. "Since we're not athletes or student presidents or anything, we wanted to be remembered for something special."

The yearbook staff was not amused.

"It's a great joke as far as she's concerned," said Jeannine Kreker, assistant editor. "But as far as Kansas alumni and everybody who's going to look at this book years from now is concerned, it makes us and the university look pretty silly."

FUNKY WINKERBEAN reprinted by permission of United Feature Syndicate.

cot should be reserved for writing about competitive situations such as sports.

◆ Use quotations that have meaning. Don't quote anyone who says, "I had a lot of fun." The quotation is short and doesn't give the reader any specific information. Ask the source for a definition of fun, and you'll get quotations that have meaning, such as, "It was fun when the senior men wore the cheerleaders' uniforms and led the cheer at the pep rally."

Figure 18.3 gives a checklist to help you evaluate your writing.

Remember, the yearbook story is the only historical record most people will ever have about this year at this school. People want to pick up their yearbooks in two or three decades and have the pictures and words take them right back to the scene. To make your writing do that, be accurate. Check the office list against another list to verify the spelling of names. Recheck every story and caption to be sure that it includes the names, dates, details and facts about each event or organization.

FIGURE 18.3
CHECKLIST FOR GOOD
WRITING

◆ Use plain words, not fancy ones. Always use the familiar word.
◆ Use mainly short words.
◆ Use descriptive adjectives, never editorial ones.
◆ Use simple sentences. Avoid compound and complex sentences.
◆ Use mainly short sentences, but vary the length.
◆ Paragraph frequently.
◆ Use the active voice.
◆ Delete all unnecessary words, sentences and paragraphs.
◆ Write clearly.
◆ Write to express, never to impress.
◆ Read copy aloud. Revise, rewrite. Read again and revise.
◆ Be satisfied only when you like what you have written.

Source: Reprinted with permission from Scholastic Yearbook Fundamentals, *2nd edition,* Columbia Scholastic Press Association, New York, NY, p. 44.

1. Write a description of the average student at your school using status details. Now add a sight-and-sound setting that students would remember, and work your "average student" into the scene.

2. Write the first paragraph for the opening copy for the theme you chose earlier in the chapter. Look at the first five words. Are they interesting, attention getting words? Do they make you want to read more?

3. Rewrite the following sentences to make more effective yearbook copy. (You may add names and facts.)

    a. Taking science classes proved to be a great way to gain knowledge about many different areas of nature.

    b. Between attending classes, participating in organizations and holding down part-time jobs, students still found time to enjoy the various events that occurred this year.

    c. The music groups kept the music department alive with activity over the year.

    d. Many individuals contributed a lot to the team standings.

    e. The 1999–2000 FBLA membership was larger than ever.

    f. Despite the 7–12 season record with nine of the 12 losses by one or two runs, the men's baseball team had an impressive year.

Why a Magazine?

Imagine that your high school journalism career has taken off like a shooting star. As a sophomore you became a prize-winning reporter for both news and sports. As a junior you were named editor of the paper, the youngest person to reach that spot in school history. Then your senior year arrives. You've already climbed the peaks. Now what?

If you're Brad Bernthal at East High School in Lincoln, Nebraska, you start something new. Brad thought a video yearbook might be a good idea, but on further reflection he realized his love of writing was his strongest motivation. So Brad decided to start a magazine.

"It would fill a void," Brad said at the time. The school newspaper was straightforward and objective, with little room for lengthy features or offbeat stories. The school literary magazine was mostly poems and short stories.

What Brad had in mind was something with a wide-open format—a magazine that could cover any kind of topic students might find interesting. What would set the magazine apart was its approach. "We write everything from our own perspective," he said. "It's very creative."

A **magazine** is usually a glossy-covered collection of articles, stories, pictures and artwork that may come out monthly, quarterly, once a semester or even once a year. The magazine is actually no stranger to the high school scene. In fact, in some schools the magazine predates the yearbook and newspaper. These magazines have strong ties to traditional journalism, but they often showcase new ventures into uncharted water.

magazine
a collection of articles, stories, pictures and artwork that is published on a regular basis

Although literary arts magazines are still the most popular type of student magazine, many others share the spotlight. Students have learned to take advantage of the magazine's longer production deadlines to develop coverage of specialized interest areas. Humor, general interest and news feature magazines are becoming increasingly popular as student publications.

Creating a New Publication

Together with a small core group of students, Brad began planning how the magazine might come into being. He needed to find enough students to fill a class, a teacher willing (or crazy enough) to serve as adviser, and administrative support to make the whole operation (including finances) work. Despite such obstacles, after about nine months of nurturing and plenty of hard labor, the first issue of *Muse,* a humor/general interest magazine, rolled off the press.

Describing the magazine as "the offspring of many fathers and mothers," Brad said the students decided not to have a single editor. Instead, the magazine used an editorial board to select the stories and articles that showed the most promise. Everybody on the staff did both writing and editing.

Muse contains 32 pages each month packaged inside a slick cover. About one-fourth of the content is given over to departments, which include the "Muse Mailroom" (letters), "A&E," (music reviews), "Movie Madness" (cinema reviews) and "College Watch" (a regular column featuring first-hand campus visits and tips on how to write application essays). The remainder of the magazine is devoted to the cover story, six or seven feature articles, a photo essay, an art page and several ads.

BYLINE

DAVID WALTERS
ART DIRECTOR, *PREMIERE*

When you open a magazine, you look first for those quick little things you can read in several minutes. You have to pull the reader into the magazine. We have a section in the front called 'Short Takes.' It's a four-page department with lots of short items. Each page maybe has three to five short pieces.

And you've got other departments in the front that pull you into the magazine. You don't want to open a magazine and jump right into a 5,000 word piece. After you bring the readers in with the cover, you have short pieces and build up into the long pieces.

Another consideration is that departments should be roughly in the same place from issue to issue. You don't want to have some section of the magazine on page 7 one month, page 47 the next month, and 97 the next month. Each week, I open *New York* magazine to the same place and quickly read through to see what's in this section, called 'Intelligencer.' 'Short Takes' is always somewhere around page 20 in *Premiere*. And the same with the other departments. These are anchors for the reader.

Source: Adapted from "Tete-á-Tete," by Carolina Lightcap, Student Press Review.

The first issue contained an interview with one of the school cooks on political turmoil in Eastern Europe. It became the first of many quirky interviews: a school secretary gave her views on nuclear disarmament, a department store Santa revealed his position on safe sex and so on. The first issue also included an in-depth report on class scheduling; a sports profile; and a few humorous pieces, such as a proposal to build a 20-minute nap into the school day.

The cover story was a team project involving a group of eight reporters who took turns shadowing a student volunteer from the time she woke at 7:02 a.m. to the moment her head finally hit the pillow that night at 11:07 p.m. They tried to find out, as one writer put it, "what goes on in the life of a normal, flag-waving, non-communist teen-age prototype." The nine-page article also included interviews with the student's parents and her boyfriend.

A Magazine for Your School

Perhaps your school already has a magazine, or you may wish to start one. You could take the *Muse's* motto to heart: "Do not follow where the path may lead. Go, instead, where there is no path and leave a trail." In any event, a magazine offers a more freewheeling and inventive format than perhaps any other kind of publication.

Magazines are generally written in a feature style with less timely news and a greater emphasis on people and personalities. This format often fits the needs of school publications with their two- to four-week production schedules much better than does the breaking news style of newspapers. The magazine format also allows more room for photos and the use of graphics to illustrate articles. Some schools have found that magazines are easier to produce in page form on small computer screens than are broadsheet newspapers.

Some schools have changed the format of their newspapers to a magazine style to help overcome the problem of long time lapses between issues. Although the school may produce fewer issues of a news magazine than it did of a newspaper, those issues may have many more pages. This helps a staff that needs more time to plan and produce each issue. It also gives readers what they want to read in the school publication—stories about people and more features on issues like AIDS and relationships—and fewer stories that have grown cold between issues.

Some schools are even producing their yearbooks in a magazine-style format. Typically, three or four installments are printed during the year. The yearbook staff then passes out a special binder with the last installment to hold everything together. The formality of a hardcover yearbook has given way to the more casual design and feel of a magazine.

Often, students who work on a magazine feel a strong sense of ownership. The students who produced the *Muse,* for example, felt they were breaking new ground with each issue. That spirit can sometimes lead to trouble, as it did with a "swimsuit issue" that began as an effort to spoof the late winter swimsuit specials but ended up offending some who didn't get the joke.

Reader's Digest Heads the List

When it comes to magazines, there are more to read than ever. About 7,000 different magazines were published 40 years ago. Today, the number is approaching 22,000.

In terms of sheer circulation, *Reader's Digest* is the largest popular magazine in the country, with over 17 million issues sold. *TV Guide* is second. Other familiar magazines on the Top 10 list include *National Geographic, Better Homes & Gardens* and *Family Circle. Sports Illustrated* ranked 23rd on one recent list.

The combined circulation of all the magazines in the United States is more than 365 million.

"We take a little bit of an off-center look at things," said staff writer Ted Genoways. Another writer, Jodi Ash, added, "There aren't many ways we can publish our kind of writing. *Muse* gives me an opportunity to do what I do best."

In any event, working on magazines is usually fun and exciting. As another *Muse* writer, Jennifer Wyatt, put it, "I love it when I can write something that makes people laugh. Anything you can do to make people enjoy being alive is worth striving for."

Does your school have a forum where student writers, designers and artists can stretch their imaginations and creativity? If not, can you imagine what that forum might look like?

Magazine Concepts

From *Traveler* to Vogue, *Premiere* to *Bon Appetit*, and *People* to *Soap Opera Update*, the nation's approximately 22,000 magazines reflect the astonishing variety and diversity of American life. You may be familiar with the major magazines that specialize in news (*Time, Newsweek* and *U.S. News and World Report*), sports (*Sports Illustrated* and *Sport*) and fashion (*Glamour, Mademoiselle* and *Seventeen,* to name just a few). However, you might be surprised to know just how wide-ranging the world of magazines is.

Virtually every hobby and interest has its own magazine, and often not just one. Think about the last time you stopped by a doctor's or dentist's office. How many different magazines could be found in the waiting room? Newsstands and book stores are other places where you can begin to sample the enormous range of magazines published every week. In fact, publishers start nearly 500 new magazines each year, though, of course, most of them don't survive.

Choosing a Format.   Different magazine formats serve the needs of different readers. Three of the most common kinds of magazines found in high schools today are the literary magazine, the general interest magazine and the special interest magazine. If you decide to start a magazine at your school, you will probably want to choose from one of these categories.

literary magazine
a magazine that publishes short stories, poetry, essays and art

creative arts magazine
a magazine that includes prose and poetry, as well as feature stories, editorials, art reviews and student surveys

general interest magazine
a magazine that includes a wide variety of articles and attempts to interest almost everyone

- **Literary magazines** publish short stories, poetry and essays. These magazines often include art in various media, such as pen-and-ink illustrations and photography. Sometimes schools publish a hybrid called a **creative arts magazine.** This format includes the traditional prose and poetry but adds lively feature stories, serious editorials, arts reviews and student surveys.
- **General interest magazines** have perhaps the broadest appeal. Such magazines usually feature a wide variety of articles in the hope of printing something of interest to everyone. *People,* one of the country's most popular magazines, carves out a broad niche in the publishing scene by claiming anyone and everyone for its subjects.

❖ **Special interest magazines** target people with a strong interest in one particular area. On the national level, for example, *Essence* features the success stories of African Americans, as well as health and beauty advice. *Model Railroading* suits those who like to work with model trains. In a school, the athletic department may publish a monthly magazine devoted to sports.

special interest magazine

a magazine that targets people with a strong interest in a particular topic

One other type of magazine may be circulating through your school as an "underground" publication. **Zines**—short for *magazines* or *fanzines* (made popular by the fans of certain punk music groups)— have proliferated as desktop publishing and photocopy machines have become available to more and more people. (*Zines* is pronounced *Zeens.*) Photocopied and often distributed hand-to-hand, the little magazines may nurture many creative ideas and design innovations. They also may contain self-indulgent rantings and ravings.

zine

a small magazine with a limited circulation that is published by a few people, often using desktop publishing programs and photocopiers; short for *magazine* or *fanzine*

Some zines are the handiwork of a single person. Others gather submissions from a wide range of guest contributors. Some are well designed using computers. Some are crude cut-and-paste efforts. Most zines come out haphazardly, as their production fits the whims, time and fiscal resources of their creators. "It's just hard for people to put them out every month," explains Garth Johnson, who runs a small record store that sells zines on the side. "Whenever people have a chunk of time or are bored or are at the copy shop, another issue comes out."

With top prices around $3, zines are cheap. Most people who produce zines are in high school or college. But there are a few older writers as well, such as the creators of *bOING bOING.* Carla Sinclair and her husband, Mark Frauenfelder, began their zine when they pasted some of their thoughts on layout boards, made photocopies, stapled the pages together and then watched the issues sell out at $2.95. The name *bOING bOING,* says Sinclair, was meant "to sound energetic and childlike."

Since that debut, the zine has added a slick cover and now has a circulation of about 17,000. Sinclair should be happy with the growth. Instead, as the only full-time employee, she sounds a bit frazzled. "It used to be fun to earn $10 a year from this thing. Now it takes all day to fill subscriptions, sell ads, market the magazine and take care of our mail orders. I don't have time to be creative anymore." Despite the zine's success, Sinclair says any further expansion might cramp her style. "The greatest part of what I do is that I can write about anything I want and nobody can tell me not to. Doing a zine really spoils you."

Soliciting Material. Let's imagine that you are a staff member of a new magazine at your school. One of your greatest challenges—a challenge perhaps even tougher than choosing a concept for your magazine or establishing a theme for a particular issue—is gathering material.

When staff members set out to gather art and articles, they should explore every potential resource for contributions. They should seek cooperation from the teachers of writing classes. The English department is an obvious possibility, but so are other departments. The science, mathematics, social studies or vocational departments could be solicited for contributions. Any courses that give students the opportunity to express themselves are potential sources for the magazine.

One student editor sent an open letter to each teacher in the school asking for the submission of any work the teacher felt was worth publishing. "What is *Coyote* material?" he asked in the letter, referring to the name of the magazine. "Obviously, it's well written. Secondly, it is accessible to the general community. Most importantly, it takes a different perspective on things than is usual or may simply be about an unusual topic. It might just be unusually insightful. It does *not* have to be satiric or even faintly amusing. Our interest is to let the unique voices of our school community speak in their own ways."

You might seek material from clubs or students who work on other campus publications. You might also provide a submissions box, where students can discreetly drop off their work. You may wish to protect an individual author's identity, but you shouldn't accept anonymous work. If you accept anonymous work, you have no way to know if the author was a student or not. Periodic contests to encourage writers to contribute to the magazine can help sometimes, too.

Magazine staff members should be keenly aware of the need for variety and should be systematic about making the most of their school's potential. The staff should brainstorm ways to make the magazine represent all kinds of talent in the student community. They might ask themselves whether the magazine is a place for all kinds of voices to be heard.

1. Imagine you are going to approach a publishing company with an idea for a new magazine. What would the magazine be called? What would some of its articles be? Who would be the intended readers? Here are a few examples to get you thinking:
   ◆ *Cue* (a magazine for people interested in theater)
   ◆ *Women in Sports*
   ◆ *Adventure* (great places to visit and things to do)
   ◆ *Movement* (the world of dance)
   ◆ *The Love Connection* (advice for singles)
   ◆ *Elite Eating* (the magazine for the modern chef)

2. Give an oral report on your favorite magazine. Plan to cover these topics:
   ◆ An analysis of its primary purpose and target audience
   ◆ A brief discussion of its history
   ◆ Some of the competitors in its particular niche. (*Writers' Market*, a resource published annually that describes virtually every magazine and journal published in the United States, gives this information)
   ◆ Any trends you can spot by looking back over the past year's issues
   ◆ What a young writer or designer can learn from this magazine.

3. Test your knowledge of the magazine market. Work in small groups, and see which group can think of the most magazine titles. List as many magazines as you can under each of the following categories:
   ◆ News magazine
   ◆ Consumer magazine
   ◆ Literary and creative arts
   ◆ Business magazine
   ◆ Men's magazine
   ◆ Women's magazine
   ◆ Technical magazine
   ◆ Medical magazine
   ◆ Special interest magazine

YEARBOOK AND MAGAZINE LAYOUT

Visual appeal is a crucial element in the success of both yearbooks and magazines. Making these publications visually appealing is the job of the designer or layout artist. In Chapter 15 we covered the terminology and fundamentals of design. In this section we'll look at the special opportunities designers have with yearbook and magazine layouts. Perhaps nowhere else in the world of school publications is there so much room for creativity.

Yearbook and magazine layouts are very similar, so we'll consider them together. For the most part, we'll refer to layouts as if we were designing a yearbook. Remember, however, that the same ideas apply to magazines. When special considerations apply to magazines only, we'll say so.

Mosaic Style

Most yearbook layouts are based on the **mosaic concept of design.** Basically, elements are arranged in a pinwheel fashion, clustered around a central focal point. What makes the design work is consistent internal margins, or spaces between elements. Each element should be the same distance—usually one or two picas—from all adjoining elements. The result is an organized and attractive page design. We will lead you through a five-step process for creating good mosaic layouts. First, though, you have some planning to do.

Before You Start. Design your magazine or yearbook two pages at a time. That is, think and plan in terms of facing pages. As we said earlier in the chapter, facing pages are referred to as a *double-page spread.* Readers usually see two pages at a time. It's almost impossible to bend a yearbook cover back upon itself, as you might with a comic book. Furthermore, two-page designs (spreads) give you twice as much room to create exciting and interesting layouts. By concentrating your design efforts on spreads, you also avoid producing pages that fight each other when placed side-by-side.

Another important consideration before you actually begin drawing a layout is to choose the number of **columns** your pages will contain. A column is the standard width you have chosen for your stories. Columns help provide order and control in your layout. They do not limit your creativity, despite what you might suppose. Almost all yearbooks and magazines use some form of column design on the next page. (See Figure 18.4.)

Once you've gained a little experience drawing layouts, you will find that there are many variations on a basic six- or eight-column format, including a strange beast called a plus column. Some layout methods even use as many as 11 columns across a single spread. You'll learn more about these strategies later in this section.

mosaic concept of design
a design concept in which all elements are arranged in a pinwheel fashion, clustered around a central focal point

column
the basis for constructing a page layout. A column is the standard width for copy chosen for a particular yearbook section or magazine

FIGURE 18.4
TYPICAL COLUMN DESIGNS

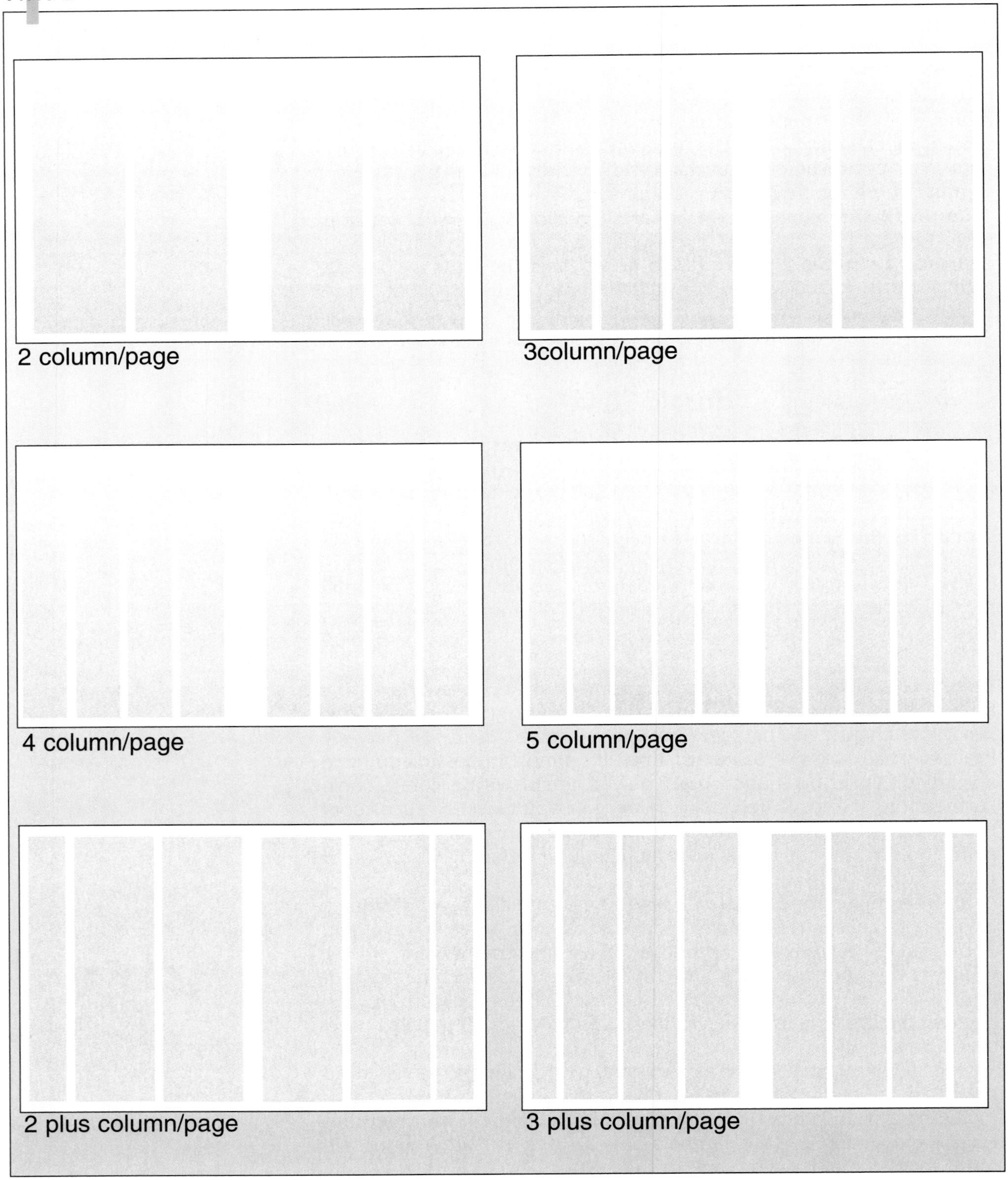

2 column/page

3column/page

4 column/page

5 column/page

2 plus column/page

3 plus column/page

You may want to gather all your materials together before you start, although you can certainly practice creating layouts with imaginary pictures and stories. The essential **elements of a spread** are

+ photos
+ a headline
+ body copy
+ cutlines and planned white space

When you have chosen the number of columns you'll use—six is a smart choice for basic layouts—gathered your materials together, and obtained a layout dummy sheet, you're ready to begin designing. The following is a five-step guide to creating good mosaic-style layouts.

Step 1: Start with a dominant photo.
Every layout should contain one photo that is at least twice as big as any other picture on the spread. A dominant photo gives the reader's eye a place to begin when looking at a page. It should be the best picture you have available for that spread—one with excellent content, sharp focus and good contrast.

The dominant photo should be tightly cropped and full of action or emotion. Generally, it should include students. Photos of pretty scenery and school buildings without people don't make good dominants. As a general rule, place the dominant photo so it touches or crosses the gutter (the gap in the middle of the book or magazine between two facing pages). Placing a picture so that it runs across the gutter is one of the simplest and most effective ways you have to unite the two facing pages. (See Figure 18.5.)

elements of a spread

things that must be included in a double-page spread, including photos, a headline, body copy, cutlines and planned white space

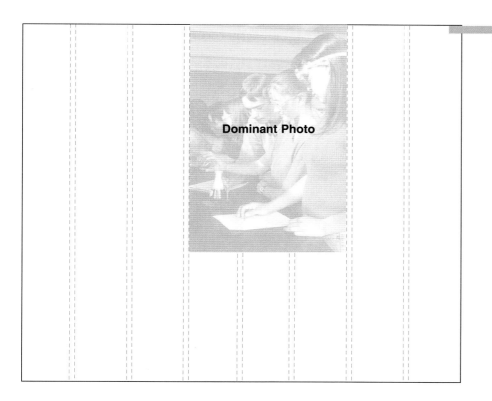

FIGURE 18.5
LAYOUT WITH ONE DOMINANT PHOTO

Dominant Photo

FIGURE 18.6
LAYOUT ESTABLISHING
EXTERNAL MARGINS

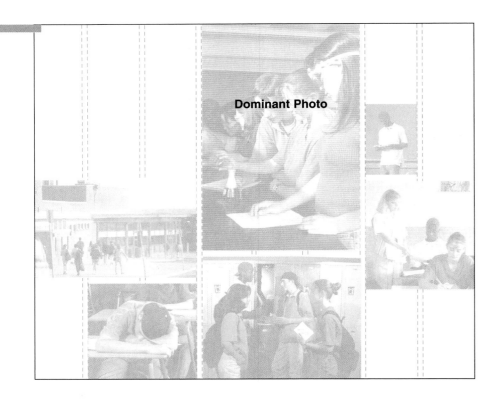

Dominant Photo

Step 2: Add other pictures, keeping consistent internal margins.
An internal margin, as we said earlier, is the space between elements (pictures, copy or graphics). The recommended spacing between each element is one pica or two picas. All the elements on the spread should be separated by the same amount of space.

Try to use a variety of picture sizes and shapes, with no two exactly alike. Mix verticals, horizontals, small pictures and large pictures. Make sure, though, that none of them is more than half as large as the dominant photo. Use only rectangular shapes. Don't use circles, ovals, stars or other unusual shapes. These shapes prevent a designer from maintaining consistent internal margins and often call too much attention to themselves.

Add these pictures one by one, working out from the center. Maintain a balance across the spread as you go. To establish the **external margin,** which is the frame around the spread, at least one element on each side of the layout must touch the outside margin. (See Figure 18.6.)

external margin

the frame around the spread

Step 3: Don't fill the spread completely; leave white space to the outside.   Every spread needs room for copy and captions. As you add pictures, think about where these elements will fall. Be sure to leave room for a caption above, next to or underneath every picture on the spread. You may group two or three captions together, but each caption

should still be either above, below or adjacent to the picture it describes. Don't allow any pictures to fall into the external margin unless they bleed off the page. To **bleed** a picture means to run it off the edge of the page. Bleed no more than one picture off the side, top or bottom of the spread. Avoid bleeding small pictures. (See Figure 18.7.)

bleed

to run a picture off the edge of the page

Step 4: Create a horizontal eyeline.

At this point, you can take a deep breath and then begin to revise your layout. Adjust your pictures to create an **eyeline**—an imaginary line running straight across the double-page spread. The eyeline is created by aligning the tops and bottoms of several pictures or of the copy blocks. Never draw the eyeline in the exact center of the spread (see the example in Figure 18.7). The dominant photo either establishes the eyeline or, for the sake of variety, breaks it.

Many yearbook companies number the pica lines on their dummy pages to make it easier to create the eyeline. A horizontal eyeline is an excellent way of uniting two facing pages, as is a dominant photo bleeding across the gutter. The use of these two techniques together is especially powerful. (See Figure 18.8 on the next page.)

eyeline

an imaginary line running straight across the double-page spread

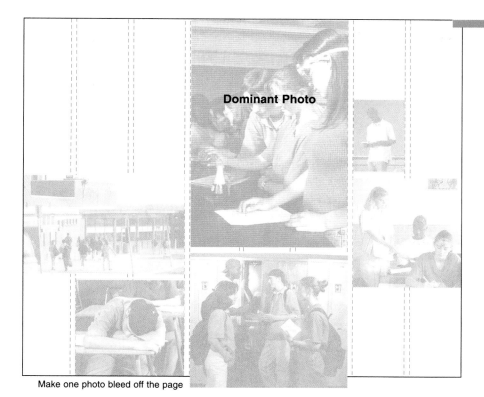

Dominant Photo

Make one photo bleed off the page

FIGURE 18.7
LAYOUT WITH BLEED PHOTO

FIGURE **18.8**
HOW TO CREATE AN EYELINE

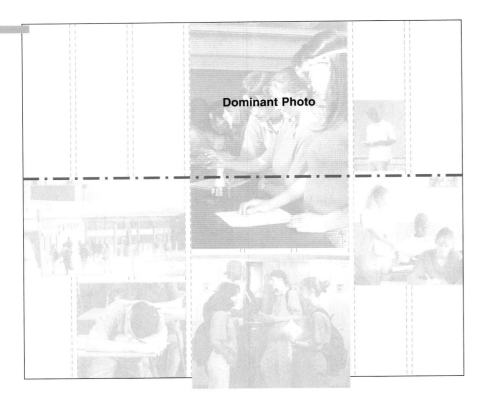

Dominant Photo

Step 5: Add copy last; keep all copy to the outside of the pictures. Use your column format to place the copy. Make sure that stories, headlines and captions span the width of one, two, three or four columns. Don't let any copy fall into the exterior margin or into the gutter. Place the copy to the outside of the pictures to focus the reader's attention squarely on the design rather than on trapped white space. (White space will be discussed in more detail later in the chapter. See Figure 18.9.)

A Few Additional Tips

+ Secondary layout elements include rule lines, tints and other graphic devices. Use these elements to help unify the spread by grouping several related elements together. Any other use is simply decoration. Make everything on your layout serve a purpose.
+ Keep column widths consistent for both copy and cutlines. The column layout method will help you accomplish this. Unless you have a special reason to do otherwise, set all copy in your magazine or in one yearbook section at a standard width. The number of columns used per spread may vary from section to section of a yearbook. However, the number should be consistent within each section.
+ Never let headlines run across the gutter. Words can get trapped in the crease, and word spacing is nearly always distorted.

Specialty Magazines

If *Cat Fancy* strikes yours, join the club. The United States leads the world in the production of special interest magazines, such as *Cat Fancy, Tattoo* and *Minitruckin.'*

The best source for locating odd or esoteric publications is the *Guide to New Magazines*, a catalog published annually by Samir Husni, a University of Mississippi journalism professor who scours newsstands in search of new titles.

A recent edition of the guide listed 584 new magazines, including *Basket Bits, Nanny Times, Scale Jets, Musky Hunter* and *Sheet Metal* (for heavy metal fans, not contractors). Some published only one issue, and some died right away.

For example, *Lottery! The Magazine for the Winning Lifestyle* faded away quickly.

Many of the more successful magazines, however, have found a unique niche in the market. This group includes *Nude & Natural,* the official magazine of the Naturist Society.

Among recent start-ups were: *Barbie Bazaar,* for adult Barbie doll collectors, and *Foxyriders,* for women who ride Harley-Davidsons.

Headline goes here

Dominant Photo

FIGURE 18.9

PLACING COPY OUTSIDE OF PICTURES

The Fine Points of Layout

Modifying the basic mosaic design, varying the number of columns, bleeding photos off a page and managing white space are all ways you can make your publications look distinctive. Remember that rules are made to be broken—if you know what you are doing.

Modifying the Mosaic Design.   You can choose any number of variations on the basic mosaic style to give each section of your yearbook its own look. We mention just a few possibilities here. (See Figure 18.10.)

- **Mondrian.** The Mondrian style (named after modernist painter Piet Mondrian) is becoming increasingly popular. To create this style, the designer draws one horizontal and one vertical line on the spread. The lines must intersect somewhere, but not in the center of the spread. The designer has now divided the layout into four separate areas. Next, a large design element is placed in the largest quadrant, and other, smaller elements are placed in the remaining three quadrants. The two crossed lines then become part of the internal margins. The Mondrian layout style holds the spread together particularly well, thanks to the creation of two eyelines.

- **Isolated element.** This style is achieved by specifically isolating one or two design elements (by surrounding them with white space) to clearly establish emphasis. This layout style is especially effective for division pages, where the designer may wish to highlight one outstanding picture by itself.

- **Modular.** A modular layout style consists of one large rectangle, which may encompass the entire double-page spread. This rectangle is subdivided into many smaller elements by the use of consistent internal margins. Headlines and copy are then placed to the outside areas of the spread. Unlike a mosaic layout, with its familiar irregular outline, the modular layout fills the pages to the margin on each side.

- **Hang it from a line.** This design style is based on the placement of an imaginary horizontal line somewhere across the top portion of a spread. The designer then places all photos and art elements above or below this imaginary line. Copy is placed on the opposite side of the line from the photos. The style may be reversed simply by changing the relationship of the copy and photos. The resulting change in design can give a distinctive personality to a special section of the yearbook or magazine.

- **Skyline.** The skyline style is accomplished by starting with a large, vertical rectangle. This element, acting as the base structure, is complemented by staggered elements to give the appearance of a city skyline. The vertical nature of the elements slows the readers down, however, as they move from left to right. Therefore, this style might be used best in mini-mags or other special pages.

DATELINE DATELINE DATELINE

LONDON AND PHILADELPHIA, July 13, 1985—An estimated worldwide audience of 1.5 billion tuned in to watch the 16-hour *Live Aid* concert broadcast simultaneously from London and Philadelphia.

Performers included Paul McCartney, David Bowie, Madonna, Tina Turner and Joan Baez. The broadcast featured film of concerts given in countries around the world and the first televised performance by a Russian rock group.

The unprecedented music marathon was broadcast to more than 80 countries simultaneously using the largest intercontinental satellite hookup that had ever been attempted up to that time.

The *Live Aid* campaign raised pledges of over $70 million for African famine relief.

FIGURE 18.10
YEARBOOK LAYOUT STYLES

Mondrian

The Mondrian style (sometimes referred to as local point) is becoming increasingly popular. First, the designer places intersecting horizontal and vertical lines anywhere on the spread, except the center. A large design element is placed in the largest quadrant, and other smaller elements are placed in the remaining three quadrants. The two crossed lines then become part of the internal margins. This layout style is particularly effective in opening and division spreads.

Isolated element

One style of layout is called "isolated element." This style is achieved by specifically isolating two or three design elements (photos, copy, or artwork) to clearly establish our desired editorial emphasis. This layout style is especially effective for division pages.

Modular

Modular layout styles consist of one large rectangle which may encompass the entire double page spread. This "large" element is then subdivided into many "smaller" elements by using a consistent internal margin. Headlines and copy are then placed to the outside.

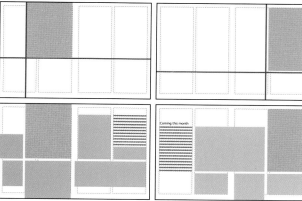
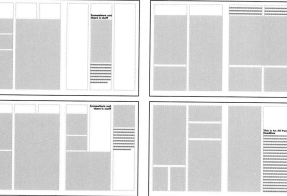

Hanging it from a line

Hanging it from a line is a design style which is based on an imaginary horizontal line being placed across the double page spread. The designer places all photos and art elements to either the top or bottom of this imaginary line, and copy is placed to the alternate side.

This may be reversed as shown by changing the copy/photo relationship. The resulting change in design is best utilized in defining different editorial sections of the book.

Dominant photo

This layout style is created by spacing one very large element anywhere on the double page spread. Smaller, less dramatic elements are then placed adjacent to the pages visually supporting the dominance of the design element.

Skyline

Similar to the dominant photo, skyline style is accomplished by starting with a large vertical rectangle. This element acting as the base structure is complemented by staggered elements giving the appearance of a city skyline. The vertical nature of the elements tend to slow the reader in this visual progression from left to right.

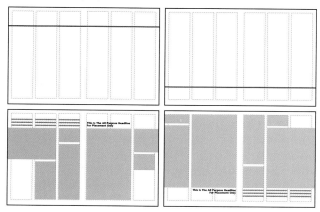
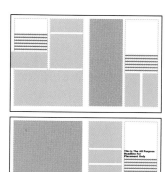
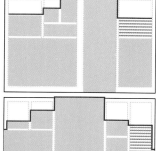

Varying the Number of Columns.   No one can say that one specific number of columns is best for all design purposes, but experience provides a few guidelines. Most designers prefer using an odd number of columns per page (usually three or five). That pattern makes it less likely that the design will be symmetrical or, in other words, have perfect balance.

If you decide to use an even number of columns (usually two or four), you can still use a clever modification to ensure a nonsymmetrical design. Try a 2 plus column approach. The idea is to divide the page into two and a half columns. Most designers use the extra column for pulled quotations, mug shots or interesting infographics. You can also use the plus column (the half column) to create an interesting shape for a photo. The photo could be one and a half or two and a half columns wide, providing that it extends into the plus column. A 4 plus column approach also works well.

Bleeding Photos.   Art school students are often told to "work to your image area." This is good advice for yearbook and magazine designers as well. Allow your creativity to stretch beyond the traditional one-inch margins that surround most published work. A photograph that slides provocatively off a page can have a dramatic effect and capture the reader's attention. But beware. As with all aspects of design, the key word with bleeds is *restraint*. A steady diet of bleeds across the gutter can become just as monotonous as no bleeds at all.

Bleeds help unify spreads and move the reader from page to page. In addition to photos, you can bleed graphics, too. A rule running across the gutter between two pages is another example of a unifying bleed. As illustrated in Figure 18.11, this can be a simple and beautiful device for creating the illusion of one page from two—if, that is, your printer and binder do a good job. If the book or magazine is not printed and bound properly, those bleeding rules will pass each other like two ships in the night.

You may turn to your computer to create a bleed. QuarkXPress, Letraset's DesignStudio and Aldus PageMaker all handle bleeds with ease. These programs include a pasteboard that allows you to position elements beyond the edges of the page. Thus, creating a bleed in these programs is as simple as extending your artwork one-eighth of an inch over the edge of the page.

Once your document is laid out, it's time to proof your work. Unfortunately, most laser printers can print only to within a quarter-inch of the paper's edge. This means that your bleeds won't print if you're trying to print a yearbook-size page on a standard 8½-by-11-inch piece of paper. One way to get around this problem is to use the page layout program's Scale option to print a reduced version of the page. In our experience, 65 percent works well. You can also select "Reduce to Fit" in some programs.

Managing White Space.   Use white space to make design elements stand out. White space provides a background that emphasizes whatever it surrounds. You can strengthen your message by using white space to focus the reader's attention on your words and ideas.

The opposite of carefully plotted and planned white space is trapped white space, white space in the middle of a page. Avoid this trapped

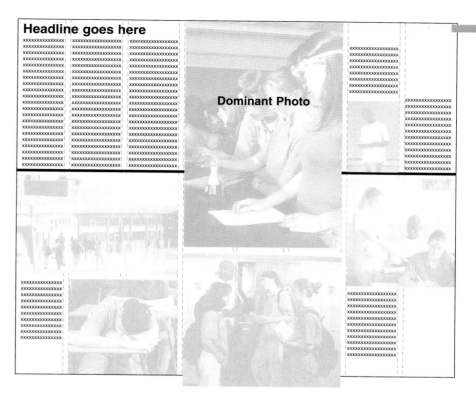

Headline goes here

Dominant Photo

FIGURE 18.11

HOW BLEEDS CAN MAKE TWO PAGES LOOK LIKE ONE

white space, as it creates unsightly holes and leads to an unfinished look.

White space also helps avoid perfectly balanced pages. Perfect balance can lead to boredom and interrupted eye movement. A moment of indecision often occurs when a reader's eyes are faced with equal-sized elements. 'What do I look at first?' the reader wonders. That's one reason a dominant photo is so important—it tells the reader where to look first as he or she turns to a spread. White space also can help create a more dynamic kind of balance (nonsymmetrical) as it creates areas of unequal size.

YOUR BEAT

● ●

1. Collect a group of five photos, and design a yearbook or magazine spread with them. You can add a headline, story (any length you like, but somewhere between five and 10 column inches) and captions to complete your design. To make the assignment more challenging, try these two ideas.

   a. Create a layout in each of these column formats: 2, 3, 4, 5 and 2 plus.

   b. Create a layout using one of these styles: Mondrian, isolated element, modular, "hang it from a line" or skyline.

2. Scan several magazines or yearbooks from other schools, if they're available. Identify a favorite and a least favorite layout. Explain your reasons to your classmates, and ask them to share their favorites with you.

CHAPTER REVIEW

KEY TERMS

Show that you know the meanings of the following key terms by correctly using them in complete sentences. Write your answers on a separate sheet of paper.

title page	signature
folio	mini-mag
table of contents	tip-in
opening section	magazine
double-page spread	literary magazine
closing section	creative arts magazine
colophon	general interest magazine
people pages	special interest magazine
mug pages	zine
panel pages	mosaic concept of design
theme	column
logo	elements of a spread
end sheets	external margin
division pages	bleed
ladder	eyeline

OPEN FORUM

1. Two students at your school are killed in a car accident after a basketball game one rainy night. It was a one-car accident. The accident report said the car hydroplaned and jetted across the highway. It rolled into the opposite ditch, and both students were thrown out of the car. They were not wearing seat belts. The alcohol levels in their blood were above the legal limit. Will you recognize their deaths in the yearbook? What facts will you use in the story? Would you omit anything? Why?

2. You are the editor of the yearbook. The staff has chosen the theme "Just Who Do We Think We ARE?" As the pages are being finished, you notice that there are no pictures of the Minority Student Union or the Association of Native American Students. You question the omissions at the next staff meeting. The organizations editor says she decided to cut them and give the extra space to the spirit squad "because more people see the spirit squad in action, and they work hard to let everyone know who we are." The staff is divided on the issue. What is the issue? How would you, as editor, decide what to do?

FINDING THE FLAW

Consider the following yearbook or magazine layouts carefully. Each has a major problem. Identify it, and show how you would correct the problem.

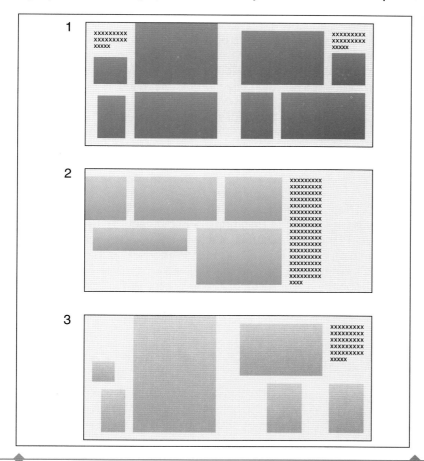

 MEDIA WATCH

1. Author Kurt Vonnegut, Jr., noted that "High school is closer to the core of the American experience than anything else I can think of." His statement is certainly true in the sense that nearly everyone—famous and nonfamous alike—passes through high school. If you really want to know the deep, dark secrets of your favorite celebrities, read their high school yearbooks.

◆ MEDIA WATCH, CONTINUED

You may find, for example, interesting pairs of classmates. Actor Robert Redford and baseball great Don Drysdale were classmates at Van Nuys High School in 1954. Golfer Arnold Palmer and "Mr." Fred Rogers of television fame were a year apart at Latrobe, Pennsylvania High School. Actors Rock Hudson and Charlton Heston were two years apart at New Trier High School in Winnetka, Illinois.

"Right now, our society is obsessed with celebrities," said Seth Poppel, the owner of more than 500 celebrity high school yearbooks. Poppel is largely responsible for the *Memories Magazine Yearbook,* a fast-selling collection of celebrities' high school graduation photos.

Poppel once paid $200 for a copy of a yearbook from Commerce High School in Commerce, Oklahoma. The yearbook contained pictures of its most famous graduate, Mickey Mantle. Poppel's prize find was Elvis Presley's yearbook from Humes High in Memphis, Tennessee. His most expensive purchase was a $4,000 copy of Lou Gehrig's yearbook. But the Holy Grail of yearbook collecting has eluded Poppel. "Babe Ruth went to high school at St. Mary's Orphanage in Baltimore," Poppel said. "He left in 1914, and I've been trying to ascertain if any yearbook was published with the graduating class." Be on the lookout—if you find the Babe's yearbook, your fortune may be made. Meanwhile, look through old yearbooks from your school to find photos of famous graduates.

String Book

To prepare for the following exercises, gather a variety of magazines to give you some raw material. Check with your journalism teacher to see if he or she has examples of yearbooks from other schools that you could borrow.

1. Select five magazine layouts that you admire. Make notes about any changes you would need to make to adapt the layouts for a school publication.
2. Clip five ads that give you ideas for yearbook themes. Highlight the words or phrases you like best. Jot down suggestions for carrying the theme throughout the book.
3. Look through yearbooks from other schools. Make a list of ideas for feature stories that you might adapt for your book.
4. From other yearbooks, copy or sketch layout ideas for theme pages and division pages, as well as for each section of your book. Note what you especially like about each layout idea and how you might change it to make it more appropriate for your book—maybe a change of typeface or a different headline treatment.

Chapter 19
Broadcast News

"We have reconstructed the Tower of Babel, and it is a television antenna."
—Ted Koppel, ABC broadcaster and host of *Nightline*

KEY TERMS

In this chapter, you will learn the meaning of these terms:

broadcast journalism
natural sound
reveal
mass media
announcer
deejay
newscaster
news package
commercial television station
public television station
syndicated programming
cable television
talent
script
pronouncer
cart
incue
outcue
total running time (TRT)
stand-up
script rundown

LEARNING OBJECTIVES

After completing this chapter, you will be able to:

◆ discuss the major differences between a news story prepared for broadcast and one written for a newspaper,

◆ explain why broadcast writing is usually informal and conversational,

◆ list the advantages radio has over other communication media,

◆ identify the crew positions needed for a typical television production,

◆ discuss the role the Federal Communications Commission plays in regulating the broadcast media,

◆ create a script for a news story in both radio and television formats.

*I*n this chapter you will learn about the unique characteristics of broadcast journalism—radio and television. Unlike print journalism (newspapers and magazines), where readers can return again and again to check facts or review a message, broadcasters have a small and fleeting window of opportunity to get their message across. Broadcast messages have a brief life. As a listener or viewer, you have one chance to catch the message, and then it's gone. The fact that broadcast news is here one second and gone the next has a great deal to do with why broadcast news takes the form it does.

HOW BROADCAST NEWS DIFFERS FROM PRINT NEWS

What if Abraham Lincoln were alive today and traveling by train from Washington, D.C., to Gettysburg to dedicate a new Civil War cemetery? What if people in the news media anticipated a major presidential address from Lincoln that would touch on issues of national importance? How would they organize their news coverage?

If the reporters worked for CNN (Cable News Network), a round-the-clock television news network, they would probably schedule a 30-minute program with live, on-the-scene reporting. They might have problems with Honest Abe, however, because the Gettysburg Address lasted only about two and a half minutes.

We can almost imagine a reporter saying to herself, "He's done already? What do we do now?" Meanwhile, an editor in a nearby command truck might be muttering, "What's that four score thing? Why doesn't he just say *87 years?*"

Thinking about how television reporters might cover the Gettysburg Address gives us a good chance to see both the strengths and weaknesses of broadcast journalism. **Broadcast journalism** is the transmission of news on television or radio. The great strength of broadcast is, of course, its immediacy—its power to give a viewer or listener the feeling that "I'm there" as news is happening. Television gives viewers the sights and motions of an event. Radio gives listeners sounds: the crack of the bat at a baseball game or the boom of an explosion.

Broadcast news segments are limited by time, not space. Many stories must be told in 30 seconds or less. That's not very long to cover a story in any detail. In fact, if you took all the words spoken during a 30-minute television news show and printed them in a newspaper, they wouldn't even cover the front page. Generally speaking, print journalism provides greater substance in its reporting. Broadcast journalism, however, often lends itself better to our fast-paced lives and short attention spans.

broadcast journalism
the transmission of news on television or radio

Writing to Pictures and Sounds

Television news broadcasting combines words and video images. In television, as one observer notes, "you can show the sunset." That means that most of the time, television news reporters write their stories to fit the pictures, a process that generally involves "underwriting." In other words, reporters don't try to describe what viewers can see for themselves but rather provide brief snippets of supplementary information. Typically, the pictures carry the story, and the words serve mainly to complement what the viewers see. "One always writes with a picture in mind," explained longtime television reporter and CBS correspondent Charles Kuralt.

Video images dominate television news. A high school broadcasting class, for example, decided to do a story on winter activities in the area. The students began with the normal interviews—talking to students who enjoyed skiing and ice skating, plus local merchants who rented or sold winter sports equipment. But one of the students thought the story wasn't exciting enough. He suggested they try a "sled cam." One of the students in the class had a toboggan, and the students made arrangements to meet at a local hill on a snowy afternoon. The student who sat in the front of the toboggan held a camcorder while the others pushed and steered. Before long, the students had enough thrilling sled cam videotape (complete with swoops and spills) to build their story. They used sound bites from the interviews to provide supporting information but made their trips down the slope the main visuals for the story.

Radio news broadcasts, like television news broadcasts, consist of more than just words. In radio news, reporters use natural sound to present a story. **Natural sound,** or *nat sound* for short, refers to the noises and voices that can be heard at the scene of a news event. Elizabeth Arnold of National Public Radio (NPR) says natural sound can be used to make a point or establish a mood. In print news, for example, you can't capture the rasp in an old man's voice when he says he doesn't want a cut in Medicare. Typically, radio news reporters work moments of natural sound into their reports every two or three sentences.

natural sound
the noises and voices that can be heard at the scene of a news event, which radio news reporters work into their reports; also called *nat sound*

CBS News anchor, Dan Rather, works in both broadcast news and print. Rather writes a weekly syndicated newspaper column.

The Dramatic Style of Broadcast Journalism

Broadcast news generally requires a little tension, a little drama, a little something extra to pull listeners or viewers in. Broadcast writers try hard to sustain the interest of the viewer or listener by creating a feeling of drama or suspense. Those who write for broadcast make an effort to find an especially dynamic verb, to avoid dense collections of facts, and especially to round off numbers so they are more listener-friendly.

Newspaper stories are top-heavy. The lead in a newspaper story gives the essentials. Then, as the story continues, the information becomes less and less important. This is because newspaper stories are designed to let readers read as much or as little as they like. Newspaper reporters don't even know where their story will end. Layout designers reserve the right to cut the bottom off a story to make it fit the space available.

In broadcast news, however, reporters try to hold a listener's interest throughout the story. That's why clever writers introduce new thoughts as the story moves along. One technique some broadcast reporters use is called a **reveal.** This technique requires the writer to hold back a key piece of information and then reveal it as the story develops. For example, a reporter might begin a broadcast news segment this way: "Maven Johnson is an airline pilot. He's been flying from Los Angeles to New York and back several days a week for the past twenty years." So far, so good, but nothing very interesting has been said. Now comes the revealing part of the story: "Johnson is blind." A typical newspaper reporter might write the same story this way: "A blind pilot has been flying the friendly skies for twenty years." That story, however, does not approach having the kind of impact or listener appeal that the broadcast version does.

A story also ends quite differently in broadcast news than in print news. "I give equal attention to the end of a story," noted Kuralt. "The way a story ends gives the thought or feeling a viewer will take away." Frequently, broadcast reporters save their most poignant piece of information for the end. No editor could afford to cut from the bottom in television or radio reporting.

The Conversational Style of Broadcast Journalism

Andy Rooney of CBS's *60 Minutes* suggests that broadcast news aims for a middle ground between how people talk and how they write.

reveal

a technique in broadcast news in which the reporter holds back a key piece of information and then reveals it as the story develops

"When we talk," Rooney says, "we repeat ourselves and beat around the bush." Those flaws can be avoided in broadcast news writing, but the sound should still be conversational. After all, on both television and radio, the announcer is still *saying* the news to an audience.

Broadcast stories must above all be clear. The viewer or listener has only one chance to grasp the meaning of a story. A newspaper reader can take five, 10 or 20 minutes to study a story, but a television or radio listener must grasp a story in as little as 30 seconds. This requires a certain simplicity in language and presentation.

In newspaper writing, reporters may use long sentences full of clauses. Consider this lead from the *Baltimore Sun,* regarding an unusual Chinese cultural custom.

> Under pressure from international animal-rights groups, the Chinese government has drafted regulations to prohibit the feeding of large mammals—such as live cows, pigs and sheep—to tigers and lions as a form of public entertainment.

That lead is more than a mouthful, especially from a broadcast perspective. The sentence is far too long and clogged with dependent clauses and participial phrases. Much of the vocabulary, too, is inappropriate for the conversational style of broadcast reporting. Words such as *drafted regulations* and *prohibited,* for example, are within most adults' reading vocabularies but are rather hard to follow in spoken conversation. A broadcast version of that story might start like this:

> Lions and tigers and bears will have to settle for pet food instead of snacking on cows and pigs if new laws in China take effect.

Clear and direct language is at the heart of effective broadcast writing. "Whenever I see 'which's,'" explains Joyce Davis of NPR, "I take them out." Davis says that besides simplifying language and shortening sentences, she tries to find a lead "as grabby as possible." You've got to hook the reader after the first five or ten seconds of the story, she says. Print journalists try to hook readers, too, but broadcast writers face a greater challenge in holding their audience's interest throughout the entire story.

DATELINE

SAN JOSE, California, 1909— The first radio station to have a regular schedule of programs was experimental station FN, owned by Charles D. "Doc" Herrold of San Jose, California.

On top of a local bank building, Herrold constructed an antenna that was so large that wires from it spread to the tops of several nearby buildings. Using a primitive microphone, he began live broadcasting in 1909 with a program of news and music every Wednesday night.

Doc built receivers and distributed them to hotel lobbies so people could hear his station. A local store placed receiving sets in a special listening room and hooked up telephone receivers so customers could listen to the music.

Herrold's wife, Sybil, may have been the first woman on radio. She hosted a music program for young people and even accepted requests for songs.

Herrold also opened a broadcasting school in 1909.

Today, station FN is San Francisco's KCBS.

YOUR BEAT

1. Tape-record a local television news show, and compare its coverage with that of a local newspaper published the next morning. Did the same stories get covered? Were some stories ignored on the television news? What differences can you detect in the way a given story was covered by each medium? If possible, record a local radio news show and make a similar comparison.

2. Take a class survey to find out where students get most of their news—both local and national. Where do they turn first to find information about a breaking story?

The World of Radio

An unknown speaker once said that "of all the peoples in the world, Americans, with their millions of television and radio sets, stand in great fear of a moment of silence." That statement certainly seems to apply to teenagers, who are perhaps the most important group of radio listeners in America. Arbitron, the company that compiles radio ratings, says its surveys show that about 97 percent of teens aged 12 through 17 listen to the radio at least once a week. "Radio is simply a part of their daily lives," concluded one study.

Not only is radio immensely popular with teens but it is also the most universal of all the **mass media** (the means of communication that can reach large audiences). Nowhere is there a patch of land or stretch of ocean so remote that it cannot be reached by radio signals beamed from more than 26,000 stations worldwide. Over a third of those stations are located in the United States, where nearly every home has at least one radio. In fact, with 500 million radios nationwide, we have an average of two radios for every citizen.

mass media

the means of communication that can reach large audiences

What Radio Does Best

Radio has a number of significant advantages over other forms of communication.

- First, radios are portable, inexpensive and convenient. You can take them with you wherever you go.
- In emergencies, radio keeps people informed. In times of extreme danger, such as blizzards, tornadoes and floods, radio can save lives.
- Radio news coverage is fast and adaptable. When a major news event occurs, radio can sometimes get the story first. Reporters armed only with cellular phones can be on the air instantly. Television reports require heavier, bulkier equipment, and most television stations have limited resources for broadcasts from remote sites. Radio reporters, in contrast, can go just about anywhere at little cost.
- People can listen to the radio while they are doing other activities, such as driving, working, housecleaning, sunbathing and even halfheartedly trying to wake up. It's impossible to be quite so free while watching television or talking on the telephone.
- Unlike television, radio doesn't need visuals to cover a story. Thus, many local radio stations can run more newscasts—sometimes at the top of every hour—than television stations do. They can therefore update information on stories more frequently.

Radio Touches Your Imagination

Radio can swiftly take you to the outer reaches of your imagination. It can put a circus, the Super Bowl or a rock concert between your ears. Radio provides the sounds, and you provide the rest. Consider this: A team of experts would need months to create the following commercial for television. Two people in a radio studio could do it in minutes:

"Fred, we're here today on the shores of Lake Michigan to witness an incredible demonstration."

"Yes, that's right, Frank. A team of scientists is about to create the world's largest cup of hot chocolate."

"It looks like they have just begun. Let's listen."

(sounds of Lake Michigan being emptied—water sucked down the drain)

"Amazing, isn't it? Look at that mud!"

(sounds of someone stepping in and out of mud.)

"Catch this, Frank. Hundreds of tankers are pulling up to the shore."

"If I don't miss my guess, Fred, they're loaded with hot chocolate."

(sounds of tankers rolling to a stop, then pumping liquid)

"Look at the steam rise. And hey, what's that?"

"We're scheduled to have a fleet of crop-dusting planes fly over next, and they're loaded with whipped topping. Here they come."

(sounds of planes flying over and then sound of a whipped cream can shooting out cream)

"That's quite a sight. A mountain of cream on top of a lake of steaming hot chocolate. What's next?"

(sound of a helicopter overhead)

"Catch this, Fred. That chopper is towing an enormous cherry. It must weigh 500 pounds. I think he's going to drop it any minute. There it goes . . ."

(sound of a giant cherry plummeting from a high altitude; sound of an enormous cherry landing on whipped topping)

"Well, there you have it. Another world first for radio."

Radio's special effects, simple and yet completely convincing, give radio a special kind of intimacy—the kind that gives listeners a feeling of being right where the action is.

Radio is probably a vital part of your life. It brings you the latest in music and keeps you up-to-date on local and national news. Radio is also a constant companion, staying with you while you wash your car, do the laundry or struggle with your homework. What you may not realize is that radio also offers some of the best opportunities to enter a broadcasting career. Many young people have found that a part-time job at a radio station can eventually lead to full-time work as a deejay or to a position in television.

Images Overwhelm Words

Former President Ronald Reagan's "media handlers" understood the power of images. When the government cut its support for nursing homes, for example, Reagan was filmed visiting a nursing home. The film appeared on television, and the bad news faded. The image was so much more powerful than the words being spoken that people—over 50 percent of the viewers, according to the television network's own survey—still believed that Reagan supported nursing homes.

Source: Adapted from Larry Gonick, Cartoon Guide to (Non) Communication (New York: HarperCollins).

This young woman might be reading a fanciful script just like the one on this page.

Working in Radio

If you're willing to start at the bottom, work hard and learn the business inside and out, you have an excellent chance to break into radio—perhaps even before you finish high school. Among the many famous people who started out in radio are Ronald Reagan, Dan Rather and George Carlin.

Beginning a Radio Career.   The radio industry currently employs over 100,000 people, a number that is likely to grow as more stations go on the air. An average-size station employs between 20 and 25 people. About a third of those will have on-air responsibilities. Entry-level positions in radio seldom pay well. In fact, many small stations may start you at little better than minimum wage. But the experience gained at these low-budget operations more than makes up for the small salaries. During the first year or two in radio, you pay your dues by learning the ropes. The small radio station provides inexperienced people with a chance to become involved in all facets of the business.

On-Air Positions.   People who speak on the air often become familiar companions as they pass the day with us on the radio. On-air positions include announcers, deejays, newscasters, sportscasters, talk show hosts and the people who lend their voices to the hundreds of commercials we hear every day.

announcer

> a person who reads commercials, public service announcements, promotions or station identifications on the radio

deejay

> the host of a radio music program; short for *disc jockey*

newscaster

> the person who reads the news over the air; in television, also called an *anchor*

- An **announcer** is anyone who reads commercials, public service announcements, promotions or station identifications. The duties of an announcer vary, depending on the size of the station. At a small station, announcers also work as writers. For example, a midday announcer who is on the air from 10 a.m. until 3 p.m. may also be responsible for writing the 4 and 5 p.m. newscasts and any commercials that are needed.
- A **deejay** is the host of a music program. Deejays must be announcers and entertainers, especially during radio's prime time (from 7 to 9 a.m. and from 5 to 7 p.m.), when people are listening in their cars driving to and from work. Deejays are actually on the air less than you might think. Music and commercials take up at least 50 minutes of every hour. A typical hour on the morning show of a full-service station may consist of 15 minutes of news, 14 minutes of commercials, six minutes of sports, 12 to 15 minutes of music and five minutes of network news. That leaves just six minutes or so for the host to speak. Many of today's most popular deejays have sidekicks, and most specialize in comedy.
- **Newscasters,** like other journalists, work hard at knowing their subjects. A newscaster is someone who reads, and often writes, the news over the air. They must study the court system, law enforcement, education and a host of other topics of public interest to give credibility to

Being a deejay takes more than a good voice and love of music. You have to have technical skills and the ability to do more than one task at a time. This Austin, Texas deejay probably serves as his own programmer, sound engineer and announcer.

their reports. Because news stories on radio are very short, the newscaster must understand their complete context to give listeners a balanced perspective.

In particular, newscasters must be familiar with the way radio news stories are put together. Most stories, for example, use natural sound (recordings made on location in the field on audiotape). Natural sounds include the noises of an event, such as the sirens of a fire engine or the chantings of a group of protesters. A radio story may also include a sound bite—a brief portion of a taped interview. Sound bites are similar to the quotations in a newspaper story. Finally, the newscaster may either prepare or introduce a **news package.** A package is a complete story, including natural sound, sound bites and the reporter's narration.

news package

a complete news story, including natural sound, sound bites and the reporter's narration

YOUR BEAT

1. Find out about the local radio stations in your area. Which station is affiliated with which network? Who owns the stations? Are any of them independent (not affiliated with a network)?
2. Take a survey to find out which radio station is the most popular among your classmates. Give the same survey to your classmates' parents. How can you account for whatever differences you find?
3. Interview a station's general manager. Ask what qualities the manager looks for when hiring young people to work at the station.

Wasted Words

On May 9, 1961, Newton Minow, chairperson of the Federal Communications Commission, stunned a meeting of professional broadcasters by denouncing the quality of television: "Sit down in front of your television set when your station goes on the air . . . and keep your eyes glued to that set until the station signs off. I can assure you that you will observe a vast wasteland." That famous critique of television came from a speech that Minow gave, in which he evoked T. S. Eliot's famous poem *The Waste Land.*

Thirty years later, Minow observed that his speech was remembered for only two words: *vast wasteland.* Those two words, however, were not the ones he wanted remembered. Minow was more concerned with the public interest. Echoing another well-known phrase—this time from John F. Kennedy—Minow explained, "To me the public interest meant, and still means, that we should constantly ask, 'What can television do for our country?'"
Source: Adapted from "'Vast Wasteland' Author Still Displeased With TV" by Tim Jones, Chicago Tribune.

THE WORLD OF TELEVISION

The word *television* comes from the Greek word *tele,* meaning "far," and the Latin word *videre,* meaning "to see." In other words, television means "to see far." And when it comes to seeing far, nothing quite approaches television, either in the sheer abundance of its programs or the vast size of its audience. It offers a mammoth handout of news, fun, art and sport—all just for turning a dial or punching a button. It is the next best thing to curling up in front of a national fireplace.

"Is that your final answer?" "Can I use a Lifeline, Regis?" If these distinctive phrases sound familiar to you, welcome to the club. The United States has become a nation of teleholics. Whether you are home alone, snowbound, bedridden or just passing the time, television is probably one of your favorite companions. It gives you the time, the weather and the latest news. It plays, sings, whistles and dances. It takes you to movies and theaters, concerts and operas, prizefights and ball games. It brings you face to face with floods, earthquakes and fires; introduces you to presidents, kings, emirs and sultans; and teaches you French, home building and first aid. Unfortunately, it is also, as many critics have observed, "chewing gum for the eyes."

At its best, television can touch your heart and mind. It delivers generous amounts of information and entertainment on command. It can bring an entire nation together to celebrate (as it did with the return of the U.S. troops from the Persian Gulf) or to mourn (as it did with the deaths of the seven *Challenger* astronauts). At its worst, television can numb us. Critics charge that it stifles conversation, teaches children the power of violence and may be one of the causes of illiteracy. "Because of television," said comedian Fred Allen, "the next generation will have eyes as big as cantaloupes—and no brains at all."

Nevertheless, television remains a tremendously important medium because it can reach enormous audiences. Consumer guides tell us that there are televisions in about 98 percent of all American homes—more homes than have bathtubs. In fact, we are rapidly nearing the day when there will be a television set for every man, woman and child in the United States. This pervasiveness has enabled television to reach amazing numbers of people. In 1969, about 125 million Americans watched Neil Armstrong as he took humanity's first step on the moon. In 1985, a worldwide audience estimated at 1.5 billion people watched a benefit for famine victims in Africa. More than any other medium of communication, television has the power to make all of us residents of a single global village.

The Tuned-In Generation

Unless you're very unusual, you're part of a tuned-in generation. Recent studies indicate that American students watch an average of 23 hours of television a week. If you keep up that pace, you will have spent a full year of your life in front of the "boob tube" by age 70. The A.C. Nielsen Company, whose powerful ratings system determines the fate of your favorite shows, reports that a television set is on at least six hours a day in the average American home.

Television journalism has changed our political process beyond recognition. Could Abraham Lincoln, for example, be elected president today, with his lanky physique and unsightly mole? After all, televised debates among political candidates are now an expected highlight of any campaign. A candidate's physical appearance is very important in such debates. News broadcasters have also given the private lives of our leaders and celebrities much greater scrutiny than ever before.

Would Abraham Lincoln's appearance help or hinder him in today's political arena?

Who Owns the Airwaves?

Approximately three-fourths of the 1,300 television stations in the United States are **commercial television stations.** That means that they depend on advertising to provide their income. Most of these stations are affiliated with one of the four major networks—ABC, NBC, CBS and Fox—that provide the great majority of their programs, including a half-hour of news each evening. Commercial stations produce some of their own shows, but they must run network programming during prime time (the evening hours from 8 to 11 p.m., Eastern Standard Time). The rest of the television stations are **public television stations.** They rely on grants and contributions to pay their operating costs.

A local station (a station based in your town or area) produces some of its own programming (such as news or local talk shows). It also takes programming from the network it's affiliated with (shows such as *Friends* or *ER* are examples). A station may also purchase **syndicated programming.** Syndicated programming refers to television shows produced by independent companies (such as *Entertainment Tonight* or *Wheel of Fortune*). Syndicated programming also includes shows that are in reruns (such as *Cheers* or *Star Trek: the Next Generation*).

The signal provided by both commercial and public stations is free to viewers, assuming they have a receiver and an antenna. Yet millions of Americans choose to pay for their television. **Cable television** is probably the fastest-growing area of the television industry. Cable television companies receive signals from many different sources and then transmit the signals via fiber optic cable to consumers. Originally, its only purpose was to bring programs to places that could not otherwise receive clear signals. People who lived in towns great distances from the nearest transmitter, for instance, needed cable television. So did those who lived in places that the signals could not reach, such as mountain valleys or homes beneath the skyscrapers of Manhattan.

Today, however, most people enjoy cable for other reasons. They like it for the improved reception it provides for regular television programs. They also like the great variety it offers. A cable system can carry a great number of different signals. Thus, a cable system can transmit regular network programs as well as special shows such as continuous news, weather and sports; programming from independent stations; first-run movies; and special events like the Olympic games or political conventions.

commercial television station
> a television station that depends on advertising to provide its income

public television station
> a television station that relies on grants and contributions to pay its operating costs

syndicated programming
> original television shows produced by independent companies. Local stations purchase this programming to use during non-network hours

cable television
> Privately-owned cable television companies receive signals from many different sources and then transmit the signals via fiber optic cable to consumers

Careers in Television

Television offers an exciting and rewarding field for ambitious young people, especially those who enjoy a competitive atmosphere. Broadcasting also provides a way to get involved in your community because television stations play a major role in the daily lives of the people they serve.

The best place for beginners to find employment in television is usually at a small commercial station, an educational station or a local cable company. Because small stations have fewer employees and jobs often overlap, working at a small station will probably give you a chance to learn several different phases of the station's operation. Beginners, however, must be prepared to work odd hours, weekends and holidays. Experience brings better working conditions and, eventually, a chance to work at a larger station.

Jobs in Programming. A programming department selects, plans and produces the programs that the station broadcasts. Nearly every station produces some of its own shows, including news and sports events. The program director not only plans the daily schedule but also develops the station's policies together with the general manager and the sales manager. Others who work in the programming department include producers, directors, writers, staff announcers and public affairs directors. Most stations also have a news staff, which includes a news director, reporters, writers and assignment editors.

Crew Positions for a Typical Production. The production of a television news program requires teamwork. It takes total cooperation from both the people who speak and perform before a camera (called the **talent**) and those behind the camera (the production staff). One of the largest staffed departments for most commercial television stations is undoubtedly the newsroom. Each member of the news team has a unique and important role within the newsroom, although at some smaller stations, the functions of staff members overlap.

talent
the people who speak and perform before a camera at a television station

+ *News Director.* In charge of newsroom operations and actually runs the show. He or she is responsible for deciding which shots the viewer will see during a newscast or production. The news director is also responsible for hiring and firing staff members, managing the budget, conducting salary reviews and determining schedules. As the head of the news operation, the news director plays a key role in editorial decisions about news content.
+ *Assignment Editor.* In charge of day-to-day assignments within the newsroom. Throughout the day, this person keeps in contact with crews in the field and communicates with producers about the status of stories. Along with other staffers, the assignment editor maintains a file of current and future news events. Traditionally, this

How do you think this news anchor contributes to her community? What are the responsibilities that go along with being a local celebrity?

DATELINE

person is also the first contact with members of the public who call with information or questions.

✦ *Producer.* Typically responsible for putting together a single newscast. He or she determines the story placement within a newscast and the amount of time to allow for each news story, weather and sports. The producer may write the news the anchors will read on the air. The producer may also be responsible for timing the show. The best producers are those who have worked as reporters or photographers. However, field experience is not always a requirement, especially at smaller stations.

✦ *Reporter.* Responsible for covering local stories within a community. Reporters work with news photographers in gathering information and conducting interviews for one or more stories. Reporters then write stories and edit videotape for broadcasts. Reporters are also responsible for live reporting and occasionally serve as fill-in anchors when the main anchor is gone. Reporters may be responsible for a specific beat (such as education or health) but may also cover a wide variety of stories outside their assigned areas.

✦ *Photographer/Editor.* A key position in a television news operation. He or she is responsible for shooting all the local videotape that the news station broadcasts. In some cases, the photographer acts as the reporter to gather information. The photographer/editor is also responsible for technical aspects of the on-air product, such as editing videotape and running live shots.

✦ *Anchor.* Responsible for reading the newscast on the air. Anchors work on the front lines in a news organization and are the people the public most identifies with. An anchor may help write some of the newscast. The anchor participates in community events and frequently speaks to the public. His or her performance may help determine news ratings.

WASHINGTON, D.C., May 1946—A government freeze on the construction of new television stations and a halt in the production of television sets during World War II slowed the momentum of the developing television industry. The number of stations broadcasting dropped from the 18 licensed on July 1, 1941, to six by the end of the war.

The rush resumed in May 1946, however, when Dumont offered television receivers for sale. RCA and Philco quickly followed. Twenty-seven companies were manufacturing television sets by the mid-1950s.

Early marketing efforts were made uncertain by high cost, lack of regulations and manufacturing standards, and the speculation that color sets would soon make black-and-white sets obsolete. Even so, in one year, 1948, the number of stations on the air jumped from 17 to 48, and the audience multiplied by 4,000 percent.

Five- to seven-inch receivers sold for $375 to $500 in 1948, plus $45 to $300 for installation. Prices dropped by almost half in the early 1950s.

The first color programming was telecast in 1953, but it was not until December 1966 that more color television sets were sold than black-and-white sets. Improved studio cameras with enhanced color quality, definition and resolution, plus the Christmas season, stimulated the year-end sales.

By 1967, about 16 percent of homes had color sets.

The Voice That Caused a Seizure

Whether you have a pleasant voice or not, you have probably never driven anyone up the wall simply by speaking. That is not the case with television personality Mary Hart, whose voice once caused an epileptic seizure.

According to Dr. Venkat Ramani, who reported the case in the *New England Journal of Medicine*, Hart's voice caused one of his patients to have seizures. In a laboratory test, Ramani said, his patient would rub her stomach and hold her head, "and then she would look confused and . . . like she was far away and out of it" when he played a tape of Hart's voice. He added that the woman has not had any seizures since she stopped watching Hart on television.

"It's the pitch and quality of the voice as a sound, rather than what she's actually saying," commented Dr. Marc Dichter of the University of Pennsylvania Medical School. Swamped with hundreds of requests for a response, Hart could only say, "My heart goes out to anyone with this problem."

Unless you sound like a piece of chalk squeaking on the blackboard, you can probably draw some confidence from this strange story. At one time, nearly all the voices in broadcasting were rich, masculine baritones. Now, however, there's room for a wide variety of voices. Yours may soon be one of them.
Source: Adapted from "That's Entertainment," Science News.

- *Technical Director.* Usually acts as crew chief and does the video switching (the process of choosing which of several camera signals to send to viewers).
- *Camera Operator.* Operates a studio camera and often takes care of lighting.
- *Floor Director.* Coordinates all studio activities, including camera operation, microphones and lighting. He or she relays the director's instructions to all studio personnel.
- *Graphic Artist.* Prepares titles, slides and other materials needed for visual presentation.
- *Character Generator.* Operates the character generator, a device used to put words on the screen.
- *Audio Engineer.* In charge of all audio operations. During a production, he or she runs the audio control board, which raises and lowers microphone levels. Finally the
- *Set Designer.* Designs and constructs the sets and provides the necessary props.

Broadcast Ethics

Explicit sex! Full frontal nudity! Blood and gore! Well, not quite. Since the television industry began, those who produce its programs have been accused of presenting material that shocks and offends. To what degree are broadcasters guilty of these charges? Are they simply giving the public what it wants? Are there guidelines, rules or restrictions that govern what can and can't be shown, said or played?

The Federal Communications Commission. Television depends on a limited resource, the airwaves, to deliver messages to its viewers. According to U.S. law, the airwaves are owned by the people. They are a natural resource, just like water or air, and they cannot be bought or sold. Because so many people would like to use a portion of the airwaves, though, some government regulation is necessary. Without the assignment of space (what we frequently call *channels*) by a central authority, communications would be chaotic.

For this reason, Congress established the Federal Communications Commission (FCC) in 1934. The FCC is an independent federal agency composed of five commissioners appointed by the president. It licenses radio and television stations and assigns frequencies for their use. It determines the call letters a station will use and regulates the amount of power a station can have.

More to the point, the FCC also sets standards that must be met if a station hopes to have its license renewed. The number of commercials a station may carry, for example, is strictly limited by the FCC. (Fortunately, there is no rule yet to prevent all of us from switching channels during those commercials.) What about the content of the programs themselves, though?

THIS JUST IN: *Portrait of a Young Journalist*
MTV's Tabitha Soren

She is MTV's top political reporter. Wait a minute. MTV's what? Tabitha Soren, youthful veteran of two presidential elections, has brightened the sometimes mundane campaign trail with her unique brand of personal reporting, a style well suited to MTV's young and restless audience. A novelty when she covered the Clinton-Bush race in 1992 at the age of 24, Soren became an accepted member of the mainstream media in the Clinton-Dole race in 1996.

"Politicians, because they notice us getting noticed," Soren explained, "are now making an effort to appeal to this voter block." MTV viewers are primarily those in the 16- to 30-year-old age bracket.

In 1992, President George Bush noted that he was not a "teeny bopper" and therefore had no business being on MTV. He changed his mind only days before the election, but by then he was already trailing MTV regular Bill Clinton. By contrast, Republican senator Bob Dole, at age 72 one of the oldest candidates for president, appeared on MTV's *Choose or Lose* election program to be interviewed by Soren.

Soren grew up in a military family that moved frequently. She developed an early interest in foreign affairs. She came to MTV from a television station in Vermont, where she anchored the late news and served as statehouse correspondent. At MTV, she has been a new kind of reporter. She deliberately avoids the sort of glamour sometimes projected by other major network reporters.

Indeed, her fingernails may sometimes be painted purple.

"I think I act differently than a lot of reporters," Soren said. "When I interview someone, it's more casual and there's not a lot of posturing. I ask different questions, they are caught off guard, and they act more human because they have to think of an answer on the spot."

During an interview in the Oval Office, for example, Soren asked President Clinton what he thought about the death of Jerry Garcia, the lead singer for the Grateful Dead. That kind of reporting may not lead to major scoops, but it can reveal the person behind the pose, a Soren specialty.

Source: Adapted from "Prime Time" by Frazier Moore. Star Express, Lincoln, NE.

Self-Censorship. The FCC is rarely involved with specific cases of censorship. When broadcasters complain that their ideas have been rejected as being unacceptable, they are usually complaining about the major television networks, which set their own standards for what is acceptable and in good taste. In the 1950s, for instance, Lucy Ricardo was never allowed to refer to herself as being "pregnant" on *I Love Lucy*, even though there was little doubt she would soon be a mother. Times have changed. In the 1990s, the cast of *Saturday Night Live* went out of its way to show off a new attitude toward censorship. In a skit set at a nudist club, the cast stood behind a bar, apparently undressed, and discussed the human anatomy in graphic terms.

But not everything is acceptable. MTV, the all-music channel, rejected a Madonna video that was too explicit. The networks all observe some rules of thumb about what should be shown during prime time (8 to 11 p.m., Eastern Standard Time) and family time (8 to 9 p.m., Eastern Standard Time). Advertisers occasionally pull their ads if they find something objectionable in a program. Parent groups have put considerable pressure on the networks to monitor the level of violence in children's cartoons.

Student broadcasters who tape their own stories may find that their "street" interviews sometimes must be carefully edited. All of us, and teenagers in particular, tend to speak in an earthier way than what is normally accepted in television, *South Park* excepted. So student reporters should expect to spend extra time doing video editing when they use unrehearsed interviews.

1. Challenge one another to bring your funniest home videos to class. Watch for technical mistakes, such as camera movement that is too rapid.

2. Keep a television viewing log for a week. Ask your parents and siblings to do so as well. Compare the viewing habits of teenagers in your class with those of the younger children and older adults.

◢ PREPARING A BROADCAST SCRIPT

Just like a newspaper reporter, a radio or television journalist will write news and feature stories that are important and interesting to the local audience. But the style in which those stories are written is different than the style for newspaper stories. In radio and television, journalists write their stories in the form of **scripts.**

script

the form in which a story is written for radio or television

Editing a Broadcast Script

Broadcast scripts must be prepared for reading aloud. Whatever the station's style, the important thing is that the script be easy to read aloud. The person who will be reading from the script may not have had time to practice it before going on the air or may be looking into the camera while reading from a scrolling teleprompter screen.

Some stations prefer scripts typed in all capital letters; some use capital and lowercase letters. Some stations double-space scripts; some prefer single-spaced or even triple-spaced scripts. Some indent paragraphs; some don't. Individual newscasters may even devise their own editing styles. The secret is to learn the station's style and use it.

Broadcast scripts are edited using special copyediting symbols. Some of the symbols for broadcast are different from those used in print journalism, because the copy is meant to be read aloud easily and with

BYLINE

PEGGY RUPRECHT
REPORTER FOR KMTV IN OMAHA, NEBRASKA

I usually work a 40-hour week, but my work-week begins Sunday evening. I'll work 1:30 to 10:30 p.m., then Monday through Thursday I work 9 a.m. to 6 p.m. However, every reporter's schedule is different. Some work weekends, some work nights.

When I come to work, I usually take a few moments to go through my mail and messages. At least once a week, I'll call sources on my beat (education) to find out what's happening around town. Sources are a good way to keep up-to-date on what's happening in the community. They can also provide good ideas for stories.

Every morning during the week, the entire news department assembles for a meeting. We talk about what's happening that day, and everyone shares information about events we should cover or stories we should do. The producers will share their ideas for the news that needs to be covered. Then the assignment editor passes out assignments for the day. While reporters make calls to set up interviews for their stories, the producers will look at network video and go through the Associated Press (AP) wire to see what other stories they're interested in. The producer works up a tentative rundown on how the newscast will look for that evening.

I then head out with a photographer into the field to work on a story. It may take me all day to work on the story. The assignment editor makes contact with sources about current or future stories. The assignment editor will also keep in touch with crews in the field about the status of a story. The producer will begin writing news copy and start thinking about what stories she wants in her show.

Afternoon reporters and photographers come in at 1:30, so assignments are made out for them. Anchors also arrive about this time and may work with the producer writing stories. Around this time, the producers and assignment editor have another meeting to talk about what stories will go in the show. The producers will make a final decision on what stories they want in their newscast. After I return from the field with my video and interviews, I must log the interviews and begin writing the story. The photographer will look through the video and decide what will be used in the final story.

After I finish writing the story, I usually have one of the producers or the assignment editor check it over. Producers read the story, checking to see that it is both clear and accurate. After the script is approved, I'll work with the photographer to edit the package. A full story is usually no more than 90 seconds long, but it may take us an hour or more to edit the story.

All this must be done before the assigned newscast. If I have the lead story for the 5 p.m. news, I must be finished by 5 p.m. No exceptions. Missing a deadline is not acceptable in the news business.

After I'm done writing the package, I may write a smaller version of the story (VO, VO/SOT) for one of the other newscasts. If I have time at the end of the day, I may make additional contacts with sources about future stories. Sometimes, breaking news will force me to work overtime, but even when I'm not at work, I'm constantly keeping my eyes open about events that would make good stories for our station.

Background. A television station in a medium-sized market can often expect candidates for positions as television news reporters to have strong writing and verbal skills. The physical requirements for the position include good vision and hearing, the willingness to endure prolonged standing, and the ability to help lift and carry camera equipment weighing approximately 25 pounds.

meaning rather than to be read by the typesetter. For instance, in editing print, one line is drawn through words to be omitted. This leaves the words still legible so that they can be reinserted later if desired. In broadcast, words to be omitted are completely blacked out so that the announcer can't possibly say them by mistake.

In print, the transposition sign is used to change the order of words or letters. The transposition sign is never used on a broadcast script, because it is confusing and might cause an announcer to hesitate or lose his or her place in the script while reading. Words or letters to be transposed should be completely crossed out and rewritten in the correct order on a broadcast script.

Other marks, called rehearsal marks, may be added to the broadcast script to assist the announcer in reading with meaning. Underline or capitalize words to be stressed. Use ellipses (. . .) or dashes (—) to indicate longer pauses:

> The doctor says the quarterback will NOT be able to play Friday
> . . . but MAY be able to return by next week.

Broadcast scripts include **pronouncers,** the phonetic spellings of unfamiliar words or names that are included to assist the announcer in pronouncing the words correctly. The pronouncer appears in parentheses above or following the correctly spelled word:

> Shots were fired in Bihac (BEE-hotch) today.
> Shaquille (sha KEEL) O'Neal
> Sinead (sha NAY) O'Connor

A pronouncer is not a substitute for the correct spelling. The names of people and places mentioned in the script are often superimposed on the television screen, and their spellings are taken from the script. Phonetic spellings have appeared on the screen unintentionally when the correct spellings weren't included in the script.

Correct spelling is as important in broadcast scripts as it is in print. Someone will be reading these scripts aloud to an audience, and misspelled words are more likely to be mispronounced. Words with the same spelling but different pronunciations, such as *wind, read, resume* and *suspect,* are also likely to be mispronounced. Avoid using them whenever possible.

Numbers in broadcast scripts are written as words from one through nine and as numerals from 10 through 999. Numbers greater than 1,000 are written as words exactly as they should be spoken, with hyphens connecting the whole number: *one-hundred-thousand-nine-hundred-fifty; three-million dollars;* or *twenty-one-year-old.* Some stations mix numerals and words: *3-million dollars* or *21-year-old.* Years are written as numerals: *1776* or *1999.*

pronouncer

the phonetic spellings of unfamiliar words or names that are included in broadcast scripts to help the announcer correctly pronounce the words

Formatting a Broadcast Script

The way a script looks—including the words a newscaster will read and instructions about when prerecorded material will be inserted and for how long—is called a format. Formatting broadcast scripts has been simplified by computer templates designed to prepare news scripts. The

templates are fill-in-the-blank forms that ask preparers to insert information such as the slug, time and script for each story. Whether the script is formatted by hand or by computer, the slug should appear in the upper left corner. It includes the one- or two-word name assigned to the story, the initials or name of the reporter, and the time of the newscast when the script will be used. The following is an example of a slug for the first page of a story:

> HOMECOMING/tws/3 p.m.

Each page of the broadcast script should be marked at the top and bottom so that the person reading the script knows, simply by glancing at the top or bottom of the page, whether the pages are in order, there is more to come or this is the last page. The slug on pages after the first page includes the page number.

> HOMECOMING/tws/3 p.m./p.2

Even if each story is typed on a separate page, which is a system that some stations prefer, the pages should be numbered so there is no confusion between the newscaster and the director or technical assistants as to what comes next. The end of each story or page in broadcast is marked with the same signals used in a print story: (more), (end), (###) or -30-.

Broadcast scripts also include instructions to directors and technical assistants. Cues must be indicated to let everyone know when a sound bite or film clip is to be inserted or when the announcer is to do a voice-over (VO). During a voice-over, the newscaster reads from a script while the viewer watches prerecorded videotape.

Radio scripts are simpler than television scripts, because they only need to cue the announcer about the insertion of voices or music recorded on tape. These insertions are on special tape cassettes called **carts.** The first five words **(incue),** the last five words **(outcue)** and the **total running time (TRT)** of the cart should be noted on the script. Total running time refers to how long the entire tape segment lasts; that way the newscaster can tell whether the correct tape is running when it comes on, as well as when the tape is about to end.

cart
> a short tape cassette that contains insertions of voices or music for use in a radio broadcast

incue
> the first five words of a cart

outcue
> the last five words of a cart

total running time (TRT)
> how long an entire tape segment lasts

Radio Script Format.   Radio scripts are usually typed across the page with margins of approximately one inch on each side. This produces a script that will take roughly four seconds per line, or 30 seconds per eight lines, to read. Figure 19.1 shows an example of a correctly formatted radio script.

Television Script Format.   Television scripts are more complicated than radio scripts, because they must include cues and instructions to the director. The television news script is divided into two columns. The left-hand column of the script contains all the information the director and crews behind the scenes need to make the production run smoothly. The right-hand column contains the news copy the talent reads, along with any sound bites from sources in the field.

In television news, there are four basic script types: the reader (RDR), the package (PKG), the voice-over (VO) and the voice-over with sound on tape (VO/SOT).

- ◆ *Reader (RDR).*This script is the most basic in broadcasting. It is the closest thing to a newspaper story. The reader contains no video, and the anchor who reads this script appears on the air the entire time. The news department uses reader scripts for visually poor stories or stories where there is no video.
- ◆ *Package (PKG):* This type of script is usually the longest and most in-depth type of script (Figure 19.2). It contains copy the reporter writes, along with natural sound and interviews (sound bites) from sources in the field. On a package, you will hear the reporter's narration and will see him or her in a stand-up. A **stand-up** is the part of the package when a reporter appears on camera, explaining information about a story.
- ◆ *Voice-Over (VO):* This script uses video during part or all of the story the anchor is reading but contains no interviews, just natural sound from the video source.

stand-up

when a reporter appears on camera to explain the information in a story

FIGURE 19.1
A WELL-FORMATTED RADIO SCRIPT

HOMECOMING/tws/3 p.m.

Homecoming royalty will be crowned at the dance following Friday's football game against Central.

Chair of the Homecoming committee, Jeanne Johnson, said she expects it to be an exciting coronation:

(CART #1, TRT - :25)

INCUE: "The king and queen will . . .

OUTCUE: "begin about 10:15 in the gym."

Parents and friends are invited to attend the coronation.

(# # #)

FIGURE 19.2
EXAMPLE OF A PACKAGE SCRIPT

PAGE 50   -<WIDE OR RAFTER OPEN>-
TIME CAPSULE   -<RELIEF>-
LORETTA

                                 IMAGINE FINDING PART OF YOUR FAMILY'S HISTORY
                                 FROM MORE THAN 70 YEARS AGO.
                                     THAT'S WHAT HAPPENED IN PAPILLION WHERE THE
                                 SCHOOL DISTRICT RECENTLY FOUND PART OF ITS
                                 PAST.
                                     CHANNEL THREE'S PEGGY SMITH SHOWS US A
                                 TIME CAPSULE AND THE TREASURES HIDDEN INSIDE.

ROLL EJ PKG   --

                                 -<N.S.5:59>-
                                 THE 74 YEAR OLD TIME CAPSULE CAME FROM AN
                                 ERA WITHOUT COMPUTERS OR TELEVISION . . .
                                 WHERE HORSES AND BUGGIES STILL OUTNUMBERED
                                 CARS.
#Linda Tafoya   -<6:38-6:46>-i saw an ad for a chevy that was $525.
#Papillion   INSIDE THE METAL BOX . . . A GLIMPSE INTO THE
                                 PAST . . . FROM OLD NEWSPAPERS TO THE NAMES OF
                                 SCHOOLCHILDREN.
                                 -<N.S.12:43>-here i am right down here . . .
#Bud Schwab   -<21:05-21:14>to see all those names . . . recognize
#79 Years Old   the ones you went to school with . . .which was a long, long
                                 time ago . . .
                                 THE BOX EVEN HELD A BALLOT FOR A THIRTY
                                 THOUSAND DOLLAR SCHOOL BOND ISSUE . . .IT
                                 PASSED BY ONE VOTE.
#Milton Fricke   -<16.59-17:06>-if they hadn't built the school i'd
#86 Years Old   been in a room with three grades in it.

#Peggy Smith   -<SNDUP 2:51-3:00>-the school district is tearing down this
#The Midlands News Channel   old building to make room for the new administrative offices.
                                 it was here . . . under the old cornerstone, where they found
                                 the time capsule.
                                 -<13:37-13:44>-bud schwab was a first grader when the cor-
#Dr. Harlan Metschke   nerstone was put in . . . he explains why there is a time cap-
#Superintendent, Papillion/LaVista sule behind the cornerstone.
                                 -<N.S.15:37>-what grade were you in . . .
                                 AND NOW, ANOTHER GENERATION OF STUDENTS
                                 HAS A CHANCE TO LEARN FROM THE PAST. WITH PHO-
                                 TOGRAPHER BOB JIMENEZ AND PEGGY SMITH CHAN-
                                 NEL THREE NEWS.
2-SHOT   --
                                     THE ITEMS IN THE TIME CAPSULE WILL BE PLACED
            loretta   ON DISPLAY IN THE DISTRICT'S NEW MEDIA CENTER
                                 ONCE THE BUILDING IS FINISHED.

◆ *Voice-Over with Sound On Tape (VO/SOT):* This script is read by the anchor (Figure 19.3). It contains video, along with an interview with a source in the field. All four kinds of television scripts may be written by a producer, an anchor or a reporter.

The director needs to know the type of script being used for each segment of a television news broadcast. Thus, the left-hand side of the script may include any of the following:

◆ When the newscaster will be reading at the same time a videotape is running (VO).

◆ When a computer graphic (CG) will be inserted.

◆ What the speakers will be saying live from the studio (O/C, which means On Camera, or LIVE).

◆ When sound and picture will be on tape (VO/SOT).

◆ When there is a live picture from a remote location (REMOTE).

◆ The time for each segment and the total time (TST/TRT).

◆ Whatever end-of-page or end-of-script marks are appropriate (for example, ###).

On the script, a cue should appear directly across from the line where a change or insertion will occur. Figure 19.4 shows an example.

FIGURE 19.3
EXAMPLE OF A VO/SOT
SCRIPT

Clinton Welfare
Reform/:45/PR/7-23-99

                   ---<Wayne reads>-----

A: Wayne

*Roll cue line tells director
when to roll video*

TAKE EJ VO------------
#Washington, D.C. Super

     The Senate has given its OK for a bill to overhaul the nation's welfare system.

     The House passed a similar version of the bill just last week.

*Super means to superimpose the
words "Washington, D.C." over
the bottom of the screen*

     The proposed bill limits lifetime welfare assistance to five years and gives states control of welfare money in the form of block grants.
     Democratic support for the bill is mixed.
     The President also has some reservations.

Cue for audio person

TAKE EJ SND FULL-------
#Bill Clinton Super
#President

EJ VO CONTINUES------

------<TAKE SOUND FULL>-----
-<soundbite>-"what we should be asking is does this weaken the protection we give children?"

     During the last Presidential campaign, Clinton promised voters welfare reform.
     Both the House and Senate must now work on a compromise to a welfare bill before handing it to the President.

HOMECOMING/tws/3 p.m.

FIGURE 19.4
A BROADCAST TELEVISION
SCRIPT SHOWING CUES

```
_____O/C                    (ANNOUNCER)
                                  HOMECOMING ROYALTY WILL BE
                                  CROWNED FRIDAY NIGHT IN
                                  KIEWIT GYMNASIUM FOLLOWING
                                  THE GAME AGAINST CENTRAL.

VO BEGINS _____                 (VO)
                                  REHEARSAL FOR THE
                                  CEREMONY WAS HELD IN THE
                                  GYM THIS MORNING. BECCA
                                  BURNETT, HOLLY HO AND
          TRT: 10                 NICOLE RUSH ARE CANDIDATES
                                  FOR QUEEN, AND JOE SCHEER
                                  (SHARE), MARIO RODRIGUEZ
                                  AND TIM HAYES ARE CANDIDATES
                                  FOR KING.

_____O/C                    (LIVE)
                                  THE PUBLIC IS INVITED TO
                                  ATTEND THE CEREMONY.
                                       (# # #)
```

Script Rundowns

Once the producer determines all the news stories that will be run in the newscast, he or she assembles them on a **script rundown.** The rundown contains a number of elements, including the initials of the anchor reading the story, the slug (name of the story), the script type (VO/SOT, VO and so on), the initials of the reporter who wrote the story and the length of the story (see Figure 19.5 on the next page).

The producer typically places hard news or spot news stories near the top of the script rundown. These are the stories that will appear first on the air. However, the producer may also lead the newscast with stories that have a broad appeal, even if those stories are human interest or feature stories. On the opening day of the College World Series in Omaha, Nebraska, for example, many of the local stations begin the newscast with events happening at the ballpark.

Specialized news stories (consumer, health or education stories, for example), may run in the second segment of the newscast (the part of the newscast that comes after the first commercial break). National or international news stories may also run in this segment. At many local news stations, weather coverage comes in the middle of the newscast, and sports runs near the end. However, some stations are experimenting with placing these segments in other locations.

script rundown

instructions prepared by a television producer that include the initials of the anchor reading the story, the slug, the script type, the initials of the reporter who wrote the story and the story's length

Television news is a fascinating, demanding and exciting enterprise. Some news shows are staged in mammoth studios with millions of dollars' worth of equipment and large crews. Other, more modest productions take place in tiny, makeshift quarters (in high schools, for instance) with a few hundred dollars' worth of equipment and a crew of two or three. In either case, the success of the production begins and ends with the producer, the person who is responsible for pulling the whole project together.

FIGURE 19.5
SCRIPT RUNDOWN

Anchor	Slug	Script	Reporter	TRT
M	Clinton Welfare Reform	PKG	PR	1:45
L	Housing Project Study	VO/SOT	WH	:45
L	Teen Pregnancy Rate	RDR	JJ	:20

1. Write and tape-record a five-minute newscast about the activities of a single day in your school (use audiotape or videotape, whichever is more readily available). Compare your decisions on the order and time allocated to each story with those of other students in your class.

2. Ask a local television station for a copy of one of its anchor scripts. Practice reading the script with as few errors as possible.

3. Watch a local late television newscast one night, and have one or two of your classmates watch the competition's newscast. Write down the order of stories in which they appeared and the format in which they were handled (VO/SOT, PKG, LIVE and so on). Notice any graphics or other distinguishing features of the newscast (for example, consumer/medical segments). Get together and compare notes. What did you like about the newscasts? Which one seemed to give the most news information? Which one was the most pleasing to watch, and why? What differences did you observe?

CHAPTER REVIEW

KEY TERMS

Show that you know the meanings of the following key terms by correctly using them in complete sentences. Write your answers on a separate sheet of paper.

broadcast journalism
natural sound
reveal
mass media
announcer
deejay
newscaster
news package
commercial television station
public television station
syndicated programming

cable television
talent
script
pronouncer
cart
incue
outcue
total running time (TRT)
stand-up
script rundown

OPEN FORUM

1. Design a schedule for one day of programming for your own experimental television station. The schedule should reflect the prime purpose of the station which is "to serve the public interest of those in the viewing area." Your schedule should cover one 24-hour day. It can include past or present programs from other networks, brand-new programs of your own creation or some combination of the two.

2. Invent your own radio station. What would your format be? What kind of listeners would you try to attract?

3. Imagine you are an alien on another planet who is somehow able to get television reception from Earth. What conclusions would you draw about American life from watching our television?

4. Should television stations pay private citizens for their home videos in cases where the videos contain newsworthy footage (an airplane crash, for instance, or a crime being committed)? Create a role-playing scenario for you and your classmates to dramatize a discussion over this issue at the station among the producer, anchor and reporters.

5. Should television stations be allowed to broadcast shocking events such as executions?

6. Andy Warhol once said that everyone in America will be famous, but only for 15 minutes. What do you think he meant? What role has television played in creating celebrities?

FINDING THE FLAW

1. Watch a live television news broadcast carefully. Try to spot any small slipups. (As with any live broadcast, there are certain to be a few.) Watch for anchors who don't look at the screen (they are looking toward the wrong camera), tapes cued improperly or tape that isn't available at all. Notice how anchors or reporters cover their mistakes. Most correct themselves immediately when they misspeak. You may gain a new appreciation for how professional most live news shows are.

2. Listen to a radio newscast to try to find any flaws. The newscaster may stumble over the script, wait for a natural sound that isn't available or have to cover when the wrong sound bite is played. How difficult is it to read through a five-minute newscast without making a single mistake?

MEDIA WATCH

1. Obtain a copy of the diary that Arbitron (the company that compiles radio ratings) asks people to keep for a week. (You can probably get a copy from a local radio station.) Have everyone in your class keep a similar diary for a week, and tabulate the class results. What conclusions can you draw from the information?

2. Arrange for your class to tour a local radio station, or invite a station manager, program director or deejay to visit your class as a guest speaker.

3. Find out what goes on behind the scenes at a television station. Many local cable television companies offer free instructional courses on television production. Sign up for one.

String Book

1. Write a five-minute newscast based on events at your school. Include short clips of interviews with key school personnel.

2. Take a story from *Time, Newsweek* or *U.S. News & World Report.* Rewrite it as a radio news story. Using a tape recorder, practice reading the story as you would read it on the air. Listen as you play it back at least twice. Make notes on the following: (a) Is the meaning of what I said clear? (b) Did I go too fast or too slowly? (c) Was my delivery smooth or choppy? (d) What vocal characteristics do I need to work on?

Chapter 20
Public Relations

"Public sentiment is everything . . . with public sentiment nothing can fail. Without it, nothing can succeed."
—President Abraham Lincoln

KEY TERMS

In this chapter, you will learn the meaning of these terms:

public relations
public
media blitz
teleconference
video news conference
photo opportunity
news release
fact sheet
video news release (VNR)
B-roll
media alert
public service
  announcement (PSA)

LEARNING OBJECTIVES

After completing this chapter, you will be able to:

◆ define public relations,
◆ understand what is involved in a public relations career,
◆ recognize the technical skills needed for a public relations career,
◆ apply public relations concepts to individual situations,
◆ write in public relations formats.

◆

Y ou like journalism, but you're not sure you want to be a reporter. You like doing desktop publishing, but you're not sure you want to spend every day in front of a computer.

You like working with people, and you want a career that will allow you to continue to use your communications and journalism skills.

You like living on the edge, moving in the fast lane, never knowing when you wake up in the morning exactly what you will be doing that day.

You like organizing things, coordinating events and taking care of details.

You'll like practicing public relations!

◤THE PRACTICE OF PUBLIC RELATIONS

Microsoft Corporation paid more than $300 million in advertising, public relations and sales promotion to launch its Windows 95 operating system. The company paid $12 million for rights to use the Rolling Stones' hit "Start Me Up" in its broadcast campaign. It paid $537,000 to sponsor the rollout day edition of the *London Times* so that 1.5 million readers could receive the day's paper at no cost. It paid late-night television host Jay Leno to be co-host with Microsoft CEO Bill Gates at the unveiling ceremony in Redmond, Washington. It paid the managers of the CN Tower in Toronto and the Empire State Building in New York City to decorate the towering buildings in red, white and blue bunting and lights for the occasion.

Microsoft's advertising campaign was supplemented by a massive public relations campaign. Promotions directed to the media got Windows 95 mentioned in every major television news and talk show and joked about in late-night monologues. The promotional campaign was such a success that by the time stores opened—many of them at 12:01 a.m.—on rollout day, Windows 95 was a household word, and computer owners around the world were waiting in line to buy it.

The advertising campaign worked, but it was the special promotions and communications with the media that made Windows 95 news and started the media talking about it. Because the media treated the debut of the new operating system as news, the public started talking about it, looking forward to it and waiting anxiously to spend their money on it.

What Is Public Relations?

Public relations is the transmission of information to the public through the media in order to make people aware of a business, organization, issue or event, in a positive way. Public relations is unpaid media exposure for a business or organization. Information from public relations sources appears as news content on television and radio and in print. It appears in public service messages promoting social issues such as health, safety and a clean environment.

Public relations messages use many of the same principles as advertising. Advertising is the way a business or organization promotes its product through paid-for messages. Public relations is the way a business or organization promotes itself. The time or space for advertising must be paid for by the product's sponsor; the time or space for public relations information is free of charge to the source.

That does not mean that public relations is free. It is paid for by the business or organization sponsoring it. The sponsor pays the public relations professionals' salaries; pays for mailings to target audiences; and pays for the production of promotional items, from letters to T-shirts to store displays. All these things provide publicity for the sponsor and the sponsor's products.

People who practice public relations have many titles. They are called communications managers, information officers, media specialists, and news service and public relations directors.

public relations
the actions and communications carried out by public relations practitioners; the department or division of a business or organization responsible for establishing and maintaining relations between a business or organization and its publics; a management function that helps define an organization's philosophy through interactions within the organization and with publics outside the organization

Public Relations Responsibilities

In today's global community, no one who does business with the public can escape having a public image or practicing public relations. Governments, companies, organizations, businesses, schools and individuals have public images and public relations responsibilities, whether they want them or not.

Every telephone call a company employee answers, every letter a company employee sends, every ad a business buys, every face-to-face or online contact between a business and a consumer becomes a public relations event. This is because it contributes to the attitudes people have about the business and the people who are associated with it.

Your school is a business. Whoever answers the telephone at the school represents the whole school as far as the caller is concerned. The coach represents the whole school when a reporter asks for an interview. You represent your whole school when you go to sell an ad for the newspaper or when you attend an event at another school. People hear and see you, and they get the idea that everyone at your school is like you. Your interactions with the public create the impressions people have of you and of your school.

From international corporations right down to your local school district, from the president of the United States to the mayor of the smallest town, people recognize the need for good relationships with the people who support them. Many employ public relations professionals to help create and maintain the positive relationships they'd like to have with the public.

Public relations professionals work hard to build favorable impressions through the publicity and information they distribute and through interpersonal contact with the media and the public. In spite of careful management, however, events happen that give people negative impressions:

- An airplane crashes, and passengers look skeptically at that airline the next time they plan a trip.
- The president of a major nonprofit organization admits having paid for parties for himself and his friends using money donated for research. Donors decide not to give any more money to that organization.
- A ride at a major amusement park collapses, and people are injured. Parents decide to take their children somewhere else this summer.

THIS JUST IN: *Portrait of a Young Journalist*
Michael Hancock, Public Relations

For Michael Hancock, having good communications skills was the key to landing an internship in the office of Denver mayor Federico Pena. During college, Hancock began sending out résumés and requesting internships. He says it was his communications skills that helped him most. "You're really judged more by your ability to communicate in speaking and in writing than anything else," he said.

Hancock, a native of Denver, worked as an adviser to the mayor on community and youth issues for about six months. He said it was a great job to get right out of college, even though some of the work was tedious.

Hancock now works as a strategic planner for the National Civic League, a national nonprofit organization, in Denver. His job includes long-term planning, consulting for local government, leadership development and research. The job also requires writing and designing publications. Most recently, he has written about youth violence and democracy.

Hancock, who majored in political science and minored in communication arts in college, says his decision to study communications was one of the single most significant decisions he made in college, because he learned many of the things that have helped him on the job.

Writing was not Hancock's favorite subject, but he says he was forced to do more of it when he went to college. "It was a pain, but I benefited tremendously from the experience," he said.

Students should not be afraid to have their work critiqued, Hancock says. "Whether it is writing or speaking, being critiqued can help students feel more confident and comfortable in the work they do.

"There are three things every student should learn: the ability to participate in and understand the information superhighway, the ability to write well and the ability to listen," Hancock said. "These three things will set you up in the world."

- Someone substitutes the word *thief* for a student's name under the football picture in the yearbook. The school gets negative publicity.
- A few students are arrested for vandalizing school property, and all students become the subjects of public suspicion.
- Three individuals encode a racist message in their personal descriptions in the yearbook. It becomes national news, and the whole community looks bad.
- A student newspaper column complains that local police officers target high school students and ticket them more often than other age groups. Police records show this assertion to be untrue, and student journalists get the reputation of being careless, irresponsible reporters.

Although none of these incidents was the fault of the school, the business or the public relations department, each created negative impressions for everyone associated with the group. That's where public relations comes in. Quick action and intense effort are needed to overcome unfavorable impressions created by such incidents.

The job of public relations professionals is to explain the mission of their employers to the public and to provide complete and honest information to the media. When an error is made or an accident happens, public relations officials tell the public what the company is going to do to fix it.

Public Relations and You

You're already on your way to being a public relations professional, because you're learning to put together messages about your school and get them out to the people who are interested in the school. When you plan the content of a yearbook or write an article for your school newspaper, you are practicing to become a public relations professional. You're thinking about the students who are your main audience, or your **public,** the people who have the most interest in your topic. You're choosing the content they'll want to see or read. You're also working hard to put out a newspaper or book that will represent your school well when parents and people in your community see it. You are a public relations professional representing your school.

You're also learning how to think like a journalist and work with the media. Today's public relations professional is an information manager—a communications specialist who knows how to get messages out to people through the media.

Public relations has become so important that its practice has grown into a multibillion-dollar business in the United States alone. Nearly 200,000 professionals—more than 50 percent of them women and about 10 percent of them minorities—will be working in public relations by the year 2,000, according to the U.S. Bureau of Labor. You could be one of them if you have strong speaking and writing skills, current computer knowledge and the ability to build positive working relationships with people.

public

a group of individuals who share a common interest or characteristic and are targeted to receive specific messages related to their common interest or characteristic

Practicing Public Relations

Public relations is an emerging profession. In today's complex global society, businesses, governments and organizations must have people who can communicate their ideas to their publics and communicate the concerns of their publics back to management.

Public relations professionals are bridge builders, according to public relations practitioner Peter F. Jeff. Jeff believes that the job of public relations professionals is to build bridges between groups such as companies and their customers, employers and their employees, celebrities and their fans, and school districts and the taxpayers who support them. The public relations person's goal is to help his or her employer establish and maintain effective relationships with consumers, employees, other businesses and the media. Messages travel back and forth, much as the traffic on a bridge goes both ways. The underpinnings that support the public relations communications bridge are basic communications skills: listening and responding.

Public relations people listen carefully to their bosses to understand what the people in charge believe the public should know about their companies. They listen to consumers by doing surveys and studying consumer trends. They listen to what employees are saying to learn about their job-related concerns. They listen to those who make the laws and regulations governing their industry. They listen to their consciences. After evaluating all the information they have gathered, they create responses that are as honest and informative as possible.

Public relations professionals create messages using basic writing and speaking skills in traditional formats (news releases, speeches and letters) and in new electronic formats (video, Internet home pages and e-mail). They make daily calls to the media and other organizations in order to build relationships that give them and their employers credibility. They work to create positive public relations for their employers in as many ways as they can.

Today's successful public relations professionals share the bad news as well as the good news. As communicators they succeed because they put complicated business problems and policies into words the average consumer can understand.

SALLY FORTH reprinted by permission of King Features Syndicate.

YOUR BEAT

• •

1. Quickly give a word or words that come to mind when you see each of these names:

Disney	Ice-T
AARP	Chicago Cubs
Red Cross	Colorado Rockies
IRS	Michael Jackson
Phillip Morris Company	Michael Jordan
Nabisco	"Magic" Johnson
The president of the United States	Washington, D.C.
	Hollywood
Motown Records	CNN

MTV	Garth Brooks
National Public Radio	Mannheim Steamroller
Elvis Presley	

Your response is the public relations image each name has for you. Compare your responses with those of your classmates. Decide if each name has a positive, negative or neutral image in your class.

2. Find examples of news, such as the airplane crash or the yearbook fiascoes described earlier, that might contribute to the public relations image of a business or individual. If the news has a negative impact, what do you think the subject can do to overcome the image created by the news?

THE ETHICAL APPROACH TO PUBLIC RELATIONS

When the Chrysler Corporation was in financial trouble, it took the problem to the public. Chrysler promised that if the public stuck with it through a rebuilding period, the company would provide buyers a quality product. Chrysler gave its promise to the public through the "Car Buyer's Bill of Rights":

1. Every American has the right to quality.
2. Every American has the right to long-term protection.
3. Every American has the right to friendly treatment, honest service and competent repairs.
4. Every American has the right to a safe vehicle.
5. Every American has the right to address grievances.
6. Every American has the right to satisfaction.

(Source: Seitel, Fraser P. *The Practice of Public Relations*, 6th ed. [Prentice-Hall: Englewood Cliffs, NJ 1995] pg. 356–357)

The company backed its "Bill of Rights" with a board to which consumers could take complaints and conducted periodic surveys to measure consumer satisfaction. The strategy worked. Chrysler is in business today because people could see that the company was trying hard and being honest with them.

The classic example of potentially negative public relations turned positive by honest communications with the public is Johnson & Johnson's handling of the Tylenol poisonings in 1982. Johnson & Johnson was faced with the news that six Tylenol users in the Chicago area had died as a result of taking Tylenol capsules that contained

This Vermont store had an immeddiate reaction to the Tylenol scare—offer alternative choices to the recalled product.

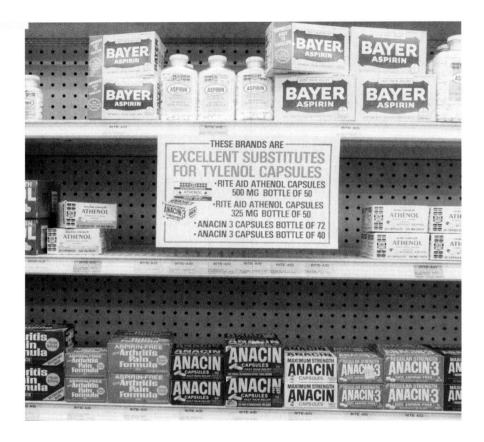

cyanide. It was later proved that the cyanide had been placed in the Tylenol capsules by one or more individuals after it left the manufacturing plant, but Johnson & Johnson's credibility had already been damaged.

Company officials listened to their instincts to be open and honest with the public. They decided they would get as much information out as quickly as they could, no matter how that information made them look. They answered thousands of calls from consumers and the media and held numerous news conferences in the next few days. Through the media, the company immediately announced a recall of 93,000 bottles of extra-strength Tylenol capsules in the Chicago area and told the public about its investigation of the manufacturing and distribution processes to try to locate the source of the problem.

Johnson & Johnson first said there was no cyanide in their plants. Then, on the second day, its public relations department announced that the information was incorrect. Cyanide was stored on the premises, but it was not used in the production of Tylenol. The company knew that having to correct the information would make it look doubly bad, but it was committed to being open and honest with the public.

Johnson & Johnson sent millions of telegrams to doctors and hospitals to warn them about the Tylenol, and they suspended all advertising to reduce consumer awareness of the product. By the second week after the crisis, Johnson & Johnson had recalled over 31 million bottles of Tylenol at a cost of over $100 million. The company also had posted a $100,000 reward for information about those responsible. Through news releases and advertisements, they offered to replace Tylenol capsules already purchased if consumers would return them.

Johnson & Johnson's willingness to take the lead in informing the public about the situation paid off. A consumer survey about two weeks into the crisis showed that 87 percent of Tylenol users realized that the company was not responsible. However, almost two-thirds said they were afraid to use the product again.

Johnson & Johnson refused to allow the incident to destroy a successful product. To overcome consumers' fears, the company designed a new triple-safety locked, tamper-resistant package. Johnson & Johnson then used an all-out **media blitz** to show the new, safer package to the public. In a media blitz, a sponsor uses many types of media simultaneously to reach as many people as possible with a message. Johnson & Johnson staged one of the world's first **teleconferences,** a satellite hookup that linked the media in 30 cities in a **video news conference.** Through the video news conference, the company was able to share information with reporters in many locations simultaneously and respond to their questions individually. The company distributed news releases; held media briefings; published ads; distributed information directly to employees and local distributors; and sent letters and telegrams to doctors, hospitals and consumers. Company officials appeared on network news and television talk shows to talk about their plans for Tylenol.

Johnson & Johnson wanted to make sure people understood that the company was more interested in consumer safety than in making money. Telling the truth, at the risk of bankrupting their own company, paid off. Within six months, Tylenol had recaptured 95 percent of its previous sales.

Johnson & Johnson's success was not yet complete, however. Four years later, a New York woman died after reportedly taking Tylenol capsules containing cyanide. This time Johnson & Johnson recalled all Tylenol capsules and replaced them with tablets that were more difficult to alter. The withdrawal of its product cost Johnson & Johnson more than $150 million, but its immediate, honest approach saved the company, its reputation, and its product.

media blitz

a public relations strategy in which a company uses many types of media simultaneously to get a message to as many people as possible

teleconference

a conference via satellite hookup that links individuals or groups at two or more locations or sites; used to share information simultaneously with multiple locations and allow persons in remote locations to interact with persons at the site from which the communication originates

video news conference

a news conference held at a location with teleconferencing capabilities so media in remote locations can interact with news conference speakers and participants; a news conference delivered simultaneously to multiple locations

1. Why do you think Chrysler's promise to the public, the "Car Buyer's Bill of Rights," was a successful strategy? What would have made it fail?

2. What other public relations options did Johnson & Johnson have in handling the first reports of Tylenol-related deaths? What options did the company have in responding to the death of another person four years later?

THE PUBLIC RELATIONS PROFESSIONAL

It takes a certain personality to handle the chaos of a public relations job. Some people thrive, and others can't survive, in the fast-paced, high-stress world of public relations.

The Public Relations Personality

Successful public relations professionals are organized, detail-minded individuals who have exceptional speaking, writing and communications skills. They are able to take leadership roles and to delegate responsibility. They are flexible, adaptable, open-minded people who can make sound judgments. They are willing to take risks based on solid research. They have creative, original ideas of their own. They believe in an ethical, honest approach and possess the integrity to stand up for it.

Among their job responsibilities are:

- working with the media
- building relationships and partnerships with other organizations
- writing news releases and preparing public service announcements
- designing and producing newsletters and company publications
- managing crises
- arranging special events
- conducting consumer surveys
- handling consumer relations
- ghostwriting speeches, articles and letters for their employers
- giving speeches and presentations
- formulating policies and procedures
- managing the image of company officials
- advising senior management
- working with volunteers
- money-raising

The Public Relations Events Planner

Planning, organization and time management skills are crucial to the success of all the activities journalists and public relations professionals do. Planning events is part of the job for many public relations professionals. Although it may not seem that planning a formal ceremony or a gala party is a job for a journalist, these activities draw on many of the same skills used in other facets of journalism. Speaking to those who will get the information and plan the event, writing invitations and knowing how to get media coverage require the same kind of organization and knowledge a reporter uses in planning, researching and writing a story.

If you find out in advance how an event is planned, you can create your own photo opportunity. This photographer positioned the camera where the Special Olympics torch bearer would light the Special Olympics Flame of Hope during opening ceremonies.

Let's say your school is going to celebrate a special anniversary, maybe 25 or 50 years. The superintendent appoints a committee to plan the event. The first thing the committee members will do is research other anniversaries and special events to see how they have been observed. They'll research schedules and calendars to find an appropriate date. They'll ask what special things the superintendent wants. After evaluating their research, they'll recommend a plan of action.

Once they have a plan, the committee members will appoint subcommittees and assign tasks. They'll get a calendar, and working backward from the date of the event to the present date, they'll set times for each step to be completed.

They'll communicate with the honored guests and speakers, write introductions and speeches for guest speakers, and make sure the media know about the event. They'll send invitations and have programs printed. They'll plan a seating arrangement and figure out how to get the cake cut to provide the best **photo opportunity**—a convenient way for photographers to get a good picture—for the media.

On the day of the anniversary celebration, the committee members will check to see that the right number of chairs are set up, test the microphone and greet the guests. They'll know who is going to clean up after the event. They'll have a plan for evaluating the success of the event. Finally, they'll make notes about what worked and what could have been improved to put in the file for future committees.

photo opportunity

an event staged or arranged in such a way that photographers can take the best possible photographs; photo opportunities may feature persons as well as events

Technical Skills in Public Relations

Writing tops the list of technical skills the public relations professional needs. Virtually every phase of public relations requires some writing, so being proficient with the mechanics of English is a must. Experience with journalistic style and editing techniques is especially helpful in writing news releases and producing company newsletters and magazines.

Public speaking is a close second in importance. Public relations professionals are called upon to make introductions, give speeches and presentations, and conduct educational seminars for company employees. As the official source of information in the company, the public relations professional may be asked to speak to a television audience as part of an on-camera interview or to narrate a series of promotional messages for radio.

Computer skills also rank near the top of the list of necessary technical skills. Public relations professionals use computers in the same ways reporters do: to write and edit, to do online searches, and to send e-mail. Many public relations departments use desktop publishing to produce company publications and promotional materials, and some have their own printing shops. Many companies have Internet home pages, which the public relations department maintains.

Knowledge of the principles of photography is helpful to those who take the photographs for their publications or who must place the photo images on the page. With scanners and digital photography replacing darkrooms, photography is becoming as much a computer skill as a camera skill.

High school journalists are learning the skills that public relations professionals use as they write stories, interview sources and use computers to produce publications that represent themselves and their schools.

1. Find out how public relations is handled in your school. If your school district has a public relations professional, invite him or her to class to talk about the job. If the school does not have someone whose job description is public relations, find out who is responsible for media relations for the school and invite that person to speak to your class. After listening to the speaker, brainstorm with your class to make a list of the public relations communications tools your school uses. These might include special activities, news releases, a district news letter, a sports information director and the students themselves.

2. After talking to someone in your school about public relations, write your definition of public relations as it pertains to you and to your school. Compare your definition with the definitions created by your classmates. List the personality traits, skills and special knowledge you think a person in a school public relations role needs to have.

3. Invite a reporter or editor to talk about what makes effective public relations people good at getting their messages in the media. Ask how a public relations person can help the media get information and create stories. Ask what actions obstruct the media in their efforts to get stories. Finally, ask what public relations professionals can do to build credibility and rapport with individuals in the media.

THE PUBLIC RELATIONS MESSAGE

Public relations professionals have to get their messages out quickly and accurately so the media can communicate those messages to the public. They use telephone, television, facsimile machines, mail, e-mail and telecommunications satellites to tell their messages to the media daily, and oftener in emergencies.

One reporter, Carla Marinucci of the *San Francisco Chronicle*, thinks they're overdoing it. In one month she received 109 pounds of "releases, videotapes, glossy magazines, posters, expensive glossy folders and plastic foam packing materials" that she classified as public relations pieces. Marinucci's experience is not unusual.

The best public relations professionals heard what Marinucci and others were saying and have stopped using cutsey approaches and glitzy promotional packages that look contrived and gimmicky. They realized that they were responsible for their own bad image. Today's professional prefers a businesslike approach to information distribution.

Still, sometimes a media blitz like the one Pepsi used in a June 1993 crisis is necessary. Ninety-five years of success almost ended for Pepsi when a consumer in the state of Washington reported finding a syringe inside a can of Diet Pepsi. A day later a hypodermic needle was reported in another can of Diet Pepsi in a nearby city. Within a few days, numerous reports of foreign objects in Pepsi cans came from locations as far apart as California, Wyoming, Pennsylvania and Louisiana.

Pepsi officials quickly formed a crisis management team. Everyone from the president of the company to local distributors worked feverishly to offset the panic that was rapidly spreading across the country.

The company knew that the way in which its cans were manufactured, filled and sealed was virtually tamper-proof. Nevertheless, it examined every step of the process, especially in the Seattle production plant. The company remained in continuous contact with bottlers and general managers in more than 400 locations. Sometimes it issued several consumer advisories and information updates each day so that local distributors would have accurate information to pass along to their customers.

Pepsi officials chose not to cease production nor to recall their product, because they truly believed the reports were false. They knew something was happening, but they were convinced it was not happening in their production plants. The media didn't see it that way, however. They perceived Pepsi's reluctance to withdraw possibly harmful products as a negligent action with possibly harmful results to consumers. The media criticized Pepsi for underestimating the power of the buying public. The company was vindicated when a man in Pennsylvania was arrested on the charge that he had fraudulently reported finding a syringe in a Pepsi can.

Throughout the crisis, Pepsi used television as its way of reaching the public. Labeling the traditional press conference a "dinosaur," the company bypassed it and the print media in favor of the much faster com-

NEW YORK, April 30, 1939— David Sarnoff chose the 1939 World's Fair for the launch of regular television broadcasting by the National Broadcasting Company.

The first telecast from the World's Fair featured President Franklin D. Roosevelt, the first president to appear on television.

The telecast was the culmination of a quarter of a century in the broadcast business for the Russian-born Sarnoff, whose name first came to the public's attention as that of the Marconi wireless radio operator who first picked up the distress signals from the *Titanic* in 1912.

Sarnoff believed radio would become a fixture in the average household. He hoped to create a radio network that would broadcast entertainment, information and education.

Sarnoff worked his way up in the Marconi Company, and when it was bought by Radio Corporation of America in 1919, he was made commercial manager. In 1930 he became president of RCA, the parent company of NBC.

Sarnoff was also one of the first to realize the value of television. In 1923 he predicted it would transform the way people communicated.

In 1932 Sarnoff built an experimental television station in the Empire State Building in New York City. The station, W2XF, became the center for RCA's experiments. By 1937 the station had mobile recording units on the streets of New York.

The first live coverage of a fire was carried on W2XF in 1938.

Communication satellite dishes are everywhere in our new global environment. Despite living in a refugee camp, this resourceful ethnic Albanian family has installed a makeshift satellite dish onto their tent.

munications satellites, which could distribute video directly to television stations. Pepsi's videotapes showed the high-speed production lines in its plants, the security measures in effect in the production plants, and finally, pictures from a convenience store surveillance camera showing a woman inserting a syringe into an open Diet Pepsi can.

Company officials appeared on the evening news and network talk shows. Videotapes of the surveillance camera pictures and a message from a Food and Drug Administration official commending the company's stance were sent to all Pepsi bottlers by overnight mail with the suggestion that they be shared with local customers.

Eventually, 55 people were arrested on charges of falsely claiming that their Pepsi cans contained foreign objects. Journalists and experts who had criticized Pepsi for standing behind its product now praised the company for its actions.

Getting Messages to the Public

Pepsi took advantage of the power of the electronic media to transmit messages to mass audiences quickly. The company bypassed the formal news conference because, it said, that was an awkward and time-consuming means of distributing information, as well as being difficult to schedule in order to suit the deadlines of newspaper and broadcast reporters. Pepsi officials didn't have time to waste, so they used the methods that today's reporters prefer. They sent information in more personal ways, such as by fax and e-mail, directly to reporters' desks. They also sent videotapes directly to local stations.

news release

information prepared in a news story format and distributed to the media to share information and generate publicity

fact sheet

a list of facts; similar to a news release in that it is a way to communicate information quickly and easily to the media

A **news release** is information from a source that has an interest in getting information out to the public. News releases come from nonmedia sources such as businesses and nonprofit organizations. They provide information to the media. Traditionally typewritten, news releases may now be sent on videotape, audio tape, floppy disc or CD and be delivered by fax or modem. A **fact sheet** is like a news release, but instead of being written in news story format it lists facts separated by white space and highlighted with bullets or check marks. News releases and fact sheets give reporters names and phone numbers of persons to contact for quotations, photographs or interviews.

Reporters should be cautious when using news releases. They are good for story ideas and basic information, but they should never be used without verifying the facts and changing the style to that of the publication or station. Quotations and information from other sources should be added to balance the story.

A **video news release (VNR)** is a news release in the form of a complete story ready to be aired. A VNR consists of video with a complete audio commentary. It is delivered free by satellite or cassette directly to the national networks and the more than 700 local television stations around the country. **B-roll** is edited videotape that stations can use to illustrate stories they write themselves. B-roll provides pictures of news events and sound bites from appropriate authorities that local stations would be unable to get for themselves. B-roll also may be accompanied by a fact sheet.

When VNRs were first introduced in the 1980s, they were a welcome novelty. Soon the media was flooded with so many VNRs, however, that the chances of one getting on the air diminished quickly. Stations found B-roll more useful, because it allowed them to illustrate stories while retaining control of the length and content of those stories.

video news release (VNR)

a news story on video delivered by satellite or cassette directly to television networks and local stations for use on news broadcasts

B-roll

extra video footage, sent separately or along with a VNR, for use by television stations in preparing their own stories

DATELINE

NEW YORK, 1904—Former *New York Times* and *New York Journal* reporter Ivy Ledbetter Lee opened a publicity firm dedicated to honest and truthful promotion of clients in New York City in 1904.

One of the first public relations professionals, Lee led the movement away from the promoter's practice of whitewashing the public to responsible public relations through a philosophy of being open and honest with the public. He is credited with having provided the public relations profession with the first code of ethics.

Lee saw his job as adjusting relationships between clients and their publics.

The movie industry, the American Tobacco Company, the American Red Cross, Standard Oil, Chrysler, the Rockefeller family, and Harvard and Princeton universities were among Lee's clients.

Another contender for the title "father of public relations" is Sigmund Freud's nephew, Edward L. Bernays.

In 1921, Bernays, 20, began to call himself a "public relations counsel." Two years later he wrote his first book on the subject and taught the first college course on public relations.

Bernays, like Lee, believed that public relations was more than just publicity and press agentry. He categorized public relations as being in the field of sociology rather than journalism because, he believed, it had more to do with influencing people's actions than with presenting information.

For instance, he convinced one company to sell bacon not by promoting the company's name but by promoting the idea of a nutritious breakfast.

Bernays was one of the first people to demonstrate that public relations could influence legislation. When short hair for women came into fashion, women stopped buying hair nets. A hair net company hired Bernays, who then emphasized the use of hair nets as a health and safety measure for food service personnel and for women working with machinery. Laws were passed requiring the hair nets, and sales increased again.

Writing a News Release or Fact Sheet

A good news release is written like a good news story. It starts with a direct lead that puts the 5 Ws and an H at the top, and it uses inverted pyramid organization. For more on organizing a news story, review basic news writing in Chapter 6.

A news release from the National Institute for Automotive Service Excellence (ASE) is shown in Figure 20.1. Note that the release has a news lead that contains the 5 Ws and an H:

- ✦ *Who:* automotive repair technicians
- ✦ *What:* want to change the image of their profession
- ✦ *Where:* Herndon, Virginia
- ✦ *When:* data released on July 12, 1995
- ✦ *Why/how:* responded to a survey by Stanford and ASE

The information is in descending order of importance. Additional information is highlighted in fact sheet style. This informative report on a survey simply states the findings. Like an objective news story, it does not state the source's opinion. If the writer had said, "ASE is proud and happy to share the results of our special survey," it would sound as though ASE were trying to make itself the center of attention rather than focusing on the information.

News releases may quote company spokespersons or experts expressing opinions or offering interpretations. Quotations should be short and punchy and not take longer than 10 seconds to read aloud if there's a possibility they may be used in a broadcast story. This news release from the National Institute for Occupational Safety and Health (NIOSH), for instance, quotes the NIOSH director:

> The National Institute for Occupational Safety and Health (NIOSH) recently released an alert which details hazardous jobs for adolescent workers. The document reveals that motor vehicle deaths accounted for the greatest number of work-related deaths of 16- and 17-year-olds between 1980–1989. Motor vehicle deaths include delivery services, road construction work, and work at gas stations. Other leading causes of death include machine related incidents, electrocutions, assaults and violent acts, and falls. Related research indicates that many adolescent workplace deaths may be associated with activities prohibited by child labor laws.
>
> "While the benefits of working are clear, we must recognize that thousands of adolescents are injured or killed in the workplace each year," said Dr. Linda Rosenstock, NIOSH Director. "Work should be a fulfilling and educational life experience for young people, not a life threatening one."

media alert

a news release that announces an upcoming event

News releases that announce upcoming events are called **media alerts.** Media alerts give data such as the time and place of the event and why it is being held. If the media alert concerns a person who will be appearing or making a speech, biographical background and the topic of the speech are important. Quotations from someone who knows the person or the person's reputation may be included.

FIGURE 20.1
SAMPLE NEWS RELEASE

NewsRelease

13505 Dulles Technology Drive, Suite 2
Herndon, Virginia 22071-3421
(703) 713-3800

**For Further information
contact:** Richard White
Nancy Guzik

And the Survey Says . . . A Profile of Today's Automotive Repair Technician

Herndon, VA -- July 12, 1995 . . . . Nearly three-fourths of automotive repair technicians are anxious to change the public's image of their profession according to a survey conducted by Stanford University Press & Consulting Psychologists Press, in conjunction with the National Institute for Automotive Service Excellence (ASE).

The survey was conducted as part of the Strong Interest Inventory used by U.S. schools. This renowned career counseling tool matches students' strengths and interests with professions. For the first time the survey included automotive mechanics in its inventory of occupations.

When technicians were asked what job features they would most like to change, 72% responded that they would like to see a change in the general public's image of the automotive repair technician. Forty-six percent would like to see a change in perks and benefits, and 45% indicated changes in the management style of their supervisors.

The survey also revealed that 89% of the technicians have at least a high school degree, 26% have post-secondary training, twenty-one percent have some college and 23% have at least an associate's degree while 2.3% hold a master's degree.

- more -

page 2 of 2
ASE News Release

...lings in the survey include:

...technicians receive 10-35 hours of update training a year, ...ree-fourths of the surveyed technicians expressed an ...eturning to school.

...en in the auto repair business between 11-20 years, 29% ...ars of experience, and 22% have been in the business ...l years.

...n at their present job 3-10 years, while 28.2% have ...present job for 11-20 years.

...ponses to the survey came from female technicians, ...her responses were generated by males.

...e of respondents, the majority fall within two groups. ...n the ages of 26-35, while 35% range between 36-45

...enter the field at age 18 or younger, while 30% ...e field between the ages of 19-25.

...reasons for seeking employment in the auto repair industry involved: 66.4% believe it is the best use of their talent, like to perform the required activities (59.2%), earn a good income (58%), can use training (55.5%), and 26.6% believe they are making an important contribution (26.6%).

The National Institute for Automotive Service Excellence (ASE), founded in 1972, is dedicated to improving the quality of automotive service and repair through the voluntary testing and certification of automotive technicians. Automobile, truck, and collision repair technicians, engine machinists, and parts specialists participate in ASE's program from all segments of the industry. More than 360,000 professionals are currently ASE certified.

# # #

The first paragraph of this media alert from a hospital gives all the facts a mother would need to participate in "Take Your Daughter to Work Day":

> The third annual TAKE YOUR DAUGHTER TO WORK DAY is scheduled for April 27. Because of the educational and occupational value associated with this event, Mary Lanning Hospital is encouraging women employees to bring their fifth through eighth grade daughters to work. A luncheon and a series of planned activities will take place between 12:15 p.m. and 3:45 p.m.

The hospital would follow "Take Your Daughter to Work Day" with a news release that told how many mothers and daughters participated and contained quotations from some of the girls about their experiences.

Formatting the News Release or Fact Sheet

The following basic information should be placed at the top of news releases and fact sheets to help editors and reporters use them easily:

- a letterhead or a heading with the source's name, address and phone number
- instructions for release: "FOR IMMEDIATE RELEASE" tells the media that the information may be used now; "FOR RELEASE AT (TIME, DATE)" means the information cannot be published or aired until after the specified time
- the date the information was prepared, either at the top of the page or in the dateline
- a dateline that tells where the story originated (optional)
- the name and phone number of one, and preferably two, contact persons

Like the format of a news story, the format for the body of a news release or fact sheet follows these basic guidelines:

- It is typed and double-spaced.
- It has 1- to 1 1/2-inch margins.
- Copy begins one-third of the way down on the first page.
- Copy is on one side of the page only.
- A slug appears at the top of each subsequent page with the story name and page number.
- Lists are indented and highlighted with bullets.
- Subheads divide and mark content changes.
- It uses journalistic editing marks, such as "more," "-30-" or "###" at the bottom of the page.
- A summary title or headline is optional but often included to tell the reader the topic.

1. Ask a local editor or station manager to save some of the most and least usable news releases he or she received this week and give them to your class. Examine the format of each news release. Decide which heading format you like best, or combine several to create one of your own from the examples. Using the heading you create, do Items 2 and 4 below.

2. Read sample media alerts. What kind of leads do they have? What organizational patterns do they use? If they use quotations, who are the sources, and where are the quotations placed in the story?

Using the model you think is best, write a media alert about an upcoming event at your school.

3. Read a news release that was written after an event. What information is in the lead? How is the story organized? If there are quotations, who are the sources? Would you include more or fewer quotations? What other sources would you quote?

4. Write a news release about an event that happened recently at your school.

5. Make a list of the media that should receive the school news release you wrote in Item 4. Compare your list with your classmates' lists, and compile a master list. Would the list be different for different stories? Why or why not?

PUBLIC SERVICE ANNOUNCEMENTS

Public service announcements (PSAs) are messages sponsored by nonprofit organizations and run at no cost to the sponsors. The brief messages in PSAs are catchy and persuasive. They are often created by public relations professionals.

PSAs focus on social, health, and safety issues. Smoky Bear, with his message about fire prevention, and the Crash Dummies, who promote the use of safety belts, are famous PSA characters (see Figure 20.2).

PSAs provide free publicity, because the media run them as a community service. Because of limited space or airtime, however, not all the PSAs distributed to the media will reach the public. Those that do will be used as the station or publication has time or space available. Local cable television stations that need to fill time between shows and on the community calendar are a new market for PSAs.

Print PSAs are sized like standard ads to fit newspaper and magazine pages. Usually several versions in different shapes and sizes are sent in one package so that the publication can choose the most convenient size. They're often accompanied by a news release or letter from the sponsor.

PSAs for radio and television run 10 to 60 seconds. Thirty seconds is the most common length. PSAs are distributed on tape ready for the station to air or as written scripts ready to read by the local announcer.

public service announcement (PSA)

an announcement promoting a public or non-profit activity; run by media at no cost to the sponsor

FIGURE 20.3
**SAMPLE PSA CAMPAIGN FOR
PRINT, RADIO AND TELEVISION**

PSAs are prepared as campaigns appropriate for all media. The message is reinforced in people's minds if they see the message on television, hear it on radio and read it in the paper within a short time period. A public relations professional needs to know how to prepare messages that all the media can use, as well as how to distribute them to the media to get the best exposure. Figure 20.3 shows an example of a PSA campaign for print, radio and television.

FIGURE 20.3, CONTINUED

THE ADVERTISING COUNCIL, INC.
GENDER EQUITY IN EDUCATION CAMPAIGN
for: Women's College Coalition, 125 Michigan Avenue, N.E. Washington, D.C. 20017

"JULIE WILLEY" :30 CNGE-5130

JULIE WILLEY: Chemistry class led me to a life of crime.

(SFX: SIREN)

I catch murderers, rapists and thieves

with a microscope.

JULIE WILLEY
Director of Delaware State
Police Crime Lab

Help your daughter

become a scientist.

YOUR BEAT

1. Prepare a fact sheet for your school. Make a list of the information the media might want to use in writing a story about your school. Start with the basics, such as enrollment, number of faculty members, and the age and size of the building. Then list the things that make your school unique. Interview authoritative sources to get the information.

2. Write the script for a 30-second PSA to encourage recycling or a cleaner environment. Target your PSA to the students if you are using it in school broadcasts. Target it to the general public if you don't have broadcast media in your school.

3. Brainstorm to come up with an idea for a PSA campaign for your school. It may be one used in student media or one designed for use by local media. Prepare a news release or fact sheet, a print promotion, a radio script and a television storyboard for the campaign.

CHAPTER REVIEW

KEY TERMS

Show that you know the meanings of the following key terms by correctly using them in complete sentences. Write your answers on a separate sheet of paper.

public relations
public
media blitz
teleconference
video news conference
photo opportunity
news release

fact sheet
video news release (VNR)
B-roll
media alert
public service announcement
   (PSA)

OPEN FORUM

1. The principal has asked your class to produce a three-minute VNR about your school to send to local television stations before school starts next fall. She knows that the opening of school is always news, and she thinks a VNR would be a good way to help out the local stations. From a public relations perspective, do you think it's a good idea? Why or why not? What other options are there for getting information about your school to the media? If you decided to do the VNR, what would you include in it? What would you not show? Why? What would you recommend to the principal?

2. A parent has challenged a book taught in a junior English class. The school has no policy for handling challenges to the curriculum. The principal has promised to "look into" the situation, but the angry parent has written a letter to the editor of the local newspaper expressing her concern about the content of the book as reading material for 16- and 17-year-olds. The school board wants to resolve the situation quickly and has asked the teacher to remove the book from his class immediately. The teacher has refused. You are the public relations director for your school. What options do you have? What would you recommend as a course of action for the school? Why?

3. Your newspaper recently published a front-page story about a student who is living with a foster family. Although removed from her home by the court at her own request, the student is undergoing counseling with her natural family and hopes to go back home soon. She was in favor of the story and gave a good interview for it. She even provided photographs of herself with both her families last Christmas (which ran on the front page). Your reporter interviewed the judge and a lawyer to make sure the story explained the legal

CHAPTER REVIEW, continued

◆ **OPEN FORUM, CONTINUED**

procedures accurately. The day after the story appeared, the superintendent called the newspaper's editor and adviser to his office and told them that the student's mother was threatening to sue the school for "washing my family's dirty laundry on the front page of your *!#*#! newspaper!" The superintendent asked the editor and adviser what they suggested should be done to avoid a lawsuit. "We don't need any more bad PR, so do something," he commanded. What do you think the newspaper should do? What should the superintendent do? What should the editor or adviser do?

4. Students elected the first minority homecoming queen in your school's history this year. The staff only got one good color photograph of the queen. The homecoming page in the yearbook is in black and white, but the opening pages are in color. Up against a deadline, the staff moves the color picture of the queen to the opening section and substitutes a picture of the first runner-up on the homecoming page. When the book comes out, the queen and her family are angry. They say it appears that the runner-up is the queen, because she is featured in the dominant photo on the homecoming page. You explain the circumstances, but they are not satisfied. A local committee for the protection of minority interests comes to the school board and demands that the book be reprinted. The committee threatens to take the issue to the media. It also threatens to take the school, the yearbook staff and the adviser to court. Most of the staff members who worked on that yearbook have graduated by now. It falls to you, the present staff, to find a solution. Could you or the school be sued for what the previous staff did? What do you recommend the school do? What do you suggest the yearbook staff do?

5. In 1993, Disney released a movie called *The Program,* which was the 12th most popular box office draw when it opened. *The Program* contained a scene in which drunken college football players lie prone in the middle of a busy highway to prove they are tough. They escape unharmed, of course, but a Pennsylvania teenager who tried the stunt after watching the movie wasn't so lucky. He was killed when a pickup truck ran over him. Within days of the movie's premier, three more teens were critically injured while lying on highways. All had just seen *The Program.*

   Disney quickly decided to delete the scene from the movie. At the time of the decision, the movie was playing in more than 1,000 theaters. *The Program* was rereleased without the offending scene, but it failed to resume its strong showing at the box office.

   The name Disney equals family entertainment. Disneyland. Disneyworld. The Disney Channel. Disney movies. Parents trust Disney, and Disney has always guarded that trust carefully.

   What would you have advised Disney to do in this situation? How do you think this incident affected Disney's public relations? Did Disney misjudge its product? Its effect on viewers? The public's response?

FINDING THE FLAW

Your publication's image is affected by every contact with your publication. Your image depends largely upon how accurately you edit. If you make errors like the ones in these examples, your reading public will begin to wonder if you check your facts as carelessly as you check your spelling, grammar and language.

Find the errors and correct them:

1. *From the cover and division pages of one yearbook:*

   m•e•m•b•e•r•s•h•i•p has it's Privleges

   Membership has its Priviledges

   Privileges of being a Vike

2. *From newspaper and yearbook copy:*

◆ Early May is the time to show our mothers all the reasons that we appreciate her.

◆ The team has greatly improved it's hitting performance throughout the season.

◆ Gliding towards the endzone for the winning touchdown, the team wins by a single point. Overjoyed with excitement, the player jumps up and down to show the satisfaction with themselves and then removes the helmet form the sweaty head under it. The crowd is simply astonished to see the long golden locks hanging from the player's head. Yes, it is a girl, you guessed right. Is that unusual?

◆ Charles Evans said that he and his wife have avoided a lot of arguments over the years by buying seperate toothpaste tubes. He likes to squeeze the tube from the bottom and role the tube up while she like to squeeze from the top, middle or any other part of it.

◆ "Masculinity is an impossible social role, no-one can do it adequately," Jenkins said. "No man feels they can fill the impossible role."

◆ It seems like all of Senior High's losses are tough one's, as of April 25, their only legitimate loss was a, 8–1, defeat courtesy of Lincoln.

◆ "We've just had a season long streak of bad luch, 2–6, is not where we planed to be," senior designated hitter Scott Athy said.

◆ "Were just not getting the two out base hits to score the runs that we need to win, were not executing", said coach Barney Cotton.

◆ After the freshmen English class received a letter from a freshman in Manitou Springs, Colo., and a cover letter from his teacher explaining the "Great Mail Race," the race was on.

   The "Great Mail Race" class members wrote to the student they received a letter from and they also chose two towns in different states to write to. Each student had to write three letters and could send one to each town if he wanted. The students sent the letters to the school in each town telling about his school,

◆ FINDING THE FLAW, continued

community and himself. Their teacher also included a cover letter telling about "The Race."

◆ "At the next meeting we want to take a look at each organizations budget and demise a plan that will enable groups to work together on activities to save money for everyone," Student ation president Gena Bagley said.

◆ If a person chooses to park illegally, they make sure they park on the city roads because the city's fines are lower than campus fines.

3. From yearbook copy written for a public who will know that the Gray Center hall windows face west:

The morning sun slips through the hall windows and beats across the red tiled hallway. Sole footfalls of Rex, the janitor, echo through the otherwise vacant building. It's 6:30 a.m., and the Gray Center is quiet.

MEDIA WATCH

1. Look through *Public Relations Journal, Advertising Age, Direct, Student Press Law Center Newsletter* or similar publications for examples of public relations problems that have been resolved. Bring an example to class

2. Identify someone in your community whose job includes public relations. Interview that person about his or her job. Find out what kinds of things the person does that could be described as public relations and what public relations problems he or she has encountered. Ask what skills that person finds most valuable and what personality traits help in the performance of the job. Compare your information with the information your classmates have gathered. What similarities and differences did you find among different public relations professionals and their jobs?

String Book

You may use any newspapers for this activity, including school newspapers. Clip the page header with the name and date of the newspaper for each article; keep it with the example.

1. Collect 10 examples of public service announcements from magazines or newspapers. Choose the three you think are best to put in your portfolio. Note whether you see the same PSA message on radio or television.

2. Write a media alert about an upcoming event at your school. Ask the public relations person in your school for a copy of the information that was sent to the media about the event. Compare your media alert with the information sent by the school.

THE STYLEBOOK

A GUIDE FOR STUDENT WRITERS AND EDITORS

*T*his stylebook provides student writers examples in correct journalistic style, alphabetized for easy reference.

Aa

abbreviations and acronyms In general, avoid abbreviations or acronyms readers would not recognize.

Guidelines:

1. Use *Dr., Mr., Mrs., the Rev., Sen., Gov., Lt. Gov., Rep., Sen,* and abbreviate certain military titles before a name outside direct quotations. Spell out president, vice president, secretary, attorney general, ambassador, chairman, professor.

> RIGHT: *Dr. Anna Rodriguez; Mr. Thomas Greene; Mrs. Ruth Cording; the Rev. Steven J. Lashbrook; Gov. Bob Kerrey*
> WRONG: *Doctor Anna Rodriguez; Mister Thomas Greene; the Reverand Steven J. Lashbrook; Governor Bob Kerrey*

For more guidelines on how to use titles, see **courtesy titles; military titles; religious titles.**

2. Abbreviate *junior* or *senior* after a person's name. Abbreviate *company, corporation, incorporated* and *limited* after a corporate title.

> RIGHT: *Douglas Henning Jr.: The Walt Disney Co.; American Broadcasting Cos.*

3. Use *A.D., B.C., a.m., p.m.,* No., and abbreviate certain months with the day of the month. See **months.**

> RIGHT: *In 220 B.C.; at 1:00 p.m.; in room No. 8; on Aug. 18.*
> WRONG: *Early this a.m. Terri asked for the No. of your room.* The abbreviations are correct only with the figures.

> RIGHT: *Early this morning Terri asked for the number of your room.*

4. Abbreviate *avenue, (Ave.) boulevard (Blvd.)* and *street (St.)* in numbered addresses: *She lives at 909 Forest Ave. She lives on Forest Ave.* See **addresses.**

5. Certain states such as, the United States are abbreviated with periods. See **states.**

6. Some organizations are recognized by their initials: *FBI, CIA, NAACP,* which are acceptable on first reference. If it fits the occasion, use *Central Intelligent Agency* instead of *CIA.*

> Don't use the abbreviation or acronym in parentheses after a full name. Do not reduce names to unfamiliar abbreviations to save words.

academic degrees If it is necessary to establish credentials avoid abbreviations. Use a phrase such as: *Mary Smith, who has a doctorate in English.*

Use an apostrophe in *bachelor's degree, master's degree, etc.* Abbreviate *B.A., M.A., Ph.D., etc.* Use the abbreviation only after a full name—never a last name.

Used after a name, an academic abbreviation is set off by commas: *Ross Carrey, Ph.D., spoke at the forum.*

Don't follow a name with a title for an academic degree and use the abbreviation for the degree in the same reference.
> RIGHT: *Dr. Nathan Lee, a biologist.*
> WRONG: *Dr. Nathan Lee, Ph.D.*

academic departments Lowercase except for proper nouns or adjectives: *department of psychology, psychology department, department of English, English department.*

academic titles Capitalize and spell out formal titles such as *professor, dean, president, chancellor, chairman, etc.,* before a name: *Professor Carol Matthews.*

accept, except *Accept* means to receive: *Tom Hanks accepts the award. Except* means to eliminate: *Take all the sweaters except the blue one.*

act numbers Use Arabic numerals and capitalize: *Act 1; Scene 2.* But: *the third act, the fourth act.*

addresses Follow the guidelines for numbered addresses from **abbreviations and acronyms.**

Spell out and capitalize addresses when they are part of a formal street name without numbers: *Main Street.*

Lowercase and spell out when used alone or with more than one street name: *Delaware and Pennsylvania avenues.*

Use the same guidelines with similar words such as, *drive, road,* etc.

Always use figures for an address number: *10 Saylor Circle.*

Spell out and capitalize *First* through *Ninth* as in street names; use figures with two letters for 10th and above: *3 Fifth Ave., 200 44th St.*

Abbreviate *north, south, east* and *west* when indicating directional ends of a street: *253 N. 44th St., 620 S. 14th St.*

affect, effect *Affect,* as a verb, means to influence: *The scores on the test will affect the class average.*

Effect, as a verb, means to cause: *Hiring him will effect the company.*

As a noun, it means result: *The effect of the fireworks captivated the crowd.*

ages Always use figures.

Hyphenate before a noun when specifying an age. Use commas to set off the ages of individuals: *The 6-year-old. Jane is 3 years old. Kimberly, 7, has a sister, 6 months old. The man is in his 50s.*

Spell out ages one through nine, use figures for 10 and above: *The boy is eight years old . . . his cousin is 15.*

alumnus, alumni, alumna, alumnae Use *alumnus* (*alumni* plural) when referring to a man who's attended school.

Use *alumna* (*alumnae* plural) when referring to a woman who's attended school.

Use *alumni* when referring to a group of men and women.

a.m., p.m. Lowercase with periods: *She woke up at 3 a.m.*

Avoid such statements as *3 a.m. this morning.*

awards Capitalize awards: *Medal of Honor, Nobel Prize, Pulitzer Prize,* etc.

Lowercase prize when it's not linked with a specific award: *The peace prize was awarded Wednesday.*

Lowercase the categories: *Pulitzer Prize for fiction.*

Bb

B.C. Acceptable in references to the period before Christ. Place *B.C.* after the year: *43 B.C.*

Bible Capitalize the book or its terms without quotation marks: *the Bible, the Gospels, Gospel of St. Matthew, the Scriptures, the Holy Scriptures.*

Lowercase as a non-religious term: *My address book is my bible.*

Don't abbreviate the individual books of the Bible.

To cite, chapter and verse(s): *Psalm 23:1, Revelation 6:3, Genesis 1:1.*

birthday Capitalize as part of the name for a holiday: *Lincoln's Birthday.* Lowercase in other situations.

book titles See **composition titles.**

brand names Capitalize them when they are used: *He smoked a Camel.*

Use a company's name in first reference when it sponsors an event, use a generic term for the event in all references: *Campbell Soup sponsored the ice-skating competition.*

Cc

capital, capitol *Capital* is the city where a seat of government is located. Do not capitalize.

In a financial sense, *capital* refers to money or property used in a business by a person or corporation.

Capitalize references to the national or state buildings and their sites. Always capitalize *the Capitol, U.S. Capitol, Capitol Hill.*

Follow the same guidelines when referring to state capitols: *The Texas Capitol is in Austin.*

Celsius Use this term rather than centigrade.

The forms: *40 degrees Celsius, or 40 C* (note the space and no period after the C). See **temperatures.**

cents Spell out *cents* and lowercase, using figures for amounts less than a dollar: *10 cents, 13 cents.* Use the $ sign and decimals for larger amounts: *$4.03, $7.50.*

church Capitalize as part of the formal name of a building, a congregation, or denomination: *the Roman Catholic Church, St. Cecilia's Church.* Lowercase these in plural: *the Catholic and Presbyterian churches.*

Also lowercase generic usage: *a Roman Catholic church, a church;* and in an institutional sense: *The priest said the church opposes abortion. They believe in separation of church and state.*

city Capitalize as part of a proper name: *Oklahoma City, New York City.*

Lowercase in other places: *a Minnesota city council, the city Board of Education* and all *city of* phrases: *the city of Cleveland.*

The form for the section of a city is lowercase: *the south side, eastern Seattle.* Capitalize recognized popular names: *Southside of Chicago, Lower East Side of New York.*

college Capitalize as part of a proper name: *Boston College.*

composition titles In books, movies, operas, plays, poems, songs, television programs, lectures, speeches and works of art capitalize the first word and all succeeding words except articles and short (four letters or less) conjunctions or prepositions. Use quotation marks for most:

"The Scarlet Letter," "To Kill a Mockingbird," "Star Wars," "The Magic Flute," "Hamlet," "The Star Spangled Banner," "Mona Lisa," "The Simpsons." See **television programs.**

Use no quotation marks for the titles of:

—A sacred book or its parts: *the Bible, The New Testament, the Koran, the Torah, the Talmud, the Apocrypha.*

—Reference works such as, catalogs, almanacs, directories, dictionaries, encyclopedias, and handbooks: *Encyclopedia Americana, The Dictionary of Slang, The Random House Thesaurus.*

county Capitalize as part of a proper name: *Saline County, Jefferson County, Montgomery County.* But: *the county Board of Health, the county.* Lowercase all *county of* and plural uses: *Lancaster and Shelby counties, the county of Boyd.*

Capitalize the names of county governments: *the Lancaster County Department of Social Services, the Boyd County Legislature.*

Capitalize as part of a title before a name: *County Commissioner Richard Gross.* Lowercase when it is not part of the title: *county Health Commissioner Carla Morales.*

courtesy titles In general, don't use *Miss, Mr., Mrs.,* or *Ms.* with first and last names of the person. Exceptions: In direct quotations and to identify relationships.

Dd

days Capitalize and do not abbreviate, except in tabular format (3 letters, without periods): *Sun, Mon, Tue, Wed, Thu, Fri, Sat.*

directions and regions Lowercase *north, south, east, west, northern,* etc., when indicating compass direction: *Hurricane Andrew is moving south.* Elsewhere:

1. Capitalize compass points that designate regions: *A heatwave developing in the Midwest is moving eastward. The storm will bring rain to the West Coast by mid-morning and to the Southeast by late afternoon. He has a Southern accent.*

2. Capitalize compass points as part of a proper name: *South America, North Pole, North Dakota, West Virginia.*

3. Lowercase compass points with other nations except to designate a politically divided nation: *northern Ireland* But: *South Korea.*

4. Lowercase compass points to describe a section of a state or city: *northern Colorado, West Idaho.* But capitalize them if a particular section is widely known: *Upper East Side of New York, Southern California.*

dollars Use figures and the $ sign in all amounts without a figure: *The compact disc cost $12. Bob, could you please loan me ten dollars?*

For amounts of more than $1 million, use the $ and figures up to two decimals: *The diamonds are worth $5.5 million.*

For amounts less than $1 million: *$5, $20, $100, $1000.*

Ee

editor in chief No hyphens. Capitalize as a formal title before a name: *Editor in Chief Garrett Anderson.*

elderly   Use elderly or senior citizen carefully. Do not use them to describe anyone under 65, and not casually for anyone beyond that age. Some general references are appropriate: *a home for the elderly.*

except   See **accept, except.**

execute   To kill in accordance with a legally imposed death sentence. See **homicide.**

exclamation point   Use it only in exceptional cases to express a high degree of surprise.

Place the exclamation mark inside quotation marks if it is part of the quoted material, outside if it isn't.

"Fire!" she yelled.

Ff

Fahrenheit   The forms, if needed: *75 degrees Fahrenheit,* or *75 F* (note the space and no period after the F). See **temperatures.**

family names   Capitalize family relationships only as part of or substitute for a person's name: *I wrote Grandma Verbeck. I sent my father a birthday card.*

foreign words   Many words and abbreviations with foreign organizations, such as *bon voyage* are accepted in English and may be used without explanation if they are clear in the context.

fraternal organizations and service clubs
Capitalize proper names: *American Legion, Lions Club, Rotary Club, Theta Chi, Sigma Epsilon*

Gg

government   Always lowercase and never abbreviate: *the U.S. government.*

An administration consists of the officials who make up the executive branch of government: *the Clinton administration.*

governmental bodies   Capitalize the full proper names of governmental agencies, departments and offices: *the U.S. Department of State, the Chicago Fire*

Department, the New Orleans City Council. Retain capitals if the specific meaning is clear without the jurisdiction: *the Department of State, the Fire Department, the City Council.*

1. Lowercase when the reference is not specific: *Nebraska has no state senate.*

2. Lowercase generic terms standing alone or in plural uses: *the New Orleans and Little Rock city councils, the department.*

Hh

historical periods   Capitalize proper nouns and adjectives in describing periods of history: *ancient Rome, the Victorian era.*

Some cultural and historical periods and events are capitalized: *the Stone Age, the Middle Ages, Boston Tea Party.*

Some are not: *the ice age, the industrial revolution.*

HIV   Acceptable on second reference for human immunodeficiency virus, the cause of AIDS.

holidays   Capitalize them: *New Year's Eve, Easter, Thanksgiving, Hanukkah, etc.*

Legal holidays in federal law are New Year's Day, Martin Luther King Jr. Day, Washington's Birthday, Memorial Day, Independence Day, Labor Day, Columbus Day, Veterans Day, Thanksgiving, Christmas.

homicide   The killing of one human by another.

Murder is malicious or premeditated homicide. Do not say a victim was murdered until someone was convicted of murder. Instead use *killed* or *slain.* Do not describe someone as a murderer until convicted of the charge in court.

Manslaughter is homicide without malice or premeditation.

A *killer* is anyone who kills with a motive of any kind.

An *assassin* is a killer of a politically important person.

To *execute* is to kill in accordance with a legally imposed sentence. See **execute.**

homosexual   Preferred over *gay* as a term for a homosexual.

Ii

initials Use periods and no space; *O.J. Simpson.* For middle initials, if used: *Michael J. Fox.* Exception: Use no periods when referring to presidents by three initials: *FDR, JFK, LBJ.*

Jj

jargon The special vocabulary of a particular class or occupational group. If jargon is used, explain it.

journalese Newswriters' jargon; words and phrases commonly used in news stories, but seldom seen elsewhere in the same context. Avoid it. Some examples:

blasted for *denounce:* The police official blasted the accusation.

blaze for *fire:* The office blaze killed 10 people.

closed-door for *private:* The counselors met behind closed doors.

designed for *purpose:* A law designed to prohibit abortion.

grilled for *questioned:* Investigators grilled the witness.

hiked for *increase:* Congress hiked taxes 3 percent.

hosted for *held:* Mrs. Nelson hosted a reception.

hurled for *made:* Accusations were hurled by the lawyers.

kicked off for *initiated:* The campaign kicked off Saturday.

probe for *investigation:* The probe lasted six months.

sprawling for *expansive:* The sprawling health center in Mississippi.

staged for *held:* The demonstration was staged at the U.S. Capitol.

triggered for *setting off:* His actions triggered the riot.

unveiled for *announced:* The general unveiled his plan.

Jr. Not set off with commas: *John F. Kennedy Jr.* See **junior, senior.**

junior, senior Spell out for a class of its members; She is a junior in high school.

Use Jr. and Sr. to designate a son or father, only with a full name. Do not set off by a comma: *Harry Connick Jr.*

jury Always lowercase. It takes singular verbs and pronouns: *The jury has been sequestered until it reaches a verdict. A jury of eight men and four women.*

Kk

kids Use children: *The children gather outside before classes begin.*

Ll

lake Capitalize as a proper name: *Lake Huron, Blue Stem Lake.* Lowercase in plural uses: *lakes Ontario and Erie.*

languages Capitalize the proper names of languages and dialects: *Cajun, English, Spanish, German, Yiddish, French, etc.*

lay, lie To *lay* is to cause to recline. To *lie* is to recline.

RIGHT: *She will lie down on the couch. She lay down the pencil.*
WRONG: *She will lay down on the couch. She lie down the pencil.*

Other forms of *lie:* She *lay* down on the couch (past tense). She has *lain* down on the couch (past participle). She is *lying* down on the couch (present participle).

Other forms of *lay:* She *laid* down the pencil (past tense). She has *laid* down the pencil (past principle). She is *laying* down the pencil (present participle).

legislative titles Capitalize formal titles before names; lowercase elsewhere: Use *Rep., Reps., Sen., Sens.* before names in regular text, but spell them out in direct quotations.

Spell out other legislative titles (assemblyman, assemblywoman, city councilor, delegate, etc.) in all uses. Other guidelines:

1. Use *U.S.* or *state* before a title only if necessary to avoid confusion: *U.S. Sen. Bob Dole spoke at the meeting.*

2. The use of a title such as *Rep.* or *Sen.* in first reference is normal but not mandatory, provided the title is given later in the story: *Bob Dole signed the bill Wednesday. The Kansas senator left briefly.*

3. Do not use legislative titles before a name on second reference unless they are part of a direct quotation.

4. Use *Congressman* and *Congresswoman* as capitalized formal titles before a name only in direct quotation.

5. Capitalize formal, organizational titles before a name: *Speaker, Majority Leader, Minority Leader.*

legislature   Capitalize plain text with or without a state name if a specific reference is clear: *the Massachusetts Legislature.* Or: *BOSTON, Mass. (AP)—Both houses of the Legislature met today on Capitol Hill.*

Lowercase legislature in all generic and in plural references: *The legislature approved the bill. The Louisiana and Arkansas legislatures are discussing the amendment.*

lesbian, lesbianism   Lowercase in reference to homosexual women, except in names of organizations.

line numbers   Use figures and lowercase: *line 1, line 20. But: the first line, the 10th line.*

literature   See **composition titles.**

Mm

magazine names   Capitalize without quotation marks. Lowercase *magazine* unless it is part of the formal publication's title: *Entertainment Weekly magazine, Redbook magazine, Harper's Magazine.* See **composition titles.**

master of arts, master of science   A *master's degree* or *a master's* is acceptable. See **academic degrees.**

mile   Use figures for amounts under 10 in dimensions: *The car slowed to 5 mph.*

Spell out below 10 in distances: *He drove nine miles.*

military academies   Capitalize *Air Force Academy, Coast Guard Academy, Military Academy, Naval Academy.*

Lowercase *academy* when it stands alone or in plural uses: *the academy, the Army, Navy and Air Force academies.*

Cadet is the title when referring to a man or woman in the Army, Air Force and Coast Guard academies. *Midshipman* is the title for men and women in the Naval Academy.

military titles   Capitalize a military rank when used as a formal title before a name. Lowercase elsewhere.

Spell out and lowercase a title when it is substituted for a name: *Gen. Paula K. Russel departed today. A soldier said the general would arrive late.*

In some cases, it may be necessary to explain the significance of a title: *Army Sgt. Maj. Jack Robinson explained the plan. Robinson, who holds the Army's highest rank for enlisted men, said the plan would be difficult.*

months   Capitalize the names of months in all uses. Use the abbreviations: *Jan., Feb., Aug., Sept., Oct., Nov.,* and *Dec.* with a specific date.

In tabular material, use three letters without a period: Jan, Feb, Mar, Apr, May, Jun, Jul, Aug, Sep, Oct, Nov, Dec.

mountains   Capitalize as part of a proper name: *Rocky Mountains, Appalachian Mountains.* Or simply: *the Rockies, the Appalachians.*

movie ratings   The following are ratings used by the Motion Picture Association of America Inc.:

G—General Audiences. All ages admitted.

PG—Parental Guidance. Some material may not be suitable for children.

PG-13—Special parental guidance strongly suggested for children under 13. Some material may be inappropriate for young children.

R—Restricted. Under 17 requires accompanying parent or guardian.

NC-17—No one under 17 admitted.

Capitalize and hyphenate adjectival forms: *an R-rated film.*

movies   See **composition titles.**

music   See **composition titles.**

Capitalize, but don't use quotation marks on titles for orchestral works: *Beethoven's Serenade for Flute, Violin and Viola. Bach's Suite No. 1 for Orchestra.* If the instrumentation is not part of the title but is added for explanation, the names of the instruments are lowercased: *Mozart's Sinfonia Concertante in E flat major for violin and viola.*

Use quotation marks for non-musical terms in a title: *Beethoven's "Eroica" Symphony.* If the work has a special full title, all of it is quoted: *"Rhapsody in Blue."*

In other references lowercase *symphony, concerto.*

Nn

nationalities Capitalize the proper names of nationalities, peoples, races, tribes, etc.: *Arab, Arabic, African, African American, American, Caucasian, Cherokee, Chinese, Eskimo, French Canadian, Japanese, Jew, Jewish, Latin, Negro (Negroes), Oriental, Sioux, Swede, etc.*

Lowercase descriptive words: *black* (noun or adjective), *white, red, mulatto.*

newspapers Capitalize *the* in a newspaper's name if that is the way a publication prefers: *The Wall Street Journal.* But lowercase *the* in a shortened name: *the Times.*

Where location is needed but is not part of the official name, use parentheses: *The Huntsville (Ala.) Times.*

No. Use this abbreviation for number with a figure to indicate position or rank: *No. 1 team, No. 2 choice.*

Do not use in street addresses, with this exception: *No. 10 Downing St., the residence of Britain's prime minister.*

Do not use *No.* in the names of schools: *Public School 20.*

Spell out, i.e. *Number 12.*

noon Don't put *12* in front of it.

numerals Roman numerals use the letters I, V, X, L, C, D and M. Use Roman numerals for wars and to show personal sequence for animals and people: *World War I, Richard III, Dancer V.*

Guidelines:

1. The general rule is to spell out numbers under 10 and use figures for those above nine. Exceptions listed below.

2. When large numbers must be spelled out, use a hyphen to connect a word ending in y to another word; do not use commas between other words that are part of one number: *twenty, twenty-one, one hundred sixty-two, one thousand five hundred seven, one million three hundred forty-three thousand eight hundred ninety-nine.*

3. Follow an organization's practice in proper names: *20th Century Fox.*

4. Always use figures for
Addresses: *500 Elm St., P.O. Box 20.*
Ages: No matter if it is a person, place or thing.
Betting odds: *4-1* (hyphenated)
Broadcast channels: *TV Channel 11*

Caliber and gauge: *.30 caliber, 10 mm, 10 gauge.*
Dates: *July 4* (not July 4th, but *the 4th day of July).*
Dimensions: *Inches, feet, yards, millimeters, etc.*
Distances: *Miles, kilometers, etc.*
Fractions and whole numbers: *2 1/2* (but *one-half* if used alone).
Governmental jurisdictions: *2nd Congressional District.*
Map coordinates: *90 degrees south latitude.*
Millions: *4 million, 8 billion.*
Military units: *3rd Fleet, 7th Air Force.*
Money: *5 cents, $3.00, 8 pounds, 12 marks.*
Nomenclature: *Title 9.*
Percentages: *6 percent* (not 6.0 percent, but *0.6 percent*)
Position or rank: *No. 1 man in the race.*
Proportions: *1 part water, to 3 parts sugar.*
Ratios: *3-to-1* (n.), *3-1* (adj.).
Rooms: *Room 14 in the Hilton Hotel.*
Scores: *50-35 victory; The Braves won 6-2.*
Sizes: *Size 6 dress, a size 7 shoe.*
Speeds and rates: *5 mph.*
Temperatures: *60 degrees F* (but *zero degrees F).*
Times: *4:15 p.m.*
Volume: *7 cubic yards.*
Votes: *Clinton defeated Bush 100-50.*
Weights: *8 pounds, 7 ounces.*

5. Always spell out:
Casual expressions: *thanks a million.*
Fourth of July: *July the Fourth* or *Fourth of July.*
Sentence openers: Spell out all numbers in the first word of a sentence except years.
From one to nine—write out: *one, two, three, and so forth.*
From 10-999—use numerals: *10, 50, 100, 900.*
Write out hundred, thousand, Million and BILLION: *25-hundred, three-thousand, seven-Million, and nine-BILLION.*

Round out all figures unless the exact one is necessary to the story.

Never say a Million. The "a" can be heard as "eight." Write it one-million.

If it necessary to begin a sentence with a figure, follow above rules for use of numerals and spelling out: *Two students tied for first place, 12 people were killed.*

Do not spell out or hyphenate years: *1965 was a good year.*

In writing dates, it is: *December 25th, 28, 31* and so forth.

Use only figures and hyphens in sports scores, odds, votes and ratios. The "to" is implied by the hyphen: *The School Board voted 7-4. Dallas shut out Buffalo 50-30.*

Oo

obscenities, profanities, vulgarities Don't use them in stories unless they are part of direct quotations or there is a reason for them.

When profanity, obscenity or vulgarity is used, flag the story at the top: *The contents may be offensive to some readers.*

Confine the offensive language in quotation marks.

In reporting profanity that uses the words *damn* or *god*, lowercase *god* and use *damn, damn it, goddamn it.* Do not change the offending words to euphemisms such as *damn it* to *darn it.*

If a quote containing profanity, obscenity or vulgarity can't be dropped but there is no reason for the offensive language, replace the letters with hyphens: the word damn, for example, would become *d---."*

OK, OK'd, OK'ing, OKs Don't use *okay.*

organizations and institutions Capitalize the names of organizations and institutions: *General Motors Corp., Harvard University, the Society of Professional Journalists, Delta Kappa, Gamma.*

Some organizations and institutions are recognized by their abbreviations: *NAACP, NATO, NASA.* See **abbreviations and acronyms.**

Pp

people, persons Use person when talking about an individual: *One person signed up for the committee meeting.*

People is preferred to persons in plural uses: *Hundreds of people attended the concert. There were 20 people at the lecture. What did people say when he announced the winner?*

Persons should be used when it's in a direct quote or as part of a title such as *Bureau of Missing Persons.*

People should be used when referring to a single race or nation: *The African-American people united.*

percent One word: *The surgeon said 20 percent of the residents passed the exam.*

planets Capitalize the names of the planets: *Jupiter, Mars, Mercury, Neptune, Pluto, Saturn, Uranus, Venus.*

Capitalize *Earth* when used as the proper name of our planet: *The space shuttle left Earth.*

p.m., a.m. Lowercase with periods.

Avoid such statements as *11 p.m. tonight.*

poetry Capitalize the first word in a line of poetry, unless the author has deliberately used lower-case for effect. See **composition titles.**

principal, principle *Principal* means someone or something in rank, authority or importance: *Ms. McIntyre is the principal of our school.*

A *principle* is a rule: *The principle reason for fighting was for respect.*

Qq

question mark Use a question mark at the end of a direct quotation.

"Who attacked the woman?" he asked. (Note the comma is not used after the question mark.) *Did he ask who attacked the woman?* Elsewhere:

1. Use a question mark at the end of a full sentence that asks a multiple question. *Did you hear him say, "What time should we attack the woman"?*

2. In a series, use a question mark after each item if you wish to emphasize each element. If no emphasis is intended, use a comma.

RIGHT: *Did they plan the attack? Pay people? Set a time?*
RIGHT: *Did they plan the attack, pay people and set a time?*

3. Do not use a quotation mark at the end of an indirect question: *He asked who attacked the woman.*

4. Do not use a question mark in parentheses to express doubt about a word, fact or number, or to indicate humor or irony.

5. In a Q-and-A format, use question marks but no quotation marks and paragraph each speaker's words.

Q. Do you know Robert, why you killed her?
A. I don't know . . . I don't know.

6. Place a question mark inside quotation marks if it applies to the quoted material, outside if they apply to the whole sentence.

Who starred in "Pretty Woman"?
She asked, "Where is the book?"

Rr

race   Use a racial identification only if it is clearly pertinent:

—In biographical and announcement stories, particularly when they involve a feat or appointment that has not been routinely associated with members of a particular race.

—When it provides readers with an insight into conflicting emotions known or likely to be involved in a demonstration or similar event.

In some stories that involve a conflict, it is equally important to specify that an issue cuts across racial lines. For example, if a demonstration by supporters of busing to achieve racial balance in schools includes substantial number of whites, that fact should be noted.

Do not use racially derogatory terms unless they are part of a quotation that is essential to the story.

religion   Lowercase religion in all uses: *the Christian religion.*

1. Lowercase all titles that describe a job: *minister, pastor, priest etc.*

Capitalize a title before a name on first reference, lowercase when standing alone or set off by commas: *Bishop Michael Taylor, the bishop; Deacon Samuel Traven, the deacon; Pope Paul VI, Pope Paul, the pope; Rabbi Daniel Ryan, the rabbi.*

Use Sister or Mother in all references before the name of a nun: *Sister Mary Teresa.* If she uses a surname, *Sister Mary Teresa Roberts* on first reference, *Sister Roberts* on second. Lowercase *sister* or *mother* without a name.

2. Capitalize references to religious orders or their members: *He is a Jesuit.*

3. Capitalize proper nouns referring to a deity: *God, Alluh, Jehova, the Father, the Son, Jesus Christ, the Holy Spirit, etc.* Lowercase words derived from God and all pronouns referring to the deity: *god-awful, goddaughter, godfather, godsend, godspeed, he , him, thee, thou, thy, thine, etc.*

4. Lowercase god in references to a deity of a polytheistic religion, but capitalize names of gods and godesses: *Zeus, Helena, Venus, Posidon.*

5. Capitalize alternate names for Mary, the mother of Jesus: *Holy Mother, Virgin Mary.* But: *virgin birth.*

6. Capitalize *Last Supper* and *Lord's Prayer*, but lowercase other rites, celebrations, sacraments or services: *baptism, bar mitzvah, confirmation, communion, mass, worship service, etc.*

7. Lowercase *angel, cherub, devil, heaven, hell, satanic, etc.*, but capitalize proper names: *Hades, Satan, Gabriel.*

Ss

school   Capitalize when part of a proper name: *Kennedy Junior High School, Lefler Middle School, Public School 2, Madison Elementary School.*

states   Lowercase in all state references: *state of Montana, the states of Rhode Island and Delaware.* Also: *state Rep. William Smith, state funds, state of confusion, state of mind.*

Four states—*Kentucky, Massachusetts, Pennsylvania and Virginia*—are legally known as *commonwealths* rather than states. The distinction is only necessary in formal uses: *The commonwealth of Pennsylvania filed for a suit.* For geographical reference: *Cotton is grown in the state of Virginia.*

Always spell out the names of the 50 U.S. states standing alone. Spell out Alaska and Hawaii and each of the 48 states with five or fewer letters. The list:

Ala.	Hawaii	Mass.	N.M.	S.D.
Alaska	Idaho	Mich.	N.Y.	Tenn.
Ariz.	Ill.	Minn.	N.C.	Texas
Ark.	Ind.	Miss.	N.D.	Utah
Calif.	Iowa	Mo.	Ohio	Va.
Colo.	Kan.	Mont.	Okla.	Vt.
Conn.	Ky.	Neb.	Ore.	Wash.
Del.	La.	Nev.	Pa.	W. Va.
Fla.	Md.	N.H.	R.I.	Wis.
Ga.	Maine	N.J.	S.C.	Wyo.

Tt

teen, teenager, teenage   Do not use *teen-aged.* Restrict use to those 13 through 17 years old, treating those 18 and over as adults.

television programs See **composition titles.**

Use quotation marks for both the series and for individual episodes: *"And Baby Makes Three,"* and episode of *"ER."*

TV is acceptable in any informal reference for television if it fits the occasion: *a TV dinner, cable TV.*

temperatures Use figures for all except zero. In stories, use a word, not a minus sign, to indicate temperatures below zero. Not: *The night's low as -20.*

RIGHT: *The low was minus 20. The low was 20 below zero. The temperature rose to zero by noon.*

Also: *5-degree temperatures, temperatures fell 5 degrees, temperatures in the 60s* (no apostrophe).

The minus sign is acceptable for below-zero temperatures in tabular material.

Temperatures get higher or lower, not warmer or cooler.
WRONG: *Temperatures are expected to cool down by Thursday.*
RIGHT: *Temperatures are expected to rise by Saturday.*

theater Use *-er* unless the theater spell its proper name *-re.*

their, there, they're *Their* is a possessive pronoun: *The couple listened to their favorite song.*

There is an adverb indicating direction: *There it is.*

There is also used with force of a pronoun for impersonal constructions in which the real subject follows the verb: *There isn't a glass in the cabinet.*

They're is a contraction for they are: *They're going to the movie.*

time Specify the time in a story if it is pertinent: *an accident at 2 p.m.* Monday gives a clearer picture than simply *an accident Monday.*

Time zones usually are not needed. In the continental United States use the time in the dateline community.

Outside the continental United States provide a conversion to Eastern time. The forms:

1. Use figures except for noon and midnight. Use a colon to separate hours from minutes: *3 a.m. EST, 10 p.m. today, 1:30 p.m. Wednesday.*

2. For sequences, use figures, colons and periods: *6:30:10.5* (hours, minutes, seconds, tenths).

3. The time zones in the United States may be abbreviated as *EST, PDT, etc.,* if linked with a clock reading: *noon EDT, 8 a.m. MST, 7 p.m. GMT.* Do not abbreviate

if there is no clock reading. Do not abbreviate other time zones outside the United States.

4. Capitalize each word of the proper name: *Omaha observes Central Daylight Time in the summer.* But: *ESTes Park is in the Mountain time zone.*

5. Do not abbreviate time zones outside the United States. Exception: *Greenwich Mean Time* may be abbreviated as *GMT* on second reference if used with a clock reading.

Uu

United States Spell out as a noun. Use *U.S.* (periods, no space) only as an adjective.

Vv

vice Two words in all uses: *vice president, vice principal.*

vs. Use this abbreviation instead of *versus* in all uses.

Ww

Who, whom Use *who* or *whom,* not *that* or *which,* to refer to humans or animals with names.

Who is the word when someone is the subject of a sentence, clause or phrase: *The man who cooked the food left it out on the table. Who is at the door?*

Whom is the word when someone is the object of a verb or preposition: *Whom do you wish to see?*

widow, widower Because *widow* has been widely used and *widower* seldom used, *widow* has often taken sexist overtones. Avoid any sexist connotations. Use *wife* and *husband* instead.

Xx

X-mas Never use this abbreviation, or any other, for Christmas.

Yy

years Use figures, without commas: *1930.* Use an *s* without an apostrophe to indicate spans of decades or centuries: *the 1700s, the 1920s.*

A year may begin a sentence: *1989 was a bad year.*

youth Applicable to boys and girls from age 13 until the 18th birthday is reached. Use man and woman for individuals 18 and older.

Zz

ZIP codes Use all-caps *ZIP* for *Zone Improvement Program,* but lowercase the word code. Run the five digits together without a comma, and do not put a comma between the state name and ZIP code: *Beverly Hills, Calif. 90210.*

THE EDITOR'S HANDBOOK

PHILOSOPHY

The authors of *Journalism Matters* conceived, planned and produced this student policy handbook as a guide for high school journalists to understand the policies and procedures of student publications.

Student publications attempt to inform and entertain readers in a responsible, accurate and objective manner on all subjects that affect readers in the areas of student life, academics, sports and organizations as well as local and national events. The target audience for student publications is the entire student body with secondary audiences including school faculty, staff and administration, community members and other scholastic journalism groups. Content focuses on coverage which will meet the wants and needs of the majority of students.

Authority for content of student publications rests solely in the hands of journalism students. Material which is libelous, legally obscene, advocates an illegal activity, physically disrupts school activities or which the editorial board and/or adviser believes is in poor taste will not be printed.

Responsibilities

A concern for truth, human decency and human betterment concurs a good student press. In order to achieve these responsibilities it must respect the standards of its own school through the following:

- Student publications will refrain from the use of negative ethnic, racial, sexual and religious references which are demeaning, degrading or offensive to the student body.
- Student journalists must always be impartial and exact in their news reports and must have facts to support their public statements. They must be responsible for everything published.
- The editor(s) will not exclude the point of view of a student, faculty, staff or administrator simply because he/she disagrees with editorial policy or educational principles of the school.
- The editor will publish corrections of all mistakes.
- Accountability for student publications pertains to student editors, staff members and the Publications Board.
- The Publications Board will hold editors and staff members accountable for meeting these responsibilities and uphold these standards. Students who fail to meet these responsibilities and standards are subject to dismissal from student publications.

Publications Board

The Publications Board is the decision-making body of student publications. The board recognizes and protects student freedom of expression while insuring student responsibility.

The following individuals constitute members of the Publications Board:

- Editor in Chief
- Production Editor
- Section Editors (News, Features, Sports, Editorial/Opinions, Entertainment)
- Photo Editor
- Business Manager

The Board will meet weekly or monthly, depending on normal operation of the publication. The meetings are required for the members listed above, but any staff member may attend. Unscheduled meetings may be called and should be attended by Board members. Any board member who must miss a scheduled meeting should notify the Editor in Chief, however, if a member of the board misses two meetings without an excuse approved prior to the miss (with the exception of illness), the Board can recommend a replacement.

Editors are subject to review by the Board if they fail to fulfill their responsibilities. The Board may dismiss a member with a majority vote and is responsible to recommend a replacement for the open position. The adviser must approve the replacement.

All Board members will vote on issues such as policy-making decisions when the need arises. A majority vote determines the decision. The adviser will not vote, but may disagree and make suggestions or comments.

Controversial issues will be discussed by the Board in order to determine what approach should be taken. The adviser may veto the decision, but the Board can overrule with a unanimous vote.

The Publications Board should decide when and where meetings will be held at the beginning of each month.

Job Descriptions

Although each school publication staff is adapted to its locality, the following jobs will be similar. Basic duties for each position are:

◆ EDITOR IN CHIEF

✓ Chairs the Publications Board.

✓ Assists section editors, staff reporters, photographers, columnists and cartoonists in all aspects concerning the content and appearance of the publication including design and production.

✓ Leads staff discussions concerning editorial stands.

✓ Calls unscheduled Board meetings.

✓ Carries out final steps in the editing process for stories and/or photos.

✓ Represents the production in outside contacts with faculty, staff, administration, community individuals or groups.

◆ PRODUCTION EDITOR

✓ Chairs the Publication Board and takes on the responsibilities of the editor in chief in his/her absence.

✓ Works with section editors on the design and layout for their pages.

✓ Provides any necessary assistance to fulfill the production needs such as layout a design on Pagemaker.

◆ BUSINESS MANAGER/ADVERTISING MANAGER

✓ Works with the editor in chief and adviser on financial planning.

✓ Keeps accounting records (accounts payable and receivable).

✓ Informs Publication Board and staff on financial situations.

✓ Supervises advertising sales and billing.

Job Descriptions, *continued*

✓ Prepares the circulation of paid subscriptions and exchange papers.

✓ Maintains a list of potential and current client listings.

✓ Works with the section editors to place ads on page layouts before the design process.

✓ Prepares the mailing of issues to advertisers.

◆ SECTION EDITOR

✓ Works with staff in developing content to fill the pages.

✓ Assigns stories and photos to staff members.

✓ Checks with reporters and photographers about the status of assignments and provides assistance if necessary.

✓ Edits all assignments before passing them on to either the editor in chief or the adviser.

✓ Consults with the production editor on design and production.

✓ Takes responsibility for completing the pages in his/her section.

◆ PHOTO EDITOR

✓ Gives photo assignments to staff.

✓ Accepts assignments from section editors.

✓ Keeps a record of photo assignments.

✓ Maintains a filing system for negatives, contact sheets and proofs.

✓ Organizes the maintenance of the darkroom facilities, photo equipment, including mixing chemicals, rolling and distributing film.

✓ Checks to make sure assignments are completed.

◆ STAFF REPORTER

✓ Brainstorms and accepts story ideas or assignments from section editors.

✓ Researches, interviews, writes and edits his/her own story.

✓ Works with section editors to complete stories.

✓ Meets deadlines with final draft.

Staff Photographer

✓ Brainstorms photo ideas and accepts photo assignments from the photo editor.

✓ Shoots and develops all assigned photos.

✓ Files negatives, contact sheets and proofs in filing system.

✓ Helps maintain the equipment and darkroom facilities.

Code of Ethics

S tudent publications serve as information carriers for students, faculty and staff. As student journalists we strive to report the truth by effectively learning and reporting our facts. This obligation requires us to perform with intelligence, objectivity, accuracy and fairness in order to carry out our responsibilities. Because of this goal, we accept the following standards of practice:

RESPONSIBILITY

Student publications focus on the students' right to know the truth concerning events of public importance and interest. In order to successfully do this, we work to gather and distribute accurate news and individual opinions. Student journalists hold the right to speak unpopular opinions and the privilege to agree with the majority.

FREEDOM OF THE PRESS

Student publications guard freedom of the press as a right of all people in a free society. It carries with it freedom and responsibility to discuss, question and challenge actions and statements of the student body, administration and other public figures. Student journalists hold the right to speak unpopular opinions and the privilege to agree with the majority.

Code of Ethics, continued

ETHICS

A newspaper is doing a special edition about drug abuse among junior high students. During an interview a 13-year-old who is recovering from a cocaine addiction admits to selling drugs to other students who attend the school. The reporter agrees to keep the source anonymous, however, after the story is published in the newspaper several calls are made by members of the community demanding to know who the source is. Although the reporter is pressured by the administration and school board members to reveal the source, she refuses. As a result, she is forced to quit writing for the newspaper.

Student journalists must be free of obligations other than the school's right to know the truth.

◆ We cannot accept special treatment or privileges in exchange for special coverage, free advertising or endorsements.

◆ We cannot publish press releases from government or private student organizations without evaluating their claims and news value.

◆ We must publish news that serves the school's interest.

◆ We must protect confidential sources of information.

ACCURACY AND OBJECTIVITY

Janet Cooke, a former reporter for The Washington Post, won the 1981 Pulitzer Prize for a story called "Jimmy's World," about an 8-year old heroin addict. When Cooke discussed the story with her editors, she said she found Jimmy's mother, who was reluctant to talk. The editors told Cooke she could keep the mother's name anonymous. After Cooke won the Pulitzer Prize and was featured in several newspapers, questions were raised about her credibility which led to the prize winning story. The result, Jimmy didn't exist and Cooke admitted that she made up the story; she resigned from the Post and was stripped of her award.

Student journalists must build trust with the school in order to have a steady foundation for a successful publication. We follow these goals as guidelines.

◆ We serve the school's right to the truth.

◆ We report our stories through objectivity, thoroughness and accuracy.

◆ Our news reports do not include opinion or bias and represent all sides of the issue.

◆ Our editorials do not purposely stray from the truth.

◆ We recognize our responsibility to offer comment and editorial opinion on public events and issues in the local community.

FAIR PLAY

A painting of a nude male, portraying a fallen angel was done by an art student and hung on display the same time the school was hosting the annual holiday basketball tournament. According to the student artist, a janitor who considered the painting "offensive" covered the private parts with a piece of paper without consent from the student, the art teacher, or the administration. The school newspaper printed the information without giving the janitor a chance to reply or tell his side of the story.

◆ Student journalists respect the privacy, rights and well-being of sources when gathering and presenting news.

◆ Student publications should not communicate unofficial facts which might affect the reputation or character of an individual, group or organization without giving the accused a chance to reply.

◆ Student publications will not invade a person's right to privacy.

◆ Student publications will promptly correct its errors, should they occur.

◆ Student journalists and the school should practice open communication.

Publication Standards

One of the hallmarks of an excellent publication is consistency. Consistency means that each issue looks similar to every other issue. This doesn't mean that designers can't use their creativity; it simply means that publications develop a personality through consistent attention to detail. Such consistency can be achieved by developing a set of publication standards and then adhering to those standards.

STANDARD DESIGN DETAILS

Headline pattern:

_____
_____
_____

Logos, graphics, artwork:

_____
_____
_____

Lines/Rules:

_____
_____
_____

Screens:

_____
_____
_____

Spot color:

_____
_____
_____

Sidebars:

_____
_____
_____

Special instructions:

_____
_____
_____

STANDARD TYPE SPECIFICATIONS

Column width:

_____
_____
_____

Masthead copy:

_____
_____
_____

Body copy:

_____
_____
_____

Byline:

_____
_____
_____

Captions:

_____
_____
_____

Pull quote:

_____
_____
_____

Special instructions:

_____
_____
_____

Assignments

K now the answers to these questions before they are asked. Jot down any ideas for stories, photos and design throughout the brainstorming, writing and production process on an assignment sheet such as the one below. Use the following topics as a guide for each story.

Assignment Worksheet

Edition:

_____

_____

_____

Section:

_____

_____

_____

Edition:

_____

_____

_____

Reporter:

_____

_____

_____

Photographer:

_____

_____

_____

Story Concept:

_____

_____

_____

Headline:

_____

_____

_____

Photos/Artwork:

_____

_____

_____

_____

_____

_____

Captions:

_____

_____

_____

_____

Due Date:

_____

_____

_____

Weekly **P**lanner

u se this planner as a guide to set deadlines, schedule meetings and to review activities completed during this week. Outline ideas for lay- outs, stories, headlines, photos and production work. Adapt it to suit your school/.

Activities by assignment, week of _____	MONDAY	TUESDAY	WEDNESDAY	THURSDAY	FRIDAY
Meetings					
Story Ideas/ Assignments					
Layouts					
Photos					
Heads					
Production Requirements					

B e sure to distribute phone numbers among all staff members. Included on the list should be: *Editor in Chief, Production Editor, Business Manager, Section Editior, Photo Editor, Reporters, Photographers* and *Faculty Advisor(s).* [Components of this list may vary, those listed above are common members of publications staffs.]

It might also be a good idea to establish a "calling tree" where one staff member, such as the editor in chief, initiates a call and the person called builds the tree by calling two other staff members, etc., until everyone is notified. Remember, phone numbers should be considered privileged information.

GLOSSARY

account executive a representative of an advertising agency who works with businesses to try to sell the agency's creative ideas to them

advance a preview of an upcoming game that compares teams and players, discusses team records and gives lineups.

advertising appeal an attempt to draw interest to an ad. Among the most common are humor, emotion, sex, testimony, bandwagon, comparison, economy and prestige.

anecdote a short account of some interesting or humorous incident.

announcer a person who reads commercials, public service announcements, promotions or station identifications on the radio.

anonymous source an unnamed source.

aperture the lens opening that admits controlled amounts of light into a camera. Its size is regulated by an iris diaphragm and expressed as an f-stop.

art photos, drawings or other kinds of illustrations in a newspaper or other publication.

attributive verb a verb used with the name of the source in an attribution.

B-roll extra video footage, sent separately or along with a VNR, for use by television stations in preparing their own stories

background information information that may be used but that can't be attributed (a source can't be given) except in a general way.

backgrounding finding out information about the sport, team, coaches, events and issues that will be covered in sportswriting.

balance to represent all sides of an issue fairly.

banner a headline that runs across the entire width of a page.

bar chart a chart or graph that consists of parallel, usually vertical, bars whose lengths represent different quantities.

bastard measure a column somewhat wider or narrower than the paper's normal column width.

beat a regular assignment given to reporters; a place reporters go regularly to get information, such as the courthouse, schools, the police department or the city council.

beat a specific area (topic or geographic region) a reporter is assigned to cover.

bias-free language inclusive language that treats individuals of different genders, races, cultures and abilities equally and that is not offensive to individuals or groups.

bleed to run a picture off the edge of the page.

body copy the text of an ad, which supports and expands what the headline says.

boldface extra dark or heavy type.

brainstorming a technique in which participants suspend critical judgment as they generate as many ideas as possible; also called *free association*.

broadcast journalism the transmission of news on television or radio.

broadsheet what today is considered a full-sized newspaper.

budget a list of the stories for the next newspaper or news broadcast. Budgets are determined by editors or producers.

byline the name of the person who wrote a story, usually printed along with the story.

cable television Privately-owned cable television companies receive signals from many different sources and then transmit the signals via fiber optic cable to consumers.

cart a short tape cassette that contains insertions of voices or music for use in a radio broadcast.

censorship removal or prohibition of material by an authority, usually governmental

circus format a standard print advertising layout that is visually very busy and filled with headlines, small illustrations and copy blocks.

classified ad an inexpensive, brief advertisement placed by individuals or businesses. The ads are classified by subject and collected in one place in the newspaper.

cliché a trite, overused word or expression.

clincher a statement in a news story that returns the reader to the opening paragraph or that reaches a conclusion necessary for complete understanding of the event or story.

closing section in a yearbook, the last double-page spread or two; reflects the opening and wraps up the theme.

colophon a technical description of a book as a product.

column an article with a byline that expresses an opinion about something and that shows individuality. Columns usually have between 450 and 1,000 words.

column inch a method of measuring space on a newspaper, yearbook or magazine page. The number of columns multiplied by the number of vertical inches in the columns equals the total number of column inches. Advertising is often sold by the column inch.

column the basis for constructing a page layout. A column is the standard width for copy chosen for a particular yearbook section or magazine.

commentary a personal view offered in a radio or TV program.

commercial television station a television station that depends on advertising to provide its income.

composition the pleasing selection and arrangement of the elements in a photograph, including the subject, foreground and background.

confidentiality the assurance of secrecy for restricted information.

conflict a characteristic of a news story that involves two sides engaged in a 'battle' from which one will emerge the winner, such as a story about war, an athletic competition or an election.

copy editing symbols standard symbol used to make a correction or change on hard copy; a symbolic language used by reporters and editors working with hard copy.

copy the written form in which a story, headline, caption or advertisement is prepared.

copy-heavy format a standard print advertising layout that emphasizes words rather than visuals.

copyright the exclusive rights to something a person has written or otherwise created.

copywriter a person at an advertising agency who writes the text for an ad.

cost analysis an itemized overview of all expenses.

creative arts magazine a magazine that includes prose and poetry, as well as feature stories, editorials, art reviews and student surveys.

credibility the belief that what someone says is true

crop test a test by which journalists determine whether a story is organized in inverted pyramid style. The journalist begins at the end of the story and decides, on a paragraph-by-paragraph basis, whether paragraphs can be cropped off without losing essential information.

crop to cut or shorten a story by cropping paragraphs from the end.

cut removed from the budget. A cut occurs when a story that is planned gets set aside because a more significant story appears before the paper is printed or the newscast is run.

cutline information about a photo or illustration.

daily newspaper a paper published once a day (except in some cases on weekends), usually in a large town or city

database a collection of information stored in a computer.

dateline the place a story was written. The dateline appears at the beginning of stories that are not written locally.

deadline the latest time a story can be finished in order to be printed in that paper or shown on that newscast.

deck a layer in a grouping of headlines.

deejay the host of a radio music program; short for *disc jockey.*

deep background information information that may be used, but only without a source indication (even an indication of a general source).

delayed lead an indirect lead in which the nut graf is placed after the first anecdote or main point. Can be used on hard or soft news stories.

depth of field the area in front of and behind the subject which appears acceptably sharp.

design the planning, or layout, stage in creating a newspaper page.

direct news lead the first paragraph or two of a hard news story. The direct news lead gives the most important facts, the 5 Ws and an H, about the story.

direct quotation the exact, word-for-word account of what a source said, enclosed in quotation marks and attributed to source.

display ad an advertisement that includes photos or images as well as headlines in large type that appear in various sizes and shapes throughout the paper.

division pages pages that separate and identify sections within a yearbook.

dominant photo a photo that is substantially larger than any other photograph on the page.

double-page spread any two facing pages in a publication.

dummy a detailed page diagram drawn in advance.

editing checking writing for accuracy, organization and writing style.

editorial   an article that states a newspaper's ideas on a particular issue.

editorial board   the group of people (usually the top editors) who decide on a plan for each editorial that will appear in a newspaper.

editorial page   the page in a newspaper that includes editorials, columns, opinion articles, reviews, cartoons and the masthead.

editorial that evaluates   an editorial that focuses on actions or situations that the editors view as being wrong or in need of improvement.

editorial that explains   an editorial that attempts to interpret or inform rather than to argue a point of view.

editorial that persuades   an editorial that offers specific solutions to a perceived problem.

elements of a spread   things that must be included in a double-page spread, including photos, a headline, body copy, cutlines and planned white space.

endsheets   heavier paper pages immediately inside the front and back covers of a book; endsheets bind the cover and the pages of the book together.

entry point   a visual element that draws a reader into the page or story. Examples include pictures, headlines, art, subheads, maps, boxes and other graphic devices.

ethics   the branch of philosophy that deals with right and wrong.

exposure   the amount of light that reaches the film in a camera. Exposure can be controlled by shutter speed, aperture and film speed.

external margin   the frame around the spread.

eyeline   an imaginary line running straight across the double-page spread.

f-stop   the setting that controls the amount of light passing through a camera's shutter. Each lens is capable of a series of aperture settings.

fact sheet   a list of facts; similar to a news release in that it is a way to communicate information quickly and easily to the media

feature   a prominent news story written like a short piece of fiction. The story is usually not related to a current event.

feature lead   an indirect lead; usually an anecdote or description that draws the reader into the scene before revealing the topic, introduces a feature story.

fever chart   a chart that plots numbers recorded over time.

film   a thin piece of plastic coated with an emulsion containing light-sensitive silver halide particles. The film can record an image as a result of exposure in a camera.

film speed   a measure of a film's sensitivity to light, measured on a scale set by the American Standards Association (ASA).

First Amendment   amendment to the U.S. Constitution that provides a right to free speech and a free press

5 Ws and an H lead   a direct news lead, so named because it answers most or all of the questions readers ask—Who? What? Where? When? Why? and How?—in the first paragraph or two.

5 Ws and an H   news cues based on the classic news questions: Who? What? When? Where? Why? and How? These cues help reporters organize questions for an interview.

flag   the newspaper's name, especially as it appears on Page 1.

flush left   the alignment of type that runs flush with the left edge of the column; also called *ragged right*.

flush right   the alignment of type that runs flush with the right edge of the column.

focusing   narrowing; in journalism, reducing a large quantity of material to a usable amount.

folio   a line showing the page number, date and name of the paper.

folio   in a yearbook, the folio is usually located at the bottom outside corner of each page and may include words describing the content of the page and/or graphic elements which reinforce the theme, in addition to a page number.

follow-up question   a question that follows a source's response to another question, intended to get the source to add to or continue with an answer or explanation. Follow-up questions usually begin with *why, how* or *what*. They cannot be planned ahead of time, as they relate to the source's statements.

font   a complete alphabet plus numbers and punctuation marks in a particular typeface and style such as bold, italic or bold italic.

fragmentary quotation   a single word or short phrase used by a source that is included in a paraphrase, enclosed in quotation marks and attributed to the source.

Freedom of Information Act   A law enacted in 1966 requiring government records except those relating to national security, confidential financial data, and law enforcement be made available to the public on request.

futures file   a list or file containing ideas for stories and dates of upcoming events for future issues of a publication or a later newscast.

gatekeepers   a label put on those individuals, such as newspaper editors and broadcast news directors, who determine what stories will be news for their communities.

general interest magazine a magazine that includes a wide variety of articles and attempts to interest almost everyone.

grid a guide to layout planning. The designer divides the page vertically by columns and horizontally by inches (or picas) to make a pattern that can then be filled by stories and photos.

gutter a narrow strip of white space between columns of text.

hammer a headline that uses a big, bold phrase to catch the reader's eye and then adds a lengthier main headline below.

hard copy copy appearing on paper, as opposed to copy on a computer screen.

hard news story a story about timely, breaking news; must run the day the event occurs or have new information added each time it appears in the news.

homer a sportswriter who becomes partisan (favors the home team) in his or her reporting.

hook a detail that draws in the reader's attention.

human element the quotations and personal interpretations gathered in an interview that make stories interesting to readers and viewers.

human interest a characteristic of a news story about people, usually those involved in some emotional struggle.

human source a person who was directly involved in an event.

identity system a newspaper's flag, labels and column heads, as well as other consistent graphic devices, that are used throughout to create a personality.

impact a characteristic of a news story based on the effect or consequence the story will have on the audience.

in-depth reporting reporting and writing in which reporters dig beneath the surface to provide a deeper understanding of a person, issue or event. In-depth reports present a thorough examination of an issue or event, drawing on many different sources of information.

incue the first five words of a cart.

index a listing of the paper's contents.

indirect lead a lead that sets a scene or introduces a character before letting the reader know the topic of the story.

infographics design elements that illustrate a story, such as a chart, map, diagram, quotation or sidebar; short for *informational graphics*.

initial cap a large capital letter set into the opening paragraph of a story to help draw the reader's attention to the beginning of the story.

internal margin a margin that keeps a consistent distance between all elements of a page, usually one or two picas.

interview a formal conversation between a reporter and a source for the purpose of gathering information and opinion.

inverted pyramid the organizational pattern in which information is presented in most news stories. Information is organized from the most important to the least important.

investigative reporting reporting that seeks to uncover something hidden. Investigative reporting requires that reporters learn the innermost details about how things work.

italic type in a style that resembles cursive handwriting.

jargon specialized words that are used exclusively by people in a particular group or activity.

journalism the gathering and reporting of the news

journalist a person who gathers and reports the news (for example, reporters, TV anchors and radio correspondents) or who provides the financial, managerial and technical support that is necessary to transmit the news (for example, publishers, station owners, directors and camera operators).

jump line a line telling the reader on what page the story continues.

justified a description of copy with straight margins at both the right and left column edges.

kerning a special kind of tracking that brings pairs of letters closer together to prevent unsightly gaps.

kicker a clever word or phrase that runs above the main headline; usually set in italics.

ladder a page-by-page plan of a yearbook that shows the proposed content of each page.

lead the beginning of a news story; conveys the main idea in a few words to several paragraphs.

lead-in information read by a newscaster to introduce a sound bite.

leading the space between two lines of type; pronounced "ledding."

leg the vertical dimension of a story (its depth).

lens the part of a camera that gathers the rays of light from the scene and transmits them to form a sharp image on the film.

libel   the printing or broadcasting of false information that damages someone's reputation.

literary magazine   a magazine that publishes short stories, poetry, essays and art.

local angle   a fact or person that connects a story which originates in another location to the local audience.

localize   to find someone or something in your community that has a tie to a story from somewhere else and then to report it in order to make the story more interesting to local readers.

logo   an easily identifiable "flag" in an advertisement that may combine art and copy and that is associated with the product.

logo   the graphic or visual element that represents the theme

magazine   a collection of articles, stories, pictures and artwork that is published on a regular basis.

mass media   the means of communication that can reach large audiences.

masthead   a statement in a newspaper that provides the details of publication.

media alert   a news release that announces an upcoming event

media blitz   a public relations strategy in which a company uses many types of media simultaneously to get a message to as many people as possible

mini-mag   a special section of a yearbook that is set aside for special topics or subject matter.

mock-up ad; spec ad   a dummy advertisement that uses information and artwork geared to a specific business made for the purpose of convincing the business to run an actual ad in a publication.

modular design   a design in which stories are arranged in rectangular shapes, or modules.

morgue   reference library that stores clippings of published articles.

mosaic concept of design   a design concept in which all elements are arranged in a pinwheel fashion, clustered around a central focal point.

mug pages   the people pages which contain rows of individual head-and-shoulders photographs, also known as mug shots.

mug shot   a small photograph of the face of someone mentioned in a story.

multipanel format   a standard print advertising layout that has at least two dominant illustrations.

natural sound   the noises and voices that can be heard at the scene of a news event, which radio news reporters work into their reports; also called *nat sound.*

news   information not previously known that is delivered through the mass media and has some impact on the audience.

news conference   a group interview planned to convey information simultaneously from one source to many reporters representing all media.

news flow   the number of news stories available to run at any one time.

news hole   the amount of space in the newspaper or time in a newscast available for news.

news judgment   a sense that experienced journalists develop about what events will make good news stories.

news package   a complete news story, including natural sound, sound bites and the reporter's narration.

news peg   the relationship of a feature to, or how a feature is pegged on, something else in the news.

news release   information prepared in a news story format and distributed to the media to share information and generate publicity.

newscaster   the person who reads the news over the air; in television, also called an *anchor.*

not for attribution   a description of information that may be used as background but whose source may not be identified.

note-taking language   a set of symbols and abbreviations used by a reporter to speed up note taking during interviews and news conferences.

nut graf   a paragraph in a lead that tells exactly what the story is about.

objectivity   a lack of personal feelings or bias.

obscenity   material that offends local community standards and lacks serious artistic purpose.

off-the-record   comments made to a reporter as background information and not for publication.

on-the-record information   information that can be used and whose source can be identified.

op-ed page   the page opposite the editorial page in a newspaper.

open-ended question   a question worded to encourage the source to give an opinion or interpretation, or to expand on basic information.

opening section   in a yearbook, the first two to four double-page spread which introduce the yearbook's theme and explain why it was chosen.

orphan   a partial line of type (the end of a paragraph) that appears at the top of a page or column.

outcue   the last five words of a cart.

outline   a special effect in some desktop publishing programs in which the insides of the letters become white or transparent.

overburn a special effect in some desktop publishing programs in which letters are printed in black on top of a colored or shaded background.

panel pages another name for mug pages, so-called because the rows of photographs resemble panels constructed by placing many small, even-sized pieces side by side.

paraphrase a summary of what the speaker said reworded by the reporter. A paraphrase does not use quotation marks but is attributed to the source.

partial quotation a combination of a direct quotation and a paraphrase, attributed to the source.

paste-up the physical process of assembling the newspaper page, either the physical process of assembling the newspaper page, either on a computer screen or with glue or wax on a full-size paste-up board.

people pages pages on which the persons who are members of the school community are featured through individual head-and-shoulders photographs and identified by name and class or job description; as a section, people pages may include candid photographs and feature stories about individuals.

person-on-the-street interview brief interviews with people passing by a location or locations the reporter chooses; usually used to gather a sampling of opinion about an issue or topic in the news.

persona the character taken on by a writer.

photo credit a line giving the photographer's name.

photo opportunity an event staged or arranged in such a way that photographers can take the best possible photographs; photo opportunities may feature persons as well as events

photojournalist a news photographer.

physical source These research tools are records, documents, reference works, newspaper clippings and direct observations.

pica a unit of measure. There are six picas to an inch.

picture-window format a standard print advertising layout in which the illustration is the dominant element.

pie graph a circle with individual wedges, each representing a different component. A pie graph divides a whole into its parts, usually by percentages.

point a unit of measure. There are 12 points in a pica, or 72 points to the inch.

point of view the vantage point from which the reader sees the action. Reporters use third person for most stories.

press box a group of seats at an athletic event that usually provide a good view of the entire field.

press row a row of seats at an athletic event that are reserved for the press, usually at courtside.

primary source a person or document essential to the meaning of a story. **secondary source** a person or document that adds information and interest to a story but that is not essential to the story.

prior review the review of a proof of a newspaper by an official before it goes to press.

profile a short, vivid character sketch.

prominence a characteristic of a news story about someone whose name or job (such as the president of the United States) is well known and easily recognized by the public.

pronouncer the phonetic spellings of unfamiliar words or names that are included in broadcast scripts to help the announcer correctly pronounce the words.

propaganda the name given to any organized, widespread attempt to influence people's thinking or behavior. It may be good or bad, according to the intensions of the originator.

proximity a characteristic of a news story that happens close to home.

public a group of individuals who share a common interest or characteristic and are targeted to receive specific messages related to their common interest or characteristic

public journalism a style of journalism that seeks to revitalize public life and to promote a sense among members of the pubic that their institutions actually belong to them.

public relations the actions and communications carried out by public relations practitioners; the department or division of a business or organization responsible for establishing and maintaining relations between a business or organization and its publics; a management function that helps define an organization's philosophy through interactions within the organization and with publics outside the organization

public service ads similar to other ads or commercials except they do not sell products or services for money. Support for activities come from non-profit organizations such as American Cancer Society or Red Cross.

public service announcement (PSA) an announcement promoting a public or non-profit activity; run by media at no cost to the sponsor

public television station a television station that relies on grants and contributions to pay its operating costs.

publication board a committee set up to help guide and advise student publications.

pulled quotation a direct quotation taken from a story and treated as a graphic to draw attention to the text.

quotation   the exact words spoken by a source and cited as such in a media story.

rapport   a harmonious, agreeable relationship between a source and a reporter established by friendly greetings and casual conversation preceding the formal interview.

raw wrap   a headline style in which the story wraps around the headline on two sides.

redundancy   repeating what's been said; usually subtle, for example 9 A.M. in the morning.

refer   a line that sends readers to a related article or item in the same issue of the paper; pronounced "reefer." removal or prohibition of material by an authority, usually governmental.

retraction   a correction in a subsequent issue of a publication.

reveal   a technique in broadcast news in which the reporter holds back a key piece of information and then reveals it as the story develops

reverse   a special effect in some desktop publishing programs in which letters appear white (for use on a dark background).

review   a column that typically comments on movies, recordings, books, television programs, concerts, plays or restaurants.

rule   a thin horizontal or vertical black line in a newspaper or other publication, notably between columns of text.

run   to appear in the media. A story is said to run the day it appears in the media: "The story will run in the Sunday edition."

sans serif type   type without tiny strokes, or serifs, at the tips of each letter.

scooped   in a situation in which another reporter has obtained a story first.

script rundown   instructions prepared by a television producer that include the initials of the anchor reading the story, the slug, the script type, the initials of the reporter who wrote the story and the story's length.

script   the form in which a story is written for radio or television.

serif type   type with tiny strokes, or serifs, at the tips of each letter.

set width   a means of scaling the width of letters. A line of type could be slightly condensed by choosing a set width of 95%.

shadow   a special effect in some desktop publishing programs in which the letters appear to cast a shadow on the page.

shutter   a dark curtain that slides back and forth across the back of the camera (across the lens) at a predetermined speed, thus controlling the length of time that light falls on the film.

sidebar   an article that accompanies and appears beside the main news story.

sidesaddle head   a headline style that sets the headline beside the story.

signature   a 16-page section of a yearbook printed on the same piece of paper during production; pages one through 16; 17–32, 33–48 and 49–60 are signatures.

sizing   calculating what the new dimensions (height and width) of a photograph will be after it has been enlarged or reduced.

slammer   a two-part headline that uses a boldface word or phrase leading into the main headline.

slander   a spoken falsehood.

slogan   a short, catchy phrase that helps an ad's audience identify the product.

slug   words that identify a story from the time it is assigned to the reporter until it is placed on the page.

soft news story   a story about individuals or lifestyle issues; less timely than a hard news story; can run anytime and still be interesting to readers.

sound bite   a taped quotation from a source used by radio and television stations in their newscasts.

special interest magazine   a magazine that targets people with a strong interest in a particular topic.

specialized column   a column that appears in a specific area of the newspaper, such as a sports column, travel column or politics column.

sponsorship   a technique for getting recommended to a source.

stand-alone   a photograph with no accompanying story.

stand-up   when a reporter appears on camera to explain the information in a story.

standing head   a label used to identify special items such as news briefs or columns.

story package   the copy for a stor and related photos or infographics.

storytelling lead   an indirect lead; another label for feature leads that begin by telling a story.

storytelling pattern   an organizational pattern that invites the reader in with an indirect lead, goes on to give the pertinent facts and information, and ends with a clincher.

structure   the organizational pattern a writer uses to establish relationships between relevant pieces of information.

student expression policy   a written directive approved by the school board or established by a school publication board to protect the rights of student expression and to establish limits on expression where needed.

style the way in writing is to be crafted to be consistent within a publication or broadcast; the general ways in which journalists format their writing.

stylebook a handbook for writers that contains rules and guidelines for writing in a particular style and in the style appropriate for a particular publication or newsroom; a manual of operations for writers.

subhead a line of type set apart from the rest of the story to break up the text and create more visual interest.

summary lead a direct news lead that begins with a paragraph summarizing the story; the second paragraph presents specific details, such as names, ages, dates and locations.

syndicated published through a syndicate, an association that acquires such things as columns, stories, articles and cartoons for simultaneous publication in numerous newspapers and periodicals.

syndicated programming original television shows produced by independent companies. Local stations purchase this programming to use during non-network hours.

table a graphic element that displays a series of numbers or words.

table of contents in a yearbook, a chart that lists each division with its beginning page number.

tabloid a half-sized newspaper.

talent the people who speak and perform before a camera at a television station.

tearsheet a copy of the page on which an advertisement appeared.

teaser a brief preview that highlights the best stories inside the newspaper.

teleconference a conference via satellite hookup that links individuals or groups at two or more locations or sites; used to share information simultaneously with multiple locations and allow persons in remote locations to interact with persons at the site from which the communication originates.

telephoto lens a camera lens that magnifies the subject so that it appears closer than it really is. Such a lens has the capability to produce a clear and large image of subjects relatively distant from the camera.

the exact words spoken by a source and cited as such in a media story.

theme in a yearbook, a word or phrase that pulls all parts together in a relationship that reflects something special about this year at this school.

third person point of view writing that uses *he, she* and *they* as subjects. Third person writing allows the writer to stand back and watch people in action, then write about their activities from a non-participating point of view.

third person question a question phrased in an impersonal manner as though someone other than the reporter were asking for the information; usually begins with a phrase such as "People say that . . ." or "What do you tell people when. . . ."

time exposure a long exposure, often necessary in conditions of low light. Usually longer than one second.

timeliness a characteristic of a news story about an event that is reported as soon as it happens.

tip an idea for a story. A tip may come from a reporter, from the public or from a beat source.

tip-in pages in a yearbook that are printed separately and attached to the book later with narrow double-stick tape.

title page page 1 in a yearbook, which contains the school's name and address, the book's name and the publication year, and identifies or reinforces the theme.

tombstoning stacking headlines alongside each other.

tone the mood of a story.

tool line a black line that can vary in thickness and length from use to use in a print advertisement.

top story the most important story of the day, usually placed at the top of the front page or at the beginning of the newscast.

total running time (TRT) how long an entire tape segment lasts.

tracking adjusting the horizontal space between letters.

transition a key word, phrase, theme or paragraph that links together the sentences and paragraphs of a story.

transition paragraph an information paragraph that links quotations from more than one source or about more than one topic.

tripod a three-part headline that includes a boldface word or phrase (often in all caps) with two smaller lines set alongside it.

type-specimen format a standard print advertising layout that usually has little copy and wants to "shout" something to the reader. Its main elements are the headline and the subhead.

typeface a distinctive set of letters (both uppercase and lowercase).

typography the art of choosing and arranging letters in a pleasing and appropriate manner.

verify to check for accuracy.

video news conference a news conference held at a location with teleconferencing capabilities so media in remote locations can interact with news conference speakers and participants; a news conference delivered simultaneously to multiple locations

video news release (VNR) a news story on video delivery by satellite or cassette directly to television networks and local stations for use on news broadcasts

weekly newspaper a paper published once a week, usually in a small town

white space an area without ink, frequently used by designers as a graphic element to define stories and give special emphasis.

wide-angle lens a camera lens with a wider angle of view than a standard lens and, in addition, greater depth of field.

widow an unacceptably short line of type (often just one word) at the end of a paragraph.

wire service a membership organization that gathers news from around the world and distributes it to local members; the way most local media outlets receive national and international news.

yes-no question a question worded to generate a response of yes or no.

zine a small magazine with a limited circulation that is published by a few people, often using desktop publishing programs and photocopiers; shorts for *magazine* or *fanzine*.

zoom lens a camera lens that allows the photographer to vary the focal length.

GLOSARIO

account executive—ejecutivo de cuentas representante de una agencia de publicidad que trabaja con diferentes firmas intentando venderles las ideas creativas de la misma.

advance—avance análisis preliminar que compara los equipos y jugadores que participarán en un partido a jugarse en fecha próxima, examina los récords de los equipos y da su alineación.

advertising appeal—atractivo publicitario recursos para atraer el interés hacia un aviso determinado. Entre los más comunes se encuentran el humor, la emoción, el sexo, los testimonios, los símbolos de éxito, las comparaciones, la economía y el prestigio.

anecdote—anécdota relato corto de un incidente interesante o humorístico.

announcer—anunciador persona que lee los avisos comerciales, los anuncios de interés público, las promociones o la identificación de las radioemisoras.

anonymous source—fuente anónima fuente no nombrada.

aperture—apertura apertura de un lente fotográfico que permite la entrada de una cantidad controlada de luz en la cámara, se regula por un diafragma de iris y se expresa como una parada-f.

art—arte fotos, dibujos u otra clase de ilustraciones de un diario o de otras publicaciones.

attributive verb—verbo atributivo verbo utilizado con el nombre de la fuente en una atribución.

background information—información básica información que puede ser usada en forma general pero sin ninguna atribución—no se puede dar fuente.

backgrounding—recopilación de datos buscar información acerca del deporte, equipo, entrenadores, eventos y temas que se deben cubrir en un artículo deportivo.

balance—imparcialidad representación justa de un acontecimiento desde el punto de vista de todas las partes involucradas.

banner—titular a toda página titular que abarca todo el ancho de una página.

bar chart—cuadro de barra un cuadro o gráfico consistente de barras paralelas, generalmente verticales, cuyos largos representan diferentes cantidades.

bastard measure—bastardo columna que es más ancha o más angosta que el ancho normal de una columna de periódico.

beat—cobertura área específica—tópico o región geográfica que se asigna a cada reportero.

beat—ronda tarea regular que se le asigna a un reportero, lugar a donde van regularmente los reporteros para obtener información, como ser tribunales de justicia, colegios, comisarías o alcaldías.

bias-free language—lenguaje libre de prejuicios lenguaje integral que trata a los individuos de diferente género, raza, cultura y habilidades en forma igualitaria y que no es ofensivo para individuos o grupos.

bleed—sangrar imprimir una ilustración sobrepasando el borde de la página.

body copy—copia del texto el texto de un aviso que apoya y expande lo que dice el título.

boldface—negrillas impresión remarcada o en tipo negritas.

brainstorming—generación de ideas una técnica mediante la cual los participantes suspenden todo juicio crítico al mismo tiempo que generan todas las ideas de que son capaces; también llamada de *libre asociación*.

broadcast journalism—locución transmisión de noticias por radio o televisión.

broadsheet—folio completo lo que hoy se considera un periódico de tamaño normal.

b-roll—cinta-b espacio no grabado de una cinta de vídeo que se deja aparte o con un VNR, para el uso de estaciones de televisión en la preparación de sus propios artículos.

budget—pauta lista de las noticias que aparecerán en el próximo periódico o noticiario. Los editores o productores son los que determinan las pautas.

byline—nombre del autor el nombre de la persona que escribió un artículo, generalmente aparece impreso junto al título del mismo.

cable television—televisión por cable compañías privadas de televisión por cable que reciben señales de diferentes fuentes y luego transmiten las señales por cable de fibra óptica a los consumidores.

cart—carrete cassette corto de cinta que contiene grabaciones de voces o música para uso en transmisiones de radio.

censorship—censura confiscación o prohibición de material por una autoridad, generalmente gubernamental.

circus format—formato tipo circo un esquema estándar para publicidad impresa que aparece atiborrada de títulos, pequeñas ilustraciones y bloques de textos.

classified ad—aviso clasificado aviso económico breve, puesto por individuos o firmas, clasificados por tema y recopilados en un lugar del periódico.

cliche—cliché palabra o expresión trillada, o de uso excesivo.

clincher—remache declaración en un artículo periodístico que vuelve al lector al primer párrafo o que llega a una conclusión necesaria para una total comprensión del hecho o relato.

closing section—sección de cierre en un anuario, el último o los dos últimos despliegues a doble página; reflejan el tema de apertura y lo resumen.

colophon—sello editorial la descripción técnica de un libro como producto.

column—columna artículo con firma del autor que expresa una opinión acerca de algo y que muestra individualidad. Las columnas tienen normalmente entre 450 a 1.000 palabras.

column inch—pulgada de columna método para medir espacio en una página de periódico, anuario o revista. El número de columnas multiplicado por el número de pulgadas verticales en las columnas equivale al número total de pulgadas de columnas. Los avisos se venden comúnmente por pulgada de columna.

commentary—comentario un punto de vista personal divulgado en un programa de radio o de televisión.

commercial television station—estación de televisión comercial estación de televisión que depende de la publicidad para obtener ingresos.

composition—fotocomposición la selección y arreglo más agradable de los elementos de una fotografía, incluyendo el tema, el primer plano y el fondo de la misma.

confidentiality—confidencialidad el compromiso de secreto para la información restringida.

conflict—conflicto característica de un artículo noticioso que involucra a dos partes que participan en una "batalla" de la cual un lado emergerá victorioso, como ser artículos sobre una guerra, una competencia atlética o una elección.

copy—original la forma escrita en que se prepara un artículo, un título, una leyenda o un aviso.

copy editing symbols—símbolos de edición del original símbolos estándar utilizados para hacer correcciones o cambios en el original impreso; lenguaje simbólico usado por reporteros y editores que trabajan con originales impresos.

copy-heavy format—formato de texto un esquema estándar de publicidad impresa que enfatiza las palabras en lugar de las imágenes.

copyright—derechos de autor derechos exclusivos sobre algo que una persona ha escrito o creado de cualquier otra forma.

copywriter—redactor de textos publicitarios persona de una agencia de publicidad que redacta el texto de un aviso.

cost analysis—análisis de costos resumen detallado de todos los gastos.

creative arts magazine—revista de arte creativo revista que incluye prosa y poesía, así como artículos destacados, editoriales, críticas de arte y encuestas de alumnos.

credibility—credibilidad la creencia que lo que dice alguien es la verdad.

crop—podar abreviar o acortar un artículo eliminando párrafos del final.

crop test—prueba de poda una prueba mediante la cual los periodistas determinan si un artículo ha sido estructurado en un estilo de pirámide invertida. El periodista empieza al final del artículo y decide, examinando párrafo por párrafo, si se pueden eliminar algunos párrafos sin perder información esencial.

cut—corte sacar de la pauta. El corte ocurre cuando se desecha una noticia que se había planificado incluir porque aparece una noticia de mayor importancia antes de que el periódico se imprima o se transmita el noticiario.

cutline—leyenda información sobre una foto o ilustración.

daily newspaper—diario periódico publicado una vez al día—excepto los fines de semana en algunos casos, normalmente en una ciudad o pueblo importante.

database—base de datos recopilación de información guardada en una computadora.

dateline—fecha y lugar de origen el lugar donde fue escrito un artículo. La fecha y el lugar de origen aparecen en el inicio de artículos que no han sido escritos localmente.

deadline—fecha de cierre el último plazo en que se puede terminar un artículo para imprimirlo en un periódico o incluido en un noticiero.

deck—cubierta capa de una agrupación de títulos.

deejay—disc jockey el animador de un programa musical de radio, abreviatura de *disc jockey*.

deep background information—información básica profundizada información que puede ser utilizada pero solamente si no se indica la fuente (ni aún una indicación de una fuente general).

delayed lead—introducción retardada introducción indirecta en la cual la idea central se coloca después de la primera anécdota o punto principal. Puede utilizarse tanto en noticias duras como blandas.

depth of field—profundidad del campo el área que va antes y después del tema que aparezca aceptablemente perspicaz.

design—diseño la etapa de bosquejo o disposición en la creación de una página de periódico.

direct news lead—introducción directa de noticias el primero o los dos primeros párrafos de una noticia dura. La introducción directa proporciona los hechos más importantes: las 5 W y la H de la noticia.

direct quotation—cita directa el relato exacto, palabra por palabra, de lo dicho por una fuente, entre comillas y atribuido a la fuente.

display ad—aviso destacado avisos con fotos o imágenes, así como con títulos en grandes letras que aparecen en diferentes tamaños y formas a través de todo el periódico.

division pages—páginas divisorias páginas que separan e identifican las diferentes secciones de un anuario.

dominant photo—foto dominante foto que es significativamente más grande que las otras fotografías de la página.

double page spread—despliegue a doble página en cualquiera publicación dos páginas que enfrentan entre sí.

dummy—maqueta diagrama detallado de una página dibujado previamente.

editing—edición revisión de un escrito para verificar su exactitud, organización y estilo.

editorial board—junta editorial grupo de personas—generalmente los editores jefes que deciden sobre un plan para cada editorial que va a aparecer en un periódico.

editorial page—página editorial la página de un periódico que incluye los editoriales, las columnas, los artículos de opinión, las críticas, caricaturas y el rótulo.

editorial that evaluates—editorial evaluador editorial que se enfoca en acciones o situaciones que, en opinión de los editores, son incorrectas o necesitan mejorarse.

editorial that explains—editorial explicativo editorial que trata de interpretar o informar más bien que discutir sobre un punto de vista.

editorial that persuades—editorial persuasivo editorial que ofrece soluciones específicas a un problema tangible.

elements of a spread—elementos de un despliegue componentes que se deben incluir en un despliegue a doble página, incluyendo fotos, título, texto, leyendas y espacio en blanco programado.

endsheets—guardas hojas de papel más grueso que van inmediatamente después de las cubiertas de un libro y que unen las tapas y las páginas entre sí.

entry point—punto de entrada elemento visual que atrae al lector hacia una página o artículo. Entre los ejemplos se incluyen las ilustraciones, títulos, trabajos artísticos, subtítulos, mapas, recuadros, y otros dispositivos gráficos.

ethics—ética la rama de la filosofía que se ocupa del bien y del mal.

exposure—exposición la cantidad de luz que llega a la película de una cámara. La exposición se puede controlar por la velocidad del obturador, la apertura y la velocidad de la película.

external margin—margen externo el marco que rodea el despliegue.

eyeline—línea visual línea imaginaria que se extiende a través de un despliegue de doble página.

fact sheet—historial enumeración de los hechos, similar a un noticiario por que constituye una forma de comunicar información a los medios en forma rápida y sencilla.

feature—artículo especializado artículo noticioso de importancia escrito como una obra breve de ficción. La historia generalmente no está relacionada con un hecho de la actualidad.

feature lead—introducción a un artículo una introducción indirecta, usualmente una anécdota o descripción que atrae al lector a la escena antes de revelar su tópico, sirve de introducción a un artículo especializado.

fever chart—cuadro febril cuadro que marca los números registrados en el tiempo.

film—película un trozo delgado de plástico cubierto con una emulsión que contiene partículas de haluro de plata sensibles a la luz. La película puede registrar una imagen si está sometida a exposición en una cámara.

film speed—velocidad de la película medida de la sensibilidad de una película a la luz, medida en una escala fijada por la Asociación Americana de Estándares—ASA.

First Amendment—Primera Enmienda enmienda a la Constitución de los Estados Unidos que estipula el derecho a la libertad de expresión y a una prensa libre.

5 Ws and H lead—introducción de las 5 W y la H una introducción directa a las noticias así llamada porque responde en el transcurso del primer o segundo párrafo a la gran mayoría o a todas las preguntas formuladas por los lectores. ¿Quién? ¿Qué? ¿Cuándo?

¿Dónde? ¿Por qué? y ¿Cómo? (en inglés cinco empiezan por la letra W y la sexta por la letra H).

5 Ws y H—5 Ws and H señales para noticias basadas en las preguntas clásicas ¿Quién? ¿Qué? ¿Cuándo? ¿Dónde? ¿Por qué? y ¿Cómo? Estas señales ayudan a los reporteros a organizar las preguntas de una entrevista.

flag—membrete el nombre del periódico, especialmente en la forma en que aparece en la primera página.

flush left—alineación a la izquierda la alineación de letras que van en línea recta con el extremo izquierdo de la columna; también llamada *derecha mellada*.

flush right—alineación a la derecha la alineación de letras que van en línea recta con el extremo derecho de la columna.

focusing—ajustando en periodismo; angostando, reducir una gran cantidad de material a una cantidad utilizable.

folio—folio en un anuario el folio está generalmente ubicado en la esquina inferior externa de cada página y puede contener, además del número de la página, palabras que describen el contenido de la misma y/o elementos gráficos que refuerzan el tema.

folio—folio una línea que muestra el número de página, la fecha y el nombre del periódico.

follow-up question—pregunta complementaria pregunta que se formula a continuación de la respuesta de una fuente con el propósito de lograr que la fuente agregue o continúe con la respuesta o la explicación. Las preguntas complementarias generalmente empiezan con *por qué, como, o que*. No se pueden planificar por adelantado ya que se relacionan a las afirmaciones de la fuente.

font—fuente de tipos alfabeto completo además de números y signos de puntuación de un tipo y estilo particular como negritas, cursivo, o negritas cursivas.

fragmentary quotation—cita inconexa una sola palabra o frase corta usada por una fuente que se incluye en una paráfrasis, entre comillas, y se atribuye a la fuente.

Freedom of Information Act—Ley de Libertad de Información Ley aprobada en 1966 que exige que los archivos del gobierno sean accesibles al público contra solicitud con la excepción de aquellos relativos a la seguridad nacional, datos financieros confidenciales y de ejecución de la ley.

f-stop—parada-f la fijación que controla la cantidad de luz que pasa a través del obturador de una cámara. Cada lente cuenta con una serie de fijaciones de apertura.

futures file—archivo del futuro lista o archivo que contiene ideas para artículos y las fechas de eventos venideros para futuros despachos en una publicación o noticiarios posteriores.

gatekeepers—guardianes de la reja apodo dado a aquellos individuos como ser editores de periódicos o directores de servicios informativos, que determinan cuales acontecimientos se convertirán noticia para sus comunidades.

general interest magazine—revista de interés general revista que incluye una gran variedad de artículos y trata de captar el interés de casi todo el mundo.

grid—cuadrícula una guía para la planificación de disposición. El diseñador divide la página verticalmente por columnas y horizontalmente por pulgadas—o picas para formar un modelo que puede ser posteriormente llenado con artículos y fotos.

gutter—margen de medianil un delgado espacio en blanco entre las columnas de un texto.

hammer—martillo titular que emplea una frase en negrillas grandes para atraer la mirada del lector y luego agrega un título más largo abajo.

hard copy—copia dura se dice de una copia impresa en contraposición a la copia que aparece en la pantalla de la computadora.

hard news story—noticia dura noticia en que el tiempo de transmisión es importante; debe transmitirse el mismo día en que ocurren los hechos y necesita de información adicional cada vez que vuelve a aparecer en el noticiario.

homer—homero se dice del periodista deportivo cuyos reportajes son parciales—favorecen al equipo local.

hook—enganche un detalle que atrae la atención del lector.

human element—elemento humano las citas e interpretaciones personales recopiladas en entrevistas que hacen que los artículos sean interesantes para los lectores y espectadores.

human interest—interés humano una característica de un artículo noticioso sobre personas que involucra alguna forma de esfuerzo emocional.

human source—fuente humana persona que estuvo directamente involucrada en un acontecimiento.

identity system—sistema de identificación el membrete, rótulo y encabezamientos de columnas, así como otros dispositivos gráficos consistentes que se utilizan todo el tiempo para crear una personalidad.

impact—impacto característica de un artículo noticioso basada en el efecto o consecuencia que la noticia va a tener en la audiencia.

incue—señal de entrada las primeras cinco palabras de un carro.

in-depth reporting—reportaje en profundidad reportaje y redacción en los cuales los reporteros investigan más allá de la superficie para proporcionar una mejor comprensión de una persona, asunto o acontecimiento. Los reportajes en profundidad representan un completo análisis de un asunto o acontecimiento, sacando información de diferentes fuentes.

index—índice listado del contenido de un periódico.

indirect lead—introducción indirecta una introducción que presenta una escena o personaje antes que el lector pueda conocer el tópico de un artículo.

infographics—infográficos elementos de diseño que ilustran un artículo como cuadros, mapas, diagramas, citas o barras laterales. Abreviatura de *gráficos informativos*.

initial cap—mayúscula inicial letra mayúscula de gran tamaño ubicada al inicio del primer párrafo de un artículo para atraer la atención del lector hacia el principio del mismo.

internal margin—margen interno margen que mantiene una distancia consistente entre todos los elementos de una página, normalmente de una o dos picas.

interview—entrevista conversación formal entre un periodista y una fuente con el propósito de recopilar información y opinión.

inverted pyramid—pirámide invertida el diseño organizativo en que se presenta la mayoría de los artículos noticiosos. Se organiza la información partiendo de los hechos más importantes hasta los de menos importancia.

investigative reporting—reportaje investigador reportaje que busca desenterrar algo oculto, el reportaje investigador requiere que los reporteros se impongan de los más mínimos detalles acerca de cómo funcionan las cosas.

italic—cursiva tipo de imprenta que se parece a la escritura a mano.

jargon—jerga vocabulario especializado utilizado en forma exclusiva en ciertas actividades o grupos sociales.

journalism—periodismo recopilación y divulgación de noticias.

journalist—periodista persona que recopila y divulga las noticias—por ejemplo, reporteros, hombres ancla de televisión y corresponsales de radio o que proporciona el apoyo financiero, administrativo y técnico necesarios para transmitir las noticias—por ejemplo, editores, propietarios de emisoras, operadores de cámaras.

jump line—línea de salto línea que informa al lector la página en que continúa el artículo.

justified—justificación descripción de un texto con márgenes rectos a ambos lados, derecho e izquierdo, de los bordes de una columna.

kerning—armonizar tipo especial de rastreo que acerca ciertos pares de letras para evitar huecos poco estéticos.

kicker—golazo palabra o frase aguda, generalmente en cursiva, que, por lo general, va sobre el título principal.

ladder—escalonamiento un programa página por página de un anuario que muestra el contenido programado para cada pagina.

lead—introducción el principio de una noticia; transmite la idea principal ya sea en pocas palabras o en varios párrafos.

lead-in—introductorio preámbulo leído por un locutor para introducir un estribillo musical.

leading—interlineación el espacio entre dos líneas tipografiadas, se pronuncia "leding".

leg—pata la dimensión vertical de una historia—su profundidad.

lens—lente la parte de una cámara que acumula los rayos de luz de la escena y los transmite para formar una imagen nítida en la película.

libel—difamación la publicación o transmisión de información falsa que daña la reputación de alguien.

literary magazine—revista literaria revista que publica cuentos cortos, poemas, ensayos y arte.

local angle—ángulo local hecho o persona que conecta a la audiencia local a una noticia originada en otra ubicación.

localize—localizar ubicar a alguien o algo de su comunidad que está vinculada con una noticia acaecida en otro lugar y luego informar sobre ello para hacer la noticia más interesante a los lectores locales.

logo—logotipo el elemento gráfico o visual que representa un tema.

logo—logotipo una "bandera" fácilmente identificable en un aviso que puede combinar arte y texto y que se asocia al producto.

magazine—revista un conjunto de artículos, historias, grabados e ilustraciones que se publica regularmente.

mass media—medios informativos los medios de comunicación con capacidad para llegar a audiencias de importancia.

masthead—cabecera información en un periódico que suministra detalles de su publicación.

media alert—alerta a los medios noticia que anuncia un evento a realizarse.

media blitz—bombardeo de medios estrategia de relaciones públicas en la cual una empresa utiliza muchos tipos de medios en forma simultánea para transmitir su mensaje a la mayor cantidad posible de personas.

mini mag—mini revista sección especial de un anuario mantenido separado y destinado a tópicos o materias especiales.

mock-up; spec ad—modelo de aviso; aviso especial maqueta de aviso que utiliza información e ilustraciones orientadas hacia empresas específicas elaboradas con el propósito de convencer a dichas empresas a poner un aviso en la publicación.

modular design—diseño modular diseño en el cual los artículos están arreglados en forma rectangular o en módulos.

morgue—morgue biblioteca de referencia que guarda los recortes de los artículos publicados.

mosaic concept of design—concepto de diseño en mosaico un concepto de diseño en el cual se ordenan todos los elementos en forma de rueda de espigas, agrupados alrededor de un foco central.

mug pages—páginas de convictos las páginas sobre personas que contienen hileras de fotografías de cabeza y de hombros también conocidas como fotos de convictos.

mug shot—foto de convicto fotografía pequeña del rostro de una persona mencionada en una noticia.

multipanel format—formato multipanel una disposición estándar de publicidad que tiene, al menos, dos ilustraciones dominantes.

natural sound—sonido natural los ruidos y voces que se pueden escuchar en la escena de un acontecimiento noticioso, que los reporteros de radio incluyen en sus despachos; también se lo conoce como *sonido nat.*

news—noticia información no conocida anteriormente que se transmite a través de los medios de comunicación y que tiene cierto impacto en la audiencia.

news conference—conferencia de prensa entrevista de grupo planificada para proporcionar información simultánea desde una fuente a muchos periodistas que representan a todos los medios.

news flow—flujo de noticias el número de noticias disponibles para transmisión en cualquier momento.

news hole—agujero noticioso la cantidad de espacio disponible para noticias en un periódico o tiempo disponible en un noticiario.

news judgement—apreciación periodística un sexto sentido que desarrollan los periodistas experimentados sobre cuáles acontecimientos se pueden transformar en buenas noticias periodísticas.

news package—paquete noticioso un artículo noticioso completo, incluyendo sonido natural, estribillos musicales y la narración del reportero.

news peg—enganche noticioso la relación de un artículo especializado o la forma en que se conecta con otras materias del noticiario.

news release—comunicado noticioso información preparada en formato de artículo noticioso y distribuido a los medios para compartir la información y generar publicidad.

newscaster—cronista noticioso persona que lee las noticias transmitidas a través del aire, en la televisión, también llamado *hombre ancla.*

not for distribution—no para distribución descripción de información que puede ser utilizada como antecedente pero cuya fuente no se puede identificar.

note-taking language—lenguaje de anotaciones conjunto de símbolos y abreviaturas utilizado por los reporteros para aumentar la velocidad de sus anotaciones durante entrevistas y conferencias de prensa.

nut graf—idea central párrafo de la introducción que dice exactamente de que se trata la noticia.

objectivity—objetividad ausencia de sentimientos personales o prejuicios.

obscenity—obscenidad material que ofende los cánones morales de la comunidad local y carece de un objetivo artístico serio.

off the record—extraoficial comentarios formulados a un reportero como información básica y no para publicación.

on-the-record information—información oficial información que puede ser utilizada y cuya fuente puede identificarse.

op-ed page—página op. ed. en un periódico la página opuesta a la página editorial.

open ended question—pregunta abierta pregunta formulada para animar a la fuente a dar su opinión o interpretación, o a ampliar la información básica.

opening section—sección de apertura en un Anuario los primeros dos a cuatro despliegues a doble página que presentan el tema del Anuario y explican la razón de su elección.

orphan—huérfano línea parcial de un texto—final de un párrafo que aparece al principio de una página o columna.

outcue—señal de partida las cinco últimas palabras de un carro.

outline—contorno efecto especial de algunos programas de edición de computadoras de escritorio en los cuales el interior de las letras se tornan blancas o transparentes.

overburn—sobrecargado efecto especial de algunos programas de edición de computadoras de escritorio en el cual las letras se imprimen en negro sobre un fondo coloreado o sombreado.

panel pages—páginas de paneles otro nombre para las páginas de convictos. Se las llama de esta forma porque las hileras de fotografías se parecen a los paneles construidos al colocar muchas piezas pequeñas del mismo tamaño una al lado de la otra.

paraphrase—paráfrasis resumen de lo que dijo un orador reformulado por un reportero. Una paráfrasis no usa comillas pero se la atribuye a la fuente.

partial quotation—cita parcial una combinación de una cita directa y una paráfrasis atribuida a la fuente.

paste-up—emplanaje el proceso físico de armar una página de periódico, ya sea en la pantalla de la computadora o en un tablero de emplanaje de tamaño completo con pegamento o cera.

people pages—páginas del público páginas en las cuales las personas miembros de la comunidad escolar aparecen fotografiadas en fotos cabeza y hombro e identificadas por nombre y clase o descripción de funciones; como sección, las páginas del público pueden incluir instantáneas y artículos especiales sobre individuos.

persona—personaje carácter asumido por el escritor.

person-on-the-street interview—entrevistas a los transeúntes entrevistas breves con personas elegidas por el reportero que pasan por un lugar o varios lugares; se usan comúnmente para recopilar muestras para encuestas de opinión sobre un asunto o tópico noticioso.

photo credit—crédito fotográfico línea donde aparece el nombre del fotógrafo.

photo opportunity—oportunidad fotográfica un acontecimiento arreglado o montado de forma tal que los fotógrafos puedan tomar las mejores fotografías posibles; las oportunidades fotográficas pueden estar relacionadas con personas o acontecimientos.

photojournalist—reportero gráfico un fotógrafo de noticias.

physical source—fuente física estas herramientas de investigación son los archivos, documentos, trabajos de referencia, recortes de diarios y observaciones directas.

pica—pica unidad de medición; una pulgada tiene seis picas.

picture-window format—formato de ventana panorámica disposición estándar de publicidad impresa en la cual la ilustración constituye el elemento dominante.

pie graph—gráfico de bizcocho un círculo con tajadas individuales, cada una de las cuales representa un componente diferente. Un gráfico de bizcocho divide un todo en partes, comúnmente sobre la base de porcentajes.

point—punto unidad de medición; cada pica tiene 12 puntos o cada pulgada tiene 72 puntos.

point of view—punto de vista posición ventajosa desde la que un lector observa la acción. Los reporteros usan la tercera persona para la mayoría de los artículos.

press box—palco de prensa grupo de asientos en un acontecimiento deportivo que normalmente proporciona una buena vista de todo el campo de juego.

press row—fila de prensa hilera de asientos en un evento de atletismo reservado para la prensa, normalmente a un costado de la cancha.

primary source—fuente primaria persona o documento esencial para el sentido de un artículo; **secondary source—fuente secundaria** persona o documento que agrega información e interés a un artículo pero que no son indispensables para el mismo.

prior review—revisión previa revisión de una prueba de periódico hecha por un funcionario antes de ir a la imprenta.

Profile—perfil un esbozo breve y vívido de un personaje.

prominence—prominencia característica de un artículo noticioso sobre alguien cuyo nombre o cargo—como ser el de Presidente de los Estados Unidos es bien conocido y fácilmente identificado por el público.

pronouncer—pronunciador inclusión del deletreo fonético de palabras o nombres extraños en el libreto de las transmisiones para ayudar al anunciador a pronunciar correctamente las palabras.

proximity—proximidad una característica de una noticia que acontece cerca del domicilio.

public—público un grupo de individuos que comparten un interés o característica común y que están señalados para recibir mensajes específicos relacionados con ese interés o característica común.

public journalism—periodismo de interés público estilo de periodismo que busca revitalizar la vida pública a promover el sentimiento entre los miembros del público que sus instituciones realmente les pertenecen.

public relations—relaciones públicas las acciones y comunicaciones llevadas a cabo por los profesionales en relaciones públicas; el departamento o división de una empresa u organización responsable del establecimiento y mantenimiento de relaciones entre una empresa u organización y sus públicos; una función administrativa que ayuda a definir la filosofía de la organización a través de interacciones dentro de la organización y con los públicos externos a la organización.

public service ads—PSA—avisos de servicio público son similares a otros avisos o anuncios comerciales con la excepción que no venden productos o servicios por dinero. Los avisos de servicios públicos buscan el apoyo de grupos sin fines de lucro.

public service ads—avisos de servicios públicos aviso que promueve actividades públicas o actividades sin fines de lucro; transmitido por los medios sin costo para el auspiciador.

public television station—emisora pública de televisión estación de televisión que depende de donaciones o contribuciones para pagar sus gastos de operación.

publication board—junta de publicaciones comité establecido para ayudar a guiar y aconsejar a las publicaciones de estudiantes.

pulled quotation—cita extraída una cita directa sacada de un artículo y tratada como gráfico para captar atención hacia el texto.

quotation—cita las palabras exactas dichas por una fuente y citadas como tales en un artículo de los medios.

rapport—afinidad relación agradable y armoniosa entre una fuente y un reportero establecida por medio de saludos amistosos y conversaciones informales que preceden una entrevista formal.

raw wrap—envoltura en bruto estilo de titular en el cual el artículo se enrolla alrededor de éste por ambos lados.

redundancy—redundancia repetición de lo ya dicho; generalmente como subtítulo.Por ejemplo: 9 A.M. En la mañana.

refer—referir una llamada que envía a los lectores a un artículo o ítem relacionado que aparece en la misma edición del periódico; pronunciado "rifer".

retraction—retractación corrección de una publicación en un ejemplar subsiguiente.

reveal—revelar técnica en la transmisión de noticias en la cual un reportero se guarda una pieza clave de información y luego la revela cuando se desarrolla la historia.

reverse—reverso efecto especial de algunos programas de edición en computadoras de escritorio mediante el cual las letras se ponen blancas (para uso contra un fondo oscuro).

review—crítica columna que típicamente comenta las películas, grabaciones, libros, programas de televisión, conciertos, obras teatrales o restaurantes.

rule—regla línea negra recta delgada, horizontal o vertical en un periódico u otras publicaciones; especialmente entre las columnas de texto.

run—publicar aparecer en los medios. Se dice que un artículo se publicó el día que aparece en los medios; "El artículo se publicará en la edición del domingo".

sans serif type—tipo sans serif modelo de escritura tipográfica que carece de líneas pequeñas o trazos, en los extremos de cada letra.

scooped—adelantarse situación en la que otro reportero obtuvo la información primero.

script—libreto la forma en que se escribe un artículo para radio o televisión.

script rundown—resumen del libreto instrucciones preparadas por un productor de televisión que incluye las iniciales del hombre ancla que lee el artículo, el lingote, el tipo de libreto, las iniciales del reportero que escribió el artículo y el largo del artículo.

serif type—tipo serif modelo de escritura tipográfica con pequeñas líneas o trazos, en los extremos de cada letra.

set width—fijación de ancho medio de graduación del ancho de las letras. Una línea de caracteres puede condensarse levemente al elegir una fijación de ancho de 95%.

shadow—sombra efecto especial en algunos programas de edición de computadoras de escritorio en los cuales las letras parecen echar una sombra sobre la página.

shutter—obturador cortina oscura que se desliza hacia adelante y hacia atrás en la parte posterior de la cámara—a través del lente a una velocidad predeterminada controlando de esta forma el lapso de tiempo en que la luz cae sobre la película.

sidebar—recuadro artículo que acompaña a un artículo principal y aparece a su lado.

sidesaddle head—título tipo silla de amazona estilo de titular que fija el título a un costado del texto del artículo.

signature—signatura sección de 16 páginas de un anuario impresas en la misma tira de papel durante su producción; las páginas 1 a 16; 17 a 32, 33 a 48 y 49 a 60 son signaturas.

sizing—dimensionado calcular el nuevo tamaño— alto y ancho de una fotografía después de su ampliación o reducción.

slammer—golpetazo título dividido en dos que utiliza una palabra o frase en negritas.

slander—difamación falsedad hablada.

slogan—lema frase corta y pegajosa que ayuda a la audiencia de un aviso a identificar el producto.

slug—chapa palabra que identifica un artículo desde el momento en que es asignado al periodista hasta su impresión en la página del diario.

soft news story—noticia blanda noticia acerca de individuos o estilos de vida; el factor tiempo es mucho menos importante que en las noticias duras; puede darse en cualquier momento y aún ser interesante para los lectores.

sound bite—estribillo de sonido cita grabada de una fuente utilizada por las emisoras de radio y televisión en sus noticiarios.

special interest magazine—revista especializada revista orientada a personas que tienen un marcado interés por un tópico determinado.

specialized column—columna especializada columna que aparece en un área específica del periódico, como ser la columna deportiva, la columna de viajes o la columna política.

sponsorship—patrocinio técnica para hacerse recomendar a una fuente.

stand-alone—solitaria fotografía que no tiene un artículo que la acompañe.

standing head—titulo permanente membrete utilizado para identificar ítems especiales, como ser noticias breves o columnas.

stand-up—tomarlo de pie cuando un periodista aparece en pantalla para explicar la información sobre un artículo.

story package—paquete de artículo el texto de un artículo con sus fotos e infográficos.

storytelling lead—introducción narrativa introducción indirecta; otro nombre para introducciones de artículos especializados que empiezan narrando una historia.

storytelling pattern—modelo narrativo modelo estructural que invita al lector a entrar por medio de una introducción indirecta; continúa dando la información y los hechos pertinentes y termina con un remache.

structure—estructura modelo de organización utilizada por el escritor para establecer una relación entre las partes pertinentes de la información.

student expression policy—política de expresión estudiantil directiva escrita aprobada por la junta de educación o establecida por una junta editora de educación para proteger los derechos de expresión de los estudiantes y establecer los límites a la expresión cuando fuese necesario.

style—estilo la manera en que el arte escribir debe perfeccionarse para ser consistente con una publicación o transmisión; el formato general que los periodistas dan a sus escritos.

stylebook—libro de estilo manual para escritores que contiene las reglas e instrucciones para escribir en un estilo determinado y en el estilo apropiado para una publicación en particular, o sala de noticias; manual de operaciones para escritores.

subhead—subtítulos una línea tipografiada separada del resto del artículo que rompe la monotonía del texto y crea un mayor interés visual.

summary lead—introducción de resumen introducción directa para una noticia que empieza con un párrafo que hace un resumen de la misma y un segundo párrafo que presenta detalles específicos como nombres, edades, fechas y lugares.

syndicated—sindicalizado publicado a través de un sindicato; asociación que adquiere cosas tales como columnas, noticias, artículos y caricaturas para publicación simultánea en numerosos diarios y periódicos.

syndicated programming—programación sindicalizada espectáculos originales de televisión producidos por compañías independientes. Las estaciones locales compran estos programas para usarlos durante las horas en que no trabajan con la red.

table—cuadro elemento gráfico que contiene una serie de cifras o palabras.

table of contents—índice de materias en un anuario, un listado que detalla cada sección con el número de la página en que ella se inicia.

tabloid—tabloide un periódico de medio folio.

talent—talentos personas que hablan o actúan ante las cámaras en un estudio de televisión.

tearsheet—página suelta una copia de la página donde apareció un aviso.

teaser—desenredo un breve avance que destaca los mejores artículos que contiene el periódico.

teleconference—teleconferencia conferencia que une a individuos o grupos ubicados en dos o más localidades conectándolos vía satélite; utilizada para compartir información simultánea con múltiples localidades y permitir a las personas en sitios remotos interactuar con las personas ubicadas en el lugar desde donde se origina la comunicación.

telephoto lens—lente de telefoto lente de cámara que agranda el sujeto de modo que aparece más cerca de lo que está. Esta lente tiene la capacidad de producir una imagen grande y clara de sujetos que están relativamente lejos de la cámara.

theme—tema en un anuario, una palabra o frase que armoniza a todas las partes en una relación que refleja algo especial en ese año y en ese colegio.

third person point of view—punto de vista en tercera persona escrito que utiliza *él, ella y ellos, ellas* como sujetos. Al escribir en tercera persona, el escritor puede mantenerse a la distancia y observar a las personas en acción para luego escribir sobre sus actividades desde un punto de vista no participativo.

third person question—pregunta en tercera persona pregunta formulada de modo impersonal como si una persona diferente al periodista estuviera solicitando la información; generalmente empiezan con una frase como "La gente dice que . . ." o "Qué les dice a las personas cuando . . .".

time exposure—tiempo de exposición en condiciones de poca luz ha menudo se necesita de un tiempo largo de exposición. Normalmente superior a un segundo.

timeliness—puntualidad característica de una noticia sobre un acontecimiento que se debe informar tan pronto como sucede.

tip—dato idea para una noticia. El dato puede provenir de un periodista, del público o de alguna fuente en los lugares de ronda.

tip-in—inserto páginas de un anuario que se imprimen por separado y se adjuntan posteriormente al libro mediante una angosta cinta adhesiva engomada en ambas caras.

title page—página titular la página 1 de un anuario, que contiene el nombre y dirección del colegio, el nombre del libro y el año de publicación e identifica y refuerza su tema.

tombstoning—lapidar apilar los títulos uno al lado del otro.

tone—tono el tono de una noticia.

tool line—línea instrumental línea negra que se usa al imprimir un aviso; su ancho y largo puede variar de acuerdo a los diferentes usos.

top story—noticia principal la más importante noticia del día; generalmente se la coloca al comienzo de la primera página y al inicio del noticiario.

total running time (TRT)—tiempo total de funcionamiento lo que dura en funcionamiento el segmento de una cinta completa.

tracking—rastreo ajuste del espacio horizontal entre las letras.

transition—transición palabra, frase, tema o párrafo clave que une a las oraciones y párrafos de un artículo.

transition paragraph—párrafo de transición párrafo informativo que une las citas de diferentes fuentes o acerca de varios tópicos.

tripod—trípode título en tres partes que incluye una palabra o frase en negrita—a menudo en mayúsculas y dos líneas más pequeñas a cada lado.

typeface—tipo de letra un juego de letras específico—tanto mayúsculas como minúsculas.

type-specimen format—formato de espécimen de tipo disposición estándar para aviso impreso que usualmente tiene poco texto y desea "gritar" algo al lector; sus principales elementos son el título y el subtítulo.

typography—tipografía el arte de elegir y arreglar las letras de modo agradable y apropiado.

verify—verificar controlar la exactitud.

video news conference—conferencia de prensa en vídeo conferencia noticiosa celebrada en una localidad que cuenta con facilidades de teleconferencia de modo que los medios de comunicación de regiones remotas pueden interactuar con los conferenciantes y los participantes; una conferencia noticiosa transmitida simultáneamente en múltiples localidades.

video news release—VNR—emisión noticiosa en vídeo artículo noticioso en vídeo transmitido directamente por satélite o cinta a las redes de televisión y estaciones locales para uso en noticiarios.

weekly newspaper—periódico semanal periódico publicado una vez por semana, generalmente en una ciudad chica.

white space—espacio en blanco área libre de tinta frecuentemente usada por los diseñadores como un elemento gráfico para definir artículos y dar un énfasis especial.

wide-angle lens—lentes granangulares lentes de cámara con un ángulo de visión más ancho que un lente estándar y, además, mayor profundidad de campo.

widow—viuda línea tipografiada inaceptablemente corta—a menudo de una sola palabra al final de un párrafo.

wire service—servicio de cable una organización de miembros que recopila noticias de todo el mundo y las distribuye a miembros locales de la misma manera en que la mayoría de las subdistribuidoras locales reciben las noticias nacionales e internacionales.

yes-no question—pregunta si-no pregunta formulada de forma que genere una respuesta de sí o no.

zine—revi revista pequeña de circulación limitada publicada por unas pocas personas, a menudo utilizando programas editores de computadoras de escritorio y fotocopiadoras; abreviatura de *revista* o de *revista de hinchas*.

zoom lens—lentes zoom lentes de cámara que permite al fotógrafo variar el largo focal.

INDEX

PHOTO CREDITS